Cycling Science

Stephen S. Cheung
Mikel Zabala

Editors

Human Kinetics

Library of Congress Cataloging-in-Publication Data

Names: Cheung, Stephen S., 1968- editor. | Zabala, Mikel, 1974- editor.

Title: Cycling science / editors Stephen S. Cheung, Mikel Zabala.

Other titles: Cycling science (Human Kinetics)

Description: Champaign, IL : Human Kinetics, 2017. | Includes bibliographical references and index.

Identifiers: LCCN 2016049270 (print) | LCCN 2016051573 (ebook) (print) | LCCN 2016051573 (ebook) | ISBN 9781450497329 (print) | ISBN 9781492551263 (ebook)

Subjects: LCSH: Cycling--Physiological aspects. | Cycling--Training. | Bicycle racing--Training.

Classification: LCC RC1220.C8 C94 2017 (print) | LCC RC1220.C8 (ebook) | DDC 796.6--dc23

LC record available at https://lccn.loc.gov/2016049270

ISBN: 978-1-4504-9732-9 (print)

This publication is written and published to provide accurate and authoritative information relevant to the subject matter presented. It is published and sold with the understanding that the author and publisher are not engaged in rendering legal, medical, or other professional services by reason of their authorship or publication of this work. If medical or other expert assistance is required, the services of a competent professional person should be sought.

The web addresses cited in this text were current as of February 2017, unless otherwise noted.

Acquisitions Editors: Tom Heine and Michelle Maloney; **Senior Developmental Editor:** Cynthia McEntire; **Managing Editor:** Caitlin Husted; **Copyeditor:** Bob Replinger; **Proofreader:** Pamela S. Johnson; **Indexer:** Michael Ferreira; **Permissions Manager:** Martha Gullo; **Graphic Designer:** Whitney Milburn; **Cover Designer:** Keith Blomberg; **Photograph (cover):** mel-nick/iStockphoto/Getty Images; **Photo Production Manager:** Jason Allen; **Senior Art Manager:** Kelly Hendren; **Illustrations:** © Human Kinetics, unless otherwise noted; **Printer:** Sheridan Books

Human Kinetics books are available at special discounts for bulk purchase. Special editions or book excerpts can also be created to specification. For details, contact the Special Sales Manager at Human Kinetics.

Printed in the United States of America   10 9 8 7 6 5 4 3 2 1

The paper in this book is certified under a sustainable forestry program.

Human Kinetics
Website: www.HumanKinetics.com

United States: Human Kinetics
P.O. Box 5076
Champaign, IL 61825-5076
800-747-4457
e-mail: info@hkusa.com

Canada: Human Kinetics
475 Devonshire Road Unit 100
Windsor, ON N8Y 2L5
800-465-7301 (in Canada only)
e-mail: info@hkcanada.com

Europe: Human Kinetics
107 Bradford Road
Stanningley
Leeds LS28 6AT, United Kingdom
+44 (0) 113 255 5665
e-mail: hk@hkeurope.com

For information about Human Kinetics' coverage in other areas of the world, please visit our website: www.HumanKinetics.com

E6316

Cycling Science

Contents

Introduction

One of the true joys of cycling is the seemingly effortless matching of human and machine. The bicycle is an incredibly efficient multiplier of human energy, allowing us to go farther and faster than most any other kind of human-powered locomotion. With the human passion for improving technology and also for pushing the envelope, it is only natural that a constant theme of our love affair with cycling has been finding ways to make both the machine and ourselves stronger and more efficient. Some of these improvements, such as improved roads, come from outside the bicycle or rider, but large improvement gains have come about thanks to the continued application of science and engineering to bicycle design and human performance.

While the bicycle has retained its traditional diamond shaped overall, even a quick perusal through back issues of magazines shows the enormous changes in bicycle engineering over the past several decades. Bicycles that were once all built from steel are now available in a wide range of materials, from aluminum to titanium and now predominantly carbon fiber. Yet while these changes have created lighter, stronger, and faster bikes, the critical factor in on-bike performance remains optimizing the fit of the rider to the bicycle along with improvements in aerodynamics. Advances in biomechanical understanding and also the engineering of bike fit technology has made this process more precise and also more time efficient, reducing though not completely eliminating the cycles of repeated trial and error.

As an endurance sport, cycling remains a sport that requires time and effort. While there remains no substitute for hard work, scientific advances in many fields related to human physiology have enabled humans to ride faster and farther. For example, improved understanding of how the human system responds to physical activity and training, along with better understanding of individual responses, have allowed coaches to better fine-tune training prescription to particular needs and goals. At the same time, improved real time performance tracking technology, notably the popularization of portable heart rate monitors in the 1980s and, more recently, the proliferation of power meters, has enabled the development of fitness tracking and prediction software.

While cycling has a strong technological aspect, it has also tended to be highly conservative, with many of the ideas surrounding training handed down through the generations and largely unchanged from the early 20th century. Indeed, with its historical emphasis on endurance and suffering, new technologies or training ideas are often looked at as being reserved only for the weak and not being worthy of true cyclists. The early Tour de France organizers derided the use of derailleurs and multiple gears as a crutch to be used only by recreational cyclists rather than true professionals. Echoes of this technological dichotomy remain today, with amateur cyclists free to purchase bicycles that are much lighter than the current arbitrary weight limit of 6.8 kilograms for professional cycling.

Despite this divide, there is no doubt that elite cyclists provide an invaluable test bed for both technology and training ideas. Understanding elite performance and improving upon it is a continuous cycle. This often starts with ideas already being used by professional cyclists, with scientists testing these ideas in a more controlled laboratory environment. In turn, this improved scientific understanding leads to better practice in the field, benefiting cyclists of all levels. A classic example of this field-to-lab-to-field cycle can be seen in the concept and practices of periodization. This idea of changing different training emphases and planning for peak performance at specific times of the year was first used by weightlifters in the former Eastern Bloc countries, gradually spreading westward beyond the Iron Curtain. Scientists have taken these ideas into the lab, and now better understand both the whole body and cellular adaptations to these different training loads, along with variations such as block periodization and the use of high-intensity training. This has led to improvements in training ideas for all levels of cyclists along with advances such as tools to predict and plan fitness based on current training loads.

We have tried to be comprehensive in our survey of cycling science. Chapters such as those on bike fit, nutrition, and training are relevant to all cyclists. We also included chapters on issues that affect all athletes, such as the impact of heat stress and pollution on physiology and performance. These chapters not only provide information on physiology, but also provide practical advice for dealing with the impact of these issues. Due to the continuing accessibility of new technology such as portable and personal hypoxic systems, we included chapters on topics such as altitude training, which is currently largely restricted to elite athletes but may become more prevalent for amateur and recreational cyclists in the future. Throughout the book, we aimed to maintain scientific rigor and an evidence-based approach to various practices, while at the same time ensuring that such knowledge is delivered in an accessible manner and with strong practical applicability.

Part I deals with basic human physiology as a way of grounding the remainder of the book in a sound understanding of the different systems involved during physical exercise. We start with a chapter on the physique of cyclists, exploring whether there is truly an ideal body type for specific cycling disciplines. This is followed by an analysis of the different metabolic pathways and genetic variability that power human exercise.

After understanding the rider part of the rider–bike interaction, part II focuses on the bicycle itself. Included are chapters on bicycle design and the influence of frame materials and geometry on the fit and feel of the bike.

With the saddle being one of the three main contact points between rider and bike—and arguably the most sensitive and tricky to perfect—we included a chapter specifically on bicycle saddle design.

With knowledge gained from understanding the cyclist and the bike, part III focuses on the all-important human–machine interface. Nothing impacts performance, comfort, and injury risk on the bike more than a proper bicycle fit. Therefore, there is a chapter on the basic biomechanics of cycling, followed by two separate chapters on achieving the perfect bicycle fit by two different authors, each bringing their own extensive work in the area. While achieving this optimized fit remains paramount, a key way to achieve "free speed" is to improve aerodynamic profile and the cyclist's ability to minimize air resistance. Therefore we take you on a tour of the latest methods in aerodynamic testing, going beyond static wind tunnel tests and into field testing. Finally, this section closes with a chapter exploring the simple yet complex art of pedaling, in order to discover practical benefits to specific training of the pedal stroke.

One of the unique and beautiful aspects of cycling is that it takes place largely outdoors on open roads or trails. However, this also means dealing with a wide range of environments. Part IV explores the impact of these environments. We begin with a chapter on dealing with the high temperatures common to many parts of the world, followed by the realities of riding in an often polluted environment. Following this, we take a detailed analysis of the impact of training at altitude, taking a historical view and also exploring the latest research into using altitude training as an ergogenic aid. Climbing hills is also an integral part of cycling, and we close this section by looking at practical tips to improve climbing performance.

Part V takes us on a tour through the critical fields of nutrition and hydration, exploring some of the latest findings in the roles and timing of different nutrients for maintaining performance throughout a long ride or over a prolonged period of training. We have tried to do our best to cut through the mass of dubious "science" and marketing pitches, as there is often so much contradictory advice and hearsay in these fields, often fueled by commercial interests rather than evidence-based practice. We close this section with a sobering look at the dark side of ergogenic aids, where the goal of improving performance may degenerate into the use of illicit substances or practices.

Many of us take up cycling with the direct or indirect goal of improving our health. Ride long enough, however, and unfortunately the odds are that you will fall off your bike or suffer some other form of injury. Part VI takes a look at cycling health issues, beginning with two chapters on the epidemiology of cycling injuries along with trauma and overuse injuries. Health can also be compromised by riding too much without adequate recovery, leading to reduced benefits from further training, prolonged fatigue, or the serious consequences of overtraining syndrome. We therefore include chapters on maximizing recovery and different tools that may benefit recovery, along with a chapter defining overtraining, including its symptoms, risk factors, and management.

To get better on the bike, there is no avoiding getting in the training itself. Part VII takes a multi-perspective approach to understanding training theory, assessment, and preparation. These chapters take a detailed view of training, notably how to use the emerging technology of power meters, manage training data, and design efficient training programs that rely on the assessment of cycling fitness. We have also taken a broader view of training with chapters on long-term athlete development and strategies for managing the relationships within a team. Part VIII covers the details of race preparation: off-the-bike training, respiratory training, warming up, and stretching.

In part IX you will find chapters scientifically analyzing diverse cycling disciplines, including road, mountain biking, track, BMX, and ultradistance cycling. No matter the preferred cycling discipline, a key attribute of elite performers is the ability to properly pace themselves throughout the event so that they neither fatigue before the line nor finish feeling as if they have something left in the tank.

One of the strengths of this book is the multidisciplinary expertise of the contributors. We have recruited to our cause some of the leading academics working today in the science of cycling. Not only are the scientists very well respected in their fields, but many, like Mikel, worked extensively with elite cyclists and other endurance athletes as coaches or sport scientists. To broaden our perspective beyond traditional laboratory science, we have recruited elite coaches, engineers, and sport scientists. Another key feature and strength of the book is the international roster of contributors. We have brought in contributors from North America, South America, Europe, and also Oceania, bringing with them a mix of ideas from many countries and their rich sporting heritages.

A love of both cycling and science has guided each of our lives. For Mikel, that path led from a professional cycling career to his current roles in the world of academia with a primary focus on cycling science, editing *The Journal of Science and Cycling* and acting as the sport scientist for the Movistar Pro Cycling Team. For Stephen, the love of cycling also led him to academia, in the process prompting a complete change in research disciplines from oceanography to exercise science. Today, he mixes scientific research with extensive popular writing on the science of cycling and consulting with various cycling industry partners. We took on the challenge of editing this book in the hopes of bringing science closer to the everyday rider regardless of fitness or goals. We hope that this book inspires you to use science to enjoy your cycling even more. May you always feel strong and ride fast.

—Stephen S. Cheung
Mikel Zabala

PART

I

The Cyclist

CHAPTER 1

The Cyclist's Physique

—Paolo Menaspà and Franco M. Impellizzeri

The cyclist's physique is unique indeed. When walking on the beach, you can easily spot a cyclist: unmistakable tan lines, shaved legs, knee and elbow scars, but more important, muscled legs paired with a wiry upper body. Even so, modern bikes make cycling an accessible sport because people of every physique can perform at the highest level on a road bike. Thanks to the evolution of materials and equipment, bike frames, seat posts, crank arms, stems, handlebars, and most bike components are available in different sizes and shapes. Hence, the physique that a cyclist is born with does not matter as long as there is a will to pedal.

Anthropometric Characteristics and Cycling Specialties

Road cycling attracts athletes of all shapes and sizes. Professional cyclists have statures between 160 and 190 centimeters, and body weight can range between 53 and 80 kilograms, as reported by Mujika and Padilla (2001). In the last decade the size of road cyclists has grown; pro riders are as tall as 197 centimeters and weigh as much as 91 kilograms (e.g., Jens Mouris). The discrepancy of almost 40 kilograms between the lightest and the heaviest pro riders makes it obvious that cyclists have different characteristics and specializations. Indeed, similar to athletes in other sports who have their own specializations (e.g., by field position in team sports), cyclists are specialized and have different roles during competitions.

Of course, physiological characteristics play a role in the determination of the specialization, but in a field in which the aerobic characteristics are equally outstanding (all the professional cyclists have high maximal oxygen consumption), anthropometric characteristics are often the determinants that distinguish different kinds of road cyclists.

For instance, in 1987 Swain and colleagues studied the effect of body size on oxygen consumption during cycling (Swain et al. 1987). They found that large cyclists had lower oxygen consumption when scaled per body weight than small cyclists. Thus, small cyclists have a performance advantage while riding uphill. But the research also showed that large cyclists have an advantage over small cyclists while riding on flat roads, because they have a lower ratio of frontal area to body weight, thus suggesting aerodynamic benefits.

The main categories of specialists within road cycling are climbers, sprinters, flat-terrain specialists, and all-rounders. Climbers excel in hilly or mountainous competitions; conversely, sprinters mainly compete for success in predominantly flat races that end at high speed and with a relatively larger number of contenders (i.e., bunch sprint). Other cyclists perform better on flat terrain, and they often have the role to control the race before the climbs or before the final sprint. Among them, the high-performing ones usually are described as specialized time trialists, which means that they are capable of winning time-trial races. The relatively few cyclists capable of succeeding in all kind of terrains are called all-rounders (Menaspà et al. 2012; Padilla et al. 1999; Impellizzeri et al. 2008). This structure, however, is a sort of simplification; in fact, cyclists fall into subcategories. For example, sprinters can be divided into riders who have a strong jump (i.e., short acceleration) and those who prefer a long progression. Among climbers, some are capable of frequent accelerations and often ride out of the saddle, whereas others prefer to ride with a more even pace.

Classic, or Traditional, Anthropometric Measures

Anthropometric characteristics play a major role in the determination of cycling specialty. Sprinters can be of virtually any size, climbers are usually short and light, and time trialists are tall and heavy. Traditionally, the most common anthropometric parameters measure stature, body weight, body mass index (BMI), percentage of fat (or sum of skinfolds), and other body measures (e.g., limb length and girth) (McLean and Parker 1989; Foley, Bird, and White 1989).

Body Composition

A cyclist's body composition can be evaluated by determining the percentage of body fat, or alternatively the sum of the skinfolds. To do that, classic methods require use of a calibrated skinfold caliper and a measuring tape. Several formulas allow the calculation of the amount of body fat, usually expressed as percentage of total mass. Describing in detail the methods and formulas to calculate the amount of fat is beyond the scope of this chapter, but to provide a reference, Jackson and Pollock's article is one of the most commonly cited (1978).

Body composition also can be evaluated by considering the sum of a certain number of skinfolds. This last method, together with the proper measuring technique, is taught by the International Society for the Advancement of Kinanthropometry (ISAK) and adopted by several sport institutes and professional cycling teams.

As reference data, some lean male cyclists have a sum of seven skinfolds (triceps, subscap, biceps, supraspinal, abdominal, front thigh, and medial calf) less than 20 millimeters. But professional male cyclists are often in the 20- to 30-millimeter range. Amateur male cyclists (e.g., U23 cyclists) are normally in the 30- to 40-millimeter range. Martin and colleagues (2001) found that internationally competitive female cyclists are generally between 38 and 51 millimeters (in sum of seven skinfolds), which corresponds to 7 to 12 percent body fat.

In general, with regard to body composition, test results should be used to monitor changes within an individual cyclist longitudinally rather than to compare between cyclists. In fact, elite riders can perform at the highest level with different body composition parameters. Also, specific body composition values may be targeted, depending on the rider's specialty. For example, climbers may benefit from being lightweight, especially when compared with flat-terrain specialists.

Body Size and Air Resistance

The main resistance that cyclists encounter while riding on flat terrain is air resistance (Davies 1980). Air resistance is related to the frontal area of the cyclist, the air density, and the velocity of the cyclist (di Prampero et al. 1979; Heil 2001). For this reason, studies report the frontal area (FA) or the total body surface area (BSA) of cyclists as anthropometric characteristics relevant to cycling performances (Mujika and Padilla 2001; Heil 2005).

The BSA can been calculated with the formula of Du Bois and Du Bois (1916):

$$BSA = 0.007184 \times BM^{0.425} \times H^{0.725}$$

in which BM is the cyclist's body mass (in kilograms) and H is the cyclist's height (in centimeters).

Several methods are used to calculate the FA of cyclists. Padilla and colleagues, assuming that FA is proportional to BSA and basing their estimate on previously published research, calculated FA as corresponding to 18.5 percent of BSA (Olds et al. 1995; Padilla et al. 1999).

Another commonly used method to determine the FA is based on the analysis of frontal pictures, which can be done with real photographs or with digital pictures and computer-based programs (Dorel et al. 2005; Heil 2002). To give a brief summary, frontal photographs of the cyclist and equipment (i.e., helmet, bike, wheels, and so on) are used to calculate the frontal area in pixel^2 using a computer program. Then the height of the front wheel is measured in pixels and used to convert pixels into meters based on a wheel's height of 0.668 meters (700c wheel with 23-millimeter tire). Other valid methods to calculate the FA are described in Debraux et al. (2009).

Modern Anthropometric Measures Relevant to Cycling Performance

More recently, other anthropometric parameters have been considered in the evaluation of cycling performance. Usually these measures require expensive laboratory devices, but valid estimates of these parameters can sometimes be made.

Body Composition

With regard to body composition, the bioelectrical impedance analysis (BIA) technique can be used to estimate body composition (Moon 2013). Bio-impedance devices can be bought for less than $110, but the high-end ones can cost several thousand dollars. BIA devices can be integrated in scales, and different models have different characteristics; for example, they may send the electrical signal from leg to leg, leg to arm, or arm to arm. To date, limited evidence supports the validity of BIA to monitor changes in athlete body composition (Loenneke et al. 2013), despite the fact that BIA is being used to assess body composition. Therefore, further studies comparing BIA equations and methods are needed before BIA can be recommended to track changes in athletes (Moon 2013).

Dual-energy X-ray absorptiometry can be considered a kind of modern gold standard in body composition science. This technique allows researchers to obtain an accurate measurement of a cyclist's lean mass, fat mass, and other important and interesting parameters such as bone density (which is, however, more interesting for health-related reasons than for performance). Knowing these values, in particular muscle mass, allows several investigations that permit a better understanding of the cyclist's physique. As an example, positive correlations have been shown between lower-body lean mass and power output in female road cyclists (Haakonssen et al. 2013). This study highlighted that attempts to reduce body weight that also reduce lower-body lean mass impair relative cycling power unless nonfunctional mass (i.e., fat mass) is also reduced considerably.

Body Shape and Air Resistance

Considering cycling performances on flat terrain, the best indicator of aerodynamic characteristics is the aerodynamic drag area (CdA). The CdA is usually measured in wind tunnels (Garcia-Lopez et al. 2008), but computational fluid dynamics (CFD) analysis has recently been used to evaluate the aerodynamic position of cyclists (Defraeye et al. 2010). CFD is the science that studies fluid flows and the interactions between fluids and surfaces. In the case of cycling, CFD can be used to analyze airflows against the surfaces of the body and bike by estimating aerodynamic characteristics using algorithms. Noticeably, field tests and procedures can validly and reliably measure a cyclist's CdA (Martin et al. 2006; Lim et al. 2011). The validity of the field assessment of the CdA depends on several variables, such as the ability to measure (or control) the weather (i.e., wind speed, air density) and the ability of the cyclist to pedal without changing speed (i.e., zero acceleration) and position on the bike for the whole duration of each measurement (about 200 meters minimum). Since the previously cited papers were published, some practical tools became available to estimate the CdA. For example, a commercially available device can be purchased and mounted on the bike handlebars. The same device measures wind speed and, when connected with a power meter by ANT+, calculates and continuously displays the CdA value on its screen. To date, no studies have validated such a device, but the theory behind the system is sound.

Another option to estimate the CdA using field data is available at no cost. In fact, the open source software Golden Cheetah (http://goldencheetah. org/) has an extension called Aero Lab that allows the user to upload power files and use the so-called virtual elevation method to find the coefficient of rolling resistance and the CdA.

Normative Anthropometric Data in Different Cycling Categories

Every research study about cycling reports in the method section data related to the anthropometric and physiological characteristics of the subjects. The study subjects are often described in detail related to their performance level, training status, and so on, but rarely is the cycling specialty of the subjects reported. To date, few researchers have examined cycling performance with the main aim to describe the cyclists' specialties. This section reports these data.

Anthropometric Characteristics of Male Professional Cyclists

Anthropometric data related to male professional cyclists belonging to different cycling specialties are shown in table 1.1; data are presented as reported in the original research or calculated using the formula mentioned in this chapter. Padilla and colleagues (1999) showed that climbers were significantly lighter than all other cyclists; they also had a higher ratio of frontal area to body mass compared with flat-terrain specialists and time trialists. These results explain the climbers' advantage while riding uphill, as well as their disadvantage in flat terrain. Similarly, other studies found that flat-terrain specialists and time trialists were significantly taller and heavier than climbers (Lucia, Hoyos, and Chicharro 2001; Sallet et al. 2006).

Table 1.1 Anthropometric Characteristics of Professional Male Cyclists

Specialty	Number of subjects	Age (years)	Stature (cm)	Body mass (kg)	BMI (kg/m^2)	BSA (m^2)	FA (m^2)	Source
Climbers	9	25 ± 4	175 ± 7	62.4 ± 4.4	20.4	1.76 ± 0.10	0.33 ± 0.02	Padilla et al. (1999)
Climbers	8	26 ± 1	176 ± 2	64.3 ± 2.2	20.5 ± 0.8	1.79	0.33	Lucia, Hoyos, and Chicharro (2001)
Climbers	24	24 ± 4	179 ± 5	67.0 ± 5.1	21.0	1.84	0.34	Sallet et al. (2006)
Time trialists	4	28 ± 5	181 ± 6	71.2 ± 6.0	21.7	1.91 ± 0.11	0.35 ± 0.02	Padilla et al. (1999)
Time trialists	8	27 ± 1	182 ± 2	72.3 ± 2.3	21.9 ± 0.2	1.92	0.36	Lucia, Hoyos, and Chicharro (2001)
Flat-terrain specialists	5	27 ± 3	186 ± 4	76.2 ± 3.2	22.3	2.00 ± 0.06	0.37 ± 0.01	Padilla et al. (1999)
Flat-terrain specialists	32	24 ± 4	181 ± 5	71.5 ± 5.0	21.9	1.91	0.35	Sallet et al. (2006)
All-terrain riders	6	25 ± 2	180 ± 2	68.0 ± 2.8	21.0	1.87 ± 0.04	0.35 ± 0.01	Padilla et al. (1999)
All-terrain riders	11	28 ± 5	178 ± 3	70.9 ± 3.2	22.4	1.88	0.35	Sallet et al. (2006)
Sprinters	6	27 ± 4	176 ± 3	71.7 ± 1.1	23.1	1.87	0.35	Menaspà et al. (2015)
Sprinters	4	20 ± 3	176 ± 2	67.3 ± 2.5	21.8	1.82	0.34	Sallet et al. (2006)

BMI = body mass index; BSA = body surface area; FA = frontal area.

Data from S. Padilla, I. Mujika, G. Cuesta, and J.J. Goiriena, 1999, "Level ground and uphill cycling ability in professional road cycling," *Medicine & Science in Sports & Exercise* 31(6): 878-885; A. Lucia, J. Hoyos, and J.L. Chicharro, 2001, "Physiology of professional road cycling," *Sports Medicine* 31(5): 325-337; P. Sallet, R. Mathieu, G. Fenech, and G. Baverel, 2006, "Physiological differences of elite and professional road cyclists related to competition level and rider specialization," *Journal of Sports Medicine and Physical Fitness* 46(3): 361-365; and P. Menaspà, M. Quod, D.T. Martin, et al., 2015, "Physical demands of sprinting in professional road cycling," *International Journal of Sports Medicine* 36(13): 1058-1062.

Anthropometric Characteristics of Elite Female and Junior Male Cyclists

To date, the literature related to cycling specialists being part of categories other than male professionals is limited. Impellizzeri and colleagues (2008) described the characteristics of elite female cyclists, and Menaspà and colleagues (2012) focused on junior (i.e., under 19) cyclists. A summary of the data presented in these studies is shown in table 1.2.

Table 1.2 Anthropometric Characteristics of Elite Female and Junior Male Cyclists

Specialty	Number of subjects	Age (years)	Stature (cm)	Body mass (kg)	BMI (kg/m²)	BSA (m²)	FA (m²)	Source
Elite female climbers	12	28 ± 5	167 ± 4	51.8 ± 3.4	18.7	1.57 ± 0.06	0.29 ± 0.01	Impellizzeri et al. (2008)
Elite female time trialists	5	23 ± 5	171 ± 6	61.6 ± 3.1	21.1	1.72 ± 0.07	0.32 ± 0.01	Impellizzeri et al. (2008)
Elite female flat-terrain riders	10	25 ± 3	165 ± 6	58.0 ± 4.6	21.2	1.64 ± 0.09	0.30 ± 0.02	Impellizzeri et al. (2008)
U19 climbers	39	17 ± 0.5	173 ± 5	59.7 ± 1.5	20.0 ± 1.5	1.71	0.32	Menaspà et al. (2012)
U19 flat-terrain riders	46	17 ± 0.7	181 ± 6	70.4 ± 5.5	21.5 ± 1.5	1.90	0.35	Menaspà et al. (2012)
U19 all-terrain riders	22	17 ± 0.7	176 ± 5	64.5 ± 4.2	20.9 ± 1.3	1.79	0.33	Menaspà et al. (2012)
U19 sprinters	25	16.9 ± 0.6	178 ± 4	70.4 ± 4.7	22.2 ± 1.0	1.88	0.35	Menaspà et al. (2012)

BMI = body mass index; BSA = body surface area; FA = frontal area.

Data from F.M. Impellizzeri, T. Ebert, A. Sassi, et al., 2008, "Level ground and uphill cycling ability in elite female mountain bikers and road cyclists," *European Journal of Applied Physiology* 102(3): 335-341; and P. Menaspà, E. Rampinini, A. Bosio, et al., 2012, "Physiological and anthropometric characteristics of junior cyclists of different specialties and performance levels," *Scandinavian Journal of Medicine and Science in Sports* 22(3): 392-398.

Scaling Different Approaches for Different Specialties and Terrain

Diverse competition terrains, or race profiles, require different and specific physiological traits. For this reason, several cycling researchers have shown the importance of scaling the physiological data (e.g., power output or oxygen consumption) to account for the effect of anthropometric characteristics on different race terrains.

Scaling for Uphill Performances

The main resistance that cyclists encounter when riding uphill is gravity. The lower the total mass traveling uphill is, the lower the necessary power output is. For this reason, to understand and describe climbing ability, power data and oxygen consumption are scaled for body weight. Nowadays, general classification (GC) contenders of cycling grand tours (Giro d'Italia, Tour de France, and Vuelta a Éspana) are commonly compared based on their ability to sustain a power output of 6 W/kg. Research has shown, however, that the more appropriate exponent to analyze uphill performance is between 0.79

and 0.91, using, for example, the power output expressed as $W \cdot kg^{-0.79}$ (Jobson et al. 2008). The use of these exponents allows researchers to magnify the differences in performance between climbers and other specialists. Padilla and colleagues (1999) reported a power output at the onset of blood lactate accumulation (OBLA) corresponding to 5.70 ± 0.46 $W \cdot kg^{-1}$ and 13.57 ± 1.14 $W \cdot kg^{-0.79}$ in professional male climbers. Their estimated maximal oxygen consumption ($\dot{V}O_2max$) was 80.9 ± 3.9 $ml \cdot kg^{-1} \cdot min^{-1}$, significantly higher than that of flat-terrain specialists (Padilla et al. 1999).

In elite female cyclists, a power output of 4.9 ± 0.5 W/kg was reported for the intensity corresponding to the respiratory compensation point (RCP). The $\dot{V}O_2max$ was 64.8 ± 2.6 $ml \cdot kg^{-1} \cdot min^{-1}$, significantly higher when compared with that of flat-terrain specialists (Impellizzeri et al. 2008).

Menaspà and colleagues (2012) reported an RCP power output of 4.8 ± 0.5 W/kg and a $\dot{V}O_2max$ of 67.5 ± 5.0 $ml \cdot kg^{-1} \cdot min^{-1}$ in junior male climbers, significantly higher than those found in flat-terrain specialists and sprinters.

The data in these studies are scaled per the cyclist's body weight, but modeling theories suggest that the total mass of cyclist plus bike should be considered (di Prampero et al. 1979). Indeed, some aspects should be considered when deciding how to scale the physiological parameters, such as the effect of the equipment weight on different cyclists. For reasons related to cycling rules, the equipment of cyclists of different sizes could potentially have similar weight (i.e., the Union Cycliste Internationale established the minimum weight for bikes, regardless of body size). In practical terms, for a light cyclist the equipment could represent more than 15 percent of his or her body mass; for a heavy cyclist, equipment could correspond to 10 percent or less of his or her body mass. This scenario clearly describes a disadvantage for small climbers that should be taken into account when evaluating their physiological parameters.

Scaling for Flat-Terrain Performances

Performances on flat terrain are often compared based on simple power output (W), but scaling for body mass with an exponent of 0.32 is recommended (Swain et al. 1987; Nevill et al. 2006). Professional male flat-terrain specialists have been able to produce 417 ± 45 W, or 104.1 ± 10.3 $W \cdot kg^{-0.32}$ at their OBLA (Padilla et al. 1999). In elite female cyclists, Impellizzeri and colleagues (2008) reported a power output of 247 ± 24 W, or 67.4 ± 5.7 $W \cdot kg^{-0.32}$ at the RCP for flat-terrain specialists.

Scaling for Time Trials and Sprints

Despite the idea that 0.32 is the commonly suggested exponent to scale physiological parameters when evaluating performances on flat terrain, when it comes to time trials or sprints, because of the exceptionally high speeds, the preferred method is to scale for frontal area or coefficient of drag, values more closely related to the cyclist's aerodynamic characteristics. As an example, studies related to the hour record have examined this unique performance considering the FA and the coefficient of drag of the contenders (Padilla et al. 2000; Bassett et al. 1999). Similarly, studies analyzing cycling road sprints have considered FA and CdA. Martin, Davidson, and Pardyjak (2007) used a forward integration model to analyze various road sprint scenarios. For example, the authors compared the effect of sprinting seated versus sprinting out of the saddle on power output (i.e., higher power when sprinting out of the saddle) and aerodynamics (i.e., lower CdA when sprinting seated). In that case, the seated sprinter would have won because the increase in power of the opponent didn't compensate for the increase in CdA (i.e., lower speed). In a different study examining the sprint performances of a professional and an under 23 (U23) cyclist, their power outputs were scaled per FA. The sprinters' peak power was 1,370 ± 51 and 1,318 ± 60 W; peak power was 3,098 ± 116 and 3,246 ± 148 W · m^{-2} for the professional and U23 cyclist, respectively.

Applying the Science

A better understanding of the distinctive characteristics of cyclists with different specializations allows researchers to evaluate their performances with ecological validity. In research, ecological validity means that the study results must be relevant for the real world to which they are related. In practical terms, to evaluate and compare laboratory performances of two or more cyclists, the best way to proceed is to use the appropriate scaling factor, according to the kind of performance of interest. For example, while comparing sprinters, the ratio of maximal power to frontal area could be used instead of simply relying on maximal power data. Similarly, to compare climbers, the threshold power output scaled by total mass (cyclist plus equipment) raised to 0.79 would ideally be used.

Also, because of the physiological differences among cyclists of different specialties, they should be compared within their own specialty groups to avoid a misinterpretation of laboratory test evaluation. As an example, a climber might be identified as a good cyclist because his relative $\dot{V}O_2$max is fairly high, but he could be below the average within his specialty group. On the other hand, a sprinter's ability could be underestimated based on mean aerobic data, but he could be within the sprinter specialty normative data. Avoiding these common errors is fundamental to preserving and guaranteeing the right support to cyclists who seem to have a predisposition to excel in their specialties.

The observations presented in this chapter should be taken into account by professionals, coaches, and cyclists themselves when analyzing laboratory and field data related to cyclists with different specializations.

CHAPTER **2**

Cycling Physiology and Genetics

—Stephen S. Cheung

The body is an incredibly complex engine, which explains why scientists are still busily exploring its inner workings after centuries of study. Great advances in genetic technology and understanding have opened new avenues for exploration of how humans respond to exercise. But the diffi- culty of piecing together genetic changes within the gene or chromosome to whole-body responses remains a challenge to overcome. In addition, the human body is incredibly versatile in the range of activities that it is capable of, so the primary mechanisms that limit exercise capacity may be different for different types of exercise. For example, the physical demands of a single 200-meter sprint on the track are quite different from those of a road sprint in the finale of the Milan–San Remo after nearly 300 kilometers of riding. Similarly, the hard efforts of a 60-minute cyclocross race, with its repeated accelerations from low speeds, can be quite different from the short, hard accelerations from high speed involved in a 60-minute road criterium, which in turn are drastically different from the steady power output required in a 40K time trial.

Compared with other animals, humans are not the fastest in a sprint, nor are they the strongest in pure muscle strength. The trump card for *homo sapiens* is being proficient at a wide variety of exercise demands. For example, cheetahs can outrun humans over short distances, but humans can easily outrun cheetahs and many predator animals over moderate distances or longer. Indeed, some anthropologists believe that the distinguishing char- acteristic that drove much of human evolution is not necessarily our upright posture or even walking, but rather the evolutionary pressure presented by endurance running to support a hunter–gatherer existence or the prolonged tracking of game (Bramble and Lieberman 2004). Furthermore, in the process of such migrations to follow food sources, humans have become uniquely

Portions of this chapter were previously published in *Cutting-Edge Cycling* by H. Allen and S.S. Cheung, 2012 (Champaign, IL: Human Kinetics), pp. 15-37.

adapted—through both physiological and behavioral responses—across a diverse range of environments on the planet, from deserts to the tropics through to the Arctic and high altitudes (Cheung 2010).

As scientific research illuminates the complexity of the body and its response to exercise and training, more questions are raised and further ideas about how to extend the limits of human potential are developed. Therefore, even a nonelite athlete interested in greater understanding and improved training cannot stick with simple definitions and generalizations when it comes to exercise physiology and the underlying mechanisms of training. Further complicating the search for meaningful information is the confusing jargon and morass of terminology, often used inaccurately by both scientists and coaches. Therefore, this chapter distills some of the basic principles in exercise science, defines the major systems and terminology, and discusses the latest concepts about what limits exercise capacity. It finishes with a look at the new wave of genetic insight into exercise performance and explores the limits of genetics as a predictive tool for identifying elite athletes.

Energy Production

The end goal of energy metabolism within the body is to produce adenosine triphosphate (ATP), which is the common currency of energy used throughout the entire body for all functions. The basic adenosine molecule can have one (adenosine monophosphate or AMP), two (adenosine diphosphate or ADP), or three (ATP) phosphates attached to it. Each of the three phosphates is attached in series to adenosine and is a store of energy. Most commonly, only the third phosphate bond is broken, and the energy stored within that bond is released to provide energy to the cell, resulting in ADP and a phosphate as by-products.

To enable varied exercise from all-out sprints to the finish line through to riding a century, the human body uses three different but interrelated energy metabolic systems to generate ATP: the alactic or phosphocreatine (ATP–PC) system, anaerobic glycolysis, and aerobic metabolism (figure 2.1).

ATP–PC System

Although it is the endpoint currency of energy, ATP is not stored in large quantities within a cell, possibly because of its relatively large size compared with glycogen and fat. Therefore, the body needs a system of replenishing ATP as quickly as possible for high-intensity efforts, like the final sprint for a mountaintop or the finish line. The ATP–PC system consists of energy stored within the phosphocreatine (PC) molecule, analogous to the high-energy bonds within the ATP. Phosphocreatine acts as an initial reservoir of accessible energy. As ATP becomes depleted to ADP (adenosine diphosphate), PC is broken down, and that released energy is then used to bind phosphate to ADP, turning it back to ATP again. The advantage of PC is that release of energy occurs rapidly with a minimum of biochemical steps. Thus, ATP

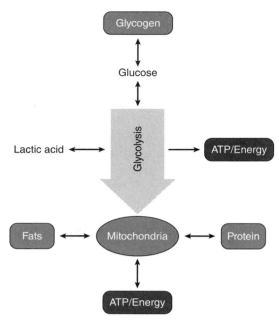

▶ **Figure 2.1** Interrelationships between energy systems.

Reprinted, by permission, from H. Allen and S.S. Cheung, Cutting-edge Cycling (Champaign, IL: Human Kinetics), 17.

levels within the muscles are fairly well preserved even during intense exercise in the time before ATP becomes readily available from glycolysis (explained in the next section). Training this system can help a cyclist extend top-end sprint speed from a short 50- to 100-meter burst to a distance up to 300 meters, greatly expanding his or her options in the finale of a race. This ability is the forte of sprinters such as Alessandro Petacchi and Mario Cipollini, who can simply outdrag their competitors to the line by keeping their speed as others fade.

The role of phosphocreatine in maintaining ATP levels during brief, intense exercise has resulted in a heavy emphasis and research on the role of creatine supplementation for resistance training and power sports such as weightlifting, American football, and many field events in athletics. Although power-based cyclists such as track sprinters may gain some advantage, the benefits of creatine supplementation for endurance cyclists is unproven, except possibly during periods of heavy resistance training (Bemben and Lamont 2005).

Anaerobic Glycolysis

Glycogen is the primary storage form of carbohydrate in the body. About 500 grams or 2,000 kilocalories are stored in the muscles and liver. This fuel is broken down for energy by both anaerobic and aerobic metabolism. Note that there is no difference in how the body treats carbohydrate when it is first broken down in a muscle. The common initial pathway is anaerobic glycolysis. In this glycolytic ("glucose breakdown") pathway to energy production, glucose or glycogen is initially broken down in the muscles without the use of oxygen (*anaerobic* means "without oxygen"). If sufficient oxygen is available to the muscle, carbohydrate can then proceed onward to aerobic (or "with oxygen") metabolism. Glycolysis of one molecule of glucose results in only two molecules of ATP. The advantage of this system, however, is that a great deal of glucose can be processed rapidly and, most important, without oxygen. This advantage is important for cyclists, because many of the efforts in cycling are short and intense. A cyclist doing a hill effort of 30 seconds to 2 minutes taxes the anaerobic system, and some people have better anaerobic systems than others. The riders with the strongest anaerobic systems will excel in races such as a criterium with a hill and six turns in it, a hard-paced breakaway in which the pulls at the front are short, and in events like cyclocross.

As related to exercise physiology, keep in mind several important points concerning glycolysis:

• **As the name implies, only carbohydrate is metabolized through glycolysis**. In contrast, fat and protein can only be converted to ATP aerobically with oxygen present. Thus, when exercising at high intensity when oxygen supply to the muscles is limited, a cyclist's body relies heavily on the limited stores of carbohydrate for energy. For that reason, among others, cyclists want to protect their limited glycogen stores during long rides or races, both by not going hard until necessary and by making sure they consume carbohydrate from early on in the ride.

• **Glycolysis takes place in both type I (slow-twitch) and type II (fast-twitch) muscle fibers, although type II fibers have higher glycolytic capacity**. The main difference between fast- and slow-twitch fibers is the degree of specialization rather than one muscle type being incapable of a particular metabolic step. For example, a top-flight sprinter is still able to climb and an elite climber is capable of an occasional sprint. Neither may be happy about it, but they can still do it!

• **The main by-product of glycolysis is lactic acid (also called lactate)**. Lactate is not a dead end, or "waste," product. When sufficient oxygen again becomes available, the lactate is converted back to pyruvate and can then continue to aerobic metabolism.

Improving the anaerobic system is a key part of training in cycling because cyclists will be challenged anaerobically many times in group rides, races, and events.

Aerobic Metabolism

With aerobic metabolism, the conversion of fuel for energy becomes much more efficient because carbohydrate can be taken beyond the initial glycolysis and be fully broken down to release more energy. In addition, the large supply of fat and the smaller supply of protein can also be converted to energy aerobically. Compared with glycolysis, aerobic metabolism is much more efficient in terms of energy return; 34 additional ATP molecules are created compared with the 2 created with glycolysis alone. A molecule of fat can produce even greater amounts of ATP than a carbohydrate molecule can. Aerobic metabolism and the burning of fat remain an important source of energy regardless of cycling speed or effort, so aerobic metabolism does not turn off and the body does not completely switch over to anaerobic metabolism. What does change, at high intensity, is how much extra anaerobic energy production is needed to meet the energy demand that aerobic metabolism alone cannot produce.

One gram of carbohydrate yields approximately 4 kilocalories of energy, whereas each gram of fat yields approximately 9 kilocalories, because of the higher number of carbon bonds within fat. This higher energy density explains why fat is a preferred fuel storage form within the body. In a lean male athlete of 70 kilograms and 5 percent body fat, 3.5 kilograms of fat, or theoretically 31,500 kilocalories of energy, may be used for aerobic metabolism. Although obviously the cyclist cannot use all of this and survive, this energy reservoir is much larger than the small supply of carbohydrate stored as glycogen. Another consideration to keep in mind with fuel use in the body is that the brain can only use carbohydrate for energy, not fat or protein. A cyclist who depletes her or his glycogen stores not only will "hit the wall" and run low on energy but also may experience impairment of mental functioning and mood as the carbohydrate supply becomes too low. Thus, keeping carbohydrate reserves as high as possible is critically important to cyclists. To achieve this, cyclists should take in carbohydrate before exercise, ingest carbohydrate early in a ride to minimize the amount of glycogen use, and start the refueling and recovery process as soon as possible after finishing a ride to prepare for the next day's ride.

Aerobic metabolism is the bedrock of cycling fitness, whether for a century rider or a points race rider on the track. When we talk about riders with big engines, what we are really saying is that they have extremely well-developed aerobic metabolic systems. Think of it this way: The stronger a cyclist's aerobic energy system is, especially his or her fat metabolism, the less reliant the cyclist will be on carbohydrate use while riding at a set workload (e.g., 200 watts) early in a race. Therefore, the cyclist can ride longer at that workload before running out of glycogen and will have more carbohydrate available for the hard attacks that require her or him to exceed that workload at the end of a race. In day-to-day training, a stronger aerobic metabolism becomes the critical foundation for improving anaerobic capacity because it permits the cyclist to do more or harder intervals. Therefore, if a cyclist can do just one thing to improve in cycling, he or she should train to improve the body's aerobic system and its efficiency at using fat, carbohydrate, and protein as fuel. Because aerobic metabolism relies on oxygen availability, an athlete's aerobic capacity can be quantified relatively simply by measuring the rate of maximal oxygen consumption, or $\dot{V}O_2$max, in the body.

Interplay Among Energy Systems

Some exercise physiology textbooks present a graph outlining the relative dominance of different metabolic pathways for events ranging from a 200-meter track sprint through a century ride. Often, these figures unintentionally give the mistaken notion that only one metabolic pathway is used at a time, implying that ATP–PC stops after 15 seconds, glycolysis begins at 15 seconds and ends at 3 minutes, and aerobic metabolism kicks in after that. This notion is false. The critical concept to take from this discussion about the various metabolic pathways is that none of them works in isolation. Rather, energy for movement is simultaneously derived from all three sources, and the relative dominance of each system depends on exercise intensity (figure 2.2). Therefore, different training workouts emphasize different metabolic systems, but all systems are trained to some extent. When a cyclist performs a $\dot{V}O_2$max interval for 5 minutes, she or he primarily taxes the aerobic system but uses the ATP–PC system in the initial sprint to start the effort. Then when a cyclist digs deep to push over the hill, he or she maxes out the anaerobic glycolysis system. Overall, however, the aerobic system got the most stress and should respond by improving, and because cycling is primarily an endurance sport, the primary emphasis is to maximize aerobic capacity. Therefore, the bulk of a well-designed training program features large doses of long rides and relatively long intervals to stress the aerobic system, supplemented with smaller doses of hard group rides and races with some purpose.

Energy Definitions

Cycling is a sport that relies on equipment, and its technocentric nature is complemented by the jargon used to describe human physiology. People commonly toss around terms such as watts, calories, and $\dot{V}O_2$max. Unfortunately, many terms are used without an intrinsic understanding of what they mean, so a great deal of confusion can arise. Moreover, some terms are used interchangeably, further hindering proper communication. This section aims to clarify the meanings of some commonly used terminology and provide some generally accepted definitions.

Units of Energy

With the development and popularization of portable power monitors, the measurement of wattage is steadily becoming the dominant metric of performance and training, taking over from heart rate, distance, speed, or volume measures. But what does wattage actually mean in terms of energy? In sport nutrition especially, the unit *kilocalorie* remains dominant. The following are some of the critical definitions of variables used in quantifying energy:

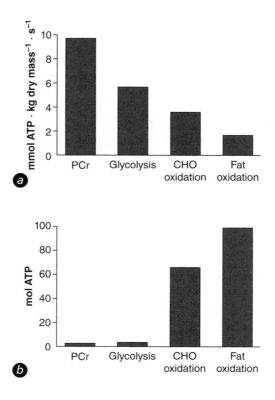

▶ **Figure 2.2**   Characteristics of different energy systems

Reprinted, by permission, from W.L. Kenney, J.H. Wilmore, and D.L. Costill, 2015, Physiology of sport and exercise, 6th ed. (Champaign, IL: Human Kinetics), 68.

• **Joule**. The metric standard unit of energy is a joule (J), which is often also quantified in kilojoules (kJ), or 1,000 joules. This unit, kilojoule, is the value also seen on power monitors, quantifying how much absolute mechanical work is performed. Because mechanical work is the actual physical load that is being imposed on the body, it can be a more accurate method of quantifying training compared with relatively crude methods such as distance or time.

• **Watt**. Wattage is a rate of energy production, and 1 watt (W) equals 1 joule per second. Therefore, a cyclist moving at 200 watts is generating 200 joules of mechanical energy each second (1 kilojoule every 5 seconds, or 720 kilojoules every hour). Although the mechanical energy is accurately quantified using such systems, power monitors do not quantify the overall energy expenditure by the body because the body is not 100 percent efficient in metabolically converting the energy stored in carbohydrate, lipids, and protein into mechanical energy. Rather, like the combustion engine in a car, the vast majority is converted to heat energy, such that the human body is only 20 to 25 percent efficient. Therefore, assuming 25 percent efficiency, to generate the 720 kilojoules of mechanical energy mentioned earlier, the body has to convert approximately three times that much, or 2,160 kilojoules of additional heat energy, for a total metabolic requirement of 2,880 kilojoules for that hour of exercise.

• **Calorie**. A calorie (cal) is an alternative unit of energy to the joule and is defined as the energy required to increase the temperature of 1 gram of water by 1 degree Celsius (C). As with joules, it can be quantified in units of 1,000 (1 kilocalorie), and kilojoules or kilocalories are the typical units of energy seen on food labels. Many exercise machines and heart rate monitor systems indirectly calculate energy expenditure in kilocalories using an algorithm that incorporates heart rate, body mass, and exercise duration. Note that although the algorithms being used are sophisticated and are constantly improving, they remain indirect estimates that are prone to error.

Frustration can arise from the fact that energy units from power monitors (W and kJ) are often not the same as those used in nutrition (kcal), making it difficult to match energy expenditure during workouts with adequate intake of food calories to achieve nutritional goals. But the conversion between the two units can be roughly assumed to work out to a 1:1 ratio because the relationship between the two is a constant ratio in which 1 kilocalorie equals 4.17 kilojoules. But if we assume that the body is 25 percent efficient in converting energy stored in nutrients to mechanical power, then we first need to multiply our mechanical energy production from the power monitor by 4 before dividing by 4.17 to obtain the number of kilocalories. Let's calculate an example:

$$200 \text{ W effort for } 1 \text{ h} = 200 \text{ J/s} \times 3{,}600 \text{ s} = 720{,}000 \text{ J} = 720 \text{ kJ}$$

$$720 \text{ kJ} \times 4 = 2{,}880 \text{ kJ total energy expenditure}$$

$$2{,}880 \text{ kJ} / 4.17 \text{ kJ/kcal} = 690.6 \text{ kcal}$$

The conversion between kilojoules and kilocalories is important to know if the cyclist is using a power meter that measures energy production in kilojoules or a heart rate monitor that calculates energy expenditure in kilocalories. The cyclist can see how much energy was burned and use that as a guide to how much he or she should eat after a ride. Many cyclists even use the kilojoule data from their power meters or the kilocalorie data from their heart rate monitors to build nutrition protocols for their events based on the energy burned along the way. The data can serve as a reminder to eat regularly during the next event or long ride to prevent running low on fuel and bonking. Of course, for those who live where food labels are provided in kilojoules (essentially anywhere other than the United States or United Kingdom), the conversion to kilocalories is unnecessary; they can simply multiply total mechanical power for a workout by four to obtain a good estimate of how much food energy has been consumed. Remember, though, that this factor of four is a general assumption and may differ across individuals and with training. The only way to get an accurate conversion factor is to do a specialized lab-based test.

Maximal Oxygen Consumption Terminology

Many athletes and coaches consider the measure of maximal aerobic capacity—or $\dot{V}O_2$max—as the gold standard test for endurance athletes. The primary purpose of quantifying this measure is to provide a good expression of the cyclist's ability to generate ATP through aerobic metabolic pathways. One important consideration is that $\dot{V}O_2$max values, as with all physiological measures of fitness, are sport specific and will differ for running, swimming, or Nordic skiing. $\dot{V}O_2$max values are typically higher for running and Nordic skiing because of the weight-bearing nature of those activities and the larger muscle mass involved. In contrast, the buoyant nature of water typically results in lower $\dot{V}O_2$max values despite the large muscle mass used. Therefore, multisport athletes need to have sport-specific fitness tests and training zones.

Maximal oxygen consumption can be quantified in a variety of ways:

• **Nonnormalized $\dot{V}O_2$max or $\dot{V}O_2$peak**. This value is the highest absolute amount of oxygen that the body can process and is generally expressed in liters per minute (L/min). This measure is the simplest and most basic way of presenting oxygen uptake capacity because it doesn't take into account any fluctuations in body weight between tests.

• **Normalized to body mass**. This value is the highest oxygen uptake during the exercise test normalized to body weight in kilograms, or milliliters per kilogram per minute ($ml \cdot kg^{-1} \cdot min^{-1}$). Thus, this number provides a better basis for comparison between two riders of different sizes and is the value that we most commonly talk about when referring to $\dot{V}O_2$max. Note that this simple division doesn't differentiate between muscle (high metabolism) and fat (minimal metabolism), and fat can be thought of as essentially dead weight. Therefore, higher $\dot{V}O_2$max values can be achieved either by increasing aerobic capacity or by decreasing body mass and fat. For example, a 70-kilogram rider with a $\dot{V}O_2$max of 4.2 L/min has a normalized value of 60 $ml \cdot kg^{-1} \cdot min^{-1}$. If he drops 2 kilograms to 68 kilograms yet maintains an oxygen uptake of 4.2 L/min, his normalized $\dot{V}O_2$max increases to 61.8 $ml \cdot kg^{-1} \cdot min^{-1}$. For that reason many pro cyclists are obsessed with dropping weight before Grand Tours and assume that their power output is not affected by the weight loss.

• **Normalized to lean body mass**. To remove the dead weight factor resulting from body fat, $\dot{V}O_2$max is sometimes normalized to lean body mass to provide a better indicator of the actual aerobic capacity of the muscles.

Genetic Factors

A classic question in sport is whether nature or nurture dominates in the making of an elite athlete, and the next frontier for exercise physiology may be in unraveling the complex genetic underpinnings of performance (Bouchard 1983). Another aspect of research into the role of genetics in sports is understanding the role of epigenetic factors, namely the expression of genetic information (genotype) into actual physical characteristics (phenotype) along with the heritability of such characteristics (Ehlert, Simon, and Moser 2013). Since the Human Genome Project first sequenced the entire human DNA, it has become exponentially easier technically to perform genetic profiling, both for clinical reasons and medical screening and for interested individuals in general. Advances in stem cell research and treatments have also opened the potential to manipulate the genome, raising the prospect of gene doping.

Out of the vast array of genes encoded in our chromosomes and their complex interactions, a single gene, or even a suite of genes, is highly unlikely to be dominant in sport performance to the exclusion of other genes or environmental factors (Rupert 2003). Nevertheless, recent interest has focused on two genetic variants, the angiotensin I-converting enzyme (ACE I/D) and the α-actinin-3 (ACTN3) R577X gene, which may be associated with either endurance or power performance, respectively (MacArthur and North 2005). The ACTN3 protein is primarily expressed in the sarcomere of type II (fast-twitch) muscle fibers. Although a strong association is present between ACE activity level and improved exercise performance or capacity across a variety of populations, the exact mechanism by which this occurs, or whether ACE is simply a coincidental marker, remains unclear (Puthucheary et al. 2011). Furthermore, each gene is polymorphic and occurs in multiple forms in the body with minor variations in composition. In a meta-analysis of 25 (ACE) and 23 (ACTN3 R577X) papers studying these gene variants and athletic performance (Ma et al. 2013), the ACE II genotype appeared to have a stronger association with endurance performance—but not power performance—than the D genotype, with a stronger association in Caucasians but no differences across sex. For the ACTN gene, the R genotype was highly associated with improved performance in power sports, with no differences across sex or ethnicity. Note, however, that such polymorphic changes are not consistently evident across all published studies. For example, elite swimmers had strong associations with different ACE forms, but the dominant forms were different between Caucasians and Asians (Wang et al. 2013). Furthermore, this same study found no association in ACTN3 R557X with swimming status in either group.

Elite performance likely includes not just a high absolute ceiling for endurance or power, as implied by this discussion, but also a high capacity for responding to training and recovering from training. A seminal study suggesting a genetic linkage to individual responsiveness to training was done as part of the HERITAGE Family Study, a long-term tracking study investigating the familial heritability of many health characteristics. As part of the study, 481 sedentary Caucasians from 98 families were tested for cycling $\dot{V}O_2max$ before and following 20 weeks of aerobic training (Bouchard et al. 1999). $\dot{V}O_2max$ increased by a mean of about 400 ml/min, but with very high variability ranging from no change to greater than 1 L/min improvement. Notably, between-family variance in response was more

Maximal Oxygen Uptake as a Performance Predictor

Is $\dot{V}O_2$max the single best predictor of endurance sport performance? Can any method predict who will be a top cyclist based on lab or field test scores? The consensus is that test scores are a broad indicator or starting point at best. Certainly, a higher $\dot{V}O_2$max is rarely a bad thing to have, and it can provide some indication of form and potential. For example, without a minimum value in at least the mid- to high 60s for $\dot{V}O_2$max in milliliters per kilogram per minute, a rider should probably not be seriously considering a professional cycling career. Beyond a basic threshold standard of $\dot{V}O_2$max, higher aerobic capacity loses its predictive ability for elite performance, as many other physical factors (e.g., recovery capacity, gross efficiency, genetics) and nonphysical factors (e.g., psychological, support network, access to opportunities) become dominant.

Testing is an important way to monitor progress, but comparing cyclists with each other is not simple and often not appropriate. Every cyclist brings a unique background and a distinctive set of physical and mental strengths and weaknesses. Therefore, regardless of racing category, $\dot{V}O_2$max and other lab-based test measures such as lactate threshold testing are more of an indirect suggestion of ability or a threshold indicator than an actual predictor of success. Think of them as the equivalent of a minimum test score needed to be admitted to a university. That is, although an applicant needs to have a particular test score even to apply to a top-level university, having the highest test score doesn't mean that she or he will become valedictorian of the graduating class after arriving on campus. Also, although $\dot{V}O_2$max stays fairly stable for a cyclist over the course of a season of training, the functional threshold power, or the highest average power that the cyclist can sustain over an hour, can change dramatically with the phases and peaks of training (see figure 2.3). Young cyclists who aspire to be pros should probably get a $\dot{V}O_2$max test to determine whether professional cycling could become a reality for them or whether golf might be a better sport. Fortunately for cyclists, the real measure of performance comes out on the open road or trail, and the strongest, smartest, and luckiest generally win.

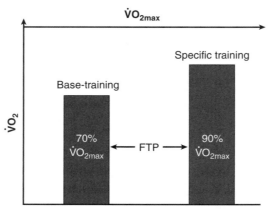

▶ **Figure 2.3** Relative changes in $\dot{V}O_2$max and functional threshold power (FTP) with training.

Reprinted, by permission, from H. Allen and S.S. Cheung, Cutting-edge Cycling (Champaign, IL: Human Kinetics), 26.

than 2.5 times greater than within-family response. Modeling suggested that responsiveness to training had a heritability index of 47 percent and that this effect was dominated by maternal transmission. Such studies also demonstrate the critical need for individualized training programs to accommodate such variability in capacity for training. Furthermore, enhanced recovery from hard training and competition is a hallmark of elite athletes, yet no analogous studies have explored either the genetic basis of athletic recovery or its heritability. Finally, although the genetic bases for many diseases are now being uncovered, minimal research exists on genetic predisposition to injury, both on a micro level at the cell or a more macro level of tissues such as the muscle or bone or through hormonal responses.

Discussion into genetics and athletic development, as with many aspects of genetics research in general, is heavily layered with ethical overtones and implications. At one extreme is the potential for countries and sporting organizations to engage in preferential selection of athletes for teams and provide enhanced training opportunities based on genetic profiling. This approach could be especially problematic if genetic information completely replaces traditional talent identification and selection. Such self-selection and streaming is already a possibility for parents; commercial genetic testing companies offer to provide recommendations on whether a child might be better specialized toward power- or endurance-based sports. Ultimately, the presence or prevalence of particular genetic patterns, even if they are indeed associated with improvements in particular aspects relevant to sport performance, cannot be considered predictive at this stage, if ever (Guth and Roth 2013). Beyond selection, an additional ethical extreme is the potential for genetic "doping" through the manipulation of genes in adults all the way through to *in utero* to produce desired performance.

Applying the Science

A sound understanding of basic exercise physiology as it relates to metabolism and energy dynamics can go a long way toward advancing a cyclist's appreciation of the various body systems at work during cycling. Even though we may not be able to alter genetic profile or makeup, cyclists and coaches should understand how genetics influence physiology so that they can know how to individualize training and nutrition. Such information is important if a cyclist is to be able to interpret the numerous claims and counterclaims out there among scientists, coaches, and companies about what works and what does not work when it comes to training and sport science. The important advice here is not to be afraid of the technical jargon of scientific literature but rather to use the basic principles in this chapter to dig deeper and examine the underlying scientific rationale and evidence for and against different training ideas. Therefore, this chapter sets the stage for subsequent chapters that examine various aspects of cycling science.

PART

II

The Bike

CHAPTER 3

Bicycle Design

—Larry Ruff

In most cases, bicycle design has been driven by the requirements of its application. Although this and the following chapter focus on road-racing bicycle frame design, some mention is also made of other competitive disciplines.

Road Bicycles

Road bicycle design has the longest history and in many cases has been driven by the requirements of competition. The modern road bicycle is a direct descendent of the Rover safety bicycle of 1886. Although the Rover did not have a diamond frame geometry, it had two equal-size wheels, chain drive from a crank to the rear wheel, and handlebars directly connected to a steerable front fork (Pridmore and Hurd 1995). From the Rover, road bicycle frames evolved in terms of geometry, materials, and joining methods.

One of the first bicycles to resemble a modern road bicycle was the Automoto Tour de France bicycle of 1926 (Heine and Praderes 2008). It had a lugged steel diamond frame of traditional geometry, drop handlebars, toe clips and straps, a rear caliper brake, but not derailleur gearing. Lugged steel frame construction involves inserting mitered frame tubes into lugs (couplings) (figure 3.1) and bonding them together using silver solder or brass.

An early derailleur geared bicycle was the Reyhand (Heine and Praderes 2005). It also had a diamond frame, but in this case it was fillet brazed. Fillet brazing involves mitering the frame tubes and then joining them together using brass and heat. The process results in large stress-distributing fillets. The Reyhand had front and rear caliper brakes, drop handlebars, toe clips and straps, and four-speed derailleur gearing.

Two early aluminum road frames were the 1950 Barra, which used welded construction, and the 1951 Caminargent, which used lugged construction in which the tubes were clamped into the lugs (Heine and Praderes 2005).

During the 1950s and 1960s higher quality road frames used lugged steel construction. The tubing was seamless butted alloy steel, such as Reynolds

▶ **Figure 3.1**   Frame lugs.

Larry Ruff

531 (Reynolds Tube Company 1972). In butted tubing the wall thickness is greater at the ends than it is in the center. This design decreases weight while providing strength at the more highly stressed tube ends. Most reduction in bicycle weight resulted from the increased use of alloy components. One of the most popular road bikes of the 1960s and 1970s was the Schwinn Paramount. The Paramount frame was built in Chicago from Reynolds 531 butted alloy steel tubing and Nervex lugs. Nervex lugs were a French lug similar to those in figure 3.1. The frames were silver soldered at approximately 1,100 degrees Fahrenheit (~593 degrees Celsius), a lower-temperature process than brazing, which requires at least 1,400 degrees Fahrenheit (760 degrees Celsius). This method made the frames less prone to failure.

During the bike boom of the 1970s, designers started investigating the use of other materials besides steel to construct frames. Although aluminum had been used by some specialty builders before this time, it now began to see more widespread use. The Italian Alan frame circa 1973 was a bonded frame made up of aluminum lugs and tubes. Gary Klein developed a welded oversize aluminum tube frame at MIT in 1973 and started producing them commercially after graduation. The Teledyne Titan, circa 1973, was one of the first titanium frames. It used welded construction

The Exxon Graftek, circa 1975, was one of the first frames to use carbon fiber in its construction. It was constructed of carbon and epoxy wrapped aluminum tubes bonded into stainless steel lugs (Exxon Graftek 1977). The Raleigh U.S. Cycling Team pursuit frame (figure 3.2) from the mid-1980s was of welded aluminum construction with a carbon fiber fairing for the rear wheel. The carbon fiber did add some structure to the seat tube.

The 1992 Schwinn Paramount (figure 3.3) was a complete carbon fiber frame with aluminum dropouts and aluminum sleeves for the seat post, head tube, and bottom bracket.

▶ **Figure 3.2**   U.S. Cycling Team pursuit frame.

Larry Ruff

▶ **Figure 3.3**   1992 Schwinn Paramount.

Larry Ruff

The evolution of the road bicycle frame has been driven by the demand for improved performance and reduced weight. The use of steel, aluminum, titanium, and finally carbon fiber in the frame is a result of this demand. The development of methods to manipulate the shape of the tubes is another result. Materials and frame geometry are discussed in more detail in chapter 4.

Although terminology may vary, the following is a list of some of the common categories of road bikes and the differences between them based on use and geometry.

Conventional road bikes usually have a frame with a horizontal top tube.

Compact road bikes usually have a frame design in which the top tube slopes down, thus requiring an extended seat post.

Endurance road bikes use a frame design in which the head tube is extended to provide a more upright riding position.

Time trial bike and triathlon bikes are designed to provide a more aerodynamic riding position and better airflow over the frame. Frame design and riding position may vary if the bike is to be used for time trials in internationally sanctioned events.

Track bikes use a fixed gear for events on a closed track and usually have a short wheelbase and a high bottom bracket.

Cyclocross bikes are designed for events ridden over a loop consisting of pavement, dirt, grass, and obstacles that have to be ridden or climbed over. Frames are often designed to be more robust and have a higher bottom bracket for better clearance over obstacles. They are also designed to accommodate wider tires.

Gravel or adventure bikes are designed for extreme road conditions. They are similar to cyclocross bikes in that they are more robust and can run wider tires, but the bottom bracket height is lower to provide better stability.

Touring bikes are designed to handle heavy loads. The frame is strong and stable and has a long wheelbase.

Some overlap can occur between some of the bicycle types described here. For example, a cyclocross bike could have compact geometry.

Mountain Bikes

Mountain bikes arrived on the cycling scene in the late 1970s and evolved from the use of balloon tire cruiser bicycles for off-road riding. The original mountain bikes had no suspension and had geometry similar to the cruisers originally used. Mountain bikes now come in a wide range of styles including rigid (no front or rear suspension), hardtail (front suspension only), and full suspension (front and rear suspension). Suspension design alone could fill a book. The designations and travel ranges listed here can differ between manufacturers. The bikes have various subcategories based on suspension travel including cross-country (1 to 4 inches [2.5 to 10.2 cm] travel), trail or all-mountain (4 to 7 inches [10.2 to 17.8 cm] travel), and downhill (8 to 12 inches [20.3 to 30.5 cm] travel).

Rigid, hardtail, and full-suspension mountain bikes can be found in various wheel sizes including 20 inch (50.8 cm), 24 inch (61.0 cm), 26 inch (66.0 cm), 650b (27.5 inch), and 29 inch (700c). A more recent wheel and frame variation, the fat bike, uses tires 4 to 5 inches (10.2 to 12.7 cm) wide. Originally developed for riding on snow, this style of mountain bike is now ridden all year on all types of surfaces.

Trials are a special subset of mountain bikes that are used for low-speed obstacle course riding. These bikes usually have a trials-specific frame design, including a high bottom bracket and no seat, and they come in two main categories: stock (26-inch [66.0 cm] wheel) and modified (20-inch [50.8 cm] wheel).

BMX Bikes

BMX has a wide range of disciplines, but this section discusses racing and the types of bikes used. BMX racing bikes are classified into frame sizes depending on the rider weight and size. The classification by frame size is shown in table 3.1.

The requirements for the bikes listed in table 3.1 are determined by the size. Some of these requirements include frame and fork construction and weight, tire and wheel size, crank length, gearing, and handlebar width and rise.

Bicycle Frame Design

A bicycle frame is a structure subjected to static and dynamic loads. Analysis can be done to assure that the frame can handle those loads. After the design and analysis is complete and the frame is fabricated, it can be tested to assure that it meets the design requirements and specifications.

Table 3.1 BMX Race Classification

Frame size	Micro-mini	Mini	Junior	Expert	Expert XL	Pro	Pro XL	Pro XXL
Top tube	15–16 in. (5.9–6.3 cm)	16–17.5 in. (6.3–6.9 cm)	17.5–18.5 in. (6.9–7.3 cm)	18.5–20 in. (7.3–7.5 cm)	19–20 in. (7.5–7.9 cm)	20–20.5 in. (7.9–8.1 cm)	20.5–21 in. (8.1–8.3 cm)	21–22 in. (8.3–8.7 cm)
Rider height	4 ft 0 in. (122 cm) and under	4 ft 0 in. –4 ft 6 in. (122–137 cm)	4 ft 4 in. –4 ft 10 in. (132–147 cm)	4 ft 8 in. –5 ft 4 in. (142–163 cm)	5 ft 2 in.–5 ft 8 in. (158–173 cm)	5 ft 6 in.–5 ft 10 in. (168–178 cm)	5 ft 10 in.–6 ft (178–183 cm)	6 ft (183 cm) and over
Rider weight	40–65 lb (18.1–29.5 kg)	50–85 lb (22.7–38.6 kg)	60–100 lb (27.2–45.4 kg)	70–110 lb (31.8–49.9 kg)	75–125 lb (34.0–56.7 kg)	100 lb (45.4 kg) and over	140 lb (63.5 kg) and over	160 lb (72.6 kg) and over

Data from USA BMX.

Frame Modeling and Analysis

The bicycle frame can be analyzed by modeling the geometry and subjecting the geometry to various loads. Several methods of modeling and analyzing the frame are described in the following sections.

Truss Analysis

Truss analysis has been used to model frames. This method of analysis calculates only the axial loads on the tubes because the joints are considered to be pinned (basically hinges). Examples can be found in Sharp (1896) and McMahon and Graham (2000).

A description of a simplified truss analysis follows. The simplification consists of analyzing the frame by ignoring the fork and extending the top tube and downtube to the intersection point in front of the head tube as shown in figure 3.4. This does change the reaction force at the front, R2. Normally, the reaction force is at the front axle. Figure 3.4 shows the distances to the points where loads (WS, WP) and reaction forces (R1, R2) are located. These points are the top of the seat tube and the bottom bracket for forces and the front and rear axles for reaction forces in the normal model. The simplified model uses the intersection point of the top tube and downtube for the front reaction force. The truss analysis forces and angles are also shown in figure 3.4.

The analysis looks at the four joints in the frame. The analysis proceeds around the frame in a clockwise direction starting at the rear axle. Note that this model is based on static loading conditions with vertical loading at the

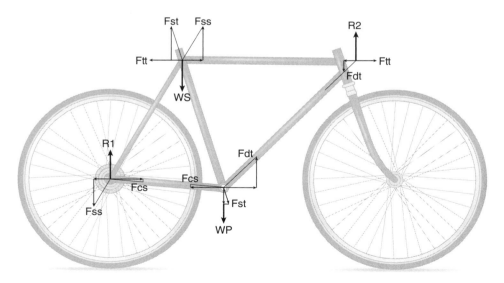

▶ **Figure 3.4** Simplified truss analysis of a frame.

top of the seat tube and at the bottom bracket. It ignores drive train forces on the chainstays and assumes that no rider weight is on the handlebars.

After the forces in the tubes are calculated, the axial stresses in the tubes can be determined based on the tube wall thicknesses. Bending stresses in the tubes can also be calculated by estimating the forces applied. An example would be the stresses in the chainstays because of the lateral loading from pedaling.

Some of the assumptions used in a bending analysis of the chainstays are shown in figure 3.5. Chainstay bridges are not found on all frames, which makes a difference in the length of the moment arm used for the analysis. One parameter used in the calculation of deflection is the moment of inertia (I), which is geometry based. As the tube diameter increases, the value of I increases. Deflection decreases as I increases. This relationship is the basis for the large diameter tubes used in some bicycles.

Finite Element Analysis

Finite element analysis (FEA) is a computer-assisted engineering (CAE) tool used, in the case of bicycles, to determine displacements, strains, and stresses under external loads. This tool requires that an accurate CAD model of a frame be generated.

Peterson and Landry (1986) described the results of early finite element modeling of three different frames. The results show the large stresses in the seat tube, downtube, and chainstays. Delph et al. (1986) presented the results of another frame finite element model in which three materials are compared. The results again show the large stresses in the bottom bracket

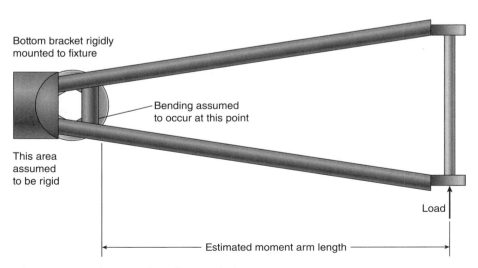

▶ **Figure 3.5** Chainstay bending analysis.

area of the frame. Since then, FEA has been used by various researchers and bicycle manufacturers to aid in the design of frames.

Design Verification

After a frame design is completed and the frame is constructed, various tests are done to verify the design. Three possible tests are deflection testing, vibration testing, and fatigue testing.

In most cases, deflection testing subjects the frame to loading that simulates the forces caused by pedaling. Lateral or torsional deflection is measured. The assumption is that reduced deflection means that more of the rider's output is put into the rear wheel.

Vibration testing measures the vibration transmitted to the rider. The results are affected by both frame design and component selection. Tires, wheels, handlebars, seat, and seat post can all affect the results. The assumption is that reducing the vibration to the rider reduces fatigue. Vibration reduction can also reduce nerve problems in the rider's hands and arms.

Fatigue testing verifies that a frame can withstand riding forces for some period of time. International standards require that a frame last for a specified number of cycles at a specified load. Fatigue failures are not uncommon in bicycle frames.

Deflection Testing

Since the early 1970s multiple studies have compared frame stiffness values. Because the values are acquired in different ways, in most cases they cannot be directly compared.

In the early 1970s Gary Klein compared his new welded oversize tube aluminum frame to other road frames on the market (table 3.2). The table shows the large improvement in stiffness at a reduced weight. The stiffness of the frame was increased through increasing the tube moment of inertia by increasing its diameter. The weight was decreased because even though the tube diameters were increased, aluminum has one-third the density of steel. The testing method is not described.

Miller (1982) documents the design of a frame rigidity test fixture and then documents the deflection measured on three different frames. Rinard (*Frame Deflection Test*) describes a method for testing frame rigidity and lists values for 62 different frames. Rinard (*Fork Deflection*) also tested 12 forks and described the testing method. On their website, Cannondale posts a lab report (2007) that lists the results of a test comparing rigidity values of their carbon frame to three competitors' frames. The test fixture is not described. In their 2008 catalog, Specialized shows the results of rigidity testing on 13 frames including 3 of their own. The test fixture and method of testing are not described. The Open University in England describes a test fixture and lists the results of rigidity testing on their website (*Bicycle Frame Testing at the Open University*). They tested 13 frames. *Velonews* describes the results

Table 3.2 Klein Stiffness Data From the 1970s

Material	Company	Model	Style	Size (cm)	Weight in lb (kg)	Bottom bracket torsional stiffness	Rear bending stiffness
Steel	Mercian	NA	Road	55	4.52 (2.05)	baseline	baseline
Steel	Colnago	NA	Road	55	4.12 (1.87)	–5%	–15%
Steel	Reynolds	Custom	Road	53	4.16 (1.89)	+5%	–10%
Titanium	Teledyne	Titan	Road	58	2.92 (1.32)	–25%	–20%
Aluminum	Fabo-Alan	NA	Road	58	3.31 (1.50)	–35%	–30%
Aluminum	Klein	Competition	Track	53	3.30 (1.50)	+115%	+75%
Aluminum	Klein	Competition	Road	58	3.83 (1.74)	+40%	+50%

Data from a Klein Company sales brochure distributed in 1973.

of rigidity testing on 13 frames in a technical report (Zinn 2006). The test fixture is also described. The magazine continues to test frames periodically.

Vibration Testing

None of the testing listed in the previous section compares the results of rigidity testing to the ride quality of the frame. Part of this ride quality is the vibration felt by the rider at the seat and the handlebars. Another part of ride quality is the perceived or actual lateral flex of the frame because of pedaling forces.

Papadopoulos (1987) alluded to some of these issues in the conclusion to his paper:

> While riders insist that bicycle flexibility reduces pedaling efficiency through the loss of the stored elastic energy, conservation-of-energy arguments indicate that there is generally no such loss. As well, cyclists seem to be inconsistent in their perceptions and choices. (For example, they claim that lightweight racing frames are stiffer than inexpensive heavy ones; and they select extra-light frames for level constant-speed races where mass would appear to be unimportant. Further, they fail to acknowledge that the seat and handlebars also contribute significantly to deflection, when transmitting reactions to pedaling loads. (Papadopoulos 1987, page 9)

Little research has been published on vibration transmitted to the rider. Three papers are summarized here.

Hastings, Blair, Culligan, and Pober (2004) describe testing done on three frames on a treadmill. The frames were set up with the same component groups. The same rider was used to test all three frames. A bump was attached to the treadmill to provide a vibration input to the frame. An accelerometer was attached to the seat post. A power meter built into the crankset was used. Heart rate and $\dot{V}O_2$max were measured as characteristics of physical fitness. The different frames showed no difference in rider performance. The data did seem to show that a stiffer bike required less power output.

Levy and Smith (2005) describe vibration testing on a mountain bike. The study includes a good description of the experimental methods and the results. This paper looked at the effectiveness of several suspension systems, so it is not directly applicable to road bicycles. The testing methods and the presentation of the results provide some good guidelines.

Champoux, Richard, and Drovet (2007) looked at road bicycle structural dynamics. Although the focus of the paper is experimental modal analysis of a road frame, a short section of the paper discusses road bike comfort. With a rider pedaling a bike on a treadmill that has a bump attached to it, the force applied on the handlebars is measured. The force is calculated from strain values measured by strain gauges attached to the stem. They propose this method to test the ride quality of various frames, forks, and components.

None of the research described here compares static stiffness values to ride quality. Researchers have approached ride quality from two directions, either measuring frame stiffness and not comparing it to ride quality or measuring ride quality and not comparing it to stiffness.

Fatigue Testing

Bicycle frame failure has always been an issue, but recently it has become a larger problem as manufacturers have been trying to build lighter frames using steel, aluminum, titanium, and carbon fiber. Before the early 1980s, most quality bicycle frames were made from alloy steel tubing with the joints reinforced by lugs. Frame failures did occur but normally only after a large number of miles (kilometers) were put on the frame. The average weight of a quality bicycle during that period was about 22 pounds (10 kg). Present-day racing bicycles of an equivalent quality weigh less than 15 pounds (6.8 kg).

Little research has been published on bicycle frame fatigue failure. Some manufacturers state they are performing research but for business reasons do not publish the results. Many manufacturers do in-house testing. Others contract with independent testing facilities. International Organization for Standardization (ISO), Deutsche Industrie Norm (DIN), and American Society for Testing and Materials (ASTM) have created bicycle standards. The ISO 4210-6:2014 standard covers safety requirements for bicycles. This standard "specifies safety and performance requirements for the design, assembly and testing of bicycles." DIN 79100 defines testing procedures for bicycle frame fatigue failure for three cases: out of saddle on pedals, rider load on saddle, and jumping. The title of the ASTM F2711-08 (2012) standards is Standard Test Methods for Bicycle Frames.

Frame Failure Examples

The most common areas of failure in a road bicycle frame are at the bottom bracket, seat tube, downtube, and chainstays. Figure 3.6 show a failure found in the field. Failures such as this can result from design issues, fabrication issues, or frame damage.

Failures commonly occur at transition areas in a frame such as at the edge of a weld as shown in figure 3.6 or at the edge of a lug or at other stress raisers such as holes in dropouts or at water bottle bosses. A rider should check a frame periodically for cracks. A good time to do this is when cleaning or overhauling a bicycle. High-stress areas such as the joints at the bottom bracket or the head tube should be checked carefully. Sometimes the start of a crack in a painted frame can be indicated by discoloration in the paint. In carbon composite frames, a crack in the paint may not necessarily indicate that the frame is failing. In some cases the frame may flex more than the paint is capable of withstanding. A manufacturer's representative should inspect a frame if any failures are suspected.

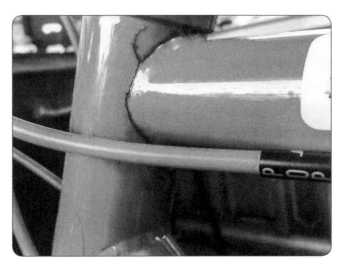

▶ **Figure 3.6** Location of cracks.

Stephen S. Cheung

Applying the Science

Bicycle design has evolved to reflect the increased number of applications. A rider can now choose from a wide range of models to fit his or her requirements. In competition, the proper frame can optimize the rider's performance.

The development of computer-aided engineering tools has allowed the bicycle designer to predict more accurately how the frame responds to various inputs and to optimize frame design. Many manufacturers use testing to verify that the physical frame characteristics match those of the model used to do the analysis. Deflection testing is a tool used by manufacturers to verify designs and to verify the quality of production frames. Third parties use deflection testing to compare frames from various manufacturers. Vibration testing is not as widely used but can be an important tool for determining ride quality. Fatigue testing is another important tool used to verify frame designs.

CHAPTER 4

Frame Materials and Geometry

—Larry Ruff

The selection of materials and the final geometry for the frame are based on the requirements and specifications of the design. Some not easily quantifiable requirements such as aesthetics may drive the selection of frame materials and joining methods. Parameters that can be calculated, such as trail, can drive the geometry specifications. The builder must define the requirements and specifications based on perceived or actual customer needs.

Frame Materials

Road bicycle frames are made from a wide range of materials or combination of materials. Since the turn of the 20th century, the most common frame material has been various steel alloys. Wood, bamboo, plastic, and magnesium have also been used at various times. The other materials commonly used today besides steel are aluminum, titanium, and carbon fiber.

Some of the terminology used to describe the mechanical properties of materials needs to be defined:

Ultimate tensile stress (UTS) is the stress at the maximum on the engineering stress-strain curve (figure 4.1). This measure indicates the strength of a material. For example, the 7005 aluminum alloy used in bicycle frames has a UTS that is 25 percent of the UTS of Reynolds 853 steel.

Density is the weight per unit volume of the material. This measure indicates the weight of a material. For example, the density of aluminum is about 33 percent of the density of steel.

Modulus (E), or modulus of elasticity, is the slope of the initial linear section, or elastic section, of the stress-strain curve (figure 4.1). This measure indicates the stiffness of a material. For example, the modulus of aluminum is about 33 percent of the modulus of steel.

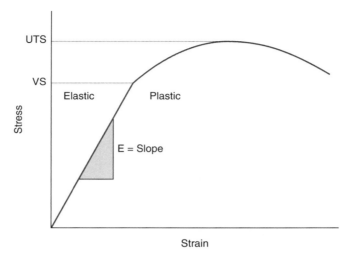

▶ **Figure 4.1** Stress-strain curve.

Elongation is a measure of ductility and is the percentage of plastic strain at fracture. This measure indicates how far a material will stretch before it fails. For example, Reynolds 853 has an elongation of 10 percent, whereas a high-modulus carbon fiber in an epoxy matrix has an elongation in the fiber direction of 0.3 percent.

Steel, Aluminum, and Titanium

A comparison of some of the steel, aluminum, and titanium alloys used for bicycle frames is shown in table 4.1. Reynolds, Columbus, and True Temper are three of the manufacturers who produce tubing for bicycle frames. Much of the data in the table comes from manufacturer product information. Ultimate tensile stress (UTS) is listed for most of the materials, but a few list only yield stress (YS). Some but not all manufacturers list percent elongation. Reynolds states, "Values lower than 5 to 7 percent would be considered brittle for bike frames" (Reynolds 1999).

Steel

Steel has the longest history in bicycle manufacturing. It is available in a wide range of alloys and tube shapes. Steel can be easily shaped. Steel tubes can be joined by a wide range of methods including silver soldering, brazing, gas metal arc welding (GMAW or MIG), and gas tungsten arc welding (GTAW or TIG). Steel tubes can be joined by adhesives, but that method is not common. In most cases steel does not require any postwelding heat treatment. Steel has great fatigue resistance, and if design and fabrication are done correctly, a steel frame should last forever. Steel has an endurance limit. As long as stresses are kept below that limit, the frame should theoretically last for an infinite number of cycles.

Table 4.1 Physical Properties of Metal Frame Materials

Material	UTS in ksi (MPa)	Density in lb/in.³ (kg/m³)	Modulus in ksi (MPa)	Elongation in %
STEEL				
1010	44 (303)	.28 (7,750)	30,000 (206,800)	
4130	87 (600)	.28 (7,750)	30,000 (206,800)	
Reynolds 531	110 (758)	.28 (7,750)	30,000 (206,800)	15
Reynolds 525	116 (800)	.28 (7,750)	30,000 (206,800)	
Columbus Zona	116 (800)	.28 (7,750)	30,000 (206,800)	12
True Temper Verus	120 (827)	.28 (7,750)	30,000 (206,800)	
Reynolds 631	125 (862)	.28 (7,750)	30,000 (206,800)	
Reynolds 725	167 (1,151)	.28 (7,750)	30,000 (206,800)	
Reynolds 753	167 (1,151)	.28 (7,750)	30,000 (206,800)	
Columbus Life	167 (1,151)	.28 (7,750)	30,000 (206,800)	14
Columbus Spirit	181 (1,248)	.28 (7,750)	30,000 (206,800)	14
Columbus XCr	196 (1,351)	.28 (7,750)	30,000 (206,800)	10
KVA Stainless	200 (1,379)	.28 (7,750)	30,000 (206,800)	14
Reynolds 853	203 (1,400)	.28 (7,750)	30,000 (206,800)	10
True Temper OX	217 (1,496)	.28 (7,750)	30,000 (206,800)	
Reynolds 953	290 (1,999)	.28 (7,750)	30,000 (206,800)	
ALUMINUM				
6061	47 (324)	.10 (2,768)	10,000 (68,900)	12
7005	49 (338)	.10 (2,768)	10,000 (68,900)	12
6066	58 (400)	.10 (2,768)	10,000 (68,900)	
Reynolds Sc-7x	58 (400)	.10 (2,768)	10,400 (71,700)	
2014	60 (YS) (413)	.10 (2,768)	10,000 (68,900)	10
Columbus Airplane	61 (421)	.10 (2,768)	10,000 (68,900)	10
7075	73 (YS) (503)	.10 (2,768)	10,000 (68,900)	11
Easton EA70	78 (YS) (538)	.10 (2,768)	10,000 (68,900)	12
Reynolds X-100	80 (551)	.10 (2,768)	10,400 (71,700)	
Reynolds X-102	102 (703)	.10 (2,768)	10,600 (73,100)	
TITANIUM				
3AL-2.5V	131 (903)	.16 (4,429)	15,500 (106,900)	15
6AL-4V	152 (1,048)	.16 (4,429)	16,700 (115,100)	

Data from Reynolds Technology Ltd., Columbus (division of Gruppo SRL), KVA Stainless Inc., and Easton Sports Inc.

Aluminum

Aluminum also comes in a range of alloys and tube shapes, although the range is not as great as that for steel. Aluminum can be shaped, but it sometimes requires annealing and then postshaping heat treating. Aluminum tubes are usually joined by TIG welding, but adhesives have been used. Aluminum frames require some kind of postwelding heat treatment that varies with the alloy. Aluminum requires careful design and fabrication to reduce the risk of frame failure. Aluminum does not have an endurance limit, and each cycle brings it closer to failure.

Titanium

Titanium has a limited number of alloys and tube shapes available. The 3/2.5 alloy is most commonly used, and 6/4 has also been used. It can be shaped; in fact, some 6/4 alloy tubes are made by shaping and welding sheet material. Titanium tubes are usually joined by TIG welding, but adhesives have also been used for titanium and carbon frames. Shielding gas is critical for welding. Titanium tubes do not corrode. Titanium has an endurance limit, so again, theoretically, the frames should last forever if they are designed and fabricated correctly.

Magnesium Alloys

Magnesium alloys have been used in bicycle frame construction. They have a low density and a high strength-to-weight ratio. The properties of one of the wrought magnesium alloys, AZ31B, include a UTS of 24 ksi (165 MPa), a density of 0.065 lb/in³ (1,800 kg/m³), and a modulus of 6,5000 ksi (44,800 MPa). Of all the metals used for frame construction, magnesium has the best capacity to dampen road vibrations. Magnesium is also easy to machine, and some of the alloys weld easily.

Metal Tube Shapes

Metal bicycle tubing can be provided shaped or butted or both. Butted tubes provide more strength at the joints in the frame where the maximum stresses occur. A picture of shaped bicycle tube sections is shown in figure 4.2. Shaped tubing is used to control the amount of frame flex, depending on the direction of loading as described in chapter 3.

Carbon Fiber

Carbon fiber is also used for bicycle frame construction. As opposed to the isotropic properties of the metals used in frame construction, in which the measured properties of the tubing materials are independent of the direction of measurement, carbon fiber tubes and structural members are anisotropic; the properties are dependent on fiber angle, number of plies, and sequence of layup as shown in figure 4.3. This feature allows the designer to tailor the ride characteristics of a frame.

Carbon fiber construction also requires an epoxy resin. The resin "fixes the fibers within a ply in a solid matrix, as well as bonds the plies to each other. A crucial second characteristic of resin is its strength to handle impacts and vibrations" (Lindsey 2010).

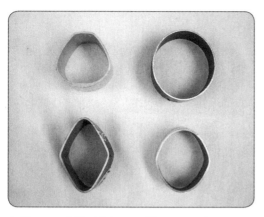

▶ **Figure 4.2** Tube profile examples.

Larry Ruff

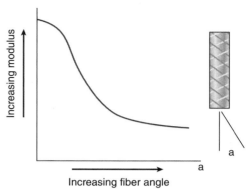

▶ **Figure 4.3** Effect of fiber orientation on modulus.

One manufacturer of the carbon fiber used in frame construction is Toray Industries (Japan). Two fibers commonly used are T700G and M60J. T700G has a tensile strength of 711 ksi (4,900 MPa), a modulus of 34,800 ksi (240,000 MPa), and a density of 0.065 lb/in³ (1,800 kg/m³). M60J has a tensile strength of 569 ksi (3,900 MPa), a modulus of 85,300 ksi (590,000 MPa), and a density of 0.07 lb/in³ (1,940 kg/m³). These values are just for the fibers in tension, and the final fabricated parts may not have a modulus or tensile strength that high. The properties are based on the rule of mixtures, mathematical expressions that give a property of the composite in terms of the properties, quantity, and arrangement of its constituents.

Bamboo

Bamboo is also being used for frame construction. Bamboo is a natural composite in which the fibers are held in place by a matrix. Bamboo does not have uniform fiber density along or across its length. As with carbon composites, bamboo's mechanical properties vary with the test direction. Properties also vary with moisture content. Bamboo is normally dried before it is used in structural applications. There are also different types of bamboo. An example of the range of mechanical properties (lengthwise) include a UTS of 16.1 to 31.8 ksi (111 to 219 MPa), density of 0.011 to 0.022 lb/in³ (305 to 610 kg/m³), and a modulus of 1,160 to 2,030 ksi (8,000 to 14,000 MPa). High-stress areas in the frame such as the headtube, bottom bracket, and dropouts are made from a stronger material such as aluminum.

Wood

Wood has been used for frame construction since the very beginning of bicycles. Wood is also a natural composite and it has unique and independent mechanical properties depending on orientation. Properties also vary with moisture content. Some use ash for frame construction. The properties of white ash with 12 percent moisture content include a shear strength parallel to the grain of 1.91 ksi (13 MPa), density of 0.022 lb/in³ (610 kg/m³), and a modulus of 1,740 ksi (12,000 MPa). As with bamboo, high-stress areas in the frame such as the headtube, bottom bracket, and dropouts are made from a stronger material such as aluminum.

Frame Geometry

The names of the tubes in a bicycle frame are shown in figure 4.4. Figure 4.5 shows the frame geometry.

Top Tube Length

Top tube length is defined as the distance between the headtube center line and the seat tube center line. Note that figure 4.5 shows that the top tube is horizontal, but that is not always the case, such as with compact or endurance frames. For road frames the top tube length is sometimes called the effective, or horizontal, top tube length, and it is measured as the horizontal distance between the headtube center line and the seat tube center line. On BMX frames the distance is measured along the center line of the top tube as shown in figure 4.6. The top tube length is related to the length of the cyclist's arms and upper torso.

Seat Tube Length

Seat tube length is defined as the distance between the center of the bottom bracket and the centerline of the top tube, known as center to center. Sometimes seat tube length is defined as the distance from the center of the bottom bracket to the top of the seat tube.

Seat tube length is related to the cyclist's leg length. The actual dimension of interest is from the center of the bottom bracket to the top of the seat. Compact frames can have short seat tubes.

Standover

Standover is the distance from the ground to the top of the top tube at the midpoint of the top tube. This dimension is the result of frame dimensions and tire size. For safety reasons the cyclist should be able to straddle the top tube.

Chainstay Length

Chainstay length is the distance from the center of the rear axle to the center of the bottom bracket. Long stays can be more flexible; short stays can be

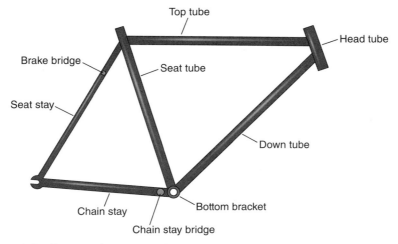

▶ **Figure 4.4** Frame tube nomenclature.

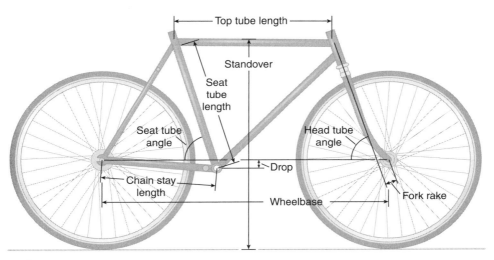

▶ **Figure 4.5** Frame geometry.

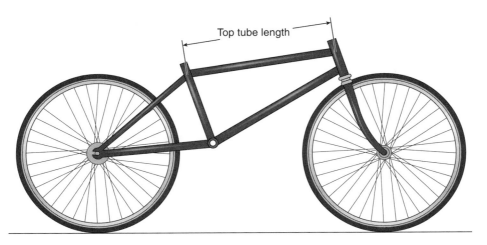

▶ **Figure 4.6** BMX geometry.

stiffer. Frame requirements such as tire and fender clearance, wheel removal, shoe heel and pannier clearance, and others can determine chainstay length. Chainstay length can also affect where the cyclist's center of gravity (CG) ends up, which determines weight distribution.

Drop

Drop is the distance from the center of the bottom bracket to the horizontal wheel axis center line. Frame requirements help determine this dimension. The larger the value is, the less the ground clearance is. Limited ground clearance could be a problem for track frames, which must offer adequate pedal clearance on a banked track, and cyclocross frames, which should facilitate clearing barriers. Changing this value also moves the CG of the cyclist vertically, which can affect handling.

Wheelbase

Wheelbase is the distance between the front and rear wheel axles. This dimension is affected by chainstay length, top tube length, headtube angle, and fork rake. Track bikes are at the short end, whereas touring bikes tend to have long wheelbases.

Seat Tube Angle

Seat tube angle is the angle between the ground and the seat tube. The most common range for this angle is 68 to 75 degrees, but triathlon and time-trial frames often have a steeper angle. Changing this angle (making it larger) moves the cyclist's CG forward and affects the biomechanics of the cyclist in terms of where the hip joint is located with respect to the center of rotation of the crank.

Headtube Angle

The headtube angle is the angle between the ground and the headtube. This dimension, along with fork rake and wheel diameter, can have a great effect on handling and a parameter called trail. This attribute is discussed later.

Fork Rake

Fork rake is the perpendicular distance between the headtube center line and the front-wheel axle. This dimension, along with the headtube angle and wheel diameter, can have a great effect on handling and a parameter called trail. This attribute is discussed later.

Headtube Angle, Rake, and Trail

The headtube angle along with the fork rake and the wheel diameter are used to determine trail. Trail, shown in figure 4.7, is the distance between a vertical line drawn from the axle centerline that intersects the ground and a line drawn through the center of the steering axis that intersects the ground. Trail can be calculated or determined from CAD. Trail can be used to determine how a bicycle will handle. Trail values of 1.97 inches (5.00 cm) to 2.48 inches (6.30 cm) work for a road bicycle. A value of approximately 2.24 inches (5.69 cm) is considered optimal.

A bicycle can have neutral steering, understeer, or oversteer. Neutral steering means that as the handlebars are turned, the fork neither rises nor drops. The equation for neutral steering is

$$Y_{neutral} = R \tan\frac{(90 \deg - a)}{2}$$

in which Y = fork rake in inches, R = wheel radius in inches, and a = head-tube angle in degrees (1 inch = 2.54 centimeters; 1 centimeter = 0.393 inches).

Oversteer means to cut a turn tighter than its true radius. Understeer means to swing wider than the true radius of the turn. A bicycle that over-steers has quicker handling and is easier to enter into a turn. Bicycles are normally designed to have some oversteer rather than neutral or understeer-ing geometry. If the headtube angle and the wheel diameter stay the same and the rake is reduced, the trail increases and the bicycle tends to oversteer. For a race bike, one recommendation is to use $Y_{quick} = Y_{neutral} - 0.75$. Touring bikes should be somewhere between Y_{quick} and $Y_{neutral}$.

▶ **Figure 4.7** Headtube angle, rake, and trail.

Applying the Science

Riders have a wide range of frame materials from which to choose. Each material has pros and cons, and manufacturers usually state their reasons for selecting a material for an application. The trend toward very light frames may have its place in competition, but for most riders a frame like this may not be the best choice. Heavier and more powerful riders may want to look at more robust frames. Touring, cyclocross, and adventure riding also usually require a more robust frame. Sometimes the environment in which a frame is used, such as in a rainy climate or near the ocean, could determine the material.

Frame geometry will affect how a rider feels on the bike. Geometry affects the fit. Stock geometries can usually be fit to the rider by component selection, such as the stem or seat post. In some cases a rider may need to have a custom frame built if a stock geometry doesn't work.

Geometry also affects handling. Some riders may not be comfortable with a quick-handling frame and may need to look for a geometry that provides slower handling. Trail, bottom bracket drop, and chainstay length are some of the parameters that can determine handling. Touring frames are usually designed to be slower handling.

Race frames have been getting stiffer in terms of lateral deflection at the bottom bracket. This attribute can be affected by geometry, such as compact frames and short chainstays. Material selection and tube profiles also determine frame stiffness. Vertical stiffness or compliance can also be affected by geometry, frame material, and tube profiles. This characteristic is important because vibration can have a major effect on rider fatigue and hand issues. In many cases component selection can have a major effect on vibration. Torsional stiffness, which is a measure of the twisting of the frame, can affect how a bicycle feels during cornering. This characteristic is also affected by geometry, material, and tube profiles. Some manufacturers have been investigating the effect of these stiffness values on rider performance, but no comprehensive scientific study has been done to date.

CHAPTER 5

Saddle Biomechanics

—Daniel Schade

Even though the health-inducing effects of cycling—such as the benefits it provides to the cardiovascular system—are well known, cyclists on all levels regularly report that they suffer from discomfort when riding. Several studies (Fröböse, Luecker, and Wittmann 2001; Schrader et al. 2002; Schwellnus and Derman 2005) have discussed the regular appearance of discomfort in cycling. In this respect, the saddle as a contact point plays a central role.

To optimize comfort and reduce problems, special attention should be paid to the saddle when analyzing the rider–bike system. Figure 5.1 presents the various contact points between rider and bike. Although other points are important for control and handling (handlebar) or force transmission (pedals), the saddle is the main weight-bearing structure. In contrast to the handlebar and pedals, the saddle surface is not divided into left and right sides. A total unloading is possible only in the out-of-the-saddle riding position. When the rider is seated, the saddle is continuously loaded. According to Potter, Sauer, and Weisshaar (2008), the load varies slightly throughout the pedaling cycle, but it is constantly present. This aspect is important to consider when analyzing this interface.

The various structures of the pelvic region bear the weight at the saddle. Several analysis methods exist to measure the exact pelvic positioning. Dynamic pressure mapping is recommended because it allows users to make an exact measurement of the intensity and location of the pressure on the saddle. These systems are already being used for scientific research (e.g., Bressel and Larson 2003; Potter, Sauer, and Weisshaar 2008; Schrader, Breitenstein, and Lowe 2008; Carpes et al. 2009). Furthermore, optical systems can be used to analyze the pelvic position on the saddle. The first part of this chapter discusses the foundations regarding anatomy and biomechanics as well as the state of knowledge on saddle discomfort. The second part considers the factors influencing the saddle as a contact point.

Pelvic Anatomy

The saddle surface is strained by several pelvic structures (figure 5.2). Concerning sensitivity, a clear distinction exists between front and rear. Whereas

▶ **Figure 5.1**   Contact points between rider and bike.

the rear of the pelvis for the most part consists of insensitive bone and muscle structures, the front is made up of more pressure-sensitive soft-tissue structures such as blood vessels and nerve tracts. The bony structures in the rear are the coccyx and the two ischial tuberosities. Because of their large surface these structures are particularly suited to bear weight. The coccyx is positioned so far back in the pelvis that it has contact with the saddle surface only in extremely upright positions, that is, with a back angle (to the horizontal) of 90 degrees or more. In sportive positions (back angle between 20 and 60 degrees), the coccyx has no contact with the saddle.

The pubic rami connect both ischial tuberosities and the pubis. The pubic rami are divided into inferior and superior, are skid shaped, and differ individually in terms of width. The pubis ends in the pubic symphysis, the cartilaginous joint uniting the superior rami of the right and left pubic bones. When viewed from below, the pelvis is thus shaped like a trapeze. The dimensions of the trapeze differ individually and depend on the width of the pubic symphysis (the upper edge of the trapeze) and the distance of the sit bones (the lower edge of the trapeze). Figure 5.3 shows a schematic summary of the undersides of two pelvises; the front is represented at the top and the back is at the bottom.

The muscles that are most strained by sitting on the saddle are the muscles of the pelvic floor. Indirectly, other surrounding muscles can be strained,

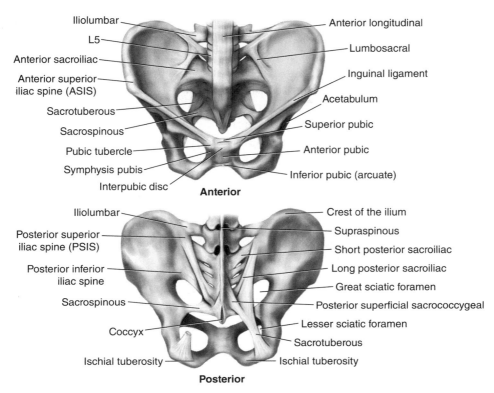

Iliolumbar — L5 — Anterior sacroiliac — Anterior superior iliac spine (ASIS) — Sacrotuberous — Sacrospinous — Pubic tubercle — Symphysis pubis — Interpubic disc

Anterior longitudinal — Lumbosacral — Inguinal ligament — Acetabulum — Superior pubic — Anterior pubic — Inferior pubic (arcuate)

Anterior

Iliolumbar — Posterior superior iliac spine (PSIS) — Posterior inferior iliac spine — Sacrospinous — Coccyx — Ischial tuberosity

Crest of the ilium — Supraspinous — Short posterior sacroiliac — Long posterior sacroiliac — Great sciatic foramen — Posterior superficial sacrococcygeal — Lesser sciatic foramen — Sacrotuberous — Ischial tuberosity

Posterior

▶ **Figure 5.2** Structure of the pelvis.

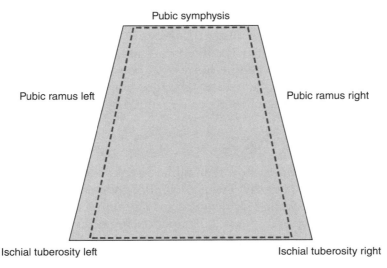

Pubic symphysis

Pubic ramus left

Pubic ramus right

Ischial tuberosity left

Ischial tuberosity right

▶ **Figure 5.3** Schematic representation of two pelvic undersides.

especially if the pressure is too high or a lot of pelvic movement is occurring. In this case, the surrounding muscles can be overstrained and can become tight. Pelvic movement is most often an evasive movement aimed at reducing punctual pressure.

Additionally, other soft-tissue structures such as nerve tracts and blood vessels can be strained. The nervus pudendus consists of multiple branches and innervates the genitals of men and women. The nerves in the perineum are compressed when strained and might develop an irritation.

Important blood vessels in this region are the pelvic arteries. Their main function is to transport blood to the leg muscles. Because of the heightened muscle usage of the legs when cycling, the arteries need to transport more blood. According to Rimpler, Hinrichs, and Wilaschek (2009), this increased blood transport, in combination with the repetitive hip flexion in the cycling position, might lead to the development of a kink in the arteries. In a study of 13 professional cyclists, 10 test subjects were diagnosed with a kink and 3 more with an occlusion of the external iliac artery. Constraining the blood flow by kinking the artery results in a performance loss under maximum load, according to Rimpler, Hinrichs, and Wilaschek. Given the population of this study, we can hypothesize that the arteries must be subject to a continuous load over several years before they lose their elasticity and develop a kink. Body position is likely related to the pressure load at the saddle.

Some general differences concerning the bone structure of the female and male pelvis can be explained by evolution. Statistically, women have a larger distance between and a stronger curvature of the hipbone and the sit bones. The underside of the pubic rami is often curved in women, but it is mostly flat in men. This difference is important when it comes to sitting on a saddle, because curved bones have less support on a flat saddle and therefore the pressure load is higher on a smaller surface. Additionally, the angle of the pubic rami toward one another when seen from the front is smaller than 90 degrees in men and larger than 90 degrees in women. This difference is especially important in sportive positions, because men and women load the saddle nose differently. Note that individual pelvic anatomy varies; all the mentioned differences are statistical averages. Some women have a rather male pelvis, and some men have a rather female pelvis.

Saddle Discomforts

Several studies with cyclists show that saddle discomforts are among the main problems in cycling. This issue seems to be independent of discipline because the studies cover road cycling (Schwellnus and Derman 2005), mountain biking (Fröböse, Luecker, and Wittmann 2001), and touring positions (Schrader et al. 2002). Figure 5.4 graphs chronic discomforts by body part. For the study by Fröböse, Luecker, and Wittmann (2001), 840 mountain bikers (83 percent male, 17 percent female) were surveyed. In total, 90 percent of respondents reported problems when mountain biking. With 45 percent, the saddle was named most frequently as causing problems. The problems mostly occur while riding (64 percent), not so much after riding (24 percent). Although mountain bikers ride out of the saddle for extended periods, the periods when in the saddle seem to cause problems. Bumps in the ground have an impact on the body and increase the symptoms related to these problems. Furthermore, scientists hypothesize that the problems may relate to bike-fitting issues, such as a saddle nose that is tilted upward or an overstretched sportive position.

The study by Schwellnus and Derman (2005) also identified the saddle as one of the most problematic regions. Eighty-five percent of the surveyed recreational cyclists indicate that they regularly have problems when cycling. When dividing this up by body part, 36.1 percent indicate problems in the sitting area and 30.3 percent have problems in the lower back. Problems in the lumbar spine may be related to suboptimal saddle positioning because evasive movements to alleviate saddle discomfort might result in changed pelvic positioning (cf. de Vey Mestdagh 1998; Marsden 2010).

In a study of 22 patrol officers, Schrader et al. (2002) identified feelings of numbness among 91 percent of the respondents. The average daily time on the bike was 5.4 hours, and the problems started at different moments (as early as after 10 minutes or as late as after 8 hours on the bike, with an average of 161 minutes).

In other studies (Mellion 1991; Weiss 1994; Guess 2006), saddle discomfort was also named as regularly occurring when cycling and as a problem that needed to be addressed when aiming to improve comfort.

These studies identify a high-pressure load as one of the main reasons for saddle discomfort. These loads occur when cycling and can cause injuries to various anatomic regions. The question of whether these damages are

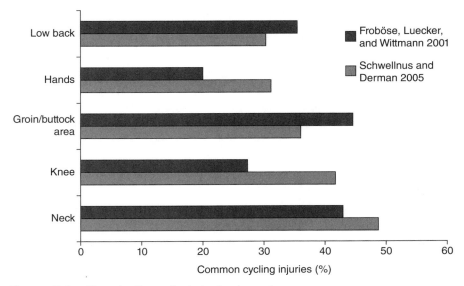

▶ **Figure 5.4** Chronic discomforts by body part.

temporary or permanent has not been sufficiently addressed. Studies of male cyclists argue that sitting on the saddle might promote erectile dysfunction. Schwarzer et al. (2002) diagnosed decreased penile blood flow in 20 test persons while cycling on an ergometer. These results show significant differences between different saddle designs. Taylor, Kao, and Albertsen (2004) analyzed the responses of 688 cyclists to an online survey on erectile dysfunctions. Within the sample, 17 percent were affected, which is considerably higher than the prevalence across noncyclists (3.9 percent according to Nayal et al. 1999). Although Taylor, Kao, and Albertsen find a clear trend, they cannot establish a statistically significant relation between cycling and erectile dysfunction. This contrasts with findings by Hollingworth, Harper, and Hamer (2014), who do not find a relationship between cycling and erectile dysfunction in their survey of 5,300 British cyclists.

Biomechanics

To improve the understanding of the pressure load on the saddle, we need to take a closer look at the biomechanics of cycling. Because the athlete has five contact points with the bike, the athlete's weight force proportionately applies to these points. Because of the gravitational acceleration, the weight force when riding in the flats applies vertically on the various contact points:

$$Force (F) = mass (m) \times acceleration (a)$$

The force distribution per contact point depends on the rider's anatomy and the setup of the position including the bike components. At every single contact point the applied force results in a pressure load. Pressure (P) is defined as force (F) per area (A).

Pressure depends on the amount of force and the size of the area it is applied to. The contact area is of decisive importance for the strength of the pressure load because the force is predefined by body weight and position. Therefore, the ultimate goal when aiming to reduce pressure is to increase the contact area. In this regard, the anatomic specificities of a person must not be ignored. Physically, distributing the force uniformly across the saddle might be ideal, but distributing the pressure equally between the sit bones and the pubic area is not efficient from a biomechanical perspective.

The force applied to the saddle depends on several other factors. It changes when the resistance is increased, such as by shifting into a harder gear: The weight force on the pedals increases, resulting in a decrease of force applied to the saddle. The highest force values on the saddle are measured on the base endurance rides, when the cyclist rides with little resistance. In a study by Potter, Sauer, and Weisshaar (2008), 22 test persons with cycling experience (11 males and 11 females) were analyzed using a saddle pressure mapping system at two different power outputs (100 watts and 200 watts). In this setting the investigators showed that the pressure applied to the saddle is significantly reduced at 200 watts. In addition, the force put on the saddle was found to vary throughout the pedaling cycle. The largest force is applied at a crank position of 160 degrees, that is, shortly before changing from the pushing phase into the pulling phase. The lowest force is applied in a crank position of 45 degrees, that is, shortly before the pushing phase begins. The force differences throughout the cycle as measured on the saddle, however, are small. Thus, no complete unloading of the saddle occurs.

Next to the vertically applied weight force, friction forces at the saddle also need to be considered. These forces mostly apply longitudinally and diagonally and occur at the seams and edges of the saddle. Increased friction can result in skin lesions and inflammations and should therefore be avoided.

Measurement Procedures to Analyze the Saddle Contact Point

Various methods and technologies can be used to quantify comfort and evaluate possible saddle discomfort. Here, the spectrum goes from a merely visual analysis to high-tech pressure sensor mats.

Visual Control and Subjective Impression

The pelvic position on the saddle can be analyzed visually by eye or by using motion capture. Where is the main weight located—more toward the front of the saddle or the back? When looking from behind, is it possible to recognize a tendency of asymmetry? In this regard, feeling for or marking the spinae iliac anterior superior (SIPS) is valuable. These bony structures at the hipbone are easily identified, and their relative position provides information on pelvic symmetry or asymmetry.

Properly analyzing the saddle also provides information on straining. Pressure spots on the saddle result in both overstraining of the human tissues and increased wear of the saddle material.

Visual analysis should be combined with the subjective feeling of the athlete. Athletes with good body awareness can indicate which areas of the saddle should be analyzed more closely. Is the discomfort correlated in time with a change of material? Did a change of saddle, cycling bib, or another component intensify the problem?

Overall, visual analysis offers limited value, because how the pelvis loads the saddle is not directly observable from the outside. It is a valuable addition, but it requires a lot of experience.

Measuring the Distance of the Sit Bones

Another method is measuring the distance of the sit bones. The athlete sits on a chair covered in a gel film, a soft foam, or corrugated board and presses the ischial tuberosities into the material. Subsequently, the distance between the two imprints is measured. Based on this measurement, the saddle width is selected. This method can be a first way to categorize the width of the pelvis, but it is meaningful only when the rider is in an upright position when the saddle is at the same height or lower than the handlebar. In this case the rider is mostly sitting on the sit bones. The saddle needs sufficient width in the back area to provide enough surface to support the sit bones. In a more sportive position, the pressure load is moved toward the front of the pelvis, and therefore the distance of the sit bones becomes less relevant. The individual form of the pelvic underside is decisive because people differ in the distance of the sit bones and the width of the pubic symphysis.

Measurement of the Pressure Distribution

Electronic measurements provide a specific and realistic account of the pressure load on the saddle. For this, a flexible measurement film consisting of pressure sensors is used to measure the pressure on the saddle (figure 5.5).

The measurement can be conducted dynamically, accounting for cadence and resistance, while the athlete pedals on the bike. With the current systems, field measurements also are possible because the data are transmitted wirelessly to a PC. Special analysis software is used to interpret the data. The raw data are represented graphically using a color scheme to represent different levels of pressure (ranging from dark to light; see figure 5.6) in predefined zones. By measuring the entire saddle surface, the anatomic structure of the pelvis becomes visible. The upper part of the pressure image shows the pubic zone; the lower part shows the two zones, left sit bone and right sit bone. Important parameters include the maximum pressure, the exact location of the main pressure points, the center of pressure, and the averages in the various zones. This method is especially helpful in visualizing eventual asymmetries or pelvic rotations. A virtual ruler enables the dynamic measurement of the distance of the sit bones and the width of the pubic symphysis.

Factors Influencing the Saddle Contact Point

When talking about the saddle contact point, we do not mean the saddle type but all elements that have an effect on the saddle (table 5.1). Table 5.1 distinguishes direct and indirect factors and is not exhaustive. Its main purpose is to visualize the complexity of this interface and its interaction with other contact points. Every change in the entire rider–bike system possibly has a consequence for the contact point saddle.

Besides the directly involved components (saddle, seat post, bib shorts), various parameters of the position influence comfort at the saddle. The

▶ **Figure 5.5** Pressure mapping system.

Daniel Schade

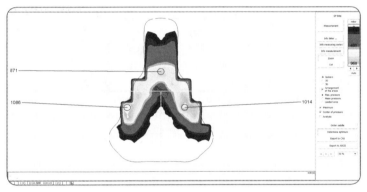

▶ **Figure 5.6** Pressure distribution on the saddle (in millibars).

Daniel Schade

main factors are saddle height, reach, fore–aft saddle position, and drop, because these variables are directly related to the saddle. But the effect of changes at other points should not be underestimated. Take the handlebar as an example. Adjusting the levers up or down will have an effect on the pelvic positioning on the saddle. A relation between hand position and pressure distribution on the saddle was demonstrated by Bressel, Cronin, and Exeter (2005). Another topic that comes up regularly in dynamic bike fittings is the position of the cleats. Unintentional differences in left–right cleat positioning possibly result in asymmetric pelvic positioning and pressure distribution on the saddle. The following section provides a closer look at the central components and main factors influencing the position in more detail.

Table 5.1 Factors Influencing the Contact Point Saddle

Direct effect	Indirect effect
COMPONENTS	
Saddle model	Handlebar shape
Bib shorts	Stem length and angle
Seat tube angle	Shoes, cleats, pedals
Seat post	
POSITIONING	
Saddle height	Brakes position
Saddle fore and aft	Handlebar position
Saddle tilt	Cleats position
Saddle–handlebar distance	Condition of cleats, shoes, pedals
Saddle–handlebar drop	

Saddle Type

Myriad saddle types are available, turning the saddle purchase into a difficult mission for every cyclist. At closer inspection, many models differ only slightly in terms of color and design. The number of truly different saddle concepts is considerably smaller. Here, the main divide is between cutout saddles and full-surface saddles, in addition to no-nose saddles (figure 5.7). Within these categories are additional differentiations, such as the material of the saddle, the size and position of the cutout, whether the rear end is heightened, and whether the rails have a cushioning effect (depending on rail material).

Because of the individuality of the pelvic structure and the different demands of the cycling disciplines, no one-size-fits-all solution is available. But some general aspects are important to consider when selecting a saddle. A well-fitting saddle offers the largest possible surface for the rider's pelvis and provides cushioning in those regions that are strained most. In this regard, the difference between the total surface of a saddle and the effectively used surface is important. Pressure analyses regularly show that only about 50 percent of the saddle surface is used for sitting. In these cases, changing to a wider saddle is not productive. Instead, improving the usage of the already available surface should be the focus.

The idea of the cutout saddle is to reduce the pressure on the perineum by moving the weight to the sides or behind the cutout. In their study of female riders, Bressel and Larson (2003) show an increased forward tilt of the pelvis on cutout saddles, which they interpret as an indicator of increased comfort. But a cutout necessarily means a decrease in the surface area, possibly resulting in higher maximum pressure to either side of the cutout. Apparently, the size and position of the cutout are of central importance.

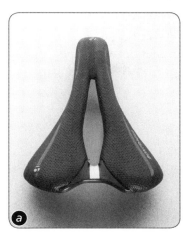

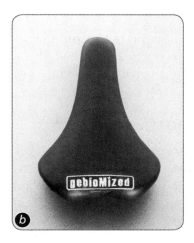

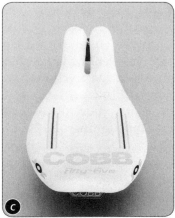

▶ **Figure 5.7**   Saddle types: (*a*) cutout saddle; (*b*) full-surface saddle; (*c*) no-nose saddle.

Daniel Schade

A full-surface saddle is based on the opposite concept. The aim is to distribute the weight equally on a large surface to prevent pressure peaks. For both of these concepts, the finishing of the saddle is highly important. Seams or edges in the loaded area result in pressure peaks that ought to be prevented because they cause friction.

Schade, Natrup, and Fritz (2006) demonstrated that customized saddles can result in a pressure reduction of up to 35 percent in the pubic area. The customization is based on dynamic pressure mapping on a raw saddle. The model is then constructed using CAD software and produced with a CNC mill.

Another widely researched concept is the so-called no-nose saddle. Here, the saddle consists of two shells that are supposed to carry the sit bones. The front area of the saddle is entirely cut off. Even though the positive effects of this saddle concept concerning comfort and pressure could be proved

(Keytel and Noakes 2002; Schwarzer et al. 2002; Schrader, Breitenstein, and Lowe 2008), it did not become a widely used solution. Possible causes are the decreased control because of the lack of contact between the thighs and the saddle and the increased strain on the upper-body musculature (cf. Bressel and Larson 2003).

Bib Shorts

The bib short constitutes the layer between rider and saddle. Its primary task is to distribute the weight on the saddle and thereby to cushion pressure peaks. Over the last years, gebioMized internal studies show that the cushioning effect of the pads is smaller than the cushioning effect of the saddle; well-fitting bib shorts can reduce maximum pressure by 15 to 25 percent, and a well-fitting saddle can reduce pressure by 30 to 40 percent.

When selecting a bib short, the rider should choose a pad wide enough to cover the pelvic bone structure. A pad that is too narrow results in high pressure at the outer edges of the cushion and seams, and the edges might further increase the pressure. In selecting the correct pad, the position should be considered. Because more sportive positions in road cycling and triathlon move the main pressure toward the saddle nose, the bib short should also cushion this area. In contrast, in a more upright position, such as in mountain biking and touring, the cushioning of the sit bones is more important.

Saddle Height

Properly adjusting the saddle height is especially important because a saddle that is too high is one of the prime reasons for saddle discomfort. To compensate for the uncomfortable saddle height, cyclists often tend to move the pelvis increasingly left and right when pedaling or place the pelvis on the saddle nose. In both cases the excessive saddle height is compensated through movements that might result in additional problems, such as overstraining of the spinal discs in the lumbar spine and increased pressure on the pubic area. To adjust the saddle to the right height, knowing the zone that is mainly strained is necessary. The effective saddle height is measured as the distance between the bottom bracket and the saddle surface at the location of the point of central force.

Let's consider an example (figure 5.8). The saddle height of two riders—A and B—is 80 centimeters measured along the seat tube. Rider A, however, mostly strains the saddle nose, and rider B sits farther back on the saddle. This positioning effectively decreases the saddle height of rider A and increases the saddle height of rider B, resulting in a nonnegligible difference. We can assume that the saddle height for rider A is not adjusted optimally.

Everyday bike fitting shows that small changes of the saddle height often have a large effect on the pressure distribution and maximum pressure. For this reason, considering the center of pressure is an important evaluation tool. From a comfort perspective, saddle height is considered optimal if the pelvis is stable on the saddle and only slight peaks in pressure occur.

Saddle Positioning

Besides selecting an individually well-fitted model, the correct positioning of the saddle must not be forgotten. The fore–aft adjustment is important in placing the pelvis stably on the pressure-insensitive structures. In earlier studies (Silberman et al. 2005; Pruitt and Matheny 2006), the saddle fore–aft positioning was recommended to adjust the knee over the pedal spindle. The use of pressure mapping in combination with motion-capturing technology, however, shows that changing the saddle position has a stronger effect on pressure distribution on the saddle than does changing the knee position relative to the spindle. This relationship, however, needs further scientific examination.

In practice, many cyclists tend to mount the saddle too far back, thereby increasing the reach. The result is a positioning of the pelvis on the saddle nose, increasing the pressure on the pubis and thus causing saddle discomfort. The example in figure 5.9 shows the pressure distribution on the saddle before and after moving the saddle toward the handlebar by 5 millimeters. Both measurements were conducted holding the hoods on a road bike, keeping cadence and resistance constant.

The maximum pressure spot on the right side of the pubis remains visible but was reduced by 41 percent. The center of pressure (black pattern) was moved back by 12 millimeters. Overall, the rider uses more of the saddle surface (an additional 6 percent), causing the decrease in the maximum pressure.

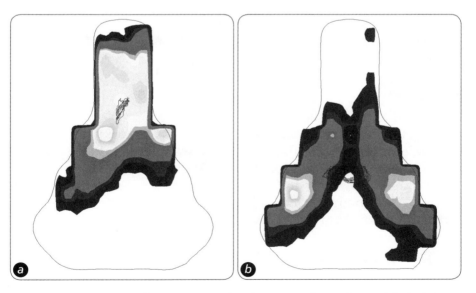

▶ **Figure 5.8** Analysis of the pressure distribution to determine saddle height.

Daniel Schade

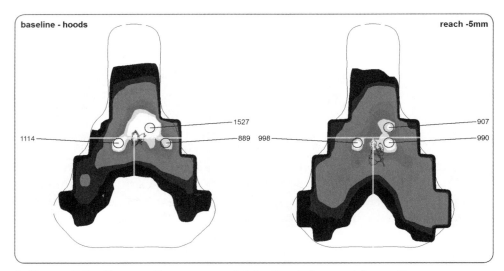

▶ **Figure 5.9** Comparative pressure distribution in two saddle positions.

Daniel Schade

A poorly fitted saddle position is possibly compensated by a wider shoulder angle and a related higher muscle tension in the shoulder girdle. Therefore, a variable to be measured in a dynamic position analysis is the tension of the upper-arm muscles. In addition, increased activation of the back muscles to pull up the shoulder is an indicator of overstraining. Both compensatory movements result from a poor saddle position and compromise the stability of the entire rider–bike system. This stability can be improved by positioning the whole bone structure of the pelvis on the saddle. Therefore, fore–aft positioning becomes an important parameter in the analysis of the position to increase comfort and stability.

Saddle Tilt

Cyclists tend to tilt the saddle nose down to decrease the pressure on the pubis. But this adjustment can result in an unstable position of the pelvis on the saddle and increase the share of the weight force that is put on the handlebar. Because the palms are not suited to be the main weight bearers, problems are merely moved, not solved. The wrong saddle height is often the cause. The recommendation is to adjust the saddle height properly with a horizontal saddle before possibly tilting the saddle nose down a little.

Discipline-Specific Differences

Discipline-specific differences in the position affect the interaction at the saddle contact point. Bini, Hume, and Croft (2014) showed significant differences in the back angle and the pelvic alignment between road cyclists and triathletes. The pressure distribution on the saddle was also different among the disciplines. Analysis of the pressure data of 150 cyclists (one-third mountain bike, one-third road bike, one-third triathlon) in the gebioMized concept lab in Münster (Germany) showed significant differences. Figures 5.10 through 5.12 show the typical pressure distribution for each of the three disciplines. The values given in the text represent the average of all riders in that discipline.

In a typical MTB position, the main load on the saddle is in a zone of 10.7 to 15.7 centimeters behind the saddle nose (figure 5.10). Accordingly, 57 percent of the main share of the force on the saddle lies on the sit bones, and the pubis is loaded with 43 percent. The center of pressure is located 13.2 centimeters behind the saddle nose.

When holding the hoods on the road bike, typically the midpart of the saddle is strained. The main load is on the zone 9.1 to 15.1 centimeters behind the nose

▶ **Figure 5.10** Typical pressure plot for MTB.

Daniel Schade

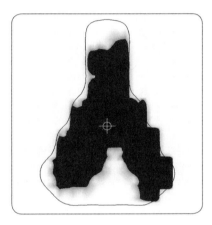

▶ **Figure 5.11** Typical pressure plot for road bike.

Daniel Schade

▶ **Figure 5.12** Typical pressure plot for triathlon.

Daniel Schade

(figure 5.11), and the center of pressure is at 12.1 centimeters. The pressure is distributed almost equally between pubis (49 percent) and sit bones (51 percent).

The typical pressure distribution in triathlon (figure 5.12) is strongly centered toward the front. Here, the pubis is strained with 73 percent of the weight, and the sit bones are strained with 27 percent. The center of pressure is positioned 7.9 centimeters behind the saddle nose, and the main loading zone starts at 4.4 centimeters and ends at 11.2 centimeters. Because of this smaller contact surface the highest maximum pressure values can be found in this position.

Applying the Science

In conclusion, the connection between the pelvis and saddle is of central importance for the entire rider–bike system. A thorough analysis and optimization of this interface helps in stabilizing the entire position and in increasing comfort on the bike. Achieving this stability and comfort will improve the athlete's well-being and performance.

PART III

The Human–Machine Interface

CHAPTER 6

Biomechanics of Cycling

—Rodrigo Rico Bini

Cycling involves the transmission of forces between human body segments and bicycle components. This link commonly involves the hands and handlebars, the saddle and pelvis, and the pedals and feet. Both the saddle (60 to 360 newtons) and handlebars (40 to 80 newtons) have been shown to transfer substantial force back to the cyclist (Stone and Hull 1995), which, over time, has been linked to wrist and hand injuries (Patterson, Jaggars, and Boyer 2003; Slane et al. 2011). Moreover, saddle–pelvis contact could be a site for overuse injuries on the perineum (Bressel and Cronin 2005).

Although force transmission at the pelvis and upper limbs is critical, muscle force is the key driver to move the bicycle and sustain motion during pedaling. To produce power to move the bicycle, skeletal muscles contract and relax at cyclical rates to transfer force toward the bicycle cranks. From anatomical design, human muscles have limitations on their ability to produce maximal force, which implies the existence of optimal combinations of motions for force production (Rassier, MacIntosh, and Herzog 1999). For that reason defining an optimal position template to fit cyclists on their bicycles has been the goal of cyclists, coaches, and scientists.

This chapter introduces the existing evidence on the potential link between changes in the human body and bicycle configuration. The intention is not to present an optimal configuration, which is discussed in a later chapter. Attention is given to the potential effect of changes in body position on force production. Along with muscle mechanics, recruitment strategies are discussed, given that the central nervous system dictates the rhythm of contractions, seeking an optimal combination between force production and energy cost.

Muscle Mechanics

The most accepted theory for contraction of skeletal muscles involves the attachment between multiple small units of myosin and actin within an individual muscle. Classic studies suggest that the number of attached myosin heads to the actin framework should determine force magnitude (Rassier,

MacIntosh, and Herzog 1999), based on the assumption that more attached actin–myosin units should lead to stronger force production (Rassier, MacIntosh, and Herzog 1999). Moreover, given the anatomical attachment of muscles wrapped around bones and joints, any force produced by a muscle is more effective for motion if that force is translated into joint torque, which will be affected by muscle length. Therefore, the overall dependence between muscle length and force production can be illustrated by the torque–angle relationship during maximal isometric contractions (see figure 6.1).

Various studies (Herzog 2007; Rassier, MacIntosh, and Herzog 1999) report that a reduction in force (and torque) occurs toward shorter and longer muscle lengths; muscles have a range of lengths where they can produce optimal force (i.e., 60 to 70 degrees for knee extensor and 20 to 30 degrees for knee flexor, as seen in figure 6.1). This range has been referred to as the optimal operational length because of the maximal possible number of active actin–myosin units (Austin, Nilwik, and Herzog 2010). Again taking the muscle as a whole, any changes in length toward maximal shortening or lengthening should lead to a reduction in maximal capacity for force production. This phenomenon has critical implication for activities such as bicycle pedaling given that joints cover a large range of changes, leading to wide change in

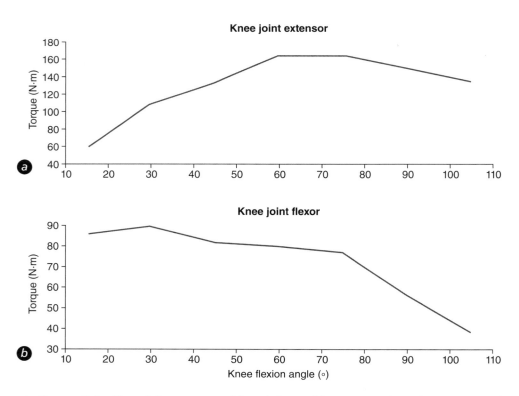

▶ **Figure 6.1**   Knee joint extensor (a) and flexor (b) torques taken during maximal isometric contraction at seven knee joint flexion angles.

muscle length. Using the knee joint as an example, it has been shown that a range of 60 to 70 degrees in joint angle could lead to a change of 20 percent in muscle length, using the model of Hawkins and Hull (1990).

Figure 6.2 illustrates the effects of changing saddle heights from preferred to low (2 percent) and high (3 percent) on vastus lateralis (VL, the main quadriceps muscle) length in 12 trained cyclists pedaling at about 250 watts and 90 revolutions per minute. Pedaling at their preferred saddle height (86 plus or minus 3 centimeters), VL length at the three o'clock crank position (90 degrees of crank cycle) changes from 66 percent of thigh length to 67 percent at the low saddle height (84 plus or minus 3 centimeters) and to 65 percent of thigh length at the high saddle height (88 plus or minus 3 centimeters). These differences are smaller than previous observations shown in other studies (2 to 4 centimeters in muscle length) using larger changes in saddle height (100 to 115 percent of leg length) (Gregor 2000). Even at the shortest muscle length, differences from changes in saddle height were about 4 percent, which may not largely affect muscle force production. This hypothesis is supported by the unchanged cycling efficiency observed when saddle height is changed in a range of plus or minus 4 percent (Connick and Li 2013). Along this line, Yoshihuku and Herzog (1996) illustrated by simulation modeling that changes in saddle height up to 4 percent of a given height could lead to changes in power produced by individual muscles. Although large reductions in crank and knee joint extensor power could be observed when lowering saddle height more than 4 centimeters, other muscle groups (e.g., hamstrings and gluteus maximus) seem to minimize the reduced crank power.

Changes in velocity of muscle contraction have been shown to play a major role in force production. Studies show that muscle force production declines

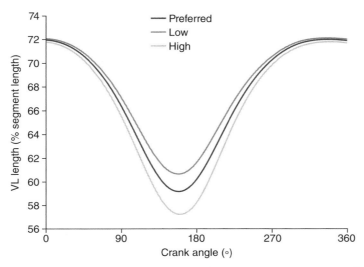

▶ **Figure 6.2** Vastus lateralis length with preferred, low, and high saddles.

exponentially with increased shortening velocity (Rassier, MacIntosh, and Herzog 1999). In figure 6.3, an example of maximal torque derived from isokinetic contractions highlights the exponential profile of muscle (and torque) production.

The main potential reason for the decline in muscle force production with increases in shortening velocity (i.e., higher cadences) has been associated with reduced capacity for maintenance of active cross-bridges (Rassier, MacIntosh, and Herzog 1999). Therefore, maximal power is a function of both a muscle's maximal force production and shortening velocity. Dorel et al. (2010) illustrated this pattern by maximal sprint cycling at different pedaling cadences. Determining a general optimal pedaling cadence for all situations is more difficult given that slow fibers have maximal efficiency at 72 revolutions per minute, whereas fast fibers work optimally at 84 revolutions per minute (Umberger, Gerritsen, and Martin 2006). Therefore, other factors (e.g., hemodynamics, inertial properties of body segments, muscle activations, and so on) seem to play an additional role in determining preferred pedaling cadence.

More recently, changes in muscle length have been assessed in terms of changes in active muscle components and noncontractile (e.g., tendons)

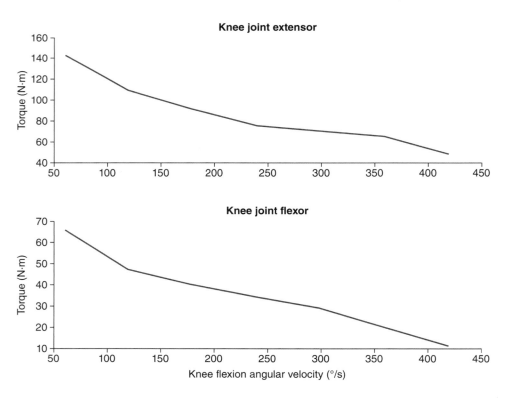

▶ **Figure 6.3** Relationship between maximal torque with knee extension and flexion speed.

components. Muraoka et al. (2001) observed a greater proportional shortening for the active muscle component of the vastus lateralis compared to its muscle–tendon unit. This finding indicates that the stiffness of the tendons could play an important role in transferring force during pedaling. This conclusion has been speculated by Sanderson and Amoroso (2009) through observations that the soleus stretches actively whereas the gastrocnemius shortens actively during the recovery phase of the crank cycle. Taken together, the existence of active stretch also lends support to the potential role of ankle joint muscles in transferring power from the legs to the crank (Kautz and Neptune 2002). The existence of active stretch and the transferring of power through tendons could have implications for the prescription of supporting training for cyclists (e.g., active stretch training) to enhance muscle–tendon stiffness. Comparison between stiffness in cyclists from varying disciplines (e.g., road, track, triathlon) could shed light on training needs for each discipline (e.g., strength or plyometrics) given that stiffness of tendons could be enhanced by training (Magnusson et al. 2008) and is critical for transferring power from muscles to bones.

Evidence has shown that active shortening before maximal force production negatively affects force production, whereas active stretching leads to enhanced muscle force capacity (Herzog 2007). Computer simulation modeling has been used to illustrate force depression after active shortening during cycling (McGowan, Neptune, and Herzog 2013). Decreases of 20 to 40 percent in crank power have been shown with a tight link to declines in force produced by the hip and knee extensors (i.e., gluteus maximus and vastii). More prominent effects were observed at the latter sections of crank power (i.e., three o'clock to six o'clock crank positions). Future research could assess whether reduction in magnitude of muscle work during shortening could reduce force depression during cycling as observed in isolated muscles (McGowan, Neptune, and Herzog 2013).

In summary, changes in muscle length and shortening velocity have a critical effect on power production during cycling. In addition, active shortening (or lengthening) before muscle force production has the potential to affect force magnitude during cycling (McGowan, Neptune, and Herzog 2013). These properties of the skeletal muscle should be the focus of upcoming design of bicycle components (e.g., noncircular chainrings) to optimize muscle function and enhance crank power.

Muscle Recruitment Strategies

Muscle force production depends on neural drive from the higher centers of the central nervous system. In cyclical movements such as pedaling, central nervous system linkages between the right and left sides of the body are such that optimal muscle control enforces minimum possible activation for the shortest possible duration to minimize energy cost (Takaishi et al. 1998).

This section briefly reviews some key aspects of muscle activation dynamics during pedaling. Figure 6.4 shows ensemble activation of some lower-limb muscles from six cyclists pedaling at the load of their ventilatory threshold (about 260 watts) and 90 revolutions per minute, measured using surface recording of electrical muscle activity (electromyography or EMG).

The recording of EMG on each graph summarizes the neural control of many muscle fibers. Although consistency in muscle activation could be expected to control energy cost (Blake and Wakeling 2013), muscle activation can be changed in terms of timing (onset and offset) and magnitude at a given point in time. The control of timing and intensity can lead to a fine-tuning of

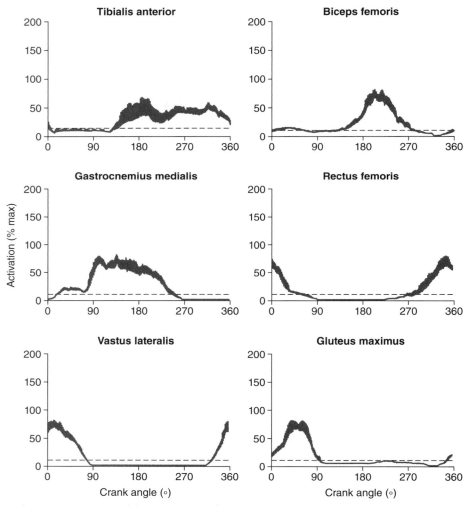

▶ **Figure 6.4** Ensemble activation of lower-limb muscles.

Reprinted from R.R. Bini, F.P. Carpes, and F. Diefenthaeler, 2011, "Effects of cycling with the knees close to the bicycle frame on the lower limb muscle activation," Brazilian Journal of Physical Education and Sport 25(1): 27-37.

energy cost given that unnecessary activation (e.g., longer or stronger) could decrease motion efficiency. This control seems to be affected by varying factors such as bicycle geometry (Savelberg, Van de Port, and Willems 2003), pedaling cadence (Lucia et al. 2004), workload (MacIntosh, Neptune, and Horton 2000), and changes in bicycle components (e.g., decoupled cranks) (Hug, Boumier, and Dorel 2013).

An additional factor in muscle activation dynamics is related to fatigue state. During short- or long-duration cycling, lower-limb muscles are subject to energy cost to move the legs and to overcome crank resistance. An effect from fatigue is the loss of muscle contraction capabilities during both high- and low-intensity exercise, requiring greater central nervous system drive to generate the same amount of force (Abbiss and Laursen 2005). This reduction in neuromuscular efficiency could indicate that muscle fibers are unable to sustain similar force production because of fatigue (Hautier et al. 2000). This lower efficiency has been reflected in anticipated large activation of main muscle drivers (e.g., gluteus maximus and vastus lateralis) (Diefenthaeler et al. 2012) when cyclists pedaled at a fixed workload and cadence to exhaustion. Suggested changes in recruitment of motor units has been inferred (Diefenthaeler, Bini, and Vaz 2012), although detecting individual changes in recruitment of motor units is not possible by surface EMG analysis. In a way, the central nervous system seems to change muscle control to cope with reduced efficiency when fatigue affects muscle actions.

Simultaneous measurements of muscle activation on both sides of the body during cycling are not commonly performed because of the limitation in the number of channels available for recording. But because asymmetry in force and torque production has been observed in some studies (Carpes et al. 2007), bilateral differences in muscle activation should be expected. Contrary to the hypothesis that bilateral asymmetries were caused by differences in neural drive, Carpes and colleagues observed that during conventional double-leg cycling (Carpes et al. 2011) or during single-leg cycling drills (Carpes et al. 2010), no differences occurred in activation of lower-limb muscles. This finding lends support to potential similarities in bilateral performance and equal capability of control of lower-limb muscles. Further research is needed in this area given that differences in joint kinematics (Edeline et al. 2004) and crank torque (Bini and Hume 2014; Carpes et al. 2007) have been observed with an unclear link to whether these differences are from different motor control for each leg or from differences in dimensions of lower-limb bones (Kanchan et al. 2008).

Applying the Science

Muscle length and shortening velocity state have a critical effect in maximal force production. During cycling, however, lower-limb muscle length effects in cycling performance from changes in body position (i.e., saddle position) seem to be controlled whenever changes in body position are within 4 percent from the optimal setup. Muscle force production is largely affected by the stretching–shortening nature of pedaling action, leading to reductions in crank power. Neural drive is affected by fatigue state, and muscle activation assessments have been sensitive in anticipating effects from fatigue in pedaling. In contrast, existing evidence does not support the link between neural control and bilateral asymmetries in pedal forces and crank power.

Training to improve noncontractile stiffness of tendons (e.g., plyometric and active stretching) and to reduce variability in activation of lower-limb muscles is required for improvements of muscle mechanics in cycling motion. Effects of changes in bicycle configuration on muscle force and power production and a suggested approach to optimizing bicycle configuration are discussed in a later chapter.

CHAPTER 7

The Science of Bike Fit

—Rodrigo Rico Bini

Body position on the bicycle has a major effect in cycling performance. This statement may seem obvious when looking back to the potential effects from changes in muscle length on maximal muscle force production. But much more comes into play regarding muscle length and crank power during pedaling. Researchers and clinicians have different views on the effects from changes in bike configuration on cycling performance and injury risk.

From a clinical perspective, an optimum configuration for bicycles should be followed to elicit maximal performance and reduce injury risk. To provide a starting step for bicycle configuration, De Vey Mestdagh (1998) presented varying methods to configure road bicycles with a focus on eliciting maximal performance and reducing injury risk. These methods were based on matching cyclists' anthropometrical measures to bicycle dimensions. Although bicycle and body dimensions are linked, later findings from Peveler et al. (2005) and Estivalet et al. (2008) showed that setting bicycles based exclusively on anthropometric measures elicited different joint angles and led to changes in the original preferred setup used by professional cyclists.

To show why the link between bicycle configuration and body position is not linear, research has defined the configuration of bicycle components based on changes in joint motion (Peveler 2008) or even based on changes from an individual preferred configuration (Bini, Hume, and Kilding 2014; Bini et al. 2014) to assess what would happen if cyclists were moved away from their existing configurations. Recall that preferred body position on the bicycle is likely matched to the optimal combination of muscle lengths for maximal force production given that muscle–tendon lengths adapt from long-term training (Savelberg and Meijer 2003).

To stress the different views from research and clinical practice, this chapter aims to show why bike fitters should not opt for small changes in bicycle configuration to seek large changes in performance.

Bike Configuration, Body Position, and Cycling Performance

Moving back to muscle mechanics, we must remember that skeletal muscles have a range of changes in length that does not elicit any effect on maximal muscle force production (i.e., plateau in force length and torque angle relationship) (Rassier, MacIntosh, and Herzog 1999). Expanding this plateau to the many muscles involved in pedaling action, Yoshihuku and Herzog (1996) developed a computer model of skeletal muscles used during pedaling and assessed what would happen if changes in bicycle configuration were performed. They showed that changes in saddle height of about 4 centimeters should not significantly affect maximal crank power production. This finding was later confirmed by Rankin and Neptune (2008) using a similar computer simulation approach in which maximal power output predicted for sprint cycling was not affected by small changes in saddle height.

Those familiar with bike fitting may be surprised that the "large" change of 4 centimeters did not affect maximal sprint performance. Indeed, Yoshihuku and Herzog (1996) illustrated that potential changes in individual muscle forces may be observed (e.g., increase in the force of hip flexors when using higher saddle height) but might also be mitigated by reduction in maximal force production from other muscle groups (e.g., reduction in the force of hip extensors when using higher saddle height). A latter study in "real cyclists" observed that indeed changes of about 4 centimeters did not affect cycling efficiency (ratio between power production by energy cost) (Connick and Li 2013), reinforcing that changes observed in joint motion when moving the saddle up or down were somewhat accommodated at the three main joints (i.e., hip, knee, and ankle; see Bini, Hume, and Kilding 2014; Bini et al. 2013; Price and Donne 1997).

Moving to the link between observed changes in joint motion and cycling injury risk, much has been said on optimal setup to reduce knee pain (Holmes, Pruitt, and Whalen 1994; Silberman et al. 2005). One of the key settings for reducing knee injuries is setting saddle height to elicit 25 to 30 degrees of knee flexion angle when the crank is at the six o'clock position (180 degrees of crank angle). Although this criterion has been largely used in a clinical perspective, research has shown that joint angles measured from a static cyclist do not replicate angles from cycling motion (Bini 2011; Ferrer-Roca et al. 2012). Along with that, changes in workload during pedaling affected knee (Peveler et al. 2012) and ankle angles (Bini et al. 2012), which reinforces that joint angles are load dependent and that bike fitting must involve the assessment of cyclists in varying exercise intensities.

Although many interventions have been advocated as effective in preventing overuse injuries in cycling, only a small percentage of these interventions have been shown to be effective in controlled trials (Dettori and Norvell 2006).

Salai et al. (1999) observed that cyclists with existing nonspecific low-back pain may benefit from a decline of 10 to 15 degrees of the anterior portion of their saddles to reduce lumbar flexion. Another effective approach involves wrist numbness, which can be reduced by using foam gloves (Slane et al. 2011). Apart from these changes, keeping saddle height within a range of about 4 percent of the preferred saddle height (i.e., about 96 percent of the trochanteric height; Bini 2012) and sustaining a fore–aft position on the saddle of about 3 or 4 degrees (Bini et al. 2013) should be sufficient to secure minimum injury risk. But these ranges should be tested in a longer prospective study to assess the number of cyclists who may reduce injury risk.

An open question on optimal saddle position configuration is related to potential effects on saddle pressure. Previous studies showed that workload, upper-body posture, and saddle type have a large effect on saddle pressure (Carpes et al. 2009a; Carpes et al. 2009b), but no study assessed the effect of changes in saddle height on saddle pressure.

Road, Triathlon, and Time-Trial Bike Configurations

Although many say that the configuration of bicycle components is of minor priority for cycling performance and injury risk, some work remains to be done on bike fitting. Taking a bottom-to-top approach for configuring bicycle components, some examples of changes in road, triathlon, and time-trial bike configurations are provided as a starting point based on existing evidence from research. The goal is to improve the proposal presented by De Vey Mestdagh (1998) and to indicate the main gaps where future research could be useful.

Shoe–Cleat Configuration

Assuming that we intend to configure a bicycle for a given cyclist, the primary link, using a bottom-to-top approach, is to fit the shoe–cleat position. Many say that we should match the cleat position to the heads of the metatarsal bones, but no research supports that suggestion. When the horizontal position of the foot on the pedal was varied (forward or backward; see figure 7.1), no significant effects on knee joint forces (Ericson and Nisell 1987), muscle activity (Litzenberger et al. 2008), pedal forces (Ericson and Nisell 1988), or oxygen uptake (Paton 2009) were observed. Therefore, no current evidence supports that the horizontal position of the foot on the pedal can be optimized to reduce the risk of overuse injuries or improve performance. Indeed, Ramos Ortega, Munuera, and Dominguez (2012) observed that cyclists opt for placing the metatarsal head 3.6 plus or minus 0.8 centimeters forward in relation to the pedal axle as the preferred fore–aft shoe-to-pedal setting.

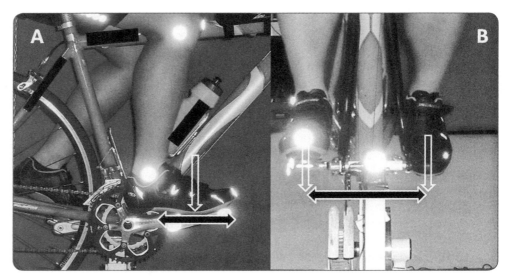

▶ **Figure 7.1** (*a*) Horizontal (fore–aft) position of the foot and shoe on the pedal (*b*) Q-factor or distance between the midpoint of the two feet.

Rodrigo Rico Bini

Preliminary findings also suggest that some degree of rotation (float) should be offered by shoe–cleat interface, given that this rotation could reduce risk of knee injury (Gregor and Wheeler 1994). But no solid link between the range of motion for rotation and knee injuries has been shown. Likewise, the knees have room for moving medially or laterally in relation to the pedal. Although this motion does not exclusively depend on bicycle setting, knee adduction and abduction could be affected by three factors. The first is mediolateral control of knee incline, which has been shown to be less developed in cyclists with anterior knee pain because of a more pronounced knee medial projection (Bailey, Maillardet, and Messenger 2003). The second is the use of shoe wedges, which force the lower leg to be inclined inward or outward. On this issue, Sanderson, Black, and Montgomery (1994) observed that cyclists produced similar lower-leg inclines even when using a 10-degree wedge (inward and outward). The third factor is a more recently explored Q-factor, which is the width from pedal to pedal in the frontal plane view (figure 7.1*b*). Disley and Li (2014) reported that reduced Q-factor (i.e., closer pedals) could lead to increased cycling efficiency (rate of power produced by energy cost).

Saddle Position

Moving focus toward the saddle, differences between road and triathlon bicycles have been limited to a greater forward saddle position for triathletes (Bini, Hume, and Croft 2014) (reduced "reach" in figure 7.2), which is in line

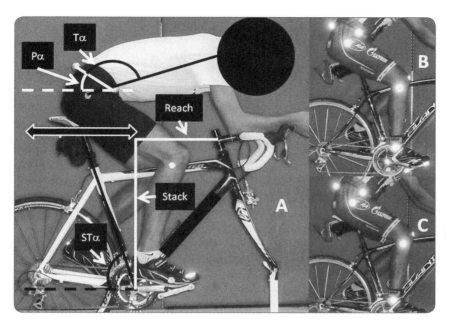

▶ **Figure 7.2** (a) Trunk (Tα) and pelvis (Pα) angles along with seat tube angle (STα). The black arrow indicates horizontal position. (b) Saddle set back such that the front of the knee is over the pedal spindle. (c) Saddle set forward with the front of the knee well forward of the pedal sindle.

Rodrigo Rico Bini

with optimal cycling efficiency (Price and Donne 1997). Ideally, saddle fore–aft position should elicit a saddle to bottom bracket angle (seat tube angle) close to 80 degrees (Price and Donne 1997; figure 7.2). This setting should be complemented by saddle height; close to 96 to 100 percent of leg length has been shown to be effective for maximal cycling efficiency (Connick and Li 2013; Price and Donne 1997).

A key goal of triathlon and time-trial bicycles is to optimize the aerodynamic profile. Therefore, a lower frontal projected area is a fundamental goal when riding in aerobars compared with riding in the hoods or drops (García-López et al. 2008). Along with that, moving the knees inward, as previously reported, could be intended by triathletes, but no research has shown the effect on reduction in drag force in moving the knee closer to the bicycle frame. The magnitude of medial knee projection is unknown, but cyclists with anterior knee pain have been shown to have 320 percent greater medial displacement than cyclists without anterior knee pain (Bailey, Maillardet, and Messenger 2003), indicating that excessive medial movement may be associated with knee pain and overload of the knee joint (Ericson, Nisell, and Ekholm 1984).

Optimal position of the handlebar in relation to the saddle is unknown. Upper-body flexion (i.e., trunk angle; see figure 7.2) should be larger for triathletes than for road cyclists (Bini, Hume, and Croft 2014). Although greater forward lean should be expected for triathletes, that should not be followed by reduced hip flexion to optimize off-bike running performance (Garside and Doran 2000). Therefore, triathletes should opt for a forward overall position on the bicycle compared with road cyclists to elicit greater trunk flexion and reduced frontal projected area. But no evidence has been done on how much the handlebar should be moved forward in relation to the saddle to elicit similar joint angles for a more forward position on the bicycle. Empirical measures have been suggested (i.e., stack and reach; see figure 7.2) that could be effective for accommodating similar configurations across different bicycles (Empfield 1999). But no studies have assessed whether changes in stack and reach measures could sustain similar joint motion.

Upper-Body Position

Upper-body position (including saddle–pelvis interface) is critical given that a sustained position has been shown to elicit reduced vascular support at the pudendal area (Bressel and Larson 2003) and hands and wrists (Patterson, Jaggars, and Boyer 2003; Slane et al. 2011). The option for saddles with a cutout relief area (Bressel, Bliss, and Cronin 2009) and for foam gloves (Slane et al. 2011) seems to mitigate the harmful effects of long-duration weight support. On this issue, more research is needed on weight distribution strategies that allow cyclists to share saddle load with the pedals. Elbow flexion is empirically used to increase upper-body support by elbow extensors contraction to reduce load directed to hands and wrists. But no evidence has assessed the effectiveness of this intervention.

Applying the Science

In summary, according to a report from Dettori and Norvell (2006), little evidence supports the existing guidelines for bike fitting. Along with that, recommendations are based on practical experience from road cyclists, which limit application to triathlon and time-trial bicycles. Novel methods (e.g., stack and reach) should be tested to ascertain whether they elicit similar joint motion when changing bicycle types.

Although optimal body position may be a dead-end search, a bottom-to-top setting approach is recommended, focusing on joint motion, given that muscle lengths and force production depend on joint angles. Therefore, a motion-based approach should be intended, assuming that joint angles are load and cadence dependent.

CHAPTER 8

Bike Fit and Body Positioning

—Todd M. Carver

Bike fit is a broad term used to describe the positioning of a rider on a bicycle. Positioning the rider involves adjusting the contact points between the rider and bike to achieve comfort and optimize performance. Many types of professionals conduct bike fits in their daily practice. Bicycle retailers, cycling coaches, and physiotherapists are the professionals who contribute most to providing this service to the cycling consumer. As bike fitting has progressed into the modern era, two categories of fit have clearly emerged: performance and clinical.

The objectives of a performance bike fit are to determine a rider's proper fit coordinates and to produce suitable frame geometry and equipment to match. A fit coordinate is a measurement that describes something about a rider's position on a bike (e.g., saddle height, handlebar reach, and so on). Measurements of frame geometry describe something about a bike's construction in terms of lengths and angles (top tube length, headtube angle, frame stack and reach, and so on).

Performance fitting, usually conducted at a bicycle shop, fitting studio, or sports medicine facility, should be accomplished at some point during the purchase process of a new bike or at any time significant changes occur in the cyclist's body or the contact points of the bicycle. Examples of the latter might include loss of flexibility with age, changing to a different saddle, or after a crash that results in major injury or broken bones. Performance fitting is popular among cyclists whose riding style demands long-distance comfort or short-distance power and efficiency.

The objective of a clinical bike fit is to resolve a problem. A certain percentage of cyclists, even when they are positioned in line with performance standards, will seek fine-tuning of the position to optimize performance or to treat a usage injury. During a clinical fit, by nature of the fact that performance fit parameters have already been achieved, the changes are viewed more as interventions with respect to the rider's functional ability to increase performance or resolve an injury. Sometimes the interventions made during a clinical fit session last for the entire career of the cyclist, if indeed a structural abnormality exists (e.g., leg-length discrepancy). Other times these same interventions are removed as the cyclist's body improves in terms of a functional limitation (e.g., flexibility and strength imbalances). The procedure for this level of fit is less recipe based and more iterative in terms of likely solutions because little scientific support exists for the methods employed.

Fit Methods

Three methods of bike fitting exist today: statistical, static, and dynamic. In the earliest days of bike fitting, the standard procedure was to predict a rider's critical fit coordinates from known relationships between rider anthropometrics and resulting fit coordinates. Through regression analysis, saddle position was proposed to be set a certain distance from the pedal spindle (Hamley and Thomas 1967) or the bottom bracket (LeMond and Gordis 1990) and the handlebar location was set a certain distance from the saddle (de vey Mestdagh 1998). Although these methods, when combined, can fit a rider in the relative ballpark, this statistical approach to fitting has lost credibility among those in the fit industry because of the imprecise relationship between rider anthropometrics and optimal cycling position.

In the 1980s a more personalized approach to bike fit emerged as a method of measuring a rider's knee angles became popular (Holmes et al. 1994). In the cycling industry this approach is called the static fitting method. By incorporating rider knee angle into the process, this method accounts for all of the rider's anthropometrics, as well as the pedal–shoe–cleat and saddle–pelvis interface adjustments that affect reach to the pedal platform. The main measurement used in this style of fitting is the extension angle of the knee at the bottom position of the pedal stroke. By this method, the optimal range for cycling has been suggested to be 25 to 30 degrees of flexion (Holmes et al. 1994; Burke and Pruitt 2003), and the best way to measure that angle is directly with a goniometer in a static position (Peveler 2008). Although this method can work well for a performance fitting at the retail level, it can lead to errors in positioning because of the differences between static and dynamic joint positions on the bike (Ferrer-Roca et al. 2012).

Modern-day bike fit has entered a new era in which technological advances in video and motion capture make it possible to obtain much more data about how a rider sits on, and pedals, a bicycle. What has become clear from the literature is that many different styles of riding exist from a kinematic and kinetic point of view. The dynamic fit process is used today by countless cyclists and triathletes to solve the interaction problems between themselves and the machine. Some of the kinematic measurements that are common in this method of fit are joint range of motion, joint angles at critical events in the pedal stroke (top and bottom dead center), movement patterns such as ankling and foot float, and alignments of various parts of the body. Kinetic measuring technologies exist such as pressure and drivetrain force and torque sensors, but currently no protocols exist for bike fitting applications.

The goal of this chapter is to introduce the current best practices in dynamic bike fitting and include scientific evidence when possible.

Foot Position

The first step in foot positioning is to set the horizontal (fore–aft) foot position on the pedal spindle. This step is accomplished by setting the cleat position so that the pedal spindle bisects a line drawn between the first and fifth metatarsal heads (figure 8.1). Changing the foot position in the horizontal direction does not change knee loads (Ruby and Hull 1993) and therefore should not affect a rider's susceptibility to injury. In addition, it has been shown that many different horizontal foot positions elicit the same cycling efficiency (Van Sickle and Hull 2007). No data exist on the effect of horizontal foot position on maximal cycling power generation. The cycling industry's stance on a neutral foot position is shown in figure 8.1.

The second step of foot positioning is to support the foot inside the shoe with an off-the-shelf cycling insole or a custom-fabricated foot orthosis. Foot support during cycling is a continual topic of debate among clinicians and bike fitters because of the high variability of preferences across cyclists. Generally, insoles and foot orthoses have been shown to change lower-extremity kinematics and kinetics in activities such as running (Mündermann et al. 2003), but no evidence exists to support the notion that this change affects risk of injury or performance. Cycling research has shown that foot orthoses have no significant effect on performance (Hice et al. 1985; Anderson and Sockler 1990; Koch et al. 2013).

The third step of foot positioning is to set the foot float angle about the pedal spindle. This process contains two steps. First, the amount of float needed for each rider must be determined. Second, the foot angles that the float rotation can allow the foot to achieve mechanically need to be set (angle of the cleat on the shoe, angle of the foot on the pedal).

Determining the exact amount of float needed for a particular rider is not easy. But luckily, this aspect is not critical because research (Ruby and

▶ **Figure 8.1** An industry-standard foot position on the pedal spindle, which should bisect a line drawn between the first and fifth metatarsal heads (marked with reflective dots).

Todd Carver

Hull 1993) suggests that excessive float does not impair performance or lead to injury. Determining the optimal foot angles within the float range (cleat rotation on shoe) is much harder. Current best practice within the fit industry is to use a moderately floating cleat (3 to 5 degrees), start with the cleat angle positioned to facilitate a neutral foot angle on the spindle, and then make subtle changes to optimize knee-tracking metrics or elicit approval from rider feedback.

The fourth step in foot positioning is to set the stance width, or Q-factor, of the foot–pedal system. Traditional pedal systems come with Q-factors of about 150 millimeters and are suitable for most recreational and competitive cyclists. During performance and clinical fitting, the common practice is to narrow the stance width for riders with medial-tracking knees and widen the stance width for lateral-tracking knees. But despite one study that showed a significant improvement in cycling efficiency by narrowing this stance width significantly (Disley and Li 2014), a void exists in the literature to support these movements during bike fitting.

The final step in foot positioning is forefoot wedging, or shimming. This step usually only occurs at the clinical level of fitting, but it can be used during some performance fitting situations as well. External (between cleat and shoe) or internal forefoot (between shoe sole and inner sole) shims can be used to augment or attenuate foot inversion or eversion at the subtalar joint of the ankle and potentially have an effect on the position and nondriving forces of the knee (Ruby and Hull 1993). Although studies have shown that this type of foot correction has no predictable effect on knee position (Sanderson, Black, and Montgomery 1994) and can even cause increases in nondriving knee torques (Gregersen, Hull, and Hakansson 2006), it must be stated that the population used for the investigations were uninjured riders. Altering the foot–pedal interface in this way may possibly have a positive effect on short-term and long-term treatments of certain usage injuries of the ankle, knee, and hip.

Crank Length

Crank length selection is important in performance and clinical fitting situations. Mechanically speaking, the length of the crank is important for leverage in the drivetrain system. Biomechanically, the length of the crank has implications on joint range of motion and therefore affects the length–tension relationship of the working muscles. Physiologically, crank length affects pedal speed at given cadences (Martin and Spirduso 2001) and therefore can potentially have an effect on muscle-shortening velocities, which have been shown to have optimal ranges (Hautier et al. 1996).

The study by Inbar et al. (1983) shows that 175-millimeter crank lengths are adequate for producing peak power during a 30-second trial but warns that failing to adjust this length across different sizes of cyclists could result in a decrease in their ability to generate optimal peak power. Note, however, that these authors' thoughts on this phenomenon have yet to be empirically supported. Crank length selection, within the commercially available range of 160 to 180 millimeters, has been shown to have no effect on maximal power production (Martin and Spirduso 2001), submaximal mechanical efficiency (McDaniel et al. 2002), or joint power coordination between the ankle, knee, and hip when cadence is adjusted to maintain optimal pedal speed (Barratt et al. 2011).

Practically speaking, though, excessively long or short crank lengths relative to the rider's leg length can change the range of motion at these two major joints. Over long-duration cycling, this change could affect performance and place a rider at risk of injury. No data, however, exist to support or refute that statement.

Most properly sized bicycles are stocked with crank lengths that facilitate adequate range of motion at the knee and hip. Ericson, Nisell, and Németh (1988) concluded that average knee range of motion in their subject population was 66 degrees. By modern standards that figure seems very low. Unpublished data from a group of 40 world-tour-level professional riders, randomly selected from four teams, suggest that a higher value of 74 degrees is the average. The discrepancy in these values is potentially indicative of the differences in saddle height between recreational and professional riders. The cyclists in the study by Ericson, Nisell, and Németh produced a minimum knee flexion angle of 46 degrees, whereas the world-tour cyclists were at 37 degrees. Nordeen-Snyder (1976) as well as the current author conclude that raising the saddle height does increase the range of motion of the knee.

To reduce range of motion at the knee and hip, crank lengths are commonly shortened. This change has become a trend over the last few years in nondrafting triathletes. Shortening the crank length can open the hip angle because the crank does not come up as high at the top of the pedal stroke. This change allows the nondrafting triathlete to maintain a low back angle for aerodynamic purposes and prevents the hip angle from closing. Although anecdotal evidence is strong in support of this change, no scientific evidence exists to support this as a performance enhancement.

Saddle Selection

The process of selecting a saddle can be daunting when riders face the numerous options available today. To simplify matters, two categories of saddle shapes have emerged: traditional and anatomical. Traditional designs are intended to distribute contact forces between the pelvis and saddle to reduce pressure points across the available surface area. Anatomical saddles are designed with cutout regions to isolate forces to certain skeletal support areas of the pelvis, the ischial tuberosities and the pubic rami.

Clinically, anatomical saddle design is gaining popularity in the industry as a way to reduce pressure in the perineal region while cycling (Lowe, Schrader, and Breitenstein 2004). But these authors' definition of a proper saddle is one without a protruding nose, which most serious cyclists will not tolerate for reasons related to bike handling and hand pressure. Beyond eliminating the nose of a saddle, performance saddle designers now experiment with changing widths and shapes in an attempt to create a better match with a rider's pelvic anatomy. In theory, better matching between saddle width and shape is intended to relieve perineal saddle pressure and attenuate the loss of penile blood flow in men. Jeong et al. (2002) showed that wider saddles are associated with less drop in penile blood flow, and Carpes et al. (2009) showed that anatomical shaping and higher torso angles reduce perineal pressure.

To complicate the matter slightly, men and women appear to sit on saddles differently and respond differently to changes in workload and hand position. A female cyclist's center of pressure is typically farther back on the saddle than a man's, and women tend to rotate the pelvis anteriorly more than men do when moving from the hood to the drop position on the bar (Potter et al. 2008).

Saddle Position

Saddle position on a bicycle can be adjusted in three ways: saddle height, effective seat tube angle, and tilt. Research has documented that saddle placement has a significant effect on cycling performance (Nordeen-Snyder 1976; Peveler 2008). Those findings, however, are contradictory to the findings of Connick and Li (2013), which suggests that large saddle height variations have little effect on mechanical efficiency.

Saddle Height

Saddle height is defined as the distance from the center of the bottom bracket to the horizontal midpoint of the saddle profile. The saddle height for any particular rider should be set in a position that eliminates the need for any major joint (ankle, knee, or hip) to reach the end of its available range of motion in either flexion or extension. Pedaling in hyperflexion or hyperextension of the ankle, knee, or hip can place physiologic strain on the muscle fibers and connective tissue that do work at these joints (Haffajee, Moritz, and Svantesson 1972).

Because of the multiple joints of the lower extremity, the dynamic method of setting saddle height has become popular with retailers and clinicians. According to the data presented in figure 8.2, anthropometric measurements (leg length) can account for most of the variability in saddle height preference, but not all. Dynamic fitting methods can record the actual movements of the cyclist's leg while pedaling and therefore can help position saddle height more accurately.

Given the rather large deviation in saddle height scores compared with the leg length measurements (figure 8.2), the dynamically recorded angles of the knee joint seem to be preserved (table 8.1). For the same group of subjects with variable saddle heights relative to overall leg length, the standard

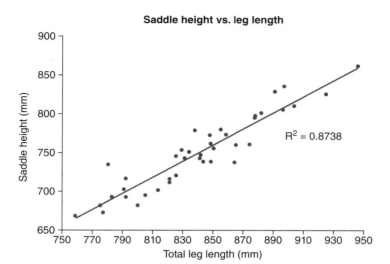

▶ **Figure 8.2** Relationship between rider leg length and resulting saddle heights for 40 world-tour riders. The large variability is a function of leg length only. Therefore, dynamic methods of saddle height placement may be better at finding the individual optimal saddle height for each rider.

Table 8.1 Lower-Extremity Kinematics of 40 World-Tour Cyclists

	Road	TT
Ankle angle maximum (degrees)	107.4 ± 6.1	112.0 ± 4.9
Ankle angle minimum (degrees)	83.9 ± 5.3	87.6 ± 4.8
Knee angle maximum (degrees)	111.0 ± 2.9	111.3 ± 2.9
Knee angle minimum (degrees)	36.7 ± 4.0	37.1 ± 3.6
Hip angle maximum (degrees)	118.2 ± 3.3	133.5 ± 3.3
Hip angle minimum (degrees)	74.1 ± 3.5	89.1 ± 3.5
Knee–foot horizontal offset (mm)	5.2 ± 18.2	77.8 ± 19.8

Data recorded with a commercially available 3D motion capture system during the 2014 season. Values are represented as mean plus or minus standard deviation. Joint angles are represented as flexion angles. Knee–foot horizontal offset describes the alignment of the knee joint over foot (fifth metatarsal head) at 90 degrees in the downstroke. Positive values represent a knee in front of the foot, and negative values represent a knee behind the foot at this particular event in the pedal stroke.

deviation for knee angles is relatively minor at 2.9 degrees and 4.0 degrees, maximum (top of stroke) and minimum (bottom of stroke), respectively.

In the same group of professional cyclists, the standard deviation of ankle angles is almost double that of the knee angles at 6.1 degrees and 5.3 degrees, maximum and minimum, respectively. These data suggest that each rider subtly adjusts ankling to preserve the knee in the adequate physiologic range. Additionally, one other place of compensation could be the horizontal position of the saddle and the position of the rider's pelvis on the saddle. The standard

▶ **Figure 8.3** Effective seat tube angle is defined as the angle between horizontal and the seat height axis.

deviation of the knee–foot horizontal offset is large at 18.2 millimeters, which suggests that riders are less sensitive to horizontal positioning than they are to changes in knee kinematics. These same trends seem to transfer between the road and time-trial (TT) positions for these riders, but the TT position is characterized by increased flexion of all these major joints (table 8.1).

Modern best practice protocol is to measure dynamic flexion and extension of the leg. A properly positioned saddle height should facilitate 35 to 40 degrees of knee flexion at maximal extension and 5 to 10 degrees of plantar flexion (extension) of the ankle. If the knee or ankle is lacking extension, the recommendation is to raise the saddle height. If the knee or ankle is overextended, the recommendation is to lower the saddle height.

Effective Seat Tube Angle or Saddle Setback

Effective seat tube angle (figure 8.3) is defined as the angle between horizontal and the seat height axis defined previously. Unlike the true seat tube angle of the bike, which is geometrically set, the effective seat tube angle is a fitting coordinate that can be adjusted. The adjustment range for the effective seat tube angle will be in the range of 71 to 75 degrees for road and mountain bikes and 75 to 85 degrees for time-trial bikes (including nondrafting triathlon bikes). Mechanically speaking, these ranges coincide with traditional thoughts about optimal bike handling and fore–aft rider positioning.

Saddle setback is another term used to describe the horizontal position of the saddle. Saddle setback is measured in millimeters and is defined as the horizontal distance from the front tip of the saddle to the bottom bracket. Because taking this measurement is easy, it is widely used in commercial bike fitting today.

Modern bicycles have become much more adjustable in this area as innovations in bike usage and therefore design have changed. Road and mountain bikes have changed little over the years in terms of achievable effective seat tube angles or saddle setbacks, but time-trial bikes have changed drastically. This change is likely in response to the growing number of participants in the sport of nondrafting triathlon and the popularity of using the time-trial style of bike for these events. Most modern time-trial bikes can achieve a larger effective seat tube angle (steeper), which allows a triathlete to position the saddle much farther forward than previously possible.

Within a geometrically determined range, effective seat tube angle (or saddle setback) is adjusted on a bicycle by moving the saddle along the rails or changing to a different seat post with a different offset between seat post axis and the saddle clamp. This adjustment mainly affects the position of the hip and knee joint over the drivetrain of the bicycle. Historically, the focus from the fit industry has been on the position of the knee joint. In 2003 Burke and Pruitt proposed a method of adjusting the horizontal position of the saddle until the patella forms a plumb relationship with the end of the crank arm when positioned at 90 degrees in the downstroke.

This method, while made popular under static fitting methods, is now being tested under modern dynamic fitting methods. This approach greatly improves the accuracy of data collection because we can now record this phenomenon under loaded cycling instead of static alignment. Logically, riders with longer femurs would ride with more saddle setback than those with shorter femurs. In figure 8.4, however, you can see the lack of statistical relationship between these variables.

Clearly, horizontal saddle position has little effect on horizontal knee position in cycling. Other factors that seem to affect this relationship dynamically

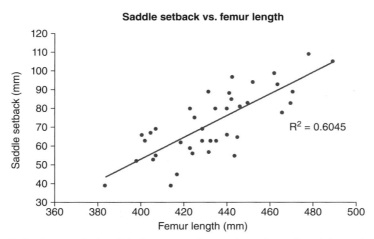

▶ **Figure 8.4** Poor relationship between femur length and saddle setback for 40 world-tour riders.

are saddle to bar drop, saddle to bar reach, and horizontal location of the center of saddle pressure (i.e., where a rider chooses to sit on a saddle). But no data exist to assess these relationships.

Much debate has ensued about the validity of this measurement because the knee landmark (patella) seems arbitrary and lacking a valid reason for being lined up with the pedal spindle as a static point in the cycle, which changes drastically as the cyclist pedals uphill or downhill. Regardless, to this day, most reputable fitters use this measurement in some fashion.

Steeper effective seat tube angles are favorable in nondrafting triathlons mainly because of the relationship between back angle and hip angle. Lower back angles are favorable for lowering aerodynamic drag, a distinct advantage during the bike portion of a nondrafting triathlon. But with lower back angles come more closed hip angles, which can be restored only by steepening the effective seat tube angle. Many athletes and coaches claim better cycling power and efficiency in this forward position, although the data of Rankin and Neptune (2010) suggest that this conclusion is practically false when kinematics and pelvic orientation are maintained (i.e., when saddle height and rotation are reset at the new effective seat tube angle).

Saddle Rotation

Saddle rotation is measured as an angle with respect to horizontal. Traditional thought was to set the saddle level. Research regarding low-back pain suggests that the saddle be angled downward 10 to 15 degrees (Salai et al. 1999). In practical experience, however, angling a saddle downward too far can place more weight on the hands, wrists, and shoulders. Practically speaking, most modern saddles are intended to be angled slightly downward. On average, in a group of 40 world-tour cyclists the average saddle angle was downward by 0.4 degree.

Grip Position

The position of the grip (road and mountain bikes) and elbow pads (time-trial bikes) is of tremendous importance in all performance and clinical fitting protocols. Generally, longer and lower grip positions, relative to the saddle, are associated with higher-performing positions. Longer and lower grip positions in recreational cyclists are associated with discomfort, increased perineal pressure (Partin et al. 2012), and reduced penile blood flow (Jeong et al. 2002).

Aggressive grip positions can place a rider at risk for low-back pain and reduced core muscle activity (Burnett et al. 2004) if time is not given for adequate adaptation to the new position (Muyor, López-Miñarro, and Alacid 2011). Therefore, best practice procedure in bike fitting is to adjust the grip location of the bicycle to facilitate appropriate spinal kinematics for each rider's riding volume and goals. Bressel and Larson (2003) have demonstrated that longer and lower grip positions increase lumbar flexion proportionally more than anterior pelvic tilt. Simply put, the back and spine tilt forward more than the pelvis in response to a longer or lower bar position. The authors proposed that the increased perineal pressure could be the reason for the limited pelvic tilt.

Also of interest is the evidence that low-back pain is the number one reason that professional cyclists miss training days (Clarsen, Krosshaug, and Bahr 2010). And although epidemiologic evidence supports raising grip locations to prevent injury risk, performance data support lowering grip locations to reduce aerodynamic drag (Lukes, Chin, and Haake 2005). Practically speaking, with respect to bike fit standards, the position of the grip and elbow pads should be related to the goals and riding volume of the individual cyclist. Although the aggressive positioning of competitive cyclists seems to be supported by the literature in terms of aerodynamics, little support exists for improvement in performance within any group of cyclists. And possibly more important to think about are the negative aspects of riding an aggressive position: increased perineal pressure, increased high lumbar and low thoracic flexion, and reduced core muscle activation.

Applying the Science

Bike fitting and rider positioning is a mixture of science and art. The science of rider positioning seems to be related to kinematic ranges of the lower extremity, pelvis, and spine. The art of rider positioning is finding the optimal setup of the contact points of the bicycle to achieve these ranges. Therefore, the best way to arrive at a good riding position is to complete an individualized motion-based fit protocol that directly measures kinematics at realistic intensities of pedaling. Relying on statistical or static approaches to rider positioning could potentially detract from optimal contact point positions by not factoring in how the cyclist sits on a saddle, how much he or she anteriorly rotates the pelvis, and the individuality of the cyclist's movement patterns such as ankling and elbow bend.

CHAPTER 9

The Aerodynamic Rider

—Andy Froncioni

Perhaps no subject is discussed more in clubhouses, in pelotons, and in online cycling forums than the topic of bicycle aerodynamics. And probably no cycling-related subject has more mystery surrounding it. Aerodynamic drag is, after all, an invisible force that can't be measured on a scale in a bicycle shop. But that doesn't mean it is not important or that it can't be used to great advantage. This chapter will increase the understanding of the fundamentals of aerodynamics and focus on what is relevant to bicycles and their riders. It may also guide riders through their own journeys to become aerodynamic cyclists.

How Important Is Aerodynamics?

Four forces determine how fast you ride: propulsion, gravity, rolling resistance, and aerodynamic drag. Riding conditions present the rider with a continuously changing mix of these forces. The relative mix of the four forces determines what is slowing down the rider the most. Figure 9.1 illustrates the force vectors on a rider going up a hill. Modifying these four forces, the course slope, wind, and rider parameters determine the relative mix of all the forces.

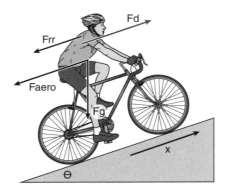

▶ **Figure 9.1**   Interaction of four forces determining bicycle speed.

Propulsion is the force that the cyclist generates from the muscles by transmitting torque to the crank. This force is transmitted by the chain to the rear wheel and, ultimately, to the ground by the rear tire.

Gravity pulls on the rider because of the component of vertical gravitational force that is in the direction of the bike. A purely flat section of road offers no gravitational pull, whereas a steep 20 percent climb creates substantial gravitational tug.

Rolling resistance is a force that comprises the drag arising from energy losses in the mechanics of the bicycle, from crank and frame flex, from chain and bearing resistance, and from energy losses in the tire rubber. The bearing drag is usually small compared with the other drag forces, and the tire rolling resistance is proportional to the vertical load on the tire. Rolling resistance is characterized by a parameter called the *coefficient of rolling resistance* that relates vertical loading of the tire to the drag force.

Aerodynamic drag is the force that pulls on a rider from behind. This force is determined by the air density (ρ), the airspeed of the bike (v), the bike and rider's aero drag coefficient (Cd), and the projected frontal area (A). We describe the aerodynamic force in detail later in this chapter.

So, compared with the other forces, how important is aerodynamic drag? To see this, let us consider a cyclist riding along a road at a power output of 300 watts and look at the relative contribution of each of the four main resistive forces on the rider. A normal 80-kilogram cyclist at a power output of 300 watts on a flat course will lose almost 90 percent of his or her power to aerodynamic losses (figure 9.2). Clearly, the greatest improvements to be made will be to refine the aerodynamic position and equipment for flat time-trial races. Rolling resistance plays a relatively minor role in the force balance. With the same rider on a 2 percent grade, gravity and aerodynamics are approximately equal in importance. Being efficient through the air is still extremely important, but rider weight is equally important. Finally, at an 8 percent grade, gravity dominates all else. Power-to-weight ratio is the primary determinant of success on steep grades. What this case illustrates is that aerodynamics plays an important role in winning on all but the steepest of grades.

Aerodynamics of Simple Shapes

The resistive force of the air rushing past the cyclist is called *aero drag*. We can learn a lot about aerodynamics just by looking at how the cylindrical shape behaves in the presence of wind. Figure 9.3 shows the streamlines that depict the path of the wind around a cylinder. Two sources of aerodynamic forces account for the rearward force on the shape: form drag and skin friction.

Important flow structures in the near field of a cylinder are shown in figure 9.3. Skin friction is generated in a small layer right next to the surface of the shape called a *boundary layer*. Form drag is mainly because of the negative pressure zone directly behind the cylinder called the *wake region*. The rearward force, F, generated by skin and form drag is given by this relation:

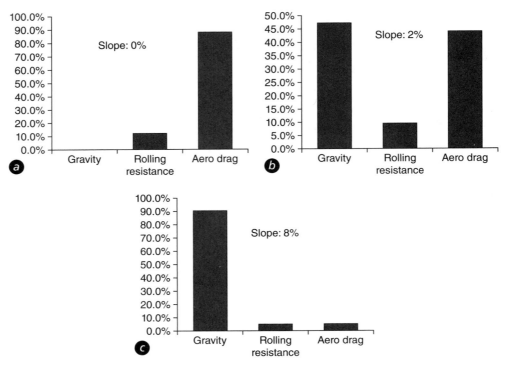

▶ **Figure 9.2** The relative influence of the forces for a 300-watt effort on (*a*) a flat grade, (*b*) a 2 percent grade, and (*c*) an 8 percent grade.

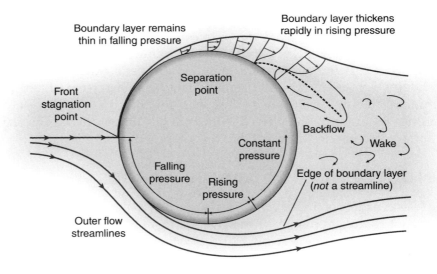

▶ **Figure 9.3** Detailed flow around a cylinder illustrating the various flow structures.

Reprinted, by permission, from A. Chowdhury, 2012, "Aerodynamics of sports fabrics and garments," PhD dissertation, School of Aerospace, Mechanical and Manufacturing Engineering, RMIT University, Melbourne, Australia. Adapted from M.M. Zdravkovich, 1997, Flow around circular cylinders: Applications (Oxford, UK: Oxford University Press).

$$F = 1/2 \, \rho \, v^2 \, Cd \, A$$

F is the force that's required to counter the aerodynamic drag. It's the total aerodynamic force that the rider is fighting.

Rho (ρ) is the density of the air. Air at sea level has a mass of 1.2 kilograms per cubic meter. Air density on earth can vary significantly, from 0.5 kilograms per cubic meter on Mt. Everest to about 1.5 kilograms per cubic meter on a very cold, dry day at sea level. Keep this range in mind; for the same airspeed, it takes up to three times less force to pull an object through the air at altitude than it does at sea level. Modern airliners make use of this fact to save fuel.

V is the speed of the air relative to the body, also called *airspeed*. All other things being equal, drag force is proportional to the square of airspeed. Ground speed, the speed of the body relative to the ground, is only one component of airspeed. For example, a headwind of 10 kilometers per hour combines with a ground speed of 40 kilometers per hour to give an airspeed of 50 kilometers per hour. Aerodynamic forces are generated according to the 50 kilometers per hour airspeed.

Cd, the aerodynamic drag coefficient, is a three-dimensional shape factor (Coggan 2011) that describes its aerodynamic efficiency. The higher the Cd is, the larger is the aerodynamic drag force that is generated when moving through air. Cd is a nondimensional parameter, which means that it is independent of the size of the object. For example, a marble and a beach ball have a similar Cd of approximately 0.47 because they both have the same shape.

A is the projected frontal area. It is the shadow that a three-dimensional body casts on a screen, as shown in figure 9.4 for six riding configurations. Note that projected frontal area for road versus time-trial positions can be significantly different. Recumbent riding confers such a large advantage in aerodynamic drag that the UCI has prohibited these positions for its races. A beach ball and a marble may have the same Cd, but the projected frontal area accounts for the fact that a beach ball is harder to push through the air. The frontal area of a marble is about 0.0001 square meters, whereas the frontal area of a beach ball is about 0.6 square meters.

The product Cd × A in our force equation can be combined into a single term, CdA. CdA is called *drag area* for short. The drag area of a beach ball is about 0.300 square meters, whereas the drag area of a marble is about 0.000047 square meters, which properly explains what we intuitively know: A beach ball offers much more air resistance than a marble does. Table 9.1 provides the Cd, A, and CdA for some common shapes.

Lesson: The aerodynamic drag of an object results from its three-dimensional shape and its projected frontal area.

▶ **Figure 9.4** Projected frontal areas of six riding positions.

Table 9.1 Aerodynamic Drag Coefficient (Cd), Projected Frontal Area (A), and Drag Area (CdA) for Common Shapes

Shape	Cd	A	CdA
Marble	0.5	0.0001	0.00005
Beach ball	0.5	0.6	0.300
Flat plate	1.0	0.6	0.600
Cylinder	0.8	0.6	0.480
Cone	0.5	0.6	0.300

Table 9.2 Cd, A, and CdA for Two Common Airfoils

Shape	Cd	A	CdA
NACA 0009	0.018	0.6	0.0108
NACA 0012	0.008	0.6	0.0048

Airfoils

Over the past 100 years, engineers have been refining the shape of the airplane wing, called an *airfoil*, and have managed to lower the Cd to an impressively small number. Table 9.2 is the same aero table as was presented for simple shapes. Data are shown for two common airfoil designs, NACA 0009 and 0012 airfoils.

Not surprisingly, modern bicycle tubing has come to look more like an airfoil than a cylinder or tube. The savings are just too good to overlook. In fact, the UCI's rulebook includes a section restricting the aero efficiency of bicycle tubing, which we have often heard referred to as the three-to-one rule of depth to width. Notably, no such restrictions apply to non-UCI races such as triathlons, and some manufacturers build frames and components that differ in compliance depending on the intended market.

Texturing or Dimpling

One of the finicky and counterintuitive anomalies of aerodynamics is that texturing or dimpling a blunt body will sometimes help it become more aerodynamically efficient. This happens because a surface layer of air, called a *turbulent boundary layer*, is created and acts to keep the flow of air attached to the surface. Figure 9.5*a* depicts air over the surface of a smooth sphere. The largest component of drag results from a large zone of negative pressure that develops behind the sphere, owing to an early detachment of the boundary layer. This effect is not as pronounced in figure 9.5*b*, where dimples

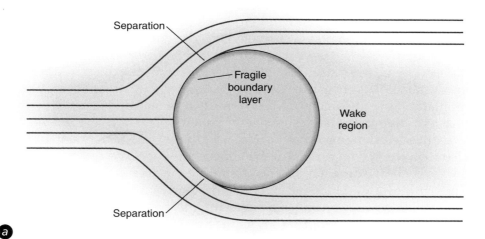

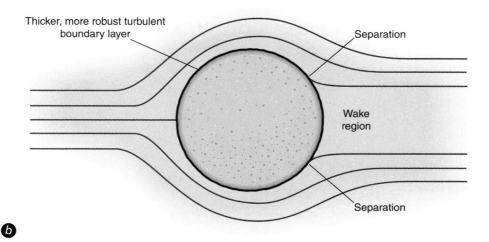

▶ **Figure 9.5**   Comparison of the flow around a (*a*) smooth and (*b*) dimpled sphere.

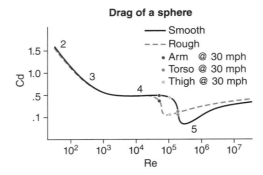

▶ **Figure 9.6** The influence of dimpling on the Cd of a sphere as a function of nondimensional airspeed, Re.

National Aeronautics and Space Administration

on the surface have stayed attached for longer. The dimples act to delay the separation of the flow from the surface, reducing the negative pressure zone directly behind the sphere and greatly reducing drag forces.

The net effect of roughness on total drag is best illustrated in figure 9.6, where smooth and rough sphere aerodynamic drag curves (Cd versus Reynolds number) demonstrate a characteristic "drag drop" at certain key speeds. The smooth sphere drag curve exhibits a more pronounced drag drop at higher speeds, whereas the rougher sphere exhibits the drag drop at a much lower speed. This effect can be used on arms, legs, and torsos to reduce drag dramatically. Studies have been performed on smooth and textured cylinders to determine optimal fabrics and weave patterns on various parts of a skinsuit to reduce aerodynamic drag. Surface roughness and stitch orientation have also been studied on vertical and inclined cylinders to determine the effects on aerodynamic drag. These studies show that fabrics with some roughness can significantly reduce aerodynamic drag on blunt shapes such as arms, legs, and torsos. As a result, a modern high-tech skinsuit can provide a 4 to 6 percent improvement in aerodynamic drag compared with a suit that has not been designed to reduce aero drag.

Rider and Bicycle: Complex Aerodynamic Shapes

Imagine a bike and rider being decomposed into a collection of simple shapes. Each shape exposed to air contributes to the overall drag force. The first step in reducing aerodynamic drag is to be able to measure it. This section describes some of the tools available to cyclists to help them measure the aero drag force.

Projected Frontal Area

Measuring projected frontal area, A, can be performed easily with a camera and an appropriately chosen background screen. The green screen technique of measuring A simply involves cutting out the outline of a photo of the rider and bike and weighing the paper on a simple pastry scale. The larger the projected frontal area is, the heavier the paper outline is. This simple technique allows anyone with steady hands to estimate A. The lower the projected frontal area is, the lower the drag area (CdA) is. A more accurate technique is to take the same photograph and subtract the background. The remaining digital pixels can simply be counted. A helpful approach is to photograph a reference shape of known frontal area alongside the subject.

Total Drag Area

A number of methods exist to measure aerodynamic drag empirically. The basic idea behind all the methods involves measuring the drag force and the airspeed to which a body is subject.

Wind Tunnel

The gold standard of aerodynamic drag estimation is probably the modern wind tunnel. The earliest wind tunnels are attributed to the Wright brothers in their attempts to improve their airplane designs. Reducing drag was an important component in keeping airplanes aloft for longer times and distances. The same goals are present in improving a rider's speed: We seek more speed for the same input power. Figure 9.7 shows a rider being aero tested at the A2 Wind Tunnel in Mooresville, North Carolina. This kind of testing is becoming increasingly popular for pro, elite amateur, and age-group riders of all skill levels.

The main components of a wind tunnel are shown in figure 9.8. The rider and bike are secured to a sled that rides on low-friction bearings. The bicycle is held to the sled by mounts. The mounts are bolted to the front and rear

▶ **Figure 9.7** Rider in the A2 wind tunnel.
Courtesy of Accelerate3 Coaching.

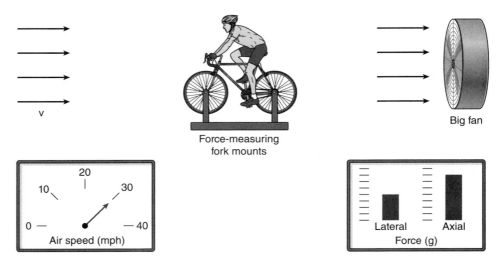

▶ **Figure 9.8** How a wind tunnel works.

dropouts of the bicycle. Airspeed is measured using a set of sensors called pitot tubes. By carefully measuring airspeed and resistive force on a load balance, the nature of aerodynamic drag can be mapped. Wind tunnel drag forces are typically reported as the mass of an equivalent weight in grams.

Besides being able to estimate the drag force variation with airspeed, some wind tunnels have a rotating stage incorporated into the sled assembly. This mechanism provides the ability to measure the effect of side winds in both axial (front and back) and lateral (side) directions. This kind of equipment has an important benefit: the ability to test the aerodynamic effect of crosswinds, or wind at a nonzero *yaw* angle, as a rider would see while riding outdoors on a windy day. Figure 9.9 illustrates the aerodynamic drag force variation with changes in yaw angle. The study aimed to understand the effect of water bottle type and placement on the aerodynamic drag at various wind angles. Notice that for wind angles under 20 degrees, the aerodynamic drag force is less than that at 0 degrees, an indication that the rider and bike are being propelled by the wind, as a sailboat would be.

Aero Field Testing

The advent of speed sensors and power meters on bicycles has opened up a whole new way of estimating drag area. Several methods exist for doing this, but its underpinnings are strongly supported by modern science. Scientific investigation has shown that the energy requirements of a rider and bike combination can be measured quite well. Figure 9.10 illustrates the excellent agreement between the theoretical power requirements of a rider and bike and actual requirements from the power equation. This finding gives us the confidence that power meter techniques can be used to measure aerodynamic drag accurately.

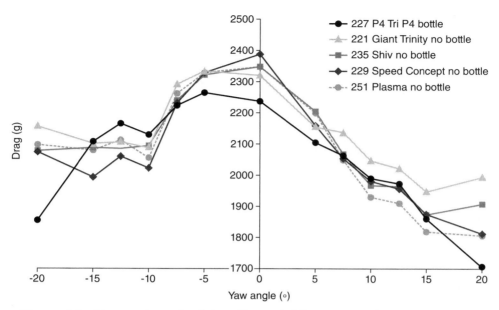

▶ **Figure 9.9** Yaw angle study of the effects of different water bottles.

Courtesy of Cervélo Cycles Inc.

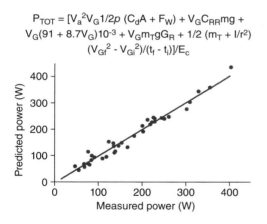

$$P_{TOT} = [V_a^2 V_G 1/2p \ (C_d A + F_W) + V_G C_{RR} mg + V_G (91 + 8.7 V_G) 10^{-3} + V_G m_T g G_R + 1/2 \ (m_T + I/r^2) (V_{Gf}^2 - V_{Gi}^2)/(t_f - t_i)]/E_c$$

▶ **Figure 9.10** Predicted versus actual power needed to ride a bike at various speeds.

Reprinted, with permission, from J.C. Martin, D.L. Milliken, J.E. Cobb, et al., 1998, "Validation of a mathematical model for road cycling power," Journal of Applied Biomechanics 14(3): 276-291.

Martin Regression Method

A popular method that has grown out of more developed use of the power meter and speed sensor is the regression method, developed by Dr. Jim Martin at the University of Utah (Martin et al. 2006). This method consists of riding a velodrome or lap-based circuit at various speeds. The average power for each lap can be plotted as a function of the square of speed (V^2), according to the graph in figure 9.11. This method can estimate both the tire rolling resistance coefficient, Crr, as well as the aerodynamic drag area, CdA.

Virtual Elevation

Another method that has grown out of the use of the cycling power meter is the *method of virtual elevation*, also known as the *Chung method*. In this method, an algorithm estimates the altitude that a rider travels. By modifying a combination of the guessed value of CdA, the user matches the estimated altitude plot with the actual altitude plot. Figure 9.12 shows the Aerolab module of the free Golden Cheetah ride analysis program. The elevation profile of three loops of an out-and-back ride are displayed in the plot window of Golden Cheetah's Aerolab module (figure 9.12). The user has selected a CdA of 0.2054 square meters, and the correct altitude plot is reproduced. In this case, the correct CdA has been found. Readers who are curious about their own drag area values can go to goldencheetah.org and try Aerolab at no cost.

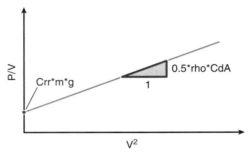

▶ **Figure 9.11** Linear dependence of force (P/V) on V^2 for a bike.

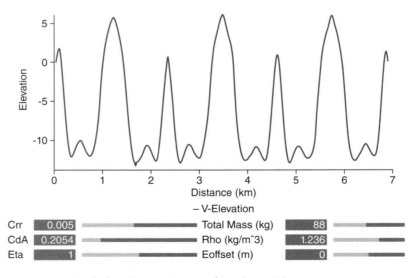

▶ **Figure 9.12** Virtual elevation estimate of a rider's CdA.

From Golden Cheetah Aerolab. Data by Tom Anhalt.

Anthropometric Estimation of Drag

Drag area can be well correlated to various anthropometric measurements: body mass, body mass index, height, sex, and so on. A number of studies that have tried to use these measurements to predict drag and frontal area of a cyclist are described in Coggan (2011).

$$A = 0.18964 \times \text{height (m)} + 0.00215 \times \text{mass (kg)} - 0.07861$$

(Bassett et al. 1999)

$$Cd = 4.45 \times \text{mass (kg)}^{-0.45}$$

(Kyle 1991)

These numbers can be combined to produce CdA.

Computational Fluid Dynamics

Computational fluid dynamics (CFD) is a field of engineering that uses computer models to solve for the velocity and pressure fields around solid bodies. Computer-aided design (CAD) models are used to describe the rider and bike. A variety of flow conditions can be created, making the method attractive to designers of bike frames and equipment. Pressure mapping can help highlight and identify areas of the flow that require improvement. CFD is flexible, because it can be used to test things that would be difficult to test in the real world.

Reducing Drag

Obviously, any time aerodynamic drag can be reduced without changing rider comfort or applied power, we have a desirable outcome. For that reason, aero benefits are often called "free speed." The reduction in aerodynamic drag can come about either because the solo aerodynamics of a rider–bike combination has been improved or because paceline or peloton formations have created drafting effects. Typically, wind tunnel tests and aero field tests make use of expert aerodynamics, bike positioning, and equipment experts to aid in the reduction of drag. Several rider and bike parameters can be adjusted to improve aero efficiency. Reductions in aerodynamic drag come from changes in position, equipment, or drafting. Because riders start at differing levels of aero optimization, predicting which changes will benefit riders the most is not always easy. But a certain priority in aerodynamic drag reduction exists. Keep in mind, however, that these rules are meant to be broken.

Position

Usually, the most significant aerodynamic reduction comes about from changes in rider position. This conclusion should not be surprising, considering that the rider makes the largest contribution to projected frontal area (recall figure 9.4).

Torso Angle

The largest gains a rider will make from positioning will likely be from lowering torso angle. The gains result mostly from a reduction in projected frontal area, but the inclination of the torso also slightly improves the drag coefficient, leading to a dramatically lower overall drag area. For example, an average male rider in a road position with a back angle of 30 degrees might have a drag area of approximately 0.320 square meters. The same rider might improve by 25 percent by riding in a TT position with a torso angle of 22 degrees, corresponding to a power saving of 25 percent to travel at the same speed. Torso angle can be changed by a combination of raising saddle height, lowering the handlebars, or increasing the distance between saddle and handlebars.

Forearm Angle

Reductions in aerodynamics drag can also result from inclining the forearm slightly. In many cases, the projected frontal area of the forearms is reduced somewhat by moving the elbow pads (or aero bars) forward. The change is equivalent to angling a vertical cylinder and often can be performed to lower the torso angle at the same time.

Posture

Posture describes what the cyclist does with his or her body after the saddle and handlebars have been locked in place. Posture can include shrugging, ("turtling") and rounding or flattening the back. Perhaps the most important skill to learn is how to shrug, or turtle. This action involves bringing the shoulders in toward the neck. The influence of shrugging is shown in figure 9.13.

Equipment

From looking at the evolution of shapes of cycling equipment in recent years, it is clear that manufacturers have not overlooked aerodynamic optimization. Every piece of equipment, from water bottles to bike frames, has undergone dramatic shape changes to favor aerodynamic efficiency. Design engineers use significant amounts of wind tunnel, CFD, and aero field testing to improve the aerodynamic shaping of their products.

▶ **Figure 9.13** Influence of shrugging on a rider's frontal area.

Andy Froncioni

Helmets

Owing to the nature of back curvature and torso angle, the selection of the optimal helmet can be personal. Helmets can be grouped into two main categories: road and aero. Typically, large torso angles will not show large differences between the different types of helmets. But the lower the back angle is, the more we begin to see improvements from the use of aero helmets, because the gap behind the rider's head is filled with the large aero tail of the helmet. Recently, we have also seen the advent of an aero road helmet, which is a cross between the two types of helmet. The aero road helmet provides the weight and cooling benefit of a road helmet with the aerodynamic efficiency of a full aero helmet.

Clothing

The 2013 Ironman World Championships introduced the world of triathlon to a new breed of ultrafast aero skinsuits. Runners-up Luke McKenzie and Rachel Joyce were among the first to use these new tri suits, which prominently featured sleeves. Aero drag savings of several percent were achieved by the careful covering of the upper arms. The adage "skin is slow" was coined by Trek engineer Paul Harder to describe the phenomenon that bare skin is often too smooth to generate a stable enough turbulent boundary layer. A small amount of texturing delays boundary layer separation on the arms and legs, as we have seen in the section on texturing.

Wheels

The highest relative airspeeds achieved on a bike are the spokes at the top of their rotation. Therefore, wheel manufacturers are extremely active in the field of aerodynamic optimization. The top of the spokes in figure 9.14 travel at about twice the ground speed, whereas those near the contact patch are nearly stationary with respect to airspeed. It makes sense that a wider rim decreases the exposure of the fast-moving spokes to the wind and presents a smoother surface. The aero drag savings can be substantial, especially for the front wheel.

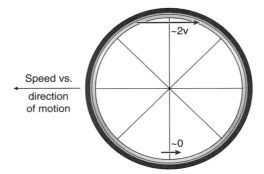

▶ **Figure 9.14** Spokes create significant drag at the top of their revolution because their airspeed is twice the ground speed.

Frame

Increasingly, aero-profiled road bikes are making their way into every stage of the Tour de France. This trend is indicative not only of the great performance improvements of aero frames in the last 15 years but also of the increased appreciation for the value of those improvements by pro riders and teams. These aero-profiled bikes are used even for Grand Tour stages that have long been considered mountain stages, for which team mechanics try to trim every gram of weight possible. The large tubing of aero frames is steadily appearing in greater numbers. Top pros have been clued in: Aerodynamics matters!

Frame tests are typically performed in wind tunnels with and without dummy riders. The most famous of these plastic, articulated riders is Cérvelo's "DZummy," so named because it was fashioned after popular rider David Zabriskie. The dummies provide a constant position that is ideal for measuring small improvements in aerodynamic frame design. Hundreds of these changes are made before a frame is manufactured.

Drafting

Paceline and peloton average speeds have long been known to be faster than the speeds attained by solo riding. The reason for the faster speed is that the aerodynamic drag forces can be shared among several riders in group rides. Solo riders must pull their negative pressure wake alone.

The technique for group riding involves each rider taking a turn at the front (called "pulling") so as to increase the net speed of the group. The pulling rider then drops to the back of the group, while another rider takes her or his place at the front. The secret to increasing group speed is that while riding behind others, riders benefit from a significant reduction in the power output required to ride at the same speed. This lower output requirement allows them to recover from their pulls.

The effects of riding directly behind another rider are obvious: The person drafting usually benefits by having to do 30 percent less work than the pulling rider does. What is more surprising is that even the pulling rider benefits from a paceline of riders behind him or her. The aerodynamic drag of the lead rider drops by 2 to 5 percent when a rider is drafting behind because the trailing riders are partially occupying the negative pressure zone, thereby reducing its effect. The group's aero efficiency increases because more of the pulling rider's power is converted into forward speed.

Aero Case Study

Let's follow the aerodynamicist's logbook, chronicling the series of steps taken to reduce a rider's aerodynamic drag. The logbook is shown in figure 9.15.

Baseline Runs

The test director begins the test by carefully measuring the rider's starting position and equipment. The drag areas of two or more runs in an identical setup are compared until they are within 1 percent of each other. The baseline runs provide the assurance that the measurement equipment is in good working order and that the rider is stably set up on the bike. Remember, even the smallest shift in position is likely to produce a measurable change in drag area! In this example, the baseline drag area was measured to be 0.285 square meters.

Position Changes and Shrugs

Following the baseline work, the next order of business is to position the rider on the bike. Aero gains from positioning are often the largest. The test director takes the rider through a series of progressively more aggressive positions (B, C, D). Significant improvements are measured from the effects of shrugging. Notably, position B with shrug produces a reduction in drag of approximately 3.5 percent, bringing the rider's drag area to 0.275 square meters.

Helmets

The positioning tests were performed with a regular road helmet. The test director now chooses to test a number of aero helmets on the rider, starting

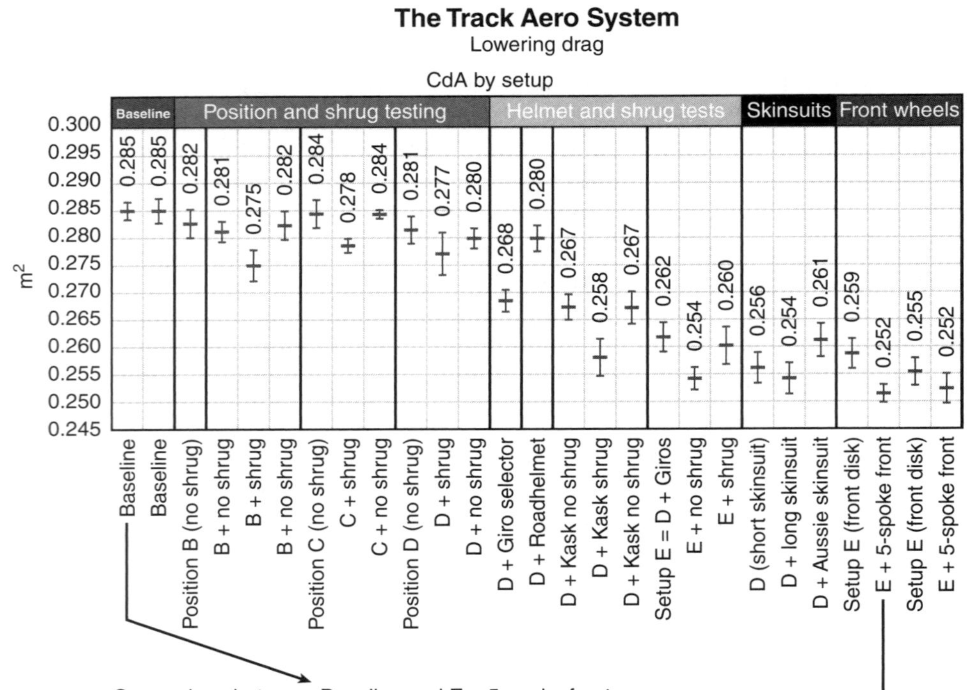

The Track Aero System

Lowering drag

CdA by setup

Setup	CdA (m²)
Baseline	0.285
Baseline	0.285
Position B (no shrug)	0.282
B + no shrug	0.281
B + shrug	0.275
B + no shrug	0.282
Position C (no shrug)	0.284
C + shrug	0.278
C + no shrug	0.284
Position D (no shrug)	0.281
D + shrug	0.277
D + no shrug	0.280
D + Giro selector	0.268
D + Roadhelmet	0.280
D + Kask no shrug	0.267
D + Kask shrug	0.258
D + Kask no shrug	0.267
Setup E = D + Giros	0.262
E + no shrug	0.254
E + shrug	0.260
D (short skinsuit)	0.256
D + long skinsuit	0.254
D + Aussie skinsuit	0.261
Setup E (front disk)	0.259
E + 5-spoke front	0.252
Setup E (front disk)	0.255
E + 5-spoke front	0.252

Column groupings: Baseline | Position and shrug testing | Helmet and shrug tests | Skinsuits | Front wheels

Comparison between Baseline and E + 5-spoke front

Wattage	Speed improvement (km/h)				Time savings by distance (mass)				
CdA	0.285m^2	0.252m^2	Variance	Secs/km	3 km	4 km	10 km	25 km	40 km
325	42.5	44.1	1.69	3.24	0:09.7	0:13.0	0:32	1:21	2:10
350	43.6	45.4	1.74	3.16	0:09.5	0:12.6	0:32	1:19	2:06
375	44.7	46.5	1.78	3.09	0:09.3	0:12.4	0:31	1:17	2:04
400	45.8	47.6	1.83	3.02	0:09.1	0:12.1	0:30	1:16	2:01
425	46.8	48.7	1.87	2.96	0:08.9	0:11.9	0:30	1:14	1:59

Comparison assumptions: Rider + bike mass: 88.0kg, Crr (DGV wood) of 0.0025,
No wind, 0% gradient (dead flat), Air density 1.18kg/m^3

▶ **Figure 9.15** An aero testing log chronicling the improvement in drag area of each setup change.

Courtesy of Alex Simmons, Aerocoach Australia and RST Sport.

from the best position found so far. With the single change from road helmet to aero helmet (Giro Selector), the rider's drag area drops to 0.268 square meters, a whopping 6.4 percent reduction in drag! Several runs with minor tweaks and a new aero helmet yield an even lower drag area of 0.254 square meters.

Skinsuits

The next tests performed involved three skinsuits. The long-sleeved skinsuit proved to be the best, but no significant drag reductions were found. The nature of aerodynamic drag is such that predicting the outcome of a given change is often difficult. In the case of skinsuits for this rider, no improvements were found.

Front Wheels

Finally, three types of wheels were tested. The five-spoke wheel proved to reduce drag the most. From the initial baseline, position E combined with the five-spoke wheel reduced drag by some 11.5 percent. This improvement in drag is dramatic!

Final Result: Great Improvement!

Looking back on the process of aero optimization, we see that enormous gains are available to riders. Translated into time and power savings, the most optimized position and equipment netted an aero drag improvement of over 2 minutes over the course of a 40K time trial.

Applying the Science

Bicycle aerodynamics is a vast topic, and we have provided only an overview of the essentials. It is also a fast-evolving area of interest; new measurement methods and sensors are coming into the market each year. Aero testing used to be only for elite pros. Today, we find many age-group and amateur riders asking some profound aerodynamic questions. In fact, many age-group triathletes and cyclists are as aero optimized as the best elite pros.

The growth of testing methods, sensors, and equipment will make cycling aerodynamics increasingly important in the future. We hope that we have provided you with the preliminary understanding you need to become a faster and more aerodynamic cyclist.

10

Pedaling Technique and Technology

—Thomas Korff, Marco Arkesteijn, and Paul Barratt

Quantifying the mechanical characteristics of cycling is important in many contexts. For example, riders, coaches, or scientists might be interested in the maximum power a rider can generate on a bicycle, the power at which the rider cycles during a ride, or the technique used to transfer forces or power from the feet to the pedals. Depending on why a rider, coach, or scientist seeks to measure mechanical variables, various technologies are available. The decision about which technology is most appropriate is usually driven by the specific purpose of the measurement and the availability of the relevant technology. A discussion of issues relevant to pedaling technology and pedaling technique can be advanced by a review of the relevant basic mechanical and anatomical concepts. Therefore, this chapter is divided into three parts. In the first part we describe the mechanical and anatomical basis of cycling, and in the second part we discuss the relevant pedaling technology. In light of these scientific and technological concepts, the third part of this chapter links the theory to selected applied issues surrounding pedaling technique.

Basic Mechanical and Scientific Principles

In most cycling events, cycling speed is the ultimate performance parameter. The athlete who cycles fastest wins the race. On a mechanical level, cycling speed is determined by the difference between resistive and propulsive forces acting on the bicycle–rider system. Regarding the former, aerodynamic drag is the most important resistive force. So from a performance point of view, minimizing this variable is important (see chapter 9). Regarding the latter, propulsive forces are those forces that are transferred from the cyclist's feet to the pedals.

During cycling, muscular forces are transferred to the pedals through the right and left feet simultaneously in an alternating fashion. On each side, the pedal force can be decomposed into a tangential and a radial component (see figure 10.1):

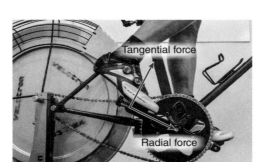

▶ **Figure 10.1** Schematic diagram of tangential and radial crank forces.

Photo by Stephen S. Cheung

- The tangential component of the force performs mechanical work (i.e., produces movement), because it is always acting in the direction of the movement.
- The radial component of the pedal force is directed toward the crank center of rotation and does not perform any work.
- The sum of the tangential forces (measured in newtons, N) produces a torque around the crank (measured in newton meters, Nm), which can be calculated by multiplying the sum of left and right tangential pedal forces by the length of the crank.
- Crank power (measured in watts, W) can then be calculated by multiplying crank torque by angular velocity.

The relationship between right and left pedal power and overall crank power is illustrated in figure 10.2. Figure 10.2a shows the power profile produced by the right leg. It can be seen that the majority of the power is produced during the downstroke (i.e., between 0 and 180 degrees of the crank cycle with a peak occurring at around 90 degrees, the three o'clock position of the crank). The shape of the left power profile (figure 10.2b) is similar but 180 degrees out of phase; the majority of left pedal power is produced during the recovery phase of the right leg (i.e., 180 to 360 degrees). Summing right and left pedal power profiles at every point in time results in the overall crank power profile depicted in figure 10.2c.

Understanding these simple mathematical relationships is important to understanding force or power measurement devices. As we will see later, many commercially available systems measure overall crank torque or power (i.e., the combined effect of forces produced on the right and left sides), which has significant implications when interpreting such data.

The relationship between force, torque, and power can be illustrated by a simple practical example. Imagine a person on a spinning bike who wishes to increase his or her power. The fact that power is the mathematical product

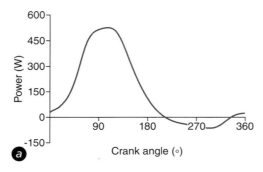

a

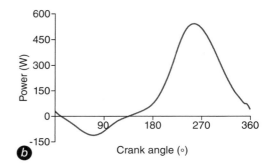

b

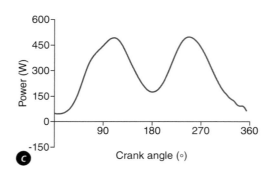

c

▶ **Figure 10.2** Relationship between pedal power and crank power. (*a*) The right pedal power is positive during the downstroke (0–180 degrees) and reaches its maximum value at around 90 degrees. (*b*) The power profile of the contralateral leg (i.e., the left leg) looks similar in shape but is 180 degrees out of phase. Thus, it is positive during the recovery phase of the right leg, between 180 and 360 degrees of the crank cycle. (*c*) Summing right and left pedal power at each data point yields crank power.

of crank torque and crank angular velocity implies that the cyclist can increase power by increasing either resistance (crank torque) or cadence (angular velocity) or both. In practice, however, the increase in resistance is often accompanied by a decrease in cadence (angular velocity), which can negate the initial goal of increasing power. Thus, in this situation, increasing resistance makes sense only if cadence does not drop below a point at which power is lower than it was during the initial situation.

Muscular Contributions to Pedal Power

Pedal power is ultimately produced by the muscles that span the hip, knee, and ankle joints. Using biomechanical analysis and modeling techniques, we can quantify extensor and flexor powers of these joints (i.e., the so-called joint action powers). Figure 10.3 illustrates the joint power profiles over one crank revolution. The majority of power is generated by the hip extensors, knee extensors, and plantar flexors. Little joint action power is produced by the hip flexors, knee flexors, and dorsiflexors.

The main function of the hip extensors and knee extensors is to generate power that is ultimately transferred to the pedal. Note that the plantar flexors (calf muscles) have two functions. In addition to directly producing

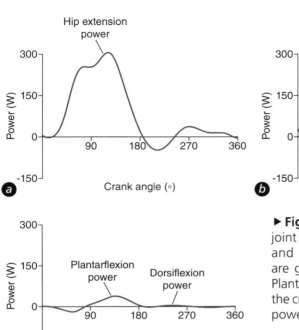

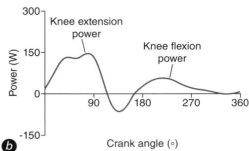

▶ Figure 10.3 Joint power profiles and joint action powers of (*a*) hip, (*b*) knee, and (*c*) ankle joints. Extension powers are generally larger than flexion powers. Plantar flexor power is produced later in the crank cycle than hip and knee extension powers.

pedal power, the plantar flexors also stiffen the ankle joint so that the power developed by the knee and hip extensors can be effectively transferred to the pedal. The simplest way to visualize this mechanism is to imagine how the leg would function if the muscles surrounding the ankle were inactive and the ankle joint had no strength at all. In this scenario, during leg extension, the power produced by the knee and hip extensors would simply cause the ankle to dorsiflex (meaning that the foot would be in an extremely heel-down, toe-up position) and the knee to hyperextend. In this scenario knee and hip extensors would accelerate the legs into a nonphysiological position and their joint action powers would not be transferred effectively to the pedal. The relative contribution of joint action powers to pedal power depends on the external cycling load. Specifically, the relative knee flexor contribution increases as the external power requirement increases, which is discussed in more detail in the section Altering Pedaling Technique.

Note that the power measured on the pedal is not only muscular in nature but also contains nonmuscular influences. Nonmuscular power results from gravity and so-called motion-dependent (i.e., centripetal and centrifugal) forces. Figure 10.4 illustrates the relationship between muscular power (the sum of knee, ankle, and hip joint powers), nonmuscular power, and total pedal power (the sum of the former two). A simple way to visualize this concept is to imagine that a skeleton is fixed to a bicycle and then pushed down a hill. In this scenario the mass of the legs would create a force measured at the pedal that, because of gravity and the motion itself, would predominantly act vertically downward on the pedal. Therefore, the pedal force (and therefore pedal power) would be positive during the leg extension phase and negative during the leg flexion phase, as seen in figure 10.4. When interpreting pedal power profiles, keep in mind these nonmuscular influences. In particular, the negative portion of the pedal power profile (see figure 10.2*a* and *b*) is often interpreted as negative or inefficient. The decomposition of pedal power into muscular and nonmuscular components, however, shows that the muscular component stays positive throughout the crank cycle. The phase of negative pedal power simply means that the pull-up force generated by the leg flexor muscles is smaller than the pushdown force caused by gravity and the mass of the leg, which is by no means inefficient.

The upper body also has a role in pedaling. During submaximal cycling with low power requirements, muscular power is produced almost exclusively by the muscles of the lower limbs. But if the power requirement increases or the lower-limb muscles start to fatigue, the muscles of the upper body are activated during pedaling. The resulting power output is transferred to the hip joint and across the leg to provide additional contribution to pedal power. The muscle activation is timed so that the vast majority of upper-body power contribution occurs within the leg extension phase. This upper-body contribution can be observed when athletes try to produce high power output by rocking the upper body back and forth or side to side.

The analysis of electrical muscle activity (termed *electromyography* or *EMG*) provides further and more detailed insight into the mechanisms by which

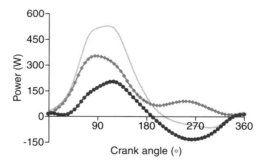

▶ **Figure 10.4** Decomposition of pedal power (solid line) into muscular (solid diamonds) and nonmuscular (solid circles) power. Nonmuscular power is positive during the downstroke, meaning that it assists in power production during this phase. During the upstroke, nonmuscular power is negative, meaning that it is acting against the movement and taking away energy during this phase of the crank cycle. Note that in spite of pedal power being negative during the upstroke, muscular power stays positive throughout the whole crank cycle.

muscular power is generated and delivered to the crank (see Hug and Dorel 2009 and So, Joseph, and Gabriel 2005 for reviews).

Before discussing the issue in more detail, we should remind ourselves about the muscles that are most important for power generation during cycling. The largest and most powerful hip extensor muscle is the gluteus maximus. The most important knee extensor is the quadriceps femoris, which is composed of four separate muscles (vastus lateralis, vastus medialis, vastus intermedius, and rectus femoris). The most important plantar flexors (calf muscles) are the gastrocnemius and soleus. The most important knee flexors in cycling are the hamstrings (biceps femoris, semimembranosus, and semitendinosus). For muscular power to be transferred to the pedal effectively, muscles have to be activated and deactivated in a timely manner. Because of the delay between muscle activation and muscular force production (termed *electromechanical delay*), the muscles have to be activated slightly before they are required to produce force. For example, the knee extensors vastus medialis (VM) and vastus lateralis (VL) are required to produce maximum force at around 90 degrees of the crank cycle. For this to happen, they need to be activated even before the pedal reaches the top dead center (TDC) position. Similarly, the gluteus maximus (Gmax) starts being active before the TDC and remains active throughout the majority of the downstroke. The plantar flexors (gastrocnemius medialis, GM; gastrocnemius lateralis, GL; and soleus, SOL) become active later in the crank cycle. This action is consistent with figure 10.3, in which the ankle power increases later in the crank cycle than knee and hip power. The tibialis anterior (TA), the most important dorsiflexor, starts being active midway through the upstroke so that it can produce force through the top dead center transition. Similarly, the knee flexors start to be active during the latter part of the downstroke to transition the pedal through the bottom dead center of the crank cycle and to produce small amounts of knee flexion power during the upstroke. The activity periods within the crank cycle of all major power-producing muscles can be seen in figure 10.5. When performing mechanical analyses of cycling performance or pedaling technique, these basic mechanical and anatomical principles must be kept in mind.

Pedal Power, Metabolic Energy Consumption, and Efficiency

To generate mechanical power, muscles have to produce forces, which requires metabolic energy (see chapter 2). Energy consumption is an important factor to consider within the context of cycling performance. From a biomechanical perspective, pedal power is the most important predictor of metabolic energy consumption (McDaniel et al. 2002). But the metabolic energy consumed by the muscles (energy in) is always greater than the energy delivered to the bicycle (energy out). Cycling efficiency can be thought

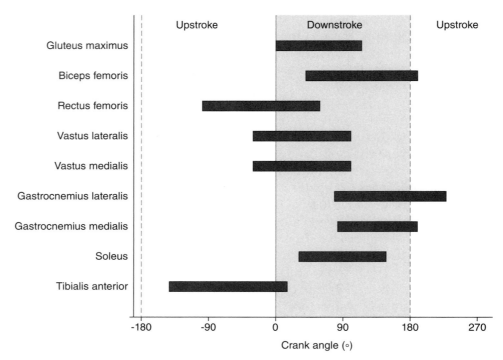

▶ **Figure 10.5** Phases of muscular activity throughout the crank cycle.

of as the ratio of crank power to the power generated by the cyclist's muscles. Because of the anatomical complexity of the cycling movement, muscular power is always greater than crank power. A typical ratio is 5:1; in other words, cycling efficiency is approximately 20 percent even in highly trained cyclists (Coyle et al. 1992).

At lower power outputs, metabolic energy is predominantly generated through the aerobic energy pathways. At higher power outputs, anaerobic energy pathways become more important. The resources to generate muscular power anaerobically are limited, which implies that cyclists fatigue more quickly if anaerobic energy sources are used. The lactate threshold is the greatest power at which the cyclist can cycle at a steady state using predominantly aerobic energy pathways. The higher the lactate threshold is, the more muscular power a cyclist can generate without fatiguing. As we will see later in this chapter, these scientific principles should be kept in mind when interpreting and measuring mechanical variables during cycling.

Pedaling Technology

When considering technology within the context of pedaling technique, the measurement of pedal or crank power is of major interest. The development of power measurement devices has, accordingly, revolutionized cycling over the last two decades. Power is delivered to the pedal by the cyclist and is transmitted to the rear wheel of the bicycle through a series of mechanical components called the drivetrain (pedal, crank, front sprocket, chain, rear sprocket, rear wheel hub, rear wheel). Therefore, power output can be measured by replacing any one of the standard drivetrain components with an instrumented component to measure force or torque and velocity (bearing in mind that power is the mathematical product of force or torque and velocity). Each potential location for instrumentation has advantages and disadvantages, and the most appropriate choice ultimately depends on the objective of the measurement.

Devices That Measure Overall Power Output

The first category of measurement devices encompasses devices that measure the total power output. This technology is appropriate in physiological or aerodynamic analyses in which information is required on the bicycle–rider system as a whole. In this instance, power is determined by using strain gauges to measure net torque output, typically at the crank spider (e.g., SRM) or at the rear wheel hub (e.g., PowerTap) along with a cadence meter to measure angular velocity. Power meters are small, noninvasive, and carry only minimal weight penalty. In addition, they allow measurement of crank power on the athlete's own bicycle. Thus, they are ideally suited for field testing and allow athletes, coaches, and scientists to assess power and thereby provide data with direct practical relevance.

Devices That Measure Independent Pedal Powers

The second category of measurement devices encompasses devices that can measure power on the right and left sides independently. Besides being able to measure overall power output, such devices allow the athlete, coach, or scientist to gain a deeper understanding of *how* the cyclist produces power. In this context, devices that record only the overall power output are clearly limited, because they measure the combined effect of both legs. During the downstroke of one leg, for example, it is not possible to say with certainty how much of the overall power output is produced by the leg pushing down and how much is produced by the opposite leg pulling up. This second category of measurement devices overcomes this limitation. Separate measures of right and left pedal powers are obtained by installing strain gauges on both crank arms (e.g., Lode), pedals (e.g., Look), or pedal spindles (e.g., Garmin Vector, PowerTap). Again, the force or torque measures obtained from the strain gauges are then multiplied by the corresponding velocity to yield right and left pedal powers. As we will see later in this chapter, this approach allows bilateral symmetry (or asymmetry) to be assessed accurately.

Devices That Measure Independent Pedal Forces in Two Dimensions

Devices falling into the first two categories measure only tangential (propulsive) forces (see figure 10.1) or their combined effect. A final category encompasses devices that are able to measure the force applied to the pedal in two (or three) dimensions. Specifically, such devices allow the measurement of both tangential and radial forces. Independent radial and tangential forces can be acquired at the crank (e.g., Pioneer, Radlabor, FES, Factor, Axis Cranks) or at the pedal (e.g., Sensix). Although the radial component of the pedal force does not produce mechanical work or power, measuring it is important because it allows sophisticated, in-depth biomechanical analyses, such as the decomposition of pedal forces into muscular and nonmuscular components (Kautz and Hull 1993) or the derivation of joint action powers. To quantify the latter, additional information about the movement is needed. This assessment is typically done by the use of video analysis or potentiometers.

Applications

In light of the mechanical and anatomical concepts, this section discusses relevant applications relating to pedaling and their uses and misuses.

Using Crank Power in Applied Contexts

The measurement of overall crank power can be useful in track sprint cycling. Sprint cycling requires an exorbitant amount of crank power produced during the initial acceleration phase. During short bursts of maximal cycling, athletes can produce up to 2,500 watts of crank power. Research has shown that athletes who can produce greater maximal power at the start are more likely to win the race, because of the high energy required to accelerate the bicycle up to speed. Dorel et al. (2005), for example, showed that maximum power was a key factor in the prediction of track sprint cycling performance in French elite cyclists. Consistent with this, Martin et al. (2006) used a modeling approach to demonstrate that maximum power capacity is a key indicator of sprint cycling performance. Maximum power assessments on stationary bikes in laboratories correlate well with maximum power produced in the field (Gardner et al. 2007). Thus, the assessment of crank power during this phase is of particular importance.

In submaximal cycling, crank power is also an important performance-related variable, particularly within the context of cycling efficiency. As will be seen in chapter 35, the monitoring of crank power can be helpful in determining the optimum pacing strategy, such as in time trials. In addition, and as described at the beginning of this chapter, cycling efficiency can be thought of as the ratio of crank power and power produced by the cyclist's muscles. Bearing this definition in mind, high cycling efficiency allows a cyclist to achieve greater cycling power for a given amount of metabolic cost. Horowitz, Sidossis, and Coyle (1994) demonstrated that higher efficiency translates into improved cycling performance. Specifically, they showed that a group of cyclists with high efficiency produced on average 9 percent more crank power than did cyclists with low efficiency. Hopker, Coleman, and Wiles (2007) demonstrated that moderately fit cyclists are more efficient than unfit cyclists. Within a moderately to highly fit population, however, cycling efficiency does not change as a function of fitness (Moseley et al. 2004). Hopker, Coleman, and Passfield (2009) and Hopker et al. (2010) further demonstrated that cycling efficiency changes as a function of time during the competitive season and that certain types of training can improve cycling efficiency.

The biomechanical mechanisms underlying between-subject differences and intervention-induced changes in cycling efficiency are multifactorial and are likely to include muscle fiber composition (i.e., muscle fiber type distribution), muscle strength, muscle coordination, and pedaling technique (Hopker et al. 2013). Discussing all these factors comprehensively is beyond the scope of this chapter, although some aspects relating to pedaling technique are discussed later in this chapter. Regardless of the exact mechanisms responsible, high cycling efficiency is undoubtedly beneficial for submaximal cycling performance. From this perspective, the measurement of crank power can be useful when monitoring (metabolic) training intensity.

Altering Pedaling Technique

As we saw at the beginning of this chapter, mechanical power is produced mainly by the hip extensors, knee extensors, and plantar flexors. These muscle groups act in synergy to deliver mechanical power to the pedals.

Submaximal Cycling

During submaximal cycling, the hip extensors, knee extensors, and plantar flexors produce almost 85 percent of the power delivered to the pedal (Elmer et al. 2011). Bearing in mind that cycling efficiency is a key factor in relation to submaximal cycling performance, it is not surprising, because these muscle groups are designed to produce large forces efficiently. In contrast, the knee flexors deliver only small amounts of power to the pedal (about 8 to 12 percent of total pedal power). One of the reasons for this is that the knee flexors (i.e., the hamstrings) are relatively weak and not designed for high force or power production. In addition, they are metabolically inefficient power producers.

Based on these muscle-specific properties, the central nervous system intuitively chooses an efficient pedaling technique during submaximal cycling. Any active attempts to alter the preferred pedaling technique generally does not increase cycling efficiency. For example, actively pulling on the pedal, or "pedaling in circles," increases the activity of the inefficient knee flexors, which has no effect or a negative effect on cycling efficiency (Mornieux, Gollhofer, and Stapelfeldt 2010; Mornieux et al. 2008; Korff et al. 2007; Theurel et al. 2012). In another study (Cannon, Kolkhorst, and Cipriani 2007), cyclists were instructed to maintain a more dorsiflexed (feet pointing upward) position. Again, this pedaling strategy resulted in a decrease in cycling efficiency.

Such results are particularly important with regard to information provided by commercially available devices that encourage riders to alter their pedaling technique. For example, many commercially available devices provide feedback about "force effectiveness" or the evenness of the torque distribution and encourage riders to pull on the pedals more actively to increase efficiency. Within the context of submaximal cycling such claims are not scientifically valid, because no scientific evidence supports the notion that altering pedaling technique positively affects either short- or long-term efficiency.

Maximal Cycling

In contrast to submaximal cycling, the goal of maximal cycling is to deliver a maximum amount of mechanical power to the pedals irrespective of metabolic cost. The fact that the knee flexors are inefficient power producers becomes less important, because the high power output does not need to be sustained for a long period. Consequently, the knee flexors play a more important role and generate almost 20 percent of total pedal power during maximal cycling (Elmer et al. 2011). Consistent with this, Dorel et al. (2012) showed large increases in knee flexor activity when cyclists moved from submaximal to maximal cycling. The researchers also demonstrated increased hip extensor activity, while knee extensor activity stayed relatively constant. Interestingly, the hip extensors were not maximally activated during the maximum cycling trial. From these results, the question about the differential roles of intermuscular coordination and muscular strength arises.

To address this question, Barratt et al. (under review) compared muscular strength and intermuscular coordination between elite and subelite track cyclists. They demonstrated that intermuscular coordination (in terms of relative joint power contributions) did not differ between the groups. In contrast, they found significant muscle-group-specific differences in strength between the two groups. Although knee extensor strength and knee flexor strength were significantly greater in the elite cyclists, no differences were found between hip extensor and hip flexor strength. These findings suggest that knee extensor and knee flexor strength might be the limiting factors to maximum cycling power and that coaches and athletes may wish to target these muscle groups with the goal of increasing sprint-cycling performance.

Bilateral Symmetry

Bilateral symmetry is present when power production is equal from the right and left across the pedal revolution. The greater the difference is between the power measured on the right and the left pedals, the greater the bilateral asymmetry is. Research has shown that bilateral symmetry is highly variable between athletes; some individuals show up to a 20 percent difference between legs in overall power contribution. Further, bilateral symmetry has been shown to be influenced by resistance as well as pedaling rate (Daly and Cavanagh 1976; Carpes et al. 2007; Sanderson 1990).

Many commercially available devices that measure crank torque and crank power provide information about cycling symmetry, claiming that increased bilateral symmetry is desirable and indicative of better cycling performance. Indeed, bilateral symmetry is intuitively attractive. If one leg produces less power than the other, strengthening the weaker leg with a view to increasing performance makes sense. Consistent with this speculation, we have some evidence (Barratt and Korff, under review) to support the notion that bilateral symmetry could be beneficial for performance in maximum cycling. We compared bilateral symmetry during a 3-second all-out sprint between elite and subelite track cyclists. Bilateral symmetry was assessed using separate force measures on the right and left pedals. Elite track cyclists showed significantly greater symmetry (4.5 percent difference between the two pedal powers) than the subelite cyclists did (15.1 percent difference between the two pedal powers). These results suggest that bilateral symmetry during maximal cycling could be beneficial for the generation of maximum power.

When interpreting bilateral symmetry data provided by commercially available measurement devices, however, caution is warranted. As we have seen in the previous section, many measurement devices measure overall torque or power. Thus, they measure the combined effect of right and left legs and ignore the fact that peak power during the downstroke of one leg is also influenced by the power production during the upstroke of the opposite leg. Indeed, Bini and Hume (2014) demonstrated that the assessment of bilateral symmetry using total crank torque is not necessarily indicative of bilateral symmetry or asymmetry obtained by the assessment of right and left pedal contributions separately. Figure 10.6 provides an example to illustrate how an asymmetrical pedaling pattern can be misinterpreted to be symmetrical when only crank power is considered. Thus, accurate measures of bilateral symmetry or asymmetry can be made only when power is measured separately on both pedals or both crank arms.

Another reason for caution lies in the lack of scientific evidence for bilateral symmetry being advantageous for submaximal cycling performance. On the contrary, previous research suggests that during submaximal cycling bilateral symmetry does not affect cycling efficiency or intermuscular

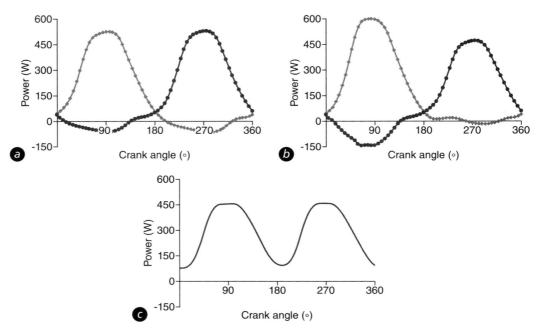

▶ **Figure 10.6** Different combinations of pedal power can result in identical crank power profile. (*a*) Two identical pedal power profiles that are 180 degrees out of phase. (*b*) Two pedal power profiles that are significantly different (asymmetrical) from each other. Specifically, the peak right pedal power (solid diamonds) is significantly greater than the peak left pedal power (solid circles). In addition, the left pedal power profile exhibits a significant negative portion during the recovery phase, whereas the negative portion of the right pedal is insignificant. (*c*) Both pairs of pedal power result in the same crank power profile. Thus, the assessment of crank power alone would not be able to detect the asymmetry that is displayed in (*b*).

coordination (Carpes et al. 2010; Korff and Romer 2012). Korff and Romer (2012), for example, found that in a group of 17 cyclists of varying fitness levels, cycling efficiency and bilateral symmetry were unrelated during submaximal cycling. This finding is perhaps not surprising, because a number of reasons may cause a cyclist to pedal asymmetrically. Specifically, interindividual differences in bilateral symmetry can be influenced by leg preference, bilateral differences in strength, bilateral leg-length discrepancies, or injury history. Bearing this in mind, caution needs to be taken when encouraging an athlete to pedal more symmetrically, because the specific cause underpinning the asymmetry should be understood.

In summary, the evidence to date suggests that bilateral symmetry may be an important performance-related feature for maximal but not for submaximal cycling. To understand the relationship between bilateral symmetry and cycling performance, longitudinal studies are necessary, which should be the subject for future research.

Pedaling Technique and Fatigue

Muscle fatigue is an important factor to consider within the context of pedaling technique. As we would expect, the power-producing muscle groups can sustain a given power output for only a limited time. This time depends, of course, on the power output itself. At high power outputs (i.e., power outputs beyond those corresponding to the lactate threshold), muscles fatigue more quickly than they do at low power outputs. Martin and Brown (2009), for example, found that overall power is reduced by more than 50 percent after a 30-second Wingate test. Results from Elmer et al. (2012) revealed that the ability to produce maximum instantaneous power is reduced by more than 30 percent after an all-out 10-minute time trial. At lower power requirements, power can be sustained much longer. Theurel et al. (2012) showed only small reductions (7 to 15 percent) in crank power during a 45-minute cycle trial at 75 percent of aerobic capacity. Bini et al. (2008) found that their subjects produced greater crank power during the later stages of a 40K time trial compared with the beginning of the race. Of course, the ability to sustain a given amount of power for an extended time depends on the training status of the athlete, among many other factors that are beyond the scope of this chapter.

The literature in relation to fatigue and pedaling technique is surprisingly scarce. In addition, studies have used different fatiguing protocols, making it difficult to compare the results of studies to each other. But some interesting commonalities are found. A common finding across the studies is that fatigue is muscle-group specific. In other words, when a rider is unable to maintain crank power, the muscle power of certain muscle groups drops more quickly than that of others. Martin and Brown (2009) quantified muscle-group powers during a 30-second Wingate test. They found that after the test, the reduction in plantar flexor power was greater than the reduction for the remaining power-producing muscle groups. This finding is consistent with results from Elmer et al. (2012). These authors measured joint action powers during an all-out maximum 3-second cycling trial before and after a 10-minute time trial. The authors found that after the time trial, the reduction in plantar flexor power was greater than the reduction for the remaining muscle groups. Both studies are also consistent in showing that the hip and knee extensors were more resistant to fatigue, showing a smaller drop in power. Together, the findings from these studies show that plantar flexors are an important muscle group to consider when designing training plans with the goal of increasing fatigue resistance in athletes.

From these studies the question arises about whether one muscle group can compensate for the power drop of another muscle group if overall power must be maintained. Research from Sanderson and Black (2003) as well as Dorel et al. (2009) provides some interesting insights within this context. Both studies used a fatiguing protocol during which participants cycled at high power output (corresponding to 80 percent of their maximum oxygen uptake) and were required to hold this power output until exhaustion. Dorel et al. (2009) found that toward the end of the cycling bout, plantar flexor muscular activity decreased while activity of the knee flexors and hip extensors increased. This finding is consistent with findings from Sanderson and Black (2003), who found that the joint moments (a surrogate measure of muscle-group force) increased in these two muscle groups. Together, these findings suggest that the knee flexors and hip extensors play an important role in producing additional power when other muscle groups are fatiguing. But note as well that Sanderson and Black also found increased plantar flexor muscle moment, which is not consistent with the results of the other three studies (Dorel et al. 2009, Elmer et al. 2012, Martin and Brown 2009). Thus, further research is needed to understand the compensatory mechanisms during muscle-group-specific fatigue during constant power cycling at high intensities.

Several studies have investigated muscle activity during submaximal fatiguing protocols. Bini et al. (2008) investigated muscle activity patterns during a 40 km time trial. These authors found a tendency for muscle activity to increase toward the end of the trial. In contrast to this finding, Theurel et al. (2012) found reductions in muscle activity toward the end of a 45-minute trial at 75 percent of aerobic capacity. The likely reason for these discrepancies is that power output was not held constant in either of the studies. To understand the role of individual muscles and muscle groups, it is necessary to investigate both muscle activity and joint moments or powers under submaximal conditions when power output is constant.

Applying the Science

We have seen that mechanical power is the major determinant of metabolic cost and maximum cycling performance. Thus, mechanical power is the obvious parameter to investigate when attempting to understand pedaling mechanics or to design interventions with the goal of increasing cycling performance. Joint action powers give us additional insights into intermuscular coordination strategies. We have also learned that during submaximal cycling, the central nervous system automatically tends to choose a pedaling technique that prioritizes cycling efficiency. Finally, power production during maximal cycling appears to be determined by muscular strength rather than intermuscular coordination strategies. Together, these results provide us with a scientific basis to evaluate the usefulness (and misuses) of the available technology to improve cycling performance.

Specifically, the assessment of crank power can be useful in monitoring maximal power capacity over time or as a function of an intervention. Monitoring crank power during submaximal cycling with a view to improving efficiency or set the desired training zones is also useful. Further, the investigation of joint powers suggests that strengthening the knee extensors and flexors may be an appropriate strategy to increase maximal cycling power. Finally, increasing the fatigue resistance of the plantar flexors may be an appropriate strategy to increase the sustainability of cycling power.

Caution must be taken when changing pedaling technique during submaximal cycling with the goal of riding more efficiently. In particular, no convincing evidence has been offered that pulling on the pedal, pedaling in circles, or increasing bilateral symmetry improves cycling efficiency. First, to date, no scientific evidence suggests that altering pedaling technique improves submaximal cycling performance. Second, in contrast to open chain movements such as running, walking, or swimming, the cycling motion is constrained by the geometrical setup of the bicycle and by the requirement of the crank to follow its prescribed circular path. As a result, pedaling technique in cycling is a far less important determinant of performance than swimming or running technique. In particular, physical fitness (maximum oxygen capacity, lactate threshold, strength) and aerodynamics are by far the best predictors of cycling performance. Thus, from a physiological and biomechanical point of view (setting aside race tactics), physical fitness, muscular strength, and an aerodynamic position on the bike are the features that athletes should focus on before trying to tweak their pedaling technique.

PART
IV

The Cycling Environment

CHAPTER 11

Dealing With Heat Stress

—Stephen S. Cheung

Part of the beauty of cycling is that it is an outdoor sport in which training and competition take place across a wide range of weather over the course of a season. Conditions can range from the cold weather associated with the spring Classics in northern Europe through to the heat typically found during the Tour de France and Vuelta a Éspana during the summer. The globalization of cycling also means that major markets for cycling are developing in many hot-weather or tropical locations such as Australia, southeast Asia, and the Middle East. At the Olympics in Atlanta in 1996 and Athens in 2004, sport scientists, coaches, and athletes alike knew that heat, humidity, and even air pollution would be environmental factors that could seriously affect the performance of the athletes. The positive aspect was that, just as the 1968 Mexico City Games kick-started scientific and applied interest in altitude training that remains strong, these recent Games spurred a lot of fundamental and applied research into ways to minimize the potentially debilitating effects of heat. The environment, therefore, becomes a major determinant of how a ride or race plays out, and it can greatly affect performance. At the same time, by understanding the effects of environmental stress on how the body responds, cyclists can minimize the negative effects and even use challenging environmental conditions to maximize their capacity.

Heat Balance

The basic heat balance equation incorporates the four major heat loss pathways (radiation, conduction, convection, and evaporation; see figure 11.1) and metabolic heat production to model the rate of heat storage ($\dot{S}$ in W·m^{-2}):

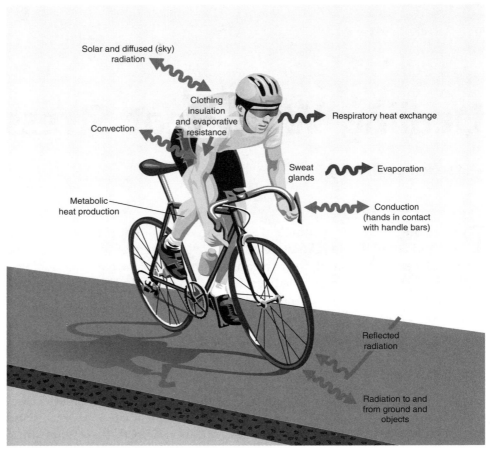

▶ **Figure 11.1** The body exchanges heat with the environment through many pathways.

Reprinted, by permission, from J.H. Wilmore, D.L. Costill, and W.L. Kenney, 2008, Physiology of sport and exercise, 4th ed. (Champaign, IL: Human Kinetics), 257. Adapted from C.V. Gisolfi and C.B. Wenger, 1984, "Temperature regulation during exercise: Old concepts, new ideas," Exercise and Sports Sciences Reviews 12(1): 339-372.

$$\dot{S} = (\dot{M} - \dot{W}) - (\dot{R} + \dot{C} + \dot{K} + \dot{E} + \dot{C}_{res} + \dot{E}_{res})$$

where

$\dot{S}$ = heat storage; a positive value represents a heat gain that could eventually lead to hyperthermia, whereas a negative value represents heat loss that could eventually lead to hypothermia.

$\dot{M}$ = metabolic heat production.

$\dot{W}$ = mechanical work.

$\dot{R}$ = radiation; this component combines direct radiation of the sun and reflected radiation from the ground. It is positive when the surrounding temperature is greater than the skin temperature.

$\dot{C}$ = conduction; this component involves direct heat transfer from one molecule to another. Its rate depends on the temperature gradient between the skin and surrounding surfaces and the thermal qualities of those surfaces. Conduction is generally not relevant for most cycling situations, because of the small contact points (saddle, handlebars, pedals) between the rider and the bike.

$\dot{K}$ = convection; this component is often discussed in combination with conduction because the effectiveness of conduction depends on the rate of heat exchange between the skin and the surroundings. As long as ambient temperature is lower than body temperature of 37 to 39 degrees Celsius, the high rate of convective flow over a cyclist moving at speed can still contribute to significant heat dissipation. But when climbing or when cycling in slower disciplines such as mountain biking, convective heat loss may be minimal, accelerating heat storage.

$\dot{E}$ = evaporation from the respiratory tract or the skin; evaporation is the main defense against hyperthermia because, as body temperature increases, the effectiveness of radiation, conduction, and convection as heat-loss mechanisms decreases. Unlike what happens with the other methods of heat exchange, the potential for evaporative heat loss is determined primarily by the water vapor pressure gradient between the body surface and the environment. A warm but humid environment can lead to much higher heat storage than a hotter but dry environment, because of the impairment of evaporative heat loss.

Effect of Heat on Performance

A consensus of scientific evidence—analyzing performance across various climatic conditions in both laboratory and field settings—has clearly demonstrated that human exercise capacity decreases in the heat. In the laboratory, Galloway and Maughan (1997) had subjects exercise to voluntary exhaustion at 70 percent of $\dot{V}O_{2peak}$ in 4, 10, 20, and 30 degrees Celsius and reported that peak tolerance time occurred at 10 degrees Celsius. Similar and shorter durations occurred at both 4 and 20 degrees Celsius, and a further decrease occurred at 30 degrees Celsius. Although the relatively limited airflow in such laboratory studies may have overamplified the negative effects of temperature in cycling studies (Morrison, Cheung, and Cotter 2014), such decrements are supported by retrospective field studies. For example, Ely et al. (2007) analyzed marathon running times across a range of finishing placings and race-day temperatures and reported the fastest running times in cool temperatures and an exponentially greater impairment in slower runners in warm temperatures. But the decrement in physiological performance is often weighed up in a cost–benefit analysis because of the potential for decreased air density—and thus lower air resistance—with increasing temperature. To take advantage of this reduced air resistance, a recent trend has been to increase velodrome temperatures to nearly 30 degrees Celsius during World Hour Record attempts.

Heat-related exercise impairment likely encompasses a wide range of physiological and psychological mechanisms (Cheung and Sleivert 2004; figure 11.2). These mechanisms include potential reductions in cerebral blood flow, decrements in neuromuscular activation in the brain, decreases in mental arousal, reduced gut blood flow leading to bacterial leakage from the gut and inflammatory response, and reduced cardiovascular efficiency while coping with increased metabolic and thermoregulatory demands. Besides causing physiological effects, higher ambient temperature may alter voluntary effort; the extra heat stress may cause the brain to reduce the willingness to work as hard as in a cooler environment to decrease the risk of heat illness and catastrophic collapse. When tasked to adjust power output to maintain a constant perceived effort similar to that needed for a 20K to 40K time-trial pace, the rate of decline in voluntary power output was higher in hot (35 degrees Celsius) compared with cooler (15 and 25 degrees Celsius) environments (Tucker et al. 2006).

Besides reducing exercise capacity, the major clinical danger with exercise in hot environments is an elevated risk of exertional heat illness such as heat exhaustion and heatstroke. An excellent book on this topic specifically for coaches and athletes was written by Dr. Lawrence Armstrong (2007) of the

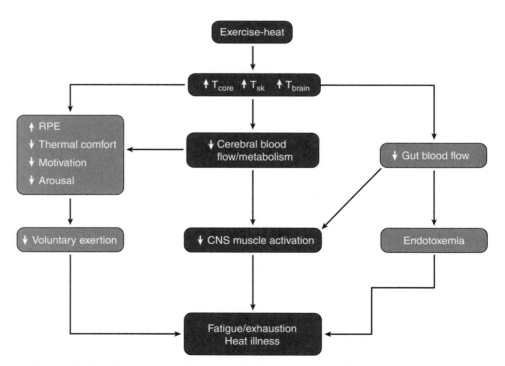

▶ **Figure 11.2** Elevated core, brain, and skin temperature during exercise-heat stress can cause fatigue through a variety of interrelated physiological and psychological factors. CNS = central nervous system; RPE = rating of perceived exertion.

University of Connecticut. An important finding is that exertional heat illness can occur even in cool weather. Dr. Armstrong led the American College of Sports Medicine Position Stand on Exertional Heat Illness (Armstrong et al. 2007), emphasizing that heat exhaustion and exertional heatstroke "occur worldwide with prolonged intense activity in almost every venue (e.g., cycling, running races, American football, soccer)" (556).

How Hot Is Too Hot?

Given that hyperthermia clearly impairs physiological function and exercise capacity, the main question for athletes is just how hot is too hot, whether that be ambient temperature or actual body temperature. This question is difficult to answer, because a slight or even significant rise in body temperature is not always an indication of problems during exercise, especially in fit or elite athletes. Ultramarathoners can exercise at maximal capacity for 4 hours in moderate ambient temperatures with only minor elevations in core temperature, suggesting strong ability to thermoregulate even under conditions of high metabolic heat production. At the same time, some endurance athletes can sustain elevated core temperatures of greater than 40 degrees Celsius throughout a marathon or triathlon without major issues (Kenefick, Cheuvront, and Sawka 2007). Especially in cycling outdoors, in which the cycling itself often generates high wind speed and thus convective cooling, high temperatures may not be as dangerous as expected. As noted previously, in certain situations a higher ambient temperature may benefit cycling performance because the lower air density reduces air resistance.

In contrast, although exertional heat illnesses occur most frequently in hot and humid conditions, such problems can occur even in cool conditions with intense or prolonged exercise. In one case study a well-trained male experienced collapse near the finish of a marathon in 6 degrees Celsius ambient conditions and presented a rectal temperature of 40.7 degrees Celsius approximately 30 minutes postcollapse (Roberts 2006). Such a wide range in responses highlights the high degree of individual variability in response to heat stress, making it difficult to develop predictive models for race organizers who are trying to protect participant safety and for coaches and sport scientists who are trying to individualize training programs or predict performance outcomes.

Protective Effects of Aerobic Fitness

Aerobic fitness provides protective physiological responses to exercise similar to those from acclimatization to hot environments (Cheung, McLellan, and Tenaglia 2000). These benefits include greater evaporative heat dissipation through improved sweating response, resulting from both lower core temperature thresholds for the initiation of sweating and greater sensitivity of sweating response to increasing core temperatures. Improved aerobic capacity also leads to elevated plasma volume and cardiac output, minimizing the competition for blood distribution between skeletal muscle and skin (heat dissipation and sweating output) during exercise and heat stress (Sawka et al. 1992). Other important benefits of aerobic fitness are a lowered resting core temperature coupled with an elevated endpoint core temperature that can be tolerated before voluntary exhaustion (Cheung and McLellan 1998). This latter effect results directly from aerobic fitness rather than body composition because differences across fitness groups remained evident when highly and moderately fit subjects were normalized for differences in body fatness (Selkirk and McLellan 2001). Therefore, fitness appears to benefit heat tolerance because of both a greater capacity for tolerating high temperatures and a slower rate of heat storage. These benefits, however, appear unique to long-term changes in aerobic fitness rather than transient changes brought about by short-term training interventions (Cheung and McLellan 1998).

Heat Adaptation

When discussing long-term responses to heat exposure, definitions of some basic terminology can help to clarify discussion and avoid confusion.

Adaptation is the overall response by humans to a different environment such as heat. Responses can be both physiological (e.g., increased sweat rate) and psychological (less perceived distress).

Acclimation is the process of adaptation through exposure to an "artificial" stimulus. An example is the training that Bradley Wiggins did for the 2011 Vuelta in his garden shed with the heaters turned up. *Acclimatization*, on the other hand, is the process of adaptation through natural exposure to the stimulus. This method would include moving to a hot environment to train and live there for several weeks before competition. Moving to a hot environment and spending the majority of the day in air conditioning, however, reduces total natural heat exposure, thus qualifying more as acclimation than acclimatization and slowing the rate of overall adaptation.

Habituation generally refers to the psychological desensitization to a stimulus. Put your hand into cold water. The first minutes feel painful and horrible, but that feeling of strong discomfort fades after a while, even though your hand itself may actually be at a lower temperature.

Scientific research on heat stress, and specifically our physiological responses and adaptation to prolonged heat exposure, is well studied. In general, humans have a high ceiling for physiological adaptation to prolonged heat exposure. Several major changes can occur:

- Resting core temperature decreases slightly, theoretically permitting more heat storage before hyperthermia-induced exercise impairments occur, along with decreasing the risk of catastrophic exertional heat illness.

- Plasma volume—the liquid component of blood—increases, resulting in greater total blood volume. Note that hemoglobin and red blood cells typically do not increase, so hematocrit generally decreases with heat adaptation.

- One consequence of higher plasma and blood volume is decreased cardiovascular strain from pumping blood to both the muscles and skin, resulting in a lowered resting and exercise heart rate.

- The beneficial sweat response adaptations include an earlier onset of sweating, a redistribution of the sweat response, and a conservation of sodium. Adapted individuals are able to dissipate heat more readily because they will begin to sweat at a lower core temperature and will sweat more from the limbs (the trunk is the main area of sweat loss for an unacclimatized person), thus making better use of the skin surface area for evaporative heat loss. Of course, the flip side of enhanced sweating is that the rate of fluid loss from the body increases.

- Sweat becomes more dilute as the sweat glands become better at reabsorption of electrolytes, which helps to minimize overall electrolyte loss with the higher sweat rate.

- Both separately and in conjunction with these physiological changes, perceptual sensitivity to heat decreases. Thermal discomfort and ratings of perceived exertion decrease while resting or exercising in the heat.

Adaptation Timeline

Generally, the rate of heat adaptation follows an exponential path, but the physiological adaptations to heat occur at differing rates (Périard, Racinais, and Sawka 2015; table 11.1). The immediate adaptation is a reduction in heart rate (HR). Most of the observed reduction occurs within 4 to 5 days, and full acclimatization appears to occur after about 7 days of exposure, coinciding with most of the beneficial core and skin temperature reductions. Thermoregulatory adaptations take a little longer than cardiovascular ones, but when following a structured acclimatization protocol, full adaptation often occurs after 10 to 14 days of exposure. Maximal sweat response improvements may take a month, and resistance to exertional heat illness may take twice that long.

Besides the occurrence of these physiological changes, important questions are whether heat adaptation is capable of eliciting improved performance to exercise in these hot conditions and how rapidly these performance changes may occur. Conversely, an interesting question is whether the adaptations caused by chronic heat exposure lead to improved response and performance when returning to a more temperate environment (Lorenzo et al. 2010). If this is the case, then heat adaptation protocols may serve a double benefit, enhancing performance across both temperate and hot environments.

Table 11.1 Magnitude of Response to Heat Adaptation Along With Comparative Timeline

Adaptation	Change from baseline
Resting heart rate	−5 bpm STHA, MTHA −12 bpm LTHA
Mean exercise heart rate	−12 bpm
Resting T_{skin}	No effect
Exercising T_{skin}	−0.57° C
Core temperature	−0.17° C STHA, MTHA −0.32° C LTHA (1 study)
Sweat rate	+5% STHA +29% MTHA, +33% LTHA
Thirst sensation	Moderate decrease
Rating of perceived exertion (RPE)	Moderate decrease
Thermal sensation	Small decrease
Exercise capacity/performance	+7% STHA +22% LTHA, +21% MTHA

STHA = short-term (< 1 week), MTHA = medium-term (8–14 days), LTHA = long-term (> 14 days) heat adaptation. Comparisons on different rows indicate significant time differences between adaptation durations.

Data from C.J. Tyler, T. Reeve, G.J. Hodges, and S.S. Cheung, 2016, "The effects of heat adaptation on physiology, perception, and exercise performance in the heat: A meta-analysis," *Sports Medicine* 46(11): 1699-1724.

A logistically challenging field experiment performed by a Qatari-Danish collaboration suggests that heat acclimatization can eventually restore performance to levels found in temperate conditions, but not exceed them (Karlsen et al. 2015a; Karlsen et al. 2015b). Highly trained Danish cyclists performed a 43.4-kilometer outdoor time trial in cool (5 degree Celsius) conditions in Denmark and then moved to Qatar (30 to 36 degrees Celsius ambient temperature) for a 2-week heat training camp. Physiological testing and a time trial of identical distance were performed at 1, 6, and 13 days into the camp. Impairment was marked upon acute exposure to heat (about 85 percent power), clearly supporting the classical consensus that heat stress severely impairs performance. Performance steadily improved over the course of the heat camp; progressive increases occurred in power output at day 6 (+14 percent) and again at day 13 (+5 percent) compared with day 1. The big caveat is that, although heat acclimatization helped performance in hot ambient temperatures, it only ever got the subjects back to square one. That is, even after 13 days, their power output only returned to nearly 100 percent of what they could do in a quite cold (5 degrees Celsius) temperature back in Denmark. Overall, then, full heat acclimatization for performance outcomes appears to require close to 2 weeks of exposure, and this timeline needs to be integrated into training and tapering programs.

The second half of the field study tested whether the increased blood volume, higher sweat rate, and other heat adaptation responses helped the cyclists when they went back to Denmark and competed in a cool environment. The interesting answer is no; no improvements occurred in time-trial performance compared with either the initial precamp test in Denmark or any of the TTs done in Qatar. This result suggests that heat acclimatization is highly specific to a hot environment and that it is not effective as an ergogenic tool for competitions in temperate environments.

Heat Acclimation Protocols

Nobody really disputes that heat adaptation occurs, but the devil is in the details for sport scientists. Specifically, what are the best and most efficient heat exposure protocols? How much daily exposure (time? intensity?) is required for optimal adaptation? How do other individual factors (e.g., fitness, hydration) affect the rate of heat adaptation?

For maximum acclimatization, exercise should be performed in elevated ambient temperatures; the primary stimulus is a sustained rise in core temperature. But no standard heat acclimatization protocol exists for frequency, duration, or intensity. A gradual increase in thermal stress is required to minimize the risks of prematurely causing exertional heat illness.

Rather than dehydration being perceived as a negative health or performance risk, recent research suggests that permitting a slight state of dehydration in conjunction with exercising in the heat may accelerate the rate of heat adaptation (Garrett et al. 2012, 2014). This effect appears to occur through either magnification of the stimulus from exercise-heat stress by dehydration or through parallel interrelated response pathways between dehydration and heat exposure.

People with high levels of aerobic fitness tend to have greater levels of heat tolerance and acclimatize much more readily than people at lower fitness levels (Pandolf, Burse, and Goldman 1977). The reasons for this differential response are likely multifactorial and linked to training-induced adaptations and increased ability to tolerate higher levels of thermal stress.

Factors such as alcohol consumption, sleep loss, and illness have all been linked to reductions in acclimatization-related benefits. Such factors should be carefully considered, especially when any acclimatization protocol causes significant disruption to the normal routine of the athlete (e.g., excessive travel and relocation associated with training camps).

The environment is also a significant component of a heat acclimation program. Wearing heavy sweat clothing in a cool environment may elicit the same increased sweating response as standard heat exposure does (Dawson 1994). Therefore, training indoors with a lower fan speed or wearing an extra clothing layer may be a useful method if training in a cold environment and traveling to a race at which hot conditions are expected. Overall, the thing to focus on with heat adaptation appears to be getting the core temperature to rise to the point at which sweating response is strongly stimulated and to maintain that high temperature and sweating for about 60 to 90 minutes a session for four to eight sessions, depending on fitness. Passive heat exposure, such as sitting in a sauna, can possibly provide the same stimulus but is not practical because staying in the sauna for long periods may be dangerous and time spent in the sauna is time not spent on training or recovering. With altitude training, maximal adaptation requires maintaining hypoxic exposure for as much of the day as possible. Currently, no research exists on whether nontraining heat exposure—such as during rest and sleep—can accelerate or optimize heat adaptation. But any benefits from nontraining exposure would likely be offset by negative consequences to recovery.

Limited data exist regarding the decay of acclimatization, but physiological adaptations may begin to subside after 3 days and may last no longer than 3 weeks. The beneficial adaptations observed in physiological parameters are lost earlier for HR than for rectal temperatures and sweat rate, so it appears that HR monitoring can be a good indicator of acclimatization decay. Differing advice can be found regarding when a "top up" of acclimatization is required. Some data suggest that one additional bout of exposure should be considered for every 5 days away from significant thermal stress (Pandolf, Burse, and Goldman 1977). Thermoregulatory research tends to separate trials by 7 days to minimize the effect of any heat acclimatization (Barnett and Maughan 1993), so a prudent recommendation is that if the adaptations are required for a sustained period following heat exposure, reexposure should take place at least once during the subsequent 7 days.

Cooling Strategies

The use of cooling protocols to improve performance or to counteract the risks of heat stress and hyperthermia has gained increasing popularity in cycling. The consistent core temperatures at the point of voluntary fatigue with a constant workload in the heat would certainly suggest that the removal of heat before exercise could increase exercise tolerance by increasing possible heat storage beforehand. Early athletic proponents include the Australian rowing teams, who used vests containing ice packs during warm-ups before competing in the 1996 Atlanta Olympics. Since then, many professional teams have used various ice vests while warming up on stationary bikes for a time trial. During riding, cyclists have used lightweight cooling collars, doused their heads with cool water, or used ice socks down their necks and backs to keep cooler.

Precooling

Although the rate of heat storage may remain unchanged with precooling, the lowered baseline temperature may enable both core temperature and heart rate to remain lower with prolonged exercise over time. Precooling also can decrease perceptions of heat stress and thereby possibly promote an upregulation of work intensity. This phenomenon has been reported in both elite runners and rowers with precooling of about 0.5 degree Celsius using cool water of about 20 degrees Celsius or ice vests (Arngrimsson et al. 2004).

Precooling is typically adopted to enhance athletic performance in hot environments rather than to increase the safety of exercising in such conditions. Decreasing core temperature before exercise or slowing the rate at which it rises during exercise can increase the time it takes to reach the high internal temperatures associated with the termination of exercise, whereas reductions in skin temperature can improve perceptions of thermal comfort. Precooling has regularly been shown to enhance endurance, exercise performance, and capacity in hot environmental conditions for moderate-duration exercise such as a 5K run (Tyler, Sunderland, and Cheung 2015; table 11.2). The improvement, however, does not always require a reduction in core temperature, which suggests that the benefit may also arise from reductions in skin temperature and the magnitude of perceived heat stress (Tyler and Sunderland 2011).

The potential benefits of precooling vary greatly across cycling disciplines, related to both their duration and their level of neuromuscular demand. Precooling does not appear to improve short-duration or sprinting exercise. Such activity is unlikely to be compromised because of thermoregulatory strain, and precooling may in fact negatively affect performance because of lowered muscle temperature and contractile capacity (Thornley, Maxwell, and Cheung 2003). Indeed, precooling before intermittent cycling sprints did not result in any improved power (Cheung and Robinson 2004; Duffield et al. 2003), and a higher ambient temperature may actually facilitate higher pedaling cadences and power outputs during maximal cycling sprints (Ball, Burrows, and Sargeant 1999). Precooling benefits may also be minimal with events such as a sportif ride or Ironman triathlon, because of the prolonged

Table 11.2   Relative Effectiveness of Precooling Overall, Broken Down by Exercise Modality, With Relative Effectiveness of Cooling During Exercise

Exercise type	Effect
PRECOOLING (23 STUDIES) ↑↑	
Sprint	↓
Intermittent	↑
Prolonged performance (e.g., TT)	↑↑
Prolonged steady rides to exhaustion	↑↑↑
COOLING DURING EXERCISE (5 STUDIES) ↑↑	

Data from C.J. Tyler, C. Sunderland, and S.S. Cheung, 2015, "The effect of cooling prior to and during exercise on exercise performance and capacity in the heat: A meta-analysis," *British Journal of Sports Medicine* 49(1): 7-13.

nature of the event and because the high metabolic heat production rapidly overwhelms any precooling-induced heat storage reduction.

Ice vests are popular for precooling because they cover the important torso region and are relatively nonconstricting during cycling compared with cooling pants. Vests also permit the legs to exercise and get the usual benefits of warming up before competition while keeping the torso as cool as possible. Research has shown that precooling the legs eliminates most of the benefits of warming up (Sleivert et al. 2001). Cooling hoods are also often used because they theoretically keep the brain cool. Furthermore, the head and face play a major role in the overall perception of thermal stress and comfort (Cotter and Taylor 2005), and head cooling by itself can be beneficial in improving high-intensity running in the heat.

Cooling During Exercise

Cooling during exercise has been studied less than precooling, but the effects and mechanisms of action (reduced core and skin temperature, heart rate, thermal sensation, and perceived exertion) appear to be similar. Although cooling during exercise can offer benefits to exercise performance, cooling jackets and vests can also increase the energy demands of exercise because of their extra mass, can create a microenvironment around the body that impairs evaporative heat dissipation, and can cause discomfort and skin irritation.

Cooling the head may achieve greater thermoregulatory advantage by directly targeting the thermoregulatory centers in the brain and the high perceptual thermosensitivity associated with the head and neck. This cooling effect may be achieved by using a cooling collar, wearing an ice sock underneath a jersey, or pouring cool or cold water over the head and neck. Cooling the head and neck region during exercise and physical activity in hot conditions has been shown to improve exercise capacity and performance (Tyler and Sunderland 2011). Physiological improvements (e.g., core temperature and HR) are equivocal, but perceptual thermal discomfort and ratings of perceived exertion are often improved. Head cooling may also protect some aspects of mental functioning when thermal strain is high, potentially a huge benefit in a sport that requires as many instantaneous decisions and carries as much risk as cycling does.

Although head and neck cooling may make athletes feel better, it is unlikely to reduce the level of thermal or cardiovascular strain experienced, so this technique should not be used as a method to lower body temperature. An important caveat and point of education with athletes is that with head and neck cooling, the improved perceptual strain in the absence of physiological improvements may provide false signals regarding the thermal state of the body and may pose a danger to the individual's health.

Applying the Science

Although some increase in body temperature during exercise is acceptable and even desirable, extreme temperatures impose extra stress on the body that diverts its focus from generating power at the muscles and delivering it to the pedals. How can you apply some of the research on heat stress and cooling strategy to cycling?

Exercise capacity is clearly reduced in both warm and hot environments. Therefore, anticipating this reduction is important in planning training and racing. For example, a cyclist who travels to a hot environment to train or race will need to adjust power or performance targets until full adaptation occurs.

Although full adaptation in physiology and performance can occur within about 2 weeks, individual responses to heat and adaptation rate can differ greatly. Therefore, cyclists need to monitor their own responses to heat. Many can do this by carefully logging training and responses during the initial heat wave of the summer.

Cyclists should keep as cool as possible before an event! They should do everything possible to stay out of the sun and heat before an event. Every bit of heat exposure is unnecessary, additional stress that detracts from training or recovery.

Precooling can be useful when competing in hot environments, but it is not universally positive as an ergogenic aid. It appears to be most effective for moderate-duration events lasting 10 to 60 minutes. Precooling appears to be counterproductive for sprint and power sports (e.g., downhill MTB, BMX, track sprinting) because of negative effects from cooling the muscles. Cooling may be effective, however, between competition heats. Precooling is also likely ineffective for long-duration events such as sportifs and many road races.

If precooling or cooling during exercise, cooling the head and torso may be the preferred strategy. The torso may strike the ideal balance between cooling the largest surface area without impeding the legs. Cooling the head and neck may improve perceptual sensations and performance despite having only minimal effect on actual heat storage.

CHAPTER 12

Air Pollution and Cyclists

—Michael Koehle and Luisa Giles

Air pollution is a mixture of gases (such as carbon monoxide and ozone) and particles (such as smoke particles and dust) that can be either emitted directly into or synthesized in the air from a variety of sources including fossil fuel combustion, wildfires, and power plants. Common air pollutants that have the potential to affect health and performance during cycling include particulate matter (PM), carbon monoxide (CO), ground-level ozone, nitrogen dioxide (NO_2), and sulfur dioxide. Smog is a common term used to describe a noxious mixture of gases and particles that make the air appear hazy. The two primary pollutants in smog are ground-level ozone and PM. The major categories of air pollutants are summarized in table 12.1.

Particulate Matter

Particulate matter (PM) is a mixture of solids and liquids that vary in size and are composed of different chemicals. Particulate matter is produced naturally from windblown dust and wildfires; it is also produced during the burning of combustibles such as wood, incense, cigarettes, and candles. Automobiles and power plants produce PM through fossil fuel combustion; older diesel engines produce higher concentrations of PM than gasoline engines. Cyclists can be exposed to PM that they would not typically think of as pollution sources, such as brake dust, road dust, and wood smoke from forest fires.

Particulate matter is typically categorized by its aerodynamic diameter, which takes into account how the particle behaves in air and plays a key role in deposition within the lungs and associated health effects. Particulate matter is typically grouped into three size ranges summarized in table 12.2. Generally, smaller particles tend to travel and deposit farther into the lungs and cause more health effects than larger particles. For example, coarse particulate matter tends to deposit in the nose and upper airways, whereas ultrafine particulate matter (UFP) deposits farther down the respiratory tree and into the alveoli. Some of the UFP may possibly cross into the bloodstream and cause effects not only in the lungs but also throughout the body.

Table 12.1 Major Categories of Airborne Pollutants

Pollutant	Source	Limits for danger to human health	Primary effects
Particulate matter	• Solid particles from a wide variety of human and natural sources • High regional and temporal variability because of weather and geography • Dust, wood smoke, pollen • Tobacco smoke, fossil fuel combustion	1,000 µg · m⁻³, 24 h average	• Effects dependent on particle size, mass, and composition, along with individual (e.g., mouth versus nasal breathing, allergies) factors • Few to no controlled studies on exercise effects in humans
Sulfur oxides (SO_x)	• Fossil fuel combustion • Sulfur dioxide (SO_2) most common	2,620 µg · m⁻³ (1.0 ppm), 24 h average	• Highly soluble gas • Respiratory irritation, bronchoconstriction, and spasms • Heightened sensitivity in asthmatics, especially with cold, dry air
Nitrogen oxides (NO_x)	• Fossil fuel combustion, cigarettes • Nitrogen dioxide (NO_2) most common	• 938 µg · m⁻³ (0.5 ppm), 24 h average • 3,750 µg · m⁻³ (2.0 ppm), 1 h average	• Soluble gas that can be absorbed by nasopharyngeal tract • Pulmonary dysfunction, respiratory irritation • Minimal evidence for major exercise impairment at low levels • Potential for acute high doses to induce prolonged pulmonary deficits
Carbon monoxide (CO)	Fossil fuel combustion	• 57.5 mg · m⁻³ (50 ppm), 8 h average • 86.3 mg · m⁻³ (75 ppm), 4 h average • 144 mg · m⁻³ (125 ppm), 1 h average	• High affinity (~230 times greater than that of O_2) for binding with hemoglobin, resulting in impaired oxygen-carrying capacity and cardiovascular function • Permanent cardiac and neural damage; ultimately fatal in high doses
Aerosols	Suspension of primary pollutants (e.g., fine particulates) in air or other (e.g., smoke, mist) gases; broad category of secondary pollutants from reactions of nitrogen oxides and sulfur oxides	• 800 µg · m⁻³ (0.4 ppm), 4 h average • 1,200 µg · m⁻³ (0.6 ppm), 2 h average • 1,400 µg · m⁻³ (0.7 ppm), 1 h average	Potentially wide range and variability of cardiovascular and respiratory responses, based on pollutant and allergy or asthma history
Ozone (O_3)	• Main component of smog • Secondary pollutant from interaction of automobile exhaust, hydrocarbons, and nitrogen oxides with sunlight and ultraviolet radiation • Highly susceptible to spikes during summers because of increased sunlight, heat, and local geography and weather	• 120 µg · m⁻³, 8 h average (World Health Organization) • 0.075 ppm, 8 h average (EPA)	• Wide range of respiratory symptoms including irritation, bronchospasms, inflammation, dyspnea, and reduced pulmonary function • Intensity of impairment during exercise dependent on concentration and effective dosage from ventilation rate • Proposed threshold of 0.20 to 0.40 ppm for significant exercise impairment

Environmental Protection Agency (EPA) of the United States unless noted.

Reprinted, by permission, from S.S. Cheung, 2010, *Advanced environmental exercise physiology* (Champaign, IL: Human Kinetics), 194-195.

Table 12.2 Size Classifications of Particulate Matter (PM)

Name	Abbreviation	Description
Coarse PM	$PM_{2.5-10}$	PM with an aerodynamic diameter between 2.5 μm and 10 μm
Fine PM	$PM_{2.5}$	PM with an aerodynamic diameter of 2.5 μm or less
Ultrafine PM	UFP or $PM_{0.1}$	PM with a diameter of 0.1 μm or less

Carbon Monoxide

Carbon monoxide is a colorless, odorless gas produced from the incomplete combustion of fuels containing carbon. Common outdoor sources of carbon monoxide include automotive exhaust (gasoline and diesel), heating and power-generating plants, smoke from fires, and cigarettes. Outdoor concentrations are highest near concentrated sources of vehicle exhaust, such as in traffic congestion and near traffic intersections (Raub et al. 2000).

Ozone

Ozone is a molecule composed of three oxygen atoms that is present high in the atmosphere (known as the ozone layer) but also occurs in the lower ranges of the atmosphere where we live (known as ground-level ozone). Ground-level ozone is a type of secondary pollutant because ozone is not emitted directly by a pollution source. Instead, it forms by chemical modification of other (primary) pollutants. For example, hydrocarbons and nitrogen oxides are modified by the sun to create ozone. Because these reactions often need sunlight as a catalyst, ozone levels increase during hot weather and are often higher later in the day.

Nitrogen Dioxide

Nitrogen dioxide is produced during fuel combustion and electricity generation. Outdoor concentrations of NO_2 near busy roadsides can be high (>0.5 ppm) but are below concentrations necessary to affect lung function in healthy adults.

Sulfur Dioxide

Sulfur dioxide is a gaseous air pollutant produced from the combustion of fuels containing sulfur. In most developed countries, the sulfur content in motor fuel tends to be low, which may mean that the likelihood of exposure is smaller. In developing countries, however, the burning of coal and the combustion of fuel containing higher sulfur content are major sources of sulfur dioxide.

Urban Versus Rural Sources of Pollution

Cyclists may be exposed to air pollution in both urban and rural settings. Urban sources of air pollution typically include traffic, emissions from off-road equipment such as leaf blowers and construction equipment, dust from construction sites, dust that is resuspended from the ground into the air from automobiles, wear from automobile brakes and tires, and windblown dust. In rural settings, cyclists may be exposed to some of the same outdoor sources of air pollution as well as outdoor air pollution transported from urban centers.

Other typical rural sources of air pollution include solid fuels (such as wood) that are used for heat and cooking, forest fires, agricultural sources such as pesticides, and large-scale use of heavy equipment (often diesel) such as tractors, harvesters, and trucks. Furthermore, pollens from grass, ash, birch, alder, hornbeam, hazel, and plantain can be present in higher concentrations in rural settings (Bosch-Cano et al. 2011). Air pollutants such as NO_2, ozone, and PM can increase allergies to pollen (Traidl-Hoffmann, Jakob, and Behrendt 2009), which may be why allergy symptoms related to hay fever occur more in urban centers than in rural settings.

Health Effects of Air Pollution Exposure

This section focuses on the health effects of air pollution from living in a polluted area or being exposed to pollution in a controlled environment while at rest, and the next section focuses directly on the risks of exercise (such as cycling) in a polluted environment. Lung function is a key concept; it refers to the ability of the lungs to breathe an adequate volume of air in and out. Narrowing of the airways through inflammation or spasm of the muscle around the airways is one of the key mechanisms that impair lung function when someone is exposed to air pollutants or other stresses.

Each of the different types of air pollutants has a slightly different health effect. Particulate matter exposure is associated with heart attacks, stroke, chronic bronchitis, and asthma (Giles and Koehle 2013). Exposure to PM can also cause the lungs to become inflamed, platelets to stick to one another (interfering with clotting), blood vessels to function improperly, blood pressure and heart rate to increase, and heart rhythms to be irregular (Giles and Koehle 2013). These health effects of PM are even more pronounced in people who have existing health conditions such as high blood pressure or heart disease. Carbon monoxide exerts a toxic effect by reducing the oxygen-carrying capacity of blood and causing tissues in the body to be deprived of oxygen (hypoxia or anoxia). Ozone irritates the lungs and causes them to be inflamed and hyperresponsive, impairing lung function and defense against other shocks and insults. Although inhalation of sulfur dioxide can rapidly impair lung function, causing wheezing and shortness of breath

(Linn et al. 1984), the concentrations used in experiments typically far exceed concentrations in the atmosphere, suggesting that sulfur dioxide may be less important than other pollutants for competing cyclists.

Health Effects of Cycling in Air Pollution

During an aerobic exercise such as cycling, the amount of air that is breathed, and therefore the amount of pollution that is ingested, increases dramatically. During intense cycling, air is breathed predominantly through the mouth, which means that the natural filtering mechanism of the nose is largely bypassed. In this section we focus on the health effects that can occur in the lungs and blood vessels and on the promotion of inflammation throughout the body from air pollution.

Studies assessing how cycling in air pollution affects inflammation in the lungs have typically occurred with people who are cycling at moderate intensity. These studies typically found that moderate cycling over longer durations (4 to 6 hours) cause lung inflammation and that people with asthma experience a significantly greater inflammatory response compared with those who are not asthmatic (Scannell et al. 1996).

Typically, ozone exposure during exercise impairs lung function, especially at higher exercise intensities. In amateur cyclists, exposure to ozone during training is associated with reductions in lung function (Brunekreef et al. 1994). Perhaps the most relevant research comes from field studies. In these studies cyclists are exposed to real pollution outdoors, not to an isolated pollutant in a laboratory setting. On balance, these field studies show that in healthy adults, exposure to air pollution while cycling impairs lung function (Brunekreef et al. 1994; Rundell et al. 2008; Spektor et al. 1988).

Being exposed to air pollution before exercise also appears to be detrimental (an example might be driving through traffic on the way to a mountain bike ride). A recent study showed that preexercise exposure to diesel exhaust negatively affects the normal lung response to cycling exercise (Giles et al. 2012).

Effects on Cycling Performance

Thus far we have mostly discussed the health effects of cycling in air pollution, but for competitive cyclists, we want to consider how cycling performance is affected. The results of research into the performance effects of air pollution are somewhat mixed (Giles and Koehle 2013), but some broad conclusions relevant to cyclists can be drawn. In general, research on athletes who are exposed to ozone, carbon monoxide, or air pollution that contains particulate matter shows that a decline occurs in cycling performance (Cutrufello et al. 2011; Koike et al. 1991; Schelegle and Adams 1986). But most of these studies test athletes over a short period (generally less than 20 minutes), and the longer exercise bouts that are more common in cyclists when training and competing have not been adequately studied. Longer exposures to pollution and correspondingly higher dosages of pollution would likely cause more profound losses in performance. To date, however, that research has yet to be conducted. In the meantime, to reduce the performance effects of pollution, cyclists and event organizers need to use some of the strategies discussed at the end of this chapter to decrease the inhaled dose of the pollutants.

Apart from direct effects of pollution on performance, pollution can affect performance by increasing symptoms. Specifically, increased symptoms and discomfort during cycling may increase the likelihood of either exercising more slowly or terminating the exercise prematurely. Studies of respiratory symptoms such as chest tightness, wheezing, and shortness of breath occur when cyclists are exposed to ozone, and these symptoms become worse when the concentration of ozone increases. Additionally, high levels of diesel exhaust exposure during cycling exercise increase the perception of effort (Giles et al. 2014). Competitive cycling is a sport of suffering. Besides having direct effects on performance, pollutants can increase the athlete's symptoms and perceived effort, which could be an important factor in performance.

Because many cycling events take place under a combination of hot and polluted conditions, the interaction between heat and air pollution is also important to consider. A variety of studies have assessed performance under these conditions (Brunekreef et al. 1994; Drinkwater et al. 1974; Gomes, Stone, and Florida-James 2010; Gong et al. 1986), and although the evidence is mixed that pollution and heat are worse than heat alone, the most important conclusion that can be made is that the negative effects of heat on exercise performance are much greater than those of air pollution. But air pollution and increased temperature often occur simultaneously. For example, later in the day, ozone levels increase with the ambient temperature; likewise, over extended periods of warm weather, smog becomes more common. So although an interaction between pollution and heat has not been substantiated, both have been shown to impair cycling performance. Fortunately, by employing strategies to reduce heat exposure, such as riding early in the day, shortening rides in extreme heat, and riding indoors in a climate-controlled environment, cyclists can reduce excessive exposure to both outdoor air pollution and heat. But cyclists need to be mindful that indoor environments are not free from pollution. For example, velodrome Derny bikes, adhesives, and paints are but a few potential sources of indoor pollutants that cyclists might encounter.

Medical Issues Related to Cycling in Pollution

Cycling is an intensely aerobic sport, so oxygen delivery is important for performance. Therefore, top cyclists demonstrate high values for $\dot{V}O_2max$, a key measurement of aerobic fitness. Common medical conditions that affect respiration and oxygen delivery to the exercising muscle can make cyclists more prone to the negative effects of air pollution.

Anemia

Anemia describes a variety of conditions that lead to low levels of red blood cells or hemoglobin in the blood. Anemia is common in endurance athletes, and if present it is a condition that could affect cycling performance in air pollution. Hemoglobin is the molecule in the blood that binds to oxygen. Athletes with anemia have less capacity to carry oxygen in their blood and will experience a decline in performance. Conversely, cyclists who are able to increase their hemoglobin content (through either permitted activities such as altitude training or prohibited methods such as blood doping) will increase their aerobic performance.

As mentioned earlier, carbon monoxide is a key constituent of air pollution that binds powerfully to hemoglobin. In fact, it binds more than 200 times more tightly than oxygen does, and in environments that have elevated levels of carbon monoxide, the oxygen molecules are displaced from the hemoglobin by carbon monoxide molecules (Giles and Koehle 2013). This displacement of oxygen results in a decrease in overall oxygen-carrying capacity of the blood and a decrease in aerobic performance. People who have anemia already have lower oxygen-carrying capacity because of their lower levels of hemoglobin; in the presence of carbon monoxide, this oxygen-carrying capacity is further diminished, exacerbating the performance decline. There are several causes and types of anemia, and the treatment for each of these conditions differs. Thus, early detection of anemia is important, so athletes planning to compete in a high-pollution environment should be screened. If the condition is present, they should work with their physicians to identify the cause of the anemia and treat it accordingly.

Asthma and Exercise-Induced Bronchoconstriction

To get large volumes of oxygen into the body, cyclists have high rates of ventilation (the volume of air breathed per minute) during peak exercise. In this population, two common conditions interfere with ventilation during exercise: exercise-induced bronchoconstriction and vocal cord dysfunction (Fitch 2012). Both conditions can be exacerbated by pollution, further interfering with exercise performance.

When a cyclist inhales, air travels through a series of airways deep into the small sacs (called alveoli) in the lungs where the transfer of oxygen into the blood occurs. The airways that carry the air in and out of the lungs are called the bronchi. Narrowing of these bronchi during or following exercise is called exercise-induced bronchoconstriction, or EIB. EIB can occur in athletes with asthma at rest, but it can also occur in those who do not have asthma symptoms outside of exercise. The key symptoms of EIB are shortness of breath, chest tightness, poor performance, and sometimes chest pain. EIB is the most common chronic medical condition in elite athletes, occurring in approximately 8 percent of Olympic athletes (Fitch 2012). This transient narrowing of the airways makes it challenging for the athlete to breathe the air out before taking the next breath, causing respiratory symptoms.

Interestingly, in endurance athletes, the proportion with EIB increases over the course of their sporting careers. The mechanism of this increase in EIB seems to be related to damage to the airways caused by high levels of ventilation over long periods. This increase in prevalence seems to be worse when the athletes are exposed to cold air or air pollutants; presumably, the cold air and the pollutants cause more accumulated damage to the airways of the lungs, in turn increasing susceptibility to EIB.

During exercise with EIB, lung function appears to be worsened by exposure to air pollutants (McCreanor et al. 2007). Note, however, that no research has looked at the effects of air pollutants on actual exercise performance in athletes with EIB. Humans have substantial reserves of lung function such that even during maximal exercise, they are not breathing close to the maximum physiological capacity. In addition, studies that use medications to improve lung function in cyclists with EIB (Koch et al. 2013) do not show that this improvement in lung function leads to an improvement in exercise performance. In summary, over time air pollution exposure seems to increase the proportion of endurance athletes who develop EIB, and air pollution exposure during exercise worsens lung function in those with EIB. But these impairments in lung function have not been definitively linked to decreases in athletic performance. Despite this lack of clear evidence for impaired performance in this group, susceptible cyclists should still consider medical treatment for their EIB (and chronic asthma, if present) to help manage the symptoms of EIB.

Two key medical treatments for EIB are worth mentioning: inhaled bronchodilators and leukotriene antagonists. The most common type of medication used by athletes with asthma (and athletes with EIB) is a bronchodilator. Examples of commonly used bronchodilators are salbutamol (called albuterol in the United States), salmeterol, and formoterol. These medications are most commonly taken using an inhaler (or puffer). They work by relaxing the muscle bands around the airways, opening up these airways, and increasing airflow. These medications have been shown to improve lung function in athletes with EIB, but they have not been shown to improve performance (Koch et al. 2013) or to reduce the symptoms of cyclists exposed to air pollutants during exercise (McKenzie et al. 1987). Furthermore, competitive cyclists need to be aware of the doping restrictions related to these medications, because the World Anti-Doping Agency (WADA) places many of these substances on their controlled list.

Some less common agents have been consistently prohibited because of their potential for increasing muscle mass. For example, clenbuterol is a bronchodilator not in widespread use in humans. But a positive test for this medication was the reason for Alberto Contador's sanction in 2010. In recent years, commonly used bronchodilators such as salbutamol, albuterol, and salmeterol have been permitted by WADA, but the status of these medications changes periodically. Therefore, cyclists competing at a sufficiently high level should check the status of these medications (and of all their medications) with the assistance of a physician.

Another class of medications that has been shown to be beneficial in preserving lung function in athletes with EIB who are exposed to pollution is leukotriene antagonists. Montelukast (trade name Singulair) has been shown to improve lung function during cycling exercise in simulated air pollution, either particulate matter or sulfur dioxide exposure (Gong et al. 2001; Rundell et al. 2005), but no attempt has been made to determine whether exercise performance was improved with this medication. Historically, montelukast has been permitted in sport, but as always, athletes need to verify that it remains permitted at the time of use.

In summary, EIB is increasingly common among cyclists and could be worsened by air pollution. Two classes of medications can improve lung function in cyclists with EIB (inhaled bronchodilators and leukotriene antagonists), but they do not demonstrate an improvement in performance. These medications should be considered in cyclists with EIB, especially when they are training and competing in conditions of high ambient pollution.

Vocal Cord Dysfunction

Vocal cord dysfunction (also called paradoxical vocal cord dysfunction, Münchhausen's stridor) is another common cause of shortness of breath during endurance exercise. It is often confused with EIB. Although vocal cord dysfunction (VCD) causes breathing symptoms, the problem occurs in the larynx (or voice box), not in the lungs. During exercise, the vocal cords normally open wider when breathing in (inspiration) to increase the airflow to the lungs. But during an attack of VCD, the vocal cords do not open during inspiration, but instead remain partially closed. This narrowing of the vocal cords reduces airflow to the lungs and can cause an audible sound as the air rushes over the narrowed vocal cords. This sound, called stridor, occurs during the inspiration phase of breathing. Along with stridor, the athlete feels chest tightness, throat tightness, and shortness of breath. VCD occurs most often during high-intensity exercise at high breathing rates and under stressful conditions (Fitch 2012). VCD can coexist with EIB and can be worsened by other conditions such as gastroesophageal reflux disease, anxiety, and postnasal drip. Exposure to air pollutants is a potential trigger for a VCD attack, possibly by direct irritation of the vocal cords.

VCD is often underdiagnosed, so the first step in management is making the proper diagnosis. Because the symptoms can be similar to EIB, athletes with VCD are often initially identified as having EIB. They then typically undergo treatment for EIB before they get the final diagnosis of VCD. The first step in managing VCD is treating underlying exacerbating conditions such as anxiety, reflux disease, and true asthma. Next, athletes are given breathing exercises to do, which are aimed at better synchronizing vocal cord function. No specific medications act on the VCD itself. Cyclists with VCD who are training or competing in a polluted environment need to ensure that their underlying conditions are managed as well as possible. They should then use a good warm-up and employ the VCD-specific breathing strategies that are most effective for them.

Applying the Science

Taking antioxidants can reduce the adverse health effects of air pollution (Sienra-Monge et al. 2004) and can protect exercisers against the acute effects of ozone on lung function and lung injury (Gomes et al. 2011). Based on these studies, cyclists could consider a diet rich in antioxidants (typical sources include beans, berries, plums, and apples), but they should be cautious about consuming high doses of antioxidants such as vitamin C and E in supplements because recent research suggests that such supplementation may interfere with the adaptation to training (Paulsen et al. 2014).

Although probably not acceptable for competitive cyclists, wearing a facemask during cycling can reduce some of the cardiovascular effects of air pollution and may have a role for commuters and those who must cycle through heavy traffic. Both the quality and fit of the facemask, along with regular inspection and replacement of the filter, are important.

Other recommendations include the following:

- Cyclists should follow local air quality forecasts and plan workouts around them.
- In the summer, cycling in the morning is preferable to minimize exposure to ozone.
- As much as possible cyclists should exercise away from traffic. Even distances as short as a few meters make a substantial difference.
- To minimize exposure to air pollution both before and during exercise, cyclists should avoid sitting in traffic while driving and plan to exercise away from traffic.
- Event organizers should consider the location and time of exercise and competition venues to minimize exposure to air pollution.
- Cyclists should shorten, postpone, or relocate workouts on smog alert days.

CHAPTER 13

Altitude and Hypoxic Training

—Randall L. Wilber

The 1968 Olympics, held at an altitude of 2,300 meters in Mexico City, ushered in the era of altitude training among athletes and interest in understanding how altitude affects human physiology among scientists. At the elite level, differences in performance are typically less than 0.5 percent, and many professional cyclists perform several extended altitude training camps over the course of a season in the hopes of gaining a legal competitive edge. Other cyclists rely on altitude simulations by using altitude houses or tents. Some of the major proposed pathways underlying altitude or hypoxic improvement are highlighted in figure 13.1.

This chapter describes the scientific basis and practical application of altitude or hypoxic training so that athletes, coaches, and applied sport scientists will come away with a better understanding of the scientific bases for altitude training and practical advice for using this unique training method.

Altitude or Hypoxic Training Models

This section focuses on the three primary altitude or hypoxic training models: live high and train high (LH + TH), live high and train low (LH + TL), and live low and train high (LL + TH). Figure 13.2 outlines the methods of altitude or hypoxic training currently used by athletes.

Live High and Train High

The original method of altitude or hypoxic training was one in which athletes lived and trained at moderate altitude (1,500 to 4,000 meters) for the purpose of increasing red blood cell (RBC) volume and ultimately enhancing sea level maximal oxygen uptake ($\dot{V}O_2$max) and endurance performance. Live high

---

Portions of this chapter are adapted, with permission, from R.L. Wilber, 2007, "Application of altitude/hypoxic training by elite athletes," *Medicine & Science in Sports & Exercise* 39(9): 1610-1624.

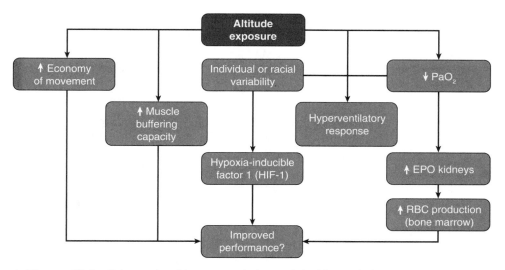

▶ **Figure 13.1** Schematic of hematopoietic model of hypoxic improvement.

Reprinted, by permission, from S.S. Cheung, 2010, Advanced environmental exercise physiology (Champaign, IL: Human Kinetics), 129.

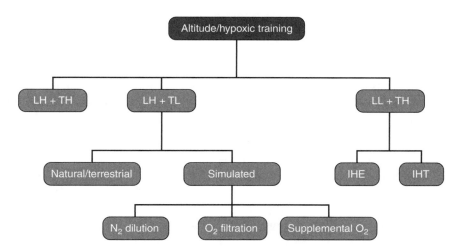

▶ **Figure 13.2** Contemporary altitude or hypoxic training models. IHE (intermittent hypoxic exposure), IHT (intermittent hypoxic training), LH + TH (live high and train high), LH + TL (live high and train low), LL + TH (live low and train high).

and train high (LH + TH) altitude training is still used today by sea-level athletes who complete altitude training camps at specific times during the training year and, of course, by high-altitude residents, such as Kenyan and Ethiopian runners. Comprehensive review articles on LH + TH can be found in Wilber (2004) and Wilber and Pitsiladis (2012).

One major conclusion drawn from both the anecdotal and scientific evidence regarding LH + TH altitude training was that endurance athletes did not seem to be able to train at an equivalent or near-equivalent training intensity (e.g., running velocity) as compared with sea-level training. Many runners and swimmers reported that they seemed to lose race fitness or form and turnover because of LH + TH altitude training. Indeed, in one of the original LH + TH altitude training studies conducted by Buskirk et al. (1967), the results suggested that collegiate distance runners who completed 63 days of LH + TH (at 4,000 meters) returned to sea level in a *detrained* state, as evidenced by 3 to 8 percent decrements in time-trial performance in the 880-yard, 1-mile, and 2-mile (800-, 1,600-, and 3,200 m) runs. More recently, it was demonstrated that absolute training intensity during base and interval workouts was significantly compromised at moderate altitude (2,500 meters) versus sea level in well-trained competitive distance runners (Levine and Stray-Gundersen 1997; Niess et al. 2003).

Live High and Train Low

As a potential solution to the training intensity limitation that appears to be inherent in the LH + TH altitude training model, the live high and train low (LH + TL) model was developed in the early 1990s (Levine 2002; Levine and Stray-Gundersen 1997). LH + TL is based on the premise that athletes can *simultaneously* experience the benefits of altitude or hypoxic acclimatization (e.g., increased RBC volume) and sea-level training (i.e., maintenance of sea-level training intensity and velocity and oxygen flux), thereby resulting in positive hematological, metabolic, and neuromuscular adaptations. Athletes who use LH + TL live or sleep at moderate altitude (2,000 to 2,500 meters) and simultaneously train at low elevation (less than 1,500 meters). This regimen can be accomplished using a number of methods and devices.

Natural, or Terrestrial, LH + TL

Initial implementation and scientific evaluation of the LH + TL model was conducted in the natural, or terrestrial, altitude environment of the Wasatch Mountains in the state of Utah, United States. The original research study by Levine and Stray-Gundersen (1997) evaluated the efficacy of LH + TL among 39 American female and male collegiate distance runners who were initially matched based on fitness level and then randomly assigned to one of three experimental groups: LL + TL, LH + TL, or LH + TH. Following a 4-week baseline period at sea level (Dallas, Texas), the LH + TL runners (n = 13) completed a 28-day training period in which they lived at 2,500 meters (Deer Valley, Utah) for approximately 22 hours per day and trained at 1,250 meters (Salt Lake City, Utah) for approximately 2 hours per day. Training consisted of alternate workouts of base training and interval training. Thirteen fitness-matched female and male collegiate runners, serving as a control group (LL + TL) followed the same training program at sea level at 150 meters (San Diego, California), as did another group of 13 female and male runners who followed a conventional LH + TH regimen at 2,500 meters (Deer Valley). Compared with prealtitude values, postaltitude sea-level tests conducted on day 3 following altitude training indicated significant improvements in the LH + TL group for RBC volume (5 percent), hemoglobin concentration (9 percent), and treadmill $\dot{V}O_2$max (4 percent). Similar changes in RBC volume, hemoglobin concentration, and $\dot{V}O_2$max were observed in the LH + TH runners, whereas no improvements in these parameters were seen in the sea-level control group. In terms of running performance, an average 1 percent improvement ($P < 0.05$) in postaltitude 5,000-meter run time was observed in the LH + TL group on day 3 postaltitude, an improvement equivalent to 13.4 seconds. Performance in the 5,000-meter run for the LH + TL runners was similar on days 7, 14, and 21 postaltitude compared with day 3 postaltitude, suggesting that the beneficial effects of LH + TL altitude training on running performance appear to last for up to 3 weeks postaltitude. In contrast, neither the sea-level control group nor the conventional LH + TH group demonstrated any significant improvements in 5,000-meter run performance at any time following the 28-day altitude training period. Collectively, these results (Levine and Stray-Gundersen 1997) suggested that living at moderate altitude (2,500 meters) resulted in significant increases in RBC volume and hemoglobin concentration in both the LH + TH and LH + TL runners. Simultaneous training at lower elevation (1,250 meters), however, allowed the LH + TL athletes to achieve running velocities and oxygen flux similar to what they achieved at sea level, thereby inducing beneficial metabolic and neuromuscular adaptations. When the runners returned to sea level, the LH + TL group was the only one that demonstrated significant improvements in both $\dot{V}O_2$max and 5,000-meter run time. These results were attributed to positive hematological adaptations (live high) as well as positive metabolic and neuromuscular adaptations (train low) resulting exclusively from 4 weeks of LH + TL altitude training (Levine and Stray-Gundersen 1997).

LH + TL through natural, or terrestrial, altitude was used effectively by U.S. national team marathon runners in preparation for the 2004 Athens Olympics. The marathon runners lived and completed their moderate-intensity training at 2,440 meters (Mammoth Lakes, California) and did their high-intensity workouts at 1,260 meters (Bishop, California). The marathoners also employed heat and humidity preacclimatization strategies while living and training in the relatively moderate-temperature, low-humidity environment of the Sierra Nevada Mountains. These combined preacclimatization strategies served to prepare them well for the harsh environmental conditions (35 to 40 degrees Celsius; 30 to 40 percent relative humidity) they eventually faced in Athens during the 2004 Olympics. U.S. Olympic team marathon runners enjoyed unprecedented success at the Athens Olympics, winning a bronze medal in the women's event (Deena Kastor) and a silver medal in the men's race (Meb Keflezighi).

Simulated LH + TL Through Nitrogen Dilution

Nitrogen apartment is a term used to describe a normobaric hypoxic apartment that simulates an altitude environment. The nitrogen apartment was developed by Dr. Heikki Rusko in Finland in the early 1990s to simulate an altitude environment in relatively low-elevation Finland, thereby allowing Finnish elite athletes to perform LH + TL without having to travel abroad to do so. The nitrogen apartment simulates elevations equivalent to approximately 2,000 meters to 3,000 meters by diluting the oxygen concentration within the apartment. A ventilation system pulls in ambient air (about 20.9 percent oxygen and about 79.0 percent nitrogen), and 100 percent nitrogen is simultaneously introduced into the ventilation system. A normobaric hypoxic environment simulating an altitude of approximately 2,500 meters is thus achieved through dilution to 15.3 percent oxygen and 84.7 percent nitrogen. Since its development, numerous elite athletes have used nitrogen apartments in conjunction with LH + TL altitude training. Typically, these athletes live and sleep in the simulated altitude environment of the nitrogen apartment for at least 12 hours per day for 4 weeks or longer, and they perform their training in natural, or terrestrial, sea-level conditions or near sea-level conditions.

Several studies have evaluated the efficacy of the nitrogen apartment on endurance athletes in Australia, Finland, and Sweden, and the details of these investigations can be reviewed elsewhere (Wilber 2007). Within this group of studies, a more limited number were conducted on elite athletes from the Australian national team (Ashenden et al. 1999; Martin et al. 2002; Saunders et al. 2004) and Finnish national team (Numella and Rusko 2000; Rusko et al. 1995), and these results have been equivocal. Whereas some researchers reported significant increases in RBC indices (Rusko et al. 1995), others have not been able to replicate those results (Ashenden et al. 1999; Saunders et al. 2004) or did not report RBC data (Martin et al. 2002; Numella and Rusko 2000). But several of these investigations on national team athletes reported significant improvements in sea-level performance following various doses of LH + TL through nitrogen dilution (Martin et al. 2002; Numella and Rusko 2000; Saunders et al. 2004).

Thus, although limited, the empirical evidence suggests that LH +TL through nitrogen dilution may enhance sea-level performance in elite athletes, provided a sufficient dose of simulated altitude is applied, that is, 12 to 16 hours per day for 3 to 4 weeks at an elevation of approximately 2,500 meters. It is not clear, however, whether the performance-enhancing effects of LH + TL through nitrogen dilution are because of accelerated RBC synthesis (Rusko et al. 1995) or because of beneficial changes in running economy (Saunders et al. 2004), skeletal muscle buffering capacity (Gore et al. 2001), hypoxic ventilatory response (Townsend et al. 2002), or skeletal muscle contraction changes (Aughey et al. 2006).

Simulated LH + TL Through Oxygen Filtration

Similar to the method of nitrogen dilution, oxygen filtration can be used to simulate an altitude or hypoxic environment. This method of LH + TL can take the form of an apartment or house or a commercially available hypoxic tent. LH + TL through oxygen filtration uses an oxygen-filtration membrane that reduces the molecular concentration of oxygen in ambient air drawn from outside the apartment or tent. The oxygen-reduced air is pumped by generator into the apartment or tent, resulting in a normobaric hypoxic living and sleeping environment.

The key research findings relative to the efficacy of LH + TL through oxygen filtration can be organized based on studies that have evaluated hypoxic apartments and hypoxic tents. All the hypoxic apartment investigations were conducted on elite endurance athletes from the French national team (athletics, biathlon, Nordic ski, swimming), whereas none of the hypoxic tent studies evaluated elite athletes. Collectively, the research findings regarding LH + TL through oxygen filtration are equivocal regarding RBC synthesis. Two studies (Brugniaux et al. 2006; Robach et al. 2006b) reported significant increases in RBC volume or total hemoglobin mass, whereas others (Hinckson and Hopkins 2005; Hinckson et al. 2005; McLean et al. 2006; Robach et al. 2006a) found no significant RBC response following LH + TL through oxygen filtration. In addition, the effect of LH + TL through oxygen filtration on performance is unclear. Significant postaltitude improvements have been reported in $\dot{V}O_2$max (Brugniaux et al. 2006), cycling peak power output (Schmitt et al. 2006), cycling power output at the respiratory compensation point (Schmitt et al. 2006), and 800-meter to 3,000-meter run time (Hinckson and Hopkins 2005). In contrast, no significant enhancement of $\dot{V}O_2$max (Robach et al. 2006a; Schmitt et al. 2006), treadmill run time to exhaustion (Robach et al. 2006a), or 2,000-meter swim time (Robach et al. 2006b) have been demonstrated following LH + TL through oxygen filtration. Thus, although athletes continue to use LH + TL through oxygen filtration to enhance performance, support appears to be as much by anecdotal evidence as by empirical evidence based on the current literature.

Simulated LH + TL Through Supplemental Oxygen

Another modification of LH + TL altitude training is one in which athletes live in a natural, hypobaric hypoxic environment but train at simulated sea level with the aid of supplemental oxygen (LH + TLO_2). LH + TLO_2 is used effectively at the U.S. Olympic Training Center in Colorado Springs, Colorado, where U.S. national team athletes live at approximately 1,900 to 2,800 meters in the foothills of the Rocky Mountain range. The average barometric pressure (P_B) in Colorado Springs is approximately 610 torr (813 hPa), which yields a partial pressure of inspired oxygen (P_IO_2) of approximately 128 torr (171 hPa). By inspiring a certified medical-grade gas with a fraction of inspired oxygen (F_IO_2) of approximately 0.26, athletes can complete high-intensity training sessions in a simulated sea-level environment at a P_IO_2 equivalent to approximately 150 torr (200 hPa).

Only a few studies have evaluated the efficacy of LH + TLO_2 on athletic performance (Morris, Kearney, and Burke 2000; Wilber et al. 2003, 2004, 2005). Wilber et al. (2003) evaluated the acute effects of supplemental oxygen on physiological responses and exercise performance during a high-intensity cycling interval workout (6×100 kilojoules [kJ]; work-to-recovery ratio of 1:1.5) in trained endurance athletes who were altitude residents (1,800 to 1,900 meters). Compared with a control trial (F_IO_2 0.21), average total time for the 100 kJ work interval was 5 percent and 8 percent ($P < 0.05$) faster in the F_IO_2 0.26 and F_IO_2 0.60 trials, respectively. Consistent with improvements in total time were increments in power output equivalent to 5 percent in the F_IO_2 0.26 trial and 9 percent in the F_IO_2 0.60 trial ($P < 0.05$). Whole-body $\dot{V}O_2$ (L/min) was higher by 7 percent and 14 percent ($P < 0.05$) in the F_IO_2 0.26 and F_IO_2 0.60 trials, respectively, and was highly correlated with the improvement in power output (r = 0.85; $P < 0.05$). Arterial oxyhemoglobin saturation (S_pO_2) was significantly higher by 5 percent (F_IO_2 0.26) and 8 percent (F_IO_2 0.60) in the supplemental oxygen trials.

The long-term training effects of $LH + TLO_2$ were evaluated by Morris, Kearney, and Burke (2000). U.S. national team junior cyclists completed a 21-day training period during which they lived and performed their moderate-intensity workouts at 1,900 meters (Colorado Springs) and performed their high-intensity interval training at simulated sea level using supplemental oxygen (F_IO_2 0.26; P_IO_2 159 torr [212 hPa]). Interval workouts were done 3 days per week, and each interval workout required the athletes to complete $5 \times$ 5-minute cycling efforts at 105 to 110 percent of maximal steady-state heart rate. A control group of fitness-matched teammates completed the same training program at 1,900 meters using normoxic gas (F_IO_2 0.21; P_IO_2 128 torr [171 hPa]). Athletes using supplemental oxygen were able to train at a significantly higher percentage of their altitude-determined lactate threshold (126 percent) versus their counterparts who trained in normoxic conditions (109 percent). Following the 21-day training period, the athletes performed a 120 kJ cycling performance time trial in simulated sea-level conditions (F_IO_2 0.26; P_IO_2 159 torr [212 hPa]). Results of the cycling performance test showed improvements of 2 seconds and 15 seconds for the normoxic-trained and $LH + TLO_2$-trained cyclists, respectively (Morris, Kearney, and Burke 2000). In agreement with Wilber et al. (2003), the results of Morris, Kearney, and Burke (2000) demonstrated that high-intensity workouts at moderate altitude (1,900 meters) are enhanced through the use of supplemental oxygen. Further, Morris, Kearney, and Burke (2000) were the first to show that sea-level endurance performance in elite athletes can be improved by $LH + TLO_2$.

Live Low and Train High

The live low and train high (LL + TH) model of altitude or hypoxic training is one in which athletes live in a natural, normobaric, normoxic environment and are exposed to discrete and relatively short intervals (5 to 180 minutes) of simulated normobaric hypoxia or hypobaric hypoxia. Normobaric hypoxia can be simulated through nitrogen dilution (e.g., Altitrainer 200 hypoxicator), oxygen filtration (e.g., Go2Altitude hypoxicator), or inspiration of hypoxic gas. LL + TH can be used by athletes in the resting state (intermittent hypoxic exposure, or IHE) or during formal training sessions (intermittent hypoxic training, or IHT) (figure 13.2). IHE and IHT are purported to enhance athletic performance by stimulating an increase in serum erythropoietin (sEPO) and RBC volume (Schmidt 2002) and can augment skeletal muscle mitochondrial density, capillary-to-fiber ratio, and fiber cross-sectional area (Vogt et al. 2001) by upregulation of hypoxia-inducible factor 1α (HIF-1α) (Vogt et al. 2001). Because of its convenience, LL + TH through IHE or IHT is used by elite athletes in several countries.

This section is limited to studies that have evaluated the effects of IHE or IHT on recreational or elite athletes and included a fitness or training-matched control group in the research design. Collectively, the empirical evidence regarding the efficacy of IHE or IHT on RBC response and athletic performance is not compelling. Only a minimal number of studies have reported increments in hemoglobin concentration (Bonetti, Hopkins, and Kilding 2006; Hamlin and Hellemans 2004). Among the few that have evaluated robust RBC markers such as soluble transferrin receptor (sTfR), RBC volume, or total hemoglobin mass, Robertson et al. (2010) reported that total hemoglobin mass was not significantly affected following 3 weeks of IHT. Furthermore, a relatively limited number of studies (n = 10; see Wilber 2007 for details) have reported that athletic performance was enhanced following IHE or IHT, including endurance performance (five studies) and anaerobic or sprint performance (five studies). In contrast, many studies (n = 27; see Wilber 2007 for details) have failed to demonstrate significant alterations in RBC markers, as well as post-IHE or post-IHT endurance or anaerobic or sprint performance.

One possible explanation for the preponderance of negative results regarding IHE or IHT and endurance performance may be related to the relatively short-duration hypoxic doses administered in the various protocols used. It has been argued that for altitude or hypoxic acclimatization to be effective in accelerating RBC synthesis and ultimately enhancing performance, the hypoxic dose must be equivalent to an altitude of 2,000 to 2,500 meters for 3 to 4 weeks at a daily hypoxic exposure of at least 22 hours a day (Levine 2002; Levine and Stray-Gundersen 2006). That argument has been countered by those who contend that the mechanism by which IHE or IHT enhances performance is nonhematological and may be because of beneficial changes in skeletal muscle mitochondrial density, capillary-to-fiber ratio, fiber cross-sectional area, and cellular enzymatic reactions favoring both endurance and sprint performance (Faiss et al. 2013; Ponsot et al. 2006; Vogt et al. 2001). Based on the current research, LL + TH through IHE or IHT may be potentially beneficial for enhancing anaerobic and sprint performance more so than endurance performance.

Practical Recommendations

A summary and cost–benefit analysis of the various models of altitude or hypoxic training are provided in table 13.1.

Table 13.1 Methods Used for LH + TL and LL + TH Altitude Training

Method	Living	Training	Pros	Cons
LH + TL				
Natural, or terrestrial	Live and sleep in a natural, or terrestrial, hypobaric hypoxic environment.	Train in a natural, or terrestrial, normobaric normoxic environment at or near sea level.	No simulated altitude equipment required. Live and train in a mountain environment.	Locations that have close proximity of high and low sites might be difficult to find or travel to.
Nitrogen apartment	Live and sleep in a normobaric hypoxic environment simulated through nitrogen dilution ($\downarrow F_IO_2$).	Train in a natural, or terrestrial, normobaric normoxic environment at or near sea level.	Convenient in terms of proximity of high and low sites.	Potential additional expense of construction, maintenance, and use of equipment. Number of hours of living and sleeping required for physiological benefits might interfere with lifestyle and multiple training sessions.
Hypoxic tent	Live and sleep in a normobaric hypoxic environment simulated through oxygen filtration ($\downarrow F_IO_2$).	Train in a natural, or terrestrial, normobaric normoxic environment at or near sea level.	Convenient in terms of proximity of high and low sites.	Potential additional expense of purchase and maintenance of equipment. Number of hours of living and sleeping required for physiological benefits might interfere with lifestyle and multiple training sessions.
Supplemental oxygen	Live and sleep in a natural, or terrestrial, hypobaric hypoxic environment.	Train in a simulated normoxic environment through use of supplemental oxygen ($\uparrow F_IO_2$).	Convenient in terms of proximity of high and low sites. Live in a mountain environment.	Potential added expense of construction, maintenance, and use of equipment.
LL + TH				
Intermittent hypoxic exposure	Live and sleep in a natural, or terrestrial, normobaric normoxic environment.	Brief exposure to simulated hypobaric hypoxia ($\downarrow PO_2$) or normobaric hypoxia ($\downarrow F_IO_2$).	Convenient in terms of proximity of high and low sites. Potential use for preacclimatization to altitude.	Potential additional expense of purchase and maintenance of equipment. Scientific support less extensive compared with LH + TL.
Intermittent hypoxic training	Live and sleep in a natural, or terrestrial, normobaric normoxic environment.	Train in simulated hypobaric hypoxia ($\downarrow PO_2$) or normobaric hypoxia ($\downarrow F_IO_2$).	Convenient in terms of proximity of high and low sites. Potential use for preacclimatization to altitude.	Potential additional expense of purchase and maintenance of equipment. Scientific support less extensive compared with LH + TL.

↑ indicates increase; ↓ indicates decrease; F_IO_2, fraction of inspired oxygen; PO_2, partial pressure of oxygen.

Adapted, by permission, from R.L. Wilber, 2007, "Live high + train low: Thinking in terms of an optimal hypoxic dose," *International Journal of Sport Physiology and Performance* 2(3): 223-238.

Athletes experience greater physiological stress when living and training at altitude compared with performing similar activity at sea level because they experience a number of physiological changes on exposure to altitude that may limit their ability to train or compete. Two of the most important physiological changes that occur are altitude-induced decrements in arterial oxyhemoglobin saturation and maximal oxygen consumption. In addition, exposure to altitude may bring about changes in heart rate, hydration status, acid–base balance, carbohydrate utilization, iron metabolism, and immune function. Collectively, these physiological changes typically force athletes to reduce their daily training volume or intensity and modify their competition and performance strategy from what they would normally do at sea level. Table 13.2 provides a summary of physiological responses and performance limitations, along with practical recommendations on how to deal with them, some of which are described in detail in the following text.

Planning an Altitude Training Camp Based on an Effective Dose

An altitude or hypoxic training block or camp must be organized around an effective hypoxic dose. In other words, the athlete must be exposed to an elevation that will be high enough to produce the desired physiological benefits (e.g., RBC synthesis), but not so high that the athlete cannot recover or have ready access to sources of food, supplies, medical assistance, and entertainment. In addition, the proper dose also takes into account how many days and hours the athlete must be exposed to altitude or hypoxia for the desired physiological effects.

Based on the current scientific research, for a performance-enhancing increase in RBC (and possibly other nonhematological changes) to occur, an effective dose seems to require the athlete to be exposed to an altitude of 2,000 to 2,500 meters for 3 to 4 weeks and for as many hours per day as possible.

Two caveats should be mentioned along with this effective dose recommendation. First, it has been shown that the altitude-induced increase in RBC volume went from approximately 4 percent after 3 weeks to approximately 8 percent after 4 weeks of altitude or hypoxic exposure (Levine and Stray-Gundersen 2006). As such, a 4-week versus a 3-week altitude training block, and a resulting doubling of RBC volume, may be worth the additional time and expense. Second, it has been shown that altitude or hypoxia exposure of 8 to 10 hours is not sufficient to stimulate RBC synthesis (Levine and Stray-Gundersen 2006). Therefore, athletes are encouraged to stay at altitude for at least 22 hours per day, which is sufficient for RBC synthesis but also allows a few hours per day to complete "train low" training, as well as attend to daily chores down in the valley.

Before Altitude Training Camp

The most important thing that an athlete can do before an altitude training camp is to ensure that iron stores are sufficient for RBC synthesis. The athlete can do this by having a blood test to measure iron status including serum ferritin, serum iron, total iron binding capacity (TIBC), transferrin saturation percent, folate, vitamin B_6, and vitamin B_{12}. This blood test should

Table 13.2 Physiological Responses and Performance Limitations at Moderate Altitude (1,525 to 3,050 Meters) and Recommendations for Exercise and Physical Performance

	Physiological responses and performance limitations	Recommendations
Heart rate	May be higher compared with sea level at rest and during submaximal exercise. May be similar or lower compared with sea level during maximal exercise.	Adjustments to heart-rate-based training zones may be necessary to avoid undertraining or overtraining.
Maximal oxygen consumption	Decreased at altitude compared with sea level.	Adjustments to exercise and physical performance will be necessary. Modifications to competition strategy need to be considered.
Hydration level	Increased respiratory and urinary water loss at altitude. Potential dehydration.	A concerted effort should be made to increase fluid intake during the day and during overnight bathroom breaks.
Carbohydrate metabolism	Increased carbohydrate utilization at altitude, particularly in men. Potential glycogen depletion.	A concerted effort should be made to replace carbohydrate before, during, and after exercise and physical activity through carbohydrate replacement drinks and solid carbohydrate.
Iron	Decrease in iron stores (ferritin) upon altitude exposure. Potential iron depletion or iron deficiency. Potential nonerythropoietic response.	Have iron status evaluated by a blood test several weeks before going to altitude. Normal iron status: serum ferritin >20 ng · ml^{-1} in females, >30 ng · ml^{-1} in males. If iron status is abnormally low before going to altitude, consult physician regarding iron supplementation.
Lactate response	Blood lactate levels increased and lactate buffering capacity reduced during first days at altitude.	Keep maximal and supramaximal exercise and physical activity to a minimum in first days at altitude.
Immune system	Potential for immunosuppression and increased chance of illness.	Ensure adequate rest and recovery. Ensure adequate postexercise carbohydrate intake to modulate training-induced stress hormone response. Ensure adequate dietary intake of the vitamins (folate, B_6, B_{12}) and minerals (zinc, selenium, copper) that affect the immune system.
Oxidative stress	Increased compared with sea level.	Antioxidant supplementation (vitamin A, C, or E).
Ultraviolet radiation	Increased compared with sea level.	Ultraviolet sunscreen and sunglasses. Antioxidant (vitamin E) supplementation.
Sleep and recovery	May be disturbed and irregular at altitude, especially the first few nights.	Afternoon naps may help until nighttime sleep disturbance subsides. Make sleeping environment as comfortable and similar to home as possible.
Body composition	Potential decrease in muscle mass at altitude but not common at elevations below 10,000 feet (3,049 m) as long as appetite is healthy.	Adequate nutrition with possible increase in caloric intake. Regular monitoring of total body mass and body composition.
Acute mountain sickness (AMS)	Potential for symptoms of headache and nausea. Not common at low altitude (<5,000 feet [< 1,525 m]), but greater risk at moderate altitude (5,000 to 10,000 feet [1,525 to 3,049 m] and above.	Use of staging, natural acclimatization, or preacclimatization in advance of ascent to altitude. Prescription acetazolamide (Diamox) or aspirin in combination with adequate rest and recovery to reduce symptoms. Elimination or significant modification to physical activity until recovery. Descend to lowest possible elevation immediately if symptoms persist or worsen and seek medical treatment.

be done 6 to 8 weeks before going to altitude. The results may indicate that the athlete needs to make dietary modifications to increase heme iron (e.g., lean red meat) and nonheme iron (e.g., iron-enriched cereal) or possibly begin using a nonprescription iron supplement (e.g., Feosol, Solgar). Upon arrival at altitude, iron stores will drop significantly because of the body's need to make more RBCs in defense of the lower oxygen partial pressure in the hypoxic environment. Therefore, the athlete needs to arrive at altitude with a healthy supply of iron in the body. Otherwise, the athlete is at risk of iron depletion, iron-deficient nonanemia, and iron-deficient anemia, all of which can have a serious negative effect on physical performance and general health. Besides checking iron stores, the athlete must not be ill (or just getting over illness) before the altitude training camp and should be in moderate or good training shape.

During Altitude Training Camp

The physiological responses and performance limitations listed in table 13.2 that athletes experience at altitude will require them to make modifications to their daily training sessions and make adjustments during competition. Training volume (e.g., total minutes or total distance) and training intensity (e.g., percentage HR max) should be reduced in the first 3 to 5 days at altitude compared with sea level. After that, training volume can be gradually increased toward sea-level training volume, but without ever necessarily matching it. Adjustments to training intensity should be ongoing and typically take two forms. First, in doing a cycling interval training workout, keep the work interval the same as at sea level but reduce the workload and increase the rest interval. A sea-level workout of 6 × 5:00 at a workload of 350 watts (W) with 1:30 recovery might be adjusted at altitude to 6 × 5:00 at 325 W with 3:00 recovery. Second, in doing a cycling interval training workout, shorten the work interval but keep the workload and rest interval the same as at sea level. A sea level workout of 6 × 5:00 at a workload of 350 W with 1:30 recovery might be adjusted at altitude to 6 × 3:30 at 350 W with 1:30 recovery. Besides training adjustments, modifications to competition pace and strategy may also be required. Finally, medical-grade supplemental oxygen might be considered as an option for use during training and competition to promote recovery and restoration of reduced oxyhemoglobin levels (Wilber et al. 2005). For example, athletes might use supplemental oxygen for recovery during a high-intensity interval training session. Supplemental oxygen might also be used during the overnight sleep period to promote optimal recovery and prevention of overtraining.

Return to Sea Level After Altitude Training Camp

Of all the questions that athletes and coaches ask about altitude training, the one that we are still not totally sure about is, "When is the best time to compete at sea level after doing an altitude training camp?" In the past, most athletes and coaches have answered this question, and acted accordingly, based on anecdotal evidence, best practices, and logistical or travel requirements. At present, we are fortunate to have some limited research-based evidence to help us make a few general recommendations on the timing of return to sea level following altitude training.

As illustrated in figure 13.3, Levine and Stray-Gundersen (1997) showed in their original LH + TL study that postaltitude 5,000-meter run performance at sea level was significantly faster (13.4 sec [1%]; $P < 0.05$) compared with pre-altitude 5,000-meter run performance in the LH + TL group when measured on day 3 in the 3 weeks following a 4-week altitude training block. In general, 5,000-meter run performance for the LH + TL group remained similar (day 7 postaltitude), slightly slower (day 14 postaltitude), and faster (day 21 postaltitude) compared with the 1 percent improvement seen on day 3 postaltitude (figure 13.3). Neither the sea-level control group nor the conventional LH + TH group demonstrated any statistically significant improvements in 5,000-meter run performance at any time following the 4-week altitude training block. Collectively, these results suggested that 5,000-meter run performance can be enhanced following a 4-week block of altitude training (LH + TL specifically) and that improvements in running performance can be generally maintained over 3 weeks after return from altitude.

Additional analysis of the postaltitude period is described in the model proposed by Millet et al. (2010) as shown in figure 13.4. This model claims that the initial 3 days postaltitude is a potentially good time for enhanced

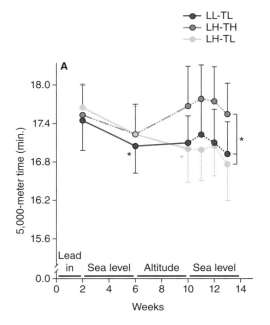

▶ **Figure 13.3** 5,000-meter time-trial results for trained collegiate runners (n = 39) at baseline, after 4 weeks of sea-level training in Dallas, and after 4 weeks of either altitude training (high-low or high-high) or sea-level training (low-low, or control). Postaltitude 5,000-meter time-trial measurements were done on days 3, 7, 14, and 21 post.

*Significantly different compared with previous time point ($P < 0.05$). *Significant difference between groups ($P < 0.05$).

Reprinted, by permission, from B.D. Levine and J. Stray-Gundersen, 1997, "'Living high—training low': Effect of moderate-altitude acclimatization with low-altitude training on performance," Journal of Applied Physiology 83(1):102-112.

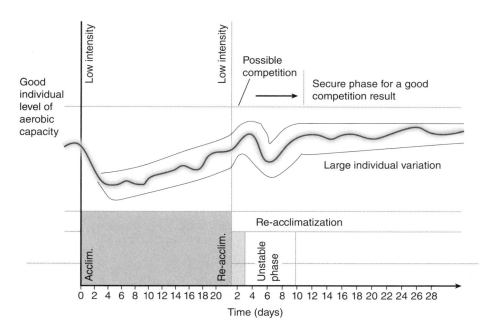

▶ **Figure 13.4**   Schematic showing potential good and unstable periods for optimal training or performance following a 3-week altitude training block. This schematic suggests that days 1 to 3 postaltitude are potentially good days for training or competition, days 4 to 10 postaltitude are unstable (not necessarily good) for optimal training or competition, and days 11 to 28 postaltitude are potentially good days for training or competition.

Reprinted from G.P. Millet, B. Roels, L. Schmitt, X. Woorons, and J.P. Richalet, 2010, "Combining hypoxic methods for peak performance," Sports Medicine 40(1): 1-25, by kind permission from Springer Science and Business Media.

training or competitive performance. The subsequent 7 days, however, represent a time when training or competitive performance may not be optimal (unstable) and therefore should probably be avoided for important races. Finally, the period from day 11 to day 28 represent a safe and secure time for good training and competitive performance. Some have argued that the unstable period from day 4 through day 10 is because of residual fatigue resulting from overzealous training by athletes who feel strong and fast coming immediately out of an altitude training block. As such, eliminating this unstable time may be possible by controlling the training load in the initial days after return to sea level to avoid the subsequent accumulation of fatigue during the period from day 4 to day 10.

In summary, although we do not have a precise and proven recommendation for the optimal time for postaltitude competitive performance, a general recommendation would be that athletes can expect good competitive results for possibly up to 3 to 4 weeks following altitude training, provided they do not exceed a moderate training load in the first few days after return to sea level. Anecdotal evidence suggests that the most important race or competition should be timed within the first 2 weeks after return to sea level. The precise timing within that 2-week window should be determined through systematic trial and error, in conjunction with objective evaluation by the athlete and coach. Finally, the previous recommendations are made based on the assumption that the athlete has completed an altitude training block that meets the criteria of an effective dose, that is, 2,000- to 2,500-meter elevation for 3 to 4 weeks and for at least 22 hours per day.

World Anti-Doping Agency (WADA) Policy on Altitude or Hypoxic Training

The use of simulated altitude by elite athletes has come under review by the World Anti-Doping Agency (WADA). WADA officials are concerned that some athletes who are exploiting illegal erythropoietic agents are making use of "utilization of simulated altitude" as a false explanation for their abnormally elevated hemoglobin and hematocrit levels, thereby circumventing WADA's List of Prohibited Substances and Methods. WADA considers "artificially induced hypoxic conditions" to include hypobaric hypoxia (barometric pressure chamber), normobaric hypoxia through nitrogen dilution (nitrogen apartment, Altitrainer 200 hypoxicator), and normobaric hypoxia through oxygen filtration (hypoxic apartment or tent, Go2Altitude hypoxicator).

For a substance or method to be placed on WADA's Prohibited List, it must meet two of the following three criteria (Levine 2006):

1. Scientific evidence or experience demonstrates that the method or substance has the potential to enhance or enhances sport performance.
2. Medical evidence or experience suggests that the use of the substance or method represents an actual or potential health risk to the athlete.
3. The use of the substance or method violates the spirit of sport.

The WADA scientific, medical, and ethics committees thoroughly evaluated the evidence regarding "artificially induced hypoxic conditions" and reached the following conclusions in May 2006 (Levine 2006):

1. Artificially induced hypoxic conditions can significantly enhance performance when properly applied by increasing the endogenous production of EPO with a subsequent elevation of red blood cell production and better oxygen transfer to the muscles.
2. Under proper medical supervision, when reliable equipment was used and when moderate altitude simulation was reproduced, no significant signs of health risk were reported.
3. Following consultations with the WADA Ethics Review Panel it was concluded unanimously that artificially induced hypoxic conditions should be considered as violating the WADA criterion regarding spirit of sport.

Collectively, these conclusions made by the WADA scientific, medical, and ethics committees indicated that criteria 1 and 3 had been satisfied and therefore that "artificially induced hypoxic conditions" were to be considered for inclusion on the WADA Prohibited List for 2007. In response to these initial conclusions, WADA conducted additional consultations throughout the summer of 2006 with its stakeholders and with scientific experts in the area of altitude or hypoxic training. The debate was amplified when several members of the international scientific community responded collectively in opposition to WADA's consideration of banning simulated altitude devices (altitudeforall.info/index.html).

The final decision regarding "artificially induced hypoxic conditions" was made in September 2006 by the WADA Executive Committee and announced by WADA Chairman Richard Pound:

> *In response to our stakeholders who requested that there be full consideration of hypoxic conditions in the context of the Prohibited List, WADA performed a scientific and ethical review of the matter and engaged in a thorough consultation with experts and stakeholders. While we do not deem this method appropriate for inclusion on the List at this time, we still wish to express the concern that, in addition to the results varying individually from case to case, use of this method may pose health risks if not properly implemented and under medical supervision. (altitudeforall. info/index.html)*

This statement indicated that WADA does not prohibit the use of "artificially induced hypoxic conditions" by elite athletes, at least through the time of publication of this chapter. Note, however, that all "hypobaric/ hypoxic practices are [currently] prohibited" in Italy, as mandated by the Italian Health Ministry in June 2005 (Decree of the Italian Ministry of Health 13.04.2005. Section 5, Subsection M.1, June 3, 2005) in response to an incident involving professional cyclists competing in the 2005 Giro d'Italia (Stage 10; 18 May 2005). The Italian law regarding simulated altitude is independent of any current and future WADA rulings and currently has judicial precedence over any WADA rulings in areas of Italian jurisdiction. Finally, the International Olympic Committee has prohibited the use of simulated altitude devices within the boundaries of the Olympic Village since the 2000 Sydney Olympics, and this mandate is expected to apply to all future Summer and Winter Olympic Games.

Applying the Science

Many contemporary elite endurance athletes in summer and winter sport incorporate some form of altitude or hypoxic training within their year-round training plans, believing that it will provide the competitive edge to succeed at the Olympic level. This chapter has presented both anecdotal and scientific evidence about the efficacy of several contemporary altitude and hypoxic training models and devices currently used by athletes to enhance performance legally. Live high, train low (LH + TL) altitude training is employed by athletes using natural, or terrestrial, altitude, simulated normobaric hypoxia through nitrogen dilution (e.g., nitrogen apartment) or oxygen filtration (e.g., hypoxic tent), and normobaric normoxia through supplemental oxygen. Research regarding several of these LH + TL strategies is either limited or equivocal, particularly regarding the optimal LH + TL hypoxic dose, as well as the physiological mechanisms that potentially affect postaltitude performance. Regarding the safety and health aspects of LH + TL, recent evidence suggests that living at a simulated altitude above 3,500 meters may have an impact on immunocompetence, but this effect may not have physiologically significant consequences.

A somewhat opposite approach to LH + TL is the altitude or hypoxic training strategy of live low, train high (LL + TH), in which athletes live in a natural normobaric normoxic environment and train for brief intervals using simulated normobaric hypoxia through nitrogen dilution (e.g., Altitrainer 200 hypoxicator), oxygen filtration (e.g., Go2Altitude hypoxicator), or hypobaric hypoxia (barometric pressure chamber). LL + TH is used by athletes in the resting state (IHE) or during formal training sessions (IHT). Collectively, the empirical evidence regarding the efficacy of LL + TH through IHE or IHT on erythropoietic response and endurance performance is not persuasive, and additional research is needed in this area. The current literature does suggest, however, that IHE or IHT may be an effective preacclimatization strategy for athletes before training or competing at altitude.

Several of these altitude and hypoxic training strategies and devices underwent critical review by WADA for the purpose of potentially banning them as illegal performance-enhancing methods. Ultimately, WADA decided to refrain from including "artificially induced hypoxic conditions" on the 2007 Prohibited List. But note that use of all hypobaric or hypoxic practices was outlawed in Italy in June 2005, and this Italian law has judicial precedence within the boundaries of Italy over any WADA rulings regarding simulated altitude. In addition, the International Olympic Committee has prohibited the use of simulated altitude devices within the boundaries of the Olympic Village since the 2000 Sydney Olympics, and this mandate is expected to apply to all future Summer and Winter Olympic Games.

CHAPTER 14

Tackling the Hills

—Hunter Allen

Climbing hills and mountains is both feared and loved by cyclists, often at the same time. Climbing ability can determine the outcome of many races and remains a central part of competitions around the world, such as the Tour de France and 1-day Classics like Liége–Bastogne–Liége and the Tour of Lombardy. Climbs are also a part of many amateur races. Riding famous or epic climbs is a major feature of many cycling holidays or Gran Fondos, and climbing is central to Strava KOMs fought over by local cyclists. Therefore, climbing is going to be a major feature of cycling no matter what the cyclist's ability or interest, so a great way to gain further enjoyment from cycling is to improve climbing.

Climbing well is a skill learned from hours of practice, but it can come naturally to riders who are physiologically gifted in the battle against gravity. Many factors play a role in determining whether a cyclist is a good climber, but chief among them is the cyclist's power-to-weight ratio. Quite simply, the lighter the cyclist is with respect to his or her power output, the faster the cyclist will go uphill. Rarely will a 190-pound (86 kg) rider climb with a 140-pound (64 kg) rider because the additional muscle mass usually does not contribute to a significantly higher power output relative to the extra weight. So first, the lighter the cyclist is, the faster he or she will go uphill.

The second most important contributor to climbing well is how effective the cyclist is at turning power into forward momentum. If climbing form is poor, the cyclist will lose energy in transferring force from the body to the rear wheel. Through good technique a cyclist may be able to add 30 watts to his or her effective power output, which could be the difference between being a good climber and a great climber.

The third factor that can make a difference in climbing is pacing ability. Pacing is a large component of all cycling events, and climbing provides an additional challenge because pacing needs to be dynamic as the gradient changes throughout a climb. Lastly, believe it or not, mental attitude toward climbing also plays a large role in success. If mental self-talk is constantly saying, "I hate climbing," then certainly the cyclist will not be a good climber. Changing self-talk and mental attitude can make a big difference in climbing ability.

Because this chapter is about strategies for climbing, we focus on the latter three factors and ignore the first main factor, power-to-weight ratio, other than stating that the higher the power-to-weight ratio is, the better climber the cyclist will be. Cyclists should strive to increase functional threshold power (FTP) to the highest level possible and then reduce body fat as far as possible while remaining healthy. Even a 5-pound (2.3 kg) weight loss can make a significant difference over a long climb. Lighter is faster.

Climbing Form

How the cyclist rides the bicycle while climbing is a critical component of success, so form while climbing should be the best it can be. To climb well, cyclists need to address five major aspects of form, in this order:

1. Center of gravity
2. Arms and shoulders
3. Action of gluteal muscles
4. Pedaling action
5. Spine and back

Climbing also has to be broken down into standing and seated climbing. Clearly, each technique requires different muscle groups, different centers of gravity, and different breathing actions. Let's tackle standing first.

Standing Climbing

Cyclists stand while climbing for several reasons: to produce more power, to handle a steeper section better, to rest the muscles used while seated, and to use body weight to help in the climb. When standing, heart rate typically rises because the cyclist uses more upper-body muscle to wobble the bike back and forth. Engaging the upper body requires the delivery of more oxygen to the working muscles, and the heart responds by pumping faster to get more blood to those critical areas. This response can be a problem if the cyclist is already at threshold. Any rise in heart rate might cause the cyclist to go over the edge and blow up, so cyclists need to know when to stand up and when to stay seated. One rule to stick with is to stay seated as long as possible when the pace is steady to help reduce heart rate and maintain pace. When the pace begins to change because of having to respond to other riders or changes in terrain, that generally signals the time to get out of the saddle to increase power.

As seen in figure 14.1, when standing, the cyclist should shift his or her body weight farther forward on the bike, both because the bike is already tilting backward from the gradient and because the forward position allows the rider to increase leverage. To do this, rather than just bending at the hips and dropping the chest toward the stem, the cyclist should think instead of pushing the pelvis

▶ **Figure 14.1**   Proper standing form. Note that the pelvis is well forward of the saddle and the rider's chest is erect, such that breathing is open and much of the body weight is on the skeleton rather than the muscle of the arms.

Courtesy of PezCyclingNews.com

toward the stem and straightening the arms to help reduce some of the energy needed by the arms to hold up the upper body. Giro 1988 winner Andy Hampsten demonstrated excellent climbing form while standing.

By standing straighter with the pelvis pushed forward, the cyclist can easily rest the upper body, almost, but not quite, locking the arms and allowing the body weight to fall on the downstroke. The cyclist should practice this when not riding at high intensity and just climbing easy to get the feel of the body weight falling on each side in slow motion. The back should be straight and elongated, and the chest should be open to help the lungs take in the maximum amount of oxygen. This action will be a little choppy with a lower cadence when first practiced, but when the cyclist gets the feeling and hang of it and then applies it to a faster cadence and higher power, he or she will be smoother while still being able to relax and apply more force than when seated.

Seated Climbing

Seated climbing allows the cyclist to reduce upper-body movement and concentrate solely on power output from the legs. By relaxing the arms and shoulders (by dropping the shoulders down from the ears) and opening the chest (by letting the chest lead), the cyclist can recruit gluteal muscles at a higher level, as well as the hamstrings and quadriceps. The seated position also provides a little more range with cadence, because pedaling faster while seated is much easier. Figure 14.2 shows an example of good seated climbing.

One of the biggest mistakes riders make while seated is that they grip the handlebars too hard and tighten their chest muscles to pull back on the handlebars. Pulling back on the handlebars is sometimes necessary to help engage the upper body to fire those leg muscles, but while climbing, having a more relaxed grip and an open chest is generally more economical. Pulling hard on the handlebars when climbing usually indicates the point at which the cyclist should get out of the saddle and climb while standing. One technique that I encourage in my athletes when they are climbing in the saddle is to slide a little farther back on the saddle and drop the heels slightly to better engage the hamstrings. This approach allows the upper legs (femurs) to act even more like a lever to concentrate force on the downward stroke of the crank arm. The result can be a 5- to 10-watt improvement in power output.

With seated climbing, one well-known piece of advice by Eddy Merckx comes to mind. When asked the best advice for climbing, he stated, "Ride on the tops of your handlebars and pretend you are playing the piano. This will relax the chest and arms and make sure you aren't pulling too hard on the bars." This suggestion makes a lot of sense, and although riding with the hands lightly touching the bars is not always reasonable, it reminds the cyclist to relax the grip, elbows, and shoulders, which helps her or him be more economical.

Two critical details can make the biggest difference in climbing ability. The first has to do with how the cyclist sits on the bike. Many riders sit on their seat as if they are sitting in an office chair. Their sit bones are pointing down, and they round the back so that they can reach the handlebars. This position causes stress on the back, and if done for many years, it may contribute to a herniated disc. The best way to sit on the seat is to roll the pelvis forward and keep the spine long and straight.

Try this experiment. Sit in a straight-back chair with your butt pushed up against the back of the chair. Now, with a flat and straight back, pivot your upper body forward and push your butt farther back in the "corner" of the chair. Rolling your pelvis forward keeps your spine straight and long, thus protecting your back while at the same time opening the gluteal muscles so that they can contribute significantly to creating power.

The second critical detail to address when climbing is allowing the chest to lead the bike. Many cyclists round their shoulders while riding, which reduces the space in which the lungs can expand. Rolling the shoulders back and down while puffing the chest out gives the lungs more space to expand. One of the best ways to learn this posture is to pretend that a thread is attached to your sternum and leading you forward. This invisible thread pulls the chest out and is attached in space about 2 meters in front of the wheel. Allowing the chest to lead the body helps to force a long, straight back and rolls the shoulders back and down. These details are critical for long-term comfort and proper pedaling.

▶ **Figure 14.2** Proper seated climbing form. Upper body is loose and weight is set back on the saddle to permit fuller leg extension.

Courtesy of PezCyclingNews.com

Speaking of comfort, rolling the pelvis forward does change where the cyclist contacts the seat. The cyclist could have more contact between the seat and the perineum (space between the anus and genitals). At no time should the genitals ever become numb when riding. If this occurs, a new seat is needed to provide a better fit for the cyclist and his or her position. I highly recommend one that has a cutout in the middle to provide relief from the perineum being pinched on the saddle.

Pacing

Pacing is a basic concept in cycling, yet it takes years to master, and many cyclists never master it (see chapter 35 for more information on pacing in cycling). Pacing during climbing is doubly important because the consequences of riding too hard can mean having to stop on the side of the road! Most likely, a cyclist won't have to stop if she or he "blows up," but the cyclist will have to reduce speed significantly, try to recover, and then start over again. If this occurs in a competitive situation, the cyclist could lose minutes on his or her rivals.

Pacing is essentially the same whatever the intensity; the cyclist should ride at a consistent intensity through the climb. Cyclists who constantly accelerate, decelerate, and ride erratically use more energy than those who ride at a consistent intensity. So the first thing to learn is to ride at a consistent intensity when climbing, which is best done at a pace below threshold. Of course, constant accelerations can be a tactic to employ in racing situations to break up the competitors' steady rhythms and force them to expend more energy than desired.

The cyclist should pick a climb that has a gradient that allows her or him to ride at tempo or upper tempo pace and focus on this pace for the entire climb. If the climb is longer than 2 kilometers, the rider can initially use heart rate to determine pace because it changes relatively slowly (as compared with wattage) and can be held within a narrow range of beats per minute, which is a great initial guide for pacing. As they gain experience, cyclists will likely use watts and perceived exertion to determine pace. For a shorter climb (less than 2 kilometers), the cyclist can use a combination of watts and heart rate to determine pace. The heart rate responds slower to increases in intensity, so in shorter climbs, the cyclist could be nearly finished with the climb before the heart rate stabilizes at a good pace, which means that using watts (which is measured instantaneously) is a better measure of pacing for short climbs.

Pacing on a long climb in a big ride can sometimes mean riding at a pace that allows the cyclist to finish climbing the climb as well as finish the ride itself. Therefore, riding at more of an endurance or upper endurance pace makes more sense to ensure completion of the ride. This pace is easier to maintain because the intensity is not extremely high and the cyclist can maintain it without much focus or desire. Again, riding at a consistent pace is more desirable than riding at an erratic pace, so the cyclist should try to find a reasonable heart rate or wattage in this endurance or upper endurance pace that allows consistency.

Pacing on other occasions means riding right at limit or threshold. This pace is difficult to maintain because the cyclist is breathing hard, the heart rate is high, the muscles are burning, and the state of being is uncomfortable. To ride right at limit, the cyclist really has to want to do it and has to push, suffer, and focus 100 percent on riding at limit. One well-known cycling coach, Neal Henderson, calls this exercise-induced discomfort, which is an accurate explanation of riding right at limit and keeping the mental self-talk positive. Learning to ride right at threshold and then maintaining the threshold power over steeper sections and flatter areas requires discipline and attention, because intensity or wattage output is based on both the force applied and the cadence. On steeper sections the cyclist needs to apply more force at a slower cadence, and on flatter sections the cyclist wants to increase cadence because the resistance to create those higher torque (force) values will decline. The cyclist has to focus to notice when wattage is dropping and then get back to threshold.

A hill climb event is essentially a time trial, so the main rule—don't start too hard—applies in all hill climbs as well. The perceived exertion feels low, but a power meter might show the cyclist doing 400 watts, even if it feels like only 300 watts. The cyclist has no chance of being able to maintain much over threshold power at 300 watts for the entire climb. So when perceived exertion finally matches actual exertion, it is too late. The cyclist has "blown up" and now needs to recover and start over. The lesson here is this: Don't start too hard!

The bigger question remains about how to determine pace on the steeper and flatter sections. Should the cyclist go harder on the steep sections? Should the cyclist save something on the steeper sections for the flatter sections? The answer depends largely on where the steeper and flatter sections are placed in the hill climb. If steep sections are followed by flatter sections, the cyclist should pace him- or herself right at functional threshold power on the steep sections, so that he or she doesn't blow up at the top of them, and then ride slowly on a faster flatter section. If the cyclist rides too hard on the steep section and gains 10 seconds on a competitor but then blows up at the top of the section and loses 30 seconds by riding at 5 miles per hour (8 km/h) instead of 10 miles per hour (16 km/h), then she or he used incorrect pacing and lost time overall. If, on the other hand, the cyclist rode right at threshold on the steep section and gained 5 seconds on a competitor, and then maintained an effort near FTP on the flatter section afterward, then he or she may gain another chunk of time there.

Let's consider the opposite situation, a long steep section followed by a short flat section and then another long steep section to the finish. In this scenario, the cyclist would want to ride at or above threshold on the first long steep section, recover on the short flatter section, and then ride above threshold again all the way to the finish.

Shorter hill climbs do not have as much pacing strategy involved as long hill climbs do because cyclists generally go all out on short climbs, not holding back at the start or during any section of the climb. The only consideration is knowing the course, so that the cyclist can go all out in the final 30 seconds.

Mental Strategies for Climbing

One of the most important ways to improve climbing and cycling overall is to improve mental self-talk. To be successful, cyclists must talk to themselves positively when thinking about climbing, while climbing, and then while mentally reviewing the climbing later. Some of the best climbers started out with a bad attitude toward climbing and at some point in their careers they decided to "love" climbing. Maybe they made a conscious choice, or maybe they found some success at it. Either way, to be good at climbing, the cyclist must at least like it, must find some joy in it. Doing that can be as simple as deciding to repeat mentally, "I love climbing" throughout the entire climb. Here are three suggestions to help focus on improving climbing by changing the mind-set.

Break it into shorter periods. All endurance athletes come to a time when they begin to test their limits in body and mind. A common game that cyclists use to improve climbing is to push themselves on the limit for longer and longer periods. As mentioned earlier, riding at the edge takes tremendous focus and motivation, so cyclists need to break the climb into small pieces and focus on them. Climb for 15 minutes, and for the entire time see whether you can ride with the highest heart rate you can maintain, the highest wattage, and the highest respiration rate. If you let your heart rate drop or find your mind wandering during the effort, start over with a shorter period and see whether you can maintain focus. Then move on to a longer period.

Create a mantra to say in your head while climbing. This refrain needs to be something positive and rhythmic to help control breathing. Come up with something easy to say that you can break into two parts; you use the first one on the inhale and the second on the exhale. My favorite mantra is to say, "Power in" on inhales and "Feeling strong" on exhales.

Visualize climbing and smiling. While riding on an endurance ride or just relaxing at home, visualize yourself climbing effortlessly and smiling the whole time. See yourself climbing out of the saddle and dropping your competitors as they are laboring all around you. You are just climbing away from them. Feel the strength in the legs and see your speed and wattage higher than before.

Descending

What goes up must come down. Descending off a mountain takes skill and nerve and is made easier by understanding the key components of descending.

Each curve or corner comprises five sections. The first one is called the *approach*. Riding on the road provides a wide area from which to choose a line, unlike mountain biking in which cyclists are generally restricted to a narrow area and only one line. The approach starts as you look far ahead into the turn, scan the road for obstacles such as rocks or sticks, and look for landmarks to help with judging the turn's sharpness or shallowness.

In general, most turns on a bicycle are called *late apex* turns. Instead of hugging the inside of the curve at the entry of the curve, you stay to the outside of the curve (far left side for a right-hand turn) until the last possible moment. You then dive to the apex of the turn and allow the bike to float back out to the outside at the exit of the turn. This path helps you use the maximum amount of road possible and is the fastest line through the turn. During the entire cornering process you keep looking with your eyes as far through the turn as possible. A mistake that newer riders often make is failing to look far enough down the road to anticipate the upcoming turn radius.

Looking ahead and assessing the sharpness of the curve determines the next component, which is *braking*. The sharper the curve appears to be, the slower you need to go to negotiate the turn. You should do all braking before the turn so that you have reduced speed enough to negotiate the turn swiftly and safely. Braking in the turn destabilizes the bike because it reduces the gyroscopic effect in the wheels and makes the bike try to stand upright.

Braking in a turn can also cause the rear wheel to begin to skid because the contact patch on the ground is much smaller when cornering, making it easier to lock up the wheel. Bottom line? Get your braking done before the turn. How much braking should you do? There's no one simple answer for that, except just enough. Each turn is different, and the more you ride, the better you will become at judging the correct entry speed for each turn.

Positioning on the bike, the third component of descending, is also super important. The outside leg needs to be down and heavily weighted. The leg itself is locked straight with the heel slightly down to generate the force needed to create more of a contact patch with the ground. Many riders think they are locking their legs, but they really do not have them locked. This is a real problem because they cannot lean deeply enough in the turn. I recommend moving the inside leg out to the side to help balance out the weight on the outside leg.

To lean the bike over correctly, you need to use a technique called *counter-steering,* as shown in figure 14.3. When making a right-hand turn, push the weight of the right hand forward in such a way that if you were stopped, you would actually turn the bike to the left; hence, the term *countersteering*. But when the wheels are spinning faster than about 14 miles per hour (23 km/h), countersteering will make the bike lean over even more than before and create a sharper turn. When descending, you need to keep your hands on the handlebar drops, not on the tops of the bars, to lower your center of gravity and give you more control of the bike. When you want to make your turn tighter—if, for example, you find yourself drifting out to the yellow line into opposing traffic—the last thing you want to do is grab brake! You need to push harder into that inside hand, countersteering even more, to make the bike carve even deeper into the turn.

The *exit* is the last component of the turn. When you begin to exit, you need to reduce your countersteering force and allow the bike to become more upright. After you are stable and exiting the turn with your gaze looking as far down the road as possible, get on top of your gear and accelerate out

▶ **Figure 14.3** Proper descending cornering form. Note the outside leg is locked with the heel down for full weight loading, and the head is up and eyes looking well forward.

Courtesy of PezCyclingNews.com

of the turn. The speed at which you exit the turn can really help you down the next straightaway, so you need to exit smoothly and in such a way to get your bike accelerating as quickly as possible.

One last topic for discussion when descending is what to do when the road surface is wet. First, you will definitely reduce your speed, but you will be surprised at just how fast you can still take the turns. Bicycle tires are so narrow that they cut through the water down to the road surface, so the bike has no chance of hydroplaning as a car does. You therefore have more grip than you might initially think, but you still need to be careful not to lean your bike too much. Keeping the bike more upright when cornering is a matter of shifting your weight from the outside leg more to the inside leg. When you first try this technique, it's very unnerving because it's not natural, but by forcing the bike to stay upright instead of leaning it over in a turn, you can maintain a larger contact patch with the ground and therefore have better grip. Practicing this technique the next time it rains will pay dividends in your next rainy event.

Applying the Science

Climbing and descending are important parts of cycling and two of the things that make cycling so interesting. The ability to climb quickly comes through hard work spent climbing, along with developing the proper form and mental attitude. Although a 190-pound (86 kg) rider will never be able to climb with a 120-pound (54 kg) rider, the heavier rider can still become a good climber using the techniques described in this chapter. Remember that becoming a good climber takes time and plenty of suffering while riding at your functional threshold power up and down the mountains. You have to put in the necessary work and take every opportunity you have to practice your climbing.

Descending also takes practice. Although you might think you need nerves of steel, you really need only the ability to control your bike precisely and the ability to read the road in front of you to assess and predict the upcoming curve and its characteristics. Practicing descending starts with practicing cornering in parking lots near home to become more familiar with exactly how much weight is needed in one hand or the opposing leg to provide the proper lean angle. Spend time working on cornering at slower speeds in parking lots before you begin fast downhills.

After years of riding, some of your favorite rides will likely include climbing and descending. At the end of the ride, you will often hear riders talking excitedly about their exploits either climbing or descending.

PART

V

Nutrition and Ergogenics

CHAPTER **15**

Cycling Nutrition

—Dina Griffin

The world of sport nutrition science and practice is continually evolving. What sport scientists and practitioners advised to athletes just two decades ago has changed with advances in research. These advances allow better examination of how nutrition influences the health and exercise performance of the human body. Today is an exciting time in nutrition science as researchers and practitioners strive to marry findings in the laboratory with real-life application to determine what enables the cyclist to maintain an optimal level of health while achieving a high level of athletic performance.

Nutrition affects many aspects of the cyclist's ability to ride recreationally or competitively. Weight management, successful completion of specific training goals, nutrient timing for racing, susceptibility to (and recovery from) injury, immune system health, and risk for chronic disease are examples where nutrition has a direct effect. Hence, cyclists of all ages and abilities need to give attention to their daily nutrition patterns as they relate to health and performance.

This chapter highlights key areas of daily nutrition and addresses some health concerns that should be on the cyclist's radar.

Daily Nutrition and the Body's Energy Sources: Fat and Carbohydrate

During rest and exercise, the body has two primary energy sources: fat and carbohydrate. The potential pool' of fat calories that the body can convert to energy is typically in the range of 30,000 to 80,000 calories. This range depends on stores in adipose tissue and intramuscular triglycerides. Stored carbohydrate (in the form of glycogen) in the skeletal muscle and liver is a limited energy source, topping out in the range of 1,200 to 2,400 calories. Therefore, the energy opportunity of fat is 10 to 40 times more than that of carbohydrate. Protein is an insignificant energy source except in chronic starvation conditions. Otherwise, protein generates less than 5 percent of daily energy.

The notion that athletes need to consume a daily high-carbohydrate diet (in the range of 50 to 65 percent of total daily calories) has been prominent in sport nutrition recommendations for quite some time. With the increasing prevalence of conditions such as overweight, obesity and metabolic syndrome, along with chronic diseases such as diabetes and cardiovascular disease from which cyclists are not immune, dietary carbohydrate consumption is under the microscope. Although research findings demonstrate performance benefits of high carbohydrate intake for athletes, a growing collection of research suggests that athletes can thrive in health and performance with more moderate daily intakes of carbohydrate. Note that there is no widely accepted definition for low- versus high-carbohydrate diets, but this classification has been proposed (Feinman et al. 2015):

- Very low (ketogenic): less than 50 grams of carbohydrate per day or less than 10 percent of total energy intake from carbohydrate
- Low: less than 130 grams of carbohydrate per day or less than 26 percent of total energy intake from carbohydrate
- Moderate: 26 to 45 percent of total energy intake from carbohydrate
- High: more than 45 percent of total energy intake from carbohydrate

Consideration of body composition goals and the cyclist's training plan strongly influence carbohydrate intake goals. Protein intake in almost all situations remains moderate at 20 to 30 percent of total energy. Dietary fat is the remaining source of calories, which can be in the range of 30 to 70 percent depending on carbohydrate intake.

The crossover concept, officially coined in 1994 (Brooks and Mercier 1994) but originating in 1930s physiology studies, proposed a model for showing how the body uses fat and carbohydrate at rest and at increasing exercise intensities. The crossover point is recognized as the exercise intensity at which the body switches from using a higher rate of fat as an energy source to using more carbohydrate as an energy source (figure 15.1).

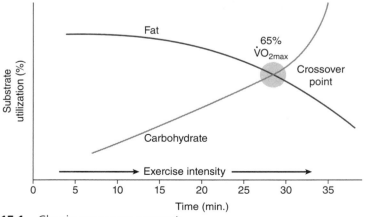

▶ **Figure 15.1** Classic crossover concept.

Years of physiological testing data have shown that the crossover typically occurs around 65 percent of $\dot{V}O_2$max. The crossover occurs because of various aerobic training adaptations that enhance mitochondrial density (where fat "burning" occurs in the cells) and increase the enzymes associated with fat oxidation. What is interesting is that not all aerobically trained athletes use a greater proportion of fat even at their supposed aerobic intensities (figure 15.2). In essence, these athletes are considered carbohydrate dependent; an assessment of daily dietary patterns will reveal this.

In contrast, athletes with low to moderate carbohydrate nutrition patterns have been shown to use fat at intensities even higher than 65 percent of $\dot{V}O_2$max (figure 15.3) and thus preserve their limited stores of carbohydrate. Their bodies are able to mobilize fatty acids as an energy source more efficiently.

No longer is the crossover point viewed as an exercise manipulation. It is viewed now as the result of both exercise and daily dietary interventions.

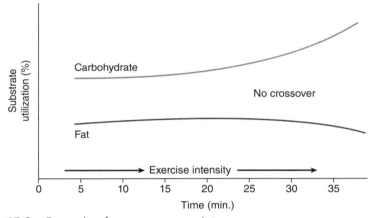

▶ **Figure 15.2** Example of no crossover point.

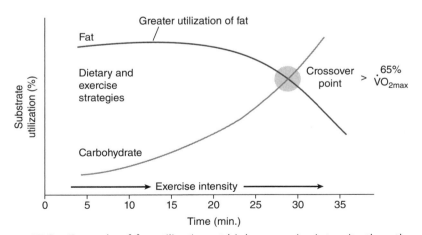

▶ **Figure 15.3** Example of fat utilization at higher exercise intensity than the classic crossover point.

Fat Adaptation

Nutrition has been recognized as a powerful influence on how an athlete's body can utilize fat and carbohydrate during exercise (Seebohar 2014; Hawley 2011). Put simply, an athlete who consumes a chronically high-carbohydrate diet will tend to be a carbohydrate burner (or sugar burner), whereas an athlete who consumes a low to moderate level of carbohydrate will be able to use more fat at aerobic intensities and push the crossover point to higher intensities. Fat adaptation can be summarized as the process of improving the body's ability to oxidize a greater proportion of fat at submaximal exercise intensities through dietary and exercise strategies. Because a person's level of fat adaptation is influenced by factors such as physical fitness, conditioning, and daily nutrition patterns, an assessment should be conducted by an expert in this area of sport and nutrition science, such as an exercise physiologist or board-certified sport dietitian. Proper testing protocols with reliable metabolic cart data and interpretation methods will reveal the status of fat adaptation and provide strategies for improvement (Seebohar 2014).

A main benefit of fat adaptation for cyclists is preservation (or sparing) of the body's limited glycogen stores for when they are needed most during training and racing, such as in a sprint finish, hill climb, or breakaway. Fat adaptation can reduce the number of hourly calories that must be consumed because the body is able to convert fat to usable energy efficiently. This adaptation has some practical implications, such as having to worry less about how to carry food on the bike and decreasing the risk for gastrointestinal distress in those who have sensitive stomachs or cannot tolerate a high hourly calorie load. Off-road cyclists, in particular, benefit because it is difficult to eat without stopping or taking the hands off the handlebars.

A common misconception among cyclists is that carbohydrate intake needs to be in the very low range for fat adaptation to occur. Although numerous research studies test the efficacy of very low-carbohydrate diets, these approaches are unnecessary to experience an enhanced level of fat adaptation. Implementing simple dietary changes with moderate carbohydrate intake levels at the appropriate time in a cyclist's training plan can be effective in increasing fat utilization during exercise.

Another concern of cyclists regarding lower carbohydrate diets is the effect on health and performance. Growing evidence suggests that controlled-carbohydrate diets can actually be more favorable to weight control, cardiovascular health, insulin resistance, and systemic inflammation (Bazzano et al. 2014). This finding is especially pertinent to cyclists who are overweight or have conditions such as prediabetes, type 2 diabetes, heart disease, or any family history that may predispose them to increased risk for chronic disease. As far as the effects of a lower carbohydrate diet on performance, the research available to date reflects mixed outcomes. More research is warranted.

Clearly, daily and training nutrition must be personalized because health and athletic goals vary significantly among athletes. In the recommendations that follow, both newer and common sport nutrition guidelines are provided so that athletes can choose which may be more applicable to their situations.

Energy Needs and Expenditure

Cyclists often want to know how many calories they need on a daily basis to support health and sport performance goals. Prescribing calorie goals, however, is a challenge, primarily because energy needs fluctuate daily depending on lifestyle, general activity level, and purposeful exercise. Because of the significant variations in energy demand from exercise, nutrition should be less focused on total calorie needs and instead focused on matching macro- and micronutrient needs to support the cyclist's health and performance-related goals during a training year. This concept, known as nutrition periodization, also includes nutrient timing principles that are discussed in chapter 16 (Seebohar 2011).

Any cyclist who uses a periodized training plan generally has three mesocycles within a typical training year:

- Preseason (also called base or preparatory): generally focused more on endurance and strength
- Competition (in season or build): focused on improving speed, power, economy
- Off-season (transition or recovery): for downtime, prehabilitation, rehabilitation

Because the physical training goals and the training protocol within each mesocycle are unique, nutrition cannot and should not be identical day to day for recreational or competitive cyclists. Aside from taking into account training plan and lifestyle differences, the design of a periodized nutrition plan should include assessments of past medical history, current medical issues, and body composition goals.

Generally, both quantitative and qualitative strategies can be used to implement nutrition periodization. The qualitative side is often neglected because of the numerous psychological, educational, and behavioral aspects that should be considered. But examining these areas is essential to identifying areas of improvement and pinpointing strengths on which to build a successful plan. These qualitative aspects include identifying the athlete's understanding of biological hunger cues and the feeling of food satiety; the effect of habitual, social, and emotional eating; basic functions of macronutrients (protein, fat, carbohydrate) and examples of those foods; reading food labels, meal planning, and grocery store navigation; and food preparation and culinary skills.

Quantitatively, the next section examines macronutrient needs in the context of the cyclist's training cycle and common goals such as weight loss and improving power-to-weight ratio. Guidance on how to include optimum foods for supporting health and athletic goals is also provided.

Macronutrients

Macronutrients are the proteins, carbohydrates, and fats in foods. This section reviews their function in the diet to reinforce the importance of variety and to demonstrate how macronutrient choices can influence cyclists' health.

Protein

Proteins have diverse structural and functional roles within the body. These roles include hormonal control, immune system support, transport of nutrients, and maintenance and repair of tissues such as tendons, muscles, and bone. The main building blocks of proteins are amino acids. Certain amino acids (referred to as indispensable or essential) must come from dietary sources because the body cannot synthesize them. Many factors influence the body's protein balance:

- Energy availability
- Daily protein intake (amount, types, and timing)
- Availability of amino acids (in the fed versus fasted state, types of amino acids in foods)
- Hormone levels to affect protein synthesis or breakdown
- Type of exercise (endurance versus resistance)
- Intensity and duration of exercise
- Gender differences (as it relates to the female menstrual cycle)

A variety of dietary protein sources are available to meet the needs of cyclists, whether the preferred source is animal based or plant based. Variety of protein intake is important because each source has a different profile of amino acids. Plant-based sources of protein have lower amino acid content, yet they should no longer be considered incomplete, as they once were. As long as adequate protein consumption occurs within a day and the sources are varied, the concern for protein deficiency is minimal.

Aside from its aforementioned roles, protein has many other benefits pertinent to cyclists. Protein provides satiety, which is especially important for cyclists who want to lose weight. The satiety factor will be noticeable when comparing the fullness level 3 to 4 hours after ingesting a meal containing 20 or more grams of protein to one that contains significantly less. Other benefits of protein include facilitating the building of lean muscle mass as well as aiding in the recovery process. This aspect is particularly critical for cyclists who are in high-volume or high-intensity training blocks or who are participating in two training sessions per day.

Another benefit to protein is that it aids in minimizing the rate of sarcopenia, which is defined as the loss of skeletal muscle mass that begins to occur after age 30.

The daily protein goals of the cyclist should include choosing a variety of proteins at meals and snacks, consuming protein evenly throughout the day (depending on training schedule), and ensuring adequate protein amounts at meals and snacks.

The recommended daily allowance (RDA) of protein for the general population is currently set at 0.8 grams per kilogram of body weight per day. Although this amount may be adequate for some recreational cyclists, it may not be optimal to promote training adaptations, maintain muscle mass, or promote fat loss (when applicable) (Phillips 2014).

Daily protein recommendations for cyclists are as follows (Seebohar 2011; Phillips 2014; Burke 2009):

- For body-fat loss: 1.5 to 2.5 grams per kilogram of body weight; recommended in the preseason or off-season when relative training intensity is low

- For preseason and in-season with no weight-loss goals: 1.2 to 2.0 grams per kilogram of body weight

- For off-season: 1.2 to 2.3 grams per kilogram of body weight

As an example, a male cyclist who weighs 70 kilograms (154 lb) wants to work on losing body fat. He would calculate his protein needs as 105 to 175 grams per day (70 kg × 1.5–2.5 g).

For maintaining protein balance and facilitating muscle protein synthesis, cyclists should consume an even distribution of protein intake throughout the day, consisting of no less than 20 to 30 grams of protein at three or four meals. Table 15.1 gives examples of protein sources and amounts per serving.

Carbohydrate

Carbohydrate has long been classified as the energy source for the body. But unlike certain amino acids and fatty acids, no particular carbohydrate is essential in the diet. The body can synthesize what it needs to function adequately. Regardless, dietary carbohydrate does supply the body with energy and come in various forms generally classified as starches, sugars, and fibers. As digestion and absorption occur, carbohydrate (with the exception of some fibers) is broken down into sugars. These sugars, namely glucose, can be immediately used for energy or converted to a stored form (as glycogen or as fat) for later use. The sugar level in the bloodstream can quickly increase as a result of the amount and type of carbohydrate consumed, depending on other macronutrients that are consumed at the same time.

Table 15.1 Protein Sources

Source	Serving size	Protein content (g)
ANIMAL-DERIVED PROTEIN		
Egg, whole	1 egg	6
Cheese	1 oz (30 g) or 1 slice	7
Egg whites	2 egg whites or about 1/3 cup	8
Cow milk	8 oz (250 g)	8
Cottage cheese	1/2 cup	14
Yogurt, Greek or plain	6 oz (175 g)	10–15
Whey protein powder	1 serving	20–25
Red meat, poultry, seafood, cooked	3 oz (90 g)	21–24
PLANT-DERIVED PROTEIN		
Chia seeds	1 Tbsp	3
Quinoa, cooked	1/2 cup	4
Spirulina	1 Tbsp	4
Broccoli, cooked	1 cup	4
Sprouted bread	1 slice	4
Tofu	1/2 cup	5
Portabella mushrooms, cooked	1 cup	5
Sunflower seeds	1/4 cup	6
Soy milk	8 oz (250 g)	7
Lentils, cooked	1/2 cup	9
Hemp hearts	3 Tbsp	10
Protein powder blends (pea, brown rice, hemp)	1 serving	15–25
Whole grains (such as barley, brown rice, amaranth, millet, oats), dry	1/4 cup	4–6
Nuts	1/4 cup	5–8
Nut butter	2 Tbsp	6–8
Beans, cooked	1/2 cup	7–8

One gram of protein provides 4 calories.

To enhance health, the cyclist should consume an abundant and diverse amount of unprocessed, unrefined carbohydrate, consisting of vegetables, fruits, and whole grains. Note that whole grains technically should not be processed into another food product to be considered whole. Food companies often use marketing claims to make packaged foods appear more wholesome than they actually are. For example, a whole-wheat bagel is a processed grain even though it may contain some whole grains.

Note also that carbohydrate is present in other foods besides fruits, vegetables, and whole grains. Foods such as nuts, seeds, yogurt, milk, beans, and soy-based foods are additional sources of carbohydrate. Expecting cyclists to avoid all processed and refined grains such as baked goods, pretzels, crackers, breads, and chips is unrealistic. But these extras should make up no more than 10 percent of a cyclist's daily intake, particularly for cyclists who have body weight and health concerns. When choosing these types of packaged foods, cyclists should look for items that have the fewest ingredients and ingredients that are identifiable.

Cyclists who consume a variety of fruits, vegetables, and whole grains will have ample carbohydrate in their daily diet. The benefits to health are numerous. Besides being a good source of vitamins and minerals, these foods are fiber rich and include many phytonutrients, which have protective health benefits such as boosting the immune system.

Optimizing the quality of carbohydrate, along with combining it with a variety of protein and healthy fat sources, is also a sound strategy to maintain weight and to promote weight loss. Including protein and fat sources with fiber-rich, unprocessed carbohydrate at meals and snacks helps to maintain a steady blood glucose level. The added benefit of satiety for 3 or 4 hours after a meal can minimize needless snacking and food cravings that typically occur in diets high in processed and refined carbohydrate.

As mentioned earlier, a new wave of sport nutrition guidelines suggests that some athletes can thrive more from moderate carbohydrate intake than from high carbohydrate intake. When considering these new guidelines, the caliber of cyclist, distance of targeted race or event, primary energy systems used in training and competition (aerobic versus anaerobic), health status, body composition goals, and training demands must be taken into account.

The daily carbohydrate goals of the cyclist should include optimizing the quality of carbohydrate consumed, pairing carbohydrate with appropriate amounts of protein and fat of high quality, and tailoring carbohydrate intake to what is needed, based on training demands and energy needs.

Daily carbohydrate recommendations for cyclists are the following (Burke 2009):

- For body-fat loss: 3 to 5 grams per kilogram of body weight; recommended in the preseason or off-season when relative training intensity is low; cyclists aiming to enhance fat adaptation can aim for the lower end of this range.

- For preseason with no fat loss: 3 to 7 grams per kilogram of body weight; the lower end is for low-intensity training or for cyclists aiming to improve fat oxidation.

- For in-season: 5 to 12 grams per kilogram of body weight; the lower range is for fat adaptation or for recreational cyclists, and the middle to upper range is for more competitive cyclists or those who are more carbohydrate dependent.

Carbohydrate needs should change daily depending on the periodized training plan or race calendar. Thus, a wide range of recommendations for in-season must be considered for each cyclist. For those experimenting with varying carbohydrate intakes, keeping a nutrition log that includes subjective observations about energy and hunger levels can be helpful. Counting calories or obsessing over exact quantitative data is not necessary, but pairing the nutrition log and training log can often reveal whether fine-tuning of the nutrition plan is needed.

Examples of optimal sources of carbohydrate for a cyclist's diet are listed in table 15.2.

Fat

Long vilified as causing weight gain and poor heart health, dietary fat is now less feared and is being promoted as part of an athlete's healthful daily diet. Fat insulates organs, absorbs and transports fat-soluble vitamins, and is essential for all cell membranes in the body. Fat has a critical role in immune system health, neural function, and anti-inflammatory responses. Fat is present in the blood (as free fatty acids and triglycerides), in adipose tissue, and within skeletal muscle. Indeed, fat is a dense energy source, providing 9 calories per gram, whereas protein and carbohydrate supply 4 calories per gram.

Fat is grouped into two main categories: unsaturated (mono and poly forms) and saturated. Fats are differentiated based on several molecular characteristics. Just as the body cannot synthesize some amino acids, certain essential fatty acids (omega-6 and omega-3 fats) must be consumed from dietary sources to prevent deficiencies.

Most noticeable to athletes who include fat as part of meals and snacks is a prolonged feeling of satiety. This sensation occurs primarily because of the slower digestion time, which is further augmented when combined with fiber-rich foods and protein. As for the general type of fat to consume, emphasis has been placed on increasing monounsaturated and polyunsaturated fat (with particular attention to omega-3 sources rich in eicosapentaenoic acid [EPA] and docosahexaenoic acid [DHA]; see table 15.3, U.S. Department of Agriculture 2016), which have been shown to have a variety of beneficial effects on health. These benefits include reduced low-grade inflammation; improvements in vascular function, lipid profile, and blood pressure; improved mood and cognitive health; and correlations with reduced risk for cardiovascular disease and sudden cardiac death (Vannice and Rasmussen 2014). Although more research is needed, omega-3 intake may affect athletic neuromuscular function, reduce muscle damage and inflammation because of exercise stress, and have therapeutic effects on traumas such as concussions and brain injuries (Bryhn 2015; Michleborough 2013; Lewis et al. 2015).

For cyclists who are in good health (without obesity or chronic disease such as type 2 diabetes and heart disease), saturated fat may be included

Table 15.2 Optimal Carbohydrate Sources

Source	Serving size	Carbohydrate content (g)
NONSTARCHY VEGETABLES		
Artichoke Broccoli Cauliflower Eggplant Onions, leeks Tomato Asparagus Brussels sprouts Celery Dark leafy greens (spinach, kale, turnip, collard, mustard, and so on) Bell pepper Zucchini Beets Cabbage Cucumber Mushrooms Radishes Summer squash	1 cup raw or 1/2 cup cooked	5
FRUIT		
Apple Cherries Nectarine Raspberries Banana Grapes Orange Strawberries Cantaloupe Kiwi Peach	1 medium piece (tennis-ball size) or 1 cup	15
Blackberries Apricots Blueberries Pineapple	3/4 cup	15
Mango Pear Pomegranate arils	1/2 cup	15
STARCHY VEGETABLES		
Corn Sweet potato, yam Beans Potato	1/2 cup	15
Winter squash	1 cup	15
WHOLE GRAINS		
Amaranth Barley Brown or wild rice Kamut Rye Farro Oats Spelt Bulgur Quinoa Teff Buckwheat	1/2 cup cooked (generally)	15

One gram of carbohydrate provides 4 calories.

Table 15.3   Sources of Omega-3 Fats Rich in EPA or DHA

Source	Serving size	Omega-3 DHA or EPA content (mg)
Salmon, Atlantic, wild Salmon, Atlantic, farmed	3 oz (90 g) cooked	1,564 1,824
Salmon, Coho, wild Salmon, Coho, farmed	3 oz (90 g) cooked	900 1,087
Salmon, canned, pink	3 oz (90 g)	916
Trout, rainbow, wild Trout, rainbow, farmed	3 oz (90 g) cooked	840 744
Halibut, Atlantic and Pacific	3 oz (90 g) cooked	200
Tuna, yellowfin Tuna, blue fin Tuna, light, canned in water	3 oz (90 g) cooked	102 1,279 230
Herring, Atlantic Herring, Pacific	3 oz (90 g) cooked	1,712 1,807
Sardines, canned in oil	3 oz (90 g)	835
Anchovies, canned in oil	1 oz (30 g)	582

more liberally in the daily diet. This source of dietary fat is no longer implicated in causes of chronic disease. Scientific recommendations generally advocate a higher dietary intake of polyunsaturated fat than saturated fat (de Souza 2015). Cyclists who remain fat-phobic should note that certain carbohydrates (namely, those high in sugar or those causing a quick rise in blood sugar) are more likely to have harmful effects on heart health than fat and are more closely correlated with chronic disease (Kuipers et al. 2011; Siri-Tarino et al. 2010, 2015).

Currently, there is little doubt that trans fat should be avoided, because it is correlated with risk for coronary heart disease, diabetes, and metabolic syndrome (Vannice and Rasmussen 2014; de Souza et al. 2015). An easy way to identify trans fat is to search for "partially hydrogenated" ingredients in packaged items. Trans fat is commonly found in fried foods and commercially prepared baked goods.

The cyclist's daily goals with respect to fat intake should include consuming a variety of fat, particularly mono- and polyunsaturated fat, yet not fearing saturated fat; avoiding trans fat; and consuming regular sources of omega-3 fat, particularly those higher in EPA and DHA.

Daily fat recommendations for cyclists are as follows:

- For body-fat loss and no fat adaptation: 0.8 to 1.0 gram per kilogram of body weight; recommended in the preseason or off-season when relative training intensity is low; also recommended for those not wanting to achieve fat adaptation through dietary strategies.

- For body-fat loss and fat adaptation: 2 or 3 grams per kilogram of body weight; recommended in the preseason or off-season when relative training intensity is low; also recommended for those wanting to achieve fat adaptation through dietary intervention; note that carbohydrate intake must be simultaneously reduced.

- For preseason with no fat loss: 0.9 to 1.3 grams per kilogram of body weight; for cyclists wanting to improve fat adaptation, this range may be much higher depending on the level of carbohydrate intake.
- For in-season: 1.0 to 1.5 grams per kilogram of body weight; depending on the type of cyclist and periodized plan, this range may increase to about 2.5 grams per kilogram of body weight for cyclists wanting to maintain a high level of fat adaptation.
- For off-season: 0.8 to 1.2 grams per kilogram of body weight, depending on health and weight-loss goals.

As described previously, a higher fat and more moderate carbohydrate intake can be implemented for cyclists wanting to use dietary strategies to promote fat adaptation. Cyclists should seek the advice of a board-certified sport dietitian to be sure that proper dietary strategies are implemented to meet macro- and micronutrient needs and support the demands of physical training.

In daily eating, cyclists should include one or more fat sources in meals and snacks. Note that foods such as dairy products and animal protein can contain fat. Additionally, wild game and grass-fed or pasture-raised sources are preferred sources of protein, because they generally provide an increased amount of all omega-3 fatty acids. For optimizing health, cyclists should also work to increase their intake of omega-3 foods rich in EPA and DHA by consuming fish two or three times per week. If fish is not tolerated or is not part of the cyclist's diet, other foods containing omega-3 should be consumed and supplementation should be evaluated. Examples of fat sources for a cyclist's diet are listed in table 15.4. See table 15.3 for sources of omega-3 fats rich in EPA or DHA.

Table 15.4 Fat Sources

Source	Serving size	Fat content (g)
Avocado	1/8 avocado	5
Coconut flakes	2 Tbsp	
Flax meal	3 Tbsp	
Green olives	10 olives	
Mayonnaise	1 tsp	
Nuts	1 or 2 Tbsp	
Oils, butter, ghee	1 tsp	
Bacon	1 slice	
Coconut milk, canned	2 Tbsp	
Cream cheese	1 Tbsp	
Pumpkin seeds, sunflower seeds	1 oz	
Chia seeds	1 Tbsp	
Black olives	8 olives	

Some meats and dairy foods contain fat.

One gram of fat provides 9 calories.

Putting the Macros Together

The preceding sections on macronutrients give quantitative guidelines for general daily eating patterns. For cyclists who may not want to assess or plan their nutrition in quantitative terms, visual representations of the food plate can be helpful (figure 15.4). Periodization plates show the proportions of foods based on the periodized training cycle (Seebohar 2011).

The qualitative and visual approach shows a model for how the food groups can be arranged to meet daily energy needs, including the training demands of a particular day or training cycle. This visual approach can make meal planning and preparation simpler and be a starting point for cyclists wanting to implement a periodized nutrition plan. The actual plate will differ from cyclist to cyclist.

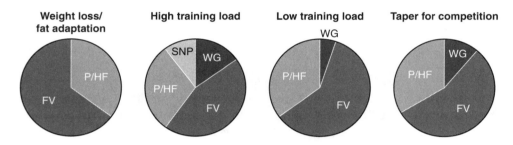

P/HF: Proteins and healthy fats
FV: Fruits and vegetables
WG: Whole grains
SNP: Sport nutrition products

▶ **Figure 15.4** Examples of periodization plates.

Courtesy of Bob Seebohar.

Body Composition and Weight Loss

Achieving low body weight and leanness is desirable among road cyclists. By simply altering the power-to-weight ratio, a cyclist can achieve faster velocities, improve functional threshold power, and climb with less effort.

Low body weight and weight-loss approaches can be a concern when trying to protect health and simultaneously maintain the performance level of the cyclist. Athletes who have suboptimal body-fat levels (less than 3 percent for males, less than 12 percent for females) likely have compromised power and a weakened immune system (Jeukendrup and Gleeson 2009). Female athletes are at risk of disrupting menstrual function and bone health because they have less energy available as a result of restricted eating or excess energy expenditure (Beals 2013). As described in detail elsewhere (Nattiv et al. 2007), the health impairments can lead to several serious health and performance consequences, such as reproductive health issues, stress fractures, and osteoporosis.

Although elite-level cyclists commonly have less body fat and more lean mass compared with recreational cyclists (Haakonssen et al. 2016; Penteado et al. 2010), cyclists in either group may undertake unsafe dietary practices to achieve quick weight loss, resulting in nutrient deficiencies. Ideally, weight loss should be undertaken in the off-season or preseason when training is generally lower in volume and intensity. Well-designed meal plans that focus on nutrient density coupled with behavior changes to minimize occurrences of overeating and mindless eating are more successful for achieving results.

Bone Health

In recent years, concern has developed that cyclists may be more prone to developing osteopenia, which can increase risk for bone fractures and lead to osteoporosis. Although factors such as dietary patterns, genetics, and hormonal flux affect bone health, we know that weight-bearing types of physical activity are more effective than cycling for achieving peak bone mass and slowing the rate of bone loss in the aging athlete (National Institutes of Health 2015; Nichols, Palmer, and Levy 2003). In general, cycling is not considered weight bearing, because less mechanical stress is placed on the skeleton and the biomechanics do not promote bone formation (Stewart and Hannan 2000; Rector et al. 2008).

Although formal guidelines have not been developed on how to prevent low bone mineral density (BMD) in cyclists, weight training, plyometrics, weight-bearing exercise, and whole-body vibration have been suggested to help maintain BMD (Mathis et al. 2013; Prioreschi et al. 2012). From a dietary perspective, low energy availability might be responsible for low BMD in cyclists (Viner et al. 2015), yet findings have been inconclusive. More research is needed.

One area in which cyclists can be proactive is with regard to calcium and vitamin D. Both play a critical role in bone formation (particularly through the age of 30) and maintenance of optimum bone health throughout the lifespan. Deficiencies are common; the prevalence of vitamin D deficiency is estimated at over 50 percent in athletes (Shuler et al. 2012). Factors contributing to deficiencies include low dietary intake; lack of adequate ultraviolet B exposure from the sun for vitamin D synthesis because of type of clothing worn, sunscreen use, or the latitude at which the cyclist lives and trains; calcium losses through sweat; and a decrease in absorption as a person ages.

Aside from their role in bone health, calcium and vitamin D are also important for their role in skeletal muscle contraction. Additionally, low levels of vitamin D have been correlated with muscle weakness, impaired injury recovery, increased inflammation, and poor immune system health, all of which can negatively affect long-term health for any type of cyclist (Close et al. 2013; Girgis et al. 2014; Larson-Meyer 2013).

Calcium and vitamin D recommendations for athletes range from 1,200 to 1,500 milligrams daily, and supplementation is recommended if needs cannot be met through food (Mountjoy et al. 2014). This is especially important for athletes with disordered eating, for females with irregular menstrual cycles, and for postmenopausal women with low estrogen levels (Burke 2009; Beals 2013). Table 15.5 provides a list of common food sources of calcium (U.S. Department of Agriculture 2015).

Optimizing vitamin D status in active people is an area of ongoing research. The RDA for vitamin D is 600 to 800 international units (IU) for adults. But groups such as the Endocrine Society recommend a daily intake between 1,500 and 5,000 IU if the person is unable to get sun exposure (Holick et al. 2011). Cyclists should routinely monitor vitamin D levels with regular blood work, but there is no consensus for what represents a deficiency in athletes. A level between 50 and 80 nanograms per milliliter is suggested for athletic peak performance (Shuler et al. 2012).

The most effective way to increase vitamin D is to have up to 30 minutes of UVB sun exposure. Duration of sun exposure varies depending on a number of factors, such as latitude, amount of skin exposed, and time of day (Vitamin D Council 2010). Good food sources of vitamin D include wild salmon, trout, ahi tuna, cod liver oil, and fortified milks and juices (Lu et al. 2007; National Institutes of Health 2014).

Table 15.5 Food Sources of Calcium

Source	Serving size	Calcium content (mg)
Beans, cooked	1/2 cup	50
Orange	1 medium	50
Almond butter, tahini	2 Tbsp	75
Tempeh	1/2 cup	75
Kale, turnip greens, cooked	1 cup	100
Broccoli, cooked	1/2 cup	100
Salmon, canned with bones	3 oz (90 g)	180
Blackstrap molasses	1 Tbsp	200
Collard greens, cooked	1/2 cup	200
Cheese	1.5 oz (45 g)	300
Non-dairy milks, fortified	8 oz (250 g)	300
Orange juice, fortified	8 oz (250 g)	300
Sardines, canned with bones	3 oz (90 g)	325
Yogurt, Greek or plain	6 oz (60 g)	150 to 300
Tofu, fortified	1/2 cup	200 to 300
Cow milk	8 oz (250 g)	275 to 300

Other Mineral Deficiencies

Daily nutrition patterns that are diverse and abundant in protein, vegetables, fruits, and whole grains should decrease the risk for mineral deficiencies. Yet for the cyclist who has restricted eating patterns, several food dislikes, or does not eat sufficient whole foods, a mineral deficiency can occur. Iron deficiency is a common concern, particularly for those who follow plant-based nutrition patterns and for menstruating women. Regular blood work is recommended, especially in the preseason, so that adjustments to food intake or supplementation can be implemented. A sports physician or sport dietitian can be consulted for recommended blood work and analysis.

Applying the Science

Sport nutrition has gone beyond the energy balance equation of counting calories in and calories out. Optimizing daily nutrition patterns must be a priority in setting the foundation for successful athletic performance, whatever the athletic ability or age of the cyclist. An emphasis on consuming a variety of whole foods and attending to nutrition periodization strategies helps to ensure that macronutrient and micronutrient needs are adequately met. Because each cyclist has unique health goals and athletic pursuits, individualized nutrition periodization strategies are also critical for meeting the physical demands of training for both short- and long-term success.

Individual dietary approaches are necessary for special circumstances, such as cyclists who have specific body-composition goals, those who desire enhanced fat adaptation, and those who are at risk for nutrient deficiencies. Because nutrition for the cyclist is no longer a one-size-fits-all approach, implementation, monitoring, and fine-tuning of the appropriate quantitative and qualitative strategies will facilitate longevity in the sport.

CHAPTER 16

Feeding During Cycling

—Dina Griffin

Nutrient timing principles for training and competition provide guidelines for preparing the body appropriately for cycling. These principles include consideration for the type, amount, and form of calories to consume during cycling. In addition, nutrient timing includes guidelines on the postexercise timeframe to restore the body with the nutrients necessary to optimize the recovery window and begin the riding cycle anew.

As explained in chapter 15, guidelines need to be adapted to the individual cyclist because numerous factors influence dietary needs and tolerances. Just as with daily nutrition patterns, the approach of a one-size-fits-all model for training and race nutrition strategies is gone. Additionally, cyclists who wish to experiment with fat adaptation can consider newer guidelines or blend some of the traditional nutrient timing guidelines, depending on nutrition knowledge and health and performance goals.

This chapter is divided into three main sections to present recommendations for before, during, and after cycling. Hydration guidelines are provided in chapter 17.

Nutrition Periodization and Nutrient Timing

Nutrition periodization for cyclists involves the planning of nutrition on a micro and macro level to meet short- and long-term health and performance goals (Seebohar 2011). Nutrition should be manipulated both daily and on a broader scale to meet the energy and nutrient demands imposed by different durations and cycling intensities within each training cycle. The process of timing nutrients before, during, and after cycling enables the body to perform optimally and recover well within an acute timeframe. Appropriate timing also promotes physiological adaptations to the stresses imposed as part of the training process.

Nutrition periodization and nutrient timing also must consider the role of individual tolerance. For example, each cyclist has unique gastrointestinal (GI) responses and preferred methods for consuming calories during cycling, both of which can affect the nutrition plan. Additionally, nutrient timing principles may be altered for cyclists who have higher carbohydrate needs compared with those who are more fat-adapted. Nutrient timing principles also will be unique for elite and more advanced cyclists compared with recreational and beginner cyclists.

Note that depending on the fat adaptation status of an athlete, the ability to use fat as an energy source more efficiently can affect the recommended fueling strategy. In the context of calories available to support training, the fat-adapted cyclist can more efficiently convert fat from the 30,000- to 80,000-calorie pool available in adipose tissue and intramuscular triglycerides (dependent on lean mass). In contrast, the carbohydrate-dependent (or "carb burner") type of cyclist relies more on the limited energy supply stored in muscle and liver glycogen, which ranges from 1,200 to 2,400 calories. This latter source can supply energy for exercise in the range of 60 to 90 minutes of moderate- to high-intensity exercise; the energy source from fat can potentially supply sufficient energy for a few days of low-intensity exercise. From a fueling perspective, depleting glycogen stores means that the cyclist will require greater amounts of exogenous (or supplemental) carbohydrate from foods or sport nutrition products. Cyclists can undergo a metabolic efficiency assessment in a reputable performance laboratory to learn their level of fat adaptation at various submaximal power outputs. This information can be used to manipulate dietary and exercise strategies to promote greater fat oxidation and assist the cyclist with training and competition fueling plans.

Cyclists who are training for a specific race or event should monitor their training nutrition successes and failures just as they monitor their physical training progress. Keeping a nutrition log for key workouts in which details such as the time of consumption and the type and amount of foods consumed, along with the type of workout intensity (or power data) and duration, is a useful tool for developing the race-day nutrition plan. An essential step is to simulate competition day a number of times 2 or 3 months before the actual race day. Cyclists should eat the foods they expect to consume on race day (before and during the event) while also training at the anticipated race effort. If possible, they should practice in the environmental conditions they expect to encounter on race day. All these simulations are important because of the blood-shunting response that occurs during exercise whereby blood flow is prioritized to the heart, peripheral working muscles, and skin while being diverted away from the GI tract (McArdle, Katch, and Katch 2009; van Wijck et al. 2012). With the diversion of blood flow from the GI tract, several changes occur in the stomach and intestinal lining that can affect food digestion and nutrient absorption. These physiological changes can lead to abdominal distress such as cramping, bloating, diarrhea, and ischemic colitis.

Heat stress and dehydration can further exacerbate GI distress. Simulating the race-day nutrition plan at goal-race effort can provide confidence that GI distress will not interfere with achieving optimal performance.

Feeding Before

Timing of nutrition before getting on the bike depends on factors such as time of day, hunger level, anticipated duration, and intensity of the ride. Cyclists must be mindful of individual GI tolerance. As such, food choices should be adjusted accordingly if the cyclist is sensitive to fiber, fat, or other allergens.

Training

For training rides that are mostly aerobic and less than 90 minutes long, consuming nutrition beforehand is not necessary. This knowledge can be useful to cyclists who want to do early morning workouts but do not have adequate time to prepare and consume a light meal beforehand. This understanding is also beneficial to cyclists who are simply not hungry and who plan a shorter, easier ride.

Fasted morning training sessions can be performed to enhance fat adaptation, but this method is more appropriate for lower-intensity training sessions. Additional consideration should be given to when the next training session is scheduled to ensure adequate time for glycogen restoration. More research is needed, but there is some indication of possible performance benefits when training is completed with low muscle glycogen stores (Hansen et al. 2005). This suggestion has sparked interest in modifying training protocols to include more fasted sessions or modifying carbohydrate intake between two training sessions to promote metabolic adaptations (Hulston et al. 2010; Marquet et al. 2016). The bottom line for the competitive athlete is not to compromise the quality of the training session, particularly in peak training cycles. For cyclists desiring weight loss, performing fasted aerobic workouts is not necessary. Recent research findings have shown that consuming a preworkout snack resulted in similar weight loss as having no snack preworkout so long as a caloric deficit was maintained (Schoenfeld et al. 2014).

For training rides that involve high-intensity work longer than 75 to 90 minutes or for endurance-oriented rides longer than 90 minutes, the recommendation for carbohydrate is 1 to 4 grams per kilogram of body weight in the 1 to 4 hours before exercise for high-carbohydrate consumers (Burke et al. 2011). For example, if a male cyclist who weighs 70 kilograms (154 lb) plans to start a training ride at 9:00 a.m. involving multiple sets at a high percentage at or above functional threshold power, he can consume a meal with 70 grams of carbohydrate by 8:00 a.m. To maintain a steady blood sugar level and to provide satiety, he should include a small amount of protein and fat in this meal. Protein or amino acids in the range of 6 to 20 grams can also be beneficial to minimize muscle catabolism for strenuous workouts. Cyclists should use whole foods when possible and save sport nutrition products for in-season when training demands are generally higher. Sample meals for the 70-kilogram male include the following:

- Smoothie made with a banana, 3/4 cup of berries, 20 grams of whey protein, and 8 ounces (250 g) of full-fat milk
- Two eggs with a large sweet potato and butter, one piece of fruit
- Two pieces of sprouted whole grain bread with almond butter and a banana
- 1 cup of cooked old-fashioned oats mixed with 3/4 cup of blueberries, 10 grams of protein powder, 2 tablespoons of chia seeds, and 1 tablespoon of maple syrup

Cyclists who are more fat adapted may find 0.5 grams per kilogram of body weight more in line with meeting their needs for preworkout carbohydrate. For the same 70-kilogram male cyclist who is fat adapted, a preworkout meal could consist of 35 grams of carbohydrate, which would be half the amount of the carbohydrate-containing foods in the previous examples. For many people, this quantity is more appealing because of the lower food volume and less potential for stomach discomfort.

A qualitative and visual representation for preride nutrition can resemble one of the following periodization food plates (figure 16.1) (Seebohar 2011):

Each wedge of the plate should be adjusted based on the type and duration of training session, the carbohydrate needs of the cyclist, and preferred food choices. Some experimentation will be necessary even with qualitative approaches to preride nutrition. Hence, the cyclist must collect feedback from training rides so that subsequent meals can be adjusted accordingly.

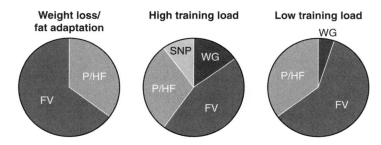

P/HF: Proteins and healthy fats
FV: Fruits and vegetables
WG: Whole grains
SNP: Sport nutrition products

▶ **Figure 16.1** Examples of periodization plates for preride nutrition.

Courtesy of Bob Seebohar.

Competition

For athletes competing in events lasting 90 to 120 minutes and who are considered more reliant on carbohydrate daily and during training, glycogen loading (or carbohydrate loading) is advised. This process results in saturation of internal muscle glycogen stores. This strategy for maximizing the capacity of muscle glycogen has been in existence for several decades, yet protocol continues to evolve. Current recommendations for supercompensating glycogen stores state that athletes should consume upward of 10 to 12 grams per kilogram of body weight in the 24 to 36 hours preceding an event that is 90 minutes long or longer (Burke et al. 2011; Bussau et al. 2002). This carbohydrate-loading strategy has replaced the 3-day loading protocol because it has been shown to be equally effective. As an example of what this loading looks like for a 70-kilogram (154 lb) cyclist, carbohydrate calories would be in the range of 2,800 to 3,360, not including any calories consumed from protein and fat. Because of this high carbohydrate intake, many athletes experience negative side effects such as bloating, stomach upset, and lethargy. To achieve this level of carbohydrate intake, athletes need to choose fewer nonstarchy vegetables (because these are lower in carbohydrate per serving) and more foods such as potatoes, rice, oats, bananas, or other grains and fruits. These foods will more easily provide high amounts of carbohydrate.

For cyclists who are fat-adapted, carbohydrate loading to the same degree may not be necessary, depending on the duration and intensity of the competition or event and what has been practiced in training. Some may see this as an advantage because they have less need to consume as many calories and have less risk for negative side effects.

When competition day arrives, cyclists need to have practiced their prerace meals and timeline sufficiently so that they are confident in their choice and combination of foods. Depending on the time of the competition and the cyclist's sleep schedule, two precompetition meals can be helpful to satisfy hunger and ensure that muscle and liver glycogen are adequately stored. The first meal can be consumed 3 to 4 hours in advance, even if it means waking up to eat and then returning to sleep. Guidelines for carbohydrate intake are identical to those listed previously for training. A second meal, 30 to 60 minutes before the event, can be consumed, depending on the length of the event, hunger level, and individual preference of the cyclist. Liquid meals or easily digestible foods that are low in fat and fiber may be better tolerated than solid foods the closer the meal is to the start of the event.

Feeding During

Current recommendations for calorie intake during cycling center on carbohydrate because this fuel source can be quickly broken down to be used for energy. Carbohydrate availability to the body has also been demonstrated to maximize performance. Remember that cycling intensity and individual fat adaptation status are two factors that influence fueling needs. For predominantly aerobic intensities, the fat-adapted cyclist needs fewer calories per hour than cyclists who are carbohydrate dependent (and therefore must have high carbohydrate availability). Note that most sport nutrition guidelines stem from research on trained or well-trained athletes, mostly male and of younger age (younger than 25 years old). Hence, recreational cyclists who ride at lower intensities may not need the same level of carbohydrate intake as elite and professional riders.

Generally, cycling durations in the range of 30 to 75 minutes with a mix of low to moderate intensity require little to no carbohydrate or other calorie sources, particularly for cyclists desiring weight loss. For more sustained high-intensity cycling of this duration, cyclists have the option to consume small amounts of carbohydrate (10 to 30 grams) or to perform a "mouth rinse." A mouth rinse involves holding a carbohydrate beverage in the mouth for 5 to 10 seconds and then spitting it out or doing sequential mouth rinses. Although the exact mechanism has yet to be elucidated, a neural response from carbohydrate receptors in the mouth seems to have an effect on certain areas of the brain. Analysis of several research studies shows a range of performance improvements from 2 to 11 percent by using this rinsing technique (de Ataide e Silva et al. 2014; Phillips et al. 2014; Sinclair et al. 2014). The act of spitting out a beverage may not seem practical or desirable, but this strategy can be useful for minimizing or avoiding GI distress during important high-intensity cycling.

The intestinal tract has limits to the amount of carbohydrate it can absorb per hour primarily because of gastric emptying rates. This circumstance is true regardless of the age, body weight, or gender of the cyclist. One strategy is to train the gut to tolerate high intakes of carbohydrate during cycling (in the range of 90 to 105 grams, or 360 to 420 calories) and to pair this with a daily diet high in carbohydrate (8 to 10 grams per kilogram of body weight) (Jeukendrup and McLaughlin 2011; Cox et al. 2010). Although this method has been shown to increase the rate of carbohydrate used during cycling, it is not clear that any significant performance difference occurs with a high daily carbohydrate diet compared with a moderate carbohydrate diet. Concern arises about the effect on health (as it relates to body weight or health markers associated with chronic disease) and whether training the gut to yield performance benefits is necessary, particularly for those who are susceptible to GI distress. This concern should be evaluated individually and adjusted based on training feedback and health goals.

Along with limitations to carbohydrate amounts that the gut can process, evidence also indicates that the source and composition of the carbohydrate influence the rate of nutrient uptake in the GI system (Jeukendrup 2010). Common carbohydrate sources include glucose, fructose, sucrose (which consists of glucose and fructose), and maltodextrin. For shorter-duration exercise (in the range of 30 minutes to 2 1/2 hours), single carbohydrate sources such as glucose can be absorbed at rates up to 60 grams (240 calories) per hour. Cyclists should not rely exclusively on fructose as a primary carbohydrate source because of its unique metabolic pathway and decreased absorption rate compared with sugars such as glucose (Goran, Tappy, and Lê 2014; Sun and Empie 2012). When combined with glucose, however, fructose is more rapidly absorbed and may be better tolerated. For more prolonged exercise (over 2 1/2 to 3 hours long), multiple transportable carbohydrate sources such as combinations of glucose and fructose or maltodextrin and fructose can be absorbed at rates up to 90 grams (360 calories) per hour (Jeukendrup 2014). Again, consideration must be given to the training status of the cyclist in addition to the specific type of training session performed. For less-trained cyclists or those performing lower-intensity riding, the 60- to 90-gram recommendation for carbohydrate intake may need to be decreased.

Cyclists can choose from a wide selection of carbohydrate foods, but the choice depends on the aforementioned factors of cycling duration, intensity, individual calorie needs, and personal gut tolerance. Carbohydrate can be solid, semisolid, or liquid and can include packaged sport nutrition products or homemade whole-food-based nutrition. Examples include the following:

- Bananas, fruit strips, or dried fruits such as dates and mango slices
- Sandwiches or tortilla roll-ups with nut butter and jam or ham and cheese
- Rice-based cakes with egg and bacon or nuts and dried fruit
- Energy bars
- Potatoes
- Energy gels, blocks, chews, or beans
- High- or low-molecular-weight starch powders

During ultraevents such as 24-hour rides, endurance cycling, or recreational multiday rides, solid mixed macronutrient foods such as sandwiches and burritos can be tolerated well. Protein or amino acid intake can minimize muscle catabolism and facilitate muscle protein synthesis in the postride window (van Loon 2014). Fat intake is not necessary but can be included based on the gut tolerance of the cyclist.

In contrast, cyclists participating in events of shorter duration and higher intensity will rely on carbohydrate-dense and easily digested sources such as energy gels and chews. Remember that because of changes in the stomach and gut during exercise, a number of factors such as the type, osmolality, and concentration of carbohydrate can affect the digestibility of food and fluids introduced during exercise. These factors can also cause dehydration and GI distress. Although the incidence of GI distress tends to occur more in sports such as running, cyclists are not immune to this potential disruptor of performance (Pfeiffer et al. 2012). This insight may further influence some cyclists to pursue improving their fat adaptation level to decrease reliance on a high amount of carbohydrate calories to sustain moderate-intensity effort. In practical terms, the cyclist will not have to transport as much food weight and will be less concerned with the effort and logistics of eating while cycling.

As previously stated, cyclists must experiment to learn what works best for them at different riding intensities and scenarios. For example, recreational off-road cyclists may not mind stopping to eat whole foods such as sandwiches, whereas competitive road cyclists need easy and accessible calorie sources. In prolonged endurance events, some cyclists experience flavor fatigue, which can result in a sudden dislike of a particular flavor or sweetness level of a calorie source. Decreased calorie consumption can result, which can certainly affect the ability to sustain power and will negatively affect performance. In these situations, having a backup nutrition plan is ideal, including either different flavors (i.e., savory and sweet) or alternative forms of the calorie source (i.e., a mix of semisolid foods and solid foods).

Another consideration for feeding during cycling concerns the weather. In cold or freezing weather, fluids and some foods can become frozen or too difficult to chew. In contrast, hot conditions can affect the palatability of certain foods. Additionally, melting can cause foods either to fall apart or to become too messy to consume. A summary of fueling recommendations and options based on cycling duration and intensity is presented in table 16.1.

Table 16.1 Recommendation Summary for Intake During Cycling

Cycling duration	Intensity	Fueling options	Notes
30 to 75 min	Low to moderate	• Nothing • Mouth rinse of carbohydrate drink for 5 to 10 s	
45 to 90 min	Sustained moderate to high	• Nothing • Small amount of carbohydrate (10 to 30 g) • Mouth rinse of carbohydrate drink for 5 to 10 s	
1 to 2.5 h	Varying	• 30 to 60 g of carbohydrate • Single or multiple transportable carbohydrate sources	Individual variance depending on cycling intensity, training status, fat adaptation level, and gut tolerance
More than 2.5 h	Varying	• 30 to 90 g of carbohydrate • Multiple transportable carbohydrate sources recommended • Mixed macronutrient foods to satisfy hunger and provide satiety • For ultraendurance events longer than 5 h, small amounts of protein or amino acids	

Feeding After

Nutrition in the postexercise window is commonly referred to as recovery nutrition. The nutrition choices made in the recovery window affect how well skeletal muscles can adapt to the stressors imposed during training and competition, the rate of muscle protein synthesis, and glycogen replenishment within the muscles. Yet recovery nutrition is not a one-size-fits-all approach. Note as well that what is consumed before a training session affects the recovery process, so recovery nutrition is not exclusive to the postworkout window.

The recovery nutrition protocol varies with factors such as duration and intensity of cycling completed, timing of subsequent training sessions, weight-loss goals, and fat adaptation status.

Glycogen restoration is a goal common to most recovery nutrition recommendations. This outcome is particularly important for those engaged in high-volume or high-intensity training blocks, for those who have multiple training sessions within a single day, and for athletes aiming to maintain a high level of carbohydrate availability (rather than implementing strategies to induce fat adaptation). Quantitative and qualitative guidelines to promote rapid and adequate recovery that is specific to various scenarios follow.

For recreational cyclists who have no formal training structure and participate in single daily rides, recovery nutrition can be in the form of actual meals. Particularly for those desiring weight loss, one strategy is to time the ride around a meal so that no extra calorie consumption is needed to support or recover from the cycling bout. For rides 30 minutes to 2 hours long that are mostly aerobic, the composition of the recovery meal can be qualitatively shown in one of the periodization plates shown in figure 16.2 (Seebohar 2011):

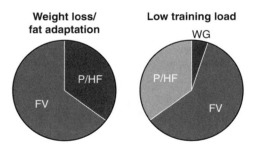

P/HF: Proteins and healthy fats
FV: Fruits and vegetables
WG: Whole grains

▶ **Figure 16.2** Example of a recovery nutrition periodization plate for cyclists desiring weight loss, seeking fat adaptation, or completing an aerobic ride of 2 hours or less.

Courtesy of Bob Seebohar.

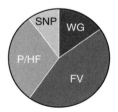

P/HF: Proteins and healthy fats
FV: Fruits and vegetables
WG: Whole grains
SNP: Sport nutrition products

▶ **Figure 16.3** Example of a recovery nutrition periodization plate for cyclists in a high-volume or high-intensity training block.

Courtesy of Bob Seebohar.

If the duration between cycling bouts is adequate (16 to 24 hours), a post-workout recovery meal is not necessary. Protein intake at the scheduled meal should be based on hunger levels but be in the 15- to 30-gram range. Carbohydrate amounts do not need to be excessive. For supporting optimal health, the postworkout meal is an opportunity to consume a mix of fiber-rich vegetables, fruits, and whole grains that will stabilize blood sugar, provide nutrient-dense foods, and offer more satiety because of a larger food volume. Notice that sport nutrition products are not necessary, because whole foods can adequately supply needed calories and nutrients.

For cyclists in the build or peak training cycles with high volume or high intensity or those who have two daily training sessions (which may include strength or resistance training) with less than 8 hours between sessions, recommendations for the recovery meal include a carbohydrate range of 1 to 1.2 grams per kilogram of body weight for 4 to 6 hours following exercise combined with 15 to 30 grams of protein (or 10 grams of essential amino acids) in the 2 hours after exercise (Burke et al. 2011; Thomas, Erdman, and Burke 2016). The periodization food plate may resemble figure 16.3.

The combination of carbohydrate and protein serves the double purpose of supporting muscle protein synthesis and glycogen repletion. For masters-level athletes, evidence suggests that 35 to 40 grams of protein (or 0.4 grams per kilogram of body weight) is more effective for muscle protein synthesis because of age-related anabolic resistance or impaired ability to repair muscle tissue (Doering et al. 2016). Some optimal carbohydrate and protein food choices are listed in chapter 15. Studies show that leucine, a branched-chain amino acid, is effective in muscle protein synthesis (Doering et al. 2016; Morton, McGlory, and Phillips 2015; Phillips 2014). Leucine-rich food sources include whey protein, cow's milk, yogurt, beef, chicken, eggs, and soymilk. Cyclists who practice a vegetarian or vegan lifestyle may need to supplement with amino acids or a plant-based protein powder to obtain an adequate amount of essential amino acids.

For female cyclists, evidence suggests that the luteal phase of the menstrual cycle (from ovulation to menstruation, which is classically defined as day 14 to day 28 of the cycle) is somewhat catabolic because of elevated progesterone levels and that estrogen can negatively affect access to glycogen stores (Hausswirth and Le Meur 2011). Muscle protein breakdown may therefore occur more in the high hormone phase and female cyclists may not be as able to perform higher-intensity exercise. Although more research is needed on female athletes and the role of the menstrual cycle on performance and recovery, some research suggests a need for increased leucine intake on days involving prolonged or double training sessions during the luteal phase (Beals 2013). Additionally, adherence to the 1-hour recovery window for proper refueling is essential for competitive female cyclists just as it is for male cyclists.

Elite competitive cyclists and cyclists who engage in stage racing have unique recovery nutrition challenges because of heavy training volume and frequent shortened nutrition windows during which to refuel. With stage racing comes the added concern of significant energy expenditure over multiple days. Combined with cumulative fatigue and energy deficits, a progressive detrimental effect on performance can occur. By having nutrient- and calorie-dense foods and liquids available, even if relying on packaged items or sport nutrition products, these cyclists can refuel rapidly, thus mitigating the potential negative effects on performance.

Applying the Science

Nutrition before, during, and after cycling varies between cyclists just as the daily nutrition patterns do. Nutrient timing and nutrition periodization principles that consider the cyclist's physical training demands and the unique health and training goals within each training cycle are key components for adequate fueling and recovery. Depending on goals such as improving body composition and enhancing fat adaptation level, cyclists can manipulate both daily and training nutrition choices to effect positive change. Although sport nutrition guidelines continue to evolve with new research findings, cyclists must engage in self-experimentation to find what formula works best to enhance their own performance and recovery, as well as support their health goals over the lifecycle.

CHAPTER 17

Hydration Science

—Stacy T. Sims

Should cyclists have a strategic drinking plan for training and competing, or should they just drink to thirst? What should cyclists drink, and how do those choices affect blood volume? Hydration is a complex topic, with even more complex physiology. In this carb-centric society, the emphasis in sport nutrition has been on carbohydrate availability in fluid form, but this focus neglects the true meaning of hydration.

What is Hydration? The Physiology of Fluid Absorption

A throw-down is happening in the sport science world. In one corner is the current dogma that "The goal of drinking during exercise is to prevent excessive dehydration (less than 2 percent body-weight loss from water deficit) and excessive changes in electrolyte balance to avert compromised performance" (Sawka et al. 2007). The challengers are Dr. Timothy Noakes and the Exercise-Associated Hyponatremia (EAH) Consensus Panel, who recommend that you "Drink to thirst, no matter how much weight you lose" (Hew-Butler et al. 2015; Noakes 2012). Both groups are trying to determine what is appropriate for performance and health, but the answer might be somewhere in the middle.

> **hy·dra·tion n.**
> 1. The addition of water to a chemical molecule without hydrolysis.
> 2. The process of providing an adequate amount of liquid to bodily tissues.

Open any exercise physiology textbook and you will find that the first factor of importance to fatigue is a drop in blood volume with its associated hormonal responses. The second, less impressive, factor is decreased carbohydrate availability. Why? Simplistically, you can fix low circulating carbohydrate effectively by eating something. You will feel the effects within minutes. A drop in blood volume is more complex, taking hours to rectify and involving a series of hormonal and electrochemical gradient feedback mechanisms.

Blood volume is a combination of the red blood cells and plasma in circulation. When discussing exercise and fluid shifts, the term *plasma volume* is often used, because this refers to the watery component of blood. As you continue exercising, a competition exists as the muscles and skin fight for circulating blood. Blood goes to the muscles for metabolic function. Blood goes to the skin to get rid of the heat produced by the working muscles. As body water drops, this competition becomes fiercer. As exercise continues and plasma volume falls through sweating, breathing, and gastrointestinal water usage, available circulating blood diminishes; the blood contains less overall water, so it is "thicker."

This redistribution cannot continue indefinitely because the demands of exercise and thermoregulation will exceed the ability of the cardiovascular system to meet those demands. Ultimately, blood distribution to the skin will decrease in favor of delivery to the exercising muscles, increasing thermal stress and eventually risking heat illness. When the body reaches this point, it becomes unable to maintain the status quo against the rising temperature of the muscles and overall core temperature. These temperature points usually signal the body to cease exercise. The first aspect of fatigue is the tipping point of muscle temperature over 102 degrees Fahrenheit (38.9 degrees Celsius), at which point the contractile proteins start to break down physically. The second point is core temperature reaching 104 to 105.8 degrees Fahrenheit (40 to 41 degrees Celsius), signaling changes to the central nervous system to slow down or cease exercise. Note here that it is not just the core temperature that dictates performance impairment but the overall thermal stress and decreased blood availability. The most trying situation for the body is the combination of hot skin, low body water, and elevated core temperature. During exercise, the most stressful physiological burden is support of high skin blood flow made worse by exercising in the heat. Skin temperature is affected more by ambient temperature; core temperature is affected by exercise intensity and is largely independent from environmental factors when heat can be offloaded effectively through the body's thermoregulatory system. With hot skin, less cooling is available to return to the body, and low body water affects blood volume, reducing sweat capacity and the body's ability to offload heat. This situation will increase heat stress and heat storage, and thus increase physiologic strain (Gagge, Stolwijk, and Hardy 1967; Sawka, Cheuvront, and Kenefick 2012). The point of contention, however, is the percentage of body mass loss where performance decline occurs.

Thermoregulation and Body Fluids

Besides vasodilation, evaporative heat loss through sweating is the other primary defense against heat storage in the body. The loss of body fluids through sweating leads to dehydration, threatening fluid balance and further challenging blood redistribution to the muscles and skin (Armstrong and Maresh 1998). Physical activity increases total metabolic rate to provide energy for skeletal muscle contraction, and 70 to almost 100 percent of this metabolically generated heat needs to be dissipated. Depending on environmental humidity and temperature, the hotter the environment is, the greater the dependence is on evaporative heat loss through sweating (Sawka et al. 1989). A reduction of the central circulating blood volume because of either reduced blood volume (hypovolemia) from the loss of water or the dilation of the peripheral blood vessels results in a decline in the cardiac filling pressure and stroke volume. If left uncompensated, cardiac output will be compromised.

Hypohydration—the sustained state of low fluid balance—inhibits thermoregulatory responses to heat stress, and both hypovolemia and plasma hyperosmolality (increased electrolyte concentration) impairs thermoregulatory responses such as vasodilation and sweating (Cheuvront and Kenefick 2014). At the onset of acute heat stress, even before any reduction in total body water through sweating, shifts in body fluid occur between the bloodstream and the surrounding tissue spaces because of blood pressure changes (figure 17.1). With sweating, a reduction of total body water occurs in particular if adequate amounts of fluid are not consumed. Hypohydration affects the water content in each of the compartments. The initial body

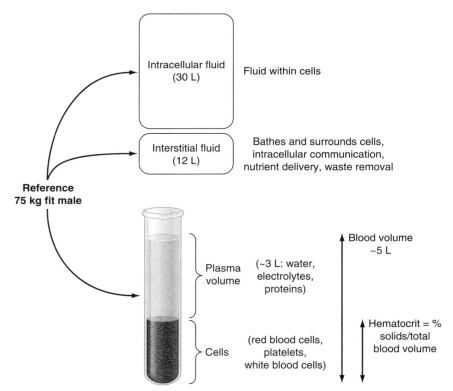

▶ **Figure 17.1** Schematic of typical body fluid compartments.

Reprinted, by permission, from S. S. Cheung, 2010, Advanced environmental exercise physiology (Champaign: Human Kinetics), 51.

water loss mostly comes from blood volume and the fluid between the cells. But as body water loss increases, a proportionately greater percentage of water deficit comes from within the cells themselves (Costill, Cote, and Fink 1976). Water appears to be lost from the plasma at a rate one to five times that of other fluid compartments, and relatively greater plasma water loss is accompanied by sodium ions lost through sweat and urine Nose and colleagues (1988) investigated the relationship between sodium [Na^+] in sweat and the distribution of body water during dehydrating exercise. A linear relationship exists between the change in extracellular fluid and the change in plasma volume, indicating that the increase in plasma concentration is what shifts fluid from the intracellular to the extracellular compartments to maintain plasma volume.

The amounts of electrolytes lost in sweat typically decline as a person acclimates to the heat because the sodium and chloride usually lost in sweat come from the extracellular compartment. A study reports that, over the course of heat acclimation, the sweat sodium concentration decreases by about 59 percent, despite an increase of sweat rate by 12 percent (Kirby and Convertino 1986). Hence, for a given sweat rate in heat-acclimated people, the solute lost from the plasma is significantly reduced, allowing a greater shift of fluid from the intracellular to the extracellular compartments, which lessens the loss of blood volume compared with unacclimated people.

Historically, dehydration has been extolled as the limiting factor to both the anaerobic and aerobic components of exercise. The longstanding view has been that critical levels of water deficit exist at which exercise performance is impaired. Early studies indicated that small (2 percent) to moderate (4 percent) body mass loss affects oxygen uptake (Sawka 1992) as well as heart rate and core temperature (Montain and Coyle 1992) in a hot environment. The traditional thinking was that the primary factor of fatigue was caused by a drop in body water, critical for thermoregulation and muscle blood flow, but hypohydration can increase several forms of physiological stress during physical activity, including metabolic (glycogen depletion), thermal, oxidative, and immune. Further, lab studies reduce the vast role of psychological and physiological behavior because of the tightly controlled study environments. We know that increased psychophysical strain is directly proportional to increased physiological strain, which, in turn, drives behavior (Tucker 2009).

To examine the prevailing theory that the interaction of skin temperature, core temperature, and hypohydration has adverse effects on exercise performance, several investigators examined the effect of high skin temperature versus high core temperature with and without dehydration on exercise performance. Cheuvront et al. (2005) tested the effect of hypohydration on aerobic performance using a protocol of 30 minutes of exercise at about 50 percent $\dot{V}O_{2peak}$ followed by a 30-minute time trial in temperate and cold environments. A small 3 percent body mass loss (5 percent body water loss) impaired performance by 8 percent in the temperate environment (T_{sk} about 29 degrees Celsius) but not in the cold environment (T_{sk} about 20 degrees

Celsius). Castellani et al. (2010) employed a similar protocol of a preload exercise at a set intensity followed by a time trial, using a T_{sk} of about 32 degrees Celsius in both hypohydration and euhydration trials. With warm skin, a 4 percent body mass loss impaired performance by 18 percent as compared with the warm skin with euhydration, and no significant differences were found in core temperature across trials. Kenefick et al. (2010) further tested the interaction between environmental conditions and hypohydration by having participants cycle for 30 minutes (at 50 percent of $\dot{V}O_{2peak}$) and then perform a 15-minute time trial in 10-, 20-, 30- and 40-degree Celsius environments (inducing stepwise increases in T_{sk} from 26 to 36 degrees Celsius) when euhydrated and when hypohydrated by 4 percent body mass. Core temperature did not differ across the hypo- and euhydration trials; hypohydration impaired aerobic performance by 12 and 23 percent when T_{sk} was 33 and 36 degrees Celsius, respectively. Collectively, these studies demonstrated that hypohydration degrades aerobic performance to a greater extent with increasing heat stress, yet note that none of these studies considered the factors differentiating the effects of hypohydration in a lab versus autonomous outdoor exercise, factors such as thirst and drive to drink, training status, airflow speed, blinding to hydration status, familiarization to the stress of the experimental trials, exercise pacing, and motivation to perform.

Thirst plays a significant role in fluid balance (because it is one of the key psychological factors to replace lost fluid) and can influence motivation as well as performance outcomes. For example, thirst can trigger decreased exercise intensity to prevent further fluid loss. In studies of dehydration, water is deliberately withheld to induce hypohydration, but when exercise-induced body mass loss to 2 to 3 percent is achieved voluntarily by drinking ad libitum, no measureable effect on exercise performance has been determined in trained people (Goulet 2011). When using realistic airflow in temperate conditions with ad libitum drinking, no effects of 2.5 percent hypohydration were found in trained cyclists over an 80-minute exercise trial, whereas indications of greater thermal strain and performance power decline was found in untrained cyclists (Merry, Ainslie, and Cotter 2010). Moreover, Mora-Rodriguez and colleagues (2013) determined that fluid ingestion reduced thermal and cardiovascular strain in unacclimated and trained cyclists, but not untrained cyclists, during moderate exercise in the heat.

Cheung and colleagues (2015) conducted a seminal study to determine the effects of thirst and dehydration on cycling performance in the heat. Participants were trained and acclimated to exercise in the heat and familiarized to the experimental sessions to reduce confounding psychological variables. The study employed either blinded sham or real IV infusion for hydration control and simultaneous thirst manipulation through the use of water mouth rise or no rinse. This design allowed four conditions to be tested: dehydrated with and without thirst sensation and euhydrated with and without thirst sensation. The participants had no clues to their actual hydration status because of the IV blinding. The final outcomes indicated that greater thermal strain occurred in the dehydrated conditions during the 20K self-paced time trial, but no performance metric (power output, 20K TT completion times, pacing profiles) was affected by either moderate dehydration (greater than 2 to 3 percent body mass loss) or thirst.

Recent research has indicated that in trained people, mild to moderate hypohydration (greater than 3 percent body mass loss) has minimal to no effect on exercise performance. Furthermore, cardiovascular strain and thermal strain are not significantly affected. Moreover, trained athletes have consistently been found to tolerate hypohydration of greater than 6 percent during competitive exercise without succumbing to heat illness or other ill effect (Beis et al. 2012). In untrained people, however, mild to moderate hypohydration does have an effect on exercise performance (Mora-Rodriguez et al. 2013), although psychological aspects of self-pacing, thirst sensation, discomfort of exercise, and heat may play a significant role in motivation. Additional research should be done to examine the effects of greater dehydration (greater than 5 percent body mass loss) on fluid balance hormones, sex differences, pacing, and autonomous outdoor exercise performance to determine the true effect of fluid intake on realistic performance measures.

Blood Volume and Fluid Absorption

What effect does the drop in blood volume have on nutrient uptake? Plenty. The intestine is the primary organ for absorption of fluids, nutrients, and electrolytes. During prolonged exercise that increases core temperature, blood flow to the gastrointestinal system may be reduced by up to 80 percent to provide sufficient blood to the working muscles and skin. As core temperature approaches 39 degrees Celsius, the intestinal temperature may be as high as 41 degrees Celsius, leading to cell damage. In addition, the shunting of blood away from the intestine causes ischemia and oxidative damage. Both results can compromise the integrity of the intestinal tract, from large-action motility to the small action of epithelial cell tight junction permeability (i.e., the seal between the intestinal cells becomes "looser"). The disruption to the tight junction proteins, the usual matrix that regulates molecules passing from one side of the intestinal cell to the other, results in increased release of luminal endotoxins (intestinal bacteria) into the blood stream. These endotoxins increase systemic immune response, inflammation, and oxidation, and perpetuate gastrointestinal dysfunction.

Endurance athletes should be concerned with how to mitigate this drop in blood volume and reduced blood flow to the gastrointestinal system. What cyclists eat and drink plays a critical part in overall performance by delaying fatigue or maintaining power because of the effects of food and fluid on fluid dynamics.

Several main factors affect fluid absorption:

- The composition of what is being drunk, such as osmolality, carbohydrate choices, and sodium content

- Gastric emptying, or how fast a solution exits the stomach and enters the small intestine
- Hypo- versus hyperosmotic changes in the intestinal lumen
- Cotransport mechanisms

Let's look at the key factors needed to pull fluid into the body's fluid spaces. Ninety-five percent of all fluid absorption occurs in the small intestine, and this organ is particular to osmotic and electrochemical gradients. Moreover, at the start of exercise, 60 to 80 percent of the blood is diverted away from the gut to meet the demands of the muscle and skin for blood. With this, the athlete needs to drink something that works with his or her physiology.

The normal osmolality of the intestinal lumen of a fasted individual sits between 270 and 290 milliosmols per kilogram, or isotonic with respect to blood. When food or fluid is consumed, the osmolality changes in accordance to the rate at which the nutrients are emptied from the stomach into the small intestine. But the proximal small intestine (duodenum and upper jejunum) are particular to osmotic and electrochemical gradients; thus, returning to isotonicity becomes the priority. The time it takes to achieve isotonicity varies with what has been consumed, and thus the composition of the solution is critical for rapid fluid absorption.

Hypertonic solutions (i.e., solutions with an osmolality greater than 290 milliosmols per kilogram) cause a net movement of water from circulation into the intestinal lumen to dilute the contents. The greater the initial osmolality is, the greater the rate of water efflux is because of the greater osmotic gradient between the contents of the lumen and the intestinal cells. Moreover, the time lapse for achieving isotonicity increases the contact time of the solution with the intestinal walls, rendering hyperosmotic solutions (solutions that increase the osmotic pressure [e.g., carbohydrate-rich sports drinks]) ineffective in promoting hydration.

To complicate the issue further, plain water is associated with a poor rate of water absorption, primarily because of the outward flow of sodium down electrochemical gradients, pulling both water and sodium into the lumen.

Studies have shown that solutions containing carbohydrate and sodium, but maintaining an osmolality less than 200 milliosmols per kilogram, achieve slower rates of water absorption than solutions of an osmolality between 200 and 260 milliosmols per kilogram (Hunt et al. 1992; Shi et al. 1994). Although this range of osmolality is tight, even the smallest differences can have significant effects on fluid absorption. For example, the comparison of three solutions composed of glucose and sodium but with different osmolalities illustrates this point succinctly.

A hypotonic solution (229 milliosmols per kilogram) produced twice as rapid net water absorption into the bloodstream compared with the isotonic (277 milliosmols per kilogram) solution and significantly less water absorption compared with the hypertonic (352 milliosmols per kilogram) solution. Moreover, an increased rate of glucose absorption is associated with the faster water absorption rates of the hypotonic solution, but there is no difference of solute absorption was seen between the isotonic and hypertonic solutions (Gisolfi et al. 1995). Further studies tested the effect of osmolality on fluid absorption. Trends for faster fluid absorption and directionally greater relative plasma volume were observed in solutions of lower osmolality for the same absolute carbohydrate content or lower carbohydrate (2 versus 6 percent) (Rogers, Summer, and Lambert 2005), respectively.

When we examine the carbohydrate used in solutions, points of contention are apparent. The sodium–glucose cotransport mechanism is critical for both fluid and glucose absorption across the cell membranes, and these are interlinked rather than separate pathways. Glucose is absorbed by the small intestine using an active process. Initially, the glucose and fluid exit the intestinal lumen through the sodium–glucose cotransporter protein and are facilitated through an additional protein "gate" of GLUT-2. With the glucose, water and sodium also enter the blood, contributing to blood volume. When fructose and glucose are ingested in combination (either as fructose plus glucose, or as sucrose), the mean oxidized amount of the mixed sugars is about 66 percent, as opposed to fructose at 29 percent (women) to 45 percent (men) and glucose at 58 percent.

But the actual absorption rate of the sugars is the contention here. Glucose is absorbed from the intestine into the plasma by more than one active glucose cotransporter protein, reducing the contact time with the gut lumen. Fructose, however, is less efficient and slower to be absorbed because of less active transport mechanisms, leading to increased contact time with the gut lumen. Why is contact time significant? With incomplete and slow absorption, fructose produces a hyperosmolar environment in the intestines. What this means is that there is more solute than water, causing increased osmotic pressure. This, in turn, signals fluid to be drawn into the intestines, producing the common feelings of bloating, gas, diarrhea, and general gastrointestinal discomfort.

Maltodextrin, a polysaccharide with the building blocks of glucose, is used in many sports drinks instead of straight glucose for several reasons. The primary rationale is that maltodextrin does not affect osmolality as significantly as glucose, fructose, or dextrose does. Because maltodextrin is a long chain of glucose molecules, it doesn't add as much to the number of solutes in a solution; thus, a solution can contain quite a bit of maltodextrin and still have a faster gastric emptying rate. From a carbohydrate availability standpoint, this attribute is appealing, because glucose molecules are absorbed through the several glucose cotransporter proteins. Here is the caveat. Although a maltodextrin solution can be hypotonic—which, in theory, should promote water absorption—the hydrolysis of maltodextrin elevates luminal osmolality, creating the same hyperosmolar environment in the intestines as fructose and slowing the rate of water absorption.

A single beverage suitable for all environmental and race conditions probably does not exist. To maximize water absorption, consideration should be given to beverages formulated with glucose and sucrose to enhance fluid uptake by cotransport mechanisms but in concentrations of 2 to 4 percent to reduce osmolality and with sodium to reduce sodium secretion in the duodenum, which serves to attenuate the osmotic flow of water from the blood into the intestinal lumen.

Exercise-Associated Hyponatremia and Sex Differences

Sodium is critical to maintaining extracellular fluid volume. When sweating takes place without fluid replacement, total body water is reduced from each fluid compartment because of the free exchange of water between compartments. A concomitant loss of electrolytes, primarily sodium, occurs. When plasma volume loss occurs because of a loss of total body water, the kidneys act to retain sodium and water to restore total extracellular fluid volume (ECFV). Sodium and other electrolytes do not act as effective vascular osmotic agents because they freely diffuse across capillary endothelium, so changes in sodium content are related to the changes in total ECFV (Harrison 1985). Therefore, the balance of sodium in the body is crucial to maintaining extracellular fluid volume. Commercially available sports drinks typically contain 20 to 40 millimoles per liter Na^+, 3 to 15 millimoles per liter K^+ and 6 percent CHO, which research has shown to be less than adequate for sodium restoration during dehydration from prolonged exercise or heat stress (Vrijens and Rehrer 1999).

Sustained, excessive intake of water, sports drinks, or other fluids can exceed the body's ability to eliminate fluids in the form of sweat and urine. The excess fluid dilutes the body's sodium level, interfering with normal regulatory processes.

▶ A hydration plan should be individualized to the athlete.

Stephen S. Cheung

Exercise-associated hyponatremia (EAH), sometimes called water intoxication, refers to reductions in the body's sodium level during or up to 24 hours after physical activity. Hyponatraemia occurs from a dilution of the extracellular fluid (ECF) with or without an excess of body water volume.

Women are at greater risk for exercise-induced hyponatremia (low blood sodium concentration). This risk has been attributed to their lower body weight and size, excess water ingestion, and longer racing times relative to men. Although these factors contribute to the greater incidence of hyponatremia in women, their greater levels of estradiol in plasma and tissue also likely play a role in increasing the risk of hyponatremia in women. The basic physiology of sodium and fluid dynamics is well understood, but plasma volume in women is highly influenced by estrogen and progesterone. Estrogen and progesterone can have profound effects on fluid dynamics, in particular the Starling forces (pressures exerted from fluids and proteins) that regulate fluid movement between the vascular and interstitial spaces altering plasma volume (Marsh and Jenkins 2002).

The hormonal influences of the menstrual cycle affect fluid dynamics by altering capillary permeability, vasomotor function, and the central set-point control of renal hormones and plasma osmolality The elevations in plasma progesterone concentrations during the luteal phase inhibit aldosterone-dependent sodium reabsorption at the kidneys because progesterone competes with aldosterone for the mineralocorticoid receptor. Stachenfeld et al. (1999) have observed that the mean concentrations of aldosterone and plasma renin activity (PRA) are greater in the midluteal phase than in the follicular phase. Thus, with the inhibition of aldosterone-dependent sodium reabsorption, a transient increase in sodium excretion ensues. This is followed by a stimulation of the renin–angiotensin–aldosterone system (RAAS) to induce slight attenuation of sodium excretion during the luteal phase. This competition, however, results in little if any overall water retention but does induce fluid shifts away from the plasma. Therefore, despite the stimulation of the RAAS during the luteal phase, plasma volume is at its lowest point midluteal.

The observed drop in plasma volume may also be attributed to the effects of estrogen on fluid dynamics across the capillary walls, characterized by vasodilation and increased capillary permeability, causing net fluid shifts out of the plasma (Oian et al. 1987). Further, a lowering of the osmotic operating point for body fluid regulation with high estrogen levels occurs, such as those found just before ovulation and again during the luteal phase of the menstrual cycle. The administration of estrogen has been shown to modulate the osmotic regulation of arginine vasopressin (AVP) and thirst, which is characterized by a shift in body water regulation to a lower plasma osmolality (P_{osm}) operating point. Thus, a higher plasma concentration of AVP for any given P_{osm} is observed, a result of a central action of estrogen. High plasma concentrations of AVP will decrease ECFV by decreasing renal free water clearance at rest and during exercise.

With these hormonal influences and physiologic perturbations in fluid balance, the signal for thirst—driven by plasma osmolality and to some extent volume with the transient hypovolemia—is dampened; the set point of osmolality is lower, and women are hypovolemic as compared with the low hormone phase. Thirst sensitivity is lessened as a physiological construct (otherwise women would go crazy with the drive to drink in the high hormone phase), yet women are closer to the clinical definition of hyponatremia in the luteal phase because of the aforementioned physiological changes.

Applying the Science

The complexity of the body extends well into the aspect of hydration and the maintenance of body fluids for health and performance. Myriad intricate responses, from cellular mechanisms to sex differences, further complicate scientific research, as does the environment in which the research is conducted. The recommendations for drinking on a schedule or drinking to thirst should be individualized, not generalized. Nevertheless, some simple categorizations of people may help guide hydration strategies:

Drink to Thirst

- If the athlete has prehydrated before the training session, drinking to thirst is warranted. Otherwise, hypohydration can predispose the athlete to tissue injury (e.g., rhabdomyolysis), decreased motivation during the session, and poor recovery (adaptations, sleep, rehydration).
- The athlete is heat acclimated for hot training or games, races, and events.
- The athlete is trained (e.g., after significant time off with lower fitness levels, hypohydration and exercise stress can exacerbate thermal strain and decrease performance metrics).
- A female athlete is in the luteal phase of her menstrual cycle or on the progestin-only minipill.
- The athlete has a history of EAH or has syndrome of inappropriate antidiuretic hormone secretion (SIADH).

Drink on a Schedule

- Do not exceed 800 milliliters per hour in a temperate environment. Smaller people need less; larger need more. In the heat, more fluid may be needed.
- The athlete is a junior athlete (i.e., has not gone through puberty).
- The athlete has two or more heavy training sessions per day (to avoid systemic dehydration).
- The athlete is unacclimated and training at altitude.
- The athlete has a history of heat illness.

CHAPTER 18

Doping's Dark Past and a New Cycling Era

—Mikel Zabala

Humans have been trying to reach higher levels of physical performance since prehistory, driven by the need to hunt animals for survival. Doping likely started with the ingestion of herbs that decreased fatigue. It is said that for some rituals an African tribe called *Kaffir* used a stimulant drink called "dop" or "dope," which could be the origin for the English word *doping*; the word is also related to an English lubricant called "dope" that later would be used as a generic term for drug.

Through the years, the use of substances such as opium, alcohol, and coffee became popular in various cultures and grew with advances in medical science. The military also became an experimental setting for testing drugs to improve health and performance in soldiers and for injury recovery. In sports, during the 8th century BC, the Greek philosopher Philostratos described special substances that some athletes used for the ancient Olympic Games. In addition, it is known that Roman gladiators took various substances to improve their performance and that the Inca tribes used coca leaves to tolerate high altitudes in the Andes better. But modern sports doping did not appear until the second half of the 19th century. In 1865 in Amsterdam, the first case of a laboratory substance being used at a swimming competition was reported. In 1886 the first stimulant-related death, that of cyclist Arthur Linton, was described. The following year, the 6-day track race in New York featured the first doping test in cycling competition. Linton's coach, "Choppy" Warburton, was found guilty of providing another cyclist an illicit substance to enhance performance, and he was removed from his role.

Uvacsek et al. (2011) stated that the use of doping substances in cycling appeared more clearly in the 1890s, when cyclists were given substances such as extra caffeine, strychnine, or cocaine to improve performance. During the 1924 Tour de France, the Pélissier brothers were interviewed in newspapers about cyclists using cocaine or chloroform. But it was not until the 1967

Tour de France that a tragedy occurred. Tom Simpson, a 29-year-old British cyclist, collapsed and died while ascending Mont Ventoux, and a postmortem examination found a mix of amphetamines and alcohol (Waddington and Smith 2009). The next events that marked the future of doping and antidoping were when Ben Johnson tested positive during the 1988 Olympic in Seoul and the Festina case of 1998, which revealed systematic doping in cycling teams (Bloodworth and McNamee 2010; Lentillon-Kaestner, Hagger, and Hardcastle 2012; Vest Christiansen 2005).

Consequently, the World Anti-Doping Agency (WADA) was established in 1999, providing a centralized body that aimed to harmonize antidoping strategies across elite sports (Catlin, Fitch, and Ljungqvist 2008). But things did not seem to change very much, and the Puerto case in 2006 (in which the Spanish doctor Fuentes and other colleagues were caught using doping substances and methods for a list of cyclists and other athletes) marked a deflection point that galvanized the fight against doping, including the landmark Lance Armstrong case that exploded in 2012. In this context, it could be said that before Puerto, cyclists and cycling itself were part of a doping culture that was normalized and many times known by some authorities. Paradoxically, although cycling was supposed to be the worst sport regarding doping, these previous cases were the reason to activate specific mechanisms, such that cycling is nowadays the most advanced sport in the antidoping fight (Morente-Sánchez and Zabala 2013).

Current Doping in Sports

Since 2004 WADA has produced an annually updated code and related documents that outline official international antidoping standards. Two of the following three criteria must be met for a substance or method to be included on the prohibited list:

- The substance enhances or has the potential to enhance performance.
- The substance threatens health or has the potential to do so.
- The substance violates the spirit of sport described in the introduction to the code.

Originally, doping was related to the use of a prohibited substance (included in a closed list) that had the aim of taking an unfair advantage by artificially enhancing performance. Today the definition of doping is "the occurrence of one or more of the anti-doping rules violations set forth in articles 2.1 through 2.10 of the code set out by WADA." This means the violation of one or more of the following (WADA code 2015):

- Presence of a prohibited substance (or metabolites or markers), defined and determined by the WADA list
- Use or attempted use of a prohibited substance or method

- Evading, refusing, or failing to submit to sample collection
- Whereabouts failures (three missed tests)
- Tampering or attempted tampering with any part of doping control
- Possession of a prohibited substance or method
- Trafficking or attempted trafficking of any prohibited substance or method
- Administration or attempted administration, in or out of competition, of any prohibited substance or method
- Complicity (assisting, encouraging, aiding, conspiring, covering up) as defined by WADA
- Prohibited association with people completing a sanction period or serving a period of ineligibility following criteria defined by WADA

So antidoping efforts are no longer about just using a specific test for a banned substance. An integrative code now tries to close all the gaps around the doping phenomenon. An athlete could fail any of the previous points regardless of ignorance about them because knowledge of the rules is the athlete's responsibility. An athlete using a contaminated nutritional supplement could fail the first point, but this mistake does not override the obligation to know what she or he is ingesting. Sometimes contamination occurs during the manufacturing process if equipment is not well cleaned after a banned substance has been processed. In addition, herbs may contain prohibited substances. As reported by Schumacher and Palfreeman (2012), from 634 different supplements purchased in 13 countries, 15 percent contained detectable steroids. In a study carried out in the United Kingdom 10.5 percent contained the same substance. Of course, in all cases this prohibited substance was not listed on the product labeling. For that reason, many labs are now marking their products with a "certified doping-free" label that assures no contamination or prohibited substances.

Reasons to Dope

Striegel, Vollkommer, and Dickhuth (2002) argued that the most frequently reported reasons for drug use were to achieve athletic success and financial gain and, to a lesser degree, to increase self-confidence and social recognition. Pitsch, Emrich, and Klein (2007) stated that athletes were encouraged to engage in doping practices by coaches, and 6.5 percent were persuaded by family members and friends. Also, various factors were acknowledged as potential reasons for use, most notably injury recovery and the economic pressures of elite sport. Nieper (2005) observed other reasons for using performance-enhancing substances (PES): to protect health, to enhance the immune system, and to improve performance. Kim et al. (2011) related the use of PES to improve recovery ability and muscle performance. Erdman et al. (2007) reported that the reasons were to increase energy, maintain health or prevent nutritional deficiency, and improve exercise recovery. In another study, subjects agreed that supplement use was necessary to be successful in sport (Bloodworth et al. 2012).

Likewise, all the young elite cyclists interviewed by Lentillon-Kaestner and Carstairs (2010) took nutritional supplements and believed that they improved performance. Hence, they were attracted to doping and admitted that they were open to using doping substances themselves if it was the key to continuing their cycling careers, but only after they became professionals. With the same sample, Lentillon-Kaestner, Hagger, and Hardcastle (2012) stated that the pressure of team staff and doctors on cyclists' use of banned substances has become less important and direct after the various doping scandals (Zabala et al. 2009).

Dunn et al. (2012) considered the false consensus effect concept. This term suggests that athletes who have a history of illicit drug use overestimate the prevalence of drug use among athletes. This idea draws attention because participants tended to report that the prevalence of drug use among athletes in general was higher than that of athletes in their sport, and these estimates appeared to be influenced by the participant's own history of drug use. In this regard, Tangen and Breivik (2001) showed that a person's decision to take banned substances is influenced by the assumption that his or her competitors are also taking drugs. Moreover, Uvacsek et al. (2011) observed that 14.6 percent of the athletes studied acknowledged using banned PES and 31.7 percent reported using recreational drugs. The results showed that those who admitted the use of banned drugs significantly overestimated the prevalence of doping in their sport (false consensus effect) compared with those who abstained from doping.

Measurement Instruments to Describe and to Detect Doping

Two main approaches are used to measure doping use. The first is for general interest to describe the overall situation. Methods can vary from less deep but easily administered methods such as interviews and questionnaires to more expensive biomedical tests of blood, urine, or genetics. The latter are cautiously developed with the aim of the second approach: to detect an individual's doping use and provide a positive case that would end in disciplinary punishment. The first approach is not valid to detect an individual case, but it could be taken into account as a valid measurement to describe an overall panoramic view.

Apart from biomedical tests that are supposed to be more quantitative and objective, a few procedures claim to detect athletes who are taking prohibited substances or at least athletes at risk of taking PES because of their attitudes. But the current research methodologies used to examine attitudes toward doping in sport seem weak. Measures such as anonymous self-reported questionnaires, developed and used for a single research project, often lack scientific rigor. Qualitative reports cannot discriminate between what athletes say and what is real, so Morente-Sánchez and Zabala (2013) suggested that data collection by questionnaire should be interpreted with caution because answers may be intentionally false. Subjects may not wish to reveal that they or their teammates use drugs, even if anonymity and confidentiality are guaranteed by the investigators. For the general description of a representative sample or a population, a combination of both qualitative and quantitative measurements (ideally including biomedical tests) should be used to make an objective determination of attitudes toward doping in sport or the estimated use of banned substances.

Complementing the previous tests done at a specific moment in or out of a race, two other effective tools for antidoping are the biological passport and tracking athletes' whereabouts.

Introduced in 2007, a biological passport is a longitudinal monitoring system for blood values for professional cyclists. Specific variables are tracked over time to detect any abnormal behavior or unexplainable values; abnormalities may be interpreted as a positive case. A biological passport is an individual document that records all the results of biological analyses (hematological parameters or urinary steroidal profile) carried out on a rider. These data track with precision the evolution of the various parameters in comparison with their baseline references. An athlete who is found to have a blood value beyond the calculated reference range is invited to offer an explanation, and if the explanation is unsatisfactory, a sanctioning procedure can be initiated. This approach guides doping detection to reveal the effects of prohibited substances rather than the substance itself (Schumacher and Palfreeman 2012). Variables taken into account include red blood cells, hematocrit, hemoglobin and its derivations, reticulocytes (absolute and percentage), mean corpuscular hemoglobin and mean corpuscular volume, and the OFF-score (hemoglobin–reticulocyte relationship). As recognized by Zorzoli (2011), the adoption of the biological passport was a major step forward in the fight against doping, allowing the efficient combination of the classical method of toxicological science with the detection of the biological consequences induced by these drugs.

All cyclists supervised by WADA must electronically update their daily locations weeks to months in advance, permitting antidoping officials to find and test athletes both in and out of competition. Three mistakes that result in missed tests within a certain period lead to sanctions. ADAMS is the online platform that tracks all data of the athletes' biological passports and their whereabouts, centralizing the information and allowing it to be shared with all stakeholders (Zorzoli 2011).

The number of athletes reported as testing positive by antidoping bodies often has been smaller than what scientific literature shows. According to Uvacsek et al. (2011), WADA's adverse analytical findings (i.e., positive doping tests) suggest that, on average, 2 percent of elite athletes use doping substances and that this number has been quite stable over the past 10 years. On the contrary, prevalence rates obtained by means of self-report usually vary between 1.2 percent and 26 percent (Morente-Sánchez and Zabala 2013). The latest data show that the relationship between the number of positive drug tests and the extent of drug use is unclear, so it is possible that drug use is widespread but positive test results are not (Waddington and Smith 2009). The substances or procedures mostly used in the past were based on blood manipulation (to improve oxygen delivery to the muscle), glucocorticoids (for their metabolic effects), and anabolic substances (to enhance muscle growth and recovery).

Recently in cycling, to complement other antidoping, a "power profile passport" has been proposed, in which the best power (wattage) average values (in different given times, from maximal power to the functional threshold power) of an athlete would be recorded to track this performance during her or his career. The ease of recording such data in cycling makes this method feasible, but this proposal is in the early stages of study and likely will not be implemented soon. Ultimately, as new substances appear, antidoping tests and controls must evolve, such as in the case of new substances discovered in blood samples of some athletes like the so-called genetic doping of GW1516 or AICAR that is supposed to act as an "exercise-in-a-pill" substance. In the future, additional tests and procedures should be developed to improve the indirect detection of other banned substances.

Separate mention is needed for those substances and procedures that are not banned but are being observed by the WADA, such as tramadol (opium painkiller), caffeine (stimulant), and SNUS (stimulant based on nicotine). From these observed substances, meldonium was studied and then put on the banned list in 2016, becoming infamous in subsequent months because of a spate of positive tests. Each athlete's ethics threshold may determine whether he or she uses substances being observed by WADA. For example, although tramadol is not prohibited, some cycling teams, but not all, consider it banned because they think it is a doping agent. In the same sense is the use of other narcotics to improve recovery, which may not improve performance acutely but are used with this aim and could be even worse than other banned substances.

Another controversial issue is related to the therapeutic use exemptions (TUEs) that officially allow athletes to use specific drugs (considered doping) under particular and assessed circumstances of medical necessity (illness, surgery, accident). Many athletes have been allowed to use specific medicines (so, formally, there is not a doping issue on this) such as glucocorticosteroids and amphetamines, although it has been suggested that misuse and abuse of these institutional permissions may have taken place in recent years. Institutions have been called on to revise and control this process.

Many believe that a new doping era is about to start, or perhaps has already started, with so-called neurodoping based on electrical transcranial stimulation that claims to affect performance by influencing the central governor in the brain (Davis 2013). Because this methodology is not well known, we should be cautious about its use because private companies are already selling this kind of stimulation device with unknown and potentially harmful effects.

Doping and Amateur Cycling

Eradicating doping is an important objective for sport governing bodies and health institutions because doping is considered a serious health issue and has an effect on sport performance (Lentillon-Kaestner, Hagger, and Hardcastle 2012; Petróczi and Aidman 2009). Anyone competing under the rules of a national or international governing body may be required to pass a doping control in competition (12 hours before competition until the time competition ends) or out of competition (any other time). Amateur or purely recreational cyclists, however, are unlikely to be tested frequently (Schumacher and Palfreeman 2012). Normally, riders competing in lower categories have never had to attend a doping control, although those who take part in international or national championships face a higher probability that could increase up to 100 percent if they are in the best positions. Regardless, cyclists must be aware of all the competing rules including the antidoping rules.

One of the most targeted sports in the fight against doping has been cycling, especially after well-known doping affairs such as the Festina case in 1998, in which a staff member of team Festina was caught delivering a huge amount of doping substances with the aim of using them systematically during the 1998 Tour de France. Most antidoping actions have focused on professional sport, leaving amateur sport at risk. In effect, antidoping controls in amateur cycling are far less common than in professional cycling, presumably because of their high cost (Zabala et al. 2016). Note, however, that the increase in nonprofessional cycling events (both competitive and noncompetitive) in recent years and the suspiciously high performance of some athletes in those events has raised concerns regarding the use of performance-enhancing drugs among amateur cyclists.

Investigating doping intention and behavior in amateur cycling is not a trivial issue because the use of performance-enhancing drugs can result, apart from an illicit performance gain, in serious health issues (Angell et al. 2012; Lentillon-Kaestner, Hagger, and Hardcastle 2012; Pope et al. 2013; Spivak 2001). Thus, one of the aims of antidoping research is to look for reliable and inexpensive ways to investigate doping intention and behavior in amateur sport. In a recent study by Outram and Stewart (2015), amateur elite cyclists' training schedules were reported as extremely demanding, frequently justifying the use of substances such as caffeine, anti-inflammatory medications, and energy boosters. Some of the subjects interviewed distanced themselves and their use of supplements and substances from actual doping, condemning the latter as unethical and objectionable, but not the former. Others appeared to empathize with professional cyclists' use of doping substances given that they rely on cycling for their income, and the amateur athletes made comparisons between doping and their own licit (not WADA-prohibited) substance use.

Statements by young cyclists in Lentillon-Kaestner, Hagger, and Hardcastle (2012) command attention. The authors often made the distinction between two generations of cyclists: cyclists of the new generation and cyclists of the old school, the generation who had commenced their cycling careers before the 1998 Festina scandal. According to Lentillon-Kaestner, Hagger, and Hardcastle (2012), doping use declined among cyclists from the professional peloton. This study pointed out that today most cyclists decide not to use banned substances. In the past, cyclists who chose not to take banned PES were marginalized. Cyclists surveyed acknowledged that doping organizations appear to have become more individualized. Hence, they concluded that although use of banned substances is less widespread, some substances used are similar to those used in institutionalized doping programs among cycling teams in the 1990s. In amateur cycling, some organized drug networks sell banned products. Police operations have revealed that sometimes athletes and coaches or doctors are involved in these kinds of organized networks (Zabala et al. 2016). The involvement of police in enforcing criminal laws related to the drug trade, public health, or what is called sporting fraud has been important in the last two decades and has been quite effective (Waddington and Smith 2009). Generally, athletes today consider punishment severity correct or not severe enough, despite differences between sports (Morente-Sánchez and Zabala 2013).

New Cycling Era

Although the 1998 Tour de France did not mark a big change in drug use in cycling, two significant changes occurred. First, since then a significant number of cyclists started to be suspended for using prohibited substances. Second, and even more important, many sponsors terminated their sponsorship in light of bad publicity, to the extent that some teams had real financial problems and struggled to survive. Cyclists and the people who support professional cycling teams suffered because everybody was paying for this created situation. Personal dramas, broken families, athletes who were rebuked in public—the social punishment was sometimes much harder than the disciplinary or economic penalty. The cycling family as a whole, not only those found guilty of using banned substances, suffered a hard situation.

Starting around 2007 some groups within professional cycling grew in public opposition to the use of banned substances and pushed for more effective antidoping actions. The so-called Movement for Credibility in Cycling (MCC), or Mouvement Pour un Cyclisme Crédible (MPCC), formed as a framework to develop fair play in professional cycling by promoting specific actions to detect and punish doping misconduct. In parallel, prevention and educational programs were started, first by national federations such as the Spanish cycling federation, which supported the "preventing to win" project (Zabala et al. 2009), and later by WADA (Athlete Learning Program About Health and Antidoping, or ALPHA), which had the aim of educating people on the doping issue. A different philosophy is shown by other concepts such as Bike-Pure and Cycling 2.0. These groups promote a new cycling culture, seeking to prevent doping by educating all stakeholders (Morente-Sánchez and Zabala 2013).

For example, Cycling 2.0 suggested the following principles (Zabala and Atkinson 2012):

- The need to seek improvement and perform better by means of ethical behavior
- Constant attitude of curiosity, learning, and teaching
- Collaborative teamwork
- Multidirectional communication
- Participation in the training plan and process in which the athlete is the main actor
- Awareness of the latest advances and technologies in the field; trust in real science
- Knowledge and understanding of what is being done; awareness of what is going on and why
- Systematic, controlled, and regular work
- Fair play and clean practices without doping

Tools and ideas must be developed with appropriate methodology that takes into account the athlete as the principal actor. For that reason, all stakeholders, from staff to media to fans, need to promote best practices among athletes. We must inspire those still affected by the worst part of the old school by promoting collaborative work that focuses on the athlete. Real teamwork is a key point, requiring collaborative work between athletes, coaches, physiotherapists, team managers, doctors, and psychologists. The common interest must be based on obtaining the best performance together.

Punishments weakened the credibility of sport, especially cycling, but sometimes to rebuild, you need to destroy part of the house. This approach seems to be the case with cycling. Cycling has tried to learn from its mistakes to create a better second version of itself, showing that "something has changed positively" (Morente-Sánchez et al. 2014). Some behaved badly, but the knowledge and context were different; before the Puerto case, some athletes were not aware of what they were doing or at least the concept regarding bad practices was not so clear and widespread. For that reason, some specialists involved in cycling and sport (journalists, sociologists, sport scientists) advocate for a reset, using 2006 as a cutting point. After the Puerto case, people became aware of the nature of the wrongdoing and the dramatic consequences that could occur.

Despite the fact that cycling is the most controlled sport today, media and fans remain skeptical. Some wish to know every detail of the athletes, even personal data regarding physiological and laboratory-based performance values, such as those who recently demanded Chris Froome's personal data. Professional cycling is a sport in which amateurs can use better material than pros, ride the same roads, even be in direct contact when ascending a climb, but it is also the only sport in which personal data of the stars is demanded to be published in the name of transparency. Sharing personal medical data is a complete transformation from the dark past of cycling. Perhaps we should consider an intermediate solution that balances athletes' privacy with antidoping control.

As recently pointed out by Zabala and Mateo (2015), the importance given to some specific variables has been so magnified that other key variables are not taken into account, distorting the total picture. Data and its analysis are useful and may explain a great percentage of athletic performance, but other variables such as tactics, decision making, tolerance to effort, and technical skills, which cannot be measured in a laboratory, have been shown to be crucial to achieving the highest competitive level. Publishing personal data is appropriate when possible, available, or voluntary, but analysis and interpretation are needed, and these must be serious (prepared and professional) and ethical. In any case, we should not be slaves of data alone.

Future of Doping in Cycling

As in sport in general or society itself, cycling is not free of cheaters who will try to take advantage by breaking rules, and not just by using banned substances. The Union Cycliste Internationale (UCI) has been working on this matter for years, trying to manage and improve the situation. Several examples are some positive test cases for newly banned substances like meldonium and the use of electric engines inside bikes, leading to a specific protocol to scan and detect this kind of mechanical doping. Sometimes the incident is more noise than reality, because some people see doping and cheating everywhere, but as it is said, "When the river sounds, water may be flowing." So the UCI asked for an independent assessment on the matter of doping that culminated in the Cycling Independent Reform Commission (CIRC). The CIRC provided a broad and interesting report that listed several key aspects to be taken into account in the future to avoid repeating mistakes. The report made several interesting points:

- UCI should work closely with governments, national authorities, and other stakeholders to make their investigative tools available in the fight against doping.
- Governments should provide a better legal framework to ensure good governance in sport organizations.
- Doctors who are found guilty of administering any banned drug should be investigated to determine whether they are fit to continue their general medical practice.
- The WADA code should be amended to provide commissions as a tool to investigate doping scandals or monitor compliance with the WADA code.
- The imposition of financial sanctions could have a deterrent effect on both riders and team staff members, and UCI should apply this rule to all stakeholders involved in cycling, concurrently educating participants on their obligation to cooperate.
- UCI should promote more antidoping research from both biomedical and psychosocial perspectives.
- UCI should set up an independent whistleblower desk. Absolute confidentiality must be guaranteed, and the attitude toward whistleblowers should be shifted to highlight their positive role in cleaning up sport.
- More information and improvement of doping test is required.
- UCI should carry out a study on their election process to make it more transparent, democratic, representative, and straightforward.
- Control and accountability for UCI should be improved in regard to its overarching management body, which has effective financial control over all actions, commissions, and bodies of UCI.
- The Ethics Commission should be revamped to ensure it is independently appointed.
- UCI should facilitate the creation of a strong riders' union to give riders a collective voice, especially on issues of ownership, revenue sharing, the racing calendar, and antidoping.
- Because doping is not the only form of cheating, UCI should investigate whether and to what extent lessons from the antidoping fight could be used to fight these new forms of cheating.
- Sanctioned riders should be used as an educational resource and make creative educational programs interesting to young athletes.
- UCI should pursue individuals through investigations as soon as a suspicion is raised.

- More attention should be paid to medical issues such as some therapeutic use exemptions.
- The feasibility of requiring that any substances used by riders during stage races (including food supplements) must be dispensed by a centralized pharmacy for the whole peloton should be studied.
- The lack of financial stability for teams and riders should be studied because financial issues could influence the decision to use banned substances to improve economic status.

Apart from these points, the report cited other recommendations such as making members of the staff of professional teams, such as coaches and physical trainers, responsible for a number of cyclists. This practice and the centralization of the information about training sessions and plans in an online platform (making it confidential but recordable and evaluable in case of necessity by the UCI) seem to be critical points that could help control the environment around cyclists, an area that has been traditionally uncontrolled (e.g., unknown coaches or doctors working behind the scenes). Some teams started to do this before any recommendations came from UCI, and today the role of coaches is starting to be standardized, while in the past this door seemed to be closed to them. We also think that the change in mentality and an objective appearance of a new cycling era is definitely seen in this circumstance.

Applying the Science

Athletes using prohibited substances mainly look for performance improvement, even though most of them acknowledge that doping is dishonest, unhealthy, and risky because of sanctions. The use of various substances or methods can be related to the lack of motivation and other factors, such as parental influence or hours spent on training. Antidoping rules are progressively becoming better known by athletes, but some still lack knowledge, which could be provided by means of educational programs. In addition, athletes lack information about dietary supplements and the side effects of some performance-enhancing substances. To minimize the phenomenon of doping, information and prevention-based programs are necessary to establish and maintain correct attitudes from the earliest ages. The support of athletes, from their personal environments to their coaches, must be carefully planned and developed as a middle- and long-term objective.

Today, the high risk of being caught and the rules implemented by the UCI in elite cycling have decreased the suspicion that cyclists are using banned substances, although in amateur cycling some individuals could still be trying to cheat because the risk is significantly lower. In any case, a few cheaters will always engage in unfair practices, so all stakeholders need to be vigilant to respect the value of fair play. Nobody should naively think that the dark history of doping is in the past. Although things have changed and cycling seems to have moved from last place to the pole position in the fight against doping, this race is not over.

Practical aspects to take into account include the following:

- Being aware of the rules (general, WADA, and UCI rules) and the consequences of using banned substances has been important since the earliest ages.
- Using ergogenic aids can be risky because they may contain prohibited substances. Also, cyclists need to be cautious with new and nonprohibited substances and methods (e.g., SNUS, tramadol, electrical transcranial stimulation).
- Tests and controls, especially ADAMS and the biological passport, have been important in the fight against doping, but the fight also has benefited from law adaptation and police intervention around traders and other people around athletes.
- Controls and tests are needed, in both professionals and amateurs, to send a message to those engaged in harmful practices. In addition, the policy on TUEs should be revised in depth to avoid potential misuse and abuse.
- New tests and prevention methods are required when new doping practices arise.
- Prevention and education are necessary for all stakeholders. Individual knowledge and responsibility make unfair and illegal practices less likely to occur.
- Collaborative work among team managers, doctors, physiotherapists, coaches, and cyclists is key to creating an environment that works against any bad practice.
- A promising new era started after a great deal of punishment and suffering, but we are all responsible for maintaining this situation and improving the culture around the sport based on fair play.

A balance must be found between the naive (doping never happens) and the negative (all cyclists are cheaters). The aim is to walk forward to find a cleaner sport and therefore a cleaner and better society. Cycling has moved forward, trying to create a new and stable situation for the majority of stakeholders. We must be optimistic but keep working without pause.

PART
VI

Cycling Health

CHAPTER 19

Epidemiology of Cycling Injuries

—Victor Lun

Like all competitive sports, competitive bicycling involves risk of injury. The patterns of injury in bicycling are unique because exposures include high speed; obstacles such as cyclists, pedestrians, and motor vehicles; and unpredictable road, environmental, and weather conditions. Furthermore, bicyclists usually do not have any external protection beyond a helmet. Cycling presents a risk of both acute traumatic injuries and overuse injuries. Injury patterns differ among the types of bicycling—road, cyclocross, off-road or mountain bike, BMX, and so on. Understanding the pattern and epidemiology of injuries suffered by competitive bicyclists can help to implement appropriate injury prevention and treatment strategies.

Most studies examining the epidemiology of injuries in competitive bicycling are retrospective questionnaire or interview in design (Bohlmann 1981; Callaghan and Jarvis 1996; Clarsen, Krosshaug, and Bahr 2010; De Bernardo et al. 2012; Pfeiffer 1993, 1994). Bicyclists are surveyed or interviewed about what injuries they suffered during a preceding period. These types of studies are easy and inexpensive to conduct but are susceptible to confounding factors such as incomplete or inaccurate details and recall and selection bias. In addition, the incidence and rates of injury cannot always be determined because accurate exposure data is not usually known. Finally, in professional and competitive bicycling, bicyclists may not accurately report injuries for strategic reasons. Nonetheless, these studies are still valuable for providing an idea of the epidemiology of competitive bicycling injuries. A few prospective injury surveillance studies have examined injuries suffered by competitive road bicyclists over periods of many years (Barrios et al. 1997, 2011) or during a single or a series of BMX and off-road bicycle races (Brøgger-Jensen, Hvass, and Bugge 1990; Chow and Kronisch 2002; Kronisch et al. 1996).

The usual outcome measures that injury studies try to quantify include the incidence, rate, location, severity, and type of traumatic and overuse injuries. The findings of bicycling injury studies to date can be difficult to compare because definitions of injury, calculations of injury incidence and rates, and descriptors of location, severity, and type of injury are not consistent.

Incidence of Injury

The overall incidence of injuries in competitive road bicyclists ranges between 58 and 86 percent (table 19.1). When examined separately, the incidence of traumatic and overuse injuries ranges between 38.4 to 48.6 percent and 51.4 to 61.6 percent, respectively. In comparison, recreational cyclists have an incidence of traumatic injuries of 24.5 percent and an incidence of overuse injuries ranging from 84.9 to 88 percent (van der Walt et al. 2014; Wilber et al. 1995).

The incidence of acute traumatic injuries at competitive off-road and BMX bicycling races has been reported to be 0.4 percent and 6.3 percent, respectively (Brøgger-Jensen, Hvass, and Bugge 1990; Kronisch et al. 1996). Kronisch et al. (1996) remarked that their study findings probably underestimated the true injury risk in competitive off-road or mountain biking because the study examined only traumatic injuries that were suffered in one race event and that pro and elite cyclists usually compete in 14 to 17 events per year and train 10 to 12 hours per week. Bohlmann (1981) evaluated the incidence of injuries suffered by 3,700 competitive bicyclists who rode different road-bicycling disciplines. Of the 77 injuries that were reported, criterium, track, and road bicyclists suffered 49.3, 29.9, and 20.8 percent, respectively, of the total injuries.

Rates of Injury

Rates of injury in competitive bicycling have been reported as number of injuries per racer, number of injuries per year, and number of injuries per kilometer by Barrios et al. (1997, 2011) and De Bernardo (2012), as seen in table 19.1. In two separate prospective injury surveillance studies, competitive road bicyclists were followed between 1983 and 1995 and between 2003 and 2009 (Barrios et al. 2011). An increase in rate of both traumatic and overuse injuries was observed in 2003 to 2009 when compared with 1983 and 1995. All three studies reported higher rates of overuse injury compared with rates of traumatic injury.

Severity of Injury

Barrios et al. (1997, 2011) and De Bernardo et al. (2012) used the Abbreviated Injury Scale (AIS) to rate the severity of injuries in competitive road bicyclists. The AIS is a 6-point injury severity ranking system in which a score of 1 means minor injury and a score of 6 means unsurvivable injury (Joint Committee on Injury Scaling 1980). These studies found that 77.9 to 94.1

Table 19.1 Summary of Epidemiology of Competitive Bicycling Injuries

Author	Study design	Subjects	Outcome measures	Injury definition	Injury incidence	Injury rates	Severity of injury: rating	Severity of injury: time loss
				ROAD BICYCLING				
Barrios et al. 1997	Prospective	65 cyclists competing on two professional European teams, followed from 1983 to 1995, mean follow-up 5 years	Incidence, location, and type of traumatic and overuse injuries and rates of injury	Overuse injury: "a complaint clearly related to an overuse condition while cycling, without previous trauma"	56 of 65 (86%) with total of 86 injuries; traumatic injuries 38.4%, overuse injuries 61.6%	Traumatic injuries: 0.54 injuries/racer, 0.11 injuries/year, 0.003/km; overuse injuries: 0.86 injuries/racer, 0.17 injuries/year, 0.005/km	Abbreviated Injury Scale: minor 41.9%, moderate 36.0, severe but not life threatening 17.4%, severe and life threatening 3.5%, severe with uncertain survival 1.2%	Days of sport activity interruption: <7 days 17.6%, 7 to 28 days 67%, >28 days 15.3%
Barrios et al. 2011	Prospective	51 elite cyclists followed from 2003 to 2009	Incidence of traumatic and overuse injuries and rates of injury		Traumatic injuries 48.6%, overuse injuries 51.4%	Traumatic injuries: 0.98 injuries/racer, 0.24 injuries/year, 0.007/km; overuse injuries: 1.04 injuries/racer, 0.26 injuries/year, 0.009/km		
Bohlmann 1981	Retrospective questionnaire and interview	3,700 competitive cyclists age 15 to 35 in the USA upper Midwest who competed in criterium, track, and road selection races leading up to and including the 1979 Junior World Championships	Incidence, location, and type of traumatic injuries		Total number of injuries 77; criterium 49.3%, track 29.9%, road 20.8%		98% of injured cyclists returned to cycling in less than 1 week and to competition within 1 month	
Callaghan and Jarvis 1996	Retrospective interview	71 elite British competitive cyclists who received medical assessments in 1995 at the British Olympic Medical Centre	Incidence of low-back pain, sciatica, other musculoskeletal problems; cause, duration and effect on training		60% incidence of low-back injury, 33% incidence of knee injury			

(continued)

Table 19.1 (continued)

Author	Study design	Subjects	Outcome measures	Injury definition	Injury incidence	Injury rates	Severity of injury: rating	Severity of injury: time loss
				ROAD BICYCLING				
Clarsen, Krosshaug, and Bahr 2010	Retrospective interview	109 cyclists from 7 pro teams	Incidence, location, and severity of overuse injuries from previous year	Overuse injury: "any pain or discomfort that was not directly related or associated with a traumatic event and was different from the normal aches and pains associated with competitive cycling"	63 of 109 (58%) injured with total of 94 injuries		Did not affect ability to complete normal training and racing 39%, led to a reduction in either racing performance or training volume 36%, caused miss of 1 or more days of training or competition 24%	Days of missed training or competition: 1–3 days 17%, 4–7 days 17%, 8–28 days 43%, >28 days 17%
Clarsen et al. 2014	Prospective survey	98 road cyclists from five semiprofessional men's teams, one professional women's team, and five junior teams	Prevalence, location, and severity of overuse injuries over a 13-week period	Any injury that was not considered an acute injury and was defined as an injury with a specific and clearly identifiable injury event	Average prevalence of injury by body part: knee 23%, lower back 16%, shoulder 7%, and anterior thigh 8%		Adjusted cumulative severity score according to body part: knee 6.98, lower back 4.45, anterior thigh 2.53, and shoulder 1.06	
de Bernardo et al. 2012	Retrospective interview	51 competitive cyclists	Incidence, location, and severity of traumatic and overuse injuries from previous 4 years	Injury: "any acute trauma or repetitive stress associated to the physical activity involved by sports practice either in competition or training sessions which causes pain, dysfunction, pathology or handicap"	43 of 51 (84%) injured with total of 103; traumatic injuries 48.5%, overuse injuries 51.5%	Total: 0.504 injuries/year/racer, 2.19 injuries/racer/year, 0.018 injuries/1,000 km; traumatic injuries: 0.245 injuries/year/racer, 0.98 injuries/racer/year, 0.008 injuries/1,000 km; overuse injuries: 0.259 injuries/year/racer, 1.039 injuries/racer/year, 0.010 injuries/1,000km	Abbreviated Injury Scale: AIS 1 64.7%, AIS 2 29.4%, AIS 3 5.9%	Days of absence from competition: 1–7 days 35.9%, 7–28 days 48.5%, >28 days 15.5%

Author	Study design	Subjects	Outcome measures	Injury definition	Injury incidence	Injury rates	Severity of injury: rating	Severity of injury: time loss
BMX								
Brøgger-Jensen, Hvass, and Bugge 1990	Prospective cohort study	976 participants of the 1989 BMX Cycling European Championships	Incidence and type of injuries		61 of 976 (6.3%)			
MOUNTAIN BIKING								
Chow and Kronisch 2002	Prospective cohort	97 riders who sustained an injury while competing at 7 different MTB races in 1994	Injury type, location, and severity	Injury severe enough to prevent continuing in a race and seek medical attention	190 injuries in 97 riders		Injury Severity Score (ISS): mean 2.9, range 1 to 17	
Kronisch et al. 1996	Prospective cohort	16 riders who sustained an injury while competing at five-event pro-elite MTB races in 1994	Injury incidence, type, location, and severity	Injury: an episode of acute trauma sustained during competition that required medical attention and rendered the rider unable to complete the event	16 of 4027 starts (0.40%), 44 injuries		Injury Severity Score (ISS): mean 3.0, range 1 to 5	
Pfeiffer 1994	Retrospective questionnaire	61 NORBA pro-elite male and female competitors in 1992	Injury incidence (injury-to-rider ratio), type, location	An accident that required the rider to stop riding and seek medical attention or first aid before being able to return to participation		Male: 4.43 injuries/rider; female: 6.5 injuries/rider		

239

percent of traumatic and overuse competitive road-bicycling injuries were AIS 1 and 2 (mild and moderate) in severity. Not unexpectedly, the studies found that overuse injuries tended to be AIS 1 in severity, whereas traumatic injuries usually ranged from AIS 2 to 5 in severity.

Although road-bicycling injuries were not severe for the most part, they could result in significant time loss; 17.6 to 35.9 percent and 43 to 67 percent of all injuries led to 1 to 7 and 7 to 28 days of lost time in training and competition, respectively. Fifteen to 17 percent of injuries led to greater than 28 days of time loss in training and competition; these injuries were usually traumatic.

Chow and Kronisch (2002) and Kronisch et al. (1996) use the Injury Severity Score (ISS) to rate the severity of injuries suffered by participants of off-road bicycling races. The ISS is an anatomical injury severity scoring system that determines an overall score for patients with multiple injuries. Scores range from 1 (minor) to 75 (most severe or unsurvivable) (Baker et al. 1974). ISS scores range, on average, between 2.9 and 3.0. The more serious injuries usually resulted from being thrown over the handlebars.

Injury Location, Type, and Diagnosis

Studies vary in how specific body locations were described or grouped. Some studies classified location of injury as upper extremity or lower extremity or just extremities. Most bicycling injuries occur in the knees and the low back, accounting for 23 to 64 percent and 16 to 60 percent, respectively, of all traumatic and overuse injuries (table 19.2). This finding is perhaps not surprising, given the body positioning and the way that biomechanical forces are exerted through the lower extremities in bicycling. Clarsen, Krosshaug, and Bahr (2010) found that knee and back injuries together caused 73.9 percent of overuse injuries that resulted in time loss from training and competition. More recently, using a novel study design to monitor overuse injuries, researchers found that the prevalence of knee, lower back, shoulder, and anterior thigh overuse problems was 23, 16, 7, and 8 percent, respectively, of semiprofessional and junior-level competitive bicyclists (Clarsen et al. 2014). Chondromalacia patella, patellar tendinitis, quadriceps tendinitis, and iliotibial band syndrome are the most common knee injury diagnoses in competitive cyclists (Barrios et al. 1997; Holmes, Pruitt, and Whalen 1994).

In competitive road bicycling, fractures and dislocations of the upper extremities are the most common type of traumatic injury, followed by contusions, abrasions, hematomas, and lacerations (table 19.2). The opposite pattern is seen in BMX and competitive off-road bicycle racing. The most common site of fractures and abrasions has been reported to be of the clavicle and the hip or elbow, respectively (Barrios et al. 1997; Bohlmann 1981).

External iliac artery endofibrosis (EIAE) is a narrowing of the artery at the anterior hip, the artery that supplies blood to the lower extremities. This

Table 19.2 Anatomic Location and Type of Injury as Percentage of All Injuries (in Descending Frequency)

Author	Anatomic location of injury	% of all injuries	Type of injury	% of all injuries
Barrios et al. 1997	Knee Ankle, Achilles, foot Lumbar spine Arm, hand, wrist	64 17 13 4	Fracture, dislocation Contusion, abrasion, hematoma, laceration Strain, sprain	63.6 24 6.1
Callaghan and Jarvis 1996	Lower back Knee Upper back Foot, ankle Head	60 33 19 11 11		
Clarsen, Krosshaug, and Bahr 2010	Shoulder, clavicle Knee C-spine Thigh	34 23 11 6		
Clarsen et al. 2014*	Knee Lower back Shoulder Anterior thigh	23 16 7 8		
De Bernardo et al. 2012	**Traumatic** Lower extremity Knee Lumbar spine **Overuse** Lower extremity Knee Lumbar spine	 34 26 16 67.9 32.1 15.1	 Fracture, dislocation Contusion, abrasion, hematoma, laceration Ruptures	 63.6 22 12
Brøgger-Jensen, Hvass, and Bugge 1990			Contusion, abrasion, hematoma, laceration Strain, sprain Fracture, dislocation	72.1 13.1 6.6
Chow and Kronisch 2002	Lower extremity Upper extremity Head and face Concussion	36.3 34.2 9.4 6.8	Contusion, abrasion, hematoma, laceration Fracture, dislocation Strain, sprain Head, TBI	64.2 17.8 11 6.8
Kronisch et al. 1996	Upper extremity Lower extremity Head and face	43.2 27.3 11.4	Contusion, abrasion, hematoma, laceration Fracture, dislocation Head, TBI Strain, sprain	75.0 13.6 9.1 2.3
Pfeiffer 1994	**Men** Knee Lower leg Thigh Shoulder **Women** Low back Lower leg Elbow Shoulder	 22.6 12.3 8.2 7.2 16.5 13.2 12.1 8.8	 Wound Bruise Strain Tendinitis Wound Bruise Strain Sprain	36.5 21.6 16.3 10.1 35.2 33.0 15.4 6.6

*Reported as average prevalence.

condition occurs primarily in bicyclists, although it is also reported in other endurance athletes. Bohlmann (1981) and Clarsen, Krosshaug, and Bahr (2010) reported one and two cases of EIAE in their studies, respectively. EIAE is discussed in more detail in chapter 20.

Chow and Kronisch (2002) reported an incidence of 13 concussions in 97 injured off-road bicyclists who were participating in seven different off-road or mountain bike races. Current studies in competitive road bicycling have reported head injuries, but none have specifically found or reported concussions or mild traumatic brain injuries. Given the significance of these types of injuries, why they have not been reported is unclear because they obviously do occur. During a bicycle race, properly assessing a bicyclist for a concussion injury is difficult because the determination of whether a bicyclist can continue riding must be made quickly and under suboptimal conditions. Nonetheless, much better adherence to the current recommendations for assessment and management of concussion, such as the most recent Consensus Statement on Concussion in Sport (McCrory et al. 2013), has been strongly recommended (Greve and Modabber 2012).

Mechanism of Injury

Most traumatic injuries are caused by falls. Barrios et al. (1997) suggested that at high speeds, bicyclists generally position their shoulders forward and then try to roll while falling, which probably explains the high incidence of clavicle fractures experienced by competitive bicyclists. Bohlmann (1981) reported that most common causes of bicycle accidents were flat tires and collision with other bicyclists. Barrios et al. (1997) found that mechanical failures caused two injuries and that other injuries were caused by falls within the peloton or fast downhill riding. In off-road bicycling races, falls over the handlebars and falls during downhill descents led to injuries that were more serious (Kronisch et al. 1996).

The cause of overuse injuries is multifactorial. Risk factors possibly include age, gender, equipment setup (namely, bike and riding shoes), years of racing experience, and training volume and intensity. Risk factors for overuse injuries in competitive cycling have not been well studied, but Wilber et al. (1995) reported that in recreational cyclists, the risk factors for male back, groin, and buttock injuries were high weekly riding mileage, lower number of bike gears, and fewer years of cycling. The risk factors for female groin and buttock injuries were more noncompetitive events per year and less precycling stretching.

Injury Prevention

Given the high speeds and unpredictable nature of bicycle racing, preventing falls and collisions can be difficult, and these occurrences can result in acute traumatic injuries such as fractures. Having a properly maintained bicycle is important to prevent mechanical failures, which may result in falls and crashes.

Proper bicycle fitting is the most common recommendation for prevention of overuse injuries of the upper and lower extremities, neck, and low back (Mellion 1991; Holmes, Pruitt, and Whalen 1994). Correct fitting includes not only having a proper frame size but also appropriately adjusted seat height and backward and forward positioning, cleat positioning, pedal float, forward reach, and handlebar and brake lever positioning. Note that many methods are used for fitting a bike including formulas, laser scanning, dynamic fitting, and 2- and 3-D motion analysis. Each method has pros and cons, and the quality of fitting usually is fitter dependent. Bike fitting may seem more of an art than a science. Moreover, the position that is optimal for power generation and aerodynamics may not be the best position for prevention of injury.

Other aspects of injury prevention include a well-thought-out training program that provides gradual and progressive increases in training volume and intensity with appropriate periods for recovery and cross-training. A complementary lower-body and core-strengthening program should be incorporated into a bicyclist's overall training program.

All bicyclists should wear a safety-approved and properly fitting bicycling helmet. Although not specifically studied in competitive bicyclists per se, evidence shows that wearing a bicycling helmet reduces the risk of head, brain, and severe brain injury by 75 to 88 percent across all age groups (Thompson, Rivara, and Thompson 1999). Furthermore, a helmet offers a protective effect of 65 percent for injuries to the upper- and midface region. Some bicycle helmet manufacturers are now incorporating a multidirectional impact system (MIPS) into the design of their helmets (www.mipshelmet.com). Helmets with MIPS technology have been shown to reduce the rotational impact forces on the head by 30 percent in the event of an oblique impact, which may further reduce the severity of a concussion injury.

Future Research

The most recent peer-reviewed study examining injuries in competitive bicycling was published by De Bernardo et al. (2012). Given the constantly evolving nature of competitive bicycling, research about the injuries in competitive bicyclists needs to be updated. Creation of multiteam or multistudy center prospective design injury surveillance studies that include consistent injury definition; calculations of injury incidence and rates; descriptors of location, severity, and type of injury; and physician diagnoses are needed to evaluate the epidemiology of injuries in all disciplines of competitive bicycling. Furthermore, cohort studies (comparison of injured and noninjured) can help to determine risk factors for injury.

Applying the Science

In summary, competitive bicycling has a high incidence of injury. The knee and low back are the most frequently injured body locations. Although the injuries that are sustained are typically minor in severity, many result in prolonged periods of reduced or stopped training and competition. Multiple strategies are required to prevent both traumatic and overuse injuries, including appropriate bicycle maintenance, proper bicycle fitting, and a progressive and comprehensive training program that includes strength and flexibility training. Wearing an approved bicycle helmet may reduce the incidence and severity of concussion and facial injuries. Additional prospective design injury surveillance studies are needed to improve the understanding of the epidemiology of injuries in competitive bicycling.

CHAPTER 20

Managing Common Cycling Injuries

—Victor Lun

As presented in chapter 19, a relatively high incidence of mild to moderate injuries occurs in competitive bicycling, many of which can lead to prolonged periods of decreased or stopped training and racing. Ideally, these injuries could be prevented, but if they do occur, optimal management may speed up the recovery of these injuries to allow bicyclists to return to training and competition. This chapter reviews the management of common competitive bicycling injuries as well as those that occur predominantly in bicycling.

Knee Injuries

The most common overuse competitive bicycling injuries involve the knee and the low back. Knee and back injuries together caused 73.9 percent of overuse injuries that resulted in time loss from training and competition (Clarsen, Krosshaug, and Bahr 2010). The high incidence of knee injuries in bicycling is not surprising given the biomechanics of force exertion through the lower extremities. Chondromalacia patella, patellar tendinitis, quadriceps tendinitis, and iliotibial band syndrome are the most common knee injury diagnoses reported in competitive cyclists (Barrios et al. 2011; Holmes, Pruitt, and Whalen 1994).

The extensor mechanism of the knee is composed of the quadriceps muscle, the quadriceps tendon at the top of the patella, the patella, and the patellar tendon at the bottom of the patella (figure 20.1). The various parts of the extensor mechanism, individually or in combination, are susceptible to injury in bicycling.

Many labels are used to describe tendon injuries, or tendinopathies, including tendinitis, tenosynovitis, and tendinosis (Jozsa and Kannus 1997). Tendinitis describes an acute tendon injury lasting 0 to 6 weeks, during

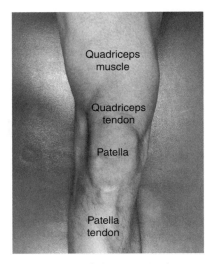

▶ **Figure 20.1** Anatomic structures of the anterior knee.

Victor Lun

which the athlete experiences an active inflammatory response and increased vascularity, leading to symptoms of pain, swelling, redness, and warmth.

As tendon injuries become more chronic, noninflammatory tendon degeneration and damage accumulates, leading to the description of tendinosis. Bicyclists are susceptible to both types of tendon injury in the quadriceps and patellar tendon. The focus of this chapter is on quadriceps and patellar tendinosis (QT and PT, respectively).

Chondromalacia patella (CP) refers to degeneration and damage of the articular cartilage covering the underside of the patella. The degree of CP can vary from mild softening of the cartilage to complete loss of articular cartilage and exposure of the bone of the undersurface of the patella or of the groove where the patella glides (femoral trochlea). CP and femoral trochlea articular cartilage degeneration can also collectively be called patellofemoral osteoarthritis (PF OA).

Patellofemoral pain syndrome (PFPS) describes patellar knee pain that is not because of tendinosis, CP, or PF OA. PFPS is considered more of a functional problem related to muscular imbalances of the hip and quadriceps muscles that leads to patellar maltracking and consequently anterior knee pain.

Diagnosis

PT and QT usually cause more localized pain at the bottom or top of the patella, respectively, as opposed to pain behind or underneath the patella for CP and PF OA. CP and PF OA can also cause a feeling of painful grinding behind the patella and even knee swelling. In PFPS, the pain is usually more generalized around the entire patella. All conditions may cause pain during riding, especially when more force is directed through the knee such as when riding in a high gear, going up inclines, sprinting, or riding while standing. Pain also is felt with deep squatting and kneeling and after sitting for a prolonged time with the knee in a flexed position. With PT, QT, and PFPS, plain X-rays are usually normal but may show enthesopathic bone changes at the insertion points of the quadriceps and patellar tendons at the patella for QT and PT, respectively. Depending on the severity of CP and PF OA, plain X-rays may show decreased patellofemoral joint space, osteophytes (bone spurs), sclerosis, and subchondral cysts. With PT and QT, depending on severity, diagnostic ultrasound may show degenerative changes including hypoechoic regions, tendon thickening, and calcific deposits. MRI is generally not required for diagnosis of PT, QT, CP, or PF OA. For PFPS, radiological investigations are usually normal.

Management

The recommendations for the initial conservative management of PT, QT, CP, PF OA, and PFPS are generally the same. These recommendations include the following:

1. **Modify training**. Training intensity and volume should be decreased to a level that does not cause symptoms.

2. **Modify riding technique**. Riding in lower gears at a higher cadence, avoiding riding while standing, and pulling up during the upstroke phase of the pedal stroke may decrease the force transferred through the extensor mechanism.

3. **Adjust bicycle positioning**. Some authors have suggested that increasing the height of the bicycle seat and pushing the bicycle seat back may help to reduce the knee joint compressive forces and, consequently, extensor mechanism knee pain (Ericson and Nisell 1986; Ericson and Nisell 1987; Mellion 1991). But a review of studies examining the effects of seating position (height and forward or backward) on knee joint compressive forces, knee injury risk, and bicycling performance found that this area is not well studied and the results of studies are conflicting (Bini, Hume, and Croft 2011). Given the uncertainty of how seating position might affect compressive forces in the knee, Bini, Hume, and Croft (2011) stated that seat positioning that allows flexion of the knee to 25 to 30 degrees with the foot at the bottom of pedal stroke may be the best position to prevent knee injuries while allowing optimal performance. A cyclist may need to try different seating positions to find the one that least aggravates knee symptoms.

4. **Use medication**. Nonsteroidal anti-inflammatory drugs (NSAIDs) can be taken orally or applied topically to reduce knee inflammation, pain, and swelling.

5. **Strengthen muscle**. Progressive strengthening exercises of the quadriceps, especially of the inner quads (vastus medialis) should be started. Quadriceps strengthening exercises include leg extension, leg press, step-down, and lunge. As symptoms improve, strengthening exercises can be performed with each leg individually. Adding or emphasizing the eccentric phase of muscle strengthening may be more beneficial for management of tendinosis compared with just doing concentric strengthening for the management of many tendinopathies (Malliaras et al. 2013; Visnes and Bahr 2007). Eccentric strengthening refers to muscle contraction while the muscle fibers are lengthening. Eccentric strengthening exercises for the quadriceps include drop squat, lunge, step-down, and dropping the weight more slowly while doing a leg extension. Initially, strength exercises should be performed with lower resistance and higher repetitions. In addition to strengthening the quadriceps, strengthening the hip and gluteal external rotation and abduction muscles and the iliotibial band may adjunctively help improve knee symptoms. The flexibility of the gluteal, hamstrings, quadriceps, and calf muscles should be maintained and improved with stretching, foam rolling, massage therapy, and yoga.

6. **Try a brace**. For CP, PF OA, and PFPS, wearing a patella brace may help promote optimal patellar tracking, and wearing a patellar strap may help symptoms of PT and QT.

7. **Try other treatments**. If quadriceps strengthening and stretching exercises, NSAID medication, and bracing do not adequately improve PT and QT symptoms, less well-studied treatment options could be tried, including nitroglycerin patches, extracorporeal shock-wave therapy, and platelet-rich plasma injections. For CP and PF OA, intraarticular corticosteroid and viscosupplementation injections could be considered. Nitroglycerin patches and the recommended intraarticular injections are not currently prohibited by antidoping organizations.

8. **Explore surgical treatment**. Surgical approaches for management of chronic tendinopathy, CP, and PF OA include open or arthroscopic debridement.

Low-Back and Neck Pain

Aerodynamic positioning on a bicycle requires bending forward at the low back and hips and maintaining the neck in an extended position to see ahead. Given the prolonged duration that bicyclists maintain this position, it is not surprising that 13 to 60 percent of competitive bicyclists complain about low-back and neck pain (Barrios et al. 2011; Callaghan and Jarvis 1996). The pathomechanical hypotheses that have been suggested to explain the development of low-back pain in bicyclists include flexion relaxation, muscle fatigue, spinal extensor overactivation, mechanical creep, and disc ischemia (Marsden and Schwellnus 2010).

Diagnosis

Fortunately, low-back and neck pain in bicycling is usually benign, involving strains of the paravertebral soft tissues or facet joints of the lumbar and cervical spine. If a cyclist experiences persistent pain when not bicycling or associated symptoms of pain radiation, numbness, or tingling down the upper or lower extremities, sensory changes in the hands and feet, muscle weakness, loss of deep tendon reflexes, or loss of control of bowel or bladder function, then more serious causes of neck and back pain, such as disc herniation, nerve root impingement, facet joint osteoarthritis, and spinal stenosis, may need to be considered. Further evaluation by a physician with diagnostic imaging, including X-rays and spine MRI, may be required.

Management

Management strategies to prevent or reduce neck and back pain include the following:

1. **Modify training**. Decrease training intensity and volume to a level that does not cause the reproduction of symptoms.

2. **Change position**. Avoid staying in one riding position for too long by regularly flexing and rotating the neck and extending and rotating the low back during a ride.

3. **Take medication**. For more severe symptoms of an acute cervical or lumbar spine strain, try oral and topical NSAIDs, oral analgesics, and muscle relaxants.

4. **Engage in therapy and muscle strengthening**. Cervical spine, lumbar spine, and pelvis core stability strengthening exercises should be incorporated into the strengthening program. Real-time ultrasound may be used to evaluate the size and activation pattern of the paraspinal stabilizing muscles of the lumbar spine and to provide biofeedback to ensure that the cyclist is performing strengthening exercises properly. Massage, chiropractic, and physiotherapy treatments can be tried. To settle more acute symptoms, spinal manipulations, manual therapy, acupuncture, and intramuscular stimulation (IMS) can also be tried.

5. **Adjust bicycle positioning**. Adjusting reach distance and saddle tilt have been suggested to be the more critical bicycle positioning adjustments for the management of low-back pain (Marsden and Schwellnus 2010). Tilting the saddle downward and thus tilting the pelvis forward may help to reduce tensile forces on the low-back tissues. Unfortunately, the optimal reach distance is debated; both increasing and decreasing reach distance may need to be tried to determine the least provocative reach distance.

Bicycle Contact Point Injuries

Not surprisingly, bicyclists are susceptible to injury at the three points of contact that a bicyclist makes with the bicycle: the hands, the feet, and the genitals and buttocks. At these points of contact, the most commonly diagnosed injuries relate to local nerve compression and inflammation at the point of contact with the bicycle. Management of these problems focuses on reducing the compression and inflammation of the affected nerves.

Hands

Bicyclists often develop pain, numbness, and tingling in their hands and fingers, possibly accompanied by a feeling of weakness of handgrip or clumsiness of the hand. These symptoms have been called cyclist's palsy or handlebar palsy. The cause of these symptoms is the compression and inflammation of the ulnar nerve at Guyon's canal (pinky side of the palm) or of the median nerve at the center of the wrist (also called carpal tunnel syndrome, CTS; figure 20.2). Arm, hand, and wrist injuries have been reported to account for 4 percent of injuries in competitive bicyclists (Barrios et al. 2011). In a prospective study, electrodiagnostic changes were found in the ulnar nerve following a 6-day, 420-mile (675 km) road bike ride (Akuthota et al. 2005). Furthermore, Slane et al. (2011) showed that riding in the drops and with the wrists extended for prolonged periods caused the most pressure on the ulnar nerve.

Diagnosis

Deciding which nerve is affected is determined by the distribution of sensory and motor symptoms. Ulnar nerve compression at Guyon's canal usually causes sensory symptoms in the pinky finger and pinky side of the ring finger. If more nerve damage occurs, a cyclist can develop motor symptoms

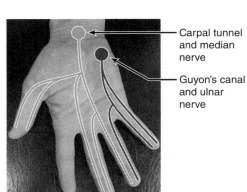

Carpal tunnel and median nerve

Guyon's canal and ulnar nerve

▶ **Figure 20.2** Nerves of the hand affected by contact point injuries.

Victor Lun

including clawing of the fourth and fifth fingers, weakness of handgrip, and pinching between the index finger and thumb. CTS causes sensory symptoms in the thumb side of the ring finger, middle finger, and index finger, and thumb and motor symptoms of weakness of handgrip, raising the thumb straight up from the palm, and squeezing between the thumb and pinky finger. If left untreated, the nerve compression and inflammation worsen, resulting in the persistence of symptoms even when not bicycle riding. Moreover, sufferers of CTS may also complain of nighttime symptoms.

Management

Minimizing direct pressure and traction of the ulnar and median nerves is the main way both to prevent and to treat cyclist's palsy. Strategies include the following:

1. **Bicycle positioning**. Lowering and shifting the bicycle seat backward will lessen the forward bent position of the upper body and thus reduce the transfer of weight onto the arms and hands onto the handlebars.
2. **For road bicycling**. Use thicker or double-layered foam or cork-type handlebar tape to provide more shock absorption, change hand position frequently, and avoid riding in the drops.
3. **For off-road and mountain biking**. Maximize the shock absorption adjustment of the front shocks, use contoured handlebar grips, and rotate the brake levers downward to reduce extension of the wrist.
4. **Gloves**. If symptoms are caused by ulnar nerve compression, try wearing bicycling gloves with padding in the area of the Guyon's canal. Slane et al. (2011) has shown that wearing gloves can reduce the pressure on the ulnar nerve by 10 to 28 percent.
5. **Splinting**. If symptoms are more related to carpal tunnel syndrome (especially if nighttime symptoms are present), wearing a volar wrist splint could be helpful. A volar wrist splint has rigid plastic material that extends from the palm of the hand to the lower forearm. Adjustable hook and loop strapping holds the splint to the wrist. These splints can be purchased from a physiotherapist, brace fitter, or medical supply store.

Oral and topical NSAIDS can reduce nerve inflammation. Corticosteroid injections of the Guyon's canal or carpal tunnel are the most direct and potent way to introduce anti-inflammatory medication around the ulnar and median nerve, respectively.

If symptoms persist despite these measures, electrodiagnostic testing (nerve conduction testing) can be performed to confirm the diagnosis and the location and degree of nerve injury. Surgical decompression of the nerves may need to be considered if more severe nerve injury is found.

Feet

Propelling a bicycle requires the transfer of power from the legs through the feet to the pedals, so cyclists may experience pain, numbness, or tingling in the forefoot area. Foot and ankle injuries account for 11 to 17 percent of injuries in competitive cyclists (Callaghan and Jarvis 1996; Barrios et al. 1997).

A common cause of forefoot symptoms in bicyclists is an interdigital, or Morton's, neuroma. The nerve that innervates the foot originates from the inner aspect of the ankle and foot and passes under the midfoot (figure 20.3). The nerve then divides into a number of branches, which extend toward the toes and between each of the knuckles of the toes (MTP joints). Then the nerves split to innervate each side of each toe. Repeated compression of the forefoot from pressure underneath the foot or from the sides of the foot can entrap and inflame the nerve at the branch point between the MTP joints.

Diagnosis

Entrapment and inflammation of the interdigital nerve result in localized pain between the affected MTP joints. Another possible symptom is an associated feeling of pain radiation, numbness, and tingling into the web space and toes of the affected nerve. After the symptoms develop during a bicycle ride, they can progressively worsen to the point that the cyclist must stop. Squeezing the foot from the sides, wearing narrow footwear or high-heeled shoes, running, jumping, and even prolonged walking often also bring on symptoms. Foot X-rays usually are normal. A diagnostic ultrasound or MRI can be used to visualize a neuroma.

Other possible causes of forefoot pain in cyclists include large toe MTP joint bunion (hallux valgus) or osteoarthritis, hammer toes, and metatarsal stress fractures.

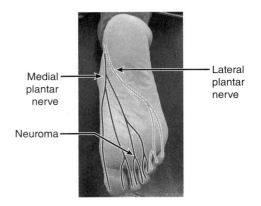

▶ **Figure 20.3** Nerves of the foot and location of Morton's neuroma.

Victor Lun

Management

The management of a Morton's neuroma is directed toward reducing the pressure in the forefoot and the inflammation around the nerve. Ways to reduce the pressure in the forefoot include the following:

1. **Foot position adjustment**. Move the shoe forward relative to the pedal axle and the side-to-side position of the cleat on the shoe.
2. **Shoes and cleats**. Select large pedals and shoe cleats, choose cycling shoes with a wider toe box, and decrease the strap tension in the forefoot area.
3. **Forefoot shimming**. Tilt the inner forefoot by placing a shim under or on top of the cycling shoe insole.
4. **Metatarsal pad**. Adhere a metatarsal pad or bar on the top of the shoe insole to dissipate the pressure to all the toes of the forefoot (figure 20.4). The pad should be positioned behind the MTP joints. Ideally, a qualified orthotist or pedorthist should do this to ensure proper placement of the pad.

▶ **Figure 20.4** Metatarsal pad on a shoe insole.

Victor Lun

Oral or topical NSAIDs can be used to reduce the inflammation of the affected nerve. If symptoms persist despite these measures, a corticosteroid injection of the neuroma could be considered. If corticosteroid injections fail or stop working after several have been performed, surgical excision of the neuroma (neurotomy) can be considered. This procedure can result in some permanent numbness of the affected toes, but no weakness of the foot or toes.

Genitals and Buttocks

Genital and perineal pain and numbness in bicyclists, also called cyclists' syndrome, is caused by compression of the pudendal nerve and artery as they pass through the perineal area (the area between the anus and base of penis or vagina), leading to nerve entrapment and decreased blood flow. Twenty-one to 61 percent of bicyclists report genital numbness, and 19 percent report erectile dysfunction (Andersen and Bovim 1997; Sommer et al. 2001). Prolonged sitting on a bicycle seat can lead to irritation of the bursa and skin that overlay the sitting bones (ischial tuberosity). Skin irritation can lead to chafing and even ulcerations.

Diagnosis

Bicyclists feel pain and numbness of the perineal area and penis or labia while bicycling, usually for more prolonged periods. The symptoms usually resolve after stopping cycling but can persist for hours or even days. With further nerve injury or vascular occlusion, erectile or sexual dysfunction and even impotence may be experienced. The ability to urinate is not usually affected.

Management

The main focus of management of cyclists' syndrome and ischial tuberosity irritation is to reduce the pressure in the perineal area and buttocks:

1. **Bicycle position adjustment**. Sitting in a more upright posture by shifting the bicycle seat forward and tilting the front of the seat downward can reduce the pressure in the perineal region (Spears et al. 2003; Gemery et al. 2007).

2. **Bicycle seat**. Bicycle seats without a protruding nose and those with a center groove have been shown to result in a significant reduction of pressure on the perineal region (Lowe, Schrader, and Breitenstein 2004; Gemery et al. 2007). Furthermore, the bicycle seat should be sufficiently wide so that the bicyclist's weight is supported directly under the ischial tuberosities. When purchasing a bicycle seat, the distance between the ischial tuberosities should be measured and matched to a seat of the appropriate width.

3. **Recumbent biking**. A cyclist having significant difficulty finding a comfortable bicycle seat or positioning on an upright bicycle could consider switching to a recumbent bike. With recumbent bikes, the sitting position generates no direct pressure on the genitals or perineum.

4. **Bicycling shorts**. To minimize ischial tuberosity and buttock skin irritation, the cyclist should wear well-padded and ventilated bicycling shorts. Shorts with seam lines that overlay the ischial tuberosity and perineum should be avoided. Applying thick cream or petroleum gel to the perineal area and buttocks can further reduce friction between the skin and lining of the shorts.

5. **Medication**. Oral or topical NSAIDs can help reduce inflammation of the pudendal nerve.

Concussion and Mild Traumatic Brain Injury

Concussions can occur in almost any sport, but the risk and severity of concussion injury can be magnified by the high-speed and unpredictable nature of bicycle racing. Unfortunately, the exact mechanisms of brain injury associated with concussion injury are not completely understood.

Diagnosis

The acute symptoms of a concussion can include dizziness, headache, nausea and vomiting, sound and light sensitivity, a feeling of being in a fog, altered vision, memory and concentration dysfunction, and poor coordination and balance. Note that a person can suffer a concussion without losing consciousness or having memory loss. After someone has experienced a concussion, another concussion injury may be more likely to occur, symptoms can become more severe, and symptoms can last longer each time a concussion is suffered.

Management

As with many sports, the decision to return to competition has to be made quickly if a concussion injury is suspected during a bicycle race. Ideally, a cyclist's condition should be assessed in a quiet area away from teammates and other distractions. A rapid assessment of a potentially concussed bicyclist's orientation, memory, concentration, and coordination can be done using the sport concussion assessment tool 3 (SCAT3), developed by the Fourth International Conference on Concussion in Sport (McCrory et al. 2013).

If a bicyclist reports any symptoms, regardless of severity, or if the SCAT3 assessment is abnormal in any way, he or she should immediately be stopped from continuing training or competition. The athlete should not be left alone and must be watched for the development of new symptoms or change of consciousness. The bicyclist should be evaluated by a physician as soon as possible. If there is any doubt, keep the bicyclist out!

Immediately after suffering a concussion, bicyclists should avoid any physical activity; consumption of alcohol or sleeping or antianxiety medication; consumption of analgesic or anti-inflammatory medications, narcotics, or other medications to treat headache pain; and driving or operating machinery, including a bicycle.

Headache symptoms should be used to monitor the possibility of a more serious head injury. If the severity of a headache progressively increases or becomes unbearable, the cyclist should immediately seek medical attention.

After a cyclist has been diagnosed with a concussion and removed from training and competition, regardless of perceived severity, safely returning to physical activity and cycling is the next critical step in properly managing a concussion. Returning to activity before symptoms have resolved usually prolongs the time required for the concussion to resolve and may lead to more chronic symptoms of concussion (also called chronic concussion or postconcussion syndrome), including chronic headache, persistent concentration and memory dysfunction, and balance problems.

A cyclist should completely rest from all physical activity including weight training and non-sport-specific crossing-training until he or she is completely symptom free for at least 24 to 48 hours. The time required to become asymptomatic can vary greatly, so a concussed bicyclist does not have to rest for any predetermined time. But he or she has to be asymptomatic before returning to physical activity. The duration of this asymptomatic period may be extended depending on a bicyclist's past concussion history. Minimizing or even stopping cognitively stimulating activities such as occupational work and schoolwork, computer work, texting, and videogames may also be needed if these activities aggravate concussion symptoms.

Ideally, the concussion should be managed by a physician who is experienced with concussion injury and clears the bicyclist to start a graduated return to exercise protocol. After symptoms have completely resolved and the cyclist has been cleared to return to physical activity, a progressive return to activity protocol can be started. The aim of such a protocol is to increase blood flow and pressure in the brain through a graduated increase in bicycling time and intensity and then add sport-specific training. Table 20.1 shows an example of a return-to-sport protocol.

Each step of the protocol should take at least 1 day. If any concussion symptoms reoccur at any step of the protocol, the athlete must stop all physical and other provocative activity until she or he is free of symptoms for at least 24 hours before restarting the protocol from step 1. Athletes may have to restart the protocol several times before successfully returning to regular training and competition.

If an athlete is unable to progress through the return-to-exercise protocol without recurrence of symptoms, a physician should reassess him or her.

Although not mandatory, web-based neuropsychological testing applications can help in return-to-exercise decision making. Competitive bicyclists should have a baseline test when they are completely free of concussion symptoms. If a cyclist suffers a concussion during the competitive season, the neuropsychological testing can be repeated to determine whether neuropsychological and cognitive function have returned to normal before the cyclist is cleared to return to physical activity.

In bicycling, essentially the only way to prevent or reduce the severity of a concussion is to wear a properly fitting safety-approved helmet (Thompson, Rivara, and Thompson 1999). In North America, the Canada Standards Association (CSA), the American National Standards Institute (ANSI), the

Table 20.1 Gradual Return to Bicycling After Concussion

Step	Activity
1	Complete rest until no symptoms are experienced for at least 24 hours.
2	Stationary bicycling (not rollers) for 15 minutes at low intensity (e.g., at less than 60% HR max)
3	Stationary cycling for 45 minutes at low intensity (e.g., at about 75% HR max)
4	Stationary cycling for 45 minutes at low intensity (e.g., at about 75% HR max) with 30-second maximum effort sprinting at minutes 25, 30, and 35
5	Solo riding on road for 45 minutes at low intensity (e.g., at about 75% HR max)
6	Solo riding on road for 45 minutes with 30-second all-out effort sprinting at minutes 25, 30, and 35
7	Solo riding on road, track, or trail for 45 to 60 minutes at sustained higher intensity (e.g., above 75% HR max) mixed with sprinting; addition of low-level technical riding with BMX and off-road bicycling
8	Group ride with sprints, climbing, pacelines, and normal technical riding

Snell Memorial Foundation, and the Consumer Products Safety Commission (CPSC) test and certify bicycle helmets. A helmet should be replaced after sustaining any significant impact, whether or not damage is obvious. Even if a helmet has never been damaged, the Snell Memorial Foundation recommends that it be replaced after 5 years.

Clavicle Fractures and Acromioclavicular Joint Separations

Cyclist often fall onto the side of the shoulder or with the arm stretched out, resulting in clavicle fractures and acromioclavicular (AC) joint injuries.

Diagnosis

Although any part of the clavicle can be broken, breaks most commonly occur in the middle of the clavicle. Diagnosing clavicle fractures and AC joint injuries is usually not difficult given the deformity that usually results from the injury. X-rays of clavicle fractures can look alarming because of how angulated the fractures can appear and the number of fracture pieces.

Among the six grades of AC joint separations, the most common are grades 1 to 3 (Rockwood, Williams, and Young 1996). Physical examination and X-rays will reveal a step deformity of the AC joint. Unless vascular or neurological injury is suspected, no other investigations are usually needed.

Management

Fortunately, despite how bad clavicle fractures may appear on X-ray, most clavicle fractures heal without surgery. Clavicle fractures usually take 6 to 8 weeks to heal and up to 3 months for the strength of the fracture site to normalize. Avoiding sport and exercise activities in which falling may be a risk is recommended for about 3 months. After the fracture heals, the clavicle usually has a cosmetic deformity, but deficits in shoulder function, motion, or strength are normally not seen. Similarly, after the acute symptoms of grade 1 to 3 AC joint separations resolve, a permanent step deformity of the AC joint will be seen, but shoulder function, motion, and strength will not be impaired. Therefore, the initial management of clavicle fractures and AC joint separations is mainly symptomatic. Analgesic medication is taken as needed, and the arm is supported with a sling. As pain symptoms improve, gentle range of motion and isometric strengthening exercises can be introduced. Stationary biking can probably be started at any time as long as the pain is tolerable.

Only a few absolute indications require a clavicle fracture to be surgically reduced and fixated, such as a break or severe tenting of the skin and secondary nerve or vascular injury. Elective indications for surgical fixation of a clavicle are significant shortening of the clavicle, cosmetic reasons, and the need to return to activity quickly. Surgical reduction and fixation of uncomplicated clavicle fractures allow faster return to physical activity and reduce the risk of a fracture nonunion. But most studies show that by 6 months, no difference in shoulder pain, range of motion, and function is seen when comparing surgery with nonoperative management (McKee et al. 2012; Virtanen et al. 2012). Moreover, a second surgery often is required to remove the surgical hardware because the skin overlying the clavicle is extremely thin.

External Iliac Artery Endofibrosis

Artery narrowing is uncommon in otherwise healthy young people. Male cyclists with leg weakness were probably the first competitive athletes to be identified with having narrowing of the external iliac artery, which is known as external iliac artery endofibrosis (EIAE). Oxygenated blood is pumped from the heart to the lower body through a large blood vessel called the aorta. The aorta splits into the right and left common iliac arteries (figure 20.5). Each common iliac artery then splits into the internal and external iliac arteries. The external iliac artery becomes the femoral artery, which supplies oxygenated blood to the leg.

The underlying cause of EIAE in bicyclists is presumed to be the prolonged and repetitive flexion and extension positioning of the hip combined with high rates of blood flow during prolonged and repetitive high-intensity cycling. Some cyclists may also have an external iliac artery that is abnormal in length or in its pathway in the hip. This condition leads to fibrosis and thickening of the inner wall of the artery, which then causes narrowing of the artery. This narrowing of the artery is different from the typical age-related atherosclerotic narrowing of arteries because there is no calcification and fewer inflammatory cells present in the EIAE (Vink et al. 2008).

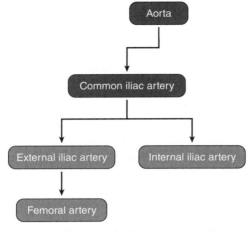

▶ **Figure 20.5** Arterial blood flow to the lower extremities.

Diagnosis

EIAE usually occurs in one leg, but it can occur in both legs. Bicyclists usually experience a feeling of thigh pain or tightness that occurs only at high cycling intensities, such as with sprinting or hill climbing. This feeling can radiate into the buttock or down to the calf. The leg then feels extremely weak or paralyzed, which forces the cyclist to decrease the intensity or stop bicycling. Routine physical examination of the affected leg is usually normal with respect to sensation, muscle power, temperature, and foot pulses (Feugier, Chevalier, and Edouard Herriot Hospital 2004). A simple and inexpensive screening test for any leg artery narrowing is to use Doppler ultrasound to compare the blood pressure measured at the elbow and ankle. This test, called the ankle-to-brachial systolic pressure index, should be performed at rest and following maximal exercise. An index less than 0.9 is considered abnormal (Aboyans et al. 2012). But with EIAE, the index can also be normal. Therefore, diagnostic imaging of the external iliac artery may help visualize EIAE. An MRI or CT angiogram is probably the most sensitive and specific way to visualize the location and extent of EIAE.

Management

To continue training and competing at a high level, the most definitive treatment for EIAE is surgical. Various surgical techniques are available and can be discussed with a vascular surgeon. Bicyclists generally return to their previous level of cycling following surgical treatment, although the postoperative rehabilitation process can take many months.

Applying the Science

In summary, bicyclists are susceptible to a variety of acute and overuse injuries. Many injuries can be related to the positioning of the bicyclist in a sitting position, force generation with leg muscles, and points of contact with the hands, buttocks, and feet. Many bicycling overuse and point of contact injuries may resolve simply with adjustments to training load, bicycling position, and equipment, or by adding strengthening and stretching exercises. Managing injuries when they first appear is better than trying to continue riding through an injury and causing it to become a chronic problem. Bicyclists should seek a professional medical assessment to ensure a systematic approach to the diagnosis and management of their injury, especially if the injury is not improving despite the recommended management strategies. The oral, topical, and injected intraarticular analgesic and anti-inflammatory medications that are usually recommended for management of musculoskeletal problems are generally not prohibited by anti-doping organizations. But cyclists who are competing at a level that requires anti-doping testing should always check medications to determine whether they are prohibited. One web-based option for checking the prohibited status of a medication is the Global Drug Reference Online (Global DRO): www.globaldro.com.

CHAPTER 21

Fatigue and Overtraining

—Romain Meeusen and Kevin De Pauw

Competitive athletes aim to improve exercise performance. The ultimate goal to ride faster is achieved by a perfect balance of training load, recovery, nutrition, sleep, social environment, and so forth. Training loads are constantly increased, and interventions are applied to speed recovery, resulting in a great amount of stress that athletes have to cope with.

Any imbalance of these components might disrupt the training plan. In an attempt to recover, imbalanced athletes tend to train harder and to recover less. When prolonged, excessive training occurs concurrent with other stressors and insufficient recovery, performance decrements can result in chronic maladaptations that might lead to overtraining syndrome (OTS). Exercise (training) is not necessarily the sole causative factor of the syndrome. OTS has many causes, characterized by physiological, biochemical, neuroendocrine, and psychological disturbances. Athletes and support staff need to follow the physiological and psychological parameters necessary to reach optimal performance and avoid OTS, because OTS frequently leads to cessation of a top sporting career.

The literature includes an abundant amount of information on overtraining. But we lack common and consistent terminology as well as a gold standard for the diagnosis of overtraining. Therefore, this chapter not only presents the current knowledge on OTS but also provides a consensus with regard to the definition of OTS, the differences between the state of overreaching (OR) and overtraining, and the diagnosis of these two states.

Overtraining Versus Overreaching

Several authors consider overtraining a status that evolves from normal training, through OR, and finally ending in OTS. Probably these states (OR or OTS) show different defining characteristics, and the overtraining continuum may be an oversimplification because it emphasizes training characteristics, whereas the features of OTS consist of more than training errors and coincide with other stressors (Meeusen et al. 2006, 2013).

As stated in the joint consensus statement of the European College of Sport Science and the American College of Sports Medicine (Meeusen et al. 2006, 2013), the difference between overtraining and OR is the amount of time needed for performance restoration, not the type or duration of training stress or degree of impairment (table 21.1). Athletes can sometimes recover from a state of OR within a 2-week period (Halson et al. 2002; Jeukendrup et al. 1992; Kreider, Fry, and O'Toole 1998; Lehmann et al. 1999; Steinacker et al. 2000). Therefore, this condition may be seen as a relatively normal and harmless stage of the training process. Athletes who are suffering from OTS, however, may take months or sometimes years to recover completely.

Some studies (e.g. Maso et al. 2003; Nindl et al. 2002; O'Connor, Morgan, and Raglin 1991; Passelergue and Lac 1999) use the term *overtraining* in the title, introduction, and discussion or as a keyword to describe the training status or state of tiredness of athletes (individual athletes or team-sport players). This incorrect use of the term *overtraining* feeds the confusion that exists in the definition.

Others (e.g., Kellmann and Gunther 2000; Knopfli et al. 2001; Maso et al. 2003) attempted to discover so-called overtraining features by monitoring athletes for short periods ranging from 3 days to 10 to 14 days of longitudinal data collection. Several possible markers, such as hormonal and psychological measurements (e.g., Kellmann and Gunther 2000; Knopfli et al. 2001; Maso et al. 2003; Morgan et al. 1988; Barron et al. 1985), were used to indicate training disturbances. Again, most authors used the term *overtraining* as an indicator of the process of increased training load, but they confounded this term with possible indicators of OTS.

In recent literature, several papers use *overtraining* as a verb and therefore indicate the process that might lead to training maladaptations (Armstrong and Van Heest 2002; Halson and Jeukendrup 2004; Meeusen et al. 2006, 2013). In many studies, *overtraining* is used to describe both the process of training excessively and the fatigue states that may develop as a consequence (Kuipers and Keizer 1988; Morgan et al. 1987; Callister et al. 1990; Meeusen et al. 2006).

Table 21.1 Stages of Training, Overreaching, and Overtraining Syndrome

Process	Training (overload)	Intensified training ⟶		
Outcome	Acute fatigue	Functional overreaching (short-term overreaching) (e.g., training camp)	Nonfunctional overreaching (extreme overreaching)	Overtraining syndrome (OTS)
Recovery	Day or days	Days to weeks	Weeks to months	Months to years
Performance	Increase	Temporary performance decrement	Stagnation or decrease	Decrease

Based on R. Meeusen, M. Duclos, M. Gleeson, et al., 2006, "Prevention, diagnosis, and treatment of the overtraining syndrome," *European Journal of Sport Science* 6(1): 1-14; and R. Meeusen, M. Duclos, C. Foster, et al., 2013, "Prevention, diagnosis, and treatment of the overtraining syndrome: Joint consensus statement of the European College of Sport Science and the American College of Sports Medicine," *Medicine & Science in Sports & Exercise* 45(1): 186-205.

In these papers, *overtraining* is clearly used to describe the process of more intensive or prolonged training. Callister et al. (1990) followed 15 judo athletes through a 10-week training period. They gradually increased the athletes' training volume and intensity and found that some but not all aspects of performance decreased without observing any sign of OTS. Several studies used a longitudinal design to register training stress in various athlete populations (Chatard et al. 2002; Maso et al. 2003; Manetta et al. 2002; Petibois et al. 2003).

More recent studies apply an intensified training period to explore the effects of progressively increased training load and therefore reveal insight into possible metabolic, hormonal, and psychological mechanisms responsible for overreaching or overtraining. These studies have the common feature that they no longer use the term *overtraining* to indicate the load put on athletes; instead, they call it *overload, intensified training, strenuous training*, and so forth. Ventura et al. (2003) had cyclists perform three additional training sessions per week for 6 weeks and included hypoxic environmental conditions. The major findings were that the increased training load did not improve endurance performance or alter metabolic parameters. Yet these authors used *overtraining* and *overreaching* as keywords, although no signs or symptoms were reported. Pichot et al. (2002) had subjects perform an intensive training period of 8 weeks, followed by 4 weeks of overload training and 2 weeks of recovery to measure heart rate variability. Hall et al. (1999) followed eight male runners and controls over 8 weeks. After 2 weeks of normal training, they increased training load by 43 percent for 2 weeks, followed that by an increase of 86 percent for the next 2 weeks, and then included a taper of 2 weeks (50 percent of normal training). Both studies registered training adaptations, but no signs or symptoms of performance decrements were observed. Halson et al. (2002, 2003) also used 2 weeks of normal training followed by 2 weeks of intensified training and 2 weeks of recovery. During the intensified training, subjects spent twice the amount of time in the intensive training zones (heart rate monitoring). In the studies of Halson et al. (2002, 2003), subjects showed signs of overreaching, manifested by a decrease in performance and disturbed mood state. Rietjens et al. (2005) investigated the central and peripheral physiological, neuroendocrine, and psychological responses to 2 weeks of increased training. Both volume and intensity of the training load were increased, creating a severe state of fatigue. The purpose was to create a state of temporary overreaching. Although they did not register performance decrements in the athletes, the authors found that reaction time, performance, and mood state were the first indicators of early overreaching. Uusitalo et al. (1998) and Uusitalo, Uusitalo, and Rusko (1998) increased training volume and intensity in nine athletes and compared the results with a control group (n = 6). The athletes were tested 2 weeks before the start of the experiment; after 4, 6, and 9 weeks of training; and after 4 and 6 weeks of recovery. The authors found marked individual differences in training and overtraining-induced hormonal changes.

These studies illustrate that athletes often use overreaching during a typical training cycle to enhance performance. Intensified training can result in a decline in performance, but when appropriate periods of recovery are provided, a supercompensation effect may occur in which the athlete exhibits enhanced performance when compared with baseline levels. In the studies that show this effect, typically the athletes go to a short training camp to create functional overreaching (FOR). The studies typically follow athletes not only during the increased training (volume or intensity) but also during recovery from this training status. Usually athletes show temporary performance decrements that disappear after a taper period. In this situation, the physiological responses counterbalance the training-related stress (Steinacker et al. 2004).

Steinacker et al. (2000) and Le Meur et al. (2013a, 2013b) made a distinction between overreaching and OTS. While following rowers and triathletes, respectively, they observed clear signs of overreaching after approximately 3 to 5 weeks of intense training. These signs were decreased performance, variations in physiological parameters (heart rate, heart rate variability, and lactatemia, or the presence of blood lactate), gonadal and hypothalamic hormone disturbances, and deterioration of recovery in the psychological questionnaire. The reason that Steinacker et al. (2000) and Le Meur et al. (2013b) called the athletes overreached was that after a tapering period the values returned to normal. This study was a typical example of FOR because here overreaching was used as an integral part of successful training, although during the intensive training period some markers already showed disturbances. Hooper, MacKinnon, and Howard (1999) showed that some physiological (norepinephrine) and psychometric variables (Profile of Mood State, or POMS) could be indicators of recovery following an 18-week training period.

When intensified training continues, the athlete can evolve into a state of extreme overreaching or nonfunctional overreaching (NFOR) that will lead to a stagnation or decrease in performance that he or she will not recover from for several weeks or months. Hooper et al. (1995) followed swimmers during a 6-month period in an attempt to determine markers of overtraining and recovery. They classified staleness based on performance criteria (decrease or stagnation in performance), poor training responses, or 7 consecutive days of high fatigue scores with no specific illness present at the time the before-mentioned criteria were registered. In a group of 14 subjects, 3 were considered stale. Stale swimmers rate fatigue and muscle soreness significantly higher than nonstale swimmers do and report significantly poorer sleep and significantly higher levels of stress. Tapering did not appear to provide the stale swimmers with sufficient time for complete recovery before competition, which could indicate that these three subjects were suffering from NFOR. Unfortunately, the authors did not report how long it took these athletes to recover fully. But these authors themselves confuse overtraining and staleness because they report on the same group of swimmers in a previous paper (Hooper et al. 1993) and identify three swimmers as overtrained and call them stale one sentence later, adding to the confusion in terminology!

Both functional and nonfunctional overreached athletes will be able to recover fully after sufficient rest. The literature also seems to suggest that in NFOR the evolution on the overtraining continuum is quantitatively determined (i.e., by the increase in training volume) and qualitative changes occur (e.g., signs and symptoms of psychological or endocrine distress). This idea is in line with neuroendocrine findings using a double-exercise test (Urhausen, Gabriel, and Kindermann 1998; Urhausen et al. 1998; Meeusen et al. 2004, 2010).

Although athletes can recover from short-term overreaching, or FOR, within a period of 2 weeks, the process of recovery from the NFOR state is less clear. Few studies have tried to define the subtle difference that exists between extreme overreaching, which needs several weeks or even months for recovery (Meeusen et al. 2006), and overtraining syndrome (OTS). Athletes who suffer from OTS may need months or even years to recover completely, leading frequently to cessation of a (top) sporting career.

The difficulty lies in the subtle difference that might exist between extreme overreached athletes and those having OTS. In using the term *syndrome*, we emphasize the many causes and acknowledge that exercise (training) is not necessarily the sole causative factor of the syndrome.

Reports on athletes suffering from OTS are mostly case studies, because training an athlete with a high training load while including other stressors is not only unethical but also probably impossible, especially because the symptoms of OTS differ by individual. Meeusen et al. (2004, 2010) reported on differences in normal training status and FOR (after a training camp) and compared the endocrinological results to a double-exercise test with an OTS athlete. Athletes were tested in a double-exercise protocol (two exercise tests 4 hours apart) to register their recovery capacity. Performance was measured as the time to voluntary exhaustion. Researchers compared the first and second exercise tests to verify whether the athletes were able to maintain the same performance. The training camp reduced exercise capacity in the athletes. Performances in the first versus the second test decreased by 3 percent, whereas in the FOR condition performance decreased by 6 percent. The OTS subject showed an 11 percent decrease in time to exhaustion. The OTS athlete also showed clear psychological and endocrinological disturbances.

Diagnosis

OTS is characterized by a sport-specific performance decrement, together with persistent fatigue and disturbances in mood state (Urhausen and Kindermann 2002; Meeusen et al. 2006, 2013; Armstrong and Van Heest 2002; Halson and Jeukendrup 2004). Thus, the key indicator of OTS can be considered an unexplainable decrease in performance. This underperformance persists, despite a period of recovery lasting several weeks or months.

Because no diagnostic tool is available to identify an athlete as suffering from OTS, diagnosis can be made only by excluding all other possible influences on changes in performance and mood state. Therefore, if no explanation for the observed changes can be found, OTS is diagnosed. Early and unequivocal recognition of OTS is virtually impossible because the only certain sign of this condition is decreased performance during competition or training. The definitive diagnosis of OTS always requires the exclusion of an organic disease, such as endocrinological disorders (thyroid or adrenal gland, diabetes), iron deficiency with anemia, or infectious diseases (Meeusen et al. 2006, 2013). Other major disorders or eating disorders, such as anorexia nervosa and bulimia, should also be excluded. But many endocrinological and clinical findings caused by NFOR and OTS can mimic other diseases. The borderline between under- and overdiagnosis is difficult to judge (Meeusen et al. 2006, 2013).

Because OTS is characterized by reduced exercise performance, an exercise performance test is considered essential for the diagnosis of OTS (Budgett et al. 2000; Lehmann et al. 1999; Urhausen, Gabriel, and Kindermann 1995). Both the type of performance test employed and the duration of the test are important in determining the changes in performance associated with OTS. Debate exists as to which performance test is the most appropriate when attempting to diagnose OR and OTS. In general, time-to-fatigue tests most likely show greater changes in exercise capacity because of OR and OTS than incremental exercise tests (Halson and Jeukendrup 2004). Additionally, they allow the assessment of substrate kinetics and hormonal responses, and submaximal measures can be made at a fixed intensity and duration. To detect subtle performance decrements, using sport-specific performance tests might be better.

Urhausen, Gabriel, and Kindermann (1998) and Meeusen et al. (2004, 2010) have shown that multiple tests or tests carried out on different days (Urhausen, Gabriel, and Kindermann 1998) or tests that use the two maximal incremental exercise tests separated by 4 hours can be valuable tools to assess the performance decrements usually seen in OTS athletes. A decrease in exercise time of at least 10 percent is necessary to be significant. Furthermore, this decrease in performance needs to be confirmed by specific changes in hormone concentrations (Meeusen et al. 2004, 2010).

Research findings (e.g. Barron et al. 1985; Urhausen et al. 1998; Meeusen et al. 2004, 2010) support that athletes experiencing maladaptive training and performance adaptation problems seem to suffer from a dysfunctional hypothalamic–pituitary–adrenal (HPA) axis response to exercise (exercise triggers the release of neuronal and circulating homeostatic signals and inflammatory signals), resulting in altered hormonal response to intense training and competition. When investigating elite athletes, the HPA axis is believed to offer valuable information about an athlete's state of adaptation

(Steinacker and Lehmann 2002). Meeusen et al. (2004, 2010) published a test protocol that used two consecutive maximal exercise tests separated by 4 hours. They found that to detect signs of OTS and distinguish them from normal training responses or FOR, this protocol might be a good indicator not only of the athlete's recovery capacity but also of the athlete's ability to perform the second bout of exercise normally. The use of two bouts of maximal exercise to study neuroendocrine variations showed an adapted exercise-induced increase of adrenocorticotropic hormone (ACTH), prolactin (PRL), and growth hormone (GH) to a two-exercise bout (Meeusen et al. 2004, 2010). Therefore, the test could be used as an indirect measure of hypothalamic–pituitary capacity. In a FOR stage, a less pronounced neuroendocrine response to a second bout of exercise on the same day is found (De Schutter et al. 2004; Meeusen et al. 2004, 2010), whereas in a NFOR stage, the hormonal response to a two-bout exercise protocol shows an extreme increased release after the second exercise trigger (Meeusen et al. 2004, 2010). With the same protocol it has been shown that athletes suffering from OTS have an extremely large increase in hormonal release in the first exercise bout, followed by a complete suppression in the second exercise bout (Meeusen et al. 2004, 2010). This finding could indicate hypersensitivity of the pituitary followed by insensitivity or exhaustion afterward. Previous reports that used a single exercise protocol found similar effects (Meeusen et al. 2004, 2010). The use of two exercise bouts appears to be more useful in detecting OR for preventing OTS.

Early detection of OR may be important in the prevention of OTS. Testing of central hypothalamic and pituitary regulation, however, requires functional tests that are considered invasive and that require diagnostic experience. These tests are time consuming and expensive.

The analysis of heart rate variability seems a promising tool in theory but needs to be standardized and at present does not provide consistent results. A performance decrease of more than 10 percent on two tests separated by 4 hours can be indicative of OTS if other signs and symptoms are present. Biochemical markers, such as lactate or urea, as well as immunological markers, do not have consistent reports in the literature to consider these as absolute indicators for OTS. Many factors affect blood hormone concentrations including factors linked to sampling conditions or conservation of the sample, stress of the sampling, and intra- and interassay coefficient of variability. Others factors such as food intake (nutrient composition or pre- versus postmeal sampling) can modify significantly either the basal concentration of some hormones (cortisol, DHEA-S, total testosterone) or their concentration change in response to exercise (cortisol, GH). Diurnal and seasonal variations of the hormones are important factors that need to be considered. In female athletes, the hormonal response depends on the phase of the menstrual cycle. Hormone concentrations at rest and following stimulation (exercise = acute stimulus) respond differently. Stress-induced measures (exercise, prohormones, and so on) need to be compared with baseline measures from the same individual. Poor reproducibility and feasibility of some techniques used to measure certain hormones can make the comparison of results difficult. Therefore, the use of two maximal performance (or time-trial) tests separated by 4 hours could help in comparing the individual results.

Researchers generally agree that OTS is characterized by psychological disturbances and negative affective states. Athletes who suffer from OTS typically experience chronic fatigue, poor sleep patterns, a drop in motivation, and episodes of depression and helplessness (Lemyre 2005). Not surprisingly, their performance is considerably impaired. Several questionnaires, such as the Profile of Mood State, or POMS (Morgan et al. 1988; Rietjens et al. 2005); Recovery-Stress Questionnaire, or RestQ-Sport (Kellmann 2002); Daily Analysis of Life Demands of Athletes, or DALDA (Halson et al. 2002); and the self-condition scale (Urhausen et al. 1998) have been used to monitor psychological parameters in athletes. Other tests, such as attention tests (finger precuing tasks; Rietjens et al. 2005) or neurocognitive tests (Kubesch et al. 2003) also serve as promising tools to detect subtle neurocognitive disturbances registered in OR or OTS athletes. Changes in mood state may be a useful indicator of OR and OTS, but mood disturbances must be combined with measures of performance.

Prevention

One general confounding factor when reviewing the literature on OTS is that the definition and diagnosis of OR and OTS are not standardized. We can even question whether subjects in most of the studies were suffering from OTS. Because OTS is difficult to diagnose, authors agree that preventing OTS is important (Foster et al. 1988). Moreover, because OTS is mainly caused by an imbalance in the training-to-recovery ratio (too much training and competition and too little recovery), athletes must record their training load daily using a training diary or training log (Foster et al. 1988; Foster 1998). The four methods most frequently used to monitor training and prevent overtraining are retrospective questionnaires, training diaries, physiological screening, and the direct observational method (Hopkins 1991). In addition, the psychological screening of athletes (Hooper et al. 1995; Urhausen et al. 1998; Morgan et al. 1988; Kellmann 2002; Steinacker and Lehmann 2002) and the ratings of perceived exertion (RPE) (Acevedo, Rinehardt, and Kraemer 1994; Callister et al. 1990; Foster et al. 1996; Foster 1998; Hooper et al. 1995) have received more attention.

Hooper et al. (1995) used daily training logs during an entire season in swimmers to detect staleness (OTS). The distances swum, the dry-land work time, and subjective self-assessment of training intensity were recorded. In addition to providing these training details, the swimmers recorded subjective ratings of quality of sleep, fatigue, stress, and muscle soreness, as well as body mass, early morning heart rate, illness, menstruation, and causes of stress. Swimmers were classified as having OTS if their profiles met five criteria. Three of these criteria were determined by items in the daily training logs: fatigue ratings in the logs of more than 5 (scale 1 to 7) lasting longer than 7 days, comments in the page provided in each log that the athlete was feeling that he or she responded poorly to training, and a negative response to a question in the swimmer's log regarding the presence of illness, together with a normal blood leukocyte count.

Foster (1998) and Foster et al. (1996) determined training load as the product of the subjective intensity of a training session using session RPE and the total duration of the training session expressed in minutes. Summarized weekly, these parameters are called the total training load of an individual. The session RPE has been shown to be related to the average percent heart rate reserve during an exercise session and to the percentage of a training session during which the heart rate is in blood-lactate-derived heart rate training zones. With this method of monitoring training, the researchers have demonstrated the utility of evaluating experimental alterations in training and have successfully related training load to its performance (Foster et al. 1996). Training load, however, is clearly not the only training-related variable contributing to the genesis of OTS. So in addition to the weekly training load, daily mean training load as well as the standard deviation of training load were calculated during each week. The daily mean divided by the standard deviation was defined as the monotony. The product of the weekly training load and monotony was calculated as strain. The incidence of simple illness and injury was noted and plotted together with the indices of training load, monotony, and strain. The author noted the correspondence between spikes in the indices of training and subsequent illness or injury, and thresholds that allowed for optimal explanation of illnesses were computed (Foster 1998).

One of the disadvantages of the traditional paper and pencil method is that data collection can be complicated and that immediate feedback is not always possible. Another problem is that when athletes are at an international training camp or competition, immediate data computing is not possible. A useful method might be to have an online training log (Cumps, Pockelé, and Meeusen 2004; Pockelé et al. 2004) that has specific features for detecting not only slight differences in training load but also the subjective parameters (muscle soreness, mental and physical well-being) that have been proved to be important in the detection of OTS.

Applying the Science

Progressive overload during a training plan is used to disturb homeostasis in an attempt to improve exercise performance. A single training session and short-term training periods (e.g., training camp) result in acute fatigue and short-term performance decrements. When full recovery takes place, functional overreaching (FOR) occurs. This state leads to improved exercise performance.

But when athletes do not sufficiently respect the balance between training and recovery, nonfunctional overreaching (NFOR) can occur. At this stage, the first signs and symptoms of prolonged training distress, such as performance decrements, psychological disturbances (decreased vigor, increased fatigue), and hormonal disturbances will be present. Athletes will need weeks or months to recover from NFOR. Several confounding factors, such as inadequate nutrition (energy or carbohydrate intake), illness (most commonly upper respiratory tract infections or URTI), psychosocial stressors (work-, team-, coach-, family-related), and sleep disorders may be present. At this stage, the distinction between NFOR and OTS is difficult to detect and will depend on the clinical outcome and exclusion diagnosis.

CHAPTER 22

Recovery Interventions

—Shona L. Halson and Nathan G. Versey

Recovery has become one of the foundations of training for athletes. Including appropriate recovery at the correct times in a training program can aid in the balance among training, stress, and fatigue. Too much training without enough recovery can lead to excessive fatigue, poor performance, and, if prolonged, overtraining syndrome. Utilizing good recovery may also reduce illness and injury and therefore improve performance by allowing consistency of training.

Because many cyclists are riding greater volumes at higher intensities than ever before, including recovery and thus balance in the training program has become increasingly common. Athletes use a number of popular methods to enhance recovery. The method used depends on the type of training, the amount of training, the time until the next training session or race, and the equipment available. Some of the most common forms of recovery for cyclists are sleep, massage, hydrotherapy, active recovery, stretching, and compression. Interesting new technologies, such as muscle stimulation devices, whole-body cryotherapy, saunas, and flotation tanks, are also becoming popular and are generally targeted at elite cyclists who have access to such equipment.

Sleep

Getting a good night's sleep can be one of the most effective ways to minimize fatigue and ensure that performance is not compromised. An appropriate quality and quantity of sleep may help reduce the risk of developing overtraining syndrome. Indeed, optimal sleep quality and quantity is considered the single best recovery strategy available to athletes.

The effects of sleep deprivation on exercise performance have been investigated in a small number of studies. Research has demonstrated decreases in performance following partial sleep deprivation. Sustained exercise appears to be more affected than single maximal efforts, and thus longer submaximal exercise tasks may be affected following sleep deprivation (Reilly and

Edwards 2007). For example, time-trial and stage-race performance may be more affected than one-off sprint efforts.

With respect to recovery, the suggested recuperative and restorative effects of sleep may have necessary beneficial effects on athletic recovery. In particular, impairments in the immune and endocrine systems that may result from sleep deprivation may impair the recovery process and hence adaptation to training. From what we know about poor sleep and performance, sleep deprivation does not seem to have any effect on pacing, cardiorespiratory, or thermoregulatory function. Following sleep deprivation, however, perception of effort is usually greater. Essentially, no real effect on physiology occurs, but people will likely think that the exercise is harder after sleep deprivation compared with after they have had a good night's sleep.

For many athletes, their training, competition, and other commitments can prevent them from obtaining sufficient nighttime sleep, so napping can be an effective way for them to catch up on sleep and gain the associated recovery benefits (Halson 2013). Despite the lack of literature on the use of napping by athletes, evidence shows that napping can improve both sprint performance and alertness (Waterhouse et al. 2007). Napping is ideally performed in the early afternoon to coincide with a dip in the circadian biological clock; athletes should avoid napping too close to bedtime because doing so may compromise nighttime sleep. The required nap duration will depend on a person's degree of sleep debt, but naps of up to 90 minutes (roughly one sleep cycle) are typically recommended.

Athletes often rank a lack of sleep as the most prominent cause of fatigue and tiredness. Thus, elite athletes and coaches often identify sleep as a vital component of the recovery process. Indeed, many athletes often have difficulties sleeping before important competitions. Getting an appropriate quality and quantity of sleep is perhaps the best recovery strategy available to cyclists. Table 22.1 outlines recommendations for getting a good night's sleep.

Massage

Massage is a widely used recovery strategy among athletes and particularly cyclists during stage races. Massage is thought to increase blood flow and therefore improve recovery by improving the clearance of metabolic waste products. Most research, however, has found no increase in blood flow or lactate removal during massage. Indeed, massage may impair blood flow and lactic acid removal. As discussed in a later section on active recovery, low-intensity cycling is an effective means of reducing lactate concentrations postexercise. Recent evidence suggests that massage may aid in reducing muscle soreness and be effective for aiding repair of damaged or injured muscles (Shroeder and Best 2015).

Massage is generally considered more effective than no recovery (i.e., passive rest) but less effective than active recovery (warm-down). In general,

Table 22.1 Practical Sleep Recommendations

Element	Recommendations
Bedroom	The bedroom should be cool (20 degrees Celsius is best), dark, quiet, and comfortable. The bed and pillows can vary in materials and softness, and their selection often comes down to individual preference, while being appropriate for the athlete's size.
Routine	Go to bed at the same time every night and wake up at the same time every morning. Create a before-bed routine (brush teeth, read a book, and so on) that starts about 30 minutes before bedtime.
Electronics	Avoid watching television or using a computer in bed. These activities can steal sleep time and form bad habits.
Clock	Avoid watching the clock. Many people who struggle with sleep tend to watch the clock too much. Frequently checking the clock during the night can wake you up, especially if you turn on a light to read the clock, and this habit may reinforce negative thoughts.
Food and fluid	Avoid caffeinated food and fluids later in the day. Do not consume too much fluid before going to bed; you may have to get up to use the bathroom.
Organization	Create a to-do list or keep a diary to ensure organization and avoid unnecessary overthinking while you are trying to sleep.
Relaxation	Try relaxation strategies such as controlled breathing techniques, guided meditation and imagery, progressive muscle relaxation, and listening to relaxing music.
Get up and try again	If you haven't been able to fall asleep after about 20 minutes, get up and do something calming or boring until you feel sleepy. Or try sitting quietly on the couch with the lights off (bright light will tell your brain it's time to wake up). Then return to bed and try again.

massage is thought to be more beneficial in improving psychological aspects of recovery than in improving functional performance. But massage may have potential benefits in injury prevention and management; therefore, massage should still be incorporated into an athlete's training program, just not with a focus on immediate recovery. The preferred type of massage depends on the timing relative to training and competition. Light massage such as Swedish massage is preferred in the couple of days before and immediately after hard exercise to relax the muscles and fascia. In contrast, deep-tissue massage is generally avoided during this time because it may cause some residual soreness that could impair performance or compromise recovery acutely following exercise.

Water Immersion

Postexercise water immersion of various types has become popular with elite athletes in many sports, including cycling, to accelerate recovery from training and competition. Four main forms of water immersion exist: cold-water immersion (CWI), hot-water immersion (HWI), contrast water therapy (CWT), and pool recovery sessions. Although substantial research has been conducted in recent years into the effectiveness of CWI, HWI, and CWT at accelerating performance recovery in cyclists, there is a paucity of research examining pool recovery. Studies that have directly compared the different forms of water immersion typically report that CWI and CWT enhance recovery more than HWI or pool recovery does when used appropriately following both cycling (Vaile et al. 2008a; Crampton et al. 2013) and resistance training (Vaile et al. 2008b). Furthermore, more studies report accelerated performance recovery following CWI and CWT than HWI or thermoneutral water immersion (TWI) (Versey, Halson, and Dawson 2013). Therefore, cyclists should consider using CWI or CWT to accelerate postexercise recovery.

When undertaking CWI, cyclists should first complete a cool-down and then aim to immerse in water of 10 to 15 degrees Celsius for 10 to 15 minutes to obtain maximal recovery benefits. Colder water temperatures are not recommended because they are likely to result in a reduction in immersion duration because of excessive discomfort and have not shown the same recovery benefits. If the water temperature is 15 to 20 degrees Celsius, increasing the immersion duration can be considered to obtain a similar cooling effect. Those unfamiliar with CWI can progressively increase the immersion duration to ensure that the body can cope when in the water and during the sustained cold sensations experienced afterward.

Recovery benefits are still likely to be obtained whether CWI is performed immediately or a few hours following the completion of exercise, but the benefits will be maximized when performed as soon as practical postexercise. This is particularly the case following exercise in the heat that has caused substantial elevation in core and muscle temperatures, because CWI will accelerate their return back to normal levels. Although cycling predominantly involves lower-body muscle contractions, for maximal benefits cyclists are encouraged to immerse in the cold water to shoulder level. Whether it is better to be active or passive when in cold water is unknown.

Contrast water therapy is performed similarly to CWI, but it involves alternating regularly between cold (10 to 15 degrees Celsius) and hot (36 to 40 degrees Celsius) water. Cyclists should spend equal or more time in the cold water compared with the hot water to promote recovery benefits. Research by Versey, Halson, and Dawson (2011) attempted to determine the optimal CWT immersion duration following cycling time-trial and sprint performance. They reported that CWT for a duration of 6 to 12 minutes enhanced recovery of high-intensity cycling performance more than a longer immersion did. Similar results were found in runners (Versey, Halson, and Dawson 2012).

The cold-water component of CWT is likely to provide most of the recovery benefits; therefore, the recommendation is to finish CWT in the cold. But when intending to exercise within 45 minutes after CWT, athletes should finish in the hot water to prevent being too cold for the subsequent exercise, which is likely to impede performance in normal conditions. Suggested CWT protocols are as follows:

1. 1 minute hot, 1 minute cold, repeat three to six times
2. 2 minutes hot, 2 minutes cold, repeat two to four times
3. 2 minutes hot, 3 minutes cold, repeat two or three times

Many athletes use hot-water immersion by itself as a recovery technique. Although a hot spa may make athletes feel good after a ride, it is likely to have no effect on recovery from performance and may even impede recovery by causing fluid loss through promoting sweat production and delaying postexercise decreases in core temperature.

Cyclists may also consider undertaking active recovery sessions in a swimming pool. Pool sessions typically involve low-intensity exercise such as walking, jogging, and swimming, as well as range-of-motion movements for 20 to 30 minutes. But little research has been conducted into the effects of pool sessions on postexercise recovery, particularly in cyclists. Theoretically, pool sessions make more sense for weight-bearing athletes such as team-sport players because the buoyancy of the water provides a means for exercise while placing limited stress on a fatigued body. An easy recovery ride is likely to be an effective substitute for cyclists.

A limiting factor in the ability of many athletes to perform water immersion is ready access to an appropriate water source. Purpose-built cold and hot pools are increasingly becoming available at athletic training facilities or swimming pools. Alternative options include portable baths and chilling or heating systems that allow temperature regulation and can be moved between venues. Athletes can add ice to a cold bath; take a shower; use a beach, river, or lake; or use water straight out of the tap in winter and cooler climates.

For recovery techniques to be useful following training, they must not only accelerate recovery but also allow adaptations to training to occur. Competition is different, because maximal recovery, not adaptation, is of primary importance. It has been suggested that CWI might impair adaptation by disrupting the mechanisms of fatigue. In contrast, recent research using elite cyclists found that CWI had no effect on adaptation during 6 weeks of training (Halson et al. 2014). At this stage, little evidence suggests that CWI can impair adaptation to training.

Active Recovery

An active recovery generally consists of low-intensity, aerobic exercise. Active recovery is considered better than passive recovery because of enhanced blood flow and the effective clearance of lactic acid and other metabolic waste products.

Findings differ on the effect of an active recovery between training sessions or following competition. But no detrimental effects on performance have been reported following an active recovery (when compared with a passive recovery) between training sessions, and a small amount of literature reports enhanced performance. Many researchers, however, use the removal of lactate as their primary indicator of recovery, and this measure may not be a valid indicator of enhanced recovery and ability to repeat performance at a previous level (Taoutaou et al. 1996; Barnett 2006).

Although the research on the benefits of active recovery beyond lactate removal is minimal, the role of active recovery in reducing muscle soreness after exercise may be an important factor for athletes. Active recovery is anecdotally reported to be one of the most common forms of recovery, and most cyclists use it.

Stretching

Stretching is one of the most widely used recovery techniques (see chapter 34 on stretching). Types of stretching include static, dynamic, ballistic, and proprioceptive neuromuscular facilitation (PNF). Static stretching is typically performed postexercise and involves holding the stretch for 30 seconds or more and repeating it a number of times. All the main muscles used during the session should be stretched.

Despite the widespread use of postexercise stretching, little evidence exists to support its ability to assist performance recovery or decrease injury risk, particularly in cycling. According to the European College of Sports Sciences position statement on the role of stretching exercises in sport (Magnusson and Renstrom 2006), passive static stretching relaxes the muscles, but the effect lasts only minutes before disappearing, suggesting that it has little effect on recovery or reducing injury risk. Furthermore, the researchers reported that preexercise stretching does not reduce injury risk. In general, evidence is insufficient to support the notion that postexercise stretching enhances recovery or reduces injury.

Despite the mixed findings that have been reported regarding the efficacy of stretching as a recovery technique, to our knowledge postexercise stretching has not been associated with any detrimental effects on performance. Stretching can improve flexibility and range of motion, and these abilities may help with the maintenance of riding position and the management of an existing injury. Therefore, routine stretching may be appropriate for some cyclists.

Compression

Many recovery strategies for elite athletes are based on medical equipment or therapies used on patients. Compression clothing is one of those strategies because it has traditionally been used to treat various lymphatic and circulatory conditions. Compression garments are thought to improve return of blood to the heart through application of graduated compression to the limbs from the ankle up. The external pressure created may reduce swelling, inflammation, and muscle soreness.

Minimal research specifically investigates cycling, but one study reported increased performance during 30 minutes of high-intensity cycling in well-trained cyclists (Driller and Halson 2013). From a specific recovery perspective, compression has been shown to improve performance between two 40K time trials performed 24 hours apart (de Glanville and Hamlin 2012). In this case the compression was worn for the full 24 hours, which may not be practical or comfortable for many riders. Compression has also been shown to improve sprint performance with a shorter recovery period (Argus et al. 2013). Maximal sprint performance was enhanced when using compression for 20 minutes between sprints.

Although only minimal research has been done on compression garments and recovery for cyclists, the small amount of data suggests that compression may be beneficial and is not harmful in any way. Compression garments should be worn for at least 60 minutes after training or racing to maximize the recovery process.

Electrical Stimulation

Electrical stimulation has been used to promote recovery, provide a training stimulus, and assist in rehabilitation. Electrodes are placed on the skin over the muscle belly or muscle nerve, and an intermittent electrical current is sent through the body. The exact location of the electrodes and characteristics of the current depend on the desired outcome; therefore, many forms of electrical stimulation exist. The sensations felt by the athlete range from nothing to moderate muscle contractions.

Neuromuscular electrical stimulation has been shown to be effective at promoting a training effect in athletic populations by stimulating visible muscle contractions (Maffiuletti 2010). The forms of electrical stimulation for recovery purposes include microcurrent electrical neuromuscular stimulation (MENS), high-volt pulsed current electrical stimulation (HVPC), monophasic high-voltage stimulation (MHVS), transcutaneous electrical nerve stimulation (TENS), and a general term of low-frequency electrical stimulation (LFES). Although electrical stimulation for recovery comes in many different forms, the two main physiological goals are to increase blood flow and reduce muscle pain (Babault et al. 2011). It is generally accepted that electrical stimulation for exercise recovery can increase blood flow to promote the removal of muscle metabolites and reduce muscle pain through an analgesic effect. Despite these physiological findings, however, the literature suggests that electrical stimulation does not assist postexercise recovery of performance. Therefore, electrical stimulation should not be used as a recovery technique unless soreness is a limiting factor in performance. But more work needs to be done to confirm this conclusion because of the wide range of electrical stimulation protocols available.

Sauna

Saunas are popular in many countries, particularly countries in Scandinavia. Although a variety of sauna types exist around the world, the traditional Finnish sauna has become most popular. This sauna is usually made of wood and contains a rock-filled heater that provides hot, dry air. The recommended temperature is 80 to 100 degrees Celsius at head level, and relative humidity should be approximately 10 to 20 percent. The apparent temperature can be increased by pouring water on the rocks, creating steam. Infrared saunas are also becoming popular; they use infrared rays to heat surfaces rather than the air. The appropriate time to spend in the sauna will vary for each person but is usually 5 to 15 minutes followed by CWI, repeated two or three times.

Sauna use is generally considered safe for healthy populations as long as appropriate temperatures and durations are maintained. A number of contraindications exist including prolonged and unstable angina, myocardial infarction or other severe cardiac event for 4 to 8 weeks postincident, severe orthostatic hypotension, severe aortic stenosis, acute infectious diseases, fever, rheumatoid arthritis in the acute inflammatory phase, and certain skin conditions. Furthermore, a sauna should not be used in conjunction with alcohol consumption (before, during, or immediately after) because it will increase the risk of hypotension and the likelihood of an adverse event.

Although saunas have been in use for more than 2,000 years, literature on their usefulness as a postexercise recovery technique is limited. Two studies have reported that sauna use after cycling increased heart rate during a subsequent bout of cycling (Ahlman and Karvonen 1961; Ridge 1986). The higher heart rate response observed following the sauna may indicate greater cardiovascular stress, or an increase in physiological work required to perform at a given load. A different study reported that, following 30 minutes of aerobic exercise, sauna recovery transiently increased free radical production, but this elicited greater antioxidant activity and overall lower oxidative stress compared to thermoneutral recovery in healthy men (Sutkowy et al. 2014).

Physiological responses to sauna use are likely to be detrimental to the acute postexercise recovery of cyclists. Exposure to the hot dry air increases skin, muscle, and core temperatures, stimulating heart rate, blood flow, and sweat production in an attempt to cool the body. When a sauna is used shortly after cycling, these physiological responses are likely to add to already elevated body temperature, heart rate, and level of dehydration. Cyclists should have a recovery period between exercise and sauna use to allow a return to normal. They should pay particular attention to maintaining fluid intake when using a sauna to avoid dehydration, particularly because athletes typically have greater thermoregulatory capacity than untrained people do and therefore have a higher sweat rate, necessitating a higher rate of fluid intake.

Note that the effect of repeated sauna bathing on endurance performance adaptation has also been investigated. Scoon et al. (2007) reported that following 3 weeks of sauna bathing completed immediately following exercise, run time to exhaustion increased by 32 percent relative to control. This increase in performance was equivalent to an enhancement of about 1.9 percent in an endurance time trial. The authors concluded that the change in endurance running performance was probably because of the increased plasma volume and total blood volume observed with sauna bathing. Although limited literature is available, repeated sauna bathing following exercise appears to be beneficial for improving endurance performance adaptation, possibly because of the additional stress placed on the body. But sauna use is not recommended during competition when acute recovery is required.

Whole-Body Cryotherapy

Whole-body cryotherapy (WBC) is a relatively new recovery technique for athletes. It involves exposure to very dry and cold air (–110 to –140 degrees Celsius), typically for 2 to 5 minutes. Participants enter either a purpose-built cold room or an individual cylinder capsule that progressively decreases in temperature during the exposure to allow acclimation. To protect the body from injury, participants wear a bathing suit, gloves, ear band, mask for the nose and mouth, shoes, and socks. To prevent frostbite, all sweat and moisture must be removed from clothing.

WBC has traditionally been used to reduce the pain and inflammation associated with chronic medical conditions such as arthritis, multiple sclerosis, and fibromyalgia. Consequently, the suggestion is that WBC may assist recovery from exercise and injury. Although no adverse responses have been reported from WBC, care should be taken with its use until more monitoring of adverse responses has taken place (Bleakley et al. 2014).

To date, no research has been published on the effect of WBC on recovery of cycling performance, but a couple of studies have recently been conducted using other forms of exercise and their findings could be relevant to cycling. One study reported that WBC had no effect on recovery of maximal single-leg strength for 96 hours following a muscle-damaging maximal eccentric single-leg press protocol (Costello, Algar, and Donnelly 2012). In contrast, another study reported that postexercise WBC enhanced recovery from 1 to 48 hours following a simulated trail run in well-trained runners (Hausswirth et al. 2011). In addition, the same study assessed physiological markers that are believed to reflect the recovery response (Pournot et al. 2011) and found that the inflammatory response decreased following WBC, which may suggest enhanced recovery.

A recent review on the use of WBC by athletes found that despite the cold temperatures used in WBC, the poor thermal conductivity of air prevents significant cooling of the body. Therefore, tissue temperature reductions are comparable to or less than those achieved with CWI (Bleakley et al. 2014). The authors also noted that although some evidence indicates that WBC could positively influence the inflammatory response, antioxidant capacity, autonomic function during recovery, and perceptions of recovery and soreness, evidence is insufficient to suggest that these mechanisms translate to recovery of performance. Until further research is conducted into WBC, cyclists should preferentially use more established techniques such as CWI to assist recovery.

Flotation Tank

The use of a flotation tank (or float tank) is another strategy that may improve recovery by promoting rest and relaxation following training or competition. The float tank strategy, a modified form of restricted environmental stimulation therapy (REST), has been found to be effective as a stress management and deep relaxation tool.

A float tank is similar to a very large covered bathtub that is dark on the inside and partially insulated from external noise. The tank is filled to a depth of approximately 35 centimeters with warm (34 degree Celsius) water containing large quantities of diluted Epsom salt. The salt increases the density of the water, which provides greater buoyancy (similar to the Dead Sea), allowing the user to float supine on the surface. Sensory deprivation occurs because the user, not needing to support his or her body weight, can relax the muscles. The environment is quiet, dark, and at a comfortable temperature. A typical float lasts 30 to 90 minutes, during which time the user may safely fall asleep. Flotation tanks are most likely found at commercial spa or relaxation facilities, but residential versions are available.

Flotation tanks reduce both psychological and physiological stress. Float tank use has been shown to decrease levels of the stress hormone cortisol (Turner and Fine 1983). Cortisol is known to increase protein degradation and decrease protein synthesis, causing catabolism, or breakdown of the muscles. Higher levels of cortisol have been linked with overtraining and may impair the repair process of muscles following exercise, negatively affecting recovery. Additionally, a recent study has reported that a 1-hour float following muscle damage resulted in reductions in blood lactate concentration and perceived pain but had no effect on maximal muscle strength, heart rate, or rating of perceived exertion (Morgan, Salacinski, and Stults-Kolehmainen 2013).

Despite the lack of literature on the use of flotation tanks by athletes, they can theoretically promote rest and relaxation, thereby reducing psychological and physiological stress and assisting recovery.

Recommendations

When developing a recovery plan for cyclists, consideration should be given to the amount of time until the next training session or race. Is recovery necessary? What can be performed in the timeframe? What strategies have been shown to be beneficial?

Is the cyclist required to perform maximal, short-duration efforts? If so, cold-water immersion before the effort will likely be detrimental. Consideration must be given to the potential change in muscle and core temperature and the possible effect of those changes on performance. Cyclists should be careful when doing cold-water immersion between two efforts when the second effort is short in duration and high in intensity.

The timing of hydrotherapy for recovery may be particularly important, specifically the time between finishing water immersion and the subsequent performance effort. When the time between exercise is short (less than 30 to 60 minutes), using cold-water immersion may reduce performance because warm muscles are needed for fast muscle contraction. Cold-water immersion may be used when the time between exercise is short if the subsequent effort is of longer duration or an appropriate warm-up is included.

Athletes need to use suitable temperatures and duration for immersion. Research that has found positive effects of water immersion use temperatures of 10 to 15 degrees Celsius for cold water and 38 to 40 degrees Celsius for hot water. Duration of 10 to 15 minutes of either cold-water immersion or contrast water therapy has been shown to improve performance. The ratio of hot to cold during contrast water therapy should be 1:1. Research that has shown positive performance effects used seven rotations of 1 minute hot and 1 minute cold.

Periodization of recovery is important in many sports, whereby recovery is minimized during intensified training to increase fatigue and potentially adaptation. But this approach may impair the quality of training and increase the risk of injury in some sports. Further, in cycling stage races and track-cycling competitions, recovery is needed to minimize fatigue and maximize recovery between races and thus should be prioritized.

Compression garments and active recovery may be beneficial for recovery in cyclists. Their use does not appear to have harmful effects, and anecdotal evidence in support is high. Sleep, however, is one of the best recovery

1. Active recovery: 5 minutes of low-intensity cycling at the end of the ride
2. Nutrition: snack to replenish energy stores and fluid levels
3. Water immersion: cold-water immersion or contrast water therapy as soon as practical posttraining, 10 to 15 minutes in 10 to 15 degree Celsius water to shoulder level
4. Compression: leg compression garments worn for more than 60 minutes after water immersion
5. Nutrition: meal to complete replenishment of energy stores and fluid levels
6. Nap: if it won't impair sleep at night
7. Massage: type of massage matched to the training and racing planned for the next few days
8. Overnight sleep: plenty of good-quality sleep

▶ **Figure 22.1** Postexercise recovery program for endurance cyclists.

strategies for athletes. Placing priority on quality and quantity of sleep is important for optimal performance, particularly for competitions.

Figure 22.1 provides an example of a recovery program for endurance cyclists.

Applying the Science

Because recovery research is a relatively new area, cyclists should experiment with a variety of strategies and approaches to identify the recovery options that work best for each individual. We do know that optimal recovery from training and racing can provide numerous benefits for cycling performance. Recovery strategies such as hydrotherapy, low-intensity active recovery, massage, compression garments, and various combinations of these methods may have merit as recovery-enhancing strategies. Incorporating these strategies into the training program can help reduce fatigue and ultimately increase cycling performance.

PART VII

Training Development and Assessment

CHAPTER 23

Long-Term Athlete Development

—Kristen Dieffenbach

In competitive cycling, the goal is to cultivate talent through training and demonstrate it in competition. Talent is considered the cornerstone of success and permeates all aspects of the sport development discussion—talent pipelines, talent pathways, talent identification, and talent selection. The underlying assumption is that talent is the key, but what is talent? Is it winning a local series, or is it winning an international event? Wearing the polka dot jersey or earning the KOM or QOM title? Or maybe it is having an off-the-chart $\dot{V}O_2$max score or blowing away teammates with amazing wattage numbers. Coaches and trainers often say they know talent when they see it, yet the path to develop talent is much less clear.

Defining talent is easy. According to the *Oxford English Dictionary*, talent is a natural aptitude or skill. It is commonly thought that talented people are born or blessed with a special ability or gift toward a particular activity. The athlete, therefore, performs well at sport, better than the average person does. But the talent label is typically accurately assigned only after performance excellence has occurred. Trying to identify elite talent early is a flawed and often detrimental exercise.

Despite the simplicity of the definition of talent, anyone who has trained and raced knows that competitive cycling is far from easy. The journey from the early stages of sport engagement to standing on the elite podium is a much more complicated endeavor than having a gift for cornering or a superhuman engine. As such, the quest to define, understand, quantify, capture, and develop talent is a multimillion dollar sport industry. Dozens of books, research articles, and self-proclaimed experts have weighed in on the subject, yet no clear path or formula has emerged.

Perhaps the best place to start is by understanding that the identification of innate skill or ability is not enough to explain how, why, or whether someone will become a successful competitor. For example, knowing that the average pace of the elite riders in a flat Tour de France stage is X or that a world class kilo rider can put out Y watts tells little about the riders' journey to the top or the ways they use their gifts to their best advantage. Further, in studies of top competitors, elite athletes have indicated that at the top level, talent alone is not enough. Because of the complex nature of performance, often the most talented athlete is not the one who walks away with the gold (Gould, Dieffenbach, and Moffett 2002). A more useful way to look at harnessing and maximizing talent is to focus on facilitating long-term athletic development and fostering expertise.

A Better Approach to Long-Term Athletic Development

Focusing on athlete development for enhancing performance is not a new concept. Traditional pathways, however, have emphasized the physical skills necessary in elite sport and overlooked or failed to address individual needs and the process required to develop the key mental, technical, and tactical skills that underpin athleticism and sport achievement. As noted by Neal Henderson (2013), the 2011 U.S. Olympic Committee Doc Counsilman Science award winner and coach of American cyclist Taylor Phinney, top performances in cycling require not only athletic skill but also drive, determination, competitiveness, focus, adaptability, balance, composure, and leadership. This concept is further supported by a strongly written consensus statement from the International Olympic Committee outlining the best practices and responsibilities for those working with athletic talent development. The statement "challenged all youth and other sport governing bodies to embrace and implement" the principles of quality evidence-based development (Bergeron et al. 2015, page 843).

As the complexities of high performance have become better understood, the thinking about "growing" talent has evolved. The latest athletic development frameworks emphasize the development of overall athleticism as a base for sport-specific achievement. Key educational and psychosocial concepts related to how and when people learn and develop (Bailey et al. 2010) as well as research from a wide range of important sport science fields including exercise physiology, motor learning, pediatric exercise physiology, motor control, and sport psychology have been used in the construction of the current top organizational models. One of the leading long-term sport development frameworks is the U.S. Olympic Committee's American development model (figure 23.1). This model is influencing athlete programming, coaching education, and development decision-making policies at all levels of athlete participation and internationally across sport organizations.

Despite being developed for different organizations, the models include remarkably similar core elements. Quality long-term athletic development is based on the idea that top performance can be achieved only by taking a lifespan approach that values early broad-based participation and develops

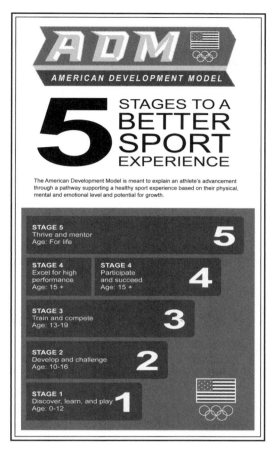

▶ **Figure 23.1** U.S. Olympic Committee American development model.

Courtesy of United States Olympic Committee (USOC).

a physical literacy foundation (Whitehead 2010), emphasizes individual developmental readiness, and uses a quality-phased approach to appropriate skill development. This approach is designed to allow all people the opportunity to develop the skills necessary to engage in healthy and meaningful physical activity across their lifespan for both physical and psychological health and well-being.

Given the high performance goals, the use of lifetime physical activity models as a means of enhancing performance may seem odd. A solid athleticism base, however, is not only beneficial for lifetime fitness but also necessary for elite performance (Balyi, Way, and Higgs 2013). By ensuring that athleticism is fully developed before competition becomes a focus and emphasizing a building-block approach to skill development, people are given the opportunity to maximize their individual growth potential as athletes. A long-term athleticism development approach not only reduces the chances of losing late-blooming talent but also has the potential to produce physically and mentally healthier athletes, thus allowing the best developmental opportunity to use innate talents and increasing the opportunities for athletic success and enjoyment.

Perhaps some of the strongest support for the use of a long-term development approach comes from the research that has been conducted on talented and successful people both in and outside sport (e.g., Csikszentmihalyi, Rathunde, and Whalen 1997; Durand-Bush and Salmela 2002; Gould, Dieffenbach, and Moffett 2002). High achievement is the result of long-term engagement and opportunities for age-appropriate growth and development in a supportive environment that provides appropriate challenges based on ability. Top achievers typically do not excel from the beginning, but they were allowed an opportunity to separate and value both the personal pride and enjoyment of participation as well as the more extrinsic or external rewards of competition. One of the most essential elements associated with developing talent is the recognition of the time, patience, and dedication necessary to develop expertise (Kaufman and Duckworth 2015).

Ideas, Attitudes, and Myths that Hamper Athletic Development in Cycling

Being seen as an expert or having talent is associated with a wide range of highly desirable outcomes ranging from social status and fame to financial security and increased access to opportunities such as college and team sponsorships. There is no denying the rewards that accompany being able to excel at something in modern culture. Unfortunately, myths, close-minded attitudes, and antiquated ideas related to performance, talent, and sport still exist and hamper the quality development and subsequent potential of many gifted riders.

The misidentification of talent and the misunderstanding of the performance pathway can cause both short- and long-term problems. Before we explore what long-term athletic development looks like in cycling and how best to facilitate it, take a moment to make sure that none of these ineffectual concepts lingers in the shadows.

One of the most common fallacies is the early misuse of the term *talent*. Young athletes are often labeled as talented or, worse, labeled as untalented. This labeling typically occurs long before it is possible to assess whether such skills and abilities really exist, often even before athletes are done with puberty. Early mislabeling can create a false sense of ability (or lack of ability), creating a wide range of negative outcomes

The label of early or emerging talent can be an incredible ego boost, but at the same time it can erode the development of valuable intrinsic motivation, work ethic, and resiliency skills needed for long-term engagement and the ability to handle the challenges of competition. Entitlement, or the attitude "I'm good, so I don't need to work that hard," is an incredibly challenging mind-set to change. Worse, the inevitable transitions into higher and more competitive fields often leaves an early talent unprepared to handle competitive challenges, resulting in frustration, poor skill development, related injuries, and sport disengagement. The early emphasis on outcome rather than skill acquisition, work ethic, and resilience often results in athletes who are unprepared for the elite levels.

The information used in the identification of early talent demands careful scrutiny. Research has found that early sport phenomes who successfully transition into adult elite competitors are the exception rather than the rule (Malina 2010). Early exposure and opportunity in a given area can allow a rider to excel at an early age, and the results may be inappropriately attributed to innate talent. When the emphasis is on outcome and giftedness over development and work ethic, young athletes are left without the skills necessary to remain competitive as others catch up to them on the experience continuum.

Another mislabeling of talent occurs because of the necessary but artificial age cutoffs used to separate youth competitors throughout adolescence. This categorization is designed to keep competition fair and balanced. What is known as the relative age effect can have a positive or negative outcome, depending on when an athlete was born during the year (e.g., Helsen, Van Winckel, and Williams 2005; Musch and Grondin 2001; Stebelsky 1991). The relative age effect occurs because a child whose birthday is in the months immediately after the youth sport cutoff date has a better chance of becoming a top athlete in a given sport. Normal puberty growth patterns during the adolescent years put these athletes ahead of their peers who were born later in the year, creating an advantage often mistaken for early talent demonstration. These early maturers are given more attention, support, and resources, and they experience more success. Athletes born later in the racing-age year may possess similar or even greater talent, but lack of early selection or success typically translates into fewer opportunities to develop and may result in lower confidence, enjoyment, and motivation.

On the flip side, and as suggested in the consideration of the relative age effect, in a system in which some are labeled as talented early, those who are not included in that group or who are told they are not in that group may face performance issues that hamper their long-term development and performance potential. Although some athletes may adopt an "I'll show you" attitude, more commonly the lack of the talent label erodes confidence and creates a motivation focus centered on self-protection from perceived failure. After all, why try if you have been told you don't have a talent for something? Identifying talent is not as easy as finding a big gold nugget shining in the desert. The reality is that most talent, like precious metals, is found through a slow and relatively tedious process. Finding, honing, and polishing talent take time. People often do not know what they really have until they are well into the process, and if they are not careful, many great opportunities may be discarded or overlooked.

The last common misconception to address is the idea that talent is everything. This mistaken notion proposes that a set of innate skills and abilities is enough to propel an athlete to the top of the performance pyramid; either you have what it takes or you don't. Although innate talent, such as a high $\dot{V}O_2$max, can be helpful when racing, an engine alone does not win races. Bike-handling skills, tactical abilities, and good decision making are crucial parts of the whole package. Innate talent may make it easy for an athlete to be a standout at lower to middle levels of the sport, even with little effort or attention paid to developing other racing skills. But living off gifts alone guarantees a cap to success potential. One of the common denominators among the most successful Olympians is that no two top athletes are gifted with a perfect set of skills and abilities necessary to be world class (Durand-Bush and Salmela 2002; Gould, Dieffenbach, and Moffett 2002). Every athlete had to work hard to bring the whole package together.

Cycling Long-Term Athletic Development

Cycling is a unique sport that has the potential to reach into all stages of life from the toddler's early use of scooters to a wide range of recreational, lifestyle, and competitive opportunities throughout adulthood. Early engagement in cycling provides an excellent opportunity to develop a range of physical motor skills, and adult engagement provides both health and well-being benefits. Learning to cycle well is an important part of long-term athletic development. But as we have seen, when seeking to maximize performance potential we need to know the difference between competence and expertise and understand the phases of long-term athletic development as they relate to competitive cycling. The Canadian Cycling Association developed a cycling-specific long-term athlete development framework that can provide a useful guide (figure 23.2).

A Healthy Start

Competence in cycling requires agility, balance, and coordination. The early stage of athletic development, the active start phase, should be based on exposure and opportunity to explore physical movement in appropriate child-safe environments, regardless of future sport aspirations. The goal is to create physical literacy, the bundle of essential movement skills that include the ability to read movement situations, move efficiently and with confidence, and move in a wide range of athletic contexts (Whitehead 2010). Emphasizing the development of these kinesthetic awareness skills through unstructured play opportunities helps develop the ABCs: agility, balance, coordination, and speed (Balyi, Way, and Higgs 2013). This development is key to developing athleticism for life.

Early essential physical literacy skills, such as balance, can be transferred from general movement activities to two wheels early in childhood through

▶ **Figure 23.2**   Canadian Cycling Association's long-term athlete development model.

Adapted, by permission, from Canadian Cycling Association, 2008, Long-term athlete development: Volume I. [Online].
Available: http://www.cyclingcanada.ca/wp-content/uploads/2012/05/CC_LTAD_Vol1_EN-2014.pdf [February 14, 2017].

free play on the bike. Advanced bike skills will be developed over time through continued play and exploration. Balance or coordination bikes, those with no pedals, are ideal starter bikes that take advantage of the natural balance moment that occurs when the child moves from a walking to a running movement. Opportunities for grass, dirt, gravel, bumpy, smooth, and paved surface exploration develop a variety of important skills.

As a child grows out of toddlerhood and into childhood, the second essential foundation stage, the fundamentals stage, is for fostering a love of movement and physical activity. At this time, the child moves beyond just exploring and begins to engage in different movement activities through more complex and coordinated movements. Real pedals can be introduced here. The emphasis should be on engagement, joy of movement and learning, and building a sense of self-confidence. Encouraging a wide range of physical activities and ensuring that the emphasis at this stage is on deliberate play over deliberate practice is essential. Deliberate play is the organic engagement in activities that are done because they are fun; participation is its own reward (Côté, Baker, and Abernethy 2007). Although adults may create opportunities or safe spaces in which deliberate play can occur, deliberate play is the product of the child's interests and imagination. Such play is crucial in the development of intrinsic motivation and creativity. Playing tag, playing sandlot baseball, and riding a bike around the neighborhood are examples of quality opportunities for deliberate play. Family-focused rides, BMX, and mountain biking are ideas for further developing athleticism and fostering a love of the sport.

Cycling Through Childhood

Toward the middle to end of childhood, many children, particularly those coming from homes in which physical activity and sports are valued, will engage more in activities organized and run by adults. On the continuum of athletic development, the learn-to-train phase begins here. Unfortunately, this phase is often overrun by adult structure, overorganization, and competition. Teams and participation in sport activities with a parent transform participation from play to deliberate practice. By definition, deliberate practice isn't as much fun, at least not in the way that deliberate play is. The benefits of deliberate practice are more abstract and often come with time as improvements are made (Ward et al. 2004).

Unlike many sports in which youth participation often follows an adult model with little to no scaling for size and ability, cycling, if introduced thoughtfully, has a multitude of possibilities to match an athlete's developmental needs. Beyond balance bikes, bikes are made in a wide range of sizes, allowing appropriate fit. To help facilitate quality long-term development, adults need to be mindful of the developmental needs of young cyclists as they ride together. Adults must try to avoid pushing an adult focus or agenda on the riding experience of the children. For example, an adult cyclist on a mountain bike ride is focused on the ride, pushing the pace, and getting his heart rate up. For a child, the same ride is full of opportunities to run over things, intentionally crash, stop and examine interesting trail finds, and sit down and eat the snacks in a backpack. The transition from deliberate play to embracing and enjoying deliberate practice takes time. Adults are cautioned not to push for an abrupt transition and are encouraged to foster opportunities for deliberate play.

Although competition at a young age provides valuable opportunities to learn about concepts such as fair play and teamwork, the emphasis must be on effort, improvement, and enjoyment. Despite the miniature gear, young participants are not miniathletes. Their motivation for participating is different from that of adults, and their overall athleticism is still developing. A premature emphasis on competition, performance, and outcome hinders the opportunities for true learning and continued skill development. The adults involved need to ensure that skill development and enjoyment remain the foci of the learn-to-train stage participation.

Becoming a Cyclist

The start of adolescence marks a turning point in the long-term athletic development model. The focus moves away from the development of physical literacy and foundational sport skills and moves toward beginning to shape an athlete from the core of athleticism. Athletes in early adolescence should continue to participate in a wide range of physical activities to ensure that their physical growth is well rounded and that they further develop a ride range of sport skills to enrich their future opportunities for physical activity. We will discuss when it is appropriate to focus on just one thing a bit later.

During adolescence, kids begin to look a bit more like adults, and their gear is catching up, too (remember eighth grade?). Still, remember that development occurs in multiple areas at different rates. Age may not be exactly what you see. Despite the yearly birthday celebration, using birth age or chronological age to determine an athlete's development timeline is a poor guide for charting a developmental pathway or determining potential.

Age can be assessed in a variety of ways beyond the standard chronological approach, including growth, maturation, development, and relative age. Some age progression, such as growth, is easier to monitor and measure by tracking changes in physical variables such as height, weight, and fat percentage. Less convenient but still measurable is maturation—structural and functional physical changes such as the change of cartilage to bone in the skeleton. Far less measurable is maturity; a person is relative to her or his same-age peers in terms of psychological, emotional, intellectual, and social skill development.

To make it all a bit more complex, things do not happen in a linear fashion or at the same rate in all adolescents. The young woman who grows tall faster than her peers may struggle with coordination or experience a time when her muscle development has not caught up to her height. The young man who is beginning to look like a young man may still act much like a boy and not quite have the emotional skills or control expected based on his appearance.

What does this mean for athletic development? The athletic development journey through the middle years of development—train to train, learn to compete, and train to compete, which cover adolescence into young adulthood—needs to be done cautiously. Athletic development occurs simultaneously with a wide range of other physical, social, and emotional changes.

Best practices for guiding athletic development during the adolescent years center on knowing and understanding the full age of the athlete as well as understanding the skill areas that should be developed. During this time, competition is certainly a part of the athlete's experience if he or she is cycling competitively. But the emphasis should still be on learning, growth, and development over the outcome of competition. The middle phase of training is an ideal time to improve handling skills, develop tactical awareness, and work on intensity and speed rather than volume.

Some of the most notable benefits of this athletic development approach are in the reduction in possible negative consequences often seen in young athletes. The dropout rate for youth sport participation, beginning at around age 14, is astounding (Fraser-Thomas, Côté, and Deakin 2008; Butcher, Lindner, and Johns 2002). Although some of that attrition can be attributed to an increase in other opportunities and activity choices and a beginning to specialize, research indicates that most of the exodus occurs because of a lack of perceived fun. By contrast, an approach that focuses on developing a racer over time at a pace appropriate for the athlete's readiness as opposed to expecting the full set of skills to emerge just because the athlete is taller and heavier helps set up athletes for success.

When to Specialize

Exactly when is the appropriate time to specialize in a sport? Given that athletes are uniquely individual in their development, trainability, and interest, this complex question has no single right answer. Cycling is classified as a late-specialization sport (Balyi, Way, and Higgs 2013) because elite performances at the top levels of competition require both peak power and endurance. These talents, no matter how great, cannot be fully realized until a person is in an adult body. Despite appearances, especially with males, physical maturation is not complete when an athlete has reached peak height. An athlete may need one to several years to complete his or her physical transformation into adulthood. And this timeline does not take into consideration mental, technical, tactical, and emotional readiness for the intensity of specialized training or competition.

Don't mistake late specialization to mean a late start. Ideally, young cyclists are on their first set of wheels early. Specialization refers to the unique point in time when an athlete chooses to focus on a single sport for training and competition (Baker, Cobley, and Fraser-Thomas 2009) and often begins to engage in year-round training. This brings back the essential question of when this choice should be made. Generally, during prepuberty and the early teen years, when a lot of physical growth and development, as well as cognitive and motor skill learning, occurs, maintaining a multisport engagement approach is optimal. This recommendation does not mean that an athlete needs to compete in multiple sports. Instead, continued participation in a wide range of activities that demand different skills should be encouraged to optimize athleticism.

The talented Taylor Phinney is a good example of a young rider who, although bikes were part of his life early on, did not specialize or even race competitively until late in his teenage years. Phinney was a soccer player and a well-rounded young athlete before taking up competitive cycling. Although scientific testing indicated innate physical talent and his parents' sport history (his mother was an Olympic gold medal cyclist and his father was a top Tour de France rider) gave him unique exposure to competitive cycling during childhood, Phinney still had an opportunity to follow a healthy athletic development pathway that allowed him to develop the mental, technical, and tactical skills necessary to maximize his physical gifts.

The decision to specialize should be carefully considered for both the potential benefits and the potential costs. And it is important to discuss what specialization means. Choosing to do just one sport competitively is often a logical option during the teenage years because the investment in both time and money goes up. But specializing doesn't have to and typically shouldn't mean an increase in pressure to perform, year-round competition, and structured training. Specialization should not be viewed as professionalization. At this stage of development, given all the growth that is still occurring, these are not part of a heathy pathway.

Premature specialization can occur when a sport system pushes for exclusivity and loyalty too early, when parents push either intentionally or unintentionally, or even because of the athlete's passion and drive. The consequences of specializing too early in a single sport can be damaging physically and psychologically (Brenner 2007). Note that before the teen years, specialization is not recommended in most sports, particularly one such as cycling. The increased pressure on young athletes that can result from knowing that family time and resources have been invested can lead to a sense of entrapment and eventual burnout (e.g. Gustafsson et al. 2007; Raedeke, Lunney, and Venables 2002). Tempering the concerns with the potential benefits is complicated by the lack of clear guidelines about when specialization should occur and often the passion of the young rider.

Pursuing the Podium

In a well-developed path, at any point after the foundation (early start, fundamentals, and learn to train), an athlete who decides not to compete should be well prepared to remain active for life, the ultimate goal. But if the competitive bug remains (or returns) and the skills within the train-to-train, learn-to-compete, and train-to-compete stages are learned, then the athlete is ready to enter the professional or advanced competition phases of learn to win and train to win. At these top stages, the emphasis shifts to competition, and the execution of the developed skills will enhance the athlete's talents. Of course, when the athlete wants to shift focus away from competition, his or her athleticism will help in maintaining a healthy, active lifestyle.

When striving to facilitate athleticism and athletic development, seeing the success of the journey takes time and patience. Piggy Lambert, the coach of famed basketball coach John Wooden at Purdue, was asked how he measured the success of his program. To this he remarked, "Ask me in 20 years and we'll see how successful these boys are. Then I'll be able to tell you if I succeeded as a coach." Given the numerous challenges that are beyond the scope of the best-designed plans—injury, bad luck, and the maze of life's twists and turns—no plan can guarantee athletic success. The biggest benefit in striving for long-term athletic development is the emphasis it places on helping a person develop the skills and ability to maximize her or his talents. These powerful skills are infinitely transferable throughout life.

Athlete Development and the Adult Rider

People sometimes falsely assume that athletic development is relevant or important only for young people seeking to be world-class athletes. Athletic development and cycling development can occur at any age. Although the development frameworks present the process as a linear one that follows age and development-based markers to guide progression, the same information can be used with adult athletes to identify gaps in development and to design a learning-based training approach that does more than just develop physical skills.

When examining an adult athlete, athletic history and training experiences, both on and off the bike, can help determine skill development strengths as well as potential deficiencies and areas for developmental focus. Like any athlete going through the developmental pathway, the adult athlete must not be rushed through the process. Unlike their younger counterparts, however, adult athletes do not have to be concerned with waiting to grow as a limitation to progression toward professional cycling. Top American cyclists Alison Dunlap and Evelyn Stevens are examples of athletes with well-developed athleticism who did not find cycling until their 20s. Through careful development, they were able to reach the top levels of their sport.

A few other considerations apply to adults in the talent development pathway. Often the athlete can draw on other areas of success to enhance cycling skills. Setting realistic goals and developing a clear well-rounded development plan is essential to maximize potential. Adult riders are cautioned not to rely only on power and engine development as indicators of competitive readiness or to rely on them alone to explore their talent. Cyclists who crash midfield or fall off the back may have powerful engines but lack the experience or skills necessary to perform or demonstrate talent.

Applying the Science

The science and knowledge about training has grown exponentially since the late 1960s. Although a lot of knowledge has been gained about the training of athletes, each athlete is an N of 1, meaning that no two athletes are exactly alike. No two athletes will respond to or benefit from a single training plan the same way, particularly as they reach elite levels.

Long-term athletic development is most likely to occur in a well-supported and intentionally constructed environment. Regardless of an athlete's age, the support of others has been noted as being an important part of the equation (Gould, Dieffenbach, and Moffett 2002). Important factors include caring, unconditional love, and support from family; financial and opportunity support from sponsors and others; and the challenge, teaching, and support that a coach can provide.

In the athletic development environment, the coach assumes many roles and is "critical for setting the standards for behavior, effort and attitude" (Hill 2007, page 28) that athletes need to become successful. But a coach does not automatically have a positive influence on the athlete's sport experience. Ultimately, the coach must intentionally create the right environment (Conroy and Coatsworth 2006; Smith, Smoll, and Cumming 2007). If the goal is a well-developed pathway for performance, the coach must understand the stages of development and be able to facilitate and monitor growth within each stage.

Here are some general guidelines for coaches and parents seeking to facilitate an athlete's development at any stage:

- Clearly define the appropriate level of challenge for the athlete. Challenges or tasks should be tailored to the developmental readiness of the athlete for maximum benefit. A challenge that is too vague is hard to tackle, one that is too hard will intimidate and demotivate, and a simple challenge will fail to inspire. Although instructions to "Win the race" and "Go out and do your best" are common, neither provides athletes a clear direction about what they should focus on or points them toward the skill to execute.

- Emphasize and value both physical and mental effort. Besides acknowledging physical gifts, emphasize hard work, resiliency, and determination.

- Provide feedback that is specific and meaningful. Give information that helps athletes grow.

- Repeat, repeat, repeat. One-time discussions or reminders rarely result in learned skills. Opportunities for practice and development should occur frequently and often.

- Display and share time and patience. The reality of the often-discussed 10-year and 10,000-hour concept that Malcom Gladwell (2008) popularized in his book *Outliers* is that there is no magic number. Although counting the hours of practice does no good, the basic premise of practice—taking the time to engage in deliberate practice aimed at maximizing talent—is solid.

- Train and evaluate every athlete individually, especially as athletes advance along the development pathway. Individual responsiveness to training or trainability, skill development, base talents, life influence, and other unique elements all need to be considered.

- Teach and foster a growth mindset. In her book *Mindset*, Carol Dweck (2006) emphasizes the importance of viewing tasks as opportunities to grow and learn rather than as indications of personal worth, ability, or value. Helping athletes focus on continuous improvement, understand elements they can influence to focus their efforts, and value the experience will serve them well, whether things are going well or not.

- Engage the athlete in the process. Training is most powerful when it is done with the athlete, not to the athlete. The athlete's contribution and engagement will help learning, commitment, and confidence.

- Set limits and guidelines. The passion and drive of a young athlete can be a powerful force. But just because an athlete can or wants to do something does not always mean it is an appropriate decision.

- Keep the professional focus where it belongs, in the professional stages. Developmental and youth sports are not professional sports. They are unique and important types of competition in their own right and should be valued and experienced.

- Proceed with caution if coaching your own child. The research is clear that this relationship can be challenging and potentially troubled. Overinvested parents can add to athlete stress and decrease enjoyment (Smoll, Cumming, and Smith 2011).

- Understand the difference between a positive parent push and a shove (Gould, Dieffenbach, and Moffett 2002). A positive push is the gentle reminder when an athlete has an occasional lull in motivation. Shoving is the consistent parental overinvolvement to ensure that training is done, that competition is properly prepared for, and so on.

- Allow youth athletes to explore and discover. If you are passionate about cycling, no matter how much your child enjoys the sport, be mindful that your adult interest does not overshadow a young athlete's opportunities to explore and discover new things during adolescence.

In a 2013 talk at the National Coaching Conference in Colorado Springs, Dr. Henderson said, "Allow athletes to express the talent and abilities they have. Remove barriers and develop strategies to help them repeatedly reach potential" (2013). This advice is perhaps the best guidance for the facilitation of long-term athletic development.

CHAPTER **24**

Psychological Strategies for Team Building

—Javier Horcajo and Mikel Zabala

The challenge of any professional cycling team is to achieve a synergistic group functioning that leads to better results collectively than could be expected from its members individually. The manager, sport directors, and other technical staff need to know how they can achieve this goal. If a team signs the nine top-ranking UCI (Union Cycliste Internationale) riders for 2016, would they make the best team for the 2017 season? Would they achieve better results both as individuals and as a team than they achieved last season? What does their success (or failure) depend on? In reality, bringing together in one team the nine best cyclists in the world would be difficult if not impossible. Clearly, this plan would not be the most desirable for their effectiveness. Instead, professional cycling teams have riders who have different individual characteristics and roles within the team but complement each other to achieve goals that would not be possible to achieve without the confluence of these differences. For example, for a team leader such as Chris Froome to win the Tour de France, he must have the help of the domestiques (i.e., the cyclists who have his back during the race and will sacrifice for him), climbers, and trialists who will provide their help in specific situations (e.g., mountain stages or team time trials).

The management of a cycling team is complex and distinctive but not exclusive to this sport. In cycling, the most important and most valuable victories are individual; that is, a rider is awarded individually, although in recent years, team awards are gaining prestige and greater status. To obtain those individual victories, however, teamwork that involves many members (e.g., coaches, sport directors, mechanics, physiotherapists, and other cyclists/ teammates) is essential. Therefore, the first factor to consider for the success of a team is its composition, that is, the individuals who make up the group and the resources they provide—characteristics, knowledge, skills, experiences, attitudes, and so on. This composition facilitates or hinders the achievement of team goals, although the ultimate success is the result of the interaction of many factors and processes including group and organizational factors (Hackman and Katz 2010). In team design, necessary resources have to be established to achieve the desired goals because a professional cycling team is conceptually a formal group. A formal group is the product of a preliminary design and plan of positions and roles, in accordance with established norms that guide appropriate and desirable behaviors aimed at performing certain tasks to achieve group goals related to those tasks. In cycling, this formal group is embedded in or may be considered an organization (Ilgen et al. 2005).

In a professional cycling team, formal and informal traits (i.e., those processes that arise spontaneously, not planned, among members, based on individual traits) form a complex network of interactions, relationships, and social psychological processes that emerge among all the individuals who make up the team over time and depending on the context that includes them. Thus, a team is a complex and constantly changing system (i.e., dynamic and adaptive; McGrath, Arrow, and Berdhal 2000). Correctly managing the various mental components (e.g., personalities, motivations, thoughts, emotions, and so on) in each person is already a complicated task that requires a rigorous and comprehensive understanding of the mental processes that influence human behavior (see Weinberg and Gould 2015, or chapter 25). Doing this in a sport in which several individuals pursue a common goal by cooperating with each other, based on individual motivations and goals, as well as with different consequences for each, is undoubtedly a titanic mission that requires deep understanding and accurate management of the variables and mechanisms operating within the team. In sum, qualified professionals should perform the psychological work with a cycling team. This work can be done directly (i.e., a sport psychologist works in person with the team to improve its group functioning) or indirectly (i.e., a sport psychologist works with the sport directors, coaches, or leaders, and they then implement that work with the whole team).

According to much theory and research on group psychology, the key to the optimal functioning of any human group—and therefore any professional cycling team—is to channel the motivations and objectives of each member toward the common goal of the group, which must be able to satisfy the specific motivations and goals of each member. In other words, the crucial question is how to integrate individuality in the group so that the group can become a positive reference point for each individual and provide the individual with a positive identity.

This chapter suggests that the success of any professional cycling team is a function of the success in the formation and permanence of the psychological group, as well as the group management that is done regarding the individualities (i.e., aptitudes, motivations, and so on) and regarding the group factors and processes, such as setting team goals and establishing roles, leadership, cohesiveness, and communication. The efficient management of all these individual and collective factors and processes results in a more effective performance and even superior results to those expected given the available resources (see Hackman and Katz 2010; Kerr and Tindale 2004; Salas et al. 2009).

The Psychological Group

In line with the self-categorization theory (Turner 1987), the primary causal factor of the formation of the psychological group is that the individual clearly defines himself or herself as a member of a particular group (ingroup, e.g., the Movistar Team) and not from another (outgroup, e.g., Team Sky). But beyond this self-categorization process, a professional cycling team is a psychological group only when that team is psychologically meaningful for its members and, therefore, is not only a belonging group (i.e., one in which they are objectively included) but also a positive reference group from which those members acquire or consolidate the values related to their profession as well as appropriate and desirable knowledge, attitudes, and behaviors for their roles and tasks. Therefore, the psychological group exists only when the team is essential for each member to define himself or herself and determines how subjectively he or she processes reality in relation to cycling, as well as how he or she behaves in his or her professional activity (Turner 1987; see Hornsey 2008 for a review).

For the success of a professional cycling team, the team must provide, as a psychological group, a positive social identity to its members (i.e., a favorable evaluation of themselves, as well as satisfaction and pride for belonging to that team and not another; see Tajfel and Turner 1986). Thus, you could say that when a cyclist belongs to one of the highest rated teams in international cycling, he or she can take up that positive evaluation of his or her team as his or her own. Accordingly, the self-categorization and associated evaluation developed by the cyclist of himself or herself (i.e., his or her self-concept and self-esteem) are better (i.e., psychologically more functional), and the evaluation that he or she makes regarding the team to which he or she belongs is more accurate and more positive. This evaluation is not made in a vacuum but in social comparison with the characteristics of other teams.

What about teams that are not in high-ranking UCI positions? Are they doomed to provide a negative (or unsatisfactory) social identity to their members? Not at all. All teams can contribute in multiple ways to the positive social identity of their members by providing them with values, norms, or roles that decrease their uncertainty or increase their self-esteem. Also, the teams that are best valued according to some aspects (e.g., UCI point ranking) could provide a negative (or unsatisfactory) social identity for some of their members based on other aspects (e.g., excessive competitiveness within the team, high uncertainty, and so on). In practice, for the sake of their long-term viability, professional cycling teams must be not only groups to which their members belong but also groups to which they want to continue belonging (see Hogg 2012; Hornsey 2008 for a review).

A theoretical (and practical) consideration is that managing a team is managing tasks and people. After the group is psychologically formed, what is to be done to keep it strongly united and effective in achieving its goals? The functioning of a group involves the technical management of factors and processes related to the tasks that it performs as well as the social emotional management of factors and processes related to the members who compose it (see Levine and Moreland 1998). This chapter suggests that both aspects (i.e., task and social emotional) must receive sufficient attention from the team, especially from those who manage or lead, because both are of great importance for achieving group goals (see LePine et al. 2008; Mathieu et al. 2008 for a review). Thus, a group might generate results that are superior to, or at least different from, the sum of its members to the extent that interactions arise among them and group structures emerge to establish, facilitate, or promote functional relationships of positive interdependence. These relationships mutually satisfy the needs, motivations, aspirations, interests, and task and social emotional goals of each member.

Thus, for example, some cyclists may be driven by the financial rewards or social status they receive from their professional activity. Others may have motivation to know and evaluate in themselves their skills as cyclists. Others may desire the sporting challenge of achieving what no other rider has achieved before. Others may be looking for personal improvement and growth in their professional activity. All these motivations and many others we attribute to cyclists must also be considered with respect to sport directors, coaches, medical staff, caregivers, mechanics, and other team members. Thus, we can say that positive interdependence exists within a cycling team when the satisfaction of the needs and goals of each member is connected to and dependent on satisfying the needs and goals of the other members. Furthermore, when this satisfaction is more likely to occur within that team (and not in another) and among those individuals (and not others), then the attraction toward that team and among its members is likely to be greater (i.e., group cohesiveness; Carron and Brawley 2000; Hogg 1992). Ultimately, team members are the bricks with which to build the group, but cohesiveness is the cement that unites them and keeps them together. In fact, the processes of interpersonal interaction and cohesiveness within the team influence the shared cognition and the identification of the members with the group (Postmes, Haslam, and Swaab 2005).

Most relevant to this chapter is the suggestion that although interdependence is a factor that influences the formation and permanence of the group, the underlying psychological process that results in a greater group cohesiveness—and under certain circumstances, a better performance in achieving group goals—is the self-categorization of the individual as a member of a collective that provides him or her with a group identity (Turner 1987). Thus, cohesiveness and cooperation among members of a cycling team for achieving group goals as well as various phenomena of shared cognition and social influence such as leadership would be the result of these members coming to regard themselves as a collective unit, coming to have the perception of a "we" (in contrast to "others") and to be united facing "our" challenges and in pursuit of "our" goals (Eckel and Grossman 2004; Hogg 2001; Turner 1987; see Postmes, Haslam, and Swaab 2005 for a discussion). In addition, in various group and organizational contexts, empirical evidence shows that the perception of group (or team) identity shared among members is a factor involved in team effectiveness (van Knippenberg and Ellemers 2003; Worchel et al. 1998), although its role as mediator or moderator of the effects is much more complex than was initially thought (Dietz et al. 2015; Swaab et al. 2007).

In this chapter we propose that building the shared group identity is, in practice, the primary work that has to be conducted with a professional cycling team to build the psychological group. Furthermore, at present, professional cycling teams face a huge challenge to the extent that they are usually composed of members with a wide variety of motivations, knowledge, abilities, attitudes, values, nationalities, languages, cultures, and so on. This complexity is a potential source of conflicts that have to be managed on the group level, and it can also provide an opportunity for innovation and development of the team (van Knippenberg and Schippers 2007). Building the psychological group is building the "we" that encompasses and transcends the characteristics of the individuals and that configures an identity of the team that is distinctive as transnational and inclusive of different cultures. Therefore, this identity could be the key factor that mediates the effects of diversity on team performance. In this sense, a basic tool that a team has for building its identity is the formation and change of beliefs, attitudes, and behaviors through communication (Turner 1987).

Team Building and Team Training

The formation of the psychological group (i.e., the "we") is suggested as a first step for the success of a professional cycling team, but it does not guarantee that team will achieve its objectives. The next step is the development of this psychological group by implementing group processes that lead to effective functioning as a team (McEwan and Beauchamp 2014). And a team is effective when it consistently and efficiently achieves its goals while maintaining high levels of satisfaction, commitment, and loyalty among members. For the development of the team and the improvement of performance in various organizational and sporting contexts, two different and compatible types of interventions have been used: team building and team training (see Delise et al. 2010; Klein et al. 2009; Martin, Carron, and Burke 2009; Shuffler, DiazGranados, and Salas 2011 for reviews).

Team building is a process that aims to promote and enhance the effectiveness of a team through interventions focused on the tasks performed or on the relationships among its members. In general, the main aspects worked on in team building are team goal setting, roles, leadership, interpersonal relationships, and problem solving. Thus, for example, by implementing a team goal-setting program, sport psychologists help to set long-term goals, establish clear paths toward those goals, involve all members, monitor the team's progress toward the established goals, reward this progress, and foster collective efficacy with respect to achieving those team goals (Widmeyer and Ducharme 1997; see Kramer, Thayer, and Salas 2013 for a review).

Team training is a process that helps team members understand, acquire, develop, and practice the knowledge, skills, and attitudes required for effective performance in the tasks they perform individually and in teamwork. In general, this process intervenes regarding cognitions (e.g., ideas related to tasks to be performed), attitudes (e.g., evaluations related to the group tasks, roles, norms, or values), and behaviors (e.g., related to the effective performance of a role within the team). In addition, team training provides an opportunity for teams not only to practice such knowledge, skills, and attitudes but also to receive feedback about areas for improvement in teamwork and obtain the necessary resources to address those areas of improvement. Thus, for example, team training can help improve shared knowledge about team goals and can be useful for identifying, understanding, and training the skills and behaviors needed to work with effectiveness within the team to achieve its goals.

Team building and team training have positive effects on team results (e.g., cognitive and affective results and actual performance) when applied in accordance with prior scientific research (Salas et al. 2012). In fact, in the field of sports teams, team building has mainly focused on cohesiveness with positive effects. In addition, positive effects have been found on the performance of the teams through direct or indirect interventions by sport psychologists. Moreover, it has been found that interventions focused on goal setting are the most effective and significantly superior to interventions involving various factors. Finally, the intervention should have a minimum duration of 2 weeks and can even be implemented throughout an entire season (see Martin, Carron, and Burke 2009 for a review on team building in sports teams). As for the evidence on team training, positive effects have been found regarding multiple criteria, although to a greater extent regarding cognitive and process-related factors (see Delise et al. 2010), supporting the hypothesis that both physical and psychological skills can be developed through practice and training (Martin, Carron, and Burke 2009).

Team Structure: Positions and Roles

When building a cycling team as a psychological group that is effective and efficient in achieving its goals, some basic elements of the structure and functioning of any sport or organizational team will be important, such as positions and roles. Positions are often the result of planning, although they may also arise because of further team development. Most professional cycling teams have the positions of general manager or team principal, sport directors, performance coaches, doctors, physiotherapists, caregivers, mechanics, office and operations personnel, and cyclists. Other positions have more recently been included, such as communication and marketing staff, nutritionists, chefs, and in some cases, sport psychologists. These positions explicitly or implicitly involve a status, thus establishing a formal or informal hierarchy within the team.

Each position has an associated role, that is, an ensemble of behaviors that are required or expected of a particular team member because of the fact that he or she occupies a position. For example, a sport director is expected to drive the team car in the race, give technical instructions to riders, make tactical and strategic decisions about the competition, and so on. These behaviors would correspond to his or her formal role, which is planned a priori. The behaviors expected from a sport director are the same regardless of the particular person who occupies that position. In practice, however, formal and informal roles can be identified within any human group. Informal roles arise and spontaneously develop from the repeated interaction between team members and depend on their individual characteristics (e.g., personalities). For instance, some members take on roles that help improve the social emotional climate within the team through behaviors aimed at promoting positive moods or group cohesiveness, yet these behaviors are not required by the position that they occupy (Cope et al. 2011). In fact, these informal roles come to fill a space required for the optimal functioning of the group and may come to be an important part of the cement that holds the team members together. Therefore, the importance of any formal or informal role lies in its ability to influence the effectiveness and efficiency of the team in achieving its goals.

Just by focusing on formal positions and roles played by riders, in a cycling team we can identify team leaders, climbers, trialists, sprinters, domestiques, and so forth. The performance of a team will increase if a domestique knows what is expected of him or her (e.g., to protect his or her team leader from the wind or provide water and food during the race) or if a climber accepts that his or her work consists of working for the team leader during the ascent of the last climb of a mountain stage. But a greater difficulty with roles in cycling arises from the fact that a single rider can play different roles depending on the competition or time of the season. Could you imagine, for example, the soccer player Cristiano Ronaldo playing defense, midfield, or forward depending on the time of year or the particular game that he plays? This flexibility is inconceivable in many team sports. In cycling, however, a team leader in a major tour (e.g., Alejandro Valverde in the Giro d'Italia) can perform the tasks of a domestique at the beginning of the season or in minor competitions. A team leader might be a climber who helps another team leader in another competition (e.g., Nairo Quintana in the Tour de France or in the Vuelta a España). A single rider (e.g., Fabian Cancellara) can even play several different roles within a major tour, such as serving as a domestique in the mountain stages or a key trialist in a team time trial, and then be the team leader in a different competition (e.g., Paris–Roubaix).

Therefore, each cyclist must know and understand with accuracy what, exactly, is expected of him or her in every competition and at each point. In this sense, research on sport and exercise psychology has shown that more role ambiguity is associated with, for example, increased anxiety, lower satisfaction of the athlete, and a decrease in performance (Beauchamp et al. 2005; Eys, Beauchamp, and Bray 2006). Thus, to increase role clarity, an athlete should know what specific behaviors are required to fulfill his or her role, understand the scope of his or her responsibilities in performing that role, have accurate information about how the performance of the role will be evaluated, and know the consequences (for the team and for him or her) of not meeting the responsibilities of the role (Eys, Beauchamp, and Bray 2006). Of course, this recommendation also applies to any other position and role within a professional cycling team (i.e., sport directors, doctors, physiotherapists, caregivers, mechanics, and so on). Psychological practice on roles and on other group factors described in this chapter includes the implementation of instruction and training, modeling, testing and reinforcement of behaviors, cognitive skills training, and group dynamics, among others. This work should be done according to available empirical evidence from scientific research.

Related to playing roles, several members who occupy the same position and play the same role can exhibit differences in how they engage in the behaviors expected of them. These small differences can be beneficial for the group in terms of positive role innovation or even positive individual differentiation (Baumeister, Ainsworth, and Vohs 2015). In this sense, Baumeister and colleagues (2015) have suggested that a group can become greater than the sum of its members to the extent that an appropriate differentiation of the individuals (i.e., differentiation of selves) occurs within the group. More specifically, they suggest that a useful approach at the start of a group is having similarities among members and, consequently, similar behaviors in the execution of similar roles. But after a group is formed and consolidated, to achieve better performance, its members should take on differentiated and distinctive roles that reflect and incorporate their individual characteristics and are considered by them to be unique and indispensable contributions. Furthermore, regarding team performance, individuals work harder and do better insofar as they are individually identified, accountable (i.e., able to justify their beliefs, feelings, and actions to others), individually competing or otherwise being evaluated, and eligible for rewards contingent on individual performance (Baumeister, Ainsworth, and Vohs 2015).

Finally, role conflict occurs when a member does not do what is required or expected, either because he or she does not have the appropriate ability or motivation, has not understood his or her role, or does not accept it. Role conflict has a significant effect on performance and satisfaction (see Eys, Beauchamp, and Bray 2006 for a review). To address these potential problems, communication is a basic and necessary tool, but it is not always enough. Sometimes profound changes in attitudes and behaviors of team members will have to occur.

Leadership

In cycling, the title "leader" usually refers to the position of team leader and the associated role in a given competition. In a more general sense, the title refers to the most outstanding rider on the team. Cyclists such as Alberto Contador, Chris Froome, Vincenzo Nibali, Nairo Quintana, and Alejandro Valverde are considered leaders on their cycling teams. But this premise should be clarified from the perspective of the psychological group.

In accordance with theory and research in social psychology, a leader is characterized mainly by the ability to influence other members of a group. A leader is able to produce positive changes of emotion or in cognition and behavior of team members as well as on various group processes, such as cohesiveness, regardless of the position occupied. A leader is able to communicate, persuade, teach, generate positive moods, motivate, be a role model for conveying norms and values, help in clarifying roles, increase group cohesiveness, or promote the creation and permanence of a positive climate and a team culture. In this regard, the team leaders can be leaders if they have such influence. This circumstance could be desirable, but this is not always the case. Sometimes other team members—not only riders but any other members—take on and play the function and role of leadership.

To illustrate this point, Pablo Lastras is a good example of a cycling leader: stage winner in the three major tours and a professional rider for 19 years, all of them in one of the most important structures of contemporary cycling (i.e., the teams led by José Miguel Echávarri and Eusebio Unzué, currently the Movistar Team). Many of the team members who have teamed with Pablo Lastras highlight his enormous capacity to influence, his charisma, and especially his commitment and involvement with the team and the group's objectives, norms, and values. Such a leader is important to helping build the psychological group because he embodies the group identity prototype. In accordance with the social identity theory of leadership (Hogg 2001; see Hogg, van Knippenberg, and Rast 2012 for a review), the leader is the main conveyor of the group identity to other members. Thus, the leader who is perceived as the most prototypical of the identity of the group is the most influential and effective in conveying that group's identity, values, and so on. In addition, a prototypical leader acts in the interests of the group, so the other members perceive him or her as "one of us," promoting greater commitment among members and better team performance. In addition, this type of leader is endowed with charisma; he or she is a visionary and transformational character who has an enormous capacity to influence the building of the psychological group, its permanence, and its transformation.

In line with the foregoing, so-called transformational leadership has proved to be effective in achieving team goals. Transformational leadership refers to influential processes with which a leader is able to change the attitudes and aspirations of group members by creating a new vision (i.e., a new formulation of collective goals), articulating a new mission (i.e., an ensemble of meaningful behaviors in accordance with the goals set), convincing them of the viability of this mission, and showing confidence that they can achieve it (Bass and Avolio 1994). In addition, such a leader is often perceived as an authentic and ethical person who can be trusted (see Beauchamp and Eys 2015 for a review on leadership in sport and exercise). Consequently, the transformational leader inspires in team members an identity that transcends their personal interests and serves the common good of the team, generating a profound effect on the psychological group.

On this point, note that leadership consists of a set of behaviors that allow a member to be perceived as a leader by other team members. Moreover, those behaviors can be learned (or developed) through training. In addition, any team can have various leaders who may hold different positions and play different roles. In fact, shared leadership can have positive effects on team performance (see D'Innocenzo, Mathieu, and Kukenberger 2016 for a review). Therefore, hypothetically, anyone could learn to be influential and to make other team members feel more confident, optimistic, and effective in performing tasks, thereby positively transforming the group and organizational atmosphere (Conger 1989). Thus, many sports teams seek people capable of exercising this leadership, of being able to influence other members, motivate them in the pursuit of group goals, and convince them of their self-efficacy to achieve them. Undoubtedly, the performance and welfare of any cycling team can be greatly benefited by the presence of these leaders. And for these reasons, in this chapter we suggest that leadership must be a process that is integrated into the social psychological interventions for the development of a professional cycling team.

The contemporary models of leadership in sports teams, such as the mediational model of leadership (Smoll and Smith 1989) and the multidimensional model of leadership (Chelladurai 1993), adopt a social psychological approach whereby the effects of leadership on the performance and satisfaction of the team members depend on the behaviors of the leader (or leaders) and the situation (or context) in which such behaviors are engaged, in which the characteristics of the other members are a key element defining the situation or context (see Chelladurai 2012 for a review). For example, the mediational model suggests that leadership by a coach (or a sport director) and its effect on an athlete in particular or on the team as a whole depends on the behaviors of that coach, determined by variables such as his or her goals and motivations; situational factors such as features of the sport or the level of competition; and the perceptions, interpretations, and affective reactions that the athletes have in relation to the behaviors of their coach (or director). This model emphasizes this third element by suggesting that the mental processing by the athletes is the mediating factor between the leader's behaviors and the corresponding effects on, for example, the performance of the athletes or team.

Moreover, several specific characteristics have been suggested regarding the behaviors of the coach as leader that are important for the functioning and performance of a team. (In cycling this could be applied to the team principal, sport directors, and so on.) For example, team cohesiveness has been found to be positively related to several leader behaviors, such as democratic coaching behavior (i.e., the extent to which the coach allows the athletes to participate in decision making), positive feedback (i.e., coaching behaviors that provide reinforcement to an athlete by recognizing and rewarding good performance), social support (i.e., behavior characterized by the coach showing concern for the welfare of the athletes by developing a positive team atmosphere and by establishing warm interpersonal relationships with the athletes), and training and instruction (i.e., coaching behaviors aimed at improving athlete performance by emphasizing hard work and strenuous training). The effects of these behaviors on performance have been more inconsistent, but leader behaviors such as positive feedback and training and instruction have been shown to be positively related to team performance (see Carron, Martin, and Loughead 2012 for a review).

Team Cohesiveness

Cohesiveness is the force that attracts members of a team to stay in it and remain together. It serves as the force of gravity of the team. Cohesiveness can result from interpersonal attraction (i.e., because of the affinity and interest generated among themselves by the team members, such as among riders); it can arise from the attraction of the tasks they perform and the goals they pursue (e.g., because of the opportunity that this offers them to achieve goals that are important to them and that would be more difficult or impossible to achieve otherwise, such as win a Tour de France); or it can arise from the attraction toward the team in and of itself (i.e., because of the fact that it gives members a distinct and positive social identity). In fact, cohesiveness is often the result of some or all of these factors interacting with each other. In general, interpersonal relationships could be as important for the cohesiveness of a team as the tasks and goals can be. But in line with the main proposal of this chapter, self-categorization and positive social identity would be the key factor in the formation and permanence of the psychological group (Hogg 1992; Turner 1987). Finally, cohesiveness is not only one of the results arising from the formation of the psychological group but also can give feedback and consolidate the team's future.

In accordance with theory and research in social psychology, some factors already described in this chapter can influence the cohesiveness of a group: positive interdependence that meets the social emotional needs and task objectives of each member, effective management of roles into which individualities are incorporated and play distinctive roles that improve group activity (i.e., performance and satisfaction), and leadership capable of uniting the ensemble of individual forces of the group and channeling them in the same direction. In addition, research has found some other variables that may enhance cohesiveness, such as the similarity of values, beliefs, and attitudes among members, frequent face-to-face communication among them, and competitiveness with other groups. Furthermore, increased cohesiveness is associated with better identification with group values, internalization of group roles, and cooperation within the team. All this can have positive effects on member performance and satisfaction. Sometimes, however, increased cohesiveness can lead to negative consequences, such as increased conformity with the values, norms, and behaviors of the group without questioning their accuracy, legitimacy, or morality; an increase in uncritical groupthink; or a tendency to develop stereotypes, prejudices, and discriminatory behaviors toward members of other groups (Hogg 1992). Finally, cohesiveness may have different components—task commitment, interpersonal attraction, and group pride—that have independent positive effects on various criteria related to behavior versus outcome measures, as well as to effectiveness versus efficiency measures (Beal et al. 2003). In sum, developing cohesiveness within a professional cycling team is complex and has to be based on scientific evidence and carefully conducted by professionals with appropriate qualifications.

Cohesiveness in the workplace has generated a lot of research, mainly because of the effect that it can have on performance (see Beal et al. 2003; Carron, Eys, and Martin 2012 for a review). In sports teams, empirical evidence has shown that cohesiveness is an important factor for predicting performance, although this relationship is much more complex than initially thought. Thus, cohesiveness, like other variables, can act as an antecedent factor that determines performance in some situations. In other situations, it may be the consequence of that performance (Martin, Carron, and Burke 2009), and in other cases it may even be the process (i.e., the mediator) that explains the effects that an antecedent variable, such as the type of leadership, has on the satisfaction and the performance of the team members (Bass et al. 2003; Loughead and Carron 2004). In addition, some studies show that greater cohesiveness, especially when it is only the result of the development of interpersonal relationships, does not necessarily lead to better performance (see Carron, Eys, and Martin 2012 for a review). Furthermore, to lead to increased performance, norms that encourage and reward productivity and high performance standards must also be consolidated within the team (Munroe et al. 1999). In other words, interpersonal attraction should serve the performance of the task—not the other way round—to give rise to positive effects on performance. In sum, regarding this complex scenario drawn about team cohesiveness (and it could be applied to any other group process) in the study of teams, several integrative models have been suggested to increase the understanding of teams based on the schema input (antecedents), process or throughput (mediators), and output (consequences; see Hardy and Crace 1997; Ilgen et al. 2005; Mathieu et al. 2008 for a review).

Applying the Science

In cycling, effective teamwork can make the difference between success and failure. A single rider is not likely to win major competitions without the cooperation and support of his or her teammates. All members of a cycling team should interact with each other, work together, cooperate in pursuit of certain goals (depending on different roles and tasks), and integrate their individual motivations and goals into the team's goals. Paradoxically, teams with lower budgets (or less athletic talent to start with) sometimes achieve better results on the road than teams with bigger budgets (or with better riders on paper). One possible explanation may be found in the group processes described in this chapter (see also Beauchamp and Eys 2014 for a review). Here we have taken the classic concept of the psychological group, incorporating some of the most relevant findings that the research on teams has accumulated over the past decades in various group and organizational contexts, and applied it to the particular case of professional road cycling. In short, the psychological group is the stage beginning and end for teams that want to reach the finish line victorious. The route is the group processes described herein.

In practice, social psychological work with a cycling team includes instruction and training about emotional, cognitive, and behavioral skills; modeling and reinforcement of behaviors; and the implementation of group dynamics to form, develop, and maintain the psychological group, as well as to set group goals, clarify roles, coach optimal leadership styles, increase team cohesiveness, and so on. This chapter has highlighted an essential element, and the fundamental tool, that underlies social psychological work on all previously analyzed group phenomena: communication. Communication processes are a key factor for building the psychological group in a professional cycling team. Through processes of interpersonal, group, and organizational communication, the basic meanings and identifying elements of the psychological group, as well as its values, norms, roles, and tasks, are conveyed to team members. In addition, the positive interdependence processes and interpersonal relationships that emerge among members also depend heavily on the communication processes that occur within the team. Likewise, leaders have to make effective use of their communication skills to bring about change in the attitudes and behaviors of team members when required to achieve group goals. Furthermore, true leaders are able to influence others through the effective use of communication by setting and rewarding appropriate team behaviors, even when they don't occupy a prominent or top position within the team structure and therefore are not in authority. Finally, some effective behaviors for enhancing the cohesiveness, performance, and welfare of a professional cycling team, such as democratic coaching behavior, positive feedback, social support, and training and instruction, are inevitably linked to communication.

Communicating is sharing meanings. It is a process of interaction among several people that reaches a shared understanding. Shared understanding, however, does not necessarily mean that members will agree or cooperate to achieve group goals. Often, dissent and conflict of individual and group interests require a more specific kind of communication: persuasive communication aimed at changing attitudes and behaviors among team members, with the essential purpose of optimizing the integration of individualities in the group and achieving both individual and group goals. In accordance with Kurt Lewin's statement that "nothing is so practical as a good theory," a contemporary scientific model of persuasion such as the elaboration likelihood model (Petty and Cacioppo 1986; see Petty and Briñol 2012 for a review) helps to describe, explain, and predict the antecedents, mediation of psychological processes, and consequences of changes in beliefs, attitudes, and behaviors as a result of persuasive communication. Recent research has shown potential applications of this model of persuasion for understanding the processes of formation and change in attitudes related to doping in sports, providing highly relevant results on how to achieve changes in those attitudes that are long-lasting and resistant, as well as predicting the behavioral intentions of the athletes (Horcajo and De la Vega 2014, 2016; Horcajo and Luttrell 2016).

In conclusion, this chapter suggests that the use of assertive, open, and sincere interpersonal and group communication as a distinctive feature of a professional cycling team will contribute to its optimum functioning to achieve the goals set, as well as promote a culture within the team in accordance with the ethical principles and values (e.g., fair play, against doping, and so on) that must characterize this wonderful sport called cycling (Zabala and Atkinson 2012).

We are grateful to our colleagues Amalio Blanco and Ramon Rico, who commented on various parts of the manuscript and provided helpful feedback.

CHAPTER 25

Motivation and Mental Training

—Jim Taylor and Kate Bennett

Contrary to what most cyclists think, regardless of competitive level, the technical and physical aspects of cycling do not usually determine the winner. Riders who compete at the same level are similar technically and physically. For example, does Chris Froome have greater stamina than Brad Wiggins? Is Marianne Vos stronger than Katie Compton? In both cases, the answer is probably no. So, on any given day, what determines who dons the Tour de France's yellow or green jersey and who doesn't make the podium? The answer lies in who wins the mental race (strong team support and a bit of luck help too, of course). When cyclists are asked what aspect of their sport seems to have the greatest effect on their performances, they almost unanimously identify the mental part. Not surprisingly, this judgment is backed by the literature. Successful cyclists who learn to create and maintain an ideal mental state thrive in performance situations (Williams and Krane 2001). But despite knowing the importance of the mind to cycling success, riders indicate that they devote little to no time to their mental preparation.

Mental Training Is Just Like Physical Training

Despite its obvious importance, mental skills training in cycling is often neglected, at least until a problem arises. The mistake that cyclists (and coaches) often make is not treating the mental side of cycling the same way they treat the physical, technical, and equipment aspects. Most cyclists do not wait until they are injured to cross-train. Nor do they wait to develop a technical flaw before working on technique. More obviously, cyclists replace tires as they wear to prevent flats versus waiting until they get a puncture. Cyclists take all these steps to prevent problems from arising. Ideally, riders should approach mental skills training in the same preventive way.

Unlike changing a tire, mental training takes time and patience. For example, cyclists working to improve their mental skills experience a process similar to changing their preference for cadence. Some riders may naturally feel inclined to push a big gear and climb with a slow cadence, but at some point they may receive feedback that using a smaller gear and spinning at a higher cadence would be more efficient. As they try to develop pedaling efficiency, they remind themselves to shift to easier gears and keep the cadence up at the base of every climb for several rides. They will likely find themselves pushing familiar old big gears up the climb on several occasions without even realizing it. They will probably need several weeks, or even months, before the lower gear and higher cadence on climbs feels natural.

Although we might wish that cyclists could simply read this chapter and instantly master the mental skills discussed, neither the physical nor the mental side of cycling works that way. Cyclists become stronger and faster only by training regularly. Likewise, developing effective mental skills requires devoted time and energy. Fortunately, with dedicated practice, all cyclists can enhance their mental skills and increase their chances of success in both training and racing.

Another characteristic that the physical and mental aspects of cycling have in common is patience. No matter how hard cyclists work, improvement does not come quickly or easily. Cyclists need to give themselves time to learn mental skills. Unfortunately, predicting how long it will take individual riders to ingrain the skills is impossible. Some cyclists may internalize new mental skills in a matter of days, whereas others need to practice consciously for several months before they can perform the skills automatically.

Step 1: Develop Motivation for Cycling Success

Motivation acts as the foundation of all riders' cycling success (Duda and Treasure 2001). Without desire and determination to improve their cycling performances and achieve their individual riding goals, all the other mental factors are meaningless. To become the best cyclists they can be, riders must feel motivated to do the work necessary to develop essential fitness for cycling success. Motivation, simply defined, is the ability and desire to initiate and persist at a task. To ride their best, cyclists must want to begin the process of improvement and must be willing to maintain those efforts until they achieve their individual goals. Motivation in cycling is crucially important because cyclists regularly face fatigue, boredom, pain, difficult conditions, and the desire to do other things. Furthermore, motivation affects everything that influences cycling performance: physical, technical, tactical, and mental training; bike preparation; and general lifestyle factors (sleep, diet, school or work, finances, and relationships).

Motivation also directly affects cycling performance. When cyclists are highly motivated to improve their performances, they willingly put in the time and effort necessary to raise the level of their riding. Additionally, motivation influences race outcomes. When riders compete against others of nearly equal fitness and skill, ability typically does not determine the outcome of the race. Rather, the cyclist who works the hardest, endures pain best, does not give up, and rides the best in critical moments prevails across the finish line. In other words, the most motivated cyclist usually wins.

Understand the Drive

To maximize individual cycling capabilities, riders must first understand what drives them to succeed. Successful cyclists might

- love being on the bike,
- enjoy competing,
- like the challenge of pushing themselves physically,
- like to improve,
- love the thrill of winning, or
- have other individual reasons.

After cyclists understand their primary motivations, they can create training and competition scenarios that inspire them to put in the time and effort necessary to achieve their unique goals. Recognizing what drives them not only enhances riders' daily motivation to get on the bike but also taps into deep intrinsic drive on tough days when staying in bed or sitting on the couch seems much more appealing than riding a bike.

Identify Individual Values

What makes cycling significant and meaningful to cyclists? How are those qualities reflected in their individual goals? Knowing how the sport represents important aspects of life to cyclists is important because value-driven goals enhance their motivation. Ultimately, riders' willingness to commit, persevere, and sacrifice will be fueled, in large part, by the value they place on cycling and the sport's relationship to other meaningful aspects of life.

Tap Into Internal and External Motivation

Cyclists are motivated intrinsically (e.g., thoughts, feelings, or goals) and extrinsically (e.g., competitors, situations, or rewards). The world's best cyclists use both internal and external motivation to propel them toward their goals. Intrinsic motivation is closely related to values. Cyclists willingly push their limits when goals are individually significant and meaningful.

Although having strong intrinsic motivation to maximize ability is essential, extrinsic motivation is also helpful. Think about group rides. Cyclists may barely drag themselves to the start of a ride, but, as the group becomes energized, they find resources to attack, bridge, and sprint. Likewise, in the final moments of a climb when everybody's legs are screaming to stop, a few cyclists always attack because they want to be the first rider to the top regardless of physical discomfort.

Respond to the Grind

Motivation is critically important when cyclists arrive at a point when time in the saddle is no longer fun. Known as the grind, this is the point at which training or racing becomes tiring, painful, and tedious. Persisting through the discomfort really counts here. The grind separates successful cyclists from those who do not achieve their goals. Many cyclists reach this point and either ease up or give up because going on is just too darned hard. But truly motivated cyclists reach the grind and keep on going.

Note here the important difference between the grind and overtraining. The grind is a psychological experience in response to a prolonged period of training or racing, when energy is low (physically and mentally) because of sustained focus in pursuit of individual goals. If they are not careful, cyclists may confuse the grind with overtraining syndrome. Overtraining syndrome is a physiological concern related to an improper balance between overloading (through intensity or volume) and recovery. Low motivation may be associated with overtraining. The key difference is that cyclists struggling

---

Defining Terms

Motivation is the ability and desire to initiate and persist at a task. It can be divided into two types:

1. Intrinsic motivation comes from within. The cyclist is internally driven to achieve pleasure and satisfaction in pursuit of a personal goal such as improving power-to-weight ratio, completing a century, racing him- or herself on a local climb, or setting a PR on a time-trial course. The cyclist finds this pursuit inherently rewarding.

2. Extrinsic motivation comes from without. The cyclist is externally driven to complete or achieve a common goal. The cyclist enjoys the external rewards such as winning races, competing for the town-line sprint in group rides, riding for a teammate, or following a coaching program.

The grind describes the point when training and racing become tiring, painful, and tedious, but tackling it is seen as necessary to achieve a personal goal.

with the grind are physiologically adapting to training and responding to recovery whereas cyclists struggling with overtraining syndrome are not responsive to periodized training or recovery.

Many people say that cyclists have to love the grind to be successful. Except for a few hypermotivated cyclists, however, love is not in the cards because there is not much to love. Responses to the grind lie along a continuum from love to hate. As just mentioned, loving the grind is rare, but cyclists who hate the grind are unlikely to stay motivated. Rather than love or hate the grind, riders can learn to accept it as part of striving toward their cycling goals. They may not find the grind enjoyable, but not achieving their personal goals (because of lack of motivation to overcome the grind and do the hard work) is much more painful. And those who confront the grind gain the sweet satisfaction of seeing their hard work pay off with success.

Set Goals

Few things are more rewarding and motivating than setting a goal, putting effort toward the goal, and achieving the goal. The sense of accomplishment and validation of the effort creates positive feelings and motivates cyclists to strive higher.

A valuable approach is to establish clear goals focused on both accomplishments in cycling (outcome goals) and steps toward achievement of those accomplishments (process goals). Additionally, setting challenging yet realistic personal goals increases the chances of success.

Focusing on long-term goals is helpful. To excel in biking, cyclists eagerly put a lot of time and effort into their training and racing. But there will be times—the grind—when motivation is sparse. When cyclists feel this way, they need to focus on their long-term goals to help them recall exactly why they are working so hard. This focus also creates the opportunity to imagine themselves achieving individual goals and reinforces the idea that hard work is the only option for success. Additionally, reflecting on goals allows cyclists to create feelings of inspiration and pride that will occur as they achieve their goals. Ultimately, this technique allows cyclists to distract themselves from discomfort, focus on future accomplishments, and generate positive thoughts and emotions. The result is increased motivation to push through the grind.

Have a Training Partner or Group

Cyclists will find it difficult to remain highly motivated on their own all the time. Regardless of competitive level, all cyclists struggle periodically with intrinsic motivation. Additionally, regardless of cyclists' willingness to push themselves, they tend to work even harder when someone pushes them. That someone can be a coach, personal trainer, parent, training partner, or team. Successful cyclists often train with partners or groups of riders at their level of ability and with similar goals. They work together to strive toward and accomplish their respective goals. Group dynamics increase the odds that at least one cyclist will be motivated and able to have a positive influence on other riders' motivation. For example, a rider who is not psyched to do hill repeats will still put in the time and effort because other cyclists exert themselves on the same hill.

Focus on Greatest Competitor

Successful cyclists maintain motivation by focusing on their greatest competitor. Riders can identify their biggest competitor and put his or her name (or photo) where it is visible daily. Each time the photo is visible, riders can ask themselves, "Am I working harder than him or her?" Cyclists must recognize that success (beating that competitor) will result only from consistent hard work.

Identify Motivational Cues

An important aspect of maintaining motivation involves generating positive emotions associated with cyclists' individual efforts and achievement of personal goals. Motivational cues, such as inspirational phrases and photographs, provide a way to maintain those feelings. For example, inspirational quotes or photos placed in visible areas (e.g., bedroom or refrigerator door) tend to elevate intrinsic motivation. Riders can use them as periodic reminders to focus their efforts and generate motivating emotions.

A final point about motivation. The techniques described are effective in increasing short-term motivation. Motivation, though, is not something that can be given to cyclists. Rather, motivation must ultimately come from within. Whether cyclists want to win the Tour, enjoy competing, focus on physical fitness, love riding with friends, or simply enjoy testing their capabilities, the drive to pedal must come from deep inside, and cyclists need to connect with that feeling every time they ride their bikes. It comes down to wanting to be the best cyclist they can be and feeling deeply connected to that desire.

Step 2: Build Confidence to Maximize Ability

Confidence is another essential mental factor in cycling. Like motivation, this mental area is also ripe for change. This section not only offers insights into how confidence affects cycling performance but also provides many practical tools for developing confidence in riding.

Confidence is defined as how strongly cyclists believe in their ability to achieve their cycling goals. This skill is incredibly important because, despite having the fitness to ride well, cyclists who do not believe in their fitness will not ride to their full ability. For example, a cyclist lacking confidence demonstrates the ability to ride a 25K time trial averaging 22 miles per hour (36 km/h) in training but struggles to reproduce those results in racing conditions for fear of bonking during the effort. With increased confidence, the rider can fully leverage her or his fitness to reproduce those results in a race. Confident cyclists are more likely to be positive, motivated, intense, focused, emotionally in control, and able to maintain their confidence in the face of struggles during training and races (Manzon et al. 2005).

Confidence Is a Skill

A common misconception among cyclists is that confidence is an inborn trait or that if it is not developed early in a cycling career, it will never develop. In reality, confidence is a skill (Zinsser, Bunker, and William 2001) that can be learned. Just as with any type of cycling skill, such as cornering aggressively or riding in a pace line, confidence is developed through focus, effort, and repetition. The problem is that cyclists have the option to practice good or bad confidence skills. Cyclists who are often negative about their cycling practice ingrain negative confidence skills. As with bad technical habits, that negativity will interfere with performance during difficult training rides or races. In other words, negatively focused cyclists become highly skilled at something—being negative—that harms their riding. Alternatively, successful cyclists develop a predisposition to focus on positive aspects of cycling and performance regardless of adversity. Seligman (1991) referred to this idea as learned optimism.

To interrupt harmful confidence skills, cyclists must retrain the way they think and speak to themselves. They should intentionally practice good confidence skills regularly until the old negative habits are broken and the new positive confidence skills are ingrained. For example, imagine a cyclist lined up with other racers at the start of a road race with a lot of climbing. As the rider compares him- or herself to the other riders (thinking error number 1), he or she might think, "Those other cyclists look like climbers. There is no way I can hang with them" (thinking error number 2). With that thought, the cyclist has already lost the race even if he or she is as objectively fit and fast as the competitors. Instead, to build confidence, the racer should focus on his or her preparation (confidence booster number 1), use positive self-talk (confidence booster number 2), identify his or her process goals for the race (confidence booster number 3), and be his or her own best ally rather than worst enemy (confidence booster number 4). This process will redirect the rider's attention toward positive self-perceptions, which further builds confidence throughout the race, increasing the chances for success.

Five Keys to Cycling Confidence

Each of the following five keys alone can enhance cyclists' confidence, but if they are used together, cyclists will find that their confidence grows stronger and more quickly. The ultimate goal for cyclists is to develop a strong and resilient belief in their riding ability so that they have the confidence to give their best effort, ride at their highest level possible, and believe that they can achieve their cycling goals in the most important races of their lives.

Preparation Breeds Confidence

Preparation is the foundation of confidence (Taylor 2001). It includes the physical, technical, tactical, equipment, and mental aspects of cycling in addition to putting in the necessary time and effort required to maximize training. When cyclists develop these areas as fully as possible, they believe that they have the capabilities to ride their best, regardless of whether they are at the start line of a race, on a long climb, or sprinting to the finish. The more that cyclists fully address their preparation, the more confidence they breed in themselves. The goal of every cyclist is to be able to say, "I'm as prepared as I can be to ride my best" at the start of every race.

Mental Skills Reinforce Confidence

Most cyclists have a toolbox that includes wrenches, oil, spare tires, and much more. This toolbox allows cyclists to keep their bikes in optimal condition and fix breakdowns when they occur. In addition to having a repair toolbox, cyclists should create a mental toolbox because development of effective mental tools is closely linked to confidence (Hanton, Mellalieu, and Hall 2004). Fortunately, a mental toolbox does not weigh anything, even when it is filled with tools!

Like a spare tube carried on the bike to repair a flat during a ride, the tools in a mental toolbox are available when psychological breakdowns occur on the bike. For example, many cyclists feel nervous before a race, despair after being dropped on a climb, or lose focus as they begin to hurt late in a race. Instead of bike parts, a mental toolbox contains essential mental tools that are critical for successful training and racing such as inspirational thoughts and images to bolster motivation, positive self-talk and body language to fortify confidence, intensity control to combat energy-depleting anxiety, keywords to maintain focus and avoid distractions, and pain-control techniques to ease discomfort during tough rides. Essentially, a mental toolbox can prevent psychological breakdowns on the bike as well as provide resources when they do occur during critical moments on the bike.

Adversity Ingrains Confidence

Most cyclists love to train in ideal weather, on courses that play to their strengths, and when they feel healthy and rested. But how often do they race under those conditions? Rarely. More often than not, the worst conditions—rain, cold, and a stiff headwind—appear during the least opportune times. But course conditions do not determine who succeeds and who fails. Instead, mental skills do. For example, two riders can face the same course and weather but view and respond to them entirely differently. Rider A sees them as a threat, which creates negativity and anxiety. Conversely, rider B views those same conditions as a challenge and becomes motivated and excited. Assuming they have equal abilities, rider B is more likely to excel that day. Successful cyclists step up to the challenge of maintaining their confidence when facing the worst possible conditions. To ingrain confidence more deeply, cyclists should expose themselves to as much adversity as possible (Cresswell and Hodge 2004) because training for adversity benefits riders in several ways (Taylor and Wilson 2005): It increases confidence in their ability to respond positively to difficult conditions, reinforces their ability to be flexible and adapt to changing race demands, and familiarizes them with harsh environmental experiences.

A common saying is that cyclists should train harder than they race. Riders should train in conditions that will be as hard as or harder than race conditions and practice responding positively to those adverse conditions. Adversity factors might include environmental obstacles, such as bad weather, rough road conditions such as cobblestones or potholes, or riding with a group slightly above their individual capabilities. Essentially, cyclists who train for adversity and subsequently face difficult race conditions simply think to themselves, "No big deal, I've trained in these conditions before." In addition, training for adversity makes cyclists feel tough!

Support Bolsters Confidence

It's difficult for cyclists to achieve success on their own. The best riders in the world have many people supporting them. When things are just not going well, having people (e.g., family, friends, coaches, and teammates) around to turn to for support and encouragement is helpful. Because confidence may wax and wane depending on how cyclists feel, as does the quality of their training and racing, riders need to have support people who provide a booster shot of confidence. For example, coaches should express belief in cyclists' abilities ("I know you can do it"), and friends should validate difficult moments ("Hang in there—things will turn around").

Success Validates Confidence

All the previous steps in building confidence will go for naught if cyclists do not ride well and achieve their goals. Success validates the confidence that riders develop in their abilities; it demonstrates that their beliefs are well founded. Success further strengthens confidence, making it more resilient in the face of setbacks and poor performance. It also rewards efforts to build confidence, encouraging cyclists to continue working hard and developing their physical and psychological capabilities.

But success does not just mean race success, such as a podium finish, at least not right away. Typically, cyclists do not experience instant success that creates confidence. Little victories during every day in training and local racing breed confidence because performance goals (goals based on individual performance regardless of training or racing outcomes) provide positive reinforcement and create an intrinsic sense of control about performance outcomes (Duda and Treasure 2001). Performance goals allow cyclists to get off their bikes after a training ride or race feeling as if they just won because they accomplished identified objectives related to personal performance (e.g., sustain specific power ranges, listen to the coach, apply specific race tactics, push through planned intervals, overcome adversity). Every small victory accumulated during training moves cyclists one step closer to that big victory, namely, achieving their cycling goals.

Step 3: Regulate Intensity for Optimal Performance

Intensity may be the most important contributor to cycling performance because all the motivation and confidence in the world will not help if cyclists' bodies are not physiologically capable of doing what needs to be done to ride their best after a race begins (Taylor 2001). Whether riders are cruising along in the peloton during a flat stage, ascending a category 1 climb, or sprinting the last 100 meters of a criterium, they must be at the right intensity to perform optimally. Simply put, intensity is the amount of physiological activity experienced in the body including heart rate, respiration, and adrenaline. Intensity exists on a continuum that ranges from sleep (very relaxed) to terror (very anxious). Somewhere between those two extremes is the intensity at which cyclists ride their best in different race situations.

Ideal Intensity

Although it may seem as if every race has an ideal level of intensity (Taylor and Kress 2006; Wilson et al. 2005), each race, in fact, has unique dynamics that play out based on course conditions, weather, and other cyclists within the peloton. In addition, each rider responds differently to those variables. Furthermore, intensity requirements vary throughout a race. So rather than trying to master an ideal intensity state, cyclists must learn how to regulate their intensity regardless of conditions (Raglin and Hanin 1999). For example, Chris Froome needs to be relaxed during the early parts of the Alpe d'Huez stage of the Tour de France to conserve energy before the big ascents that lie ahead. Fabian Cancellara must be at moderate intensity as he speeds through a time trial. Katie Compton moderates her intensity as she races toward another cyclocross national championship. Marcel Kittel must be a nuclear reactor of intensity in the final sprint to the finish in Marseilles.

Different types of races as well as varying race situations call for different levels of intensity. Short races require cyclists to be mentally and physically psyched up at the start line. For example, track races explode from the start, whereas road races begin with a neutral start and often vacillate between periods of high intensity (attacks and counterattacks) and low intensity (feed zones and long stretches of flat roads). Managing intensity during a road race requires cyclists to be constantly aware of moderating their energy efficiently and maintaining reserves for critical moments throughout the race. After determining the optimal intensity for a specific race situation, cyclists must recognize their intensity at any given moment to determine whether it is at an ideal level (Ravizza 2001). Several factors reflect the current level of intensity: breathing, heart rate, muscle tension, body position on the bike, pedal stroke, thoughts, and emotions (Taylor and Kress 2006).

Psych-Down Tools

Indicators of being on the high side of intensity include rapid or shallow breathing, a racing heart, muscle tension, and rigidity on the bike (locked elbows, stiff arms, or tight back). Cadence also provides feedback: Spinning furiously or stomping on the pedals while other racers seem relaxed likely indicates that it is time to calm down. Finally, cyclists might notice themselves feeling worried or experiencing racing thoughts because lack of confidence correlates with overintensity (Taylor and Wilson 2002).

Most cyclists naturally experience an increase in intensity before a race. Racing is the ultimate way for riders to test their fitness and training efforts. But when intensity turns to anxiety, performance deteriorates. Anxiety creates muscle tension, inhibits oxygen intake, and creates physical discomfort, all of which slow cyclists down on the bike. But, rather than just resigning themselves to feeling nervous and expecting a bad ride, cyclists can take active steps to reach and maintain their ideal intensity to perform optimally. Cyclists can use a number of simple psych-down techniques to regain control of their intensity.

Deep Breathing

One of the first things disrupted by overintensity is breathing. It becomes short and choppy, inhibiting the uptake of oxygen that the body needs. The most basic way to lower intensity is for cyclists to take control of their breathing by taking slow, deep breaths. Conscious regulation of breathing results in more positive and consistent performances (Williams and Krane 2001). Deep breathing has several important benefits (Taylor and Wilson 2002). It ensures that cyclists get enough oxygen for their bodies to function well. Increased oxygen uptake allows anxious bodies to relax and feel better as well as reestablishes a sense of control. This increased comfort also enhances confidence and helps cyclists combat negative thoughts, which are often the cause of overintensity. In addition, deep breathing allows cyclists

---

Benefits of Deep Breathing

Circulates oxygen throughout the body for optimal functioning

Relaxes anxious bodies or tense muscles

Establishes a sense of control within oneself

Increases self-confidence

Grounds the mind in the present moment

Creates opportunities to challenge negative self-talk and manage emotional reactions

---

to let go of negative emotions, such as fear or frustration, and creates room for positive emotions such as excitement. Finally, focusing on breathing creates opportunities for cyclists to redirect their attention away from factors that cause overintensity. Taking conscious deep breaths before the start of a race is a simple and easy way for cyclists to settle themselves down and prepare for the start. Likewise, deep breathing during races, such as when starting a climb, allows cyclists to regulate their intensity.

Muscle Relaxation

Muscle tension is another common and debilitating symptom of overintensity (Landers and Boucher 1986). This physical symptom is crippling because tight, stiff muscles interfere with cycling performance. Two muscle relaxation techniques support healthy levels of muscle activation during training rides and races: passive relaxation and active relaxation (Jacobson 1938). Similar to deep breathing, muscle relaxation enables cyclists to regain control of their bodies and increase their physical comfort, and it offers the same mental and emotional advantages.

To perform passive relaxation, cyclists simply focus on their muscles and allow them to relax. When cyclists feel tense and cannot relax passively, active relaxation becomes a better option. Although the method may seem counterintuitive, cyclists tighten their muscles for a brief period (for example, 5 seconds) and then relax them. Active relaxation typically involves tightening and relaxing four major muscle groups: face and neck, arms and shoulders, chest and back, and buttocks and legs. People can also individualize active relaxation to focus on particular muscles that trouble them the most. The neck and shoulders seem to be the important muscle groups for cyclists because tightness in those muscles raises their center of gravity and reduces oxygen, power, and stamina.

Smile

The last technique for lowering intensity is seemingly strange yet surprisingly effective. A few years ago, Jim worked with a young professional cyclist who was having a terrible training ride. He was riding poorly, and his coach expressed frustration toward the rider. He dropped back to Jim feeling angry and depressed. His body was in knots. He asked Jim what he could do. Jim did not have a good answer until an idea just popped into his head. Jim told him to smile. The rider said, "I don't want to smile." Jim told him to smile. He said he was not happy and did not want to smile. Jim told him again to smile. This time, just to get Jim off his back, the rider smiled. Jim told him to hold the smile. During the next 2 minutes an amazing transformation occurred. As he rode along with the smile on his face, the tension began to drain out of his body. His breathing became slow and deep. He said that he was feeling better. In a short time, the rider looked more relaxed and happier. He returned to his training pace, rode with improved performance, and made some progress during the remainder of ride.

The cyclist's response was so dramatic that Jim wanted to learn how such a change could occur. When Jim returned to his office, he researched the effects of smiling and learned two things. First, as people grow up, they become conditioned to the positive effects of smiling. In other words, people learn that when they smile, they are happy and life is good. Second, smiling directly affects brain chemistry. The research revealed that outward facial expressions provide feedback to the brain (Laird 1974). Furthermore, when people smile, the act of smiling releases brain chemicals called endorphins, the body's natural relaxants, which create a physiologically relaxing effect (Zajonc 1965). Essentially, when cyclists choose to smile (regardless of mood state), their facial expressions send messages to their brains that they are happy, which results in a more relaxed state and leads to a more positive experience on the bike.

Psych-Up Tools

Underintensity tends to be related to overconfidence, lack of interest, and boredom (Taylor and Wilson 2002). Although less common than overintensity (Williams and Harris 1988), letdowns in intensity also negatively affect cycling performance. A decrease in intensity causes all the things that enable cyclists to excel to disappear. Physically, cyclists no longer have optimal blood flow, oxygen, or adrenaline needed for strength and stamina during races. Mentally, they lose the motivation and focus that enables them to ride well. Similar to the psych-down tools used when intensity is too high, cyclists can use psych-up tools to elevate their intensity when it drops.

Intense Breathing

Just as deep breathing reduces intensity, intense breathing increases it. When cyclists find their intensity dropping, several hard exhalations elevate cyclists' minds and bodies to more intense levels. Cyclists should practice taking two intense breaths before a race. Excitatory breaths are also great cues during races to amp up intensity as the peloton approaches a difficult climb (think Tejay van Garderen) or sprint finish (think Mark Cavendish).

High-Energy Self-Talk

A main cause of drops in intensity is letdown thoughts. Cyclists' internal thoughts such as "I've got this won," "I've bonked," or "I can't believe I've been dropped" all result in decreased intensity (Caudill, Weinberg, and Jackson 1983; Williams and Harris 1988) because their minds send the message to their bodies that they no longer need to exert effort. This language creates a sure bet that their riding will decline. When cyclists notice these thoughts, they need to replace them with high-energy self-talk (Edwards and Hardy 1996). Self-talk such as "Keep attacking!" "Go, go go!" and "Stay pumped!" helps cyclists stay motivated and focused.

Step 4: Master the Pain of Training and Racing

Pain is, without a doubt, the most pervasive obstacle for cyclists as they strive for their greatest gains in training and best competitive performances in races. Pain has profound physical, psychological, and emotional effects on cyclists (Taylor and Kress 2006). Despite this importance, riders spend little time educating themselves about what pain is, how it affects them, and how they can manage it. Fortunately, considerable scientific evidence suggests that simple psychological techniques can significantly increase cyclists' pain tolerance.

Differentiating Pain

The first step to mastering pain in training and racing is for cyclists to differentiate between performance pain and warning pain. Performance pain (Taylor and Taylor 1998) is typically perceived as dull and generalized, does not persist after physical exertion, exists without localized swelling or tenderness, and is not associated with sustained soreness. In contrast, warning pain (Catalano 1987) is sharp, localized, and experienced during and after exertion. Additionally, it creates swelling, tenderness, and, possibly, prolonged soreness (Rian 1990).

Cyclists' experiences of the two types of pain while riding lead to different perceptions and responses. Fortunately, riders have a choice in how they interpret and respond to pain (Taylor and Kress 2006). Cyclists usually view performance pain as positive, short-lived, voluntary, and controllable (Kress 1998; Taylor and Kress 2006). As a result, performance pain typically leads to feelings of satisfaction and inspiration, facilitates performance, and enhances riders' overall sense of well-being (Heil 1993). Conversely, cyclists perceive warning pain as negative, chronic, uncontrollable, and indicative of danger to their physical health. These perceptions cause a loss of confidence, interfere with motivation to train and race, and increase anxiety about the underlying cause of pain.

Pain as Information

Typically, pain is viewed as an unpleasant experience meant to be avoided. Pain, however, provides valuable information for cyclists to use throughout their season, including information about their training schedules (e.g., overtraining), their training intensity (e.g., too high), their recovery (e.g., not enough rest), and the presence of injuries (e.g., serious and chronic). With a clear understanding of the type of pain they are experiencing, successful cyclists use a variety of pain mastery techniques to control pain on the bike. Pain mastery techniques can be classified into two general categories: pain reduction and pain focusing (Heil 1993).

Pain Reduction Techniques

Pain reduction techniques act directly on the physiological aspects of the pain, decreasing the actual amount of pain that is present. Specifically, they work to reduce sympathetic nervous system activity such as norepinephrine release (Heil 1993), shallow breathing, and muscle tension, all of which intensify the experience of pain. Cyclists accomplish these outcomes by inducing greater states of relaxation, which are associated with an increased sense of control in a negative situation, increased pain tolerance, and decreased reports of pain (Thompson 1981). Pain reduction techniques commonly used during and following training and racing include deep breathing, muscle relaxation, and therapeutic massage.

Deep breathing   Perhaps the simplest, most essential, yet most neglected technique to reduce pain is deep breathing (Catalano 1987). Pain inhibits breathing, lessens blood flow, and causes muscle tension and bracing, which exacerbate pain (Cousins and Phillips 1985). Deep breathing diminishes pain by transporting sufficient oxygen throughout the body, relaxing muscles, and decreasing generalized sympathetic nervous system activity. Deep breathing also acts as a distraction; when cyclists focus on their breathing, they pay less attention to their pain. Incorporating deep breathing into all aspects of training and racing increases cyclists' chances of success because the skill helps them reduce their experience of pain.

Muscle relaxation   Muscle tension and bracing in response to pain is common among cyclists (Taylor and Kress 2006). This response is often seen in tight neck and shoulder muscles or clenched hands on the handlebars. Refer to the section Psych-Down Tools earlier in the chapter for practical steps to reduce pain related to muscle tension and bracing. Muscle relaxation training and therapeutic massage are also comforting tools to use after training and racing when pain is high and resources to manage the discomfort are low. When used after rides, these skills and techniques decrease pain and restore a general sense of physical comfort and well-being.

Therapeutic massage   Therapeutic massage aids recovery from regular training and racing as well as recovery from injury. The most well-known form of massage involves a masseuse providing deep-tissue massage to a cyclist. On professional cycling teams, this person is often referred to as the soigneur. For athletes who do not have regular access to traditional massage, foam rollers provide an effective way to roll out muscles before and after riding.

Pain-Focusing Techniques

Pain-focusing techniques involve directing attention to (association) or away from (dissociation) the pain as a means of reducing or altering the awareness of pain (Leventhal and Everhart 1979). These strategies do not directly affect the physiological effect of pain; instead, they decrease the perception of pain.

External focus   External focus involves directing attention externally away from the experience of pain. Examples of external focus include looking at the scenery during a training ride or focusing on other riders during a race. If cyclists are not attending to their pain, they perceive the pain as less discomforting.

Rhythmic cognitive activity   This technique involves focusing on a repetitious or structured task (Taylor and Taylor 1998). Rhythmic cognitive activity is commonly used by cyclists in the form of counting breaths or pedal revolutions. By becoming absorbed in the repetition of these tasks, cyclists pay less attention to the pain they experience.

Dramatic coping   Dramatic coping consists of putting the pain in a different context, in this case, seeing training and racing pain as part of a grand challenge (Taylor and Taylor 1998). Putting pain in a heroic context can be real or imagined. For example, a cyclist training for the Olympics is, indeed, challenging the pain in pursuit of an Olympic berth. Similarly, a weekend cyclist on a training ride can imagine that he or she is competing in the Tour de France, thus making experiencing the pain seem like a worthy sacrifice.

Situational assessment   This technique involves evaluating the causes of pain and using that information to make adjustments to relieve the pain (Taylor and Taylor 1998). Situational assessment is an essential tool for optimal performance on the bike because it allows cyclists to recognize the presence of pain and identify its source. Potential sources of pain in cycling include too slow a cadence, inadequate pace adjustment on climbs, improper bike fit, saddle sores, or the occurrence of an injury such as a strained back muscle. Active steps to manage the pain depend on whether cyclists experience performance pain or warning pain. In response to performance pain, riders make adjustments related to the cause. For example, they modify cadence or body position on the bike to reduce the pain. Alternatively, cyclists practice pain mastery techniques to reduce the performance pain. To address warning pain, cyclists either reduce intensity or interrupt riding to prevent aggravation of an injury. Increased understanding of the presence of pain is an invaluable tool to maximize performances. The development of awareness and control allows cyclists to acknowledge pain, identify its type, and directly reduce the experience and perception of pain when training and racing.

Applying the Science

All things being equal, the mental aspect of cycling typically elevates riders to the top of the podium. Although most cyclists recognize the importance of mental skills, they rarely take time to develop this critical aspect of performance. Learning to develop and maintain an ideal mental state increases the chances of success regardless of cycling discipline. Similar to physical training, mental skills training requires time, dedication, patience, and regular practice.

First, cyclists must maximize their motivation to develop a competitive mental edge. Motivation, when linked to values, provides a driving force to push limits and persist through the grind. Goal setting, group training, focusing techniques, and motivational cues all enhance motivation.

Second, riders need to develop a solid foundation for confidence. Contrary to popular belief, confidence is a learned skill. The five keys to developing cycling confidence include preparing for rides and races, creating a mental toolbox, training through adversity, utilizing support, and experiencing success.

Next, commitment to intensity regulation is essential. Regulating physiological activity before and during races is critical for excelling in the sport. Although intensity requirements vary based on conditions and individual needs, every cyclist has an ideal intensity for any given moment on the bike. To psych-down, cyclists can practice deep breathing, muscle relaxation, and smiling. To psych-up, although the need to do so is less common, riders should practice intense breathing and high-energy self-talk.

Finally, mastering pain in cycling is crucial for optimal performances. Performance pain leads to positive experiences that reinforce cyclists' efforts on the bike. Warning pain creates negative experiences and warrants modifications to alleviate the discomfort. To increase pain tolerance, cyclists can practice pain reduction techniques, which focus on physical relaxation, or pain-focusing techniques, which engage distraction skills.

CHAPTER 26

Assessing Cycling Fitness

—James Hopker and Simon Jobson

The most beneficial training program is the one that is specific to the athlete. A generic training program often facilitates performance improvements simply because it offers an increased training structure. An individualized approach is more beneficial as it takes account of the athlete's specific strengths and weaknesses. Of course, before such an individualized program can be developed, these strengths and weaknesses must be identified. For many years, such questions have been best answered with carefully controlled exercise tests conducted in a laboratory environment. Although laboratory testing continues to be an important part of the committed cyclist's regular test battery, the combination of inexpensive heart rate monitors and increasingly affordable power meters means that more cyclists are able to complete regular self-tests on the turbo trainer and on the road. Indeed, the proliferation of robust power meters for mountain bikes, cyclocross bikes, and BMX bikes means that self-testing for a variety of cycling disciplines can be completed in the field.

In chapter 2 the physiological requirements of different cycling disciplines were described. From this you have developed an awareness of the physiological attributes that determine performance in your corner of the cycling world. In this chapter we focus on a range of self-administered tests that can establish a cyclist's strengths and weaknesses in relation to those attributes. This information can then be used in the design of an individualized training program. The inclusion of regular retesting (every 1 to 2 months) within a program will allow the cyclist to avoid training stagnation and adjust to new race goals.

Although field-based testing is more viable than ever before, a number of key test principles must be observed to maximize the reliability of self-tests. For example, when using a power meter, ensure that, before each test, you carry out manufacturer-recommended calibration or zero-offset procedures. When testing on the road, in each test try to use the same stretch of road in the same weather and at the same time of day. Try to standardize your routine (e.g., sleep, physical activity, and nutrition) in the 24 hours before each test to maximize the probability of a good test and to ensure a fair comparison between tests. By carrying out regular self-tests in these ways, fitness assessment will become a key part of your performance program instead of a rare and therefore relatively unhelpful treat.

What Is Your Power Profile?

Success in sprint cycling requires a rider to produce very high power output (greater than 1,000 watts) for a short time (about 5 seconds). In contrast, time-trial success requires a cyclist to sustain moderate power output (250 to 500 watts) for a more sustained period (typically between 18 and 120 minutes). Cyclists tend to focus on the type of cycling (sprinting, time trialing, and so on) that they are good at. For most, however, the greatest performance gains will be achieved by focusing on areas of weakness. A power profile approach can provide vital information about where to focus training by establishing peak performance over a range of durations.

Sport scientists have developed power profiles using a range of test durations. Hunter Allen and Andrew Coggan (2010) described a power profile test that evaluates maximal performance over durations of 5 seconds, 1 minute, and 5 minutes. Following a 45-minute warm-up (including a 5-minute effort at threshold power output and three 1-minute fast pedaling efforts), the test begins with a 5-minute all-out (i.e., maximal) effort. This effort is followed by 10 minutes of recovery at endurance pace, 1 minute all out, 5 minutes of recovery, 1 minute all out, 5 minutes of recovery, 15 seconds all out, 2 minutes of recovery, and 15 seconds all out. The test ends with an easy warm-down.

A power profile is defined as the highest power outputs from a test over durations of 5 seconds, 1 minute, 5 minutes, and 60 minutes, the latter being established during the functional threshold power test described in the section Where Is Your Threshold? By comparing the results to Allen and Coggan's power profile table (see figure 26.1), you can see where your relative strengths and weaknesses lie. For example, within your road race category you might have high 1-, 5-, and 60-minute values but a low 5-second value. In this instance, focused sprint training would likely lead to a much bigger improvement in road race performance than would a continued focus on threshold training.

Determining Your Critical Power

Critical power (CP) is an indication of a cyclist's ability to produce power output over time. It is based on the fact that the length of time for which a cyclist can ride depends on how hard she or he is riding. The relationship between sustainable power output and time can be modeled by using three or more separate cycling time-trial-type efforts. This relationship can be described through the construction of a power–time curve similar to that represented in figure 26.2. This curve can be used directly to guide power targets for individual race efforts or training sessions. For example, when

	MEN				WOMEN			
	5 s	1 min	5 min	FT	5 s	1 min	5 min	FT
World class **(e.g., international pro)**	25.18	11.50	7.60	6.40	19.42	9.29	6.74	5.69
	24.88	11.39	7.50	6.31	19.20	9.20	6.64	5.61
	24.59	11.27	7.39	6.22	18.99	9.11	6.55	5.53
	24.29	11.16	7.29	6.13	18.77	9.02	6.45	5.44
	24.00	11.04	7.19	6.04	18.56	8.93	6.36	5.36
	23.70	10.93	7.08	5.96	18.34	8.84	6.26	5.28
	23.40	10.81	6.98	5.87	18.13	8.75	6.17	5.20
Exceptional **(e.g., domestic pro)**	23.11	10.70	6.88	5.78	17.91	8.66	6.07	5.12
	22.81	10.58	6.77	5.69	17.70	8.56	5.98	5.03
	22.51	10.47	6.67	5.60	17.48	8.47	5.88	4.95
	22.22	10.35	6.57	5.51	17.26	8.38	5.79	4.87
	21.92	10.24	6.46	5.42	17.05	8.29	5.69	4.79
	21.63	10.12	6.36	5.33	16.83	8.20	5.60	4.70
Excellent (e.g., cat. 1)	21.33	10.01	6.26	5.24	16.62	8.11	5.50	4.62
	21.03	9.89	6.15	5.15	16.40	8.02	5.41	4.54
	20.74	9.78	6.05	5.07	16.19	7.93	5.31	4.46
	20.44	9.66	5.95	4.98	15.97	7.84	5.21	4.38
	20.15	9.55	5.84	4.89	15.76	7.75	5.12	4.29
	19.85	9.43	5.74	4.80	15.54	7.66	5.02	4.21
Very good (e.g., cat. 2)	19.55	9.32	5.64	4.71	15.32	7.57	4.93	4.13
	19.26	9.20	5.53	4.62	15.11	7.48	4.83	4.05
	18.96	9.09	**5.43**	4.53	14.89	7.39	4.74	3.97
	18.66	8.97	5.33	**4.44**	14.68	7.30	4.64	3.88
	18.37	8.86	5.22	4.35	14.46	7.21	4.55	3.80
	18.07	8.74	5.12	4.27	14.25	**7.11**	4.45	3.72
	17.78	8.63	5.01	4.18	14.03	7.02	4.36	3.64
Good (e.g., cat. 3)	17.48	**8.51**	4.91	4.09	13.82	6.93	**4.26**	3.55
	17.18	8.40	4.81	4.00	**13.60**	6.84	4.17	3.47
	16.89	8.28	4.70	3.91	13.39	6.75	4.07	**3.39**
	16.59	8.17	4.60	3.82	13.17	6.66	3.98	3.31
	16.29	8.05	4.50	3.73	12.95	6.57	3.88	3.23
Moderate (e.g., cat. 4)	16.00	7.94	4.39	3.64	12.74	6.48	3.79	3.14
	15.70	7.82	4.29	3.55	12.52	6.39	3.69	3.06
	15.41	7.71	4.19	3.47	12.31	6.30	3.59	2.98
	15.11	7.59	4.08	3.38	12.09	6.21	3.50	2.90
	14.81	7.48	3.98	3.29	11.88	6.12	3.40	2.82
	14.52	7.36	3.88	3.20	11.66	6.03	3.31	2.73
Fair (e.g., cat. 5)	14.22	7.25	3.77	3.11	11.45	5.94	3.21	2.65
	13.93	7.13	3.67	3.02	11.23	5.85	3.12	2.57
	13.63	7.02	3.57	2.93	11.01	5.76	3.02	2.49
	13.33	6.90	3.46	2.84	10.80	5.66	2.93	2.40
	13.04	6.79	3.36	2.75	10.58	5.57	2.83	2.32
	12.74	6.67	3.26	2.66	10.37	5.48	2.74	2.24
	12.44	6.56	3.15	2.58	10.15	5.39	2.64	2.16
Untrained (non-racer)	12.15	6.44	3.05	2.49	9.94	5.30	2.55	2.08
	11.85	6.33	2.95	2.40	9.72	5.21	2.45	1.99
	11.56	6.21	2.84	2.31	9.51	5.12	2.36	1.91
	11.26	6.10	2.74	2.22	9.29	5.03	2.26	1.83
	10.96	5.99	2.64	2.13	9.07	4.94	2.16	1.75
	10.67	5.87	2.53	2.04	8.86	4.85	2.07	1.67
	10.37	5.76	2.43	1.95	8.64	4.76	1.97	1.58
	10.08	5.64	2.33	1.86	8.43	4.67	1.88	1.50

▶ **Figure 26.1** Power profile chart.

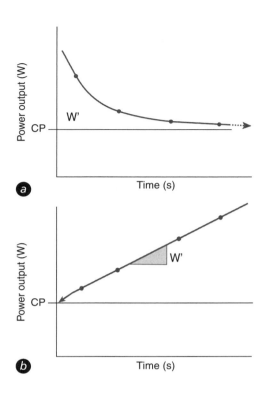

▶**Figure 26.2** (a) Schematic showing the power–time (P–t) relationship for high-intensity exercise. Numbers 1 to 4 indicate time to exhaustion for independent tests at the power designated for each. Notice that although it has become customary to illustrate the nonlinear model using reversed axes, time remains the dependent variable. (b) Determination of parameters CP and W' from the linear P–1/t transform.

designing interval training sessions, you could use the curve to identify the power output that could be sustained for the desired duration of each interval. This approach would maximize the effect of each interval and therefore maximize training gains.

The equation of the power–time curve can also be used to quantify the separate aerobic and anaerobic contributions to exercise. Instead of fitting a curve to the data, power output (or work done) can be plotted against time using a linear regression. Two parameters can be extracted from this relationship, CP and a finite, or fixed, amount of anaerobic work that can be performed above CP, known as W prime (W'). The intercept of the regression corresponds to CP, whereas W' is described by the slope of the relationship, giving the equation $P = W'/t + CP$. Here sustainable power output (P) depends on anaerobic capacity (W') divided by time (t), added to critical power (CP). Because the anaerobic component is divided by time, you can see that W' cannot last forever; that is, everyone has a finite anaerobic capacity. We have only so many matches to burn! In contrast, the aerobic component of the equation, CP, is not divided by time. We could then say that CP denotes a power output that could be maintained forever. Of course, this solution is unrealistic, so we instead say that CP is the maximum rate of work that can be sustained for a very long time without fatigue.

Establishing a cyclist's critical power curve with a power meter is relatively simple. The drawback is that three to five maximal all-out efforts are required to derive accurate estimates of CP and W'. In a research setting the conventional wisdom is to allow 24 to 48 hours of recovery between trials to ensure that participants are adequately rested before the subsequent effort. But we have recently started to use a much shorter 30-minute recovery period of low-intensity riding between maximal efforts. Research led by Bettina Karsten demonstrated that the CP and W' obtained using a 30-minute recovery were no different from trials using a 48-hour recovery (Karsten et al. 2014). Therefore, if you want to assess CP and W', you can do so as part of one training ride or on a turbo trainer in one session.

To ensure that power output measurements are accurate and that the test is repeatable (i.e., if you are intending to test at multiple time points throughout the season), you need to make sure that you are using an appropriately calibrated power meter. You must also have undertaken an appropriate warm-up that should be standardized before each test. The duration of each all-out effort should be different to provide a good power–time range. Typically, all-out efforts should last between 3 and 12 minutes, although time trials of up to 30 minutes can be used. Data from the longer trials will enhance the accuracy of the model but will likely reduce the possibility of being able to fit all the efforts into a single training session. If you are conducting CP testing as part of a training session, the intensity of the 30-minute recovery ride between efforts should also be standardized to ensure that the test is repeatable over time.

Calculating CP and W' values requires the mean power output for each all-out trial duration. These data can then be plotted in Excel or a similar program using either an inverse of time model or a power–time curve, as shown in figure 26.2.

Assessing Changes in Performance

To extend the CP model, a more elaborate model can be used whereby the relationship between power output and time is modeled over durations from 7 minutes to 4 hours using data collected during training and racing efforts. Thus, the power profile of a cyclist, defined as the record power profile (RPP), corresponds to the relationship between different sequential records of power output and the corresponding time durations during a whole race season. The method, described by Pinot and Grappe (2011), builds on the power profile approaches described by Allen and Coggan (2010; described earlier) and Quod and colleagues (2010). The RPP uses 13 maximal power outputs over durations of 1, 5, 30, and 60 seconds, and 5, 10, 20, 30, 45, 60, 120, 180, and 240 minutes, all recorded during normal training and racing. The RPP of a cyclist is then modeled as the relationship between the 13 maximal power outputs, expressed relative to the cyclist's body mass (W/kg) and the various durations. The maximal power outputs for the various durations can be calculated in Excel or by using specialized data analysis software such as TrainingPeaks. Using this approach we have modeled some data from a cyclist in two phases of the cycling season—the precompetitive period (January to March) and the competitive period (April to September)—at

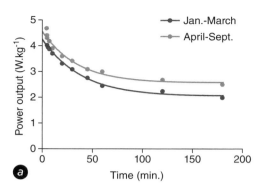
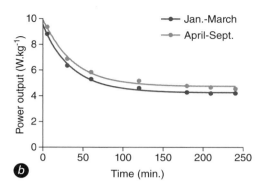

▶ **Figure 26.3** (a) Changes in a cyclist's RPP between the precompetitive and competitive period at durations of 1 second to 5 minutes. (b) Changes in a cyclist's RPP between the precompetitive and competitive season at durations of 5 minutes to 4 hours.

durations of 1 second to 5 minutes and between 5 minutes and 4 hours (see figure 26.3). You can clearly see that the relationship between power output and time changes over the course of the cycling season in that the cyclist is able to produce more power over the range of durations evaluated. Therefore, after you have developed a database of training sessions over time, you can optimize the training process using this approach; for example, by varying training loads and duration, you can see how the RPP changes over time.

Moreover, the RPP allows you to quantify your training power output in five exercise intensity zones: moderate exercise intensity (zone 1, between 2 and 4 hours), heavy exercise intensity (zone 2, between 20 and 60 minutes), lower severe intensity (zone 3, 5 to 10 minutes), upper severe intensity (zone 4, 30 to 60 seconds), and force velocity or sprint (zone 5, 1 to 5 seconds). Therefore, training zones can be established, monitored, and adjusted by assessing the RPP over time.

Where Is Your Threshold?

All exercise requires energy to fuel body movement. A variety of chemical reactions take place to produce and use this energy. A lack of energy reduces the number of energy-consuming reactions that can take place. Many of the reactions involved in the energy production pathways also produce metabolic by-products, such as hydrogen ions, that have a direct negative effect on muscle function and slow the further production of energy. If this happens during cycling, the cyclist experiences fatigue and therefore a drop in performance.

The human body is constantly producing metabolic by-products and, at the same time, is constantly working to remove them. At relatively low cycling speeds, the body has no difficulty removing all the by-products produced. But when the body reaches the point at which it is no longer able to remove all the by-products, they begin to accumulate. At this point, the cyclist has passed a threshold beyond which metabolic by-products cause fatigue and reduce performance.

Many threshold types have been defined, and the most well known is lactate threshold. Knowledge of threshold allows a cyclist to know the intensity beyond which he or she will be unable to sustain a given level of performance. Sport scientists have shown many times that threshold is a better predictor of endurance performance than $\dot{V}O_2$max (Loftin and Warren 1994).

Although lactate threshold is usually measured in a laboratory setting, the availability of heart rate monitors and, particularly, mobile power meters now allows cyclists to establish their threshold outside the laboratory, that is, on a turbo trainer or on the road. Ed Coyle and colleagues (1988) have shown that performance in a laboratory-based 1-hour time trial is highly correlated with performance in a road-based 40K time trial. Furthermore, they have shown that the maximal mean power output that can be maintained for 1 hour is also closely correlated with various scientific thresholds. The highest power output that a cyclist can maintain in a quasi-steady state without fatiguing for approximately 1 hour is therefore a valid field-based measure of threshold. Andrew Coggan named this alternative functional threshold power (FTP) (Allen and Coggan 2010).

Although FTP can be estimated from an analysis of training and racing power data, the most accurate determination of FTP requires the calculation of average power output during a maximal 1-hour time-trial. A 1-hour time-trial is demanding, however, and in our experience the alternative threshold test described by Allen and Coggan (2010) is often more suitable for regular self-administered testing.

The threshold test begins with a 30-minute moderate-pace (i.e., 65 percent of maximum heart rate) warm-up that includes three 1-minute fast pedaling (i.e., 100 rpm) efforts between minutes 20 and 25. A 5-minute all-out effort is next, followed by 10 minutes at moderate pace. This leads into the main part of the test, which consists of a maximal all-out 20-minute time trial. The goal is to produce the highest possible average power output. Finally, the test ends with 15 minutes at moderate pace and a further 15 minutes of easy warm-down. Functional threshold power is calculated as 95 percent of average power output during the 20-minute time-trial phase of the test.

Monitoring the Balance Between Training Load and Recovery

Training responses are related to training stimuli during different phases of the cycling season. Too much training leads to overtraining, and too little training results in a detraining effect. Fitness and fatigue responses must be closely monitored during training phases so that training load and recovery time can be adjusted to ensure optimal training response.

One test used for this purpose is the Lamberts Submaximal Cycling Test (LSCT; Lamberts et al. 2011). The LSCT uses set submaximal exercise intensities that require the cyclist to achieve a heart rate of 60, 80, and 90 percent of maximal heart rate (HR_{max}). (Estimate maximal heart rate by using the equation $HR_{max} = 220 - age$.) The test lasts for 17 minutes. Cycle for 6 minutes at 60 percent and 80 percent of HR_{max}, 3 minutes at 90 percent of HR_{max}, and then a final 1.5 minutes with monitoring of heart rate recovery. If you have time to monitor only one of the test stages, go for 90 percent of HR_{max} because this intensity demonstrates the lowest day-to-day variation. The idea of the test is to assess heart rate at these submaximal exercise intensities and during recovery every 4 to 6 weeks. After downloading heart rate data, exclude the first minute of each stage because it takes time for heart rate to respond to changes in power output such that the cyclist cannot achieve the target value immediately. Next, obtain average heart rate for the remaining time in each stage of the test and throughout the whole recovery period. Store this data so that when you have performed the test a few times you can start to track training adaptation. Generally, a change of submaximal exercise heart rate of more than 3 beats per minute, or a change in heart rate recovery of more than 6 beats per minute, can be regarded as meaningful, provided the tests have been completed under exactly the same conditions. These changes can be caused by an increased or decreased training status or by the accumulation of fatigue following periods of intensive training.

But monitoring heart rate provides only part of the picture. On some days on the bike, reaching target heart rates feels easy; on other days, it feels like a real struggle. This is true for many other physiological parameters, and only when you take the perception of effort into account can you can make decisions about current training status. The LSCT requires the cyclist to rate how hard she or he finds the exercise during the last 30 seconds of each work stage. This assessment of perception of effort depends on how hard the cyclist feels that he or she is driving the legs, how heavy the breathing is, and how strenuous the overall sensation of performing the exercise is. The Rating of Perceived Exertion (RPE) Scale was first developed by Gunnar Borg in the 1970s. The Borg scale (Borg 1998) uses a range of values from 6 to 20 to correspond to healthy adult heart rates by multiples of 10. For example, a rating of 6 means "no exertion at all" and is expected to correspond to a heart rate of 60 beats per minute. A rating of 9 corresponds to "very light exercise," such as turning a light gear slowly at your preferred cadence for some minutes. A rating of 13 means "somewhat hard exercise," but you are OK to continue. A rating of 17, which is "very hard," means that you can continue but have to push yourself. Your legs feel very heavy and you feel very tired. A rating of 19, "extremely hard," on the scale roughly coincides with a heart rate of 190 beats per minute and is described as "extremely hard" near-maximal exercise.

To compare RPEs over several repeated tests separated by prolonged periods, you need to appraise feelings of exertion as honestly as possible without thought for the actual physical load (i.e., the power output, speed, heart rate).

As training status improves, heart rate should decrease during exercise at equivalent work rates. Such an effect would be shown by the LSCT because cycling at the same percentage of maximal heart rate would elicit an increase in recorded power output. An increase in mean power output in stages 2 and 3 of the test with no change, or even a decrease, in RPE might be suggestive of changes in training status and increased fitness. Conversely, suboptimal adaptation because of doing too much (i.e., overtraining) might cause increased power output and RPE during stages 2 and 3 of the test because the prescribed submaximal heart rates were harder to achieve. Finally, the assessment of heart rate during the recovery phase of the LSCT can be used to indicate the development of training-induced chronic fatigue, a situation that would be signaled by a slower than normal recovery toward resting heart rate. A lower heart rate and a higher RPE during the exercise part of the LSCT alongside a normal heart rate response during the recovery stage might indicate a bit of residual fatigue that normally would be overcome quite quickly. But if heart rate is lower and RPE is higher in both exercise and recovery parts of the test, the cyclist might be in a state of longer-lasting fatigue or overtraining.

Assessing Sprint Ability

Although road racing often involves several hours of submaximal cycling, the decisive moments of a race are often determined by maximal sprint efforts (breaking away from a group, sprinting for the finish line, and so on). This type of effort requires very high power output to be sustained for a relatively short time, often no longer than 5 or 6 seconds.

We tend to perform sprint tests in a carefully controlled laboratory environment on a cycle ergometer. In this setting the cyclist sprints against a fixed resistance equivalent to a percentage of her or his body mass, often 7.5 percent, or at a fixed cadence. Following the test, the total amount of work produced over the test, defined as the anaerobic capacity, is calculated. In addition, the highest 1-second power output is recorded as the peak power output.

At a minimum, power output should be recorded during the test once every second, something that is now possible with most commercially available power meters. Therefore, sprint testing is also possible on a turbo trainer or on the road. As outlined earlier in the chapter, sprint testing requires the power meter to be appropriately calibrated to ensure that accurate and reliable data are obtained. Using a set gear ratio and sprint resistance and a rolling start from the same power output and cadence further enhances test repeatability. If you are testing on the road, then the added factors of weather, road, and traffic conditions should also be considered.

After a short warm-up (about 10 minutes) at moderate intensity, which should be kept constant for all subsequent tests, the cyclist performs an all-out effort for 5 to 10 seconds, remaining in the saddle for the duration. If the test is performed on a turbo trainer, the bike must be adequately secured to the turbo trainer and the trainer must be fixed to the floor to allow safe sprinting. If the test is performed on the road, the best setting is a short, steep hill of approximately 6 to 8 percent gradient and long enough so that the sprint lasts 5 to 10 seconds. Use a standardized rolling start by approaching the hill at a set speed, such as 20 kilometers per hour. Perform approximately three attempts with a break of about 5 minutes after each. After the test, obtain average power output over the first 5 or 6 seconds of the sprint and identify the highest 1-second data point (usually achieved within the first 3 seconds). Divide this number by body weight to calculate maximal power-to-weight ratio.

Applying the Science

Until recently, the assessment of cycling fitness has been confined to the sport science laboratory. But the combination of affordable measurement devices (e.g., power meters) and scientifically validated field-based test protocols means that you can now accurately assess fitness more frequently than ever before. Such assessments can be used to provide information about relative strengths and weaknesses, allowing the development of a training program specific to the needs of the cyclist. Regular retesting allows tracking of areas of improvement and stagnation, information that can be used to fine-tune training activities on an ongoing basis.

To ensure that any assessment of cycling fitness is reliable and therefore useful, care must be taken to ensure that conditions are standardized between tests. Although doing this is easy in a laboratory setting, the self-testing cyclist might have to make some compromises. Nevertheless, when possible, attempt to use the same route or trainer, avoid drastically different weather and traffic conditions, make sure that the power meter or turbo trainer is correctly calibrated, and perform zero-offset procedures before testing.

For the well-organized cyclist, self-testing offers the possibility of assessing all aspects of cycling fitness. Individual fitness components such as peak power output and threshold can be evaluated using a sprint test and Allen and Coggan's functional threshold power test. Beyond this, power profiling and critical power testing can be used to provide a more global assessment of cycling fitness. The extension of the power profiling and critical power concepts, in the form of the record power profile, can then be used to track performance changes over time across the full range of cycling intensities. By combining this information with the awareness of freshness provided by the Lamberts Submaximal Cycling Test, you will have all of the information required to optimize a training and racing program.

CHAPTER 27

Designing Training Programs

—Paul B. Laursen, Daniel J. Plews, and Rodney Siegel

We write this chapter as both cycling coaches and applied exercise physiologists who work in the high-performance sector. In our world, having a plan is critical. Athletes and coaches who have some form of a plan are likely to perform better than those who do not. Plans not only help to keep athletes and teams on track, in terms of providing the performance gains we strive for in a step-by-step manner, but also instill confidence as athletes attain the progressive smaller goals as the plan is implemented.

This chapter describes why and how the cycling coach or athlete might want to design a training program. Here, we outline the basic principles of planning and training. We begin by outlining the training program principles we'll work with alongside periodization theory. After we're ready to get to the nuts and bolts of making the program, we'll start with a needs analysis of the targeted event, establish the rider's capacity, and then build an appropriate plan to enhance the physiological systems of importance for the event in question. The chapter concludes by offering examples to help you design your own training template plan to target your objectives.

Principles

Ultimately, a training program for any cyclist is a systematic plan that will prepare the cyclist for a particular physical or performance goal. More specifically, each training session and training phase should have a purpose, whereby the response to the training stimulus applied should enable the physiological adaptations that assist to limit the fatigue that will be experienced and improve performance for the event in question.

The exercise training process uses the principle of biological adaptation, whereby an acute disturbance in the body's homeostasis caused by an exer-

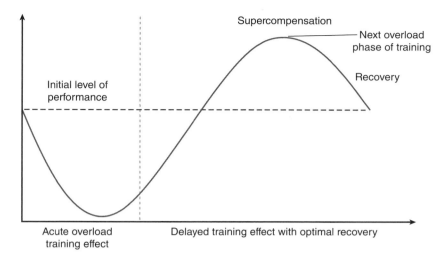

▶ **Figure 27.1** Fundamental concept of biological adaptation, in which an overload exercise stimulus causes a delay in performance ability because of acute fatigue but produces a supercompensation recovery response that increases fitness and performance ability.

cise session initiates a rebound adjustment, or supercompensation, that leads to less disturbance during the next exercise session (figure 27.1). Inevitably, this individual adaptation permits the higher cycling power and improved cycling performance we all desire.

A number of principles should be considered when planning a training program for cycling to maximize the rider's adaptation and performance. These include the principles of progressive overload, duration, intensity, frequency, recovery, and specificity. We impart these principles through the concept of periodization, which breaks the training process up into microcycles, mesocycles, and macrocycles. For high-performing cyclists who focus on endurance training and therefore perform a substantial volume of training, we also need to discuss another important principle that has emerged in recent years, called polarized training. We'll define these principles and concepts first before we begin the planning process.

Progressive Overload

Following the principle of biological adaptation (figure 27.1), progressive overload is the foundation of nearly all exercise training programs. Overload can be achieved by increasing duration (how long the ride in a training session is), intensity (how hard the session is), frequency (how often training is performed), and the amount of recovery or rest that occurs within and between training sessions.

Duration or Training Volume

Exercising for long durations is a critical aspect of training for endurance cyclists. When exercise is prolonged, reliance on aerobic energy or oxidative metabolism is critical. Important adaptations occur following long-duration training, including enhancements in blood plasma volume, cardiac stroke volume, cardiac hypertrophy, and skeletal muscle mitochondrial content, as well as changes in substrate handling kinetics that allow greater fat oxidation to occur in subsequent sessions, thereby sparing carbohydrate for high-intensity cycling. Thus, a training program that is high in volume is likely to stimulate these important adaptations.

Intensity

Training intensity seems to have the quickest effect on short-term improvements in fitness. The high-power outputs required to perform high-intensity cycling recruit the large type II muscle fibers. Using these fibers regularly, in the form of high-intensity interval training, is known to elicit rapid improvement in the ability to produce power, including increased muscle mitochondrial content of the larger type II fibers, enhanced buffering capacity, and a greater capacity to uptake and process glucose and fatty acids in the muscle. Although the short-term benefits of high-intensity training are impressive, the ability to perform this type of training is limited, and too much training in the high-intensity domain can result in a syndrome known as overtraining (see chapter 21).

Frequency

Frequency relates to how often training sessions occur. Highly trained cyclists tend to train often (i.e., daily) and have few rest or recovery days. Training in this way can enhance performance by increasing how often the signals that cause training adaptation occur. But the ability to handle this high frequency of training repetition relates to fitness and, of course, the length and intensity of the training sessions. Rest and recovery periods should be planned to allow the training supercompensation process to occur; failure to do so can result in maladaptation and stagnation in performance gains.

Specificity

The principle of specificity states simply that you get what you train for. In other words, loads of beach volleyball training, while potentially providing some strength gains, is not going to go too far toward improving cycling performance. The simple message is that you need to ride the bike a fair bit to get better at it because riding targets the specific muscle groups and motor patterns required to perform at a high level. But this guidance doesn't mean that you should spend all training time at, or close to, race intensity.

Covering a broad spectrum of intensities is extremely important in a training program, because each intensity provides a slightly different stimulus and specific adaptation that will improve cycling performance (Laursen 2010; Stoggl and Sperlich 2014).

Periodization

Periodization is the systematic planning of short- and long-term training programs by varying the training intensity of a session, its duration, its frequency, and rest and recovery performed after each session. Essentially, periodization refers to targeting the specific abilities required for the event, which become more specific as race day approaches. The act of scheduling these sessions by cycling coaches is often thought of as being somewhat of an art. Successful plans originate through years of trial and error by coaches from various sports throughout the world.

The process of periodization has evolved to use the terms microcyles, mesocyles, and macrocyles to help plan training to elicit the desired training adaptation and peak performance. Microcycles are the shortest period of training, typically planned as 1 week (although they can vary from 4 to 10 days). A mesocyle is a group of microcyles and varies from 2 to 6 weeks, targeting a specific set of abilities. A macrocyle is a small group of mesocyles, which typically form a purposefully targeted performance output.

Traditional Versus Block Periodization

In recent times, two distinct models of periodization have arisen, known as traditional periodization and block periodization (figure 27.2). The traditional periodization model is typically divided into two specific periods, the preparation period and the competition period. These two periods are further subdivided into the general preparation phase, the specific preparation phase, the precompetitive phase, and finally the competitive phase. Although different terms are used for these phases, traditional periodized programs typically begin with a long aerobic base phase characterized by training sessions consisting of long-duration, low-intensity cycling. This phase is usually followed by the specific preparation phase, consisting of a concentrated period of training characterized by high-intensity and high-volume training (i.e., long, hard riding and preparation racing). During the competition phase, training volume may be lowered to facilitate recovery, but training intensity is maintained or increased. This phase typically includes a taper, or reduction in training load, before the pinnacle event of the season. This key event marks the transition to the recovery phase, which typically consists of a couple weeks without training and another few weeks of an alternate training form. This period is typically prescribed to allow a mental (and physical) break from the heavy demands of repetitive endurance training.

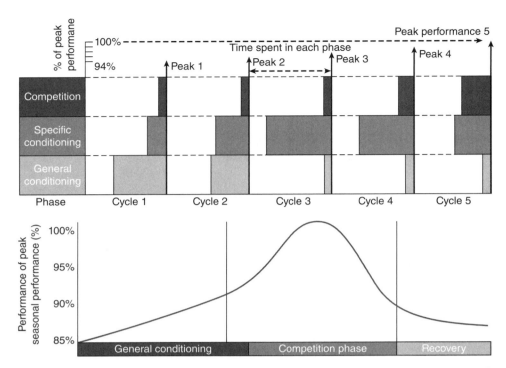

▶ **Figure 27.2** Comparison of classic (lower panel) versus block (upper panel) periodization planning.

Recently, the lucrative appeal of elite sport to mass audiences through the media has increased the demand on athletes to perform more frequently at pinnacle events. This higher frequency of competition has made coaches rethink their periodization methods, and a new form of training periodization, the block periodization model, has been formed (figure 27.2). The block periodization model uses a similar training philosophy as the classic periodization model but shortens the phases so that peak performances can occur more often. In shortening the training phases, fewer abilities can be targeted in each mesocycle. In contrast, traditional periodization tends to focus on more abilities simultaneously. A major drawback of traditional periodization is that it may not allow optimal development of each targeted ability because of the time constraints inherent within the model. Likewise, training interference may occur between competing abilities (e.g., neuromuscular power versus aerobic endurance). Taken together, this method may result in stagnation in gains and increased fatigue because of its longer mesocycle. Block periodization helps to resolve these issues by focusing on fewer abilities at a time in an attempt to optimize their development, takes into consideration potential interference, as well as accounting for residual training effects (i.e., how long it takes for gains to diminish) before moving on to the next set of abilities (Issurin 2008). Another advantage of block periodization is that it generally results in the commencement of high-intensity training earlier in the season, which is believed to be an important factor related to enhancing performance even later in the season near the likely more critical events.

Polarized Training

Polarized training was recognized by exercise physiologist Stephen Seiler in the late 1990s. The polarized training concept refers to the balance within a training program with periods of low-, moderate- and high-intensity training (Seiler and Kjerland 2006). In this context, low-intensity training refers to training performed below the aerobic threshold, whereas high-intensity training refers to training above the anaerobic threshold. Moderate-intensity training refers to training completed between these thresholds. When an athlete performs polarized training, the majority of training (about 80 percent) is performed below the aerobic threshold, most of the remaining 20 percent is performed above the anaerobic threshold, and a limited amount of training is performed between the thresholds. Attainment of polarized training likely implies that the training performed within the specified period has achieved segments of aerobic development, with limited quantities of autonomic (central nervous system) disturbance, that in return have allowed the achievement of high-intensity (i.e., quality) training sessions (figure 27.3). A common occurrence for amateur cyclists performing a substantial training volume is spending too much training time between thresholds, training time designed to be dedicated to low-intensity training. This practice

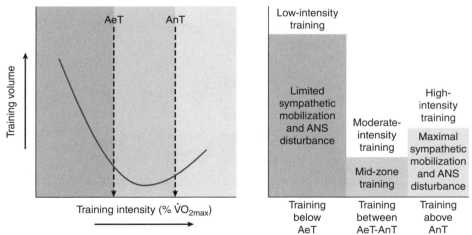

▶ **Figure 27.3**   Polarized training model. During high-volume training programs, roughly 80 percent of the training volume is performed below the aerobic threshold (AeT) and most of the remaining 20 percent of training volume is performed above the anaerobic threshold (AnT). $\dot{V}O_2max$ = maximal oxygen uptake; ANS = autonomic nervous system.

often leads to an increase in fatigue, causing key high-intensity training to be performed below the optimal intensity. Suboptimal training adaptation and performance ensue, which can result in nonfunctional overreaching and overtraining if sustained for too long.

Recovery and Microcycle Distribution

The microcycle is the shortest defined training block, typically 4 to 10 days long. It is normally established by the number days that occur until the next rest day. The microcycle tends to be individual and dependent on life demands and the number of key workouts that the training program requires. In general, most successful training programs for endurance cyclists consist of three or four key high-intensity workouts each microcycle. Thus, the planning, distribution, and variation within each microcycle is important to ensure that the cyclist can complete each session to the best of his or her ability. For example, the high training load apparent with a demanding high-intensity interval training session typically should be followed by low-intensity training (below the aerobic threshold) to permit autonomic nervous system recovery and subsequent adaptation that allows the cyclist to complete the next high-intensity session at a high level (Plews et al. 2014).

Figure 27.4 shows the average time needed to recover from typical training sessions (low intensity, threshold, and high intensity). These data are taken from the time needed to recover, shown from heart-rate variability

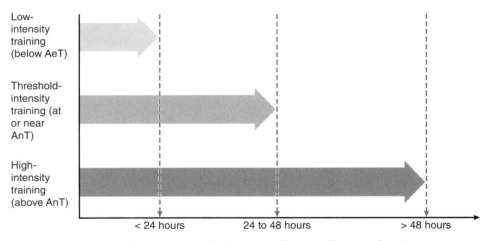

Average time needed to recover from specific types of sessions

▶ **Figure 27.4** Average time needed to recover adequately from specific training sessions. Recovery from high-intensity sessions (greater than anaerobic threshold, AnT) should be spaced by more than 48 hours. Threshold type training (at or slightly below or above the anaerobic threshold, AnT) should be spaced by 24 to 48 hours. Low-intensity sessions (below the aerobic threshold) generally should be spaced between these sessions to support recovery.

research (Stanley, Peake, and Buchheit 2013). Although this duration may not reflect the recovery of all physiological systems (e.g., energy stores and neuromuscular system), it does provide a proxy measure of recovery and thus provides a good general guideline to maximize the day-to-day distribution of microcycle training content. Accordingly, threshold (at or slightly below or above the anaerobic threshold) sessions should be spaced by 24 to 48 hours, and high-intensity sessions (greater than anaerobic threshold) should be spaced by more than 48 hours. Accordingly, low-intensity sessions (below the aerobic threshold) should generally be spaced between these sessions, which allows larger training volumes and likely maximal adaptation (Laursen 2010).

Taking this into account, the number and type of key sessions as well as the individual time needed to recover likely determine the recommended length of the microcycle for an individual. For example, a training program consisting of three key sessions (two high-intensity sessions and one threshold session) fits nicely into a 7-day microcycle. Conversely, fitting four high-intensity key sessions into such a small microcycle becomes more difficult, so a larger one may be required. Even so, other sessions within the microcycle can include some form of intensity (e.g., fartlek sessions), but the total volume of intensity within each session should be taken into account.

Planning

Now that we've established some terminology and principles, we're ready to make a plan. To begin, we're going to need to know a bit about the event we're targeting and its likely performance demands. We'll also need to know a bit more about the athlete in terms of her or his performance and physiological profile. We then put the two together, in the context of the strengths and weaknesses of the rider's profile relative to the event in question. Together, our assessments give us insight into the physiological systems we need to target to maximize performance for the race. Figure 27.5 outlines a schematic flow chart of the general planning process.

Event-Specific Needs Analysis

When starting out (figure 27.5), we first need to analyze and break down the specific event. What is the event, and what will it entail? Are we talking about a 1-hour intermittent high-intensity criterium race, an individual 20K time trial, a multiday stage race over consecutive days, a hilly single-day 4-hour Granfondo event, or a short kilo sprint on the track? As shown in figure 27.5, we need to start with a general idea about the intensity, duration, and technical aspects of the event before we move to the next step. For example, track riders require high maximal anaerobic power; sprinters require the ability to produce very high power outputs over short durations (i.e., 10 seconds) at intermediate and final stages of long endurance races; criterium racers need

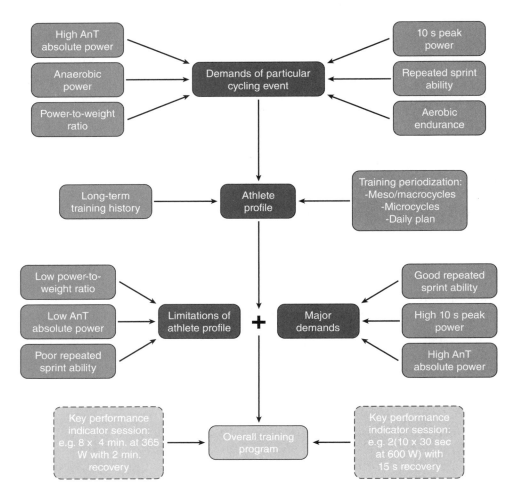

▶ **Figure 27.5** Schematic flow chart of the planning process, which takes the demands of the targeted event and individual rider profile and capacity into consideration. AnT = anaerobic threshold.

to be able to sprint multiple times during an event; time trialers require a high anaerobic threshold; hill climbers require a high power-to-weight ratio; and ultradistance cyclists require a high aerobic threshold. Of course, other events require a mixture of abilities, such as cross-country mountain biking and cyclocross, which require a blend of repeated high-intensity performance and a high anaerobic threshold combined with savvy technical riding skills.

Whatever the event, we need to ask ourselves some important planning questions. What is the approximate duration of the event? How is it typically performed from a pacing standpoint (all out, evenly paced, variably paced)? What does the typical maximal mean power curve look like for this rider

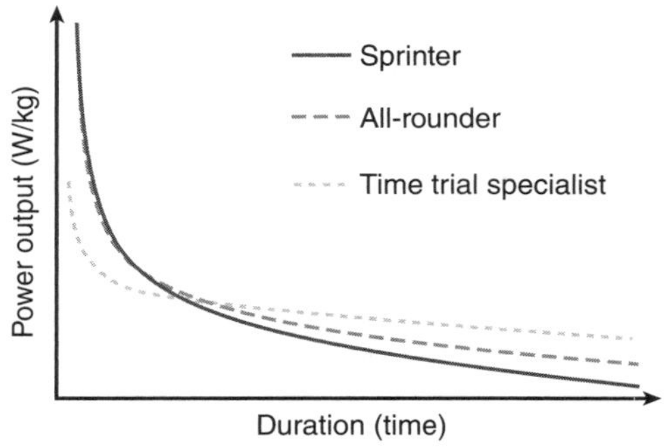

▶ **Figure 27.6** Hypothetical power profiles depicting the power–time capacities of various cycling specialists.

(figure 27.6)? After we know this, how does the intensity and duration of the required power outputs for the targeted performance relate to the likely contributing energy systems?

After we know these elements, along with the rider's individual capacity (see chapter 26) and the day of the event, we can work backward from the event date and put a plan in place to give our athlete the physiological resiliency to compete in that event to his or her potential.

Assessing Rider Capacity and Physiology

The ins and outs of testing are described in chapter 26. When we are interested in assessing a cyclist's performance parameters and physiology, we tend to use two main tests—a progressive exercise test and a power profile. Fortunately, technological advances in power meters, heart rate monitors, and software analysis programs allow us to test for these various anchor points from field data.

Power Profile

The power profile is both a laboratory and a field test that assesses a cyclist's maximum capacity to produce power over durations that are typically encountered during cycling (Quod et al. 2010). Consequently, the power profile test may provide a platform for evaluation of the power-producing capacity of cyclists that can be directly compared to the power that a cyclist produces during competition. A laboratory-based power profile requires only 1 hour to be completed and is conducted in standard laboratory conditions. But field-based data collected from the power meter of a cyclist's own road bike can also be validly used to assess a cyclist's power profile (Quod et al. 2010).

The likely critical power–time continuum markers arising from the athlete's power profile (watts per kilogram) can then be assessed in relation to the predicted demands of the targeted event. Hypothetical power profiles of various specialist cyclists are shown in figure 27.6.

Progressive Exercise Test

The specifics of progressive exercise tests for cycling are described in chapter 26. Reviewing briefly, progressive exercise tests are useful for determining the physiological anchor points associated with the performance power outputs determined in the power profile. As mentioned, the power outputs and heart rates associated with the aerobic threshold, anaerobic thresholds, and maximal oxygen consumption levels can conveniently help determine the amount of training time performed at, below, or above these points. Together, these assessments can assist us in determining the degree of polarization in a training program, the appropriateness of the training performed relative to the training prescribed, and the athlete profile, as well as potentially offering indicators of fatigue, overreaching, or overtraining. Ideally, the principles of testing and monitoring run alongside the training program plan and are used to adjust training according to the athlete response on a weekly and daily basis.

Individuality

Although we may be tempted to tailor the training program to suit the event, one important aspect is the principle of individuality. It is often said that we should aim to train the athlete, not the event. In reality, however, we should likely train a combination of the two. For example, during testing we may have identified a cyclist as being anaerobically weak. Although training for anaerobic development may be important, focusing too much on this aspect could lead to limited gains or overtraining. In contrast, if an athlete appears to be aerobically deficient, making this a larger focus of the program would be prudent because of the well-known plasticity of the aerobic system, although total load or volume must still be considered.

Aspects such as the age of maturation, the cyclist's training age, and the individual recovery characteristics are all traits that should be taken into consideration when planning and adjusting programs for individual athletes.

Applying the Science

In this chapter, we described the foundational principles and theories you can use to develop a successful plan to maximize cycling performance. Figures 27.1 through 27.4 illustrated the key planning principles, and figures 27.5 and 27.6 described the planning process and the way it should be shaped with both the athlete and event demands in mind.

We end this chapter with an example of a plan that might be formed from this information (figure 27.7). Our athlete is an experienced semielite

Weeks	12	11	10	9	8	7	6	5	4	3	2	1
Training phase	General preparation				Specific preparation				Competition			
Main emphasis	Build volume, strength, endurance, build AnT				Aerobic development, build AnT				$\dot{V}O_{2max}$ power, max power, technical			
Sub emphasis	Anaerobic power production, testing				Repeated high power, $\dot{V}O_{2max}$, testing				Freshness, adapt, recover			

Emphasis	Training ride	E.g. workout		Emphasis	Training ride	E.g. workout		Emphasis	Training ride	E.g. workout	
Volume	2 x long rides <AeT 2 x rec rides	3-5 h <AeT 1.5-2.5 h easy	Recovery week	Volume	2 x long rides <AeT 2 x rec rides	3-5 h <AeT 1.5-2.5 h easy	Recovery week	Volume	2 x long rides <AeT 2 x rec rides	3-5 h <AeT 1.5-2.5 h easy	Taper/race
Strength endurance	1 x hill reps over-geared	6-8 x 8" 3" RI		Anaerobic threshold	2 x threshold reps at AnT	3 x 20', 5' RI 4 x 12' build, 3' RI		Anaerobic threshold	1 x threshold reps at AnT	8-10 x 4 min.; 2 min. RI	
Anaerobic threshold	1 x threshold reps at AnT	5/6 x 10, 2 RI		Repeated high power	1 x RHP >$\dot{V}O_{2max}$	4(6 x 1'1' RI) 3(8 x 40"20" RI)		Repeated high power	1 x RHP >$\dot{V}O_{2max}$	4(6 x 1'1' RI) 3(8 x 40"20" RI)	
Anaerobic power production	2 x anaerobic max intensity	E.g. 8-10 x 30", 5' RI		$\dot{V}O_{2max}$	1 x $\dot{V}O_{2max}$	3 x 3'; 3' RI		$\dot{V}O_{2max}$	1 x $\dot{V}O_{2max}$	5-6 x 2.5' 2.5 RI	

▶ **Figure 27.7** Sample plan for a semielite endurance cyclist using a 7-day microcycle and targeting a hilly Granfondo pinnacle event. AeT = aerobic threshold; AnT = anaerobic threshold; $\dot{V}O_2$max = maximal oxygen uptake; RI = recovery interval; rec = recovery; RHP = repeated high power output.

endurance cyclist who prefers a common 7-day microcycle format because of work commitments. The rider is targeting a hilly Gran Fondo event as his pinnacle race for the season. The plan illustrated shows a single block periodized phase (see figure 27.2) beginning 12 weeks out from the key competition. General preparation, specific preparation, and competition mesocycles are shown. Each emphasis and subemphasis of the mesocycle is also illustrated, along with the key workouts and example training rides. Note that the specific placement of training sessions for each microcycle should be spaced in accordance with the individual recovery characteristics inherent with the session and specific to the cyclist (see figure 27.4). The final 7 to 10 days out from competition end with a taper in training, when training volume should be reduced but intensity of training sessions should be maintained or increased slightly.

After the plan is in place, the cyclist must get out there and ride it. The cycling coach or athlete should monitor progress with heart rate, power output, and perceptions and adjust the future training content accordingly.

CHAPTER 28

Training Periodization

—Bent R. Rønnestad and Mikel Zabala

At the end of the season, each cyclist should sit down with his or her coach to analyze what happened and why, which goals were achieved and which were not, to answer questions related to performance and the results reached during the season. This conversation should be the first step to achieving a better start to the following season. Answer questions like these: Where are we? Where do we want to go? How are we going to do this? These questions are obligatory to answer before any season starts. Preferably, these questions are asked and answered weeks before the season begins so that time is available to move things. If the cyclist wants to improve any aspect related to performance, she or he will look for an orderly, systematic program. Periodization is a concept that normally appears. After understanding the relationship between training and improvement, factors such as genetic influence, previous history, and psychological capacities should be taken into account. A plan is developed based on a realistic starting point and achievable goals (both short- and long-term goals that are specific, measurable, time limited, realistic, yet challenging) for the coming season. Periodization is a method for outlining training plans.

Training periodization can be defined as systematic planning and structuring of training variables in defined timeframes in an attempt to optimize training adaptations and performance and minimize risk of injury. Basic training principles such as overload, variation, specificity, and reversibility are important in periodization training. Periodization is the foundation of an athlete's training plan (Bompa and Haff 2009). Other authors, such as Mujika and Laursen (2012), define training periodization as systematic planning of the short term (months) and middle (years) term by varying training intensity, duration, frequency, and recovery.

Periodization has been shown to be an effective tool not only for elite athletes but also for those seeking augmented performance by gaining strength, endurance, flexibility, and technique. Advantages of periodization training include more efficient use of time with more rest and recovery, increased consistency in attaining objectives, and the avoidance of injuries. Beyond elite training, periodization appears to be a feasible way to prescribe exercise for sedentary subjects with more guarantee of successful health outcomes (Strohacker et al. 2015).

One of the first periodization models, and the most typical, was presented by Matveyev (1977) in his book *Fundamentals of Sport Training*. Matveyev introduced a training structure that progressively segmented transitions from high to low volume and from low to high intensity, along with increased specificity as the main competition approached. Since this publication, several periodization models have been presented as alternative approaches to Matveyev`s periodization model. But Matveyev seemed to support concepts used in some of the alternative models such as focusing on development of specific abilities while maintaining others, shock cycles, and recovery.

As Chapple (2006) pointed out, "Periodization is based on the idea that you cannot improve all aspects of fitness [we would say *performance* instead of *fitness*] at the same time, and that you cannot maintain peak fitness year-round." This idea makes sense especially for cyclists who attempt to be at the highest levels during the complete season, such as some professional road cyclists who compete from the first classics through the Tour of Spain or the world championships in September, or even Lombardia in October. A cyclist cannot possibly be at the highest level from January through October. Not many years ago, some professional cyclists rode 30,000 kilometers per year or completed 6- to 7-hour workouts without a real training plan, sometimes without the knowledge of which races would be included.

Although the origins of periodization are unknown, the concept is not new. In the 1940s Soviet sport scientists discovered that athletic performance improved when training stresses were varied throughout the year (Friel 1996). Nowadays, cycling teams pay special attention to training plans to get the best performance from their cyclists; training periodization is a key aspect to get the best results.

Periodization supports two main aspects of training (Bompa and Haff 2009):

1. It divides the annual training plan into smaller phases, making it easier to structure the needed work and plan a training program to ensure that the desired performance takes place in the intended moment.

2. It structures phases to target and allow the athlete to improve speed, power, agility, and endurance as needed.

In general, each annual plan is divided into three phases: preparatory, competitive, and transition. The preparatory phase is divided into two subphases, general and specific, according to the differing tasks. The competitive phase is divided into precompetitive and competitive subphases.

One of the most relevant aspects for the success of any plan is to integrate training factors from an interdisciplinary point of view. Collaboration among experts such as doctors, biomechanists, and nutritionists is desirable to reach the highest level. The coach often directs or coordinates this collaboration.

Training Principles

The combination of training duration, intensity, and frequency is considered seriously. Training needs to be systematic and orderly. For this purpose, several training concepts or training principles need to be considered:

- Timing: all the events scheduled for specific moments
- Overload: a stressful stimulus that takes the cyclist out of comfort status
- Adaptation: proper recovery from overload to produce better status or adaptation
- Individuality: different treatments and considerations for each cyclist
- Specificity: training for cycling, not, for example, rowing
- Reversibility: recognition that all gains can be lost if training stops
- Load–recovery balance: finding the overload that can be converted into desired adaptations by means of appropriate recovery, recognizing that the more a cyclist trains, the more recovery is needed, although each person is different
- Pedagogic principle: understanding of the plan by both the athlete and the coach or any other agent involved in the training process; collaborative learning by athletes and their coaches, sharing the coaching process and building all the related steps together

Timing

Set primary, secondary, and other kinds of races according to their importance so that the cyclist's fitness will peak at the important races. At this point, the input of the team manager, sponsor, and so on can be used to guide both the cyclist and the coach. Some authors relate this principle to another they call periodization but add the concept that, over a year, different seasons or periods may occur. These seasons or periods may include winter (cyclocross) or summer (road) seasons, classics and grand tours, track and road seasons, and so on. Also, periodic recovery is related to this periodization principle, but recovery emphasis is needed between longer in-season periods or between load stimuli. Without periodic recoveries athletes could feel tired, perform inadequately, and ultimately be at risk of overtraining.

Overload

Overload is based on the training concepts of supercompensation and adaptation to improve performance. Load needs to progress as the cyclist adapts for improvement to continue. Some authors point to progression as another principle of training.

Adaptation

Adaptation relates to the cyclist's previous training load. After adaptation occurs, performance improves. Again, progression should be taken into account. This principle relies on the load–recovery balance principle, because if recovery is not appropriate for a given load, the intended adaptation would lead to maladaptation, fatigue, and ultimately to an injury or illness.

A hot topic in the recent literature is tapering (Mujika 2009; Rønnestad et al. 2016). Although this idea may seem new, historically it has been just a matter of seeking the best adaptation for a specific event. *Tapering* is the term used when the recovery after a related and previous load is specially focused on to allow supercompensation (not just physical but also psychological) for a given competition or event. Tapering allows the athlete to recover from the previous training load before the event while maintaining gains and the competing rhythm required for the event. Normally, the number of sessions is maintained but the overall training volume is reduced 60 to 80 percent, depending on the previous load and fatigue. High-intensity intervals are used with longer recoveries than usual, replicating the intensities that will be necessary in the competition. In addition, because the total amount of work is dramatically reduced, the quantity of food must be reduced as well to avoid putting on excess body weight.

Individuality

Each cyclist is different in many ways because of factors such as genetics, social environment, material, economy, and motivation, and others such as buffering capacity, recovery level, technical abilities, and so on. Therefore, priorities can be quite different among cyclists competing at the same level of overall performance. We say, "Each cyclist is a different world."

Specificity

As juniors, cyclists can practice track, mountain bike, or road, but if they want to be their best in one of these disciplines, they should eventually specialize so that practice and work is more specific for that discipline. During a season, specificity relates to training that is less general, or cross-training, but it progressively becomes more specific to cycling. For example, as a cyclist starts the season he or she practices trekking, swimming, and cross-country skiing but later introduces the bicycle and the primary racing discipline, focusing increasingly on this until it is the most important and prioritized training content. Complementary training and variety are necessary to keep the cyclist from getting used to the training load and thus violating the progression principle.

Reversibility

Any fitness or training gains can be lost; they don't last forever. Normally, more time is needed to gain fitness than to lose it. The faster a cyclist conditions (for example, by losing fat), the faster he or she can surrender this gain if the stimulus is lost because of a recovery period, injury, or other reason. Continuity in training is needed to make any gain or to maintain it. A cyclist who doesn't train with the minimum frequency should not expect any improvement. Cramming all the training hours of a week into two workouts and spending the rest of the week resting does not make sense.

Load–Recovery Balance

Cyclists should not train so much that they are unable to recover or so little that even with no recovery they don't get enough training stimulus. They should train and load the amount that, with an appropriate recovery, leads to higher performance gains. Both training load and recovery status should be monitored to ensure more than the minimum stimulus but less than a nonsustainable one. Cyclists are said to be like popcorn because the more watts and the more time they train, the more appetizing they are. But as with popcorn, a range of watts and time is optimal; too much causes the popcorn to become harder and darker until it is ultimately inedible.

Pedagogic Principle

Cyclists should always be aware of what they are doing and why. A coach's role is not just to train for performance but also to teach and explain to cyclists any aspect that could improve this relationship and, ultimately, performance.

Types of Periodization

In general, two training periodization approaches are used: classic, or traditional, periodization and block periodization.

Classic, or traditional, periodization uses longer periods called mesocycles (months) that include these phases: wide aerobic base training with long-duration and low-intensity workouts; specific conditioning with a high intensity and high volume of training; competitive phase with low volume and high intensity, including tapering; and recovery of approximately 15 passive days and 15 semiactive days. This classic periodization was used by Miguel Indurain, who focused his entire season on the Tour de France, using the prior races to prepare him progressively for the peak of performance at the Tour de France.

Normally, cyclists use block periodization when they need to compete at a high level of performance multiple times throughout the training cycle or cannot afford to have just one or two peaks in a season. Block periodization is based on the same principles as classic periodization, but shorter phases allow more times of peak performance. Block periodization is typical of disciplines based on a cup model such as the Mountain Bike World Cup; riders need to earn points in various races spread widely throughout the season.

The periodization approach doesn't need to be black or white; cyclists sometimes combine both approaches depending on the structure and objectives of the season. For example, Alejandro Valverde tends to use block periodization at the beginning of the season so that he is fit for the classics, but he trains under a traditional model in the second half of the season to be competitive for a grand tour (Tour de France or Vuelta a España). A different and complex situation occurs during an Olympic year. Overall, as the number of main objectives in a season increases, block periodization becomes more necessary. Also, riders having a grand tour as the main goal tend to use classic periodization, whereas riders who point toward winning the UCI ProTour overall classification at the end of the year favor block periodization.

Among other proposals of periodization types, we need to point out the one called reverse periodization. This proposal suggests that the traditional approach of starting the season with more volume and less intensity and progressing to more intensity and less volume should be inverted. Therefore, the season would start with short, high-intensity efforts. This kind of work was famous years ago in the cycling world because Team Sky coaches suggested that the key for their success was this revolutionary type of training. In our opinion this approach is neither good nor bad; its effectiveness depends on the individualization principle of training. The method could be useful for veteran riders who have a good endurance base, but in general we don't recommend its use for younger cyclists or those who do not have a strong endurance background. Although the reverse periodization concept can be interesting for experienced and mature riders, if a young cyclist does not build a sufficient endurance base, starting the season with high-intensity training could lead to poor performance later or even to an injury. In an alternative middle program, a cyclist could start with a shorter endurance base and then include high-intensity training; this plan would not be pure reverse periodization.

Block Periodization

In the concept of block periodization, a complementary and more particular approach emphasizes the concentration of a specific stimulus for a limited period. Vladimir Issurin aroused interest in this concept with his publications about block periodization (Issurin 2008), so we now look at the findings in the scientific literature.

Both continuous low-intensity training (LIT) and high-intensity aerobic interval training (HIT, also known as high-intensity interval training, or HIIT) are frequently used to improve cycling performance. As the endurance athlete's performance level increases, increasing the intensity of aerobic endurance training is necessary to obtain further improvements in lactate threshold and maximal oxygen consumption ($\dot{V}O_2$max) (e.g., Shephard 1968; Wenger and Bell 1986; Midgley, McNaughton, and Wilkinson 2006). Therefore, it has been recommended that endurance athletes perform 75 to 80 percent of their endurance training as LIT, 10 to 15 percent as HIT, and the remaining endurance training time near threshold intensity (Seiler and Kjerland 2006; Seiler 2010). But it remains unclear how to organize LIT and HIT to achieve optimal training outcomes and endurance performance. The traditional organization of the training has been two weekly HIT sessions interspersed with low-intensity training. Another way of organizing the training is the block periodization model, in which training periods are divided into shorter periods (1 to 3 weeks) with the focus on improving a few specific abilities such as $\dot{V}O_2$max while maintaining other abilities. The idea of block periodization is to provide a concentrated stimulus to achieve further adaptations in well-trained athletes, which is not always possible when placing equal focus on too many abilities important for performance (Issurin 2010).

The first studies indicating superiority of block periodization had a larger volume of HIT, which made it somewhat challenging to determine whether the positive effect was because of the block periodization per se or because of a larger volume of HIT (Breil et al. 2010; García-Pallarés et al. 2010). In trained cyclists, however, block periodization was observed to be superior to the traditional organization of training when total training volumes of HIT and LIT were matched (Rønnestad et al. 2014; Rønnestad, Hansen, and Ellefsen 2014). A 1-week five-session HIT block separated by 3 weeks of one HIT session per week and a general focus on LIT during a 12-week intervention period (see figure 28.1) resulted in superior adaptations compared with a traditional organization of two weekly HIT sessions interspersed with low-

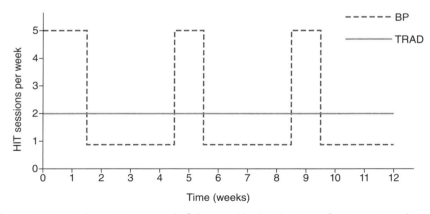

▶ **Figure 28.1** Schematic protocol of the weekly distribution of HIT sessions during the 12-week intervention in a block periodization group (BP) and a group with traditional distribution of the training (TRAD).

Data from B.R. Rønnestad, S. Ellefsen, H. Nygaard, et al., 2014, "Effects of 12 weeks of block periodization on performance and performance indices in well-trained cyclists," Scandinavian Journal of Medicine & Science in Sports 24(2): 327-335.

intensity training, despite similar total volume and intensity distribution. This result was evident from the effect size of the relative improvement of $\dot{V}O_2$max (maximal aerobic power), power output at a blood lactate concentration of 2 millimoles per liter, and mean power output during a 40-minute all-out trial, which revealed a moderate effect of block periodization versus traditional training (see figure 28.2). Superiority of concentrating the training stimulus was also indicated in the study of Clark et al. (2014). Whether the intensity distribution was similar between the groups seems to be a bit unclear. Nevertheless, the researchers observed that trained cyclists who performed seven HIT sessions in a week achieved a superior improvement in a 20K time trial 14 days after the last HIT session compared with a control group who continued their normal cycling training (Clark et al. 2014).

If trying the method with concentrated training stimulus, be aware of the cyclist's response to the concentrated stimulus. Large individual differences occur in response to a concentrated and large stimulus, especially when multiple HIT sessions are performed in a short period. Some cyclists can handle six HIT sessions in a week, whereas others struggle with three. Among others factors, this individual difference depends on training status, genetics, daily life stressors, and nutrition. Nevertheless, getting heavy legs during intense training periods is common. This is shown in figure 28.3 in which five HIT sessions are performed every 4th week for a 12-week training

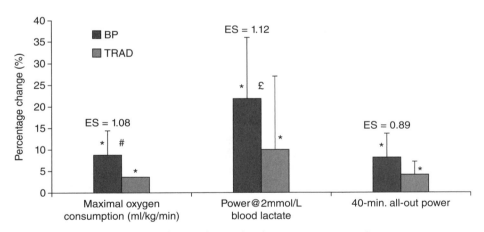

▶ **Figure 28.2** Percentage change in maximal oxygen consumption, power output at a blood lactate concentration of 2 millimoles per liter, and mean power output during a 40-minute all-out trial after a 12-week intervention period for a block periodization group (BP) and a traditional group (TRAD). * Larger than at pre ($p < 0.05$). # The relative change from pre is larger than in TRAD ($p < 0.05$). £ The relative change from pre tends to be larger than in TRAD ($p = 0.054$). The magnitude of improvements of BP versus TRAD is shown as effect size (ES).

Data from B.R. Rønnestad, S. Ellefsen, H. Nygaard, et al., 2014, "Effects of 12 weeks of block periodization on performance and performance indices in well-trained cyclists," Scandinavian Journal of Medicine & Science in Sports 24(2): 327-335.

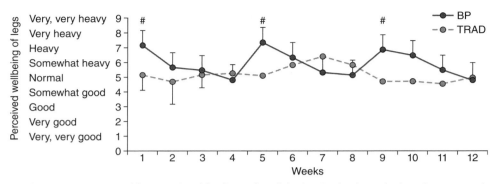

▶ **Figure 28.3**   Weekly perceived feeling of well-being in the legs during the 12-week intervention period for a block periodization group (BP) and a traditional group (TRAD). Difference between groups (p < 0.05).

Adapted, by permission, from B.R. Rønnestad, S. Ellefsen, H. Nygaard, et al., 2014, "Effects of 12 weeks of block periodization on performance and performance indices in well-trained cyclists," Scandinavian Journal of Medicine & Science in Sports 24(2): 327-335.

period (Rønnestad et al. 2014). Between the HIT weeks the focus was on LIT and one HIT session per week. Having a training period with normal legs is important before performing a new training period during which the cyclist wants to induce heavy legs.

A critique of many previous periodization studies is that because the control group had no variation in the training program within the microcycles (e.g., training week), the studies investigated the effect of interjecting training novelty into habituated patterns instead of block periodization per se (Kiely 2012). Although it lasted only 5 weeks, a recent study on well-trained cross-country skiers also included some variation in the weekly number of HIT sessions in the control group and simultaneously matched the volume of HIT and LIT between the block-training group and the control group. In that study, a 5-week block periodization approach to endurance training demonstrated superior effects on indices of endurance performance (maximal aerobic power and power output at lactate threshold) compared with traditional organization in well-trained cross-country skiers approaching competition season. The effect sizes of the relative improvement in $\dot{V}O_2$max, maximal aerobic power, and power output at a blood lactate of 4 millimoles per liter revealed moderate effects of block periodization versus more traditional organization of the training.

Recently, Issurin (2016) pointed out that block periodization is an effective alternative to traditional periodization, using highly concentrated training workloads as a main point, and with the possibility of developing his block periodization in two versions: the concentrated unidirectional version and the multitargeted version. In the main recommendations in his recent review, Issurin (2016) suggested that concentrated unidirectional training is more suitable for athletic disciplines that require one fitness component (e.g., jumping performance) and that multitargeted block periodization is more suitable for sports that require many athletic abilities, such as endurance sports, team sports, and combat sports. The focus of overall fitness and health also make multitargeted block periodization a suitable system for recreational athletes.

In well-trained endurance athletes, indications are that changes in the training pattern per se provide important stimuli that have positive effects on performance and physiological responses. It may be theorized that organizing endurance training into HIT blocks interspersed with weeks with one HIT session per week and a general focus on LIT results in superior adaptations compared with traditional organization. A more even distribution of HIT sessions induces superior adaptations in already highly trained athletes. Therefore, in certain periods of the training year, using block periodization and focusing on developing a small number of abilities can be a good alternative training plan.

Applying the Science

Periodization is essential to directing the training process and to reaching key moments in the best shape and fitness. Training principles must be respected and taken into account to avoid mistakes. Tapering is an important concept because it summarizes how well an athlete has trained and adjusted to training to get the best adaptations and can make improvements to produce the best performance possible at a specific competition.

Whether to use block periodization or traditional periodization depends on the situation. Both approaches have pros and cons. Cyclists and coaches must take into account all the variables in relation to the athlete's competing context (types and dates of competitions, goals and specific objectives, and so on).

Block periodization as the concentration of specific stimulus for a limited period can be an interesting approach, depending on the case. The use of reverse periodization may not be the most appropriate for every athlete. Again, individual characteristics and necessities must be considered.

CHAPTER 29

Using a Power Meter

—Hunter Allen

Training with power means using the most effective tool in the cycling industry today to maximize athletic potential. A power meter is a measuring device on a bicycle that determines the amount of wattage produced by the cyclist while pedaling the bicycle. Wattage measures the amount of work done on the bicycle. As the cyclist improves, the wattage, or the amount of work, goes up and is easily quantified.

Power meters can measure the wattage produced by the rider in the hub of the bicycle wheel, the spider of the crank arm, the crank arm itself, the pedals, the axle of the bottom bracket, or even the tension of the bicycle chain. The power meter head unit looks just like a larger, more complex bicycle speedometer, and it records every few seconds while the cyclist rides. It records many metrics from the rider including watts, heart rate, speed, cadence, torque, temperature, GPS location, and distance that the rider has traveled. Some power meters and head units also permit detailed analysis of each leg or the pedal stroke itself in real time. This complete historical record of a ride is then available for download to a computer and can be analyzed postride to determine optimal training or racing performance.

Although power training involves seven steps, in this chapter I focus on only four: testing functional threshold power (FTP), establishing training zones, building a power profile, and creating power-zone-based workouts.

Testing Functional Threshold Power

The first thing to do is to start riding with a power meter every day during riding and racing. Do this without any specific power-based plan; the only goal is to obtain as much power data as possible during typical rides. Begin to understand what the wattage number means in the real world and then start to associate those numbers with rides. A downloaded power meter file is literally a second-by-second graphical recreation, or diary, of a ride. Therefore, download the data and then analyze it to get a sense of what 300 watts (W) means in relation to heart rate, cadence, speed, elevation gain, and so on. These data are especially useful when combined with a GPS map of the

> ## Seven Steps to Power Training
>
> 1. Test functional threshold power (FTP).
> 2. Establish training zones.
> 3. Build a power profile to understand strengths and limitations.
> 4. Set goals based on target events or races.
> 5. Build a periodized power plan focused on peaking at key events.
> 6. Build power-zone-based workouts to ensure training efficiency and effectiveness.
> 7. Track fitness and progress through performance manager charting.

ride. Associate areas of riding in crosswinds, long climbs, short butt-kicking hills, and stops along the way to understand your cycling better.

After completing some rides and learning to operate the computer on the bike, schedule the first testing session to begin to determine training zones so that you can correctly focus your efforts. The first test to do is a test to learn how many watts you produce at functional threshold power (FTP) and establish a fitness baseline. I call this the threshold test. By doing the test every 6 weeks, you can track changes in fitness, assess current fitness, and then decide whether to make changes to the training program based on the test results.

An important thing to remember before and during the test is always to test on the same stretch of road or do the test on an indoor trainer. You should also do the test at similar times during the day and with similar weather. You want to minimize external influences on the test so that you can be confident when comparing test results. Before you begin the test, you may want to understand why this test is important and learn some background.

Defining Functional Threshold Power (FTP)

What exactly is functional threshold power, and why is it important to test it? The term *threshold* has become synonymous with the word *confusion* in the minds of many athletes! Several words are used for essentially the same thing: anaerobic threshold (AT), lactate threshold (LT), maximal lactate steady state (MLSS), onset of blood lactate (OBLA), and just plain old threshold. It seems that there are so many possible definitions based on heart rate, blood lactate, wattage, and other indicators that even in many scientific articles, the authors have to present their own definitions to the reader.

For more than 30 years, exercise physiologists have known that the exercise intensity at which lactate begins to accumulate in a person's blood—that is, functional lactate threshold (LT)—is a powerful predictor of the person's endurance performance ability. Although a person's cardiovascular fitness (i.e., maximal oxygen uptake, or $\dot{V}O_2$max) sets the upper limit to his or her rate of aerobic energy production, it is metabolic fitness (i.e., LT) that determines the percentage, or fraction, of $\dot{V}O_2$max that can be used for any given period. The physiological factors that determine functional lactate threshold are complex, but in this context blood lactate levels essentially serve as an indirect marker for biochemical events within exercising muscle. More specifically, a person's LT reflects the ability of the muscles to match energy supply to energy demand, which in turn determines the fuel mix (i.e., carbohydrate versus fat) used and the development of muscle fatigue.

Consequently, functional lactate threshold—especially when expressed as a power output, which also takes into account cycling efficiency—is the single most important physiological determinant of performance in events ranging from as short as a 3-kilometer pursuit to as long as a 3-week stage race. Just as important, because the effort experienced by an athlete when exercising at any given intensity depends on her or his power output relative to power at LT, this parameter provides a physiologically sound basis around which to design any power-meter-based training program.

Therefore, the definition of functional threshold power (FTP) is the maximal average power in watts that the cyclist can maintain in a quasi-steady state without fatiguing for 60 minutes.

How do you determine threshold power? Obviously, one way is by laboratory testing with invasive blood sampling, but few people have access to such testing on a regular basis. In addition, power at LT as determined in this manner is often significantly below what athletes and coaches tend to think of as a threshold. A more convenient and possibly more accurate way of determining functional threshold power is to rely on data collected using a power meter in the field. There are a number of different ways of doing so, each of which has its advantages and disadvantages, but all of which provide similar estimates of threshold power. I recommend doing the simplest thing that you can repeat on a regular basis—the 20-minute threshold test.

Protocol for 20-Minute Threshold Test

The goal of this initial test is to sustain the highest average wattage possible for the entire period. When getting to the effort, the cyclist must be sure to set an appropriate pace so that he or she does not blow up prematurely.

Start with a 20-minute warm-up, riding at a moderate pace of about 65 percent of maximum heart rate (HR), or at what would be called endurance pace. Again, be sure to do the warm-up at the same intensity each time you do the test.

After the warm-up, perform three fast pedaling efforts at 100 revolutions per minute for 1 minute each with 1 minute of easy recovery pedaling after each effort to prepare the muscles further. After these efforts, ride for 5 minutes at an easy pace of 65 percent of maximum HR. Then the true test begins.

Ride for 5 minutes all out. Punch it and hold it! Start at a high pace but not so high that you die at the end. Have a little in reserve to kick it to the finish line in the last minute. The goal of this stage is twofold: to open up the legs for the next efforts and to glimpse your ability to produce watts in what is called $\dot{V}O_2$max power, or level 5, discussed a bit later in the chapter. This initial 5-minute effort helps get rid of any initial freshness present at the beginning of the ride so that for the next effort, you are able to produce what is more likely to be truly representative of your FTP. Recover with 10 minutes of easy riding at endurance pace, at 65 percent of maximum HR.

Perform a 20-minute time trial. Try to do this on a road that is flat and allows a strong, steady effort for the entire 20 minutes. Do not start out too hard! That is a common mistake, so make sure to get up to speed and then try to hold that speed as best you can. If you have never done one of these efforts before, I suggest trying this on a steady climb or into a slight headwind so that you have to do it at maximum effort for the entire 20 minutes. The test is less useful if you go out too hard and then explode, unable to produce true maximal steady-state power for the entire duration. A better approach is to start out in the first 2 minutes a little under what you believe to be FTP and then build up along the way, riding at maximum in the last 3 minutes.

Pedal easy for about 10 to 15 minutes at endurance pace, at 65 percent of maximum HR. Finish the ride and cool down for an additional 10 to 15 minutes. To estimate your FTP, take 95 percent of this 20-min wattage, reflecting that you cannot sustain teat same 20-min wattage over a full 60 minutes (e.g., a 20-min wattage of 300 W would give a FTP of 285 W).

To reiterate, the goal in the 20-minute test is to produce the highest average watts over the entire 20-minute period. Because one goal of any training program is to increase power at threshold, the value entered into cycling power analysis software such as TrainingPeaks WKO+ should be periodically reassessed to be certain it is still accurate. How often threshold power significantly changes depends in part on a person's training history and habits. For example, someone who is just beginning or is returning to cycling may see large rapid changes in threshold power, whereas an experienced rider who has been training for many years or an athlete who maintains a high level of conditioning year round will probably experience much less variation. In general, however, assessing threshold power a few times per year (e.g., near the start of training as a baseline, partway through the precompetition period to track improvement, and during the season to determine peak fitness achieved) is probably sufficient.

Establishing Training Zones

Because more cyclists are using power meters, the need has clearly developed for power-based training programs akin to those used with heart rate monitors. To help alleviate this demand, Dr. Andrew R. Coggan developed a system of power-based training levels, or zones. These training levels (table 29.1) were developed by drawing on fundamental principles of exercise physiology as well as approximately two decades of experience with power-based

Table 29.1 Power-Based Training Levels (Coggan Power Zones)

Level	Name or purpose	% of threshold power	% of threshold HR	Perceived exertion	Time to exhaustion
1	Active recovery	≤55%	≤68%	<2	70 to 80 minutes
2	Endurance	56 to 75%	69 to 83%	2 or 3	2.5 hours to 14 days
3	Tempo	76 to 90%	84 to 94%	3 or 4	2.5 to 8 hours
4	Lactate threshold	91 to 105%	95 to 105%	4 or 5	10 to 60 minutes
5	V̇O₂max	106 to 120%	≥106%	6 or 7	3 to 8 minutes
6	Anaerobic capacity	121 to 150%	Not applicable	>7	30 seconds to 2 minutes
7	Neuromuscular power	Not applicable	Not applicable	Maximal	5 to 15 seconds

Adapted, by permission, from H. Allen and A. Coggan, 2010, *Training and racing with a power meter*, 2nd ed. (Boulder, CO: VeloPress), 49.

training in both laboratory and field settings. These training levels are all based on FTP; after completing FTP testing, take the 100 percent number and calculate training levels from it.

Building a Power Profile

Beyond the FTP test, cyclists must learn individual strengths and weaknesses. Dr. Coggan and I created a test for this as well, called the power profile test (Allen and Coggan 2010). This test not only helps determine personal strengths and weaknesses but also allows comparison of cyclists. The power profile itself was created from the world's best cyclists and then compared with more than 300 others to assess the various categories. The power profile includes categories for both men and women (figure 29.1), and it has been revised over the years to reflect more accurate data. The power profile test is the next set of tests to perform to continue on the power trip.

The test consists of evaluating three different periods: 5 seconds, which is representative of neuromuscular power (level 7); 1 minute, which is a good representation of anaerobic ability (level 6); and 5 minutes, which is close to V̇O₂max (level 5). The goal is to do your best in each test to determine which of the energy systems could be limiting performance. Always start with the 1-minute test because this test relies on anaerobic capacity, which is at its maximum when you are fresh. So before you are hardly even warmed up, perform the 1-minute test.

Power Profile Test

Warm-Up
Warm up for 10 minutes with three efforts of 1-minute fast pedal intervals (pedal at 120 revolutions per minute for 1 minute and then at 80 revolutions per minute for 1 minute).

		Average power output in watts per kilogram							
Level	Cat	Men				Women			
		5 s	1 min.	5 min.	FTP	5 s	1 min.	5 min.	FTP
World record		25.18	11.5	7.6	6.4	19.42	9.29	6.74	5.69
World class	Int. pro	24	11.21	7.34	6.17	18.87	9.06	6.36	5.36
Exceptional	Pro	22.22	10.48	6.68	5.61	17.5	8.48	5.79	4.87
Excellent	Cat 1	20.44	9.75	6.02	5.04	16.13	7.91	5.21	4.38
Very good	Cat 2	18.66	9.02	5.37	4.48	14.77	7.33	4.64	3.88
Good	Cat 3	16.59	8.29	4.71	3.91	13.4	6.76	3.98	3.21
Moderate	Cat 4	14.81	7.56	4.05	3.35	12.03	6.18	3.44	2.82
Fair	Cat 5	13.04	6.83	3.4	2.78	10.66	5.61	2.83	2.32
Untrained		11.26	6.1	2.74	2.22	9.29	5.03	2.26	1.83

▶ **Figure 29.1** The power profile chart uses the best power data from world champion cyclists to establish the highest bar. Each level has been determined by studying more than 300 riders.

Main Set 1: 1-Minute Max

After you are warmed up, test 1-minute max. Kill it and go as hard as possible! Do this test on an uphill, if possible, preferably something with a 4 to 8 percent gradient. Perform the test for 1 minute and 5 seconds, to compensate for a possible slow start.

Main Set 2: Sprints

To test 5-second power, perform four total sprints. The first two sprints should be in the small chainring. Start from a slow speed (8 to 10 miles per hour [13 to 16 km/h]), jump on the pedals, and accelerate as fast as possible, shifting down each time after you wind out that gear. Sprint for 50 to 75 meters. Recover for 3 to 5 minutes after each effort. The second set of sprints should be in the big chainring, starting at 18 to 20 miles per hour (30 to 34 km/h). Using the 53 × 17 or 50 × 16, begin and sprint for at least 200 meters, shifting down one gear at a time as you accelerate. Again, rest by riding easy for 5 minutes after each effort.

Main Set 3: 5-Minute Max

Rest for 10 to 20 minutes with some easy riding and then test 5-minute max. Go as hard as you can! You need to pace yourself a little more here, so don't start out at the same pace as you did in the 1-minute test. If possible, do this test on a hill. As with main set 1, push yourself for 5 extra seconds to make sure you get 5 minutes of all-out effort.

Cool-Down

Cool down with 10 to 12 minutes of easy spinning.

Creating Power-Zone-Based Workouts

One of the keys to effective and efficient cycling training is to ensure that the cyclist is working at the proper exertion for the desired effect. Now that you have tested FTP and established training zones, you can set the big goal, outline an annual training plan, and start to build workouts that have a specific focus. This means thinking about the specific energy system to be targeted. For example, for a race that requires a high FTP with steady-state power, such as climbing or a sustained breakaway, you should perform threshold intervals in level 4, like 4 efforts of 15 minutes at 100 to 105 percent of FTP.

Another example might be a criterium; the cyclist needs to be ready to do hard sprints out of each turn each lap, which could be four to six sprints per lap. After each sprint out of the corner, the cyclist gets up to speed and then coasts to the next corner with lower power. To prepare for this race, perform intervals like the microbursts workout described later with 15 seconds at 150 percent of FTP and then 15 seconds at 50 percent of FTP. Another example might be for a 100-mile (160 km) Gran Fondo; in this case, the cyclist needs to be able to complete the 100 miles and climb a 5,000-foot (1,500 m) mountain. The corresponding workout might be to do 4 or 5 hours on the road at endurance pace, including an hour of steady climbing at tempo (level 3) pace. Ultimately, the key is to tailor workouts to the specific demands of the cycling required.

Here are examples of one workout in each level to help you better understand how each workout addresses each energy system. The sample is done for a rider with an FTP of 290 watts; remember to base workouts on the cyclist's FTP.

Level 1: Active Recovery Total time: 1.5 hours. Warm up for 15 minutes under 150 watts (48 to 51 percent of FTP) and then ride for the next hour with wattage under 180 (62 percent), keeping cadence nice and smooth at 90 to 95 revolutions per minute. Cool down for 15 minutes with wattage under 140 (48 percent of FTP).

Level 2: Endurance Total time: 3.5 hours. Warm up for 15 minutes at less than 190 watts and then ride with watts at 200 to 220 (69 to 75 percent) for 2 hours, performing short bursts (8 seconds, seated, taking revolutions per minute to 130 and watts to 300) every 10 minutes. The rest of the ride is at normal self-selected cadence. Cool down for 15 minutes at less than 150 watts.

Level 3: Tempo Total time: 2.5 hours. Warm up for 15 minutes at less than 200 watts. Then nail it between 76 and 90 percent of FTP, at about 220 to 260 watts. Try your best to hold in this range over hills, on flats, and even downhills. Emphasize spending as much time as possible in the 240 to 260 (82 to 90 percent) range. Keep cadence normal and meter your efforts on hills. If you have to go over 260 watts, that is fine, but avoid sprinting up the hills. Do not underestimate the strong effort and mental focus that this ride requires!

Level 4: Threshold   Total time: 2 to 2.5 hours. Warm up well for 15 minutes below 200 watts and then do a 5-minute blowout effort at 290 watts, or 100 percent of FTP. This effort prepares the body for some solid work. After 5 minutes of easy riding, perform two efforts of 20 minutes at 290 watts, at approximately 100 percent of FTP. You need to stay in this range as best you can. Rest for 15 minutes between efforts. Use a gear that allows you to keep your cadence in your self-selected range or challenge yourself to pedal just a touch faster than you would normally. Finish the workout with 1-minute fast pedaling efforts with cadence over 105 revolutions per minute, holding watts under 280. Rest for 2 minutes after each effort. The goal is not to go superhard but to spin a high cadence at FTP. Try for 8 to 10 of these and then cool down.

An alternative: Start with three efforts of 10 minutes and build to four efforts of 10 minutes. Start over at three efforts of 12 minutes, build to three efforts of 15 minutes, and then move to two efforts of 20 minutes. A category 3 bike racer should not need to do more than two efforts of 20 minutes, but higher category racers should strive to build to four efforts of 20 minutes.

Level 5: Race-Winning Intervals   Total time: 2 to 2.5 hours. These are race-winning efforts, a simulation of an attack during a race or what is needed to win solo! Do five to eight sets. Begin each set with a 30-second sprint (15 seconds out of the saddle); average 600 watts (200 percent of FTP) in these first 30 seconds with a peak of at least 900 to 1,000 watts (300 percent). Then perform 3 minutes of hammering at 300 watts, or 100 percent of FTP, finishing each with a 10-second burst at the end, trying to reach 600 to 700 watts. Rest for 5 to 6 minutes. Finish with eight 1-minute fast pedaling efforts at a cadence greater than 130 revolutions per minute.

Level 6: Anaerobic Capacity   Total time: 2 hours. Perform a standard warm-up and then set your power meter so that you can see the average mode in interval or lap mode. Perform eight efforts of 2 minutes as hard as possible, using your average watts as a carrot to push all the way to the end. The goal is to average more than 390 watts (130 percent of threshold power). Reach for that. Stop when you can't reach 355 watts (118 percent) in your average. Recover for at least 2 minutes, more if needed. Finish with five 1-minute efforts and try to average over 420 watts (140 percent). Do all of them, unless you can't even get over 390 watts. Also, set a goal for your best 5 seconds in these 1-minute efforts. Maybe you can get your max over 1,000 watts and your best 5 seconds at 800 watts.

Level 7: Neuromuscular Power   Total time: 2 hours. Get ready for micro-bursts! Perform a standard warm-up and then do three 10-minute efforts of microbursts: 15 seconds on and 15 seconds off. Each block is 15 seconds on (go to 450 watts, or 150 percent) and 15 seconds off (150 watts, or 50 percent). Repeat continually for 10 minutes. Perform 5 minutes of easy spinning before the next block. Cruise for 15 minutes easy and then do 10 sprints of 10 seconds out of the saddle, with at least 2 minutes after each sprint. Try to reach 300 to 350 percent of FTP as your max wattage. Cool down for 15 minutes.

Applying the Science

Training with a power meter is a great adventure that will expand a cyclist's knowledge of his or her body and its response to training. This kind of training will be more efficient and effective. For cyclists who have been riding for a long time, using a power meter will open up a new dimension of cycling, as they learn about power meter data, charts, and graphs and are able to quantify improvements. If you would like to learn more, I suggest reading the book I wrote with Dr. Coggan, *Training and Racing With a Power Meter*.

CHAPTER 30

Data Management for Cyclists

—Dirk Friel

Cycling today in many ways is a leader among Olympic sports when it comes to tracking and analyzing training and competition data. High-tech carbon bikes equipped with power meters that can measure everything from watts to kilojoules have attracted athletes and coaches who are analytical and innovative.

The argument could be made that sports that rely less on technology could monitor and track training more easily because there are fewer metrics to capture and a smaller technology gap between elite athletes and beginners. Runners and cyclists track much of the same data (time, distance, heart rate, speed), but cyclists can track additional metrics such as watts, kilojoules, torque, and more. These additional metrics are often leveraged to create advanced metrics such as chronic training load (CTL), acute training load (ATL), training stress balance (TSB), functional reserve capacity (FRC), and more (Allen and Coggan 2010).

Just a short decade ago few cyclists downloaded their power meters daily. Cycling has seen a revolution that seems to have started in the early 2000s and is directly tied to knowledge gained from the use of power meters. Power meters were certainly available in the 1990s, but their widespread adoption and the knowledge gained by coaches and athletes emphasized the need to capture as much data as possible. Web, mobile, and connectivity advancements such as Bluetooth and ANT+ technology have made it almost effortless to capture and store data. The ease of use of GPS cyclometers and power meters along with the reduction in price has caused a cultural evolution in cycling. Today, top professionals and beginning amateurs have access to the same technology, which has democratized access to cutting-edge training techniques. It could even be said that many amateur masters riders a decade ago were training smarter and more effectively than top professional athletes. Those tech-savvy amateur riders started experimenting with all the new metrics being collected by power meters and applying the principles of cutting-edge coaches and physiologists. Most of the first cyclists to use new metrics such as training stress score, normalized power, chronic training load, and so on weren't Tour de France riders but masters club riders who simply wanted to go faster in their local events. Those pioneers of a new wave of knowledge pushed cycling training methods forward faster than it had progressed at any other time in history.

Even as amateur cyclists were setting the groundwork for new ways to quantify training, professional athletes rarely downloaded data from their power meters. From the 1990s to the mid-2000s, pros typically used their power meters only during training rides. Downloading data afterward seemed too complicated and not worth the effort. Few teams, if any, mandated that riders download their workouts and races to provide their employers with access to the data. In fact, few professional cyclists traveled with a computer. This practice started to change around 2007 when a few professional teams sought to change their culture in an effort to combat the use of performance-enhancing drugs. Teams and athletes realized that performance gains should be sought through better training rather than better pharmacology. The culture of cycling finally started to change, and it slowly broke free from the ways of the past, enabling the sport to become a leader for other sports to learn from.

Leveraging large data to improve performance has only just begun. We don't know what secrets future algorithms may uncover, but one thing is certain. If an athlete doesn't collect and save training and race data, no algorithm or any amount of new science will work at all. Technology and knowledge have dramatically shaped the way that coaches track, analyze, and plan training programs, and this process will continue to evolve (Borden and Lambert 2006).

The evolution of tracking training data started thousands of years ago and remained more or less the same until personal computers came along. Training logs and training diaries hold the secrets to many athlete training programs throughout the ages. But pen and paper are rapidly being replaced by mobile devices. Instead of storing training diaries on a shelf, training statistics and athlete comments are stored in large databases in a digital cloud.

No matter where the data sit, recorded comments and training metrics are invaluable to an athlete and a coach. Technology is rapidly adding more value to an athlete's training log. Coaches are becoming more efficient through the use of technology, which allows them to spot trends, quantify race demands more accurately (Ebert et al. 2006), and apply advanced analytics to quantitate training load (Hayes and Quinn 2009), endeavors unimaginable just a decade ago.

At the end of the day, cyclists who don't track their training and racing data are at a distinct disadvantage when it comes to maximizing their potential. This disadvantage becomes ever more evident as an athlete progresses. The influence of technology as it relates to performance gains becomes more profound as the athlete improves. Elite and Olympic-level athletes rely heavily on their collected training data to make decisions on how to train as well as how to race. Training diaries will take on even more importance as big data start to shape sport even more (Halson 2014). Like it or not, elite cyclists can't rely only on their intuition and traditional training practices to stay competitive.

Although much of sport science relies on objective data, the importance of subjective feelings, sensations, changes in mood, sleep quality, and so on should not be ignored. In fact, a current trend is to quantify non-performance-related data and cross-reference it with performance data to help make better sense of how physical training, perceived exertion, and recovery techniques affect performance (Martin and Andersen 2000). No two athletes are the same, and no single perfect training formula can be computed for every athlete. The art of training and coaching is difficult to replace with a computer program. In fact, it might be argued that coaching practices are often ahead of science and that the scientists often try to prove why certain training protocols work. In many ways, a training program is one large experiment managed by a coach and aided by technology and science.

Training Individualization Starts With Tracking

The starting point for any individualization of training starts with historical data; otherwise, decisions are simply guesswork. Attempting to create physical and psychological peak performance is complex, and many variables are involved, but a well-documented training program can remove many of the unknowns. Sport analytics can get us only so far, but coaches and athletes can gain valuable insight by reviewing what has happened in the past. Athletes improve by adapting to stress, but each athlete responds in a slightly different way to the same stress (Manzi et al. 2009b). The better we can quantify the stress (both physiologically and psychologically) and the better we can measure the adaptation to that stress, the better an athlete can decide what to do to improve.

Keeping good records helps objectify progress because perception is often wrong. Hard data can show true progress and, unfortunately, regression. Using collected training data to assess progress objectively can be correlated along with the subjective input of how the athlete feels. Subjective input collected from an athlete can override decision making even if it conflicts with performance-related data. The fact that performance statistics have been collected doesn't mean that an athlete's mood, rating of perceived exertion (RPE), stress level, sleep quality, motivation, and so on are to be ignored. Evidence-based data along with subjective input need to be balanced (Borresen and Lambert 2008).

Athletes should also keep in mind that a training program isn't just the physical workouts they endure but also the recovery techniques they allocate after training sessions. Training programs should have a macro view of the training, which includes nutrition, psychology, and recovery. Historically, training analysis was focused on single-workout data with little insight into the relationship to previous training. Now, of course, we know that improvements in performance are directly related to how an athlete has adapted to training (Manzi et al. 2009a). Therefore, training logs need to measure and compare a multitude of metrics over time. Traditional pen and paper training logs fall short here, because creating quick and accessible reports from handwritten training diaries is too difficult.

As mentioned earlier, intuition is often a poor gauge of how an athlete is performing. Self-coached athletes who don't consult with an experienced coach often miss obvious signs of overtraining and push through training sessions without enough rest (Foster 1998). A training log that can provide a daily snapshot of key indicators can be invaluable to such athletes because they may see signs of overtraining that they would otherwise ignore.

Accurate and complete training records can also help athletes gain confidence in their training programs. Personal records can often be set when the athlete doesn't realize it. The pain and suffering of training or racing can sometimes overshadow a personal record such as a peak power value. A quick analysis can show how a new peak performance may have been set even if the athlete didn't finish with a top result. This outcome can be especially common for road cyclists who race in support of teammates when top results aren't the goal for the individual. An athlete's performance isn't always directly related to race results. A good postride routine that includes downloading and saving data to an electronic training software program can reveal true fitness and performance independent of race results.

Besides helping athletes build confidence, capturing training data also educates athletes and builds self-knowledge so that they can make more informed decisions themselves based on their unique experiences. Athletes can learn and review lessons more easier when training is well documented.

Training logs can also help athletes get inspired by reviewing past performances. Preparing for an event isn't just a physical endeavor; the winner often has a psychological edge. Training logs can capture how an athlete was thinking and what decisions he or she made before and during a competition. When reviewed, this information can move the person into a desired psychological state of mind before competition. Visualization techniques may be enhanced by reviewing past training-log entries. This process can be especially effective if the athlete is working with a sport psychologist.

Cloud-Based Training Logs

Modern-day athletes are starting to rely on a team approach to coaching whereby sharing of data is becoming more important. Traditionally, handwritten training logs weren't shared, and they were intended only for the use of one athlete. But as documenting training data and regimes became more important, training logs needed to be shared between people. At first, coaches reviewed their athletes' handwritten logbooks in person, and later they studied faxed or e-mailed journal entries and spreadsheets. Starting in the 1990s coaches started asking athletes to e-mail their daily workout files from their heart rate monitors and power meters so that the coach could enter them into desktop software programs for analysis. Nowadays, powerful and accessible web-based and mobile applications allow a team of experts to work with an individual athlete. Sharing of data is easy, and e-mailing of file attachments is being replaced by shared databases. Accessibility can be controlled and leveraged by as many people as needed. Many teams and national governing bodies are embracing a team-of-experts approach to coaching because they realize the value of leveraging experts in multiple fields. A coach cannot be the expert in all areas of high performance, but a head coach can coordinate with several assistants or experts such as a strength coach, nutrition coach, sport psychologist, team manager, and others.

The process of collecting data in this new age of technology is progressing rapidly as new wireless protocols are being leveraged within training devices. Downloading is being replaced by automated upload procedures through WiFi and cellular networks. The days of cumbersome download cables attached to a personal computer are being replaced by almost seamless collection processes. In fact, performance can now be tracked and monitored in real time. As this technology advances, coaches will be able to monitor training as it happens and be able to give immediate feedback even if they aren't at the same location as the athlete.

Another technology trend is leveraging and sharing data between multiple web and mobile applications. Data (for example, nutrition) can be collected through one application and automatically synced to another. This linkage allows athletes to use multiple applications that perform specific tasks well instead of expecting one application to do everything they may need. For example, an athlete may record nutrition data within one mobile application, recovery metrics within another, and training and performance data within a third. All the applications can be synced to share data as needed. Coaches and athletes can also sync data to desktop applications that allow them to use the information even when disconnected from the web. This trend will continue to advance as more applications are built that realize the benefits of application program interfaces (API).

Algorithms and Modeling of Fitness

As athlete data become more accessible, advanced metrics and modeling formulas are being developed to run against larger data sets. Rapid advancements in wearable technology have the potential to inform the athlete and coach by quantifying recovery, movement patterns (Balouchestani and Krishnan 2014), and performance data. Making sense of all the incoming information is the challenge now that we can easily capture almost all aspects of performance. The ability to make fast, accurate decisions based on incoming data, which can be acted on to improve both training and racing, is where science and technology is helping coaches the most. The result will lead not to one homogenous method of training, but instead to training individualization. Determining an athlete's weaknesses and the demands of competition through software analysis will become even more prevalent. The same analysis will help guide the coach and athlete as they make daily training decisions that will inevitably lead to new world records being set as a direct result of data analysis, not performance-enhancing drugs.

Referring to her training log, American cyclist Kristin Armstrong (three-time Olympic gold medalist) wrote, "Thanks for keeping me honest." She attributed part of her success to decisions made directly because of knowledge gained from her training log. She and her coach relied heavily on technology and software to make training decisions daily.

Team selections will evolve to take into account past data and future mathematical models, which will help selection committees forecast who might be in peak form on race day. National governing bodies have started to use data to help with athlete development and talent identification, especially as technology continues to become more widely accessible. The next generation of athletes won't ask why they are being asked to track their data as past generations have. Many of today's young athletes have started collecting their own performance data before they have even entered a high-performance program. Technology and education efforts are bringing cutting-edge knowledge to anyone who cares to learn.

What to Track

Now that we've discussed the importance of keeping track of training and race data, let's discuss what can be tracked. Power meters, heart rate monitors, and GPS devices collect a multitude of metrics. But other metrics, such as weather, soreness, injury, psychological mood, perceived exertion, blood parameters, and many more, should be tracked and analyzed as well.

The list of what can be monitored and analyzed is almost endless. Here is a summary of options to consider tracking by category. An athlete and coach may choose to track different metrics at different times of the year depending on the emphasis and the athlete's phase of training. Remember an old rule of thumb that holds true when trying to decide what to measure: "You can't control what you don't measure."

Planned Workout and Completed Comments

- What was the planned workout and goal for the day?
- How did the workout progress, and how did the athlete feel? Record any completed intervals and associated metrics as well as the rate of perceived exertion.

Basic Metrics

- Date and time of day of workout
- Duration of workout
- Distance

- Elevation gain
- Speed: average, max, and time series data

Performance Data Collected by Training Devices

- Power meter: watts (average, max, normalized power, training stress score, and time series data), kilojoules, right and left leg output
- Heart rate monitor: heart rate average, max, and time series data

Psychological Metrics

- Mood and motivation
- Stress levels

Daily Metrics

- Body weight
- Fatigue level
- Soreness
- Injury report
- Morning resting pulse
- Heart rate variability
- Hours of sleep
- Quality of sleep
- Sleep elevation

Recovery Techniques
All recovery techniques should be recorded to help the athlete better understand which protocols work the best. Recovery techniques may include massage, stretching, ice baths, compression clothing and machines, and so on.

Nutrition

- Nutrition and meals to be analyzed for macro- and micronutrients and correlated with performance data
- Preexercise, exercise, and postexercise nutrition to be reviewed by a sport nutritionist
- Hydration
- Additional supplementation

Blood Parameters
A history of complete blood counts (CBC) can be useful in helping athletes determine when and whether overtraining has occurred and how they can avoid overtraining in the future. CBCs can also be used to see how peak performance related to changes in blood chemistry. A CBC history can be invaluable for medical professionals when the athlete consults with a doctor on any issues or general health concerns.

Other

- Exercise stress tests: Results collected from lab tests should be stored as a way to record performance markers and quantify changes in fitness. Blood lactate readings collected from lactate testing should be stored along with any training protocols and performance data.
- Weather can play a big part in performance. Temperature, humidity, and wind can all be recorded or archived with the help of weather applications. Performance prediction software that takes into account weather forecasts is now available to help cyclists with pacing strategies.
- Video is becoming used more as a way to help with technique, pacing, and strategy. Video can be valuable in analyzing race performances and providing visual feedback about positioning on the bike.
- Race results should also be recorded, and links to official result web pages can be added to training logs for future reference.

Methods of Tracking

The key to tracking and gathering consistent data is to create a routine before, during, and after each training session and race. Good habits learned within the early years of an athlete's career create behaviors that can lead to a complete training history. Many of today's athletes already have access to affordable training devices that can store hundreds of hours' worth of training data. Saving that data and making it accessible to a knowledgeable coach is the key step to communicate to the athlete. Cloud-based (web and mobile) training-log applications have become almost a commodity now that so many are available free with limitless storage capacity. If you have a smartphone with a data plan, you have no more excuses not to track training. Many mobile apps can now record the GPS track of a workout, again at no cost.

As mentioned earlier the evolution of tracking data has changed dramatically within the past two decades. Not too long ago, manually writing completed workout descriptions and metrics within paper notebooks was the norm. Then came digital spreadsheets that allowed the viewing of data over time through the graphing of any quantifiable metric. Next came files that were created by training devices, which also needed to be saved and shared.

At first e-mail became the way to share spreadsheets and device files, but any coach with more than a few athletes quickly found the process cumbersome. Access to reports and data was one-directional; the coach received all the data and the athlete tended to be left isolated from the vast information being collected on her- or himself. Another downside to e-mailing files and spreadsheets is that data are saved only on a hard drive, which has the risk of being lost, stolen, or corrupted.

Some desktop analysis software applications do sync to web databases, which helps reduce the risk of data loss and facilitates data sharing. Recent trends have been to upload device files directly to web-based management systems, which can later be downloaded for offline access if needed.

Smartphones are playing a bigger role within data management systems as wireless technologies are integrated into new training devices. Some of these technologies include ANT+, Bluetooth Low Energy, and WiFi capabilities. This innovation led to the ability to pair peripherals such as power meters, heart rate monitors, cadence sensors, and more to a main collection device or a smartphone. Training devices can now upload to an online database as soon as a local WiFi network has been detected. This process saves the athlete quite a few steps and ensures quick and easy access immediately after a workout is completed.

In the future we will inevitably see the collection of data becoming even easier. Onboard video cameras are becoming more common on bikes, as is the ability to transmit live data. Future technology will make race coverage more exciting, and this new technology coupled with additional scientific knowledge will improve training practices even more.

Applying the Science

Leveraging the latest in sport science research and theory within a training regime depends on the creation and application of beliefs and assumptions that often can't be proved. An athlete's training log certainly has a wealth of data, but it often does not have sufficient data to prove or disprove the value of all training methods and protocols. Similarly, science doesn't hold all the answers in the question of nature versus nurture, and coaches and athletes often simply know that certain training regimes work independent of any scientific proof.

The best use of a training log and collected training data may be to give the athlete insight into the overall trends occurring with his or her fitness. Also, keep in mind that data analysis should not replace intuition and experiential decision making, especially because athletes are also managing psychological stress, mood swings, emotions, hormones, and many other factors that are hard to measure or quantify within a training log. Data can be valuable in informing the decision-making process and confirming that progress is (or isn't) being made.

Making decisions faster and with a higher degree of accuracy and success should be the intent of monitoring an athlete's training program. Collecting large amounts of data and asking the athlete to record as much as possible every day is simply a waste of time if the data are not used to drive decisions. The data collection process can also demotivate some athletes if the process is too difficult or time consuming.

Too much data analysis, or simply bad data, can be more dangerous than having no data at all. Analyzing data simply for analysis purposes doesn't lead to more efficient and effective training. A problem thesis or belief to solve must drive the experiment and analysis process. Before embarking on a data-driven approach to training, coaches and athletes should first understand what they are trying to confirm or deny. Making training decisions is essentially a real-life science experiment, and applying the principles of science theory can lead the way. Questions to ask that can inform what to track include the following:

- When was the athlete's peak performance, and what could be tracked to help predict future peaks?
- Is the current training focus and load resulting in a desired outcome?
- What are the demands of the highest priority events, and how do they relate to the athlete's individual weaknesses?
- After a limiter is chosen to improve, what key performance indicators (KPIs) can be monitored to track progress?
- What training or circumstances consistently lead to poor performance, and can any prior KPIs help predict poor performance?

After you know what you are looking for, the process of data interpretation will become more focused and valuable. Key performance indicators can be monitored at a micro, meso, and macro level. Keep in mind that athletes often tend to focus on individual training session numbers and lack a meso or macro view of their training. The coach's role is to keep things in perspective, focus on the long-term goals, and understand that progress often takes years. Trends mean more than outliers do, and this perspective must be continually communicated to the athlete. Along the journey, data can boost confidence that progress is being made. But to progress, the athlete may at times need to revert to focusing on an underlying weakness. Progress toward a larger goal may require a loss of sport-specific fitness to make gains somewhere else (for example, a focus on injury prevention). The data can help the athlete understand why the drop in fitness may be necessary, yet data can also set a new target to achieve after competition training is resumed.

The key to making the scientific data-driven process work is to understand how the information collected will be leveraged to lead decision making. Data alone will not provide solutions unless a belief or thesis to prove or disprove is proposed. Yet no matter how much effort is placed on trying to objectify the process of training load and the resulting adaptation, assumptions and a belief in a theory sometimes outweigh the lack of evidence or results. The coach and athlete have the advantage of experimenting without regard to accountability of evidence, yet the preferred road to follow, the one that reduces the unknowns and has the highest likelihood of success, has its roots in the scientific method.

PART

VIII

Preparing to Race

CHAPTER 31

Off-the-Bike Training

—Bent R. Rønnestad

Among elite cyclists, differences in performance are extremely small. Therefore, coaches and athletes strive for the optimal training strategies. This interest in optimizing training is present not only within the elite group but also among cyclists and coaches operating at a lower performance level. Consequently, training off the bike, as a mean of optimizing performance on the bike, has gradually received more attention during the last decade. The effects of adding strength training to the normal endurance training on the bike have been a particular topic of interest among both scientists and practitioners. Hickson, Rosenkoetter, and Brown (1980) were among the first to give us the idea that heavy strength training could positively affect cycling performance. Their study was performed on untrained persons, but lately the knowledge of the effects of adding strength training to endurance training in recreational, well-trained, and elite cyclists has increased. The purpose of this chapter is to describe the effects of concurrent strength and endurance training on basic strength-training adaptations, explain how strength training influences important determinants of endurance performance, present potential mechanisms behind the effects of strength training on cycling performance, and provide practical recommendations.

Effects of Concurrent Strength and Endurance Training on Basic Strength-Training Adaptations

According to the principle of training specificity, strength training and endurance training induce quite different muscular adaptations. Endurance training has been associated with lower maximum shortening velocity of the initially fast type II muscle fibers, peak tension development in all fiber types (Fitts, Costill, and Gardetto 1989), lowered vertical jumping ability and strength (Costill 1967), and unchanged or slightly reduced cross-sectional area of muscle fibers (Fitts, Costill, and Gardetto 1989). On the other hand, strength training improves these measurements (Kraemer et al. 1995). Based on the finding that endurance training and strength training have contrasting effects, an interesting investigation is to explore how concurrent training affects strength performance and to compare those effects with the effects of strength training alone. Most studies investigating the effect of concurrent training in endurance-trained people include participants with little or no experience in strength training during the 6 months before the start of the intervention. When the strength training is combined with a relatively low volume of endurance training (two or three endurance sessions per week), the endurance training seems to have no or only minor negative effect on strength-training adaptations (e.g., McCarthy et al. 1995). When heavy strength training is combined with a larger volume of endurance training (four or more sessions per week), the increase in strength and hypertrophy seems to be impaired (Jones et al. 2013; Kraemer et al. 1995; Rønnestad, Hansen, and Raastad 2012), likely because of a negative effect of endurance training on intracellular pathways important for myofibrillar protein synthesis (reviewed in Hawley 2009). Even so, a small increase, about 2 to 6 percent, seems to occur in measurements of muscle hypertrophy of the main target muscles after 8 to 16 weeks of concurrent training (Rønnestad, Hansen, and Raastad 2010a, 2012; Rønnestad et al. 2015; Taipale et al. 2010; Losnegard et al. 2011; Aagaard et al. 2011). An important finding is that despite the observation of a small muscle hypertrophy, total body mass does not increase (Bishop et al. 1999; Levin, Mcguigan, and Laursen 2009; Rønnestad, Hansen, and Raastad 2010a, 2010b; Sunde et al. 2010; Aagaard et al. 2011). The latter indicates that some fat mass has been exchanged with muscle mass during the preparation period. When only heavy strength training is performed, researchers commonly observe a reduced proportion of the fast type IIX muscle fibers that are rapidly fatigued and a concomitant increase in the proportion of the slower but more fatigue resistant type IIA muscle fibers. This outcome has also been observed in well-trained and elite cyclists after concurrent strength and endurance training (Aagaard et al. 2011; Vikmoen et al. 2014).

Effects of Strength Training on Important Determinants of Endurance Performance

Let's take a closer look at how the addition of strength training to ongoing endurance training affects endurance performance. Anaerobic capacity combined with the interaction of maximal oxygen consumption ($\dot{V}O_2max$) and lactate threshold (percentage of $\dot{V}O_2max$) explains how long a given rate of aerobic and anaerobic metabolism can be sustained, which altogether determines the performance $\dot{V}O_2$ (figure 31.1). The efficiency then determines the

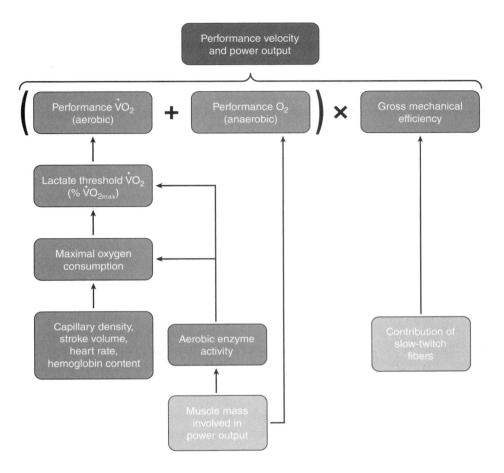

▶ **Figure 31.1** Important physiological factors that interact as determinants of performance power output.

Adapted, by permission, from M.J. Joyner and E.F. Cole, 2008, "Endurance exercise performance: The physiology of champions," Journal of Physiology 586(1): 35-44.

power output at a given amount of energy consumption and thus primarily determines the performance (Joyner and Cole 2008). We will now look closer at how strength training affects these performance determinants and, most important, cycling performance.

Combining heavy strength training with normal endurance training seems to have neither a positive nor a negative effect on the development of $\dot{V}O_2max$ (Hickson et al. 1988; Bishop et al. 1999; Bastiaans et al. 2001; Levin, Mcguigan, and Laursen 2009; Rønnestad, Hansen, and Raastad 2010a, 2010b; Rønnestad et al. 2015; Sunde et al. 2010; Aagaard et al. 2011; Barrett-O'Keefe et al. 2012; Louis et al. 2012). When it comes to cycling economy and efficiency, the findings are more equivocal. When cycling economy is measured by the traditional method (i.e., short, 3- to 5-minute, submaximal bouts of cycling), there is no observed additional effect of combining heavy strength training with endurance training in well-trained and elite cyclists (Rønnestad, Hansen, and Raastad 2010a, 2010b; Rønnestad et al. 2015; Aagaard et al. 2011). But by using the same approach to measure cycling economy, improvements have been observed after adding heavy strength training in moderately trained cyclists (Barrett-O'Keefe et al. 2012; Louis et al. 2012; Sunde et al. 2010). During 3 hours of submaximal cycling by well-trained male and female cyclists, no effects of heavy strength training on cycling economy during the first 1 to 2 hours were observed, but during the last hour cycling economy in the strength-training group improved (Rønnestad, Hansen, and Raastad 2011; Vikmoen et al. 2014). The latter finding indicates that well-trained cyclists may also improve cycling economy when measured during a longer ride (which might be more relevant for cyclists).

Lactate threshold is often used to express the relationship between blood lactate concentration ([la⁻]) and fraction of $\dot{V}O_2$max. Lactate threshold describes an estimation of a breakpoint on the [la⁻] curve as a function of exercise intensity (Tokmakidis, Leger, and Pilianidis 1998). Lactate threshold expressed as a percentage of $\dot{V}O_2$max is largely unaffected by exercise economy and $\dot{V}O_2$max, which might explain the small correlation between lactate threshold expressed as percentage of $\dot{V}O_2$max and time-trial cycling performance in cyclists (Støren et al. 2013). The studies that have reported the effect of strength training on lactate threshold expressed as percentage of $\dot{V}O_2$max observed neither a positive nor a negative effect (Sunde et al. 2010; Rønnestad et al. 2015). There are numerous ways to determine the power output at the lactate threshold, resulting in diverse thresholds on the [la⁻] versus power curve, which all seem to correlate well with long-term endurance performance (Tokmakidis, Leger, and Pilianidis 1998). Among other factors, the power output at lactate threshold is affected by cycling economy. Because improved cycling economy is often observed after strength training, improved lactate threshold power output is also frequently observed after strength training (Koninckx, Van Leemputte, and Hespel 2010; Rønnestad, Hansen, and Raastad 2010a, 2010b; Rønnestad et al. 2015).

The traditional way of measuring cycling performance is to perform time trials lasting 30 to 60 minutes. When positive effects of concurrent training are reported, heavy strength training is performed with multiple leg exercises during a minimum of 8 weeks (Hickson et al. 1988; Koninckx, Van Leemputte, and Hespel 2010; Rønnestad, Hansen, and Raastad 2010b; Rønnestad et al. 2015; Aagaard et al. 2011). In contrast, studies failing to show much improvement were typically short in duration and used a low volume of strength training or explosive strength training (Bishop et al. 1999; Bastiaans et al. 2001; Levin, Mcguigan, and Laursen 2009). A measurement that can be looked at as a performance measurement is the power output at $\dot{V}O_2$max (W_{max}), which is influenced by $\dot{V}O_2$max, cycling economy, anaerobic capacity, and neuromuscular characteristics (Jones and Carter 2000). Accordingly, W_{max} has been shown to predict endurance performance in cyclists (Hawley and Noakes 1992; Lucia et al. 1998) and to distinguish the endurance performance in well-trained cyclists (Lucia et al. 1998). Concurrent endurance and heavy strength training are reported to increase W_{max} or time to exhaustion at W_{max} (Hickson et al. 1988; Sunde et al. 2010; Rønnestad, Hansen, and Raastad 2010a, 2010b; Rønnestad et al. 2015). But this positive effect does not seem to be present when explosive strength training (Bastiaans et al. 2001) or short-term (6 weeks) strength training (Levin, Mcguigan, and Laursen 2009) is used (figure 31.2). A relatively new way of assessing cycling performance in

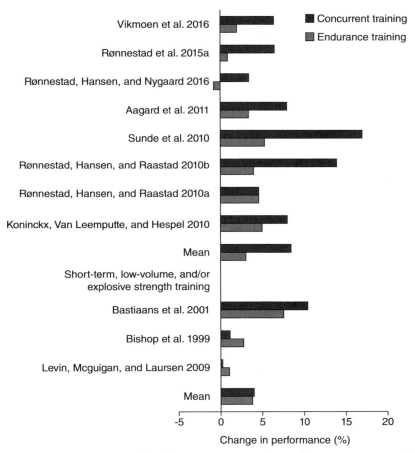

▶ **Figure 31.2** The upper studies show percentage change in measurements of cycling performance after at least 8 weeks of combined heavy strength training (moderate training volume) and endurance training (concurrent training) versus endurance training only (endurance training). The lower studies show percentage change in measurements of cycling performance after less than 8 weeks of combined low-volume heavy strength training or explosive strength training and endurance training (concurrent training) versus endurance training only (endurance training).

the lab is an attempt to imitate road-cycling competitions by performing a rather long duration of submaximal cycling followed by a 5-minute all-out trial. Combining heavy strength training with standard endurance training has improved 5-minute all-out power after 3 hours of submaximal cycling in well-trained cyclists, both female and male (Rønnestad, Hansen, and Raastad 2011; Vikmoen et al. 2014).

Another factor important for the outcome of a cycling race is the ability to close a gap, break away from the pack, or perform well in the final sprint. The outcome of these crucial moments of a race is decided primarily by the size of the involved muscle mass and the maximal leg strength (Izquierdo et al. 2004). The ability to generate high power output for a short period is often measured in the lab as mean and peak power output in a 30-second all-out test. Based on the known effects of heavy strength training on muscle strength and muscle mass, concurrent training is expected to improve the ability to generate high power output for a short period (Rønnestad, Hansen, and Raastad 2010a, 2010b; Rønnestad et al. 2015). This finding has practical implications, because the ability to generate high power output during a short period is an important aspect of overall cycling performance (Atkinson et al. 2003).

Potential Mechanisms Behind the Effects of Strength Training on Cycling Performance

Multiple potential mechanisms are behind the positive effects on cycling performance of combining heavy strength training with the ongoing endurance training. Figure 31.3 summarizes some of the possible mechanisms that are discussed in this section.

A potential mechanism for improved performance after combined strength and endurance training is increased maximal strength in the efficient type I muscle fibers, thus postponing activation of the less efficient type II muscle fibers, resulting in improved cycling economy and performance. Because mainly type I fibers are activated during traditional submaximal measurements of cycling economy, this might explain why the literature is equivocal on improvements in cycling economy in well-trained cyclists using this assessment. Postponed activation of type II muscle fibers is a plausible explanation for the findings of improved cycling economy in well-trained cyclists after 2 hours of submaximal cycling after a period of concurrent training (Rønnestad, Hansen, and Raastad 2011; Vikmoen et al. 2014). Prolonged cycling likely exhausts some of the type I fibers, so the postponed activation of the less efficient type II fibers may explain the improved cycling economy. The latter may have a glycogen-sparing effect that might explain

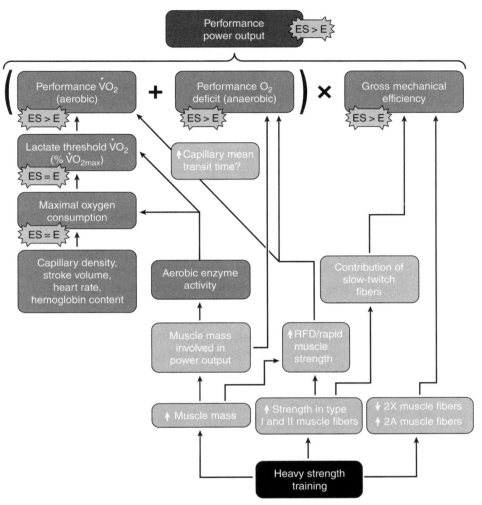

▶ **Figure 31.3** Proposed mechanisms for improved performance power output in cyclists after adding heavy strength training to ongoing endurance training (ES). The arrows indicate links between each factor and proposed strength-training effects. The overall findings in the literature of the effects of concurrent heavy strength and endurance training versus endurance training only (E) on the main determinants of endurance performance are presented in the 12-pointed stars.

improved 5-minute all-out performance after 3 hours submaximal cycling after 12 weeks of concurrent training (Rønnestad, Hansen, and Raastad 2011; Vikmoen et al. 2014).

Another potential mechanism related to muscle fiber recruitment is an increased proportion of type IIA fibers at the expense of type IIX fibers. An increased proportion of type IIA fibers at the expense of type IIX fibers has been observed after 12 to 16 weeks of heavy strength training in both well-trained female cyclists and top-level male cyclists (Aagaard et al. 2011; Vikmoen et al. 2016). The increase in the type IIA fibers, which are more resistant to fatigue yet capable of higher power output, may contribute to improved endurance performance. Indeed, recent data from our lab reveal a large correlation between change in mean power output during a 40-minute all-out test and change in IIX fibers ($r = -0.63$, $p < 0.05$). The reduced proportion of type IIX fibers after 12 weeks of heavy strength training (and endurance training) was associated with improved power output during a 40-minute all-out trial in well-trained female cyclists.

Another putative mechanism explaining improvement in endurance-related measurements after concurrent training is increased maximum force, or increased rate of force development (RFD), which facilitates better blood flow to exercising muscles (Heggelund et al. 2013; Sunde et al. 2010; Aagaard et al. 2011). Improvement in maximum force or RFD might lower the relative exercise intensity and induce less constriction of the blood flow. Alternatively, improved RFD may reduce time needed to reach the desired force in each movement cycle, thereby potentially increasing the relaxation phase with improved blood flow. Twenty-five weeks of combined strength and endurance training in elite cyclists led to earlier occurrence of peak torque during the pedal stroke, whereas endurance training alone did not (Rønnestad et al. 2015). Whether blood flow is enhanced after a period of concurrent training has not been thoroughly investigated, but in theory an increase in blood flow will lead to increased delivery of oxygen and substrates to working muscles and thus contribute to increased power output at a fixed [la⁻], but not necessarily to better cycling economy. Accordingly, it has been observed that improvement in power output at 4 millimoles per liter [la⁻] and mean power in a 40-minute all-out trial correlated well with changes toward earlier peak torque during the pedal stroke ($r = -0.50$ and $r = -0.63$, respectively, $p < 0.05$; Rønnestad et al. 2015). On the other hand, a study on moderately trained cyclists by Barrett-O'Keefe et al. (2012) showed that 8 weeks of heavy strength training improved work economy at a cadence of

Muscle Fibers

Human skeletal muscle contains three types of muscle fibers. Each fiber type has different qualities in how they perform and how quickly they fatigue.

Type I fibers have the slowest shortening velocity but the highest resistance to fatigue. They are thought to be the most work-efficient fibers.

Type IIX fibers have the highest shortening velocity but the lowest resistance to muscle fatigue.

Type IIA fibers are a hybrid of type I and IIX fibers. They have a faster shortening velocity than type I fibers but are generally more prone to fatigue than type I fibers.

60 revolutions per minute and reduced muscular blood flow while maintaining muscular arterial–venous oxygen difference. The latter finding indicates that improvement in muscular efficiency is an important mechanism behind improved work economy and improved endurance performance.

Coyle et al. (1991) observed a relationship between lean body mass and 1-hour all-out power output in well-trained and elite cyclists, suggesting that improved ability to recruit a relatively large quantity of muscle mass in each pedal stroke was associated with elite performance. Furthermore, cyclists who use a larger amount of their muscle mass had a larger fractional utilization of $\dot{V}O_2$max (Coyle et al. 1991). This outcome was related to recruitment of increased amounts of mitochondria, sharing the power production and leading to less metabolic strain at a given power output. Increased fractional utilization was indicated in another study in which elite cyclists improved 45-minute all-out performance after 16 weeks of adding heavy strength training. The authors estimated that the power output during the test had increased from 76 percent to 83 percent of the power output at $\dot{V}O_2$max (Aagaard et al. 2011). We might thus speculate that increased lean mass and increased absolute amounts of aerobic enzymes, with no change in the concentration of aerobic enzymes, could contribute to improved performance after adding heavy strength training to normal endurance training. This speculation is in agreement with the recent findings of a large correlation between change in mean power output during the 40-minute all-out test, change in the cross-sectional area of the quadriceps (r = 0.73, p < 0.05), and improved fractional utilization of $\dot{V}O_2$max (Vikmoen et al. 2016).

Practical Recommendations for Implementing Strength Training

This chapter explains that adding heavy strength training to normal endurance training seems to have a positive effect on cycling performance. Nevertheless, endurance training on the bike is the most important focus for a cyclist. If only three training sessions are available during the week, the cyclist will experience the largest performance increments by spending those sessions on the bike. If more time is available, however, the scientific literature indicates that adding some heavy strength training can improve cycling performance.

When choosing strength-training exercises, keep the specificity principle in mind. The muscle action, the muscles engaged, and the movement pattern should be somewhat similar to the action on the bike. Specificity is advocated partly because of adaptations in the neural system (like optimal activation of the involved muscles) and partly because of structural adaptations (like optimizing the number of active cross-bridges in the particular range of motion). The force developed during maximal contractions with both legs is generally smaller than the sum of the forces developed separately by the two legs. Because cyclists use each leg alternately when cycling, single-legged exercises should be chosen when practical. The major contribution to the power output during cycling is achieved from concentric muscle action during the pedaling downstroke. Peak force during pedaling occurs when the crank arm reaches an angle of approximately 90 degrees, which is usually equal to a knee angle of approximately 100 degrees. Therefore, a general rule is to focus on strength-training exercises that include a knee angle between 90 degrees and almost full knee extension. That being said, the exercises should not be so difficult to perform that the mechanical loading and muscle mass involved is too low. Mechanical loading is an important stimulus for strength-training adaptations. For instance, what some call strength training on the bike, or power pedaling, which consists of cycling at a low cadence (40 revolutions per minute) with relatively high force, has no effect on either maximal force capacity of the legs or cycling performance (Kristoffersen et al. 2014).

The intended velocity rather than the actual velocity seems to determine the velocity-specific training response. Therefore, although the actual movement velocity may be quite low, a cyclist can increase RFD by focusing on performing the lift as quickly as possible. Therefore, cyclists should use maximal effort in the concentric, cycling-specific phase. They should perform the concentric phase as quickly as possible and the eccentric, noncycling specific phase more slowly (lasting around 2 or 3 seconds). A slow muscle action during the eccentric phase reduces the risk of injury and muscle damage.

Maximal strength should be built during the first phase of the preparatory period leading up to the competition season. Two strength-training sessions per week is normally enough to achieve a sufficient increase in strength during an 8- to 12-week period (Rønnestad, Hansen, and Raastad 2010a; Rønnestad et al. 2015; Sunde et al. 2010; Vikmoen et al. 2016). We have seen an increase in maximum strength of 23 to 26 percent after 10 to 12 weeks with a strength-training program designed as a daily undulating periodized program with progression in intensity, starting with 10-repetition maximum (10RM) and ending at 4RM. This program varies the training load from session to session and progresses toward heavier loads and fewer repetitions. Cyclists should perform between 10RM and 4RM and two or three sets with approximately 2 to 3 minutes of rest between sets. Before starting with heavy loads, cyclists must first develop a proper lifting technique with lower loads.

The repetition maximum approach makes it easy to control strength-training intensity and progression. For example, 10RM means to use the maximum weight that allows 10 repetitions. When strength increases, the resistance also increases to ensure a true RM target. Alternatively, strength training can be prescribed by using a number of repetitions at a certain percentage of 1RM.

Note that at the beginning of the strength-training period, cyclists commonly experience heavy and sore legs after strength-training sessions.

Therefore, they need to take it easy with endurance training during the first 2 to 3 weeks of strength training. A good approach is to start strength training rather quickly after the end of a competition season, when endurance training has lower priority.

Some exercises to choose from when designing a strength-training program are half squat, single-leg half squat, step-up, leg press with one foot at a time, single-legged hip flexion (imitating the pedaling upstroke), and toe raise (to ensure proper force transmission from the large thigh muscles into the pedal). Cyclists should perform 5 to 10 minutes of general warm-up followed by a specific warm-up with a gradual increase in loading of the strength-training exercises. The session should begin with the exercise that involves the largest muscle mass, often the most coordinative demanding exercise. Thereafter, cyclists should complete two or three more exercises that focus on the important muscles for the pedaling action. Strength-training sessions to increase cycling performance do not have to be time consuming; including the warm-up, a session can be completed in 45 minutes. Finally, cyclists should perform some core training for the back and abdominal muscles to prevent injury. Based on individual needs, other upper-body exercises can also be useful.

During the preparatory period, the focus should be on endurance training in some phases. In these phases, cyclists should try to maintain strength-training adaptations. This can be done by performing one heavy strength-training session every 7th to 10th day (Rønnestad, Hansen, Raastad 2010b; Rønnestad et al. 2015). To avoid detraining effects, high-intensity muscle actions and maximal mobilization should be performed in the concentric phase, but the repetition maximum principle does not need to be followed. For example, cyclists can perform two or three sets of five repetitions at a load that allows 8 to 10 RM. Table 31.1 presents a sample strength-training

Table 31.1 Sample Strength-Training Program

	PREPARATORY PERIOD						COMPETITION PERIOD
	Weeks 1–3		Weeks 4–6		Weeks 7–12		Weeks 13–25
	Session 1	Session 2	Session 1	Session 2	Session 1	Session 2	Session 1
Half squat	3 x 10RM	3 x 6RM	3 x 8RM	3 x 5RM	3 x 6RM	3 x 4RM	2 x 5 at 80 to 85% of 1RM
Single-leg leg press	3 x 10RM	3 x 6RM	3 x 8RM	3 x 5RM	3 x 6RM	3 x 4RM	2 x 5 at 80 to 85% of 1RM
Single-leg hip flexion	3 x 10RM	3 x 6RM	3 x 8RM	3 x 5RM	3 x 6RM	3 x 4RM	1 x 6RM
Ankle plantar flexion	3 x 10RM	3 x 6RM	3 x 8RM	3 x 5RM	3 x 6RM	3 x 4RM	1 x 6RM

For the single-leg leg press, single-leg hip flexion, and ankle plantar flexion, the repetitions given are for each side.

program that has been shown to improve muscle strength and cycling performance during the preparatory period and maintain initial strength gains into the competition period (Rønnestad et al. 2010b, 2015). Cyclists should perform strength maintenance training during the competition season, as stopping all strength training over the course of the competitive season may result in losing most of the strength-training adaptation.

Applying the Science

A large amount of endurance training reduces the normal muscle hypertrophy after heavy strength training. Nevertheless, strength gains and some muscle hypertrophy occur after 10 to 12 weeks of combined heavy strength training and endurance training. The overall finding in the scientific literature is that supplementing endurance training with heavy strength training seems to improve power output at the lactate threshold and cycling economy with no negative effect on $\dot{V}O_2$max. Because of those improvements, the added heavy strength training has a positive influence on both prolonged endurance performance and short-duration, high-power performance.

Potential mechanisms for improved endurance performance include postponed activation of less efficient type II muscle fibers, conversion of type IIX fibers into more fatigue resistant IIA fibers, and increased muscle mass and rate of force development.

Here are some practical recommendations:

- Use strength exercises that imitate the pedaling action.
- Focus on maximal mobilization in the concentric phase of the lift.
- To develop muscle strength, perform two strength sessions per week with multiple exercises for the lower body. Do three sets per exercise, rest 2 to 3 minutes between sets, and perform 10RM to 4RM.
- To maintain strength, perform one strength session per week with high intensity.
- Perform core training for the back and abdominal muscles to prevent injury.

CHAPTER 32

Respiratory Training

—A. William Sheel and Carli M. Peters

The physiological demands of cycling are substantive and involve highly coordinated interplay among the respiratory, cardiovascular, muscular, and metabolic systems. Most cycling events require a high fractional usage of maximal oxygen consumption ($\dot{V}O_2$max). As such, any improvement in the steps that transport oxygen from the atmosphere to the working muscles would likely serve to improve exercise performance. In fact, much of what is done during the course of a training period serves to improve oxygen delivery and utilization. For example, effective training will increase maximal cardiac output (i.e., oxygen delivery) and dramatically change the profile of skeletal muscle metabolism (i.e., oxygen utilization). In this chapter we are primarily concerned with the first step in oxygen transport, namely the respiratory system.

The respiratory system is responsible for the continuous flow of air in and out of the body and can be divided into three major parts: the airways, the lungs, and the respiratory muscles. The first two parts of the respiratory system, the airways and lungs, do not respond appreciably to training; no improvements are seen in lung volumes, lung function, or ability to transfer oxygen from the lungs to the blood after training. The respiratory muscles, however, do respond positively to training stimuli.

The purpose of this chapter is twofold. First, we provide a brief overview of the respiratory system and the physiological rationale for why specific training of the respiratory musculature could improve cycling performance. To further the discussion of specific respiratory muscle training and the effects on cycling performance, we first review the basic physiology of exercise with respect to the respiratory muscles. Second, we synthesize those studies that have sought to determine the effects of respiratory muscle training on cycling performance.

Muscles of Respiration

The movement of fresh air into the lungs occurs when the inspiratory muscles contract. The diaphragm (figure 32.1), a thin, dome-shaped muscle

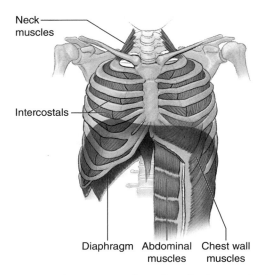

Neck muscles

Intercostals

Diaphragm Abdominal Chest wall
              muscles   muscles

▶ **Figure 32.1** Human respiratory muscles. The diaphragm is the most important muscle of inspiration, and the external intercostal and neck muscles serve as accessory inspiratory muscles. The main expiratory muscles, those of the abdominal wall, are assisted by the internal intercostal muscles.

that separates the abdominal and thoracic cavities, is the primary muscle of inspiration. Other inspiratory muscles include the external intercostals, the scalenes, and the sternocleidomastoid. Contraction of the inspiratory muscles leads to an increase in the volume of the thoracic cavity and induces airflow into the lungs. Unlike inspiration, which is always an active process, expiration is passive at rest. After actively expanding during inspiration, the lungs and chest wall tend to return to their equilibrium positions. Exercise and voluntary hyperventilation cause a shift from passive to active expiration. The expiratory muscles are recruited to remove air forcefully and return the lungs to their resting volume. The primary muscles of expiration are the abdominal muscles, including the rectus abdominis, internal and external oblique muscles, and the transverse abdominis. Contraction of the abdominal muscles increases the pressure in the abdomen and causes the diaphragm to be pushed upward, thereby moving air out of the lungs.

Breathing During Exercise

A proportional relationship exists between metabolic rate and minute ventilation ($\dot{V}E$). With the onset of exercise, $\dot{V}E$ increases immediately and increases further as intensity progresses. The rise in ventilation during low levels of exercise intensity occurs because of increases in both the frequency of breathing (b) and tidal volume (VT). With more strenuous exercise, VT expands into both inspiratory and expiratory reserve volumes with little or no further increase in b. With heavy exercise, after VT reaches approximately 50 to 60 percent of vital capacity (i.e., the maximal amount of air that can be expelled), a plateau occurs in VT and any further increases in $\dot{V}E$ are accomplished by increases in b. The additional rise in ventilation caused by increases in b is commonly referred to as the tachypneic breathing pattern of heavy exercise. Increases in b are achieved by reductions in both inspiratory and expiratory time.

Minute ventilation ranges from 6 to 8 liters per minute in healthy people at rest and reaches values of 120 to 130 liters per minute in untrained people during heavy exercise. Well-trained endurance athletes are capable of minute ventilations exceeding 200 liters per minute. Exercise-induced alterations in breathing pattern are not without cost, however. At rest, breathing accounts for approximately 2 percent of the body's total $\dot{V}O_2$. This cost increases to 3 to 5 percent of total $\dot{V}O_2$ as breathing becomes deeper and more rapid during moderate-intensity exercise. During heavy exercise, the circulatory and metabolic costs of hyperventilation can account for 10 percent of total $\dot{V}O_2$ in untrained people and up to 15 percent in trained people (Aaron et al. 1992). As such, the working muscles of respiration require a significant portion of the total oxygen consumed and a high fraction of blood pumped by the heart (i.e., cardiac output). What controls exercise hyperpnea and breathing patterns is beyond the scope of this chapter and is related to myriad feedforward and feedback mechanisms (see Sheel and Romer 2012 for a review). But the ventilatory pattern adopted during exercise is generally believed to be governed by the so-called principle of minimal effort.

Effect of Cycling Posture and Exercise Mode on Breathing Mechanics

The ventilatory pattern adopted during exercise depends on several factors including body position and exercise modality. Cyclists commonly use three main postures: upright or brake hoods, leaning forward onto drop handlebars, and crouched forward over aerobars (i.e., time-trial position). When cyclists lean forward onto drop handlebars or over aerobars, they reduce the volume of their abdomens. Large organs of the abdominal compartment are immediately below the diaphragm and act as a noncompressible mass that must be moved each time the cyclist breathes in. A reduction in abdominal volume may thus hinder the movement of the diaphragm and increase inspiratory muscle work. Because of the possibility of altered breathing mechanics in the aerobar position, the ventilatory responses may be different relative to upright cycling. But when male cyclists performed upright and aerobar cycle ergometer exercise, no differences in $\dot{V}O_2$max, $\dot{V}E$, $\dot{V}T$, or b were observed (Origenes, Blank, and Schoene 1993). This finding suggests that energy expenditure and ventilatory mechanics are unchanged when the cyclist is in the aerobar position. But that study was conducted indoors and did not consider the need to overcome wind resistance. In an outdoor field study of trained cyclists who maintained a speed of 30 kilometers per hour in either brake hood, dropbar, or aerobar cycling postures when exposed to wind resistance, whole-body $\dot{V}O_2$, $\dot{V}E$, and heart rate were found to be significantly lower in the aerobar position relative to the brake hood position (Sheel et al. 1996). The results of these studies suggest that the aerobar posture does not limit breathing mechanics and is the most energetically efficient cycling position.

The type of exercise performed influences breathing mechanics. Both treadmill running and cycle ergometry are common exercise modalities undertaken in laboratory settings to study ventilatory patterns and evaluate respiratory muscle training. For example, what are the breathing patterns when the same subjects perform incremental cycling or treadmill running to the point of voluntary exhaustion? At comparable levels of ventilation, a higher $\dot{V}T$ and a larger portion of the ventilatory capacity appear to be used during cycling compared with running (Elliott and Grace 2010). In addition, ventilatory efficiency (the relationship between $\dot{V}E$ and CO_2 production: $\dot{V}E / \dot{V}CO_2$) is greater during cycling. More recently, others have reported differences in the respiratory response to cycling versus treadmill running; ventilatory efficiency, arterial oxygen saturation, and operational lung volumes were all greater during cycling (Tanner, Duke, and Stager 2014). Collectively, these studies highlight the importance of considering exercise mode when studying breathing mechanics and demonstrate the uniqueness of breathing during cycling.

Respiratory Muscle Fatigue

Because contraction of the diaphragm is required throughout life, the muscle was long believed to be highly resistant to fatigue. In the 1980s, however, fatigue of the diaphragm was reported after strenuous cycling exercise among other endurance activities. Fatigue of the diaphragm is intensity dependent and appears to occur only at intensities greater than 80 to 85 percent of $\dot{V}O_2$max (Johnson et al. 1993). Expiratory muscle fatigue has received less attention, but these muscles are also susceptible to exercise-induced fatigue (Taylor and Romer 2008).

Does fatigue of the respiratory musculature have an effect on cycling performance? This question has been addressed in laboratory-based studies. Harms et al. (2000) hypothesized that if respiratory muscle fatigue can negatively influence cycling performance, then unloading the muscles of respiration should result in longer endurance time and "loading" the respiratory muscles should cause reduced endurance time. Trained cyclists cycled at 90 percent of $\dot{V}O_2$max to the point of exhaustion under three different conditions: control, breathing with an increased resistive load, and respiratory musculature unloaded with a ventilator. Unloading the respiratory muscles increased endurance time by 14 percent, whereas loading the respiratory muscles reduced endurance time by 15 percent. Loading and unloading of the respiratory muscles also influenced the cyclists' perceived effort when the perception of limb and breathing discomfort was increased during loading trials and decreased during unloading. The link between respiratory muscle work and endurance exercise performance lies in a reflex effect from fatiguing respiratory muscles, which increases sympathetic vasoconstrictor outflow and reduces limb blood flow during prolonged exercise (Dempsey et al. 2006). When respiratory muscles are subjected to a high amount of work and begin to fatigue, by-products of metabolism accumulate within the muscle. This increase in local metabolite concentration stimulates nerves traveling from the muscle to the brain, leading to a decrease in limb blood flow and oxygen transport to locomotor muscles. The reduced blood flow and available oxygen is associated with significant fatigue of the quadriceps muscle and decrements in exercise performance. Presumably, sensory

The Side-Stitch Phenomenon

Most athletes, including cyclists, are familiar with the side-stitch. A side-stitch is a transient, exercise-induced increase in abdominal pain. This pain can occur in any region of the abdomen but is most common in the lateral portion of the midabdomen just under the ribcage (Morton and Callister 2000). Severe side-stiches are often described as stabbing or sharp pains, whereas less intense stiches are described as an aching, pulling, or cramping sensation.

Factors potentially influencing side-stitch, including age, gender, body mass index (BMI), training status, and sporting activity, were investigated in a large study of 965 regular sporting participants (Morton and Callister 2002). Participants from six different sporting events—running, swimming, cycling, aerobics, basketball, and horse riding—were surveyed for the study. Based on survey findings, the researchers concluded that the prevalence and severity of side-stitch was not related to training status, gender, or BMI. They also found that younger respondents were more likely than older subjects to report stitches. Controlling for all other factors, side-stitch was 10.5 times more common in running than in cycling (Morton and Callister 2002).

Currently, the cause or causes of side-stitch remain speculative. Several strategies have been suggested to prevent stitches or relieve them when they are present. These strategies include not consuming large volumes of food and drink for 2 hours before exercise to avoid pain and trying to breathe deeply, push on the affected area, and stretch the affected side if a stitch develops. Without a definitive cause of the abdominal pain, however, these management techniques remain conjecture. Fortunately for cyclists, side-stiches are far less common than they are in other sporting events.

feedback from blood-deficient fatiguing leg and respiratory muscles to the higher central nervous system would occur and cause the athlete to slow his or her pace (Amann et al. 2008).

Training the Muscles of Respiration

To this point, we have provided a brief summary of the demands placed on the respiratory muscles during exercise. The question relevant to this chapter is this: Does specific respiratory muscle training improve cycling performance and, if so, how? Most respiratory muscle training studies have been designed with the goal of improving respiratory muscle strength or endurance. One method to improve respiratory muscle strength is inspiratory pressure threshold loading using a commercially available handheld device. Athletes breathe through the device with a one-way valve that can be loaded during inspiration to a variable degree to achieve the desired inspiratory pressure. The one-way valve opens during expiration so that no load is imposed during the expiratory phase of respiration. These devices can also generally be used for expiratory muscle training. Also available are flow-resistive devices that increase the inspiratory load by using holes of different diameters. The expiratory side of the circuit is also unloaded.

A number of studies have used voluntary hyperventilation in which subjects maintain a target level of ventilation for more than 40 minutes to improve respiratory muscle endurance. A rebreathing circuit or additional carbon dioxide must be added to prevent a significant loss of carbon dioxide. The most commonly used method to improve respiratory muscle strength is inspiratory pressure threshold loading. Recent studies that have used pressure threshold loading have typically been of good quality by using suitable research design (i.e., including a control, or sham, group) and measuring cycling-related performance outcomes in athletes rather than healthy but untrained subjects. Other well-controlled studies, however, have used voluntary hyperpnea. We have limited our treatment of the topic to those studies that have used appropriate control groups and have incorporated a measure of cycling performance.

How Can the Muscles of Respiration be Trained?

With whole-body exercise training such as cycling, skeletal muscles undergo many adaptations including structural, enzymatic, neural, and functional (strength and endurance). The muscles of respiration, as with all skeletal muscles, can show improvements with application of an appropriate stimulus. The general principles of exercise training can be applied to respiratory muscle training and include individuality, specificity, reversibility, progressive overload, and periodization (Romer and McConnell 2003). Published protocols to elicit favorable changes to the respiratory muscles vary widely, and there is no clear consensus on best practices. Many studies, however, use a variation of a protocol that includes inspiring at 50 percent of maximal inspiratory pressure for 30 breaths twice daily for a period of 5 to 12 weeks. As the inspiratory muscles adapt to the training stimulus, the target pressure must be increased to maintain an overload stimulus. These types of training regimes have consistently been shown to yield improvements in maximal inspiratory pressure (i.e., a global index of respiratory muscle strength) in the range of 8 to 45 percent. Studies that have used the highest percentage of maximal inspiratory pressure during training and have had the longest duration of training tend to report the highest change in maximal inspiratory pressure. Although we might be tempted to speculate that the respiratory muscles, like other muscles, respond in a dose–response fashion to a given training stimulus, the available data are too few to make such a conclusion. Respiratory muscle endurance training can also elicit significant improvements. For example, 20 training sessions (30 minutes per session) over 4 or 5 weeks has been shown to improve respiratory muscle endurance significantly (Verges et al. 2007).

Does Training the Muscles of Respiration Improve Cycling Performance?

Contradictory findings were found in early studies because of inadequate research designs and inappropriate outcome measures. A number of more contemporary studies that have used controlled experimental designs have shown that inspiratory muscle training can improve endurance performance. The collective results of this body of work have been summarized in two recent meta-analyses (HajGhanbari et al. 2013; Illi et al. 2012). The changes in performance induced by respiratory muscle training have been varied and relate, in part, to the type of performance measure used. Several studies have used incremental tests and found no change because of respiratory muscle training. This result is perhaps not surprising given that the diaphragm does not fatigue during these types of tests. Other studies that have used constant load or time trials, which are more relevant to cyclists, have reported improvements. Because we cannot summarize all studies, we provide an example of a well-conducted study to show the effects of respiratory muscle training on cycling.

Romer, McConnell, and Jones (2002a) used a rigorous experimental design, which included random assignment to either a training or a placebo group. Pressure threshold respiratory muscle training was performed for 6 weeks, and adherence to the training program was closely monitored. Following training, cycling performance was improved in simulated 20K (3.8 plus or minus 1.7 percent) and 40K (4.6 plus or minus 1.9 percent) cycling time trials. These improvements can be considered a worthwhile change and are of practical importance for cyclists. Important features of this study were that no effect was observed in the control (sham training) group and that competitive cyclists were used as subjects. These considerations add confidence in the observed improvements in cycling performance. Controlled trials of respiratory muscle endurance training show larger improvements in exercise tolerance during constant-load exercise tasks, which is a function of task specificity.

Endurance training of the respiratory muscles has been shown to have variable effects on cycling performance. Verges et al. (2007) had moderately trained subjects perform constant-load cycling (85 percent maximal power output) to exhaustion before and after 4 to 5 weeks of respiratory muscle endurance training or sham training. Cycling performance was improved in only those subjects who exhibited fatigue of the diaphragm before the training regime. This result suggests that endurance training may be of benefit for some subjects and not others. Further study is required to assess the effects of endurance training of the respiratory muscles and cycling performance and those factors that contribute to the absence, or presence, of a training effect.

Why Does Training the Muscles of Respiration Improve Cycling Performance?

The mechanisms for the effect of respiratory muscle training on exercise performance have been shown to be unrelated to increases in $\dot{V}O_2$max or maximal lactate steady state. Instead, the ergogenic effect could be because of a lessening of respiratory muscle fatigue (Romer, McConnell, and Jones 2002b) or limb muscle fatigue (McConnell and Lomax 2006), perhaps by increasing the threshold for activation of the respiratory muscle metaboreflex (Witt et al. 2007).

The physiological hypothesis can be summarized as follows. Respiratory muscle training would increase the strength or endurance performance of the inspiratory and expiratory muscles. Moreover, they would be more fatigue resistant during strenuous exercise. The musculature might possibly become more metabolically efficient and require a smaller portion of cardiac output during exercise or accumulate metabolites less readily. Equally possible is that the ergogenic effect of respiratory muscle training is related to the perceptual benefit obtained by relieving the discomfort associated with high levels of respiratory muscle work (McConnell and Romer 2004). Possible mechanisms of how respiratory muscle training may improve performance are shown in figure 32.2. In sum, attenuation of the metaboreflex and decreases in the ratings of perceived breathlessness and exertion are proposed mechanisms to explain how specific training of the respiratory muscles can lead to performance improvements. Although this rationale is appealing, further well-designed studies are required to study the mechanistic basis of respiratory muscle training.

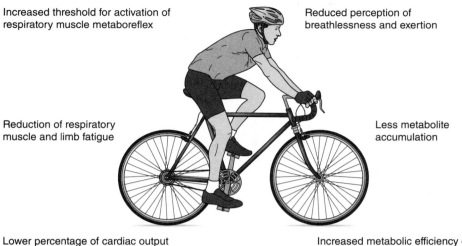

Increased threshold for activation of
respiratory muscle metaboreflex

Reduced perception of
breathlessness and exertion

Reduction of respiratory
muscle and limb fatigue

Less metabolite
accumulation

Lower percentage of cardiac output
required by respiratory muscles

Increased metabolic efficiency of
respiratory muscles

▶ **Figure 32.2** Overview of mechanisms proposed to explain performance benefits resulting from respiratory muscle training.

Applying the Science

In this chapter we discussed the muscles of respiration, breathing patterns adopted during exercise, and cycling-specific breathing mechanics. We also highlighted the fact that respiratory muscles fatigue in response to high-intensity exercise and that this fatigue adversely affects performance. The fact that the respiratory muscles fatigue leads athletes and physiologists alike to ask what would happen if respiratory muscles could be trained not to fatigue. Specific respiratory muscle training has been investigated for years as a means to surpass the plateau that cyclists reach with traditional training. Incorporating specific training of the respiratory muscles into a well-developed overall training plan has been shown to improve cycling performance. We emphasize, however, that the performance gains are likely to be relatively small in relation to the gains obtained in other systems (i.e., heart, circulatory, metabolic, neural, psychological) as a result of yearly and systematic training. Said differently, training the respiratory muscles is not a substitute for the more traditional approaches to cycle training. The causal factors of why respiratory muscle training improves performance require additional study, and the possibility of a placebo effect needs to be appropriately addressed. Despite the mentioned caveats, given the miniscule range of performance times among elite cyclists, respiratory muscle training may be a worthwhile addition to traditional cycle training.

CHAPTER 33

Warming Up

—José M. Muyor

In sport, a warm-up protocol is a set of measures carried out before per-forming a physical sport activity for training or competition. The goal is to create an optimal state of preparation from a physical, psychological, coordinative, and kinesthetic point of view to improve athletic performance and prevent injuries (Hedrick 1992).

Traditionally, the warm-up protocol has been associated with a series of metabolic, physical, and psychological effects, and positive consequences have also been observed regarding injury prevention (table 33.1).

Often, a warm-up protocol is based more on practical training and compe-tition experience than on scientific evidence. Normally, the typical warm-up protocol is based on a brief period of low-intensity aerobic exercises followed by joint movement exercises, stretching, and specific (low-intensity) sport exercises (Safran, Seaber, and Garrett 1989).

As the name indicates, many of the effects of warming up have been associ-ated with mechanisms related to a change in body temperature (Bishop and Maxwell 2009; Faulkner et al. 2013; Lee et al. 2015; Levels et al. 2013; Racinais, Blonc, and Hue 2005). Several studies have also reported that a warm-up protocol produces metabolic and physiological changes in athletes, preparing them for the principal sport activity they will perform (Burnley et al. 2001; Burnley, Doust, and Jones 2002; Burnley et al. 2000; Gray and Nimmo 2001; Gray, Devito, and Nimmo 2002; Wittekind et al. 2012).

In theory, these changes in body temperature and the metabolic or physi-ological state will benefit athletic performance because of the postponement of fatigue or the increased energy efficiency (aerobic–anaerobic) used during the exercise. Fradkin, Zazryn, and Smoliga (2010) conducted a systematic review and meta-analysis on this subject and found that warming up improved physical performance in 79 percent of the criteria examined, and only a few studies have observed that warming up reduced performance.

Normally, a reduction in performance results from inadequate warm-up intensity or duration (Tomaras and MacIntosh 2011). Excessive intensity in the warm-up limits the energy available for performing the physical activity (Wittekind et al. 2012). In contrast, adequate intensity of the warm-up

Table 33.1 Effects Attributed to a Warm-Up Protocol on Physiological, Physical, and Psychological Variables and Injury Prevention

	SYSTEMS			
	Metabolic	**Muscle and tendon**	**Cardiovascular**	**Respiratory**
Physiological reactions	Increase in body temperature and baseline oxygen consumption ($\dot{V}O_2$) Improvement in oxygen delivery Activation of the sympathetic system	Decrease in tissue irritation Improvement in elasticity and joint movement	Increase in systolic volume Activation of circulatory system Opening of blood capillaries	Increase in pulmonary ventilation (frequency and depth of respiration)
Physical responses	Improvement in intra- and intermuscular and body segment coordination Adaptation to specific athletic movements and actions			
Psychological responses	Creation of a state of optimal stimulation Improvement of concentration during the principal task			
Injury prevention	Increase in the extensibility of musculature and joint flexibility Greater reactive capacity with increased concentration on the task			

improves athletic performance because of a reduction of the anaerobic glycolytic metabolism and an increase in the aerobic metabolism, potentially induced by greater oxygen consumption ($\dot{V}O_2$) kinetics, which postpones fatigue.

With regard to the duration of the warm-up protocol, Tomaras and MacIntosh (2011) found that a moderate-intensity 17-minute warm-up (without exceeding 70 percent of the maximum heart rate [HR_{max}]) led to better performance in the Wingate test than a 51.5-minute warm-up that reached intensities of up to 95 percent of the HR_{max}. The Wingate test is an anaerobic test performed on a cycle ergometer. The subject cycles for 30 seconds to maximal velocity against a determined resistance. This test may be the most popular way to assess peak anaerobic power, anaerobic fatigue, and total anaerobic capacity. The optimal combination of intensity, duration, and types of exercise performed during the warm-up, as well as the duration of rest before the athletic event, will determine the maximum performance obtained (Jones, Koppo, and Burnley 2003).

Recently, Christensen and Bangsbo (2015) observed that a moderate-intensity warm-up protocol produced significant improvements in the performance of a maximal 4-minute test in highly trained cyclists. But a high-intensity warm-up protocol with a short recovery period (6 minutes) reduced performance. Although incorporating a longer break (20 minutes) improved performance in the last minute of the test, the high-intensity warm-up did not present an improvement in performance relative to a moderate-intensity warm-up.

The warm-up protocol is usually based on two distinct techniques: passive warm-up and active warm-up. Passive warm-up tries to increase body temperature using various systems or external devices (for example, hot showers or baths, electric blankets, saunas). Although passive warm-up increases muscle temperature, it does not affect the oxygen consumption response (Burnley, Doust, and Jones 2002).

Active warm-up tries to increase body temperature by moving the most muscle groups possible, induces a greater metabolic and muscular change than passive warm-up (Bishop 2003), increases the contraction speed of muscle fibers and the muscular potential generated (Stewart, Macaluso, and De Vito 2003), and reduces postexercise muscular pain (Olsen et al. 2012).

After the cyclist has reached adequate muscle temperature through the warm-up protocol, the time lapse between this phase and the principal activity must be short to avoid losing body temperature, which will result in a reduction in performance. In this regard, Faulkner et al. (2013) found that using a system of passive heating pads on the legs attenuated the reduction of body temperature in the time between the warm-up and the principal exercise and improved sprint performance in cyclists.

Each sport has its own peculiarities and unique characteristics. Therefore, one type of warm-up can be useful in one sport discipline but not in others (Fradkin, Zazryn, and Smoliga 2010). Even in the same sport, such as cycling, different modalities exist, such as road racing, time trials, track cycling, mountain biking, downhill biking, and BMX. Each type of warm-up has its own duration, intensity, and regulation characteristics.

Various studies have investigated the effects of warming up on different cycling tests. This chapter attempts to highlight the most relevant studies that have investigated the effects of warming up on different variables in cycling, in addition to highlighting the warm-up protocols used (table 33.2).

Metabolic and Performance Effects

Passfield and Doust (2000) observed that carrying out a 6-minute moderate-intensity warm-up (60 percent of peak oxygen consumption [$\dot{V}O_2peak$]) produced a significant increase in $\dot{V}O_2$ and a reduction in the respiratory exchange ratio and the blood lactate level during a 60-minute exercise performed at the same intensity as the warm-up. This warm-up, however, did not produce an improvement in performance during a maximal 5-minute exercise. Moreover, the authors observed that a 10-minute warm-up (60 percent of $\dot{V}O_2peak$; 100 rpm) that ended with a 30-second sprint caused a significant increase in $\dot{V}O_2$ and a decrease in the respiratory exchange ratio and blood lactate level during a 60-minute exercise (60 percent of $\dot{V}O_2peak$). However, this reduced the power generated (in watts) during the 30-second sprint, possibly because of the fatigue produced during the exercise.

Gray and Nimmo (2001) reported that although the increase in body temperature through active warm-up influenced the metabolic responses during exercise, an increase in muscular temperature alone was not sufficient for athletic performance improvement in a high-intensity, short-duration cycling exercise. Afterward, Gray, Devito, and Nimmo (2002) observed that an active warm-up protocol produced a reduction in the accumulation of lactate in

Table 33.2 Principal Studies That Analyzed the Effects of Various Warm-Up Protocols on Different Cycling Exercises

Study	Subjects	Warm up protocol	Main exercise
Atkinson et al. 2005	8 male cyclists	Experimental warm-up 1: 5 min cycling (preferred intensity and cadence) followed by 5 min rest before performance trial	16.1 km cycling time trial at 7:30 h and 17:30 h
		Experimental warm-up 2: 25 min cycling (60% of PO_{max}; preferred cadence) followed by 5 min rest before performance trial	
Bishop and Maxwell 2009	8 trained males	No warm-up: Subjects sat on bike for 10 min.	36 min cycling of intermittent sprint exercise
		Experimental warm-up 1: 5 min cycling (50% of $\dot{V}O_2max$) + 2 x (30 sec [70% of $\dot{V}O_2max$] + 30 sec passive rest) + 2 x (4 sec all-out sprint with 2 min cycling [35% of $\dot{V}O_2max$] after each sprint)	
		Experimental warm-up 2: 10 min cycling (50% of $\dot{V}O_2max$) + 2 x (30 sec [70% of $\dot{V}O_2max$] + 30 sec passive rest) + 2 x (4 sec all-out sprint with 2 min cycling [35% of $\dot{V}O_2max$] after each sprint)	
Burnley, Doust, and Jones 2005	12 well-trained cyclists	Experimental warm-up 1: 6 min bouts of heavy exercise followed by 10 min rest before performance trial	7 min cycling performance trial
		Experimental warm-up 2: moderate exercise performed for 10 to 12 min to complete the same amount of external work as done during heavy exercise followed by 10 min rest before performance trial	
		Experimental warm-up 3: 30 sec all-out sprint followed by 10 min rest before performance trial	
Christensen and Bangsbo 2015	28 trained male cyclists	Warm-up: 20 min cycling (50% of iPPO) followed by 6 min recovery before maximal performance test	4 min performance test mimicking 400 m individual pursuit in track cycling
		Progressive high-intensity warm-up (HI6): 3 min cycling (25% of iPPO) + 3 min cycling (55% of iPPO) + 1 min active recovery (10% of iPPO) + 2 min cycling (75% of iPPO) + 1 min active recovery (10% of iPPO) + 1 min cycling (100% of iPPO) + 2 x (2 min and 40 sec cycling [10% of iPPO] + 20 sec sprint [~160% of iPPO]) + 3 min cycling (10% of iPPO) followed by 6 min recovery before performance test	
		Progressive high-intensity warm-up (HI20): Same as HI6 but last sprint was followed with 20 min recovery before performance test.	
Dos-Santos et al. 2014	9 untrained males	Control protocol: no warm-up; rest for 3 min	Incremental cycle ergometer test
		Warm-up protocol: 3 min cycling (70 W; 60 rpm)	
		Ballistic stretch protocol: 6 sets of 30 sec ballistic stretching (stretched abdominals, lower back, hamstrings, gluteals, hip adductors, quadriceps femoris, gastrocnemius, and soleus)	
Faulkner et al. 2013	11 male competitive cyclists and triathletes	Standardized warm-up: 5 min (100 W) + 5 x 10 sec maximal sprints with 1 min, 50 sec cycling at 75 W (85 rpm) after each sprint	30 sec maximal sprint test
Faulkner et al. 2015	10 endurance-trained competitive male cyclists and triathletes	Standardized 9 min warm-up: 3 min at 150 W + 3 min at 200 W + 3 min at 250 W	1 h cycling at 75% of W_{max}
Gray and Nimmo 2001	8 healthy males	Active warm-up: 5 min cycling (40% of PO_{max}; 60 rpm) + 1 min rest + 4 x (15 sec sprints [120% of PO_{max}; 120 rpm]) with 15 sec rest after each sprint	30 sec maximal cycling sprint test
		Passive warm-up: Subjects sit quietly in environmental chamber maintained at constant temperature (45 °C) and relative humidity (70%) until musculature temperature reaches same value achieved during active warm-up.	
		Control trial: Subjects remain on examination couch in lab for same time spent in active warm-up.	

(continued)

Table 33.2 *(continued)*

Study	Subjects	Warm up protocol	Main exercise
Gray, Devito, and Nimmo 2002	6 female subjects	Experimental trial (active warm-up): 5 min cycling (40% of PO_{max} ; 60 rpm) + 1 min rest + 4 x (15 sec sprints [120% of PO_{max}; 120 rpm]) with 15 sec rest after each sprint	30 sec maximal cycling sprint test
		Control trial: Subjects' legs passively heated (electric heat blanket) to temperature induced by active warm-up	
Hajoglou et al. 2005	8 well-trained cyclists	No warm-up: Subjects sat on ergometer for 6 min and then began performance trial.	3K cycling time trial
		Easy warm-up: 5 min at a PO of 70% of VT + 5 min at a PO of 80% of VT + 5 min at a PO of 90% of VT followed by 2 min rest before performance trial	
		Hard warm-up: 5 min at a PO of 70% of VT + 5 min at a PO of 80% of VT + 5 min at a PO of 90% of VT + 6 min at the intensity of RCT followed by 6 min rest before performance trial	
Johnson et al. 2014	10 trained competitive road cyclists	No warm-up: Subjects sat at rest for 19 min.	10K cycling time trial
		Experimental warm-up 1: 5 min cycling (70% of gas exchange threshold) + 5 min cycling (80% of gas exchange threshold) + 5 min cycling (90% of gas exchange threshold) followed by 2 min rest before time trial	
Levels et al. 2013	10 male recreational cyclists	Active warm-up (WARM-UP): 10 min cycling (moderate power of 2 W/kg BM)	15K cycling time trial in the heat
		Scalp cooling + active warm up (SC + WARM UP): 10 min cycling (moderate power of 2 W/kg BM) while wearing a neoprene-covered silicone cooling cap connected to a cooling machine (–9 °C to –10 °C) for 30 min	
		Precooling trial with ice-slurry ingestion (ICE): Subjects ingested 2 g/kg BM ice slurry within 5 min, syrup (containing ~6 g of carbohydrate).	
		Scalp cooling + ice-slurry ingestion (SC + ICE)	
Passfield and Doust 2000	10 male competitive cyclists	Experimental warm-up 1: 6 min cycling (60% of $\dot{V}O_2max$; preferred cadence)	5 min cycling performance test
		Experimental warm-up 2: 10 min cycling (60% of $\dot{V}O_2max$; 95 rpm)	30 sec maximal cycling sprint test
Racinais, Blonc, and Hue 2005	8 male physical education students	Experimental warm-up: 12 min cycling (50% of $\dot{V}O_2max$) with brief 5 sec accelerations at 4, 7, and 10 min followed by 6 min rest before performance trial	7 sec maximal sprint test
Teles et al. 2015	10 recreationally trained men	Experimental warm-up: 5 min cycling (60% of HR_{max}) + 5 min cycling (65% of HR_{max}) + 5 min cycling (70% of HR_{max}) + progressive acceleration to 35 km/h during 30 sec + 6 sec sprint followed by 1.24 min active recovery	30 sec Wingate test
		LED irradiation warm-up (LED): Application performed through direct skin contact at angle of 90°; plate kept stationary for 23 sec in each area. The areas were irradiated separately in following order: right triceps surae, left triceps surae, right hamstring, left hamstring, right gluteus, left gluteus, right quadriceps, left quadriceps.	
		Whole-body vibration warm-up (WBV): Subjects performed a squat exercise (knee flexion of 10° to 90°) for 6 sec each repetition during 5 min.	
		LED + WBV warm-up: All parameters used in the LED and vibration treatments were the same. Subjects were subjected to vibration followed by LED application, and the time taken for the application of the two techniques combined was approximately 10 min.	
		No warm-up: All procedures were the same as those used in the other experimental conditions, but after the 15 min rest period, subjects remained at rest in the supine position for an additional 10 min.	

Study	Subjects	Warm up protocol	Main exercise
Tomaras and MacIntosh (2011)	10 highly trained male track cyclists	Traditional warm-up: 18 min cycling from 60% to 80% of self-reported HR_{max} + 2 min acceleration from 80% to 95% of HR_{max} + 4 x (6 sec sprint with 1.5 min active recovery) followed by 6.5 min rest period, seated on a chair	30 sec Wingate test
		Experimental warm-up: 15.5 min cycling from 60% to 80% of self-reported HR_{max} + 2 min acceleration progressively to 35 km/h + 6 sec sprint, followed by 24 min active recovery	
Wittekind and Beneke 2011	11 trained male cyclists	Easy warm-up: 6 min cycling (40% of PAP)	1 min sprint cycling test
		Moderate warm-up: 5 min cycling (40% of PAP) + 1 min cycling (80% of PAP)	
		Hard warm-up: 5 min cycling (40% of PAP) + 1 min cycling (110% of PAP)	
Wittekind et al. 2012	8 trained male cyclists or triathletes	Easy warm-up: 6 min cycling (40% of PAP) at 60 rpm	30 sec sprint cycling test
		Moderate warm-up: 5 min cycling (40% of PAP) + 1 min cycling (80% of PAP) at 80 rpm	
		Hard warm-up: 5 min cycling (40% of PAP) + 1 min cycling (110% of PAP) at 80 rpm	

BM = body mass

HR_{max} = maximal heart rate

iPPO = incremental test peak power output

MIP = maximal inspiratory pressure

PAP = peak aerobic power

PO = power output (W)

PO_{max} = maximal power output (W)

RCT = respiratory compensatory threshold

rpm = revolutions (number of pedaling) per minute

$\dot{V}O_{2max}$ = maximal oxygen consumption

VT = ventilatory threshold

W_{max} = maximal power output

the blood and muscles because of an accumulation of acetylcarnitine before the exercise, which increased athletic performance. These authors indicated that further studies in this area are necessary.

Atkinson et al. (2005) analyzed the effect of a warm-up protocol on the performance of a 16.1-kilometer cycling activity as a function of the time of day (7:30 hours versus 17:30 hours). These authors concluded that although performing a 25-minute warm-up at 60 percent of the peak power output (PPO) produced a small but statistically significant improvement in performance in the 16.1-kilometer activity, this protocol did not improve the performance during the morning compared with the afternoon. Moreover, the time of day had a greater effect on the results obtained in the study than did performing a 5-minute or 25-minute warm-up at 60 percent of PPO.

In addition, with regard to the time of day that an exercise was performed, Racinais, Blonc, and Hue (2005) observed that performing an active warm-up protocol increased muscle temperature and muscular power in a 7-second cycling split. The authors also found that the increase in muscle temperature did not cause an increase in force; instead, the time of day influenced the muscular performance of the exercise.

Burnley, Doust, and Jones (2005) determined the effects of various warm-up protocols on the output produced in a 7-minute cycling exercise. This study showed that moderate-intensity (without altering the baseline blood lactate) and high-intensity (that increased lactate to about 3 millimoles) warm-up were equally effective for performance improvement at extreme intensity in a sample of high-level cyclists. The authors associated the performance improvement with a moderate- or elevated-intensity warm-up that increased the range of the initial $\dot{V}O_2$.

Hajoglou et al. (2005) designed a study to determine whether

- a warm-up protocol would improve the performance of a 3-kilometer time-trial exercise in cycling;
- a more intense warm-up protocol would be more effective than a less intense warm-up protocol in this exercise; and
- a warm-up protocol would produce an acceleration in the $\dot{V}O_2$ kinetics while maintaining the anaerobic energy reserves.

Those authors found that the warm-up protocol produced a 2 to 3 percent improvement in performance, although they did not observe significant differences in the performance obtained by conducting a less intense warm-up compared with an elevated-intensity warm-up. The improvement in performance was more closely associated with the increase in aerobic metabolism than with the anaerobic energy reserve.

Wittekind and Beneke (2011) examined the effect of warm-up intensity on metabolism and performance in a 1-minute sprint. They detailed three types of warm-up protocols (table 33.2): an easy warm-up (WE), a moderate warm-up (WM), and a hard warm-up (WH). These authors found that the concentrations of blood lactate after warming up were 1.2 ± 0.3 millimoles per liter for the WE, 2.0 ± 0.3 millimoles per liter for the WM, and 4.2 ± 0.9 millimoles per liter for the WH ($p < 0.001$). They also observed, however, that during the 1-minute sprint, the WH reduced the production of lactate compared with the other warm-up protocols (WE, 11.6 ± 1.6; WM, 10.9 ± 1.9; and WH: 9.2 ± 1.4 millimoles per liter [$p < 0.05$]). In contrast, they found that in spite of the lower glycolytic level produced by the WH compared with the other warm-up protocols, the average power generated was not affected by the increase in oxygen in the WH group during the sprint. The authors therefore concluded that a high-intensity warm-up that induces a reduction in the range of glycolytic energy production does not negatively affect athletic performance, at least for a long-duration sprint (1 minute), because the intensity can be maintained due to the increase in oxygen consumption.

Subsequently, Wittekind et al. (2012) analyzed the effect of three types of warm-ups (moderate, elevated, and very intense) on the performance of a 30-second sprint. All the warm-up protocols had a duration of 6 minutes. These authors found that the average power and the peak power during the 30-second sprint test were reduced by 2.5 and 4.5 percent, respectively, after a very intense warm-up compared with a moderate-intensity warm-up. These authors concluded that although the muscular oxygenation did not seem to be altered by performing different warm-ups at distinct intensities, the very intense warm-up reduced the production of power, mostly because of the initial reduction of the production of anaerobic–glycolytic energy. Thus, the warm-up intensity and its effects on the production of glycolytic energy are important to consider for sprint performance (30 seconds), particularly when the duration of the sprint is too short for the aerobic metabolism. In this case, the metabolism cannot adequately compensate for the deficit in glycolytic energy production, which seems to be the case in the previous study that used 1-minute sprints (Wittekind and Beneke 2011).

As was observed in previous studies, different warm-up protocols aim to activate muscles, increase temperature, and adapt to different energetic systems. Another variable to consider, however, is the activation of the respiratory musculature, which participates in the ventilation processes of athletes. Johnson et al. (2014) examined the effects of an active warm-up with and without an added warm-up for the inspiratory musculature on a 10K time-trial cycling exercise. These authors observed that exercise performance was not improved by specifically warming up the inspiratory musculature. They concluded that an adequate active warm-up on the bicycle is sufficient to prepare the inspiratory muscles sufficiently for a cycling exercise of approximately 15 minutes.

Recently, Teles et al. (2015) confirmed that warming up is effective for the optimization of performance of a high-intensity, short-duration cycling exercise. In addition, they observed that a combined warm-up application of light-emitting diode irradiation with whole-body vibration or whole-body vibration alone was as effective as a traditional 17-minute warm-up protocol consisting of pedaling at increasing intensity.

Body Temperature

In resistance sports, such as cycling, athletic performance progressively lessens as the ambient temperature increases (Galloway and Maughan 1997), and this effect worsens when high temperatures are combined with high humidity (Maughan, Otani, and Watson 2012).

Bishop and Maxwell (2009) examined the effect of active warm-up protocols on thermoregulation and performance in an intermittent sprint with a total duration of 36 minutes, which was performed in high temperatures (35.5 ± 0.6 degrees Celsius; relative humidity, 48.7 ± 3.4 percent). These authors found that a long duration (20 minute) active warm-up increased rectal temperature but did not improve performance in intermittent sprint tests of less than 40 minutes. In these types of tests, body overheating must be reduced during training and competitions that are carried out in hot environments.

Recently, Lee et al. (2015) found that an increase in skin temperature from 24 degrees Celsius to approximately 34 degrees Celsius increases the core temperature, heart rate, cutaneous blood flow, and cardiac output. The ejection volume is reduced only when the core temperature is higher than 38 degrees Celsius; then, the heart beat increases such that the time for cardiac filling is reduced, thus reducing the ejection volume.

Levels et al. (2013) analyzed the effect of warming up and precooling on the rhythm developed in a 15K cycling time trial in a hot environment (30 degrees Celsius). They developed four protocols:

1. An active 10-minute warm-up (WARM-UP) pedaling at a moderate power of 2 watts per kilogram of body mass
2. Use of scalp cooling (SC) for 30 minutes at a temperature of −9 to −10 degrees Celsius plus 10 minutes of pedaling at a moderate power of 2 watts per kilogram of body mass (SC + WARM-UP)
3. Ingestion of 2 grams per kilogram of body weight of ice slurry (ICE) for 5 minutes
4. Use of SC for 30 minutes at a temperature of −9 to −10 degrees Celsius plus 10 minutes of pedaling at a moderate power of 2 watts per kilogram of body weight plus ingestion of 2 grams per kilogram of body weight of ice slurry (ICE) for 5 minutes (SC + ICE)

This study showed that the WARM-UP protocol produced a greater subjective perception of effort and generated lower power (in watts) than the SC + ICE protocol did. In addition, with the SC + ICE protocol, a lower body temperature (rectal and skin) and a revitalized sensation at the beginning of the time trial were observed, which produced greater benefit in the rhythm profile at the final stages of the activity. Overall, however, the different precooling strategies produced no effects on performance. According to the authors, this lack of effect was because of the limited duration of the exercise.

As mentioned throughout this chapter, one of the principal objectives of the warm-up is to increase body temperature to improve athletic performance. Although it seems paradoxical, the use of clothing (vests, shorts, and so on) during warm-ups to cool the body and avoid rewarming, which can cause a decrease in athletic performance, has recently increased. Faulkner et al. (2015) demonstrated that the use of clothing that cools the body with ice plates for 30 minutes, including the warm-up (which consisted of three phases of 3 minutes of pedaling at 150, 200, and 250 watts), significantly reduced skin temperature, producing greater pedaling power (in watts). Athletic performance improved significantly by 5.8 percent or 2.6 percent, in a 1-hour cycling exercise at 35 degrees Celsius and approximately 50 percent relative humidity, by the use of clothing that had been cooled through immersion in water and freezing, in comparison with using a vest cooled only by immersion in water.

Stretching

Although chapter 34 discusses stretching in depth, we note here that few studies have analyzed the use of stretching exercises in a cycling warm-up protocol. Dos-Santos et al. (2014) evaluated the effectiveness of different components of a warm-up session, such as performing a low-intensity aerobic warm-up or ballistic exercises before incremental and maximal cycling exercises. These authors found that the use of ballistic stretching warm-up exercises reduced the performance of the activity. In contrast to previous researchers, they did not observe a significant improvement in the performance obtained during incremental exercise after performing a 3-minute warm-up protocol by pedaling at 70 watts. The sample utilized in this study included nine untrained men, and the authors indicated that more studies on this subject were necessary.

Applying the Science

No consensus has emerged from the scientific literature regarding which warm-up protocol should be performed to optimize athletic performance. This lack of consensus is reflected in table 33.2, which lists a multitude of warm-up protocols with respect to the study objectives.

A consensus exists for the idea that warming up should focus on the characteristics of the activity that will be performed. A progressive warm-up that finishes at an elevated intensity can be beneficial when the exercise is maximal and the duration is sufficient for the aerobic system that will be used. But if the exercise is relatively short or if the rest period between the warm-up and the principal exercise is insufficient, such a warm-up could have a negative effect because of increased fatigue of the cyclist.

On the other hand, a warm-up carried out with the objective of increasing body temperature could be useful when the weather is cold. In contrast, if a cycling exercise is to be performed in a warm environment, the use of systems that cool the cyclist's body (ingestion of an ice slush or wearing cooling clothing) is recommended to avoid overheating, which can result in a loss in athletic performance.

In addition, warming up should be optimized and included in a long-term development process according to individual needs to produce optimum effects on athletic performance.

Before competitions, the training methods should not be modified in intensity and volume relative to the preparation methods. Any change in the warm-up protocol could result in a lack of adaptation and a consequent reduction in athletic performance.

Finally, only through personal experience and with the aid of the scientific literature can the type of warm-up that is most appropriate for an individual athlete be tested. This testing should be performed during athletic exercise or training by adapting the intensity and volume so that the athletic performance is optimized.

CHAPTER 34

Stretching

—José M. Muyor

Joint mobility is the quality that allows athletes to perform large-range movements by themselves or under the influence of external forces. Traditionally, stretching has been considered an important component of physical fitness and athletic performance. It is generally practiced as part of warm-up and cool-down to increase flexibility (joint mobility) and performance, prevent injury, and decrease postexercise muscle soreness (Ratamess 2012; Taylor et al. 1990), thereby accelerating recovery for further training or competition.

This chapter presents the main arguments for stretching in cycling, both pre- and postexercise. In addition, several methodological questions are raised regarding the proper and effective implementation of stretching after training or competition.

Stretching to Improve Performance and Prevent Injury

Although most athletes and coaches accept stretching as a means to improve performance and prevent sports injuries, studies regarding this issue offer conflicting conclusions (Andersen 2005; Ingraham 2003; McHugh and Cosgrave 2010). Ingraham (2003) reported that stretching performed to develop flexibility beyond the needs of specific sport movements can cause muscle injury and thus diminish athletic performance. After a systematic review of the literature on stretching, Andersen (2005) determined that the scientific evidence was insufficient to support the idea that stretching before exercise would reduce the risk of injury or lead to a decline in postexercise muscle soreness. McHugh and Cosgrave (2010) stated that stretching had an immediate and acute detrimental effect on performance and maximum force production. But these effects were less obvious in muscle strength tests and appeared to be absent when stretching was combined with low-intensity exercise in a warm-up protocol.

Focusing specifically on cycling, Wolfe et al. (2011) demonstrated that static stretching produced an acute effect during the first 25 minutes, increasing submaximal $\dot{V}O_2$ and thus decreasing pedaling efficiency. Similarly, Esposito, Cè, and Limonta (2012) found that static stretching produced an acute immediate effect with a 4 percent decrease in mechanical efficiency and a 26 percent decrease in the duration of the constant-intensity cycling test at 85 percent of $\dot{V}O_2$max. Behm et al. (2004) found that the use of static stretching to warm up produced an acute effect that adversely affected balance and reaction time. Other studies, such as the work by O'Connor, Crowe, and Spinks (2006), observed that the inclusion of static stretching exercises in the warm-up protocol increased anaerobic power compared with a warm-up protocol that did not include these stretching exercises.

Recently, Kingsley et al. (2013) examined the effects of static stretching and motor imagery on anaerobic performance in trained cyclists. Motor imagery was defined as the visualization of simple or complex motor activities in the absence of physical movement. These authors found that neither static stretching nor motor imagery negatively affected anaerobic performance in trained cyclists when the anaerobic test lasted less than 30 seconds.

Curry et al. (2009) compared the effects of three types of warm-up protocols (static stretching, dynamic stretching, and light aerobic exercise) on the range of motion and muscle strength in untrained women. These authors found no significant differences among the three protocols evaluated regarding range of motion or muscle strength, although they did find that dynamic stretching improves performance and muscle strength compared to static stretching.

As is apparent from the cited studies, the influence of stretching on athletic performance and the prevention of muscle injury is not yet clear. The methodological difficulty of designing a longitudinal study showing the long-term effects of stretching on these variables may be the reason that most of the studies published in the scientific literature have been designed to assess a particular effect in a specific context, generally the acute effect of stretching on muscle strength or on anaerobic performance.

Regarding cool-down, few studies have evaluated the effects of stretching as a recovery method after finishing a workout or cycling competition. Miladi et al. (2011) observed that dynamic stretching is an effective method for improving performance, cardiorespiratory measures, and lactate levels during intermittent supramaximal intensity tests in cycling. Other studies have reported that low-intensity aerobic exercise, such as cycling at 20 percent of $\dot{V}O_2$max, is a method that facilitates performance recovery during intermittent high-intensity cycling exercise (Dorado, Sanchís-Moysi, and Calbet 2004) or after the completion of dynamic exercise to fatigue (Mika et al. 2007).

In this regard, dynamic stretching is recommended as a part of warm-up, immediately before the main part of the training, or as a recovery method between high-intensity series. In contrast, passive stretching should be performed after the main activity as a cool-down or relaxation method after exercise (Peck et al. 2014).

In road cycling, low-intensity cycling for the first part of the ride could be used as a specific warm-up without the need to perform dynamic stretching exercises. Although not formally considered stretching, the cat–camel exercise (figure 34.1) is a motion exercise recommended for cyclists to use before mounting the

▶ **Figure 34.1** Cyclist performing the cat–camel exercise: (a) cat; (b) camel.

José M. Muyor

bicycle to decrease the intraarticular viscosity of the spine (internal resistance and friction), improve spinal load distribution, and minimize spinal stress. The emphasis is on motion in the ranges of flexion and extension with the integration of the cervical, thoracic, and lumbar spine. The recommendation is to perform five to eight cycles to reduce most viscous-frictional stresses (McGill 2007).

In contrast, passive stretching exercises should be performed after training or competition to promote muscle recovery.

Stretching and Cyclist Posture

The cyclist's posture on the bicycle is characterized by sustained forward trunk flexion to reach the handlebars. Studies have reported that the cyclist maintains greater alignment of the thoracic spine on the bicycle than in the standing posture, regardless of the handlebar grip used or the type of activity (Muyor, López-Miñarro, and Alacid 2011a, 2011b, 2011c). The lumbar spine changes from its standing lumbar lordosis to lumbar kyphosis on the bicycle (Usabiaga et al. 2007), resulting in higher lumbar flexion the lower and more distal the handlebar support is relative to the seat position (Muyor, López-Miñarro, and Alacid 2013a). The hamstring muscle length, however, does not appear to affect the cyclist's spinal posture on the bicycle (Muyor, López-Miñarro, and Alacid 2011d, 2013a) because slight knee flexion is always maintained in pedaling kinematics (Bini and Diefenthaeler 2010). Therefore, the hamstrings would not suffer excessive tension.

In contrast, studies have found that the cyclist has greater thoracic kyphosis in a standing position compared with nonathletes (Muyor, López-Miñarro, and Alacid 2011a; Rajabi, Freemont, and Doherty 2000), and thoracic flexion increases as the cyclist ages (Muyor et al. 2012).

Positions that maintain the spine in flexion have been associated with increased intradiscal pressure of the thoracic (Polga et al. 2004) and lumbar (Wilke et al. 1999) spine, greater deformation of the spinal tissues

(Solomonow et al. 2003), and high spinal stress (Beach et al. 2005), increasing the likelihood of injury or the development of spinal pain. Back pain is one of the most common overuse injuries in cycling (Asplund, Webb, and Barkdull 2005; Marsden 2010; Salai et al. 1999), possibly because of the unnatural body position assumed on the bicycle (de Vey Mesdagh, 1998).

For this reason, stretching exercises have been positively associated with a decrease in thoracic kyphosis and spinal pain at the cervical, thoracic (Cunha et al. 2008; Yoo 2013), and lumbar (Khalil et al. 1992) levels, as well as with good posture in activities of maximal trunk flexion (Muyor, López-Miñarro, and Alacid 2013b).

Passive Stretching Exercises

As mentioned previously, passive stretching exercises should be performed after training or competition to promote muscle recovery after exercise. To prevent increased spinal stress, the spine should be aligned during all stretching exercises, maintaining its physiological curvatures. The cyclist should perform three sets of each exercise, maintaining tension (stretching posture) for 15 to 20 seconds. Stretching should be performed gradually to the point of muscle tightness, but not soreness.

Soleus   Stand with hands resting on a wall or other surface. Begin extension at the hip, keeping the knee slightly flexed and the entire sole of the foot on the ground (figure 34.2). To increase the intensity of the stretch, shift body weight back onto the leg being stretched. The lower opposite leg will be in a forward position, and the knee will be semiflexed, supporting the body and creating stability.

▶ **Figure 34.2**   Soleus stretch.

José M. Muyor

Gastrocnemius   The body position is similar to the position for soleus stretching, but the leg to be stretched is the leg with the knee extended and the sole of the foot touching the ground completely (figure 34.3). In this exercise, body weight can be shifted forward to increase the intensity of stretching.

▶ **Figure 34.3**   Gastrocnemius stretch.

José M. Muyor

Tibialis Anterior   Sit on a chair or other surface with a straight back. Cross the leg to be stretched over the thigh of the other leg (figure 34.4). The ankle is passively extended by manual manipulation of the foot.

▶ **Figure 34.4**   Tibialis anterior stretch.

José M. Muyor

▶ **Figure 34.5**   Quadriceps stretch.

José M. Muyor

Quadriceps   Stand with one hand on a wall or other surface. Flex the knee of the leg to be stretched and hold the ankle or foot with the hand on the same side (figure 34.5). Pelvic retroversion can generate greater muscle tension during stretching. The back should be kept straight throughout the stretch.

▶ **Figure 34.6**   Hamstring stretch.

José M. Muyor

Hamstrings   Stand with the heel resting on one stair (height depends on the cyclist's degree of hamstring extensibility). Lean the trunk forward slightly, keeping the spine aligned throughout the exercise (figure 34.6). Pelvic anteversion can generate greater muscle tension. Touching the toes with the hands is unnecessary, because this movement promotes lumbar kyphosis and thereby increases spinal stress.

Tensor Fascia Latae and Iliotibial Band   In a supine position, with one leg crossed over the knee of the other leg, perform lateral hip rotation toward the side where the upper knee is located (figure 34.7). Slight knee extension of the leg being stretched, while exerting downward pressure with the other leg, can generate greater muscle tension during the stretch.

▶ **Figure 34.7**   Tensor fascia latae and iliotibial band stretch.

José M. Muyor

Adductors   In the supine position, with knees and hips flexed, thighs parallel, and the soles of the feet flat on the ground, abduct the thighs, bringing both knees toward the ground while keeping the soles of the feet in contact with each other (figure 34.8). To increase muscle tension, apply pressure toward the ground with both hands, favoring the abduction of both thighs. This exercise should not be performed in a seated position, which favors lumbar kyphosis and thereby increases spinal stress.

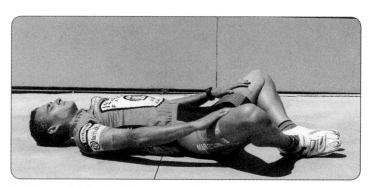

▶ **Figure 34.8**   Adductor stretch.

José M. Muyor

Psoas and Iliacus   Stand with one foot forward and the knee and hip flexed. Extend the other leg from the hip and rest it on the ground (figure 34.9). Hip extension can be increased to increase muscle tension, intentionally limiting extension to the knee of the front foot to prevent knee hyperflexion and thereby increased patellar tendon stress.

▶ **Figure 34.9**   Psoas and iliacus stretch.

José M. Muyor

Gluteus   In the supine position, with knees and hips flexed, thighs parallel, and the soles of the feet flat on the ground, rotate the hips to one side, bringing the knee of the upper leg toward the chest (figure 34.10). Hold the thigh on the popliteal area and not on the anterior tibial area to prevent hyperflexion of the knee and greater resulting stress on the patellar tendon.

▶ **Figure 34.10**   Gluteus stretch.

José M. Muyor

Gluteus and Lumbar Muscles   In the supine position, with knees and hips flexed, thighs parallel, and the soles of the feet flat on the ground, flex at the hips, bringing both knees to the chest (figure 34.11). Thighs should be held on the popliteal area and not on the anterior tibial area to prevent hyperflexion of the knee and greater resulting stress on the patellar tendon.

▶ **Figure 34.11**   Gluteus and lumbar muscles stretch.

José M. Muyor

Lumbar Muscles and Latissimus Dorsi   Stand with hands on a wall or other surface. Bend forward at the hips, keeping the back aligned at all times (figure 32.12). Pelvic anteversion can increase muscle tension. Forward trunk flexion greater than 60 degrees should not be performed, because the flexion–relaxation phenomenon would occur (McGorry and Lin 2012) and increase spinal stress.

▶ **Figure 34.12**   Lumbar muscles and latissimus dorsi stretch.

José M. Muyor

Pectoralis and Anterior Deltoid
Stand with one hand on a wall or other surface. Extend the scapular–humeral girdle and externally rotate the humerus (figure 34.13). Rotate the lateral trunk to the opposite side of the wall support.

▶ **Figure 34.13** Pectoralis and anterior deltoid stretch.

José M. Muyor

Biceps Brachii Stand with one hand on a wall or other surface. Extend the scapular–humeral girdle and internally rotate the humerus (figure 34.14). The lateral trunk rotates to the opposite side of the wall support.

▶ **Figure 34.14** Biceps brachii stretch.

José M. Muyor

Triceps Brachii Stand with shoulders flexed. The flexed elbow of the arm to be stretched should be secured with the opposite hand while the scapular–humeral girdle is flexed, bringing the elbow to the side of the head (figure 34.15).

▶ **Figure 34.15** Triceps brachii stretch.

José M. Muyor

Neck Muscles   Stand and hold one side of the head. Laterally flex the cervical spine, inclining the head away from the muscle (sternocleidomastoid) to be stretched (figure 34.16*a* and *c*). A forward flexion of the cervical spine (figure 34.16*b*) is also performed, bringing the chin toward the sternum to stretch the splenius and trapezius muscles. The cervical spine can be rotated, but always in a slow and controlled manner, avoiding cervical hyperextension.

▶ **Figure 34.16**   Neck muscles stretch: (*a*) left side; (*b*) back; (*c*) right side.

José M. Muyor

Applying the Science

In cycling, stretching before training or competition is not necessary. If stretches are performed before training or competition, they should be active dynamic stretching exercises. To prepare for training or competition, the cat–camel exercise should be performed before mounting the bicycle.

Passive stretching exercises should be performed after cycling to improve the recovery processes. All stretching exercises should be completed with the back aligned (maintaining the physiological curvature of the spine), avoiding maximum trunk flexion.

PART

IX

Racing Your Bike

CHAPTER 35

The Science of Pacing

—Chris R. Abbiss

Pacing refers to the distribution of speed or energy expenditure throughout an exercise task. This factor is considered extremely important in the successful execution of any race (Abbiss and Laursen 2008; Foster et al. 2005; Foster et al. 1994). Indeed, at some stage all cyclists have probably misjudged an attack up a hill or the distance to a sprint finish, blowing up well before the finish line. Alternatively, if cyclists are too cautious they may fail to distribute their efforts appropriately and consequently have plenty of energy stores remaining as they cross the finish line. Even if a cyclist completes an event completely exhausted, she or he may wonder whether pacing was optimal through the entire event. Could the cyclist have improved performance by taking it a bit easy in the first half of the race?

Understanding the pacing strategy that results in the best possible performance during a particular event is an extremely complicated process that may be influenced by several important factors, including but not limited to race format, fitness, fatigue, age, sex, environmental conditions, and race duration (Abbiss and Laursen 2005; Atkinson and Brunskill 2000; de Koning, Bobbert, and Foster 1999; Le Meur et al. 2009; Swain 1997). Over recent years, a rapid increase has occurred in scientific research that examines and models these factors in an attempt to prepare athletes for competition.

Cycling typically has two distinct race formats or tasks, and these have a significant influence on pacing:

1. Mass-start events in which other competitors largely dictate an athlete's pace
2. Individual or solo events in which athletes have considerable control over their individual pacing

During individual cycling tasks, which include time trials, solo breakaways, and certain mountain bike or cyclocross events, cyclists are usually required to complete a given distance as quickly as possible. Alternatively, cyclists may be required to complete the greatest distance possible in a given time, as in the 1-hour track-cycling record. Because of the simplicity of this race format and the ability to replicate race scenarios in the laboratory, most pacing research to date has been conducted using such trials. This research has made it clear that pacing is influenced by several intrinsic (i.e., physiological, biomechanical, and cognitive) and extrinsic (i.e., environmental, race dynamics) factors (Abbiss and Laursen 2008; Edwards and Polman 2013; Noakes, St. Clair Gibson, and Lambert 2005; St. Clair Gibson et al. 2006). Cyclists often assume that during such individual tasks they should focus on intrinsic factors, forget about other competitors, and ride at their own pace. For instance, I'm sure that most people reading this book know the feeling of being dropped by a peloton when cycling uphill and, rather than bury themselves to stay with the group, instead decide to maintain a manageable pace for the remainder of the climb in the hope that they will eventually join back on.

Note that although intrinsic factors are important to pacing during solo cycling tasks, the actions of competitors are still likely to have an influence on both self-selected and optimal pacing strategies (Baron et al. 2011). For instance, athletes who begin a time trial later in the day may be at an advantage over other competitors, because they are able to pace the event based on the performance of the riders before them. Clearly, however, competitors, race dynamics, and tactics have a much greater influence on pacing and ultimately overall success during head-to-head competitive events (Abbiss et al. 2013b). A prime example of this is the complex tactics played out during the individual track sprint whereby athletes play a tactical game of cat-and-mouse before the sprint. During such events an appropriate distribution of pace is important in being able to judge the precise time to attack and the effort to give during the sprint.

Monitoring Pacing

With the recent advancements in the methods used to capture, monitor, and analyze training and race data, the amount of information (i.e., speed, heart rate, GPS, power) available to athletes and coaches has exploded. This information can be extremely beneficial in training prescription and performance monitoring (see chapter 30), but it can quickly become confusing, complicated, and even distracting during competition. Regardless, this information can be valuable in performance analysis and the optimization of individualized pacing strategies.

With the recent development of cycling power meters, cyclists and coaches can quantify not only the mechanical power generated but also the physiological strain induced (i.e., heart rate) and the resulting speed (i.e., GPS and speedometers). Many systems now also provide information on elevation change, which can be extremely important in understanding the resistive forces experienced during many cycling events (Menaspà et al. 2014). Although each of these factors is important to performance, the term *pacing* strictly refers to changes in speed throughout an event. Indeed, speed is ultimately the most important variable to overall performance during cycling. This is not to say that power output and heart rate are not important to pacing. Of course, the speed of a cyclist is dictated by several factors, including the mechanical power generated, momentum, and resistive forces experienced (Candau et al. 1999; de Koning, Bobbert, and Foster 1999; Swain 1997). Note that although power output is often used to examine and monitor pacing during cycling, its relationship with speed and velocity is not linear. This point is especially important during conditions in which resistive forces vary because of wind, incline, or acceleration (discussed later in this chapter).

Because of limitations with each method used to monitor intensity (i.e., speed, power output, or heart rate), one method is often considered better than the others when it comes to pacing. Indeed a considerable lag (20 to 30 seconds) occurs in heart rate when compared with measures of power and speed. Furthermore, heart rate can be influenced by fluid volume and hydration status, resulting in a gradual increase in heart rate (called cardiovascular drift). Likewise, speed can be drastically influenced by environmental factors such as wind and elevation. From this, it is often suggested that all cyclists need a power meter if they want to be able to monitor their pacing. But for some this might not be the case. Races are not necessarily won by the athlete who produces the highest power output; ultimately, speed is the most important factor in success. Therefore, we need to examine the strengths and weaknesses of each type of monitoring and the association between data collected by them. For instance, power output gives extremely valuable data on the energy produced by the athlete, but how and where this energy is distributed and how it influences speed is what is important to pacing. Although heart rate may be considered a poor indicator of pacing because of the previously mentioned limitations, it is a good indicator of the physiological strain induced by the exercise demands. Therefore, heart rate can provide useful information on how an athlete is coping with the exercise task. Regardless of the speed or power output, if heart rate begins to increase to the athlete's maximum heart rate during a prolonged time trial, the cyclist should probably reduce intensity. In the remainder of the chapter, these variables are discussed in relation to performance during short, middle-distance, and prolonged cycling events.

Pacing During Sprinting: All-Out Strategy

Because of the relatively stable resistive forces (i.e., coefficient of drag and body weight) during individual track-cycling events, pacing and performance can be accurately modeled (Candau et al. 1999; de Koning, Bobbert, and Foster 1999; Swain 1997). Such research clearly shows that performance during short events (less than or equal to 30 seconds) benefits from an all-out strategy (figure 35.1), whereby athletes give maximal effort from the beginning of the event (Abbiss and Laursen 2008; Keller 1974).

Such a strategy is considered optimal because of the considerable energy cost associated with accelerating from rest. Indeed, during the 1-kilometer track sprint, 20 to 40 percent of the race can be spent in the acceleration phase. As a result, a considerable proportion of the total energy demand during this event may be required simply to alter the body's kinetic energy from rest. Because expending the energy required to accelerate is inevitable, doing this at the beginning of the event is ideal. Despite this, the prolonged time spent in the acceleration phase (at relatively low speeds) during short events results in a negative-split performance time, whereby the first half of the event is performed slower than the second (figure 35.2). Evidence from sprinting research, however, indicates that continuing to accelerate until reaching the finish line is not always ideal. Instead, after an athlete reaches peak velocity using an all-out strategy, speed often declines slightly (figure 35.1; Wilberg and Pratt 1988). This occurs because any energy or momentum carried over the finish line is essentially wasted kinetic energy. As such, during short-duration efforts (less than or equal to 30 seconds), the optimal

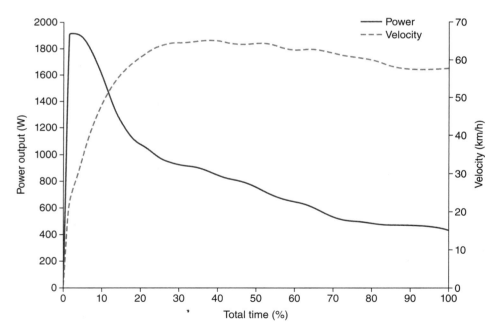

▶ **Figure 35.1** Example of power output and speed during a 1,000-meter track-cycling event. Note the high power output needed to alter the kinetic energy from rest and the gradual decline in velocity beyond 40 percent (about 25 seconds) of the overall trial time.

Reprinted, by permission, from C.R. Abbiss and P.B. Laursen, 2008, "Describing and understanding pacing strategies during athletic competition," Sports Medicine 38(3): 239-252, by kind permission from Springer Science and Business Media.

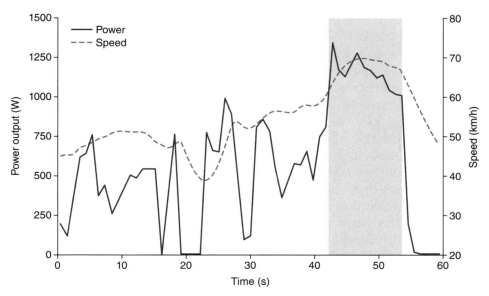

▶ **Figure 35.2** Example of power output and speed at the end of a professional road race. The final sprint is highlighted in grey.

approach appears to be to accelerate rapidly to maximal speed, even if this effort results in a minor reduction in speed because of fatigue closer to the finish line.

The metabolic cost of acceleration is also extremely important to road sprint cycling performance. Although factors such as momentum, fatigue, tactics, wind, and geography make it difficult to model performance during road sprinting, the optimal sprint duration appears to range from 12 to 15 seconds (Menaspà et al. 2013). These durations are similar to those required to establish a breakaway in road cycling (Abbiss et al. 2013a). An important difference, however, is the necessity to maintain high power output (400 to 500 watts) for a further 30 seconds to 5 minutes when establishing a break- away. The shorter duration of such all-out efforts, when compared with track cycling, is likely to be associated with high speeds (50 to 70 kilometers per hour) and thus considerable momentum but also metabolic fatigue are experienced by road cyclists before the all-out effort.

Middle-Distance Events: Positive Pacing

Within middle-distance cycling events (1.5 to 6 minutes), the ideal approach appears to be to adopt a positive pacing strategy, whereby speed gradually declines throughout the event. This strategy is especially evident in swim- ming events in which relatively little energy is required to accelerate at the beginning of the event because of the dive start. Within middle-distance cycling events, however, cyclists are required to accelerate not only their own mass but also the mass of the bicycle, resulting in a relatively slow start. Regardless, athletes appear to benefit by being able to accelerate rapidly to maximal speed and then gradually slow in the second half of the event (van Ingen Schenau, de Koning, and de Groot 1992). The adoption of such a positive pacing strategy may enhance performance because of faster oxygen uptake kinetics, resulting in greater energy supply from aerobic metabolism, thus possibly preserving anaerobic energy capacity until later in the event (Aisbett et al. 2009a, 2009b; Bishop, Bonetti, and Dawson 2002). Indeed, numerous studies have shown that a relatively high power output at commencement of middle-distance cycling events (750 to 4,000 meters) may increase overall oxygen consumption and improve performance, when compared with slow or even-start strategies (Aisbett et al. 2009a, 2009b; Hettinga, de Koning, and Foster 2009).

Note, however, that the adoption of a positive pacing strategy may be less ideal and evidence of unrealistic or overambitious starting speeds. Indeed, cyclists may begin a race at a speed they believe is necessary to finish among the medalists or in a personal best time but gradually fade because of increasing fatigue. It is interesting to consider whether such a strategy is suboptimal given that the particular athlete is unlikely to finish in the desired placing unless she or he rides at the selected intensity from the beginning of the race. During a single individual time trial, cyclists may adopt such a strategy because the chance of success outweighs the risk of finishing in a lower place. During a multistage event, however, in which overall performance time for a tour leader is important not only to the individual stage but also to the general classification, an athlete may be less likely to adopt such an aggressive starting strategy.

Prolonged Exercise: Even Pacing

As race duration increases, the energy cost of acceleration and the energy lost when crossing the finish have less influence on overall performance times. Consequently, during such events, maintaining an even or constant distribution of pace is thought to be optimal (Abbiss and Laursen 2008; de Koning, Bobbert, and Foster 1999). This approach differs from maintaining an even distribution of effort or power output, which is discussed later in this chapter.

The theoretical support for an even pacing strategy stems from mathematical laws of motion and the critical power concept. This model indicates that the highest maintainable speed of a cyclist is dictated by the athlete's physiological limitations (i.e., lactate or ventilation threshold) along with the resistive forces he or she experiences (Billat, Koralsztein, and Morton 1999; di Prampero et al. 1979; Fukuba and Whipp 1999; Morton 2006). Because the relationship between power output and speed is nonlinear, greater energy expenditure is required to overcome air resistance at faster speeds. Therefore, deviating from an even distribution of speed results in greater energy loss to overcome wind resistance, resulting in suboptimal performance times. The maximal maintainable speed of a cyclist is therefore ultimately dictated by her or his biomechanical positioning and physiological and metabolic limitations. Physiological testing for maximal oxygen consumption, lactate threshold, or ventilation threshold has long been the preferred method to obtain information regarding a cyclist's metabolic limitations. Many of the training and power analysis software programs (e.g., TrainingPeaks, WKO+) now provide detailed and novel analytical methods that can be used to obtain such data (i.e., functional threshold power, or FTP; see chapter 29 and Allen and Coggan 2010). This information is not only important in training prescription but also valuable in understanding the maximal mean power output that a cyclist can maintain over a given exercise duration.

Pacing in the Real World: Variable Pacing

Although an even pacing strategy is considered ideal during prolonged cycling trials, varying external conditions such as wind or hills make this difficult to achieve during outdoor cycling. For instance, we all know that variable wind or terrain in road or mountain bike cycling make it impossible to maintain a constant speed, regardless of the race distance. Indeed, if we download a data file from a race or training session, we quickly notice variability in heart rate, speed, and power output, even if we are riding alone and attempting to maintain a constant speed (figure 35.3). Could we

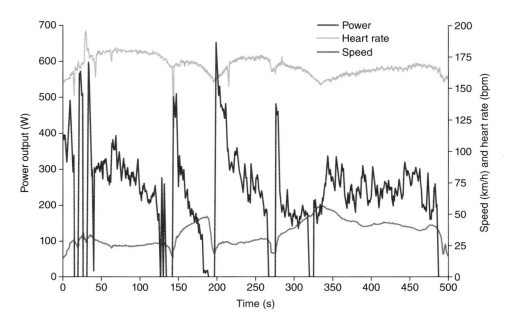

▶ **Figure 35.3** Example of power output, heart rate, and speed during a section of an individual time trial event performed outdoors.

have improved performance with more or less variability? Would it have been better to adopt a more aggressive speed up the hill and recover on the downhill?

When cycling under varying external conditions, the optimal pacing strategy to select is still underpinned by the same mathematical laws of motion and physiological and metabolic limitations previously discussed. But during outdoor cycling, the constantly varying environmental conditions make it difficult to quantify the resistive forces experienced by the cyclist. Note as well that the physiological limitations to exercise performance are not consistent and can change dramatically with fatigue or under varying environmental conditions (such as at altitude or in the heat). As a result, modeling optimal pacing strategies during such events is extremely complicated. But by focusing on the most significant factors that influence resistive forces (i.e., bike and body mass, wind, and gradient) along with many other factors (i.e., air density, drive chain efficiency, coefficient of drag, and rolling resistance), many studies have improved our understanding of the pacing patterns that best enhance performance (Simmons 2008). These studies have found that performance can be enhanced by increasing power output during periods of high external resistance (i.e., into a headwind or uphill) and reducing power output during periods of low resistance (i.e., with a tailwind or downhill) (Atkinson, Peacock, and Law 2007; Atkinson, Peacock, and Passfield 2007; Swain 1997). Here again the nonlinear relationship between power output and speed comes into play. Because of this nonlinear relationship, expending considerable energy to go extremely fast on descents is not beneficial because much of this energy is wasted in overcoming the high resistive forces. A better strategy is to increase energy expenditure uphill when speed and wind resistance is low. Supporting this idea, research has shown that better-placed finishers during cross-country mountain bike events spend a lower percentage of time on technical uphill sections of the course and a greater percentage of time on downhill and nontechnical flat sections (Abbiss et al. 2013b). Interestingly, when compared with open category elite male cyclists, both junior and female cyclists spend a greater percentage of time on technical uphill sections of the course. Such differences are likely to be the result of differences in physiological characteristics (i.e., power-to-weight ratio) among junior, female, and male cyclists.

Indeed, the degree to which a cyclist should increase or decrease power output to accommodate varying external conditions is largely based on that cyclist's physiological limitations. For that reason, increasing intensity to push competitors to their physiological limits when attempting to establish a breakaway is much more likely to be successful during periods of high external resistance (i.e., into a headwind or uphill). Success in dropping riders during downhill sections of a course is usually the result of superior technical descending skills or greater risk taking rather than enhanced physiological characteristics. As such, altering both cycling proficiency and physiological characteristics, such as strength, anaerobic capacity, $\dot{V}O_2$max, or lactate threshold, will enhance a cyclist's ability to maintain power output for a given exercise duration and therefore will be extremely important in modeling optimal pacing. By examining the power output distribution over various segments of a course, a number of models have been established to assess and improve pacing for individual athletes (CyclingPowerLab 2008-2014; Simmons 2008). These models provide useful methods to review previous race profiles to determine whether pacing could have been improved (i.e., postevent performance analysis) and to examine what could be an optimal pacing strategy in future events based on predicted power outputs. Further refining of these models will allow athletes to individualize a race strategy based on the event, environmental conditions, and their own physiological characteristics.

Applying the Science

Pacing strategies have a considerable influence on performance during cycling. Clearly, the optimal pacing strategy to select during cycling is influenced by numerous factors, but the characteristics of the race are paramount. In mass-start events, pacing is dictated largely by the peloton, so individual cyclists tend to have less control over their own pace. With that said, athletes are continuously making important decisions that influence their energy distribution during such events. For instance, in mass-start events, cyclists can spend a greater amount of time in the middle of a peloton to conserve energy for later in the event.

During individual events, athletes have much greater control over their pacing. In such events, the duration of the event is one of the most important factors in determining the best pacing strategy because the duration often has considerable influence on the cost of acceleration and development of fatigue. In extremely short sprint events, the cyclist must quickly accelerate the mass of the bicycle and his or her body weight. During longer events, however, the cost of acceleration has less influence on performance because wind resistance becomes the most influential factor in optimizing pacing. Based on mathematical models, performance during prolonged endurance events is thought to be optimized with an even pacing strategy. Using this strategy, energy loss can be minimized by balancing the cyclist's highest maintainable power output with the resistive forces experienced. Although an even pacing strategy may be optimal during competitions such as the 1-hour track-cycling record, few events in cycling have consistent resistive forces. Instead, when competing in races with varying external resistance (i.e., wind and hills), performance can be improved by increasing power output uphill and into headwinds and reducing power output downhill and with a tailwind. Clearly, the degree to which cyclists should vary power output is influenced by the duration and slope of the hill, the strength of the wind, and individual physiological capacities.

Note as well that the highest power output that a cyclist can maintain for a given duration is not consistent and can be considerably influenced by factors such as body position, fitness, fatigue, altitude, and environmental temperature. Indeed, the oxygen content in the atmosphere is highest at sea level and decreases as elevation increases, particularly when above 1,500 to 2,000 meters. As a result, performance may be optimized by adopting a slightly higher power output at the base of a climb rather than near the summit, when less oxygen is available to muscles. Most research that models optimal pacing during cycling has not considered this and assumes that the cyclist's ability to produce power for a given duration is consistent. Further research is needed to enhance understanding of the influence that varying environmental conditions have on fatigue, exercise capacity, and resistive forces. Given the complexity of the way in which the body regulates pace and the constant changes that occur in environmental conditions, we need to try various pacing strategies in training to optimize pacing and performance in competition.

CHAPTER 36

Road Racing

—Hunter Allen

Winning a bicycle race is always a challenge. The description of bicycle racing as chess on wheels applies to nearly every race, and smart tacticians are always thinking one move ahead. A rider might race in 30 to 40 races and finally get into the winning position only to watch in shock as the real winner moves ahead.

During that first experience, a newbie is happy just to be there and thinking only of how not to get dropped rather than how to win, but a winning mind-set comes with experience and confidence. An experienced rider has been in the winning situation before and is thinking through five different scenarios of how he or she can win with multiple contingencies for each one. A clear understanding of how to win a race can be taught, learned, and used if the opportunity is recognized. This chapter will help you focus on the finish and help you finish first.

If you are not on a team and do not have a teammate in the peloton, your breakaway tactics are generally the same, but you don't have the benefit of working with a teammate to help one of you win. In most breakaway situations, you'll be flying solo whether you are on a team or not, because you most likely won't have a teammate there.

Winning Solo

The first and foremost tactic you should consider, after you are in the winning break, is to try to escape solo and ride by yourself to the finish line. This guarantees you the win, a perfect win that demonstrates superior fitness and smarts. But that tactic might not be possible because you might not be feeling that strong, you fancy the sprint among a small group, or the chasing peloton is too close to risk capture if your horsepower gets you away from the break but is not enough to hold off the field.

Getting away cleanly from the breakaway requires proper timing, a strong attack so that no one gets on your wheel, proper pacing after you are off the front, and 100 percent commitment. When you make your attack, the best approach is to attack from the back of the breakaway, gaining an element of surprise and at the same time coming by the other riders at a speed that discourages the chase.

Try to time it so that your main competitor—the strongest or next strongest rider in the peloton—is just finishing taking a pull at the front when you attack. For that to happen, he or she needs to be behind you in the order of the breakaway. To get your rival two riders behind you, you need to get to the back of the peloton and sit out a few turns so that you change up the order of the breakaway to your advantage. After your competitor is the second rider behind you, you'll want to make sure that he or she doesn't know that you feel strong when you take a pull, so take a normal or mediocre pull at the front leading up to your surprise attack. You want to get your rival two riders behind you, not right behind you, because when you make your attack, you'll be at the back and get the rider who is right behind you and who just took a pull to drop in, giving you just a little extra rest in the legs before your attack. Drop slightly off the back (maybe 5 feet [1.5 m] or so) and carefully watch the strongest rider at the front. Then when he or she pulls off to one side, you launch your sprint up the other side of the breakaway, making it that much more difficult for him or her to respond quickly. If done correctly, you should come flying by the front of the breakaway at 30 miles per hour (48 km/h) or more, creating a solid gap and deflating all the other riders with the ferocity of your effort.

At this point, you need to keep driving your effort hard in a near all-out sprint for 10 seconds, settle down to a very hard pace for the next 20 seconds, and then settle into a pace that you can maintain to the finish line. Now, this pace depends on the distance to the finish line, because if you are only 3 to 8 minutes out from the line, you will want to push your intensity at $\dot{V}O_2$max pace or 105 to 120 percent of your functional threshold power (FTP). FTP is the highest average power you can maintain in a quasi-steady state without fatiguing for 1 hour. If your effort will have to be longer than 8 minutes, you'll need to keep your pace right at and just above your FTP, or 100 to 105 percent of FTP.

You have to go faster than the breakaway is going as a collective group, of course, but your attack may cause the other riders to react by chasing you, thus increasing their pace and causing counterattacks that could actually end up decreasing their pace. An interesting dynamic occurs when one rider attacks away from a breakaway and the others try attacking to get the rider back. The initial chaser might attack, but when another rider gets on her or his wheel, the chaser stops chasing, not wanting to bring back the rider by her- or himself. This action causes a reduction in speed, which ultimately is good for you as the solo rider off the front because your speed is constantly high. Any small hesitation by the chasers allows the gap to grow larger. On the other hand, a highly motivated group of chasers can launch repeated counterattacks, all leap frogging themselves up to you and neutralizing your brilliantly planned winning move. After you have opened the attacks with your attack and been caught, prepare for more attacks and counterattacks. At this point, you will have to follow a chaser, hoping to catch some brief recovery and then launch a counterattack on your own. You are now playing a game of attack and counterattack that, if done correctly, will have you arriving at the finish line off the front.

A couple additional pieces of advice might be helpful here. If you find yourself chasing back an attacker, you may gain an advantage by doing it somewhat slowly, so that you catch the leader closer to the line. This tactic, if executed by a few riders, will prevent more counterattacking and gives you one last chance close to the finish line. Another tactic that can be successful after you are caught is to follow wheels of the chasers for a while, refuse to help chase, and then launch a decisive attack near the end. This tactic can be difficult to pull off because many chasers will refuse to drag you closer to the line unless you do some of the work.

Key Workout: Race-Winning Intervals   To improve your $\dot{V}O_2$max and your ability to win races, try these race-winning intervals. These workouts simulate what a wattage file would show for a rider attacking in a race for the race win.

Total time: 1.5 hours. Warm up for 20 minutes, keeping your effort in the endurance zone (56 to 75 percent of threshold power or 69 to 83 percent of threshold heart rate). Start with five 1-minute fast pedaling efforts in which you get your cadence to at least 110 revolutions per minute and hold there for 1 minute. The amount of force on the pedals is relatively low, but do enough to avoid bouncing in the saddle. Perform easy pedaling and recovery for 1 minute after each set. Ride at endurance pace for 5 minutes and then get ready for the race-winning intervals. Try for at least five efforts and up to eight in one session. Each interval begins with a 30-second sprint (15 seconds out of the saddle), and you must average 200 percent of threshold power in these first 30 seconds with a peak of at least 300 percent. (If you are using a computer without power, try to reach at least 28 to 30 miles per hour [45 to 48 km/h] and hold for 30 seconds.) Ride for 3 minutes and really hammer at 100 to 110 percent of threshold power or the best speed you think you can maintain for an hour. Then finish with an out-of-the-saddle 10-second burst after the 3 minutes is over and try to reach 200 percent of threshold power again, or 28 to 30 miles per hour. Rest for 5 or 6 minutes after each interval.

If you haven't had enough, finish with eight 1-minute fast pedaling efforts, with 1 minute of rest after each set. Keep your cadence over 110 revolutions per minute. Cool down for 15 minutes.

Small Breakaway and the Sprint

If your sprint is better than most and you are not interested in winning solo, then making sure the breakaway comes down to a small group sprint is more desirable for you. Of course, getting this to happen is a completely different story! In this scenario, you believe yourself to be the fastest finisher in the group and you want to be able to battle it out with the rest in a sprint. Of course, the riders who do not have a sprint will be attacking you, trying to drop you and win solo, or just taking you out of the equation. Your strategy is to do as little work as possible in the final 15 minutes of the race, taking easy pulls, or sitting in all together and then marking the strongest riders, only following attacks and neutralizing them.

One key element in this scenario is to be decisive with your efforts; you are the sprinter and don't want to be caught trying to bring back someone attacking off the front. Think of yourself as the shark; you are ready to jump immediately on the wheel of anyone who goes up the road. In this scenario, you need to use your sprint to your advantage, so that might mean you have to do a bunch of little sprints in those last 15 minutes leading up to the final sprint. The job of the other riders in the breakaway is to get rid of you by attacking and riding as hard as possible on all difficult sections leading to the finish. If there is a hill before the end, you can be sure that they will try to drop you! In these areas you have to be 100 percent committed and willing to suffer a thousand deaths to stay on the wheels. Push yourself as hard as you can here. If you do get dropped, you should try to get back to the breakaway as quickly as possible, so that you don't spend the next 10 minutes time trialing behind them. Make a big effort to get back on as soon as possible.

You will have to play the sprint itself correctly too. Knowing your strengths and weaknesses as a sprinter is critical to your success. If you are an explosive sprinter who has an incredible snap but poor fatigue resistance after 10 seconds, the sprint should be a short one at a relatively slow speed. You want to use your explosiveness to jump away quickly and distance yourself before you fatigue. You can do this by riding at the front of the breakaway in the last kilometer and slowing the breakaway on purpose in a game of cat and mouse. This tactic works well when it is just you and one other rider, but it can also work in a small group. The key here is to ride at the front and drop the speed so that you aren't doing any real work and are bringing the group to the finish line at a slow speed. If someone tries to go from 300 meters out, you can instantly jump on his or her wheel and then come around in the last 50 meters. If no one goes before 200 meters, then you'll need to open the sprint at 175 to 150 meters and just go for it, because you are within your striking range of winning the race. Your best tactic is to hide from the wind as much as possible, pop out with only 100 meters to go, and sprint to the finish line with all you have. Save your energy and then explode with everything when you go!

If you are more of a diesel sprinter, you will need a higher speed from which to start your sprint. A diesel sprinter does not have an explosive initial jump but can produce extremely high power output and hold it for up to 30 seconds. Initiate the sprint from at least 350 meters out from the finish, ensure that no one easily gets on your wheel, and then drive it all the way to the finish, doing your absolute maximum to maintain your power output. If others start to come around you, just keep driving it, because you will likely outlast them. You want to get in a long drag race with the others because you'll be able to win through superior resistance to fatigue. If you are in the final kilometers and the pace is slowing too much, you'll need to be willing to take the pace at the front to keep the pace high. In this case, you'll also want to ride close to one edge of the road to force other riders to come around you into the wind or just on one side. Do not let the sprint come down to a slow, short sprint, or you'll likely get beaten. Spend a little energy, keep the pace high, and sprint from the front of the group rather than have it come down to a short sprint that does not favor your strengths.

Key Workout: Sprints   To improve your sprint for this season, try this sprint workout. Make sure you have a smooth road with plenty of visibility and ideally a flat to gently downhill straight section of road. The shorter sprints are to work on your explosiveness, and the longer ones are to help you improve your fatigue resistance.

Total time: 2 hours. Warm up for 20 minutes, keeping your effort in the endurance zone (56 to 75 percent of threshold power or 69 to 83 percent of threshold heart rate). Start with three 1-minute fast pedaling efforts in which you get your cadence to at least 110 revolutions per minute and hold there for 1 minute. The amount of force on the pedals is relatively low, but do enough to prevent bouncing in the saddle. Perform easy pedaling and recovery for 1 minute after each set. Ride at endurance pace for 5 minutes and then get ready for the sprints. Start with small-ring sprints, beginning at a slow speed of about 10 miles per hour (16 km/h). Your goal is to emphasize the initial jump, wind out that gear as best you can, and spin the legs. Do six small-ring sprints in your small ring and two cogs down from the hardest gear on the rear wheel, 50 meters with no gear changes; wind out the gears! Rest for 1 to 2 minutes after each sprint, which is the time it usually takes to ride leisurely back to the starting line of your sprint. After the small-ring sprints, get ready for the big-ring sprints. Do six big-ring sprints, about 250 meters, with only one gear change. Try starting with 53:17 from 20 miles per hour (32 km/h). When you wind out this gear, shift to the 53:16 and wind it out to the finish line. Again, rest at least 2 minutes if not longer for these intervals. Finish with four more sprints, starting from a slightly harder gear and a faster speed. Do three more big-ring sprints from 53:16 at 23 miles per hour (37 km/h). This time you can shift gears twice so that you finish at 53:14. The final sprint of the day is in the big ring from 30 miles per hour (48 km/h). Start at 53:15 and give yourself two gear changes so that you finish at 53:13. Remember that for each sprint you need to wind out each gear until you have nothing left to wind out. Cool down for at least 20 minutes.

Breakaway Tactics to Use as a Team

In many situations you can use a team to your advantage to win a race, but for this chapter, let's focus on the most common ones that will help you win: (1) ensuring a field sprint and leading out the sprinter and (2) putting two riders in a breakaway. To put two riders in a breakaway, they can attack together in a coordinated effort to get both riders in the break, they can attack and counterattack, or one can help the other slip away by gapping her or him.

Ensuring a field sprint is somewhat course dependent, but if the course will likely force a field sprint, then having a team that chases down breakaway attempts or rides on the front to keep the pace high and discourage attacks is a huge advantage. The team must have complete confidence in their sprinter to get the job done, because they are sacrificing their placing to put their sprinter on the top step of the podium. The most important things in a team lead-out are communication between teammates and practice! Teams that are successful in executing a team lead-out practice it regularly. They practice lining up the correct riders in order, making sure that the final lead-out rider before the sprinter can be smooth in the lead-out to minimize hard efforts by the designated sprinter. They also learn how to communicate up and down the paceline. I have worked with many teams over the past 20 years, teaching them to lead out a sprinter properly, and the first three or four tries are always chaotic because some riders ride too hard at the front, creating an accordion effect at the back. Other times riders ride too long at the front, allowing the speed to drop; in a race, the team would be swarmed. Each rider has to learn to be as smooth as possible in the final lead-out and know when to pull off the front and let someone else take a pull. The sprinter, along with his final lead-out rider, must communicate clearly and loudly to make sure that the riders are aligned correctly on the road to provide maximum shelter from the wind. The final lead-out rider must pull off from the paceline on the correct side to give the sprinter a nice hole to jump through. The best teams open a hole at the last minute to allow only the final lead-out rider and sprinter through and then close that hole so that anyone else will have to go around the long way and into the wind.

Putting two riders in a breakaway isn't as hard as it seems. If you go to enough bike races, you'll soon see two riders from the same team in a breakaway. This scenario is favorable because as long as the riders work together and are skilled in tactics, it should be a sure win for one of them. The first part of achieving this goal is getting both riders to attack at the same time so that they go up the road simultaneously or one right after the other.

For the double attack to work, the timing has to be right. The attack needs to be done when the breakaway can succeed (in the correct part of the course, or during a hard part of the race) and when both riders are able to work together quickly to establish a gap with other riders. The scenario won't work if two teammates go up the road and no one else comes with them, or if the attack is launched during a time in the race when the peloton is sure to catch them. Some of the most successful double-rider attacks occur when a teammate attacks from each side of the peloton. That way, additional riders come with each of them. They all come together up the road and instantly start working together as well. Another successful tactic is to have two or three teammates designated to follow each successive attack. If a rider attacks, a teammate follows the attack up the road. Then in the next attack, the other teammate follows it up the road so that when things come together off the front, two teammates are in the breakaway.

After you have two teammates in the breakaway, it becomes a matter of how best to win the race. One rider might lead out the other in a sprint finish, or one rider might attack solo. Then the other rider counterattacks if the first rider is chased down and caught. On a difficult section, one rider might casually open a gap to his or her teammate at the front. Before the other riders in the breakaway realize it, the first rider has a gap on the group. The tactic depends on what the strengths of the riders are and how they are feeling. How confident are you in winning the race? If neither rider is a good sprinter, the attack and counterattack strategy is the best one to follow. When one teammate is off the front, the other is sitting on the second wheel and forcing one of the breakaway companions to chase down the teammate. As soon as that teammate is caught, then the teammate that has been blocking instantly counterattacks and tries a turn at staying away solo. Opening a gap for one rider can be particularly effective if one rider feels confident and strong and the final 10 to 15 minutes of the race includes some hard hills. This tactic takes some coordination. The weaker rider needs to be behind the stronger rider in the order of the breakaway and then carefully open a gap to the stronger rider. Teammates can also create a gap in a criterium when they enter a fast and technical turn. The second rider slows up a little bit and allows the rider in front to gain a quick 10- to 20-meter gap on the breakaway.

One word of caution about having two teammates in the breakaway is that both riders need to work because the other riders in the break will be reluctant to pull or will not pull at all if one teammate is sitting on. The key piece of advice here is to make sure that neither cyclist becomes the workhorse in the break (unless one rider knows that she or he will get dropped and is willing to sacrifice her or his chances for the other one) and that both evenly share the workload. As the end of the race approaches, communication between teammates is critical. If one rider is feeling particularly strong compared with the other rider, the role that each will play to win the race is more obvious.

Key Workout: FTP Work With Bursts   This workout is designed to simulate a breakaway with some hard sprints and attacks near the beginning and end of the workout.

Total time: 2.5 hours. Warm up for 15 to 30 minutes, steady and smooth. For the main set, do 10 hard attacks of 1 minute each. Rest for 1 minute after each attack at 80 revolutions per minute. Now do three efforts of 20 minutes with watts at 95 to 100 percent of FTP. Every 2 minutes during each 20-minute interval, push your watts up to 120 percent of FTP, hold for 20 seconds, and then recover to 95 to 100 percent of FTP. Rest for 5 minutes after each 20-minute block. You will perform solid work at your threshold with some bursts above it! Finish with three race-winning intervals. Make these efforts strong! Cool down for 15 minutes.

Applying the Science

The more experience you have in bike racing, the more chances you have to win. Practicing some of the various race-finishing scenarios can be one of the most helpful ways to learn how to win. Put together a group of riders, find a quiet section of the road at least 5 kilometers long, and split up into teams. Each team should have a specific assignment of how to win the race. Assign each rider a role such as designated sprinter, lead-out, attacker, and so on. Play around with team roles. One team might try the team lead-out, and another team might attack and counterattack the entire time. These short practice races are lots of fun. They allow you to try various scenarios and learn the best way to win a race. Focusing on the finish before you race can help you identify and change your mind-set from one of survival in the breakaway to one of deciding how you will win the race.

CHAPTER 37

Mountain Biking

—Howard T. Hurst

Although mountain biking (MTB) includes several subdisciplines, Olympic cross-country (XCO) and individual downhill (DHI) are the most high-profile events and have received much research interest over the past decade. Both XCO and DHI are raced over trails that include grassy fields, rocky paths, and forestry tracks. XCO courses include a significant amount of climbing, typically around 40 percent of lap distance. Elite XCO races involve mass starts, last between 1.5 and 1.75 hours, and are competed over laps of 4 to 6 kilometers. These events focus primarily on aerobic fitness. In contrast, elite DHI races are conducted in a time-trial format and last 2 to 5 minutes. Course lengths typically vary from 1.5 to 3.5 kilometers. Although aerobic fitness is important, the Union Cycliste Internationale (UCI) states that the emphasis of these races should be on technical skill.

Cross-country and downhill have been described as high intensity and intermittent in nature and place demands on the whole body (Hurst and Atkins 2006). But differences in modern MTB course profiles and the duration of XCO and DHI events have led to discipline-specific developments in both training and equipment design that result in different competition demands. As a result, riders generally specialize in either the endurance or the gravity-based MTB disciplines.

Cross-Country Mountain Biking

Cross-country mountain biking involves mass starts, often with as many 100 riders taking part. Although the focus is primarily on aerobic fitness and races tend to suit athletes who are lighter and slight of build, riders are still required to perform numerous short anaerobic efforts to gain position at the start of the race or to negotiate short, steep climbs. Additionally, high levels of agility, coordination, and balance are needed to overcome obstacles on the course. Subsequently, the demands of XCO racing are unique in comparison with other cycling disciplines.

Cardiovascular Demands

Cross-country racing requires a highly developed aerobic capacity, and early studies found elite XCO riders to be comparable to elite road cyclists in this respect (Padilla et al. 1999; Lucía, Hoyos, and Chicharro 2001). Wilber et al. (1997) reported mean laboratory-based maximal oxygen uptake ($\dot{V}O_2$max) values relative to body mass of about 70 milliliters per kilogram per minute in both U.S. national-level male XCO racers and national-level road cyclists. But they found significant differences in $\dot{V}O_2$max between elite female XCO and road cyclists, potentially because of differences in annual training volume. Furthermore, the aerobic capacity of subelite amateur riders has been shown to be lower, although they still demonstrate a high level of aerobic fitness. Table 37.1 summaries the aerobic capacities of XCO riders at elite and amateur levels.

Field-based data on oxygen uptake during XCO competition is scarce, largely because of the intrusive nature of gas analysis and race regulations that forbid such testing. But MacRae, Hise, and Allen (2000) looked at the relationship between power output and oxygen uptake in mountain bikers during noncompetitive field-based isolated climbing time trials. Average oxygen uptake during the climbs was about 50 milliliters per kilogram per minute, equating to 84 percent of laboratory-based $\dot{V}O_2$max. Because XCO racing includes a significant amount of ascending, it is fair to assume that typical races would be performed at an average intensity somewhere between 80 and 90 percent of $\dot{V}O_2$max values, supporting the notion that high aerobic capacity is a requirement of XCO racing. Additionally, they found average power outputs of about 270 to 340 watts, depending on whether suspension systems were used or not. Use of suspensions resulted in the higher power outputs.

Heart rate (HR) has also been used to quantify the exercise intensity of mountain bike racing. Impellizzeri et al. (2002) observed four elite XCO races and found mean heart rate to be 191 beats per minute, equating to

Table 37.1 Aerobic Capacity of XCO Athletes

Study	Category	L/min	ml·kg^{-1}·min^{-1}	HR$_{max}$ (beats/min)
Gregory, Johns, and Walls 2007	Amateur	4.50 ± 0.5	64.8 ± 8.2	191 ± 7
Impellizzeri and Marcora 2007	Elite	4.9 ± 0.42	75.9 ± 5.0	191 ± 5
Impellizzeri et al. 2005	Elite	4.6 ± 0.47	72.1 ± 7.4	190 ± 7
Lee et al. 2002	Elite	5.1 ± 0.5	78.3 ± 4.4	189 ± 5
Stapelfeldt et al. 2004	Elite		66.5 (M) 58.2 (F)	193 178
Warner, Shaw, and Dalsky 2002	Expert	4.8 ± 0.36	67.4 ± 4.6	
Wilber et al. 1997	Elite	4.9 ± 0.44 (M) 3.3 ± 0.27 (F)	70.0 ± 3.7 (M) 57.9 ± 2.8 (F)	192 ± 12 (M) 178 ± 70 (F)

M = male; F = female.

90 percent of HR_{max} and 84 percent of $\dot{V}O_2max$. They also found that over 82 percent of race durations were performed above lactate threshold (LT), with LT occurring between 75 and 77 percent of $\dot{V}O_2max$. Similar results have been reported elsewhere (Stapelfeldt et al. 2004; Gregory, Johns, and Walls 2007). Gregory, Johns, and Walls went further by splitting a typical XCO course into different sections: ascents of 5 to 10 percent gradient, 10 to 15 percent gradient, and 15 to 20 percent gradient; flat postascent; flat posttechnical; and downhills of 5 to 10 percent gradient, 10 to 15 percent gradient, and 15 to 20 percent gradient. This classification allowed a more detailed analysis of the physiological responses during different phases of a race. Unsurprisingly, HR was highest during the steepest gradient ascents, 179 beats per minute, or about 94 percent of HR_{max}, and lowest during the steepest descents, 150 beats per minute, although this still equated to about 78 percent of HR_{max}, potentially indicating significant isometric contractions of upper-body musculature and the possible influence of stimulation of the adrenal cortex and the release of adrenaline, both of which would aid the maintenance of elevated heart rates. Hurst and Atkins (2002) demonstrated remarkably stable heart rate responses to downhill riding in a group of XCO and DHI riders. Such increase in total muscle contribution to performance may partly explain the higher workloads seen in XCO racing compared with those observed in road cycling.

Power Output and Cadence

The ability to produce high power outputs is critical to XCO performance, because races require riders to perform numerous short-duration bursts of high intensity for climbing, maneuvering over obstacles, and sprinting for position. Laboratory-based incremental tests have shown elite male riders to have maximal aerobic power (MAP) in excess of 420 watts or, when expressed relative to body mass, greater than 5.5 watts per kilogram. Power at LT is about 286 watts for male competitors (Baron 2001; Impellizzeri et al. 2005). Trained subelite riders generally have slightly lower MAP values, between 360 and 400 watts, and the MAP of elite female XCO racers has been shown to be approximately 313 to 320 watts, or about 5 watts per kilogram (Wilber et al. 1997; Stapelfeldt et al. 2004), although power at LT has not been reported for female mountain bikers. Peak power output (PPO) when expressed relative to body mass is around 14 watts per kilogram for male XCO racers, but data on females have yet to be reported.

Unlike road cycling time trials in which power output has been shown to vary by only about 7 percent, XCO racing requires a large range of power output, showing coefficients of variation of 69 percent (Stapelfeldt et al. 2004). Average power output during field-based XCO racing has been shown to be significantly lower than laboratory-based maximal values at about 246 watts, or 3.5 watts per kilogram (Stapelfeldt et al. 2004). The lower power output observed during racing may be attributed to the numerous periods of nonpedaling when either descending or negotiating obstacles.

Stapelfeldt et al. (2004) analyzed power output at various thresholds: time spent below aerobic threshold (AT); time spent between AT and individual aerobic threshold (IAT), defined as 1.5 millimoles per liter lactate above AT; time spent above IAT and below MAP; and time spent above MAP. They found that 39 percent of race duration was spent below AT, 19 percent between AT and IAT, 20 percent between IAT and MAP, and 22 percent above MAP. This range demonstrates the high degree of variance in power output required to complete an XCO race and further demonstrates the need for both high aerobic capacity and high anaerobic capacity.

Concerning cadence choice, Hurst et al. (2012a) found that the optimal cadence for producing peak power was about 108 revolutions per minute in a group of six elite XCO riders. A high cadence has been shown to aid in reducing peripheral muscle fatigue in road cycling from pushing overlarge gears (Patterson and Moreno 1990). The cadence choice of XCO riders, however, may be more indicative of the lower gear ratios used because of the terrain encountered and subsequently the result of specific training methods to maintain high speeds.

Pacing Strategy in XCO Racing

Blood lactate data from XCO racing are at present limited. But of the studies that have determined lactate levels, all have shown a progressive decrease in concentration from 9 to 11 millimoles per liter during the initial stages of an XCO race to 4 to 6 millimoles per liter during the latter stages of the race (Impellizzeri et al. 2002; Stapelfeldt et al. 2004; Wingo et al. 2004). These decreases in lactate levels would indicate a pacing strategy that involves a fast start followed by subsequent decreases in pace and increases in lap time as the race progresses. Although an even pace has often been shown to be beneficial for road-cycling time trials, such a strategy is not possible during XCO racing. Because XCO races are mass-start events in which starting positions are determined by rider ranking, a high-intensity sprint start is usually observed as riders aim to reach the first corner toward the front of the field to avoid bottlenecks and a slowing of pace. Following these high-intensity starts, when heart rate, power output, and lactate can reach near peak levels, pace gradually decreases over the remainder of the race. Additionally, unlike road racing during which riders can draft behind other riders to conserve energy, XCO racing does not allow such tactics. Because of the terrain encountered, riders are frequently required to make high-intensity efforts to climb short, steep inclines and to overcome trail obstacles. Therefore, riders rarely get a period of sustained low-intensity effort. This lack of a break could explain why several studies have reported overall exercise intensity to be greater in XCO racing than that observed in road racing.

Downhill Mountain Biking

Downhill mountain biking demands higher levels of skill and technical ability than those required for XCO racing. But because athletes are required to perform numerous runs over the course of a race weekend, aerobic fitness is still an important element to performance. Over the past decade, courses have become increasingly more technical in nature, and developments in equipment have led to higher speeds. Therefore, these events tend to suit riders who are more powerfully built than XCO athletes. In addition, although environmental factors and equipment choice are important considerations to XCO, they are likely to play a greater role in DHI racing, given the nature of the courses.

Cardiovascular Demands

Like XCO racing, DHI can be characterized as intermittent in nature, although unlike XCO, the efforts required of DHI racing are much shorter in duration. Despite the popularity of DHI racing, limited research exists about the physiological demands of the sport, particularly the aerobic requirements. Hurst and Atkins (2002) were the first to evaluate the demands of DHI riding, although we did not report oxygen uptake of the participants. Instead, we used heart rate as a marker of exercise intensity. As with XCO racing, this choice was largely because of the intrusive nature of gas analysis and possible health and safety implications of such testing. As indicated by other studies, the use of such systems may impede rider vision because of the wearing of masks. In addition, the weight and restrictive nature of the harness may influence the natural biomechanics of the riders (Sperlich et al. 2012).

Sperlich and colleagues currently provide the only available data on the aerobic capacity of elite DHI racers. During laboratory-based testing they found that mean peak oxygen uptake was 59 milliliters per kilogram per minute. This value is significantly lower than that reported for elite XCO riders. The peak oxygen uptake levels reported by Sperlich et al. (2012) indicate that aerobic capacity is important to DHI racing, although not to the same extent as for XCO racing. The lower values reported most likely reflect differences in training modalities between DHI and XCO riders and the more sprint-based nature of DHI. Therefore, training will likely focus more on brief high-intensity efforts rather than the more sustained though still high-intensity efforts characteristic of XCO racing. Despite the high-intensity nature of DHI, riders are required to perform numerous practice runs followed by a qualification run and final during the course of a race meeting. Therefore, good aerobic capacity is potentially advantageous to aid recovery between runs, although the correlation between aerobic capacity and DHI performance has yet to be determined.

Despite the inherent difficulties of field-based assessments of aerobic capacity in DHI riders, Burr et al. (2012) are the only group currently to have established such field-based data. They tested a mixed gender group of experienced but subelite downhill riders and reported average $\dot{V}O_2$ during field-based downhill riding of 23 milliliters per kilogram per minute, equating to 52 percent of the riders' laboratory-derived maximal values (45 milliliters per kilogram per minute). But values ranged between 19 and 75 percent of maximal values, thus indicating the diverse nature of the sample group. Therefore, aerobic contributions may be significantly higher in elite riders. Burr and colleagues also found mean HR during the downhill runs to be 146 beats per minute. This value was significantly lower than that reported in our studies of 176 and 168 beats per minute (Hurst and Atkins 2002; Hurst and Atkins 2006, respectively) and also lower than that of Sperlich et al. (2012), who reported a mean value of 183 beats per minute in elite German DHI racers. These absolute values indicate significant differences between elite and subelite riders, but when expressed as a percentage of maximal HR, all the reviewed studies reported intensities greater than 80 percent of maximal heart rate irrespective of ability and above 90 percent for elite riders.

Despite those findings and the relative ease of heart rate monitoring, heart rate values do not reflect the intermittent nature of the sport. In both our study and that of Sperlich et al., heart rates remained stable following an initial rapid increase at the start of the runs. This finding is somewhat paradoxical to the observed stochastic nature of the event and is potentially influenced by increased upper-body isometric contractions to stabilize the rider and maneuver the bike down the course. In addition, the psychologically stressful nature of such extreme sports may influence heart rate. Indeed, Sperlich and colleagues investigated the psychophysiological responses to DHI racing and found that both pre- and postrace salivary cortisol levels, used as a marker of stress, were more than double those recorded during baseline testing the day before the German National Championships. This finding supports the notion that DHI racing induces stress and therefore may elevate heart rate response. Because of this paradox our research group has sought to use power output to determine the demands of downhill racing.

Power Output and Cadence

Hurst and Atkins (2006) used an SRM power meter to determine the field-based power output of 17 trained subelite male DHI racers. Mean peak power output during the runs was 834 watts and ranged between 518 and 1,064 watts. Peak power was achieved within an average of 4 seconds (range of 2 to 8 seconds). Although this interval is somewhat less than that recorded for track cyclists, this result again likely occurs because of the course terrain used in this study and the relatively bumpy initial few meters out of the start ramp being followed by a smoother section. Therefore, time to peak power is likely to differ considerably depending on course design. When peak power was adjusted for body mass, relative peak power equated to 10.7 watts per kilogram. But these values were lower than those we recorded for elite DHI racers from the Swedish national DHI team during laboratory testing. They recorded a mean peak power output of 1,137 watts, which when expressed relative to body mass equated to 15 watts per kilogram (Hurst et al. 2012a). The data currently available for both elite and subelite DHI riders suggest that PPO is not significantly different from that of comparable XCO riders. This finding may suggest that high peak power outputs for DHI are not a key contributor to performance and that skill may be more important. In addition, the relatively low peak power outputs of DHI racers, when compared with those of other sprint-cycling disciplines, likely reflect the influence of course profiles on power production and therefore do not reflect a lower physical ability of the riders.

Hurst and Atkins (2006) observed that mean power output of subelite riders over the course of a whole DHI run was only 75 watts, equating to only 9 percent of the peak values. Again, however, pedaling opportunities in DHI are largely determined by course design. When riders are not pedaling, the SRM power meter would naturally record a zero value. In the course used in our 2006 study, 55 percent of the mean run time was spent not pedaling, which likely explains the low mean power outputs observed.

With respect to optimal cadence at peak power output, both elite and subelite riders appear to select comparable cadences, 114 and 128 revolutions per minute, respectively, irrespective of whether testing was field based or laboratory based. Again, this result may reflect the sprint-based training that these athletes perform. Figure 37.1 shows the mean HR, power output, and cadence data of the 17 DHI riders monitored in the Hurst and Atkins (2006) study.

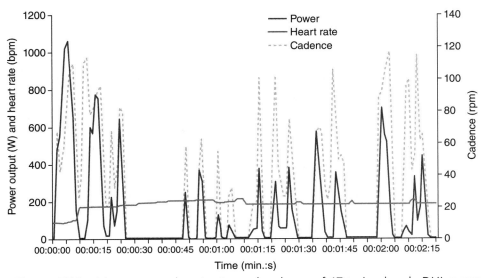

▶ **Figure 37.1** Mean power, heart rate, and cadence of 17 trained male DHI racers during a downhill race. Data were recorded at 5-second intervals.

Other Factors Influencing MTB Performance

As alluded to previously, course profile plays a significant role in the demands of both XCO and DHI racing. Both XCO and DHI include numerous sections in which pedaling is often not possible. Nevertheless, heart rate remains elevated while power output is relatively low during these phases. Therefore, these methods may not provide the optimal means of determining the true energetics of these sports, particularly during descents. Newer technologies such as global positioning systems (GPS), accelerometry, and assessment of the muscles' electrical activity (by surface electromyography [sEMG]) may prove more insightful.

Hurst et al. (2012b, 2013) investigated the muscle activity of elite DHI and XCO racers from the Swedish national teams during descents on courses of differing difficulties. These courses were categorized as either manmade (MM) or natural terrain (NT). The manmade courses were more sculptured, had a somewhat smoother surface, and included several manmade jumps and obstacles, whereas the natural terrain course followed a more direct route down the mountain and used the surrounding landscape to provide technical challenges. Electrical activity of the biceps, triceps, forearm, and latissimus was monitored throughout the runs. We found no significant differences in the amplitude of muscle activity between courses or between groups, but when we compared each muscle group against each other, significant differences were revealed with respect to which muscles were activated the most between DHI and XCO riders.

For the DHI riders, the triceps was activated to a significantly greater degree than either the biceps or latissimus for both courses when expressed as a percentage of maximal voluntary isometric contraction force (MVIC). For XCO riders, no differences were found between courses, although this time the forearm was recruited to a greater extent than the other muscles. Results of this study can be seen in figures 37.2 and 37.3. We conclude that these findings may be due in part to the differences in bicycle design and setup. As a result, XCO and DHI riders should consider adopting training practices that specifically target those muscles to increase strength and potentially reduce the risk of injury because of muscle fatigue.

Although assessment of muscle activity may provide further information to supplement power and HR data, this method is somewhat intrusive, even with newer wireless systems, and it may interfere with the natural movement of the riders. In addition, assessment of muscle sEMG is costly, prohibiting its use for most riders. GPS and accelerometry, however, are rapidly becoming more affordable and can potentially provide a more useable means of determining the activity profile of DHI and XCO racing and training on different courses. Hurst et al. (2013) used GPS and accelerometry technology to determine acceleration, deceleration, and instantaneous and accumulated rider

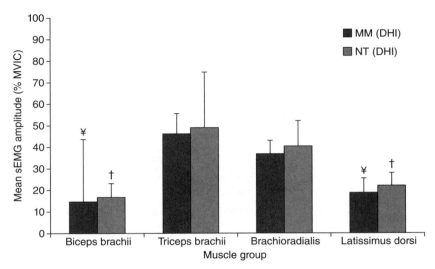

▶**Figure 37.2** Mean plus or minus standard deviation of mean sEMG amplitude as a percentage of maximal voluntary isometric contraction for DHI riders during NT and MM downhill runs. ¥ significantly different from triceps (MM); † significantly different from triceps (NT).

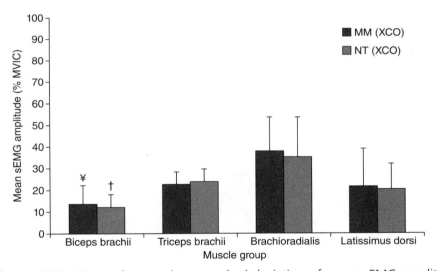

▶**Figure 37.3** Mean plus or minus standard deviation of mean sEMG amplitude as a percentage of maximal voluntary isometric contraction for XCO riders during NT and MM downhill runs. ¥ significantly different from forearm (MM); † significantly different from forearm (NT).

loads, along with time spent in different velocity bands and the number of efforts and distance per effort within these bands performed by DHI riders. We looked at these responses over different courses and showed that this technology is sensitive and accurate enough to monitor DHI, and probably XCO, performance in various environments and, more important, during the numerous nonpedaling phases of those events. Such technology may enable riders and coaches to target training and bicycle setup for specific courses and pinpoint the demands at specific points on a course, thereby providing a more powerful diagnostic and training tool. Figure 37.4 shows a screen shot of the GPS and accelerometry software, illustrating how video footage can be synchronized with the data to enable pinpointing of rider loads at any point on a course.

With respect to bicycle setup, downhill bikes generally have greater suspension travel, larger-diameter disc brakes, and slacker head tube angles than those found on XCO bikes. Hurst et al. (2012b) proposed that these differences may lead to the differences in muscle recruitment between the disciplines. Because of the slacker head tube angles of downhill bikes (typically between 63 and 67 degrees) and the significantly wider handlebars than those on XCO bikes, the rider would potentially be in a more rearward position on the bike when descending, therefore placing more stress on the triceps brachii muscles. In contrast, the steeper angles seen on XCO bikes (69 to 72 degrees) potentially force the rider's mass farther forward and over the handlebars, resulting in the greater forearm activity seen in the XCO riders. In addition to frame geometry, the greater degree of suspension travel on downhill bikes most likely reduces the forces transferred to the forearms, and larger disc brakes may result in less force being required to decelerate the bicycle. But fitting larger brakes to XCO bikes would increase the overall mass of rider and bicycle, therefore requiring more energy to ride uphill, something that DHI riders are less concerned with.

The optimal balance between the level of suspension travel and brake diameter, and therefore mass, to reduce upper-body stress before perfor-

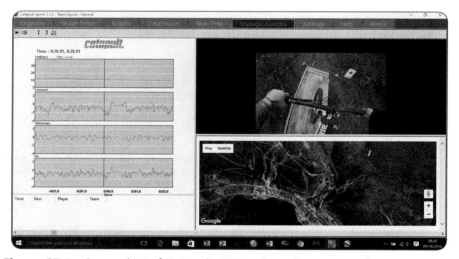

▶ **Figure 37.4** Screenshot of Catapult GPS and accelerometry software.

Howard Hurst. Used with permission of Catapult.

mance is compromised has yet to be determined. Similarly, the exact extent of suspension travel on upper-body activity has yet to be investigated in a more controlled environment that has the same riders performing trials on both long- and short-travel bicycles. Future research might seek to test riders using different suspension setups to get a more complete indication of the effectiveness of these systems. Studies have looked at the effects of suspension on heart rate and oxygen uptake (MacRae, Hise, and Allen 2000; Seifert et al. 1997) and have found that suspension increases the energy cost of muscles, although how much more the muscles are activated because of different suspension setups has not been reported.

Applying the Science

XCO and DHI are both high-intensity, intermittent activities that require high levels of aerobic and anaerobic ability, at both elite and subelite levels. Course terrain largely determines the energy demands of these races, because some courses are more technically challenging than others. Current research, however, indicates that the different demands of the two primary MTB disciplines require athletes to specialize in one event or the other. Cross-country riders should focus on developing power at the lactate threshold, because these races are performed largely at or above this intensity, along with the ability to perform repeated short-duration near-maximal efforts. In contrast, DHI riders should focus on developing rapid acceleration and time to peak power to get a fast start and accelerate out of corners, although skill is likely to play a greater role in overall performance by facilitating speed through technical sections. Despite the predominantly anaerobic nature of DHI, riders should not neglect aerobic conditioning, which may influence recovery between race runs. With respect to strength, both XCO and DHI riders should aim to develop good core stability, which may help in reducing fatigue, maintaining good body position, and maneuvering the bicycle. Finally, current research suggests that the differences in bike design and setup influence muscular activity and that riders would benefit from upper-body strength training that emphasizes lower-arm strength in XCO riders and upper-arm and back strength in DHI riders. Further research in this area is warranted.

CHAPTER 38

Track Cycling

—Chris R. Abbiss and Paolo Menaspà

The first track-cycling competitions date back to the late 19th century (i.e., 1870). Track cycling has been an Olympic sport since the first edition of the modern Olympic Games in 1896, with the exception of the 1912 edition, when the organizing committee decided not to build a velodrome.

In recent years, the Olympic Games track-cycling program has considerably changed with the inclusion of new competitions and the loss of more traditional events. Since the London 2012 Games, the Games have had 10 events, 5 for men and 5 for women.

Track cyclists could be classified into two distinct categories based on their anthropometric and physiological characteristics, which suit different races. Indeed, many short competitions are designed for sprinters; longer races, sometimes involving bunch riding, are specifically intended for endurance cyclists.

Velodromes have a characteristic oval shape consisting of two straights and two turns. Both the straights and the turns are banked, though with differing slopes. Velodromes can be categorized into the following types: indoor or outdoor; short or long based on their lengths, ranging from about 180 meters to more than 600 meters; and fast or slow based on their surfaces (i.e., wood or concrete). Shorter velodromes typically have steeper banking when compared with longer velodromes. Recent Track World Championships and Olympic Games typically have been organized on indoor, 250-meter wooden velodromes. In the last century more than 100 velodromes have been built by Schuermann Architects.

Track Cycling for Sprinters

This section briefly describes the main characteristics of track-cycling competitions dedicated to sprinters, riders who excel in short, fast competitions.

Individual Sprint

The individual sprint is among the oldest of the track competitions and was part of the Athens 1896 Olympic Games. In the modern format, the race starts with a 200-meter time-trial race, used to select and rank the participants. In this flying effort, riders have 3.5 laps to reach the desired speed and position on the track. Athletes are able to use the track banking to reach maximal speed during the timed flying 200 meters. The individual sprint race itself is a competition between two (in particular cases up to four) riders over the length of 750 meters (3 laps). The individual sprint tournament is organized in heats, and the starting position is determined by drawing lots. Rules guarantee fairness for all the competitors, but the most important is that the winner is the first rider to cross the finish line.

Keirin

The keirin race is a competition in which five to seven riders sprint to the finish line after having completed a number of laps behind a motorized pacer. As with other sprint races, the winner is the first rider to cross the finish line. At the start the riders follow a motorized pacer, who gradually increases the speed to 45 kilometers per hour for women and 50 kilometers per hour for men and eventually leaves the track with 2.5 laps to go. The competition is organized with qualifying rounds, heats, and finals. The finals always have six riders.

Team Sprint

The team sprint was introduced in the Olympic program at the Sydney 2000 Games. The competition has a standing start, and the winning team is the one that covers the distance in the shorter time. In this race two opposing teams contest each other over a fixed distance. Each rider leads for one lap and then drops off, leaving the final rider to race the last lap solo. The men's event is run by three riders over 3 laps (750 meters), whereas the women's event involves two cyclists over 2 laps (500 meters). The event is organized with qualifying rounds and finals.

Time Trial

The time-trial races were not part of the Rio Olympic program, despite previously being Olympic events. At cycling Track World Championships the time trials are 1,000 meters for men and 500 meters for women. These races begin from a standing start, and the final ranking is based on riding time.

Track Cycling for Endurance Riders

This section briefly describes the main characteristics of track-cycling competitions dedicated to endurance cyclists. These riders specialize in efforts that take approximately 4 minutes to 1 hour.

Team Pursuit

The team pursuit has been in the Olympic program since London 1908. In the team pursuit two teams of four riders compete on a fixed distance of 4,000 meters, starting on opposite sides of the track. The winning team is the one with the fastest time or the team that catches the team that started on the other side of the track. Four cyclists start the race, but only three are required to finish. Time stops when the third cyclist crosses the finish line. The event has qualifying rounds and finals. Up until 2013 the women's competition covered a distance of 3,000 meters by three riders, but has since also been standardized to 4,000 meters and four riders per team.

　　The team pursuit is an important competition in which various nations participating in World Championships and Olympic Games can compare performance. Success in such events is determined by the consistent performance of the whole team, not the talent of a single outstanding cyclist. Given the complex relationship of team tactics, physiological fitness, aerodynamics, and other factors that are important to success in the team pursuit, this race is an interesting event when trying to understand what is involved in high-level sport performance (e.g., coaching, equipment, sport science). Indeed, several studies have analyzed practical and theoretical aspects of the 4,000-meter team pursuit races, highlighting the power demand of the teams participating in the 1996 and 2000 Olympic Games (Broker, Kyle, and Burke 1999; Schumacher and Mueller 2002).

Omnium

The omnium is a single competition consisting of six different events held over 2 consecutive days. It is the newest Olympic track-cycling event, first included in the Olympic program in London 2012. The cycling event includes six races: scratch, individual pursuit, elimination, time trial, flying lap, and points race. The events are always performed in that order. For each of the first five events, the winner earns 40 points, second place earns 38 points, third place earns 36 points, and so on. The total points scored in the fifth event are used as starting points for the final event, the points race, which has a different point system (for details, see the later section Omnium Points Race). The cyclist with the highest number of points at the end of the sixth and final event is the winner of the omnium. Given the complexity of various races that may be important in overall success of the omnium, research has examined the use of statistics and machine-learning techniques to analyze the scoring system of the event to improve the decision-making process toward successful participation in competition (Ofoghi et al. 2013).

Omnium Scratch Race

The scratch race is the track-cycling competition that most closely resembles a road race. It is an individual race over a specified distance. Men compete over a distance of 15 kilometers, and women compete at 10 kilometers.

Omnium Individual Pursuit

In the individual pursuit, two riders compete over a fixed distance, starting on the opposite sides of the track. The race begins with a standing start, and the cyclists are ranked based on their race time: The faster rider is the winner. Male cyclists ride 4,000 meters, and female cyclists ride 3,000 meters.

Omnium Elimination Race

The elimination is an individual race that includes intermediate sprints every two laps. The biggest difference when compared with a traditional race is that during the elimination race riders don't sprint to cross the finish line in first position. Instead, riders sprint to avoid crossing the finish line in last position. As the name suggests, the rider who finishes last during each intermediate sprint is eliminated from the race.

Omnium Time Trial

In the omnium competition, time trials have a similar format to the individual pursuit; the main difference is the race length. During the time-trial events, men compete over 1,000 meters, and women race over 500 meters. As with the individual pursuit, these events begin from a standing start.

Omnium Flying Lap

The flying lap is a race against the clock over a length of 250 meters (one lap). Cyclists are allowed to use the banking of the velodrome to maximize their starting speed.

Omnium Points Race

In the points race cyclists can score points with intermediate sprints (i.e., 5, 3, 2, and 1 point for the first four classified) or by laps (i.e., 20 points each time a cyclist can break away and reach the tail of the main bunch). The final ranking is determined by the sum of the points scored during the event plus the initial points (sum of the points for the first five events of the omnium). The event is raced over 40 kilometers in the men's events and 25 kilometers in the women's events. The points race is the final event of the omnium, so the winner of the points race is the overall winner.

Individual Pursuit

The individual pursuit competition was previously a traditional Olympic event but nowadays has been removed from the Olympic program. The event is still part of the Track World Championship program and similar to the event held in the omnium race (see previous section). The difference with the omnium event is that a complete individual pursuit event involves both qualification rounds and finals.

Points Race

The points race is a relatively new competition, first included in the Olympic program at the Los Angeles 1984 Games, but it's not part of the current Olympic program. The points race has similar rules to the event run within the omnium competition. The main difference is that all the cyclists start with zero points. The ranking is determined by the sum of the points won by the cyclists during intermediate sprints or by laps.

Scratch

The scratch race is part of the Track World Championships program and is similar to a road-cycling race. The scratch is an individual race over a specified distance. Men race 15 kilometers, and women race 10 kilometers.

Madison

The Madison has been part of several Olympic programs from Sydney 2000 to Beijing 2008. It is not currently an event in the Olympic program, but it remains an important event in the Track World Cup and World Championship programs. The Madison is a competition similar (but not identical) to the points race. The difference is that the Madison involves a pair of cyclists of which only one at a time actively participates in the race. The final ranking is determined by distance (i.e., laps are accounted for in a different way) plus total points scored.

The Hour Record

The hour record is a unique track-cycling event that involves cyclists traveling the longest distance possible on a bike in 1 hour from a standing start. Several hour record holders have been successful road cyclists, even though the event is and has always been a track-cycling affair.

History of the Hour Record

The first hour record was set in 1876 by an American who rode 26.5 kilometers on a penny-farthing bike. The first record to be officially approved by the Union Cycliste Internationale (UCI) was recorded 17 years later in 1893, when Henri Desgrange of France rode 35.2 kilometers in Paris. In the 1930s and 1940s the Italians Olmo (45.1 kilometers) and Coppi (45.8 kilometers) broke the record while riding on the famous Vigorelli velodrome in Milan. In the 1950s, 1960s, and 1970s several Tour de France winners established new records; for example, Jacques Anquetil rode 46.2 kilometers in 1956 and Eddy Merckx rode 49.4 kilometers in 1972. In the meantime, the Russian Tamara Novikova set the women's record with a distance of 38.5 kilometers in 1955.

The hour record has always been an interesting event, often used to test new frontiers in equipment, aerodynamics, physiology (e.g., altitude attempts), sport science support, and training.

The Record and Rule Changes

The evolution of the hour record is strongly connected with changes in UCI regulations. In particular, in 1997 the UCI established two categories for the record: the UCI World Record, with several restrictions in equipment and a standardized cycling positioning, and the UCI Absolute Record, in which cyclists can use more modern cycling equipment. (In 1996 Chris Boardman rode 56.4 kilometers to set the Men's Absolute Record and Jeannie Longo-Ciprelli rode 48.2 kilometers to set the Women's Absolute Record.) The establishment of this new rule reduced the number of attempts. Following the 1990s when the hour record was extremely popular, interest in the event waned. But in 2014 the regulations for the hour record were changed. From 2014 onward, cyclists were allowed to use aerodynamic bikes, basically the same equipment that can be used during regular track competitions.

Modern Hour Record

Since the 2014 rule change, several male and female cyclists have attempted to set new hour records. Currently, the men's record is held by Sir Bradley Wiggins at a distance of 54.526 kilometers, and the women's record is held by Evelyn Stevens at 47.980 kilometers. As mentioned previously, the hour record could be considered a showcase of physiology, technology, and science. In fact, research has shown that when going from the standard Merckx position to the futuristic Obree position, a cyclist could travel at the same speed with 20 percent less power (about 80 watts) (Bassett et al. 1999).

To date, little data have been published detailing the power output during hour record attempts, but it was estimated that when Tony Rominger rode 55.291 kilometers in 1994 under the old Hour Record rules, he produced an average power output of 7.0 watts per kilogram (power: 456 watts, mass: 65 kilograms) (Padilla et al. 2000).

Characteristics of Track Cyclists

The nature of track-cycling competitions, with durations ranging between a few seconds and 2 days, allows a broad spectrum of cyclists to excel in velodrome racing. Because of the obvious lack of climbs, track cyclists are generally taller and heavier than their road or off-road colleagues. In recent history, cyclists switching their focus from road to track (and vice versa) have recorded body weight changes in the magnitude of approximately 10 kilograms of lean mass.

Sprinters

Sprint track-cycling events are unique in that athletes are required to produce extremely high power outputs for relatively short periods. Elite male sprint track cyclists produce in excess of 1,600 to 1,800 watts (19 to 20 watts per kilogram) (Dorel et al. 2005; Gardner et al. 2007), and elite females produce 1,300 to 1,500 watts (18 to 20 watts per kilogram). This high power output is needed to accelerate the athlete and the bicycle to maximal velocities from a standing, rolling, or flying start, depending on the particular sprint event. Because of the unique requirements, the anthropometric and physiological requirements of successful sprint track cyclists differ from those of most other competitive cyclists.

Although the duration of a sprint event is relatively short, the physiological requirements of track sprinting are complex. Indeed, cyclists are required to produce high power over a range of muscle contraction velocities and in different bike positions (i.e., standing versus sitting). For instance, at the start of standing-start events cyclists produce high torques (more than 200 to 300 newton meters) (Gardner et al. 2007) to accelerate the bicycle in the shortest possible time. Because track bicycles do not have gears, this high torque is produced at very low cadences. The acceleration phase is critical in sprint cycling and requires athletes to have well-developed muscular strength.

At later stages in the event, cyclists are required to produce high power output at extremely rapid contraction velocities. Peak power output is typically produced at cadences of approximately 125 to 135 revolutions per minute (Dorel et al. 2005; Gardner et al. 2007), and peak cadences reach over 200 revolutions per minute (figure 38.1). Because of this wide range in physical requirements, the physical, physiological, and performance characteristics of cyclists competing in the same sprint events may differ greatly, even if they finish within 1000s of a second from each other.

For example, one sprinter may be extremely strong and rapidly accelerate to peak velocity but not possess the neuromuscular characteristics necessary to maintain the high cadences later in the event. The rider is eventually overtaken by a weaker but more fatigue-resistant cyclist. Such differences highlight the variety of training techniques and foci (i.e., hypertrophy,

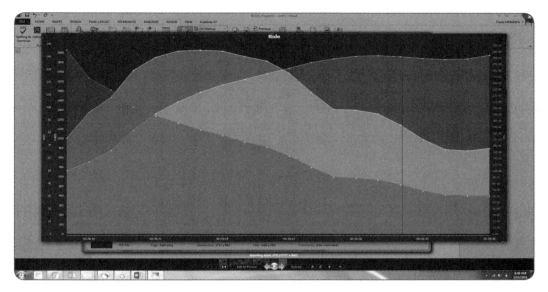

▶ **Figure 38.1** Cadence (increasing all the way during the effort), torque (decreasing), and power (bell-shaped curve) profiles of a standing 250-meter sprint event. Note that the registration starts when the rider reaches 50 revolutions per minute.

Chris R. Abbiss and Paolo Menaspà

strength, power, endurance, and fatigue resistance) that may be manipulated to maximize sprint track-cycling performance.

Trained track sprinters not only have greater thigh and calf girths than endurance cyclists have but also typically have greater chest and arm girth, highlighting the importance of upper-body strength in sprint cycling (McLean and Parker 1989). The high muscle mass of a sprint track cyclist allows greater force development and powerful extension of the hip, knee, and ankle, particularly in the acceleration phase of the sprint. Note that during such events track cyclists are required to accelerate their own mass. Furthermore, a larger surface area will increase the aerodynamic drag experienced by the athlete, particularly at the high speeds reached later in the event. As such, a tradeoff occurs between high muscle mass, which is required to produce the high force necessary to accelerate the bicycle to peak velocities, and low overall body mass, which reduces the energy cost of acceleration, rolling resistance, and projected frontal area.

Yet given the importance of the acceleration phase, hypertrophy (increased muscle mass) is generally believed to be an extremely important aspect to maximizing functional muscle strength and performance in sprint cycling. Indeed, successful track cyclists spend a considerable portion of their training in resistance training to increase muscle mass and maximize strength. But because body weight and body surface area are important aspects of sprint-cycling performance, such athletes also try to minimize nonfunctional mass (i.e., additional body fat). Consequently, professional sprint cyclists have an extremely low body fat percentage (males less than 12 percent and females less than 20 percent) (Dorel et al. 2005).

In addition to high muscular strength, sprint track cyclists also possess other specific neuromuscular characteristics that further allow a rapid rate of force development. The rate at which the muscles can produce force is influenced by several factors including muscle fiber type and the stiffness of the muscle–tendon unit (Driss and Vandewalle 2013). An important aspect associated with muscle fiber type is the aerobic and anaerobic characteristics of the athlete. As expected, sprint cyclists possess extremely high anaerobic capacities that facilitate the rapid supply of energy (ATP) through anaerobic pathways. Furthermore, such anaerobic capacities are typically higher than those in their endurance counterparts (Craig et al. 1995a).

To date, limited research has described the aerobic characteristics of sprint cyclists. Given the duration of sprint-cycling events, however, absolute aerobic capacity is likely an important aspect to success, particularly in the longer competitions. Of particular importance is the athlete's upper capacity for aerobic metabolism ($\dot{V}O_2$max) and the rate at which the athlete is able to increase oxygen uptake at commencement of exercise, known as $\dot{V}O_2$ kinetics.

Endurance Riders

When compared with sprint track cycling, endurance track cycling has far different competition demands because of the longer duration of the events. As a result, the anthropometric and physiological characteristics of endurance track cyclists differ considerably. Indeed, the physical characteristics of endurance track cyclists are much more similar to those of road cyclists. In fact, many cyclists often compete in both endurance track and road-cycling competitions throughout a season or between seasons. But some evidence indicates that the anthropometric characteristics of such cyclists differ slightly; world-class road cyclists are slightly leaner and lighter than endurance track cyclists (Haakonssen et al. 2016). These differences are likely because of notable differences between these events.

Endurance track-cycling events are typically shorter in duration than most road-cycling competitions. In addition, track cyclists are not required to perform the same volume of uphill climbing (cycling against gravity). Therefore, absolute power output rather than relative (watts per kilogram) power output becomes slightly more important to endurance track cyclists, who may benefit from having a slightly higher muscle mass compared with competitive road cyclists.

Because the demands of each endurance track-cycling event differ, the physiological characteristics of athletes who compete in these events can vary. Yet given the nature of these events, aerobic capacity appears to be incredibly important to success. Indeed, endurance track cyclists often spend considerable time at their maximal aerobic capacity ($\dot{V}O_2$max). As a result, they have some of the highest values recorded (90 milliliters per kilogram per minute) (Craig and Norton 2001).

Note that $\dot{V}O_2$max is extremely important in recovery during the many intermittent high-intensity endurance track-cycling events. Indeed, in endurance events, extremely high power outputs may be reached when accelerating, when riding as the lead cyclist in the team pursuit (figure 38.2), or during repeat sprints in the points or elimination races. Craig and Norton (2001) and Jeukendrup, Craig, and Hawley (2000) have reported case studies on the power output of elite team pursuit cyclists during competition. In these studies, instantaneous power outputs of 1,000 to 1,250 watts were observed for the first 10 seconds. Thereafter, outputs fluctuated between 650 and 700 watts for the lead position and 350 to 400 watts when positioned behind team members. At velocities approaching the world record (greater than or equal to 65 kilometers per hour), lead power outputs of between 700 and 800 watts are required within the team pursuit.

Such power outputs surpass the athletes' aerobic limits, so they rely heavily on anaerobic energy pathways during the efforts (ATP–PC and glycolysis). Yet the recovery from such efforts depends highly on the athletes' aerobic capacity (Balsom et al. 1992; Glaister et al. 2006). Consequently, successful endurance track cyclists are required to possess high aerobic (greater than or equal to 70 milliliters per kilogram per minute) and anaerobic (greater than or equal to 61 milliliters per kilogram) capacities, the magnitude of which are positively correlated to power output and overall performance time (Craig et al. 1993; 1995b; Craig, Pyke, and Norton 1989). Besides maximal aerobic and anaerobic capacities, many other factors can influence endurance track-cycling performance, including lactate kinetics, threshold power,

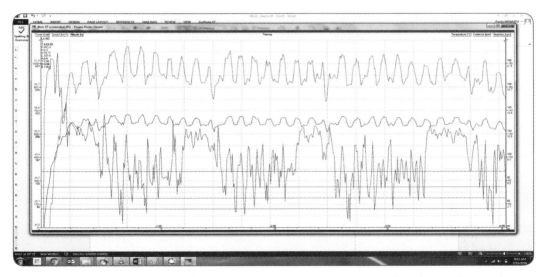

▶ **Figure 38.2** Example of the intermittent power output and cadence during the 4,000-meter team pursuit. The three lines in the graph are (from the top) speed, cadence, and power, respectively.

Chris R. Abbiss and Paolo Menaspà

critical power, and exercise economy (Coyle et al. 1991; Jeukendrup, Craig, and Hawley 2000; Mujika and Padilla 2001).

An additional physiological characteristic that has been shown to be important to many endurance track events is the rate at which athletes are able to increase oxygen uptake (known as $\dot{V}O_2$ kinetics). Indeed, adopting a relatively faster start during the first 10 to 15 seconds of exercise has been found to increase $\dot{V}O_2$ kinetics in cycling bouts lasting 54 seconds to 6 minutes (Aisbett et al. 2009b; Hettinga, De Koning, and Foster 2009; Hettinga et al. 2007) and can result in a 25 percent increase in $\dot{V}O_2$ in the first 60 seconds of the event compared with a more conservative start (Aisbett et al. 2009b). The same effect has been shown to occur when cycling bouts of 1.5 to 10 minutes are preceded by an intense warm-up phase (Palmer et al. 2009). Both techniques result in improved performance (Aisbett et al. 2009a, 2009b; Miura et al. 2009; Palmer et al. 2009). The increase in $\dot{V}O_2$ with either an intense warm-up (Palmer et al. 2009) or an all-out start (Aisbett et al. 2009b) reduces demands on anaerobic energy until later in the event, thereby allowing the cyclist to maintain higher power output later in the event.

Applying the Science

Track cycling has the reputation of being the university of cycling. The track is where cyclists learn basic skills, racing tactics, and strategies. With the ease of measuring and comparing splits and therefore performance, cyclists in their development phase are pushed to focus on details that are sometimes overlooked in road and off-road cycling programs (especially at young ages). These aspects include aerodynamics, gear selection, and equipment choices. Furthermore, within track cycling, every training session is completed under the supervision of a coach, which is logistically impossible in other disciplines of cycling.

Track competitions have profoundly changed over the last century and will keep progressing to adapt to modern times and to attract new generations of talent. Although several endurance medals were awarded in the past, the current Olympic format is skewed toward sprinters; 60 percent of the medals are awarded for sprint events. This bias may indicate the direction in which track cycling is evolving.

Sprint and endurance track cyclists generally have different career paths. Sprint cyclists usually dedicate their full careers to track cycling (with a few rare exceptions). Endurance cyclists often use track as a step in their cycling careers, and several renowned road cyclists have earned world titles and Olympic medals as track cyclists before signing professional road-cycling contracts.

CHAPTER 39

BMX

—Manuel Mateo-March and Cristina Blasco-Lafarga

In 2003 the International Olympic Committee decided that bicycle motocross (BMX) should join the Olympic disciplines, giving BMX riders, coaches, technicians, researchers, manufacturers, and others the opportunity to develop the sport and reach new heights. Beijing 2008 was the first Games in which people could enjoy BMX riders' ability to negotiate seemingly impossible tracks, by both men and women, confirming the International Olympic Committee's expectation about public attendance and media interest.

BMX consists of speed racing across an always-different small track (figure 39.1): 300 to 400 meters of an explosive speed race interspersed with jumps, banked turns, and other obstacles (120 to 160 meters long by 50 to 60 meters wide if a single start ramp is used; 120 to 160 meters long by 70 to 80 meters if a double start ramp is used). Each race lasts about 40 to 45 seconds, requires close to maximal anaerobic power, and is full of neuromuscular requirements, although aerobic power might be crucial as well, as we will explain later.

Summarizing, the technique, strength, and stamina demands are high, and the race time is short. Success and failure in elite athletes is often determined by a margin between first and second as narrow as 1 percent. No time is available to recover from even a small technical or tactical mistake. For example, at the London 2012 Olympic Games, the first four positions in the BMX men's individual final were decided by less than 1 second. Keep in mind as well that riders have to warm up and compete in qualifying rounds until the eight best compete in the final, which gives the aerobic pathway paramount importance.

BMX rules accept several differences in track design. As a result, tracks vary considerably, and track characteristics increase in difficulty as the level increases, from low difficulty in conventional tracks at national and continental levels to maximum difficulty in UCI Supercross tracks (Mateo-March et al. 2012a). The UCI BMX track design guidelines (UCI 2014) describe these features and their legal considerations. This freedom in the rules allows great creativity in design and highlights the importance of technical mastery and plasticity among BMX riders.

Figure 39.1 shows the structure of a basic track layout and some important minimum distances to ensure rider security. According to this structure and the performance profile, we can distinguish three phases in the BMX race (Mateo, Blasco-Lafarga, and Zabala 2011).

First is the gate start phase, an acceleration phase determined by the gradient of the start ramp and largely conditioned by the values of maximum strength and the resulting rate of force development, or RFD (Mateo, Blasco-Lafarga, and Zabala 2011; Mateo-March et al. 2012b; Mateo and Zabala 2007; Zabala, Sánchez-Muñoz, and Mateo 2009), which are important capacities for reaching maximum acceleration (Rylands and Roberts 2014). We include the start ramp and the 5 or so meters until the first obstacle. The length of the start ramp may change from a minimum of 2.5 meters in C1 and national events to 5 meters in UCI-certified BMX World Challenge and a maximum height of 8 meters in Continental and World Championships and Olympics. This initial phase is crucial for success, because it is important to be at the front of the race from the very beginning of the competition and to choose the best lines to gain advantage over opponents (Mateo, Blasco-Lafarga, and Zabala 2011; Mateo et al. 2012a).

Immediately afterward is a large and mixed central phase in which riders have to combine impulse actions without pedaling when tackling

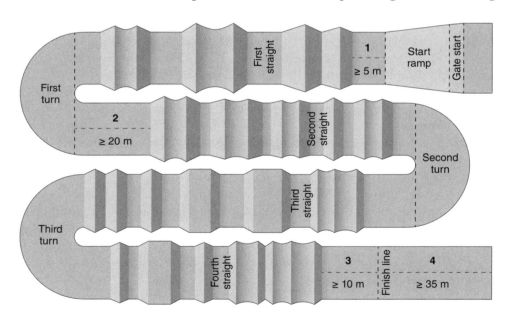

120 m-160 m length × 50 m-60 m wide (single start ramp)

▶ **Figure 39.1** Basic track layout and minimum distances to ensure rider security.

Adapted, by permission, from Union Cycliste Internationale, 2014, BMX track guide. [Online]. Available: http://www.uci.ch/ mm/Document/News/NewsGeneral/16/58/58/UCIBMXtrackdesignguideline_v5_140326_Neutral.pdf [January 10, 2017].

the obstacles—acyclic actions with high demands on balance, isometric strength, and coordination—with short pedaling bouts, when possible, aimed to achieve or recover maximum power for increasing or maintaining the speed already gained. This phase includes the track from the first obstacle in the first straight, the two following straights, and the banked turns that follow them (figure 39.1).

The first straight is 45 to 70 meters long and includes two or three large- to medium-sized obstacles, according to its length and the height of the start ramp. The straight aligns the first banked turn with the start ramp. The first jump is at least 5 meters from the foot of the ramp to ensure security (figure 39.1). Increasing speed when the start ramp is not extremely sloped and coming out of the turn without losing speed while being properly placed in the race are the main objectives in this segment. Only the best riders can achieve these goals.

In the second straight jumps can be big and technical to complement the high speed coming out of the first turn. When the start ramp is high, we need big jumps at the first straight, but when the ramp is lower, the biggest jumps are placed in this second segment of the race.

One more banked turn and here it comes—the third straight, probably the most technical one. There are few opportunities for pedaling now but many technical challenges through various combinations of jumps. Only the most technical riders are able to increase speed in this segment. In fact, although the performance of most riders starts to deteriorate, some are able to increase speed and even compensate for the better exit of the more powerful opponents.

At the end is the final stamina phase, including the last straight and the finish line, in which athletes try to maintain maximum speed and avoid losing strength and coordination. A combination of pedaling and other nonaerial techniques leads riders through a group of small single, double, or even triple jumps and obstacles until the last sprint, 10 meters before the finish line. Velocity, stamina, and the capacity to maintain high power outputs make the difference here.

Summarizing, at the beginning of the race, at the top of the start ramp, riders stand on the gate start waiting for the fence to fall. Balance and proprioception, as well as external attentional processes and concentration, play their role in initiating pedaling as quickly and explosively as possible. These first maneuvers are important. As the gate start falls, riders must choose the techniques that allow them to maintain or even enhance velocity despite the scarce possibility of pedaling, because they have many other possibilities of moving quickly. Riding economy (which is not only a pedaling economy) is paramount throughout the whole race, and stamina becomes crucial at the end of the race.

Let's look through some main issues in optimizing performance in this discipline. We first review some technical and neuromuscular requirements, because the technical domain is extremely important for racing success.

Neuromuscular Profile and BMX Technique

In 2012 our research group (Mateo-March et al. 2012a) established a technical taxonomy according to the rider's possibility of pedaling and the bicycle's contact with the ground. Tables 39.1 and 39.2 summarize this taxonomy and the main BMX technical repertory. Table 39.1 distinguishes aerial techniques that require both wheels to lose contact with the ground, from nonaerial techniques, those actions during which at least one wheel remains in con-

Table 39.1 Technical Taxonomy of BMX Comprising Aerial and Nonaerial Techniques

Aerial techniques: both wheels losing contact with the ground	Nonaerial techniques: at least one wheel remaining in contact with the ground
Simple jump: passing over an obstacle without making ground contact, following the natural angle of flight	Pedaling: cyclical action consisting of pushing the pedals with the feet
Technical jump: tracing the parabola in the shape of the obstacle to minimize loss of speed and gain maximum speed after the drop; includes level jumps (both wheels remaining parallel to the ground during flight) and drawing jumps (both wheels leaving the ground and adapting the angle of flight to the draw of the obstacle)	Pull: coordinated pulling action of the legs and arms used when descending obstacles
	Curve pass: taking the best curve line path around the track to maximize performance
	Gate start technique: first maneuvers to start the race after the gate is released
	Manual: maintaining the back wheel on the ground and the front wheel balanced in the air from the final part of the takeoff until landing
	Linking obstacle manual: action resulting from the pull in which the descending gradient of the obstacle produces the action of lifting the front wheel (manual) to pass or overshoot the next obstacle
	Nose manual: rounding the obstacle with the front wheel to propel the bike during descent
	Absorption: technical maneuver that keeps the bicycle on the ground, avoiding unnecessary flight; corresponds to the action of lifting the front wheel and keeping it balanced from the front of the jump ramp until it makes contact with the top of the ramp or at the start of the descent
	Complete absorption: lifting the front wheel and keeping it balanced from the front part of the jump ramp until landing on the back wheel (manual), achieving an increase of speed

Table 39.2 Mixed Techniques: Actions That Combine Aerial and Nonaerial Requirements

Aero–terrestrial techniques: combining an aerial technique with the action of landing on the back wheel	Terrestrial–aerial techniques: combining a nonaerial technique with a taking-off action
Aero–manual: combining any aerial technique with a landing manual action	Bump jump: jump actions starting from the manual technique in a jump slope
Jump plus nose manual: combining a jump action with a nose manual technique at landing	Complete absorption and jump: combining the complete absorption technique with a jump at the end
	Top manual: jump actions starting from the manual technique from a plane obstacle

tact with the ground when tackling the obstacles. Table 39.2 adds a list of the technical requirements that combine both, which we have called mixed techniques.

Of course, this technical repertoire depends on the type of track. In low-difficulty tracks (LD) where riders compete at the beginning of their professional careers, the design favors the nonaerial pedaling actions, because riders still have difficulty increasing speed without pedaling. The gradient and length of the starting ramp are often lower in the medium- and low-difficulty tracks (MD and LD), and the distances are larger between fewer and simpler obstacles. The possibility of pedaling increases, and powerful athletes with greater pedaling ability can aspire to be successful despite being less technically skilled. Conversely, as riders improve, tracks make pedaling almost impossible in professional and elite categories, and the aerial abilities become the most important. A significantly higher ramp at the gate start in these high-difficulty (HD) tracks, as well as a greater number of obstacles—more difficult most of the time—encourages greater initial speed but reduces the possibilities for developing maximum power in the acceleration phase. Riders face longer flight times when tackling obstacles, as well as demanding aerial technical actions.

In previous studies (Mateo, Blasco-Lafarga, and Zabala 2011), we analyzed power and speed outcomes regarding technique (i.e., the possibility of pedaling) and the difficulty of the track. We compared three types of races—non-pedaling (NP), gate start pedaling (GSP), and free pedaling (FP)—through three levels of difficulty in the design (HD, MD, and LD tracks). NP races consisted of completing the whole race at the maximum velocity achieved by means of the impulse and other acyclic actions. In GSP races, riders were allowed to start pedaling freely along the ramp, but not any more until the end of the track. FP races had no pedaling limits, thus simulating a competition. Through this three-by-three experimental protocol, we calculated that up to 83.3 percent of the riding performance (measured as mean velocity in the race) resulted just from impulse actions, without pedaling (NP).

An additional 4.4 percent resulted from the possibility of pedaling through the descending line in the gate start ramp, and the remaining 12.3 percent was the consequence of pedaling freely through the straights (figure 39.2).

In addition, we demonstrated that the cyclic pedaling actions were replaced by acyclic propelling actions to reach higher velocities when increasing the track difficulty (i.e., HD or in elite tracks). Even more, when pedaling was forbidden (NP), riders managed to achieve the best results for mean velocity in the HD tracks, followed by MD and LD tracks, with statistically significant differences among them. This finding confirmed that the HD designs favor the use of acyclic aerial techniques; just the opposite occurred in FP races, in which riders were significantly quicker at LD and worst in HD.

The bigger slope in the HD gate start might explain this higher mean velocity as well as the fact that the time to reach peak velocity again occurred sooner in the HD track when pedaling was totally forbidden (8.59 plus or minus 2.88, 22.58 plus or minus 2.88, and 19.79 plus or minus 4.49 seconds for HD, MD, and LD, respectively). The bigger obstacles in the HD tracks may contribute to keeping these higher velocities, showing that pedaling is not the key regarding velocity in elite BMX races. BMX cyclists should pay special attention to the use of the upper limbs and momentum without relying on pedaling techniques (Mateo-March et al. 2012a) to reach top performance.

On the other hand, as we expected, LD showed larger mean power outcomes, linking pedaling to power production. We also found that the peak power appeared very soon, because cyclists tried to accelerate to maximum and reach the highest speed as soon as possible. Maximizing peak power and

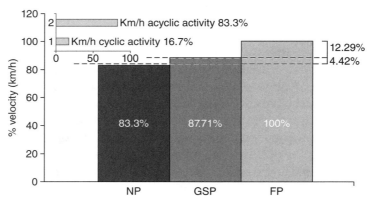

▶ **Figure 39.2** Percentage for cyclic and acyclic activity derived from the technical options in BMX.

Reprinted, by permission, from M. Mateo, C. Blasco-Lafarga, and M. Zabala, 2011, "Pedaling power and speed production vs. technical factors and track difficulty in bicycle motocross cycling," Journal of Strength and Conditioning Research 25(12): 3248-3256.

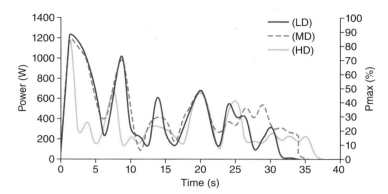

▶ **Figure 39.3**   Absolute (watts) and relative (P$_{max}$) power–time curve along the bicycle motocross (BMX) race regarding the technical difficulty of the track. LD = low difficulty; MD = medium difficulty; HD = high difficulty.

Reprinted, by permission, from M. Mateo, C. Blasco-Lafarga, and M. Zabala, 2011, "Pedaling power and speed production vs. technical factors and track difficulty in bicycle motocross cycling," Journal of Strength and Conditioning Research 25(12): 3248-3256.

RFD while pedaling is crucial to taking advantage at the beginning, but not so much to keep the mean velocity in the race, because the power outcomes decrease as velocity increases through the race (figure 39.3).

But despite this decrease in power production and despite the fact that 83.3 percent of the velocity in the race results from acyclic impulse actions, the remaining 16.7 percent, and mostly the 4.4 percent accomplished by pedaling in the start ramp, is decisive for success. The minimal performance differences among the BMX cyclists and the limited number of rounds through the track give this small advantage at the starting phase its importance. Overtaking opponents through the many obstacles and turns in such a short race is complicated, whatever the difficulty of the track.

Riders in our study came close to an average peak power of 1,200 watts, which is 85 percent of their maximum power, and they got it in an average time of only 1.44 seconds (figure 39.3). These outcomes came from a national-level team, but other studies have shown that the peak power can reach from 1,600 to 2,000 watts (Bertucci and Hourde 2011; Chiementin, Crequy, and Bertucci 2012; Debraux et al. 2013; Rylands, Roberts, and Hurst 2016). Of note is the peak power of 2,087 plus or minus 156.8 watts at 1.6 seconds revealed by Herman et al. (2009) in a small sample of elite BMX male riders, also in field-testing conditions.

After the rider is outside the start ramp, pedaling is hindered and the relative power decreases to an average score of 73 percent (already close to an average score of 51 percent in the first straight). For that reason, the transition from high to low power productions without losing velocity is important. Again, figure 39.4 confirms that the power outcomes were lower as the difficulty of the track became higher (figure 39.3).

In the second phase of the race, generating large power outcomes is complicated, so riders need to increase velocity through changes in the center of pressure (COP) when tackling obstacles. They look to increase inertial forces in the jumps while reducing any loss of linear velocity during the continuous takeoffs and landings. The domain of absorptions and the increasing velocity while falling in the obstacles make the difference, as does the proper use of the banked turns. Choosing the best strategies to benefit from the inertial forces involved in turning, which change according to the cant of the curve and the speed and angle of entry into those turns, may be meaningful for success.

At the end of the race, over 25 to 30 seconds, power declines dramatically, despite athletes' attempts to maintain speed. Coordination and technique, more than power, are the important factors in keeping enough velocity and stamina in this third phase.

Summarizing, a mean power of around 330 watts in our study, lower in HD tracks, confirmed that BMX, despite its short duration, is more than a power discipline or just a cyclic sport. In fact, the power frequency chart in figure 39.4 reflects that in only 11.22 percent of race duration was the average mean power over 50 percent of maximum power. Conversely, close to 75 percent of race time featured relative power under 35 percent of maximum. This conclusion might explain why Cristian Becerine and other powerful riders showed both the capacity to be first at the beginning of the race and some difficulties in keeping this position in the final meters, where riders with better endurance capacities, such as Kyle Bennett, overtook them. Nowadays, the great BMX champions try to become overall riders and improve all these neuromuscular requirements. Olympic champions Maris Strombergs, Liam Phillips, and Sam Willoughby are able to win the position on the first line and then maintain it.

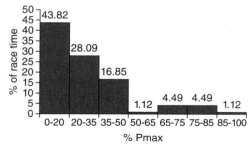

▶ **Figure 39.4** Mean power frequency chart.

Data from M. Mateo, C. Blasco-Lafarga, and M. Zabala, 2011, "Pedaling power and speed production vs. technical factors and track difficulty in bicycle motocross cycling," Journal of Strength and Conditioning Research 25(12): 3248-3256.

To conclude this section, remember that neuromuscular capacities are strongly related to technique, the improvement of which is a main objective for the industry. Recently, our research group has conducted some studies (Mateo-March et al. 2014; Mateo-March, Zabala, and González-Badillo 2012) to discover whether technological breakthroughs like the eccentric Q-Ring chainring, designed to minimize the loss of pedaling power in the dead spots (Córdova et al. 2009), improves BMX performance. The more powerful cyclists in the elite group in our study significantly improved the distance covered with a noncircular Q-Ring chainring (1.12 percent), an average improvement of 0.26 meters achieved during the short 3.95 seconds of the starting sprint (p = 0.02). Although not statistically significant, the mean efficiency index was also better with the eccentric Q-Ring in the elite group. The cadet group, however, was not able to cover greater distances, even though they enhanced power significantly from the traditional circular chain ring (p < 0.05), pointing to the need to be very powerful to manage the higher load requirements during the downstroke with the eccentric devices.

Similarly, Rylands, Roberts, and Hurst (2016) have recently confirmed that peak power and peak torque outcomes in the first phase of the race are related to gear ratio. Their eight national-level male BMX riders achieved a mean peak power of 1,658 plus or minus 20 watts with a 45:16 tooth, significantly larger than with the traditional 43:16 tooth (p = 0.010) or the smaller 41:16 tooth (1,437 plus or minus 20 and 1,381 plus or minus 20 watts, respectively). Because no significant differences were found in the time to this peak power (1.00 plus or minus 0.53 seconds for 45:16 tooth versus 0.88 plus or minus 0.44 seconds for the traditional gear ratio), they concluded that the selection of a proper gear ratio might result in higher power output in this first phase of acceleration. Herman at al. (2009) previously suggested that gear ratio might be a conditioning factor for the acceleration capacity in the starting sprint, although they found only some differences regarding performance time or pedaling cadence, but not in power outcomes, when comparing different sprint start situations in field-testing conditions.

Whatever the technological device or bicycle equipment improvement, any change oriented to enhance the neuromuscular capacities of the BMX cyclist requires a deep and individualized analysis of the cyclist's needs and capacities.

Physiological Profile

After BMX cyclists have reached the minimum technical level to face the neuromuscular requirements of the race, coaches should work hard to improve the cyclists' physiological responses. We propose holistic improvement of tactics and specific bioenergetics built on a good neuromuscular foundation, so we need to understand bioenergetics and the way in which it is mediated by tactical approaches. Bioenergetics encompasses the energetic demands of BMX competition resulting from neuromuscular demands, work–rest intervals within those demands, overall race duration, number of races or warm-up periods per day, the cyclist's mood and psychological stress associated with competition, and other factors. For example, higher psychological stress means higher energy demands and less neuromuscular economy while racing.

Few studies have analyzed the constraints of elite BMX, and most have focused on biomechanical characteristics (Bertucci et al. 2007; Bertucci and Hourde 2011; Campillo, Doremus, and Hespel 2007; Chiementin et al. 2012; Debraux et al. 2013; Herman et al. 2009; Mateo-March et al. 2014, 2012b; Mateo and Zabala 2007; Romero-Rodríguez, Mateo-March, and Zabala 2013), but Mateo-March et al. (2012b) agree that during exercise lasting 10 to 40 seconds, the metabolic pathways are involved in a nonsequential way, and the degradation of phosphate and carbohydrate, but also aerobic metabolism, contributes simultaneously to energy provision. The already described combination of acyclic and cyclic techniques, alternated in short periods, predominately stresses the anaerobic pathways during the race, that is, phosphocreatine and glycolytic pathways (Mateo et al. 2012b; Zabala et al. 2008; Zabala, Sánchez-Muñoz, and Gutiérrez 2009). The short 40- to 45-second duration of each race contributes to this predominance, so we need to optimize anaerobic power. But because of the series of interspersed complex terrestrial and aerial skills that differ largely according to the technical level of each track, we also need well-trained cyclists who are adapted to respond to such metabolic differences and alternations (Mateo, Blasco-Lafarga, and Zabala 2011; Mateo et al. 2012a).

Louis et al. (2013) observed that during a BMX race simulation in the laboratory, riders were able to reach an average of 94.3 plus or minus 1.2 percent of $\dot{V}O_2$max, with a mean blood lactate production of 14.5 plus or minus 4.5 millimoles per liter, similar to the 13 to 16 millimoles per liter recorded with 400-meter track athletics (Blasco-Lafarga et al. 2013). This finding confirms that both aerobic and anaerobic glycolytic pathways are strongly demanded. Furthermore, the repetition of six cycling races separated by 30 minutes of recovery—simulating the classifying bouts in the competition (Louis et al. 2013)—led to a significant impairment of acid–base balance from the third to the sixth race (mean decrease in the base excess [BE]: 18.8 plus or minus 7.5 percent, $p < 0.05$). A significant association was found between the decrease in BE and $\dot{V}O_2$peak ($r = 0.73$, $p < 0.05$) in the same study (Louis et al. 2013), indicating that $\dot{V}O_2$peak could explain 54 percent of the variation in BMX performance. These results suggest again that both oxygen-dependent and oxygen-independent fuel substrate pathways are important determinants of BMX performance.

On the other hand, in the neuromuscular section we confirmed that power outcomes during a BMX race were not constant. Extremely brief periods of high power production occurred in the initial phases of the race (Mateo,

Blasco-Lafarga, and Zabala 2011), followed by an important decrease after a few seconds, and some additional peaks of power interspersed until the end. Acyclic efforts (i.e., nonpedaling efforts) account for greater percentages during the race (greater even in elite BMX competitions), so we can conclude that the capacity to produce high levels of power and RFD needs to be combined with all the acyclic technical skills, many of them developed with the upper limbs. BMX riders need to be able to alternate quasi-isometric phases of work with explosive movements along the whole race. Economy while pedaling, but also while landing, taking off, or handling the turns, must be an important target of BMX training. The upper limbs, like the lower limbs, must be specifically trained.

Rider training should look to enhance muscular capacity to relax while developing optimum levels of strength, power, and velocity stamina. At the same time, riders need to enhance their aerobic capacity to sustain maximum efficiency, and high aerobic capacity and the glycolytic anaerobic pathway will ensure maximal and quick energy supply. The aerobic contribution to total energy provision in BMX is significant, suggesting that $\dot{V}O_2$max could be an important determinant of performance despite the short duration of the races. A high-intensity interval training (HIIT) approach might be an interesting solution to the BMX mixed profile. The consecutive repetition of short and powerful sprints, performed at supramaximal intensities and interspersed with incomplete recovery periods, involves gains in the neuromuscular domain accompanied by great improvement of aerobic and anaerobic capacities.

Power Outcomes and Pedaling Cadence

Recent results from Rylands et al. (2016) shed light on the influence of pedaling cadence in BMX riders' power outcomes (peak power production and time to peak power). The pedaling cadence links the neuromuscular and the bioenergetics requirements. Rylands at al. (2016) found no differences when comparing 80, 100, 120, and 140 revolutions per minute, neither for peak power (p = 0.424) nor for the time to peak power (p = 0.532). As they recognize in their background statement, the influence of the pedaling rate on cycling performance is well documented in the cycling disciplines in which pedaling is the main technical resource to produce power and where pedaling economy is decisive because of the long duration. But this is not the case with BMX. Attending to previous studies, the ratio between peak power and the optimal cadence changes with the duration of the race—the higher the cadence is, the shorter the discipline is: 70 to 90 revolutions per minute for cycling events lasting more than 4 hours, 90 to 100 revolutions per minute for endurance races lasting less than 4 hours, and 100 to 120 revolutions per minute for track sprint cyclists (Rylands et al. 2016). But as previously suggested by Herman et al. (2009), BMX does not have one optimal cadence.

Although BMX riders might benefit from higher pedaling cadences, they may be making individual choices as a resource to optimize their performance. And higher cadences would not be reasonable for all of them.

Applying the Science

BMX consists of speed racing across an always-different small track, 300 to 400 meters of an explosive speed race interspersed with jumps, banked turns, and other obstacles that is more difficult at the higher levels of competition. At the elite level, the difficulty of these tracks makes the continuity of the pedaling almost impossible after the gate start ramp, so aerial abilities can make the difference. Only the most technical riders are able to increase or even maintain speed when pedaling is prevented.

In this highly demanding neuromuscular discipline, bioenergetics improvement must be subjected to the training of the technical domain as well as to the possibility of reaching the maximum rate of force development in the first seconds of the race. Riders need to be at the front of the race at the end of its first phase, comprising the start ramp and more or less the 5 meters until the first obstacle. Riding economy, which is not only a pedaling economy, becomes paramount from that point throughout the whole race, and stamina becomes crucial at the end of the race.

BMX cyclists ride close to their maximum anaerobic power in these 40- to 45-second races, and aerobic power becomes important because of the number of races in the overall competition. Any technological improvement must be oriented to enhance the neuromuscular capacities of the BMX rider without affecting riding economy or stamina capacity. This step requires previous familiarization, individualization, and research.

Technical and physical conditioning training of BMX riders must be designed so that they can achieve maximum peak power and maximum peak torque in the minimum time, always within the first second of the race, and riders must then be able to maintain maximum speed and the first position until the end. A differential and specific training approach is recommended to improve the technical domain as well as possibly to increase speed by taking advantage of obstacles, drafts, and other technical challenges. BMX thus becomes an amazing and spectacular sport show.

CHAPTER 40

Ultradistance

—Beat Knechtle and Pantelis Theodoros Nikolaidis

An ultraendurance competition is defined as any event exceeding 6 hours in duration (Zaryski and Smith 2005). Regarding cycling, the shortest race in ultracycling is therefore, by definition, the 6-hour challenge (Ultra Marathon Cycling Association, ultracycling.com). Various kinds of ultracycling races are offered worldwide. These races can be classified as distance-limited cycling races (e.g., held in kilometers or miles), time-limited cycling races (e.g., 6 to 48 hours), cycling races across a country or a continent, and cycling races around a country. The most famous ultracycling race in the world is the Race Across America, also called the RAAM (www.raceacrossamerica.org). Most ultracycling races held worldwide aim to prepare or to qualify cyclists for the Race Across America (for RAAM series races, see www.raamchallenge.com). This chapter presents existing knowledge in ultracycling such as where these races are held, performance in ultracycling, the age of the best ultracycling performance, sex difference in ultracycling performance, and aspects of nutrition and fluid intake during ultracycling racing.

Race Locations

Although most ultracycling races are held in the United States, several European ultracycling races exist. Most ultracycling races held worldwide are part of the Ultra Marathon Cycling Association (UMCA). The UMCA was founded in 1980 by John Marino, Michael Shermer, and Lon Haldeman, pioneers in ultracycling and successful finishers in the Race Across America.

The UMCA is the leading international organization dedicated to ultracycling. UMCA has a calendar of ultracycling events at which riders earn points for a placement in the Ultracycling Cup and the World Cup of Ultracycling, the Ultra-500 Race Series, and mileage toward the UMCA 6-, 12-, and 24-hour challenges. The UMCA also sanctions ultracycling records, including national, state, timed, and distance records.

Generally, the rather short ultradistance races such as 200 and 400 miles and 12 and 24 hours are more popular than the longer races during which athletes cross a state, country, or continent. For the distance-limited races, the 200-mile

(322 km) distance seems to be the most popular (table 40.1), probably because of the RAAM Challenges (RAAM Series Races), the races to qualify for the Race Across America (RAAM) that are held in Texas, Oregon, Minnesota, North California, Ohio, South California, and Florida. Among time-limited races (table 40.2), the 12- and 24-hour challenges are the most frequently offered races.

Furthermore, races crossing a certain region such as a state, province, country, or even a continent are offered (table 40.3). The longest ultracycling race held in the world is the Race Across America, followed by the Race Across Europe and the BC Explorer.

Apart from crossing a country, there are also races around a country (table 40.4). These races around a country seem to be a domain of the Europeans since all these races are held in Europe where the longest events are the Race Around Austria and the Race Around Ireland. Overall, most of these ultracycling races intend to prepare or qualify riders for the Race Across America, with the Race Across America considered the ultimate ultracycling challenge.

Ultracyclists

To date, little is known about demographic aspects of ultracyclists in comparison with ultramarathoners (Hoffman and Fogard 2012). A recent study investigated participation and performance trends in both an American qualifier (i.e., the Furnace Creek 508) and a European qualifier (i.e., the Swiss Cycling Marathon) for the Race Across America and the Race Across America itself (Shoak et al. 2013). This study showed that ultraendurance cycling is highly selective. On average, about 41 percent of participants did not finish the Race Across America or the Furnace Creek 508, and about 26 percent did not finish the Swiss Cycling Marathon (Shoak et al. 2013). For these three races, 26 to 40 percent of starters were unable to finish; the percentage of female finishers was 3 to 11 percent. Generally, women are slower than men; the difference in performance is 18 to 28 percent. Ultracycling seems to be a domain of older athletes because about 46 percent of the successful finishers were masters athletes (Shoak et al. 2013).

In the beginning, the Race Across America was dominated by American cyclists (Sigg et al. 2012), but in recent years, European athletes, especially central European athletes, started to dominate (Sigg et al. 2012). Of the top three male finishers in the Race Across America for each year from 1982 to 1997 (i.e., a first period of 16 years), 42 (87.5 percent) originated from the United States, 4 (8.3 percent) originated from Austria, and 2 (4.2 percent) originated from Australia. From 1998 to 2012 (i.e., a second period of 15 years), only 12 of the annual top three male finishers (26.7 percent) were American cyclists, and 30 finishers (66.7 percent) originated from Europe. These European athletes originated from countries in central Europe such as Austria, Slovenia, Switzerland, Germany, Italy, and Liechtenstein (Sigg et al. 2012).

Ultracyclists typically seem to prepare for their planned race based on the race distance. A recent study compared participants in a qualifier

Table 40.1 Distance-Limited Races From 100 to 500 Miles

Race	Country	Website
100 MILES (161 KM)		
Sebring Century	USA	www.bikesebring.org
Calvin's Century Challenge	USA	www.calvinschallenge.com
Willamette Gran Fondo	USA	http://willamettegranfondo.com
Gran Fondo Las Vegas	USA	http://planetultra.com
Tour of the Unknown Coast	USA	http://tuccycle.org
High Cascades 100	USA	http://highcascades100.com
Mid-Atlantic 100-Mile TT	USA	www.midatlanticultrasports.com
200 MILES (322 KM)		
RAAM Challenge Texas	USA	www.raamchallenge.com
RAAM Challenge Oregon	USA	www.raamchallenge.com
RAAM Challenge South California	USA	www.raamchallenge.com
RAAM Challenge Minnesota	USA	www.raamchallenge.com
RAAM Challenge North California	USA	www.raamchallenge.com
RAAM Challenge Ohio	USA	www.raamchallenge.com
RAAM Challenge Florida	USA	www.raamchallenge.com
Eastern Sierra Double Century	USA	http://planetultra.com
Solvang Double Century	USA	http://planetultra.com
Mulholland Double Century	USA	http://planetultra.com
Terrible Two Double Century	USA	http://srcc.memberlodge.com
Nightmare Tour Double Century	USA	http://dreamrideprojects.org
White Mountain Double Century	USA	http://ndzone.com/white-mountain-double/
Solvang Autumn Double Century	USA	http://planetultra.com
Mulholland Double Century	USA	http://planetultra.com
Death Valley Double Century—Spring	USA	www.adventurecorps.com/dvspring
Death Valley Double Century—Fall	USA	www.adventurecorps.com/dvfall
Heartbreak Double Century	USA	http://planetultra.com
Great Alaska Double Century	USA	www.fireweed400.com
Race Across Oregon 200	USA	www.raceacrossoregon.com
Lake Taupo Cycle Challenge	New Zealand	www.cyclechallenge.com
Balltown Classic Double Century	USA	www.ultramidwest.com
Metamora 4 x 50 Double Century	USA	www.ultramidwest.com
300 MILES (483 KM)		
Hoodoo 300	USA	http://planetultra.com
400 MILES (644 KM)		
RAAM Challenge Texas	USA	www.raamchallenge.com
RAAM Challenge Oregon	USA	www.raamchallenge.com
RAAM Challenge South California	USA	www.raamchallenge.com
RAAM Challenge Minnesota	USA	www.raamchallenge.com
RAAM Challenge North California	USA	www.raamchallenge.com

(continued)

Table 40.1 *(continued)*

Race	Country	Website
400 MILES (644 KM)		
RAAM Challenge Ohio	USA	www.raamchallenge.com
The Fireweed—The Race Across Alaska	USA	www.fireweed400.com
Montreal Double Double	USA	www.adkultracycling.com
500 MILES (805 KM)		
Race Across Oregon	USA	www.raceacrossoregon.com
Hoodoo 500	USA	http://planetultra.com
Tejas 500	USA	http://tt24tt.com
Swiss Cycling Marathon	Switzerland	www.swisscyclingmarathon.ch
Furnace Creek 508	USA	www.adventurecorps.com
Cascade Ultra	USA	www.cascadeultra.org

Table 40.2 Time-Limited Races From 6 to 24 Hours

Race	Country	Website
6 HOURS		
Ultra TT Series #1, 6-Hour TT	USA	http://pro251.wix.com/cdcultrattseries
Ultra TT Series #2, 6-Hour TT	Ireland	http://pro251.wix.com/cdcultrattseries
Ultra TT Series #3, 6-Hour TT	Ireland	http://pro251.wix.com/cdcultrattseries
Ultra TT Series #4, 6-Hour TT	Ireland	http://pro251.wix.com/cdcultrattseries
Bessies Creek 6 Hour	USA	http://bessiescreek24.com
Texas Ultra Spirit 6-Hour TT	USA	www.texasultraspirit.com
Calvin's 6-Hour Challenge	USA	www.calvinschallenge.com
6 Hours in the Canyon	USA	www.24hoursinthecanyon.org
Texas 6-Hour Shoot Out	USA	http://tt24tt.com
6-Hour World TT Championship	USA	www.souleventsusa.com
Sacandaga 6-Hour TT	USA	www.sacandaga61224hrchallenge.com
12 HOURS		
Ultra TT Series #1, 12-Hour TT	USA	http://pro251.wix.com/cdcultrattseries
Ultra TT Series #2, 12-Hour TT	Ireland	http://pro251.wix.com/cdcultrattseries
Ultra TT Series #3, 12-Hour TT	Ireland	http://pro251.wix.com/cdcultrattseries
Ultra TT Series #4, 12-Hour TT	Ireland	http://pro251.wix.com/cdcultrattseries
Bike Sebring 12 Hour	USA	www.bikesebring.org
Bessies Creek 12 Hour	USA	http://bessiescreek24.com
Texas Ultra Spirit 12-Hour TT	USA	www.texasultraspirit.com
Calvin's 12-Hour Challenge	USA	www.calvinschallenge.com
Lewis and Clark 12 Hour	USA	http://lacultra.com
12 Hours in the Canyon	USA	www.24hoursinthecanyon.org
Bianchi Melfar 12-Hour Cycling Challenge	Denmark	www.bianchi-melfar24.dk
UK 12-Hour Championship	England	www.cyclingtimetrials.org.uk
Nightmare 12-Hour TT	USA	http://dreamrideprojects.org
Mid-Atlantic 12 Hour	USA	www.midatlanticultrasports.com
Ring of Fire 12 Hour	USA	www.raceacrossoregon.com
Texas 12 Hour	USA	http://tt24tt.com
12-Hour World TT Championship	USA	www.souleventsusa.com

Table 40.2 *(continued)*

Race	Country	Website
12 HOURS		
Sacandaga 12-Hour TT	USA	www.sacandaga61224hrchallenge.com
Saratoga 12/24: Hudson River Ramble 12	USA	www.adkultracycling.com
Saratoga 12/24: Nighthawk Nighttime 12	USA	www.adkultracycling.com
24 HOURS		
Bike Sebring 24 Hour	USA	www.bikesebring.org
Bessies Creek 24 Hour	USA	http://bessiescreek24.com
Texas Ultra Spirit 24-Hour TT	USA	www.texasultraspirit.com
24 Hours in the Canyon	USA	www.24hoursinthecanyon.org
Bianchi Melfar 24-Hour Cycling Challenge	Denmark	www.bianchi-melfar24.dk
National 24-Hour Challenge	USA	www.n24hc.org
Oregon MTB 24	USA	http://oregonmtb24.com
Le Mans 24	France	www.24heuresvelo.fr
Mersey UK 24-Hour Championship	England	www.cyclingtimetrials.org.uk
Nightmare 24-Hour TT	USA	http://dreamrideprojects.org
Mid-Atlantic 24	USA	www.midatlanticultrasports.com
Ring of Fire 24 Hour	USA	www.raceacrossoregon.com
Texas 24 Hour	USA	http://tt24tt.com
24-Hour World TT Championship	USA	www.souleventsusa.com
Sacandaga 24-Hour TT	USA	www.sacandaga61224hrchallenge.com
Saratoga 12/24: Saratoga Challenge 24	USA	www.adkultracycling.com
Ultra Midwest 24 Hour	USA	www.ultramidwest.com

for Paris–Brest–Paris with participants in a qualifier for the Race Across America (Knechtle et al. 2012a). The Race Across America is four times longer than Paris–Brest–Paris, it requires support teams, and racers typically get little sleep. Therefore, the qualifiers for the Race Across America should be substantially more highly trained than those intending to qualify for Paris–Brest–Paris. The qualifiers for the Race Across America cycled at a greater intensity in training, whereas the qualifiers for Paris–Brest–Paris relied more on training volume. Different strategies and types of training seem to reflect the different demands of the races.

Women in Ultracycling and Sex Differences in Ultracycling Performance

To date, ultracycling races have largely been the domain of men; the percentage of female ultracyclists is rather low (Rüst et al. 2013; Shoak et al. 2013; Zingg et al. 2013). Female finishers accounted for about 11 percent in both the Race Across America and the Furnace Creek 508 but only about 3 percent in the Swiss Cycling Marathon (Shoak et al. 2013).

Table 40.3 Race Across a Part of a Country, Whole Country, or Continent

Distance	Race	Country	Website
112 miles (180 km)	Tri States Gran Fondo	USA	http://planetultra.com
125 miles (201 km)	Cincinnati to Cleveland: Stage 2	USA	https://bike-ohio.wildapricot.org/
194 miles (312 km)	Cincinnati to Cleveland: Stage 1	USA	https://bike-ohio.wildapricot.org/
412 miles (663 km)	Gut Check 212	USA	http://gutcheck212.com
452 miles (727 km)	Cascade Ultra	USA	www.cascadeultra.org
508 miles (818 km)	The 508	USA	www.the508.com
520 miles (837 km)	Race Across Oregon	USA	www.raceacrossoregon.com
544 miles (875 km)	Adirondack 540	USA	www.adkultracycling.com/adk540
824 miles (1,326 km)	Gut Check: Hell and Back—Race Across South Dakota	USA	http://gutcheck212.com
860 miles (1,384 km)	Race Across the West	USA	www.raceacrossthewest.org
2,933 miles (4,720 km)	Race Across Europe	Europe	www.theraceacrosseurope.com
3,100 miles (4,989 km)	Race Across America	USA	www.raceacrossamerica.org
333 kilometers	Wysam	Switzerland	www.wysam333.ch
540 kilometers	Race across the Alps	Austria	http://www.raceacrossthealps.com
550 kilometers	Ultracycling Dolomitica	Italy	www.ultracyclingdolomitica.com
715 kilometers	Swiss Cycling Marathon	Switzerland	www.swisscyclingmarathon.ch
927 kilometers	Swiss Cycling Marathon	Switzerland	www.swisscyclingmarathon.ch
1,000 kilometers	Tor Tour	Switzerland	www.tortour.com
1,015 kilometers	Glocknerman	Austria	www.glocknerman.at
1,200 kilometers	Paris–Brest–Paris	France	www.paris-brest-paris.org
2,820 kilometers	BC Explorer	Canada	http://bcexplorer.ca
5,145 kilometers	Tour of BC	Canada	http://bcexplorer.ca

Table 40.4 Race Around a Country

Distance	Race	Country	Website
560 kilometers	Race Around Austria Challenge	Austria	www.racearoundaustria.at
1,100 kilometers	Irish Ultra Challenge	Ireland	http://racearoundireland.com
1,231 kilometers	Race Around Slovenia	Slovenia	www.dos-extreme.si
2,200 kilometers	Race Around Austria	Austria	www.racearoundaustria.at
2,200 kilometers	Race Around Ireland	Ireland	http://racearoundireland.com

Generally, women are slower than men in ultracycling (Rüst et al. 2013; Zingg et al. 2013; Rüst et al. 2015). In the Swiss Cycling Marathon during the period from 2001 to 2012 (Zingg et al. 2013), the sex difference in performance was 13.6 percent for the fastest cyclists ever, 13.9 ± 0.5 percent for the three fastest cyclists ever, and 19.1 ± 3.7 percent for the 10 fastest cyclists ever. Women became faster, however, over the years. The annual top three women improved cycling speed from 20.3 ± 3.1 kilometers per hour (in 2003) to 24.8 ± 2.4 kilometers per hour (in 2012). The cycling speed of the annual top three men remained unchanged at 30.2 ± 0.6 kilometers per hour. The corresponding sex difference in performance for the annual top three women and men decreased from 35.0 ± 9.5 percent (in 2001) to 20.4 ± 7.7 percent (in 2012) (Zingg et al. 2013). In the Race Across America, men crossed America faster than women in the last 30 years, and women are unlikely to overtake men in the near future (Rüst et al. 2013). Mean cycling speed was 19.4 ± 2.0 kilometers per hour for men and 17.5 ± 2.0 kilometers per hour for women between 1982 and 2012. Men were riding 1.9 ± 2.0 kilometers per hour (10.9 percent) faster than women were. During this period, the fastest cycling speed ever was 24.77 kilometers per hour for men and 21.27 kilometers per hour for women, a difference of 14.2 percent. Between 1982 and 2012, cycling speed was 22.7 ± 1.1 kilometers per hour for the annual fastest men and 18.4 ± 1.6 kilometers per hour for the annual fastest women, a difference of 19.4 ± 7.3 percent. For the annual top three men, cycling speed was 21.8 ± 0.9 kilometers per hour with no change across years. The annual top three women achieved a cycling speed of 16.6 ± 1.0 kilometer per hour with no change over time. The difference between the sexes of 24.6 ± 3.0 percent showed no change across years.

Sex differences in performance might be influenced by drafting, that is, cycling behind other cyclists to save energy (Salihu et al. 2016). The assumption might be that women benefit from drafting behind men in a draft-legal ultracycling event. In a 24-hour draft-legal cycling event, the mean cycling distance achieved by the male winners of 960.5 ± 51.9 kilometers was significantly greater than the distance covered by the female winners of 769.7 ± 65.7 kilometers. The sex difference in performance for the annual winners of 19.7 ± 7.8 percent remained unchanged across years (Pozzi et al. 2014). A sex difference in performance of about 20 percent seems to remain in ultracycling when cyclists are allowed to draft.

Optimum Age for Ultracycling Performance

Little is known about the age of the best ultracycling performance. The fastest ultracyclists seem to be masters athletes (a masters athlete is typically defined as an athlete older than 35 years of age) who are systematically training for and competing in organized forms of sport specifically designed for older adults (Reaburn and Dascombe 2008). In the Swiss Cycling Marathon, the age of peak ultracycling speed was 35.9 ± 9.6 years for men and 38.7 ± 7.8 years for women for the 10 fastest finishers ever (Zingg et al. 2013). In a 24-hour draft-legal cycling event held between 2000 and 2011, the age of peak cycling speed remained unchanged at 37.3 ± 8.5 years and 38.3 ± 5.4 years for the annual fastest women and men, respectively (Pozzi et al. 2014). In shorter ultracycling races such as the Swiss Bike Masters, the fastest cyclists seemed to be younger than in longer ultracycling races. The age of the top ten men was 30.0 ± 1.6 years (Haupt et al. 2013). Unfortunately, the age of the fastest finishers in the Race Across America is not investigated because only age groups of the athletes, not their actual ages, are indicated on the race results.

Energy Deficit and Nutrition in Ultracycling

The aspect of energy intake, energy expenditure, and energy deficit is a well-investigated topic in ultraendurance performance such as ultracycling. Competing in an ultracycling race leads to a considerable energy deficit (Armstrong et al. 2012; Bescós et al. 2012a, 2012b; Francescato and Di Prampero 2002) because ultraendurance cyclists are unable to self-regulate their diet or exercise intensity to prevent a negative energy balance (Stewart and Stewart 2007). During ultraendurance cycling, the overall energy expenditure increases as a function of the accumulated performance time. The daily energy expenditure, however, decreases with increasing race duration (Francescato and Di Prampero 2002).

The problem of the energy deficit in ultracycling has been investigated in various case reports and field studies. For example, in a 164-kilometer road-cycling event with 42 men and 6 women, men voluntarily underconsumed food energy with a deficit of 2,594 kilocalories (Armstrong et al. 2012). During a 24-hour ultracycling race, a cyclist expended about 15,533 kilocalories and energy intake was about 5,571 kilocalories, resulting in an energy deficit of about 9,915 kilocalories (Bescós et al. 2012b). During 2 days of stationary cycling, a cyclist expended 14,486 kilocalories and consumed 11,098 kilocalories, resulting in an energy deficit of 3,290 kilocalories and a weight loss of 0.55 kilograms (Stewart and Stewart 2007). During a 1,230-kilometer bike marathon, food and fluid intake were monitored in a group of 14 participants. Energy intake of 19,749 ± 4,502 kilocalories was lower than energy expenditure of 25,303 ± 2,436 kilocalories in 12 of 14 athletes. Energy and average carbohydrate intake of 57.1 ± 17.7 grams per hour decreased significantly after 618 kilometers (Geesman, Mester, and Koehler 2014). A cyclist was investigated during the ultraendurance cycling race XX Alps 2004 covering a distance of 2,272 kilometers and 55,455 meters of altitude that he had completed in 5 days and 7 hours (Bircher et al. 2006). The cyclist lost about 2.0 kilograms of body mass, corresponding to about 11,950 kilocalories. Fat mass was reduced by about 790 grams (7,110 kilocalories), and fat-free mass decreased by about 1.21 kilograms (4,840 kilocalories). The energy deficit estimated using continuous heart rate monitoring was about 29,554 kilocalories.

The problem of the energy deficit has also been investigated in the Race Across America. A case report described the energy turnover in a cyclist competing in the Race Across America (Knechtle, Enggist, and Jehle 2005).

The cyclist completed 470 ± 73 kilometers (range 372 to 541 kilometers) per day with a daily change in altitude of 2,582 ± 1,576 meters (range 683 to 5,047 meters). During the race, he expended a total energy of 179,650 kilocalories with a daily mean of 17,965 ± 2,165 kilocalories (range 15,100 to 23,280 kilocalories). Total energy intake was 96,124 kilocalories with a daily average of 9,612 ± 1,500 kilocalories (range 7,513 to 12,735 kilocalories). Of the total ingested calories, 75.2 percent was derived from carbohydrate, 16.2 percent from fat, and 8.6 percent from protein. His diet consisted of 1,814 ± 310 grams (range 1,336 to 2,354 grams) of carbohydrate, 172 ± 47 grams (range 88 to 251 grams) of fat, and 207 ± 52 grams (range 128 to 286 grams) of protein. The average daily energy deficit amounted to 8,352 ± 2,523 kilocalories (range 4,425 to 13,631 kilocalories). A total deficiency of 83,526 kilocalories resulted after the race, and the athlete lost 5 kilograms of body weight (Knechtle, Enggist, and Jehle 2005). In a field study investigating a team of four cyclists who finished the Race Across America, total mean energy expenditure was 43,401 kilocalories with a mean daily energy expenditure of 6,420 kilocalories. Total mean energy intake from all food and drink consumed was 29,506 kilocalories with a mean daily energy intake of 4,918 kilocalories. The total mean energy deficit was 13,878 kilocalories, and the mean daily energy deficit was 1,503 kilocalories (Hulton et al. 2010).

For endurance exercise lasting 30 minutes or more, the most likely contributors to fatigue are dehydration and carbohydrate depletion. Gastrointestinal problems, hyperthermia, and exercise-associated hyponatremia can reduce endurance exercise performance and are potentially health threatening, especially in longer events (Jeukendrup 2011). Dehydration can be associated with a deteriorated mood state and perceptual ratings during a 161-kilometer race (Moyen et al. 2015). To manage dehydration, cyclists should use an individualized drinking plan that takes into account sweat rate (Armstrong et al. 2015a, 2015b). The high energy demands during ultraendurance racing cannot be compensated by the energy intake of the athletes. This energy deficit seems to be covered by a reduction of the body's own stores in fat (Bischof et al. 2013; Knechtle et al. 2009). In a 600-kilometer ultracycling race, body mass decreased by 1.5 ± 1.2 kilograms, fat mass decreased by 1.5 ± 1.1 kilograms, and skeletal muscle mass remained unchanged. The decrease in body mass correlated to the decrease in fat mass. The skinfolds at pectoral, abdominal, and thigh sites showed the largest decrease. The decrease in abdominal skinfold was significantly and negatively related to cycling speed during the race (Bischof et al. 2013). The adipose subcutaneous tissue of the belly is probably the best energy source for ultracyclists.

Generally, ultraendurance cyclists ingest mainly a carbohydrate-rich diet (Black, Skidmore, and Brown 2012; García-Rovés et al. 1998; Knechtle, Enggist, and Jehle 2005; Wirnitzer and Kornexl 2014). Typically, male cyclists who undertake intensive training programs report a high energy intake of 250 kilojoules per kilogram per day and carbohydrate intake of 8 to 11 grams per kilogram per day (Burke 2001). The intake of macronutrients such as carbohydrate, protein, and fat in ultraendurance cyclists has been investigated in case reports and field studies. During a 24-hour team relay, the nutritional strategy of eight men was investigated. The mean ingestion of macronutrients during the event was 943 ± 245 grams (13.1 ± 4.0 grams per kilogram) of carbohydrate, 174 ± 146 grams (2.4 ± 1.9 grams per kilogram) of protein, and 107 ± 56 grams (1.5 ± 0.7 grams per kilogram) of lipids, respectively (Bescós et al. 2012a). During a 24-hour period during a real 3-week competition, the average intake of macronutrients was 841.4 ± 66.2 grams per day period in carbohydrate, 201.8 ± 17.7 grams per day period in protein, and 158.6 ± 16.3 grams per day period in fat. The carbohydrate, protein, and fat contributions to energy were 60.0, 14.5, and 25.5 percent, respectively (García-Rovés et al. 1998). In an observational study including 18 cyclists competing in a 384-kilometer cycle race, mean carbohydrate, fat, and protein intakes were 52 ± 27 grams per hour, 15.84 ± 56.43 grams per hour, and 2.94 ± 7.25 grams per hour, respectively (Black, Skidmore, and Brown 2012). A case study investigated the nutrient intake of a cyclist training for and competing in the Race Across America. Carbohydrate accounted for 65 percent of the calories consumed during training (4,743 kilocalories), 75 percent of the calories consumed during 24-hour races (10,343 kilocalories), and 78 percent of the calories consumed during the Race Across America (8,429 kilocalories) (Lindeman 1991).

The relationship between energy intake and performance suggests that reducing the energy deficit may be advantageous (Black, Skidmore, and Brown 2012). Given the high carbohydrate intakes of these athletes, increasing energy intake from fat should be investigated as a means of decreasing energy deficits (Black, Skidmore, and Brown 2012).

Exercise-Associated Hyponatremia

Exercise-associated hyponatremia, defined as a plasma sodium concentration less than 135 millimoles per liter, is an electrolyte disorder frequently found in endurance athletes such as marathoners (Almond et al. 2005; Kipps, Sharma, and Pedoe 2011). In ultraendurance athletes, however, the prevalence of exercise-associated hyponatremia was no higher compared with that reported for marathoners (Chlíbková et al. 2014; Knechtle et al. 2011). Indeed, in ultracyclists, no case of exercise-associated hyponatremia was found in a 720-kilometer ultracycling marathon, the Swiss Cycling Marathon, in which 65 ultraendurance road cyclists were investigated (Rüst et al. 2012). But fluid intake and exercise-associated hyponatremia has not been investigated to date in the Race Across America.

Performance-Limiting Factors

Athletes competing in nonstop ultracycling races covering days or even weeks such as the RAAM will face the problem of sleep deprivation (Lahart et al. 2013). Lahart et al. (2013) reported that sleep and sleep efficiency were better maintained when using longer rest periods, highlighting the importance of a race strategy that seeks to optimize the balance between average cycling velocities and sleep time. For shorter ultraraces, taking breaks for sleeping seemed not to enhance performance. In a 600-kilometer qualifier for Paris–Brest–Paris, finishers who took power naps were not faster than finishers who did not take power naps (Knechtle et al. 2012b).

Another performance-limiting factor is the effect of ultracycling on the immune system. For instance, it has been reported that after cycling for 164 kilometers, faster cyclists showed more acute transient immune suppression than their slower counterparts (Luk et al. 2016). Cycling such distance might also result in increased levels of growth hormone and cortisol, especially in faster cyclists (Vingren et al 2016). Performance in ultracycling might be influenced by pacing, and positive pacing (i.e., speed gradually declining through a race) has been recommended as the optimal strategy in the RAAM (Heidenfelder et al 2016). A similar conclusion has been drawn in a case study in which a cyclist covered 896 kilometers within 24 hours by adopting positive pacing (Knechtle et al. 2015).

Designing a Monthly Training Program

Designing training should consider the basic training principles: sport specificity of exercises, going from easy to hard exercise intensity, interindividual differences, and periodization. An example of a monthly training program is depicted in table 40.5. Because ultracycling relies mostly on aerobic capacity,

Table 40.5. Sample Monthly Training Program for Beginners

Day	Training program
WEEK 1	
1	20 min x low, 20 min x moderate, 20 min x low
2	20 min x low, 5 x (1 min x high, 2 min x low), 20 min x low
3	80 min x low
WEEK 2	
1	20 min x low, 30 min x moderate, 20 min x low
2	20 min x low, 5 x (1.5 min x high, 2 min x low), 20 min x low
3	100 min x low
WEEK 3	
1	20 min x low, 40 min x moderate, 20 min x low
2	20 min x low, 5 x (2 min x high, 2 min x low), 20 min x low
3	120 min x low
WEEK 4	
1	20 min x low, 20 min x moderate, 20 min x low
2	20 min x low, 5 x (1 min x high, 2 min x low), 20 min x low
3	80 min x low

Low, moderate, and high describe exercise intensity.

performing a $\dot{V}O_2$max test in a sport science laboratory is crucial for prescribing exercise intensity. The results of this test identify important performance parameters such as $\dot{V}O_2$max and anaerobic threshold and provide information about individualized training zones of exercise intensity in beats per minute and watts (e.g., fat burn, aerobic capacity, anaerobic threshold, and $\dot{V}O_2$max).

With increasing experience in training and competition, the locomotor system of the lower extremity will become more used to the load. Experienced ultracyclists increase duration and distance of their daily training up to 200 to 300 kilometers during intense training weeks (personal communications).

Applying the Science

The most investigated aspects in ultradistance cycling are the energy deficit and intake of nutrients. The sex difference and age group of the fastest finishers in ultracycling performance are also well investigated. Little is known, however, about what motivates these athletes. Furthermore, aspects of fluid intake and exercise-associated hyponatremia are not known in very long ultracycling races such as the Race Across America. Future studies should investigate the motivation for athletes to compete in the Race Across America, the age of the fastest finishers, and the aspects of fluid intake and exercise-associated hyponatremia in this race.

In summary, the research to date shows that in ultraendurance cycling, the fastest finishers are about 35 years of age and originate mainly from Europe. Women are about 20 percent slower than men, and women seem unlikely to be able to outperform men in long-distance cycling races. Ultracyclists face an increasing energy deficit with increasing race distance, which seems to be covered by a decrease in body mass, mainly by a decrease in fat mass.

References

Chapter 1

Bassett, D.R., Jr., C.R. Kyle, L. Passfield, J.P. Broker, and E.R. Burke. 1999. Comparing cycling world hour records, 1967-1996: Modeling with empirical data. *Medicine and Science in Sports and Exercise*, 31(11): 1665-1676.

Davies, C.T. 1980. Effect of air resistance on the metabolic cost and performance of cycling. *European Journal of Applied Physiology and Occupational Physiology*, 45(2-3): 245-254.

Debraux, P., W. Bertucci, A.V. Manolova, S. Rogier, and A. Lodini. 2009. New method to estimate the cycling frontal area. *International Journal of Sports Medicine*, 30(4): 266-272.

Defraeye, T., B. Blocken, E. Koninckx, P. Hespel, and J. Carmeliet. 2010. Aerodynamic study of different cyclist positions: CFD analysis and full-scale wind-tunnel tests. *Journal of Biomechanics*, 43(7): 1262-1268.

di Prampero, P.E., G. Cortili, P. Mognoni, and F. Saibene. 1979. Equation of motion of a cyclist. *Journal of Applied Physiology: Respiratory, Environmental and Exercise Physiology*, 47(1): 201-206.

Dorel, S., C.A. Hautier, O. Rambaud, D. Rouffet, E. Van Praagh, J.R. Lacour, and M. Bourdin. 2005. Torque and power-velocity relationships in cycling: relevance to track sprint performance in world-class cyclists. *International Journal of Sports Medicine*, 26(9): 739-746.

Du Bois, D., and E.F. Du Bois. 1916. A formula to estimate the approximate surface area if height and weight be known. 1916. *Nutrition*, 5(5): 303-311; discussion 312-313.

Foley, J.P., S.R. Bird, and J.A. White. 1989. Anthropometric comparison of cyclists from different events. *British Journal of Sports Medicine*, 23(1): 30-33.

Garcia-Lopez, J., J.A. Rodriguez-Marroyo, C.E. Juneau, J. Peleteiro, A.C. Martinez, and J.G. Villa. 2008. Reference values and improvement of aerodynamic drag in professional cyclists. *Journal of Sports Sciences*, 26(3): 277-286.

Haakonssen, E.C., D.T. Martin, J.C. Martin, L.M. Burke, and D.G. Jenkins. 2013. Muscle mass-cycling power relationships in female road cyclists. 60th Annual Meeting of the American College of Sports Medicine, Indianapolis, IN.

Heil, D.P. 2001. Body mass scaling of projected frontal area in competitive cyclists. *European Journal of Applied Physiology*, 85(3-4): 358-366.

Heil, D.P. 2002. Body mass scaling of frontal area in competitive cyclists not using aero-handlebars. *European Journal of Applied Physiology*, 87(6): 520-528.

Heil, D.P. 2005. Body size as a determinant of the 1-h cycling record at sea level and altitude. *European Journal of Applied Physiology*, 93(5-6): 547-554.

Impellizzeri, F.M., T. Ebert, A. Sassi, P. Menaspa, E. Rampinini, and D.T. Martin. 2008. Level ground and uphill cycling ability in elite female mountain bikers and road cyclists. *European Journal of Applied Physiology*, 102(3): 335-341.

Jackson, A.S., and M.L. Pollock. 1978. Generalized equations for predicting body density of men. *British Journal of Nutrition*, 40(3): 497-504.

Jobson, S.A., J. Woodside, L. Passfield, and A.M. Nevill. 2008. Allometric scaling of uphill cycling performance. *International Journal of Sports Medicine*, 29(9): 753-757.

Lim, A.C., E.P. Homestead, A.G. Edwards, T.C. Carver, R. Kram, and W.C. Byrnes. 2011. Measuring changes in aerodynamic/rolling resistances by cycle-mounted power meters. *Medicine and Science in Sports and Exercise*, 43(5): 853-860.

Loenneke, J.P., M.E. Wray, J.M. Wilson, J.T. Barnes, M.L. Kearney, and T.J. Pujol. 2013. Accuracy of field methods in assessing body fat in collegiate baseball players. *Research in Sports Medicine*, 21(3): 286-291.

Lucia, A., J. Hoyos, and J.L. Chicharro. 2001. Physiology of professional road cycling. *Sports Medicine*, 31(5): 325-337.

Martin, D.T., B. McLean, C. Trewin, H. Lee, J. Victor, and A.G. Hahn. 2001. Physiological characteristics of nationally competitive female road cyclists and demands of competition. *Sports Medicine*, 31(7): 469-477.

Martin, J.C., C.J. Davidson, and E.R. Pardyjak. 2007. Understanding sprint-cycling performance: The integration of muscle power, resistance, and modeling. *International Journal of Sports Physiology and Performance*, 2(1): 5-21.

Martin, J.C., A.S. Gardner, M. Barras, and D.T. Martin. 2006. Modeling sprint cycling using field-derived parameters and forward integration. *Medicine and Science in Sports and Exercise*, 38(3): 592-597.

McLean, B.D., and A.W. Parker. 1989. An anthropometric analysis of elite Australian track cyclists. *Journal of Sports Sciences*, 7(3): 247-255.

Menaspà, P., E. Rampinini, A. Bosio, D. Carlomagno, M. Riggio, and A. Sassi. 2012. Physiological and anthropometric characteristics of junior cyclists of different specialties and performance levels. *Scandinavian Journal of Medicine and Science in Sports*, 22(3): 392-398.

Menaspà, P., M. Quod, D.T. Martin, J.J. Peiffer, C.R. Abbiss. 2015. Physical demands of sprinting in professional road cycling. *International Journal of Sports Medicine*, 36(13): 1058-1062.

Moon, J.R. 2013. Body composition in athletes and sports nutrition: an examination of the bioimpedance analysis technique. *European Journal of Clinical Nutrition*, 67 (suppl 1): S54-S59.

Mujika, I., and S. Padilla. 2001. Physiological and performance characteristics of male professional road cyclists. *Sports Medicine*, 31(7): 479-487.

Nevill, A.M., S.A. Jobson, R.C. Davison, and A.E. Jeukendrup. 2006. Optimal power-to-mass ratios when predicting flat and hill-climbing time-trial cycling. *European Journal of Applied Physiology*, 97(4): 424-431.

Olds, T.S., K.I. Norton, E.L. Lowe, S. Olive, F. Reay, and S. Ly. 1995. Modeling road-cycling performance. *Journal of Applied Physiology (1985)*, 78(4): 1596-1611.

Padilla, S., I. Mujika, F. Angulo, and J.J. Goiriena. 2000. Scientific approach to the 1-h cycling world record: A case study. *Journal of Applied Physiology*, 89(4): 1522-1527.

Padilla, S., I. Mujika, G. Cuesta, and J.J. Goiriena. 1999. Level ground and uphill cycling ability in professional road cycling. *Medicine and Science in Sports and Exercise*, 31(6): 878-885.

Sallet, P., R. Mathieu, G. Fenech, and G. Baverel. 2006. Physiological differences of elite and professional road cyclists related to competition level and rider specialization. *Journal of Sports Medicine and Physical Fitness*, 46(3): 361-365.

Swain, D.P., J.R. Coast, P.S. Clifford, M.C. Milliken, and J. Stray-Gundersen. 1987. Influence of body size on oxygen consumption during bicycling. *Journal of Applied Physiology*, 62(2): 668-672.

Chapter 2

Bemben, M.G., and H.S. Lamont. 2005. Creatine supplementation and exercise performance: Recent findings. *Sports Medicine*, 35: 107-125.

Bouchard, C. 1983. Genetics of physiological fitness and motor performance. *Exercise and Sport Sciences Review*, 11: 306-339.

Bouchard C., P. An, T. Rice, J.S. Skinner, J.H. Wilmore, J. Gagnon, L. Pérusse, A.S. Leon, and D.C. Rao. 1999. Familial aggregation of VO_2max response to exercise training: Results from the HERITAGE family study. *Journal of Applied Physiology*, 87: 1003-1008.

Bramble D.M., and D.E. Lieberman. 2004. Endurance running and the evolution of homo. *Nature*, 432: 345-352.

Cheung, S.S. 2010. *Advanced environmental exercise physiology*. Champaign, IL: Human Kinetics.

Ehlert T., P. Simon, and D.A. Moser. 2013. Epigenetics in sports. *Sports Medicine*, 43: 93-110.

Guth, L.M., and S.M. Roth. 2013. Genetic influence on athletic performance. *Current Opinion in Pediatrics*, 25: 653-658.

Ma, F., Y. Yang, X. Li, F. Zhou, C. Gao, M. Li, and L. Gao. 2013. The association of sport performance with ACE and ACTN3 genetic polymorphisms: A systematic review and meta-analysis. *PloS One*, 8: e54685.

MacArthur, D.G., and K.N. North. 2005. Genes and human elite athletic performance. *Human Genetics*, 116: 331-339.

Puthucheary, Z., J.R. Skipworth, J. Rawal, M. Loosemore, K. Van Someren, and H.E. Montgomery. 2011. The ACE gene and human performance: 12 years on. *Sports Medicine*, 41: 433-448.

Rupert, J.L. 2003. The search for genotypes that underlie human performance phenotypes. *Comparative Biochemistry and Physiology. Part A, Molecular and Integrative Physiology*, 136: 191-203.

Wang, G., E. Mikami, L.L. Chiu, A. DE Perini, M. Deason, N. Fuku, M. Miyachi, K. Kaneoka, H. Murakami, M. Tanaka, L.L. Hsieh, S.S. Hsieh, D. Caporossi, F. Pigozzi, A. Hilley, R. Lee, S.D. Galloway, J. Gulbin, V.A. Rogozkin, I.I. Ahmetov, N. Yang, K.N. North, S. Ploutarhos, H.E. Montgomery, M.E. Bailey, and Y.P. Pitsiladis. 2013. Association analysis of ACE and ACTN3 in elite Caucasian and East Asian swimmers. *Medicine and Science in Sports and Exercise*, 45: 892-900.

Chapter 3

Bicycle frame testing at the Open University. http://materials.open.ac.uk/bikeframes/bikeframe.htm.

Cannondale. 2007. *Cannondale lab report: Competitive testing/performance bicycles-synapse*. www.cannondale.com/lab_report/synapse.html.

Champoux, Y., S. Richard, and J.M. Drovet. 2007. Bicycle structural dynamics. *Sound and Vibration*, July: 16-22.

Delph, T., W. Kim, R. Flower, and J. Redcay. 1986. Bicycle frame stress analysis. *Bike Tech*, 5: 1-4.

Exxon Graftek. 1977. Sales brochure.

Hastings, A.Z., K.B. Blair, K.F. Culligan, and D.M. Pober. 2004. Measuring the transmitted road vibration on cycling performance. In *The engineering of sport 5*, ed. M. Hubbard, R.D. Mehta, and J.M. Pallis. Sheffield, England: International Sports Engineering Association.

Heine, J., and J.P. Praderes. 2005. *The golden age of handbuilt bicycles*. Seattle, WA: Vintage Bicycle Press.

Heine, J., and J.P. Praderes. 2008. *The competition bicycle*. Seattle, WA: Vintage Bicycle Press. page 28.

Levy, M., and G. Smith. 2005. Effectiveness of vibration damping with bicycle suspension systems. *Sports Engineering*, 8(2): 99-106.

McMahon, C.J., and C.D. Graham. 2000. *Introduction to engineering materials: The bicycle and the walkman*. 2nd ed. Philadelphia: Merion Books.

Miller, C.M. 1982. Frame rigidity. *Bike Tech*, 1(1): 1-5.

Papadopoulos, J. 1987. Forces in bicycle pedaling. In *Biomechanics in sport: A 1987 update*, ed. R. Rekow, V.G. Thacker, and A.G. Erdman. New York: American Society of Mechanical Engineers.

Peterson, L.A., and K.J. Landry. 1986. Finite element structural analysis: A new tool for bicycle frame design. *Bike Tech*, 5(2): 1-9.

Pridmore, J., and J. Hurd. 1995. *The American bicycle*, 39. Osceola, WI: Motorbooks International.

Reynolds Tube Company. 1972. *Top tubes by Reynolds*. Birmingham, England: Reynolds Tube.

Rinard, D. *Fork deflection*. www.sheldonbrown.com/rinard_forktest.html

Rinard, D. *Frame deflection test*. www.sheldonbrown.com/rinard/rinard_frametest.html

Sharp, A. 1896. The frame: Stresses. In *Bicycles and tricycles: An elementary treatise on their design and construction*, 303-336. London: Longmans, Green.

Specialized. 2008. *Specialized 2008 fact bikes and equipment*, 12-13.

Zinn, L. 2006. Flexing their muscles: Does a superlight frame come with a sacrifice in stiffness? *Velonews*, March 27, 35(5): 48-50.

Chapter 4

Easton Sports. *Easton technology report #1: Materials/aluminum*. Van Nuys, CA: Easton Sports.

KVA Stainless. www.kvastainless.com. Escondido, CA: KVA Stainless.

Lindsey, J. 2010. Black magic. In *Mountain bike 2010 buyer's guide*, 26-33.

Reynolds. 1999. *Comparative mechanical properties of commonly used cycle tube materials*. Reynolds USA.

Chapter 5

Bini, R., P. Hume, and J. Croft. 2014. Cyclists and triathletes have different body positions on the bicycle. *European Journal of Sport Science*, 14 (sup1): 109-115.

Bressel, E., J. Cronin, and A. Exeter. 2005. Bicycle seat interface pressure: Reliability, validity, and influence of hand position and workload. *Journal of Biomechanics*, 38(6): 1325-1331.

Bressel, E., and B.J. Larson. 2003. Bicycle seat designs and their effect on pelvic angle, trunk angle, and comfort. *Medicine and Science in Sports and Exercise*, 35(2): 327-332.

Carpes, F.P., F. Dagnese, J.F. Kleinpaul, A. Martins Ede, and C.B. Mota. 2009. Bicycle saddle pressure: Effects of trunk position and saddle design on healthy subjects. *Urologia Internationalis*, 82: 8-11.

De Vey Mestdagh, K. 1998. Personal perspective: In search of an optimum cycling posture. *Applied Ergonomics*, 29(5): 325-334.

Fröböse, I., B. Luecker, and K. Wittmann. 2001. Overuse symptoms in mountain bikers: A study with an empirical questionnaire. *Deutsche Zeitschrift für Sportmedizin*, 52(11): 311-315.

Guess, M.K., K. Connell, S. Schrader, S. Reutman, A. Wang, J. LaCombe, C. Toennis, B. Lowe, A. Melman, and M. Mikhail. 2006. Genital sensation and sexual function in women bicyclists and run- ners: Are your feet safer than your seat? *Journal of Sexual Medicine*, 3(6): 1018-1027.

Hollingworth, M., A. Harper, and M. Hamer. 2014. An observational study of erectile dysfunction, infertility, and prostate cancer in regular cyclists. *Journal of Men's Health*, 11(2): 75-79.

Keytel, L.R., and T.D. Noakes. 2002. Effects of a novel bicycle saddle on symptoms and comfort in cyclists. *South African Medical Journal*, 92(4): 295-298.

Marsden, M. 2010. Lower back pain in cyclists: A review of epidemiology, pathomechanics and risk factors. *International SportMed Journal*, 11(1): 216 -225.

Mellion, M.B. 1991. Common cycling injuries: Management and prevention. *Sports Medicine*, 11(1): 52-70.

Nayal, W., U. Schwarzer, T. Klotz, A. Heidenreich, and U. Engelmann. 1999. Transcutaneous penile oxygen pressure during bicycling. *BJU International*, 83(6): 623-625.

Potter, J., J.L. Sauer, and C.L. Weisshaar. 2008. Gender differences in bicycle saddle pressure distribution during seated cycling. *Medicine and Science in Sports and Exercise*, 40(6): 1126-1134.

Pruitt, A., and F. Matheny. 2006. *Andy Pruitt's complete medical guide for cyclists*. Boulder, CO: VeloPress.

Rimpler, H., A. Hinrichs, and M. Wilaschek. 2009. Development of pelvic artery occlusion in professional athletes. *Gefässchirurgie*, 14: 308-313.

Schade, D., J. Natrup, and M. Fritz. 2006. Druckverteilung auf Fahrradsätteln nach Maß. *Orthopädieschuhtechnik*, 7/8: 28-31.

Schrader, S.M., M.J. Breitenstein, J.C. Clark, et al. 2002. Nocturnal penile tumescence and rigidity testing in bicycling patrol officers. *Journal of Andrology*, 23(6): 927-934.

Schrader, S.M., M.J. Breitenstein, and B.D. Lowe. 2008. Cutting off the nose to save the penis. *Journal of Sexual Medicine*, 5: 1932-1940.

Schwarzer, U., F. Sommer, T. Klotz, C. Cremer, and U. Engelmann. 2002. Cycling and penile oxygen pressure: The type of saddle matters. *European Urology*, 41(2): 139-143.

Schwellnus, M.P., and E.W. Derman. 2005. Common injuries in cycling: Prevention, diagnosis and management. *South African Family Practice* 47(7): 14-19.

Silberman, M.R., D. Webner, S. Collina, B.J. Shiple. 2005. Road bicycle fit. *Clinical Journal of Sports Medicine*, 15(4): 271-276.

Taylor, J.A., T.C. Kao, and P. Albertsen. 2004. Bicycling riding and its relationship to the development of erectile dysfunction. *Journal of Urology*, 172: 1028-1031.

Weiss, B.D. 1994. Clinical syndromes associated with bicycle seats. *Clinics in Sports Medicine*, 13(1): 175-186.

Chapter 6

Abbiss, C.R., and P.B. Laursen. 2005. Models to explain fatigue during prolonged endurance cycling. *Sports Medicine*, 35: 865-898.

Austin, N., R. Nilwik, and W. Herzog. 2010. In vivo operational fascicle lengths of vastus lateralis during sub-maximal and maximal cycling. *Journal of Biomechanics*, 43: 2394-2399.

Bini, R., P. Hume, and A. Kilding. 2014. Saddle height effects on pedal forces, joint mechanical work and kinematics of cyclists and triathletes. *European Journal of Sport Science*, 14: 44-52.

Bini, R.R., F.P. Carpes, and F. Diefenthaeler. 2011. Effects of cycling with the knees close to the bicycle frame on the lower limb muscle activation. *Brazilian Journal of Physical Education and Sport*, 25: 27-37.

Bini, R.R., and P.A. Hume. 2014. Assessment of bilateral asymmetry in cycling using a commercial instrumented crank system and instrumented pedals. *International Journal of Sports Physiology and Performance*, 9(5): 876-881.

Blake, O.M., and J.M. Wakeling. 2013. Estimating changes in metabolic power from EMG. *Springerplus*, 2: 229.

Bressel, E., and J. Cronin. 2005. Bicycle seat interface pressure: Reliability, validity, and influence of hand position and workload. *Journal of Biomechanics*, 38: 1325-1331.

Carpes, F.P., F. Diefenthaeler, R.R. Bini, D. Stefanyshyn, I.E. Faria, and C.B. Mota. 2010. Does leg preference affect muscle activation and efficiency? *Journal of Electromyography and Kinesiology*, 20: 1230-1236.

Carpes, F.P., F. Diefenthaeler, R.R. Bini, D.J. Stefanyshyn, I.E. Faria, and C.B. Mota. 2011. Influence of leg preference on bilateral muscle activation during cycling. *Journal of Sports Sciences*, 29: 151-159.

Carpes, F.P., M. Rossato, I.E. Faria, and C.B. Mota. 2007. Bilateral pedaling asymmetry during a simulated 40-km cycling time-trial. *Journal of Sports Medicine and Physical Fitness*, 47: 51-57.

Connick, M.J., and F.X. Li. 2013. The impact of altered task mechanics on timing and duration of eccentric bi-articular muscle contractions during cycling. *Journal of Electromyography and Kinesiology*, 23: 223-229.

Diefenthaeler, F., R.R. Bini, and M.A. Vaz. 2012. Frequency band analysis of muscle activation during cycling to exhaustion. *Brazilian Journal of Kineanthropometry and Human Performance*, 14: 243-253.

Diefenthaeler, F., E.F. Coyle, R.R. Bini, F.P. Carpes, and M.A. Vaz. 2012. Muscle activity and pedal force profile of triathletes during cycling to exhaustion. *Sports Biomechanics*, 11: 10-19.

Dorel, S., A. Couturier, J.R. Lacour, H. Vandewalle, C. Hautier, and F. Hug. 2010. Force-velocity relationship in cycling revisited: Benefit of two-dimensional pedal forces analysis. *Medicine and Science in Sports and Exercise*, 42: 1174-1183.

Edeline, O., D. Polin, C. Tourny-Chollet, and J. Weber. 2004. Effect of workload on bilateral pedaling kinematics in non-trained cyclists. *Journal of Human Movement Studies*, 46: 493-517.

Gregor, R.J. 2000. Biomechanics of cycling. In *Exercise and sports science*, ed. W.E. Garret and D.T. Kirkendall, 549-571. Philadelphia: Lippincott Williams & Wilkins.

Hautier, C.A., L.M. Arsac, K. Deghdegh, J. Souquet, A. Belli, and J.R. Lacour. 2000. Influence of fatigue on EMG/force ratio and cocontraction in cycling. *Medicine and Science in Sports and Exercise*, 32: 839-843.

Hawkins, D., and M.L. Hull. 1990. A method for determining lower extremity muscle-tendon lengths during flexion/extension movements. *Journal of Biomechanics*, 23: 487-494.

Herzog, W. 2007. Muscle. In *Biomechanics of the musculoskeletal system*, 3rd ed., vol. 1, ed. B.M. Nigg and W. Herzog, 169-225. Chichester: Wiley.

Hug, F., F. Boumier, and S. Dorel. 2013. Altered muscle coordination when pedaling with independent cranks. *Frontiers in Physiology*, 4: 232.

Kanchan, T., T.S. Mohan Kumar, G. Pradeep Kumar, and K. Yoganarasimha. 2008. Skeletal asymmetry. *Journal of Forensic and Legal Medicine*, 15: 177-179.

Kautz, S.A., and R.R. Neptune. 2002. Biomechanical determinants of pedaling energetics: Internal and external work are not independent. *Exercise and Sport Sciences Reviews*, 30: 159-165.

Lucia, A., A.F. San Juan, M. Montilla, S. Canete, A. Santalla, C. Earnest, and M. Perez. 2004. In professional road cyclists, low pedaling cadences are less efficient. *Medicine and Science in Sports and Exercise*, 36: 1048-1054.

MacIntosh, B.R., R.R. Neptune, and J.F. Horton. 2000. Cadence, power, and muscle activation in cycle ergometry. *Medicine and Science in Sports and Exercise*, 32: 1281-1287.

Magnusson, S.P., M.V. Narici, C.N. Maganaris, and M. Kjaer. 2008. Human tendon behaviour and adaptation, in vivo. *Journal of Physiology*, 586: 71-81.

McGowan, C.P., R.R. Neptune, and W. Herzog. 2013. A phenomenological muscle model to assess history dependent effects in human movement. *Journal of Biomechanics*, 46: 151-157.

Muraoka, T., Y. Kawakami, M. Tachi, and T. Fukunaga. 2001. Muscle fiber and tendon length changes in the human vastus lateralis during slow pedaling. *Journal of Applied Physiology*, 91: 2035-2040.

Patterson, J.M.M., M.M. Jaggars, and M.I. Boyer. 2003. Ulnar and median nerve palsy in long-distance cyclists a prospective study. *American Journal of Sports Medicine*, 31: 585-589.

Rassier, D.E., B.R. MacIntosh, and W. Herzog. 1999. Length dependence of active force production in skeletal muscle. *Journal of Applied Physiology*, 86: 1445-1457.

Sanderson, D.J., and A.T. Amoroso. 2009. The influence of seat height on the mechanical function of the triceps surae muscles during steady-rate cycling.

Journal of Electromyography and Kinesiology, 19: e465-e471.

Savelberg, H.H.C.M., I.G.L. Van de Port, and P.J.B. Willems. 2003. Body configuration in cycling affects muscle recruitment and movement pattern. *Journal of Applied Biomechanics*, 19: 310-324.

Slane, J., M. Timmerman, H.-L. Ploeg, and D.G. Thelen. 2011. The influence of glove and hand position on pressure over the ulnar nerve during cycling. *Clinical Biomechanics*, 26: 642-648.

Stone, C., and M.L. Hull. 1995. The effect of rider weight on rider-induced loads during common cycling situations. *Journal of Biomechanics*, 28: 365-375.

Takaishi, T., T. Yamamoto, T. Ono, T. Ito, and T. Moritani. 1998. Neuromuscular, metabolic, and kinetic adaptations for skilled pedaling performance in cyclists. *Medicine and Science in Sports and Exercise*, 30: 442-449.

Umberger, B.R., K.G. Gerritsen, and P.E. Martin. 2006. Muscle fiber type effects on energetically optimal cadences in cycling. *Journal of Biomechanics*, 39: 1472-1479.

Yoshihuku, Y., and W. Herzog. 1996. Maximal muscle power output in cycling: A modelling approach. *Journal of Sports Sciences*, 14: 139-157.

Chapter 7

Bailey, M.P., F.J. Maillardet, and N. Messenger. 2003. Kinematics of cycling in relation to anterior knee pain and patellar tendinitis. *Journal of Sports Sciences*, 21: 649-657.

Bini, R., P. Hume, and A. Kilding. 2014. Saddle height effects on pedal forces, joint mechanical work and kinematics of cyclists and triathletes. *European Journal of Sport Science*, 14: 44-52.

Bini, R.R. 2011. Effects of saddle position on pedalling technique and methods to assess pedalling kinetics and kinematics of cyclists and triathletes. Doctoral thesis, AUT University, Auckland, NZ.

Bini, R.R. 2012. Patellofemoral and tibiofemoral forces in cyclists and triathletes: Effects of saddle height. *Journal of Science and Cycling*, 1: 9-14.

Bini, R.R., P.A. Hume, and J.L. Croft. 2014. Cyclists and triathletes have different body positions on the bicycle. *European Journal of Sport Science*, 14: S109-S115.

Bini, R.R., P.A. Hume, F.J. Lanferdini, and M.A. Vaz. 2013. Effects of moving forward or backward on the saddle on knee joint forces during cycling. *Physical Therapy in Sport*, 14: 23-27.

Bini, R.R., P.A. Hume, F.J. Lanferdini, and M.A. Vaz. 2014. Effects of body positions on the saddle on pedalling technique for cyclists and triathletes. *European Journal of Sport Science*, 14: S413-S420.

Bini, R.R., D. Senger, F.J. Lanferdini, and A.L. Lopes. 2012. Joint kinematics assessment during cycling incremental test to exhaustion. *Isokinetics and Exercise Science*, 20: 99-105.

Bressel, E., S. Bliss, and J. Cronin. 2009. A field-based approach for examining bicycle seat design effects on seat pressure and perceived stability. *Applied Ergonomics*, 40: 472-476.

Bressel, E., and B.J. Larson. 2003. Bicycle seat designs and their effect on pelvic angle, trunk angle, and comfort. *Medicine and Science in Sports and Exercise*, 35: 327-332.

Carpes, F.P., F. Dagnese, J.F. Kleinpaul, E. De Assis Martins, and C. Bolli Mota. 2009a. Bicycle saddle pressure: Effects of trunk position and saddle design on healthy subjects. *Urologia Internationalis*, 82: 8-11.

Carpes, F.P., F. Dagnese, J.F. Kleinpaul, E.D.A. Martins, and C.B. Mota. 2009b. Effects of workload on seat pressure while cycling with two different saddles. *Journal of Sexual Medicine*, 6: 2728-2735.

Connick, M.J., and F.X. Li. 2013. The impact of altered task mechanics on timing and duration of eccentric bi-articular muscle contractions during cycling. *Journal of Electromyography and Kinesiology*, 23: 223-229.

De Vey Mestdagh, K. 1998. Personal perspective: In search of an optimum cycling posture. *Applied Ergonomics*, 29: 325-334.

Dettori, N.J., and D.C. Norvell. 2006. Non-traumatic bicycle injuries: A review of the literature. *Sports Medicine*, 36: 7-18.

Disley, B.X., and F.X. Li. 2014. Metabolic and kinematic effects of self-selected Q factor during bike fit. *Research in Sports Medicine*, 22: 12-22.

Empfield, D. 1999. *Slowtwitch*. www.slowtwitch.com

Ericson, M.O., and R. Nisell. 1987. Patellofemoral joint forces during ergometric cycling. *Physical Therapy*, 67: 1365-1369.

Ericson, M.O., and R. Nisell. 1988. Efficiency of pedal forces during ergometer cycling. *International Journal of Sports Medicine*, 9: 118-122.

Ericson, M.O., R. Nisell, and J. Ekholm. 1984. Varus and valgus loads on the knee joint during ergometer cycling. *Scandinavian Journal of Sports Sciences*, 6: 39-45.

Estivalet, M., P. Brisson, J. Iriberri, X. Muriel, and I. Larrazabal. 2008. The bike fit of the road professional cyclist related to anthropometric measurements and the torque of de crank (P242). In *The engineering of sport 7*, vol. 1, ed. M. Estivalet and P. Brisson, 483-488. Paris: Springer.

Ferrer-Roca, V., A. Roig, P. Galilea, and J. García-López. 2012. Influence of saddle height on lower limb kinematics in well-trained cyclists: Static versus dynamic evaluation in bike fitting. *Journal of Strength and Conditioning Research*, 26: 3025-3029.

García-López, J., J.A. Rodríguez-Marroyo, C.E. Juneau, J. Peleteiro, A.C. Martínez, and J.G. Villa. 2008. Reference values and improvement of aerodynamic drag in professional cyclists. *Journal of Sports Sciences*, 26: 277-286.

Garside, I., and D.A. Doran. 2000. Effects of bicycle frame ergonomics on triathlon 10-km running performance. *Journal of Sports Sciences*, 18: 825-833.

Gregor, R.J., and J.B. Wheeler. 1994. Biomechanical factors associated with shoe/pedal interfaces: Implications for injury. *Sports Medicine*, 17: 117-131.

Holmes, J.C., A.L. Pruitt, and N.J. Whalen. 1994. Lower extremity overuse in bicycling. *Clinics in Sports Medicine*, 13: 187-203.

Litzenberger, S., S. Illes, M. Hren, M. Reichel, and M. Sabo. 2008. Influence of pedal foot position on muscular activity during ergometer cycling (P242). In *The engineering of sport 7*, vol. 1, ed. M. Estivalet and P. Brisson, 215-222. Paris: Springer.

Paton, C.D. 2009. Effects of shoe cleat position on physiology and performance of competitive cyclists. *International Journal of Sports Physiology and Performance*, 4: 517-523.

Patterson, J.M.M., M.M. Jaggars, and M.I. Boyer. 2003. Ulnar and median nerve palsy in long-distance cyclists a prospective study. *American Journal of Sports Medicine*, 31: 585-589.

Peveler, W.W. 2008. Effects of saddle height on economy in cycling. *Journal of Strength and Conditioning Research*, 22: 1355-1359.

Peveler, W.W., P. Bishop, J. Smith, M. Richardson, and E. Whitehorn. 2005. Comparing methods for setting saddle height in trained cyclists. *Journal of Exercise Physiology Online*, 8: 51-55.

Peveler, W.W., B. Shew, S. Johnson, and T.G. Palmer. 2012. A kinematic comparison of alterations to knee and ankle angles from resting measures to active pedaling during a graded exercise protocol. *Journal of Strength and Conditioning Research*, 26: 3004-3009.

Price, D., and B. Donne. 1997. Effect of variation in seat tube angle at different seat heights on submaximal cycling performance in man. *Journal of Sports Sciences*, 15: 395-402.

Ramos Ortega, J., P.V. Munuera, and G. Dominguez. 2012. Antero-posterior position of the cleat for road cycling. *Science and Sports*, 27: e55-e61.

Rankin, J.W., and R.R. Neptune. (2008). *Determination of the optimal seat position that maximizes average crank power: A theoretical study*. Paper presented at the North American Congress on Biomechanics, Michigan, USA.

Rassier, D.E., B.R. MacIntosh, and W. Herzog. 1999. Length dependence of active force production in skeletal muscle. *Journal of Applied Physiology*, 86: 1445-1457.

Salai, M., T. Brosh, A. Blankstein, A. Oran, and A. Chechik. 1999. Effect of changing the saddle angle on the incidence of low back pain in recreational bicyclists. *British Journal of Sports Medicine*, 33: 398-400.

Sanderson, D.J., A.H. Black, and J. Montgomery. 1994. The effect of varus and valgus wedges on coronal plane knee motion during steady-rate cycling. *Clinical Journal of Sport Medicine*, 4: 120-124.

Savelberg, H.H.C.M., and K. Meijer. 2003. Contribution of mono- and biarticular muscles to extending knee joint moments in runners and cyclists. *Journal of Applied Physiology*, 94: 2241-2248.

Silberman, M.R., D. Webner, S. Collina, and B.J. Shiple. 2005. Road bicycle fit. *Clinical Journal of Sport Medicine*, 15: 271-276.

Slane, J., M. Timmerman, H.-L. Ploeg, and D.G. Thelen. 2011. The influence of glove and hand position on pressure over the ulnar nerve during cycling. *Clinical Biomechanics*, 26: 642-648.

Yoshihuku, Y., and W. Herzog. 1996. Maximal muscle power output in cycling: A modelling approach. *Journal of Sports Sciences*, 14: 139-157.

Chapter 8

Anderson, J.C., and J.M. Sockler. 1990. Effects of orthoses on selected physiologic parameters in cycling. *Journal of the American Podiatric Medical Association*, 80(3): 161-166.

Barratt, P.R., T. Korff, S.J. Elmer, and J.C. Martin. 2011. Effect of crank length on joint-specific power during maximal cycling. *Medicine and Science in Sports and Exercise*, 43(9): 1689-1697.

Bressel, E., and B.J. Larson. 2003. Bicycle seat designs and their effect on pelvic angle, trunk angle, and comfort. *Medicine and Science in Sports and Exercise*, 35(2): 327-332.

Burnett, A.F., M.W. Cornelius, W. Dankaerts, and P.B. O'Sullivan. 2004. Spinal kinematics and trunk muscle activity in cyclists: A comparison between healthy controls and non-specific chronic low back pain subjects—a pilot investigation. *Manual Therapy*, 9(4): 211-219.

Burke, E.R., and A.L. Pruitt. 2003. Body positioning for cycling. In *High tech cycling*, 2nd ed., ed. E.R. Burke, 69-92. Champaign, IL: Humans Kinetics.

Carpes, F.P., F. Dagnese, J.F. Kleinpaul, A. Martins Ede, and C.B. Mota. 2009. Bicycle saddle pressure: Effects of trunk position and saddle design on healthy subjects. *Urologia Internationalis*, 82(1): 8-11.

Clarsen, B., T. Krosshaug, and R. Bahr. 2010. Overuse injuries in professional road cyclists. *The American Journal of Sports Medicine*, 38(12): 2494-2501.

Connick, M.J., and F.X. Li. 2013. The impact of altered task mechanics on timing and duration of eccentric bi-articular muscle contractions during cycling. *Journal of Electromyography and Kinesiology*, 23(1): 223-229.

de Vey Mestdagh, K. 1998. Personal perspective in search of an optimum cycling posture. *Applied Ergonomics*, 29(5): 325-334.

Disley, B.X., and F.X. Li. 2014. The effect of Q Factor on gross mechanical efficiency and muscular activation in cycling. *Scandinavian Journal of Medicine and Science in Sports*, 24(1): 117-121.

Ericson, M.O., R. Nisell, and G. Németh. 1988. Joint motions of the lower limb during ergometer cycling. *Journal of Orthopaedic and Sports Physical Therapy*, 9(8): 273-278.

Ferrer-Roca, V., A. Roig, P. Galilea, and J. García-López. 2012. Influence of saddle height on lower limb kinematics in well-trained cyclists: Static vs. dynamic evaluation in bike fitting. *Journal of Strength and Conditioning Research*, 26(11): 3025-3029.

Gregersen, C.S., M.L. Hull, and N.A. Hakansson. 2006. How changing the inversion/eversion foot angle affects the nondriving intersegmental knee moments and the relative activation of the vastii muscles in cycling. *Journal of Biomechanical Engineering*, 128(3): 391-398.

Haffajee, D., U. Moritz, and G. Svantesson. 1972. Isometric knee extension strength as a function of joint angle, muscle length and motor unit activity. *Acta Orthopaedica*, 43(2): 138-147.

Hamley, E.Y., and V. Thomas. 1967. Physiological and postural factors in the calibration of the bicycle ergometer. *Journal of Physiology*, 191(2): 55P-56P.

Hautier, C.A., M.T. Linossier, A. Belli, J.R. Lacour, and L.M. Arsac. 1996. Optimal velocity for maximal power production in non-isokinetic cycling is related to muscle fibre type composition. *European Journal of Applied Physiology and Occupational Physiology*, 74(1-2): 114-118.

Hice, G.A., Z. Kendrick, K. Weeber, and J. Bray. 1985. The effect of foot orthoses on oxygen consumption while cycling. *Journal of the American Podiatric Medical Association*, 75(10): 513-516.

Holmes, J.C., A.L. Pruitt, and N.J. Whalen. 1994. Lower extremity overuse in bicycling. *Clinics in Sports Medicine*, 13(1): 187-205

Inbar, O., R. Dotan, T. Trosil, and Z. Dvir. 1983. The effect of bicycle crank-length variation upon power performance. *Ergonomics*, 26(12): 1139-1146.

Jeong, S.J., K. Park, J.D. Moon, and S.B. Ryu. 2002. Bicycle saddle shape affects penile blood flow. *International Journal of Impotence Research*, 14(6): 513-517.

Koch, M., M. Fröhlich, E. Emrich, and A. Urhausen. 2013. The impact of carbon insoles in cycling on performance in the Wingate Anaerobic Test. *Journal of Science and Cycling*, 2(2): 2-5.

LeMond, G. and Gordis, K., 1987. *Greg LeMond's complete book of bicycling*. Putnam Pub Group.

Lowe, B.D., S.M. Schrader, and M.J. Breitenstein. 2004. Effect of bicycle saddle designs on the pressure to the perineum of the bicyclist. *Medicine and Science in Sports and Exercise*, 36(6): 1055-1062.

Lukes, R.A., S.B. Chin, and S.J. Haake. 2005. The understanding and development of cycling aerodynamics. *Sports Engineering*, 8(2): 59-74.

Martin, J.C., and W.W. Spirduso. 2001. Determinants of maximal cycling power: Crank length, pedaling rate and pedal speed. *European Journal of Applied Physiology*, 84(5): 413-418.

McDaniel, J., J.L. Durstine, G.A. Hand, and J.C. Martin. 2002. Determinants of metabolic cost during submaximal cycling. *Journal of Applied Physiology*, 93(3): 823-828.

Mündermann, A., B.M. Nigg, R. Neil Humble, and D.J. Stefanyshyn. 2003. Foot orthotics affect lower extremity kinematics and kinetics during running. *Clinical Biomechanics*, 18(3): 254-262.

Muyor, J.M., P.A. López-Miñarro, and F. Alacid. 2011. Spinal posture of thoracic and lumbar spine and pelvic tilt in highly trained cyclists. *Journal of Sports Science and Medicine*, 10(2): 355.

Nordeen-Snyder, K.S. 1976. The effect of bicycle seat height variation upon oxygen consumption and lower limb kinematics. *Medicine and Science in Sports*, 9(2): 113-117.

Partin, S.N., K.A. Connell, S. Schrader, J. LaCombe, B. Lowe, A. Sweeney, S. Reutman, A. Wang, C. Toennnis, A. Melman, M. Mikhail, and M.K. Guess. 2012. The bar sinister: Does handlebar level damage the pelvic floor in female cyclists? *Journal of Sexual Medicine*, 9(5): 1367-1373.

Peveler, W.W. 2008. Effects of saddle height on economy in cycling. *Journal of Strength and Conditioning Research*, 22(4): 1355-1359.

Potter, J.J., J.L. Sauer, C.L. Weisshaar, H. Ploeg, and D.G. Thelen. 2008. Gender differences in bicycle saddle pressure distribution during seated cycling. *Medicine and Science in Sports and Exercise*, 40(6): 1126.

Rankin, J.W., and R.R. Neptune. 2010. The influence of seat configuration on maximal average crank power during pedaling: A simulation study. *Journal of Applied Biomechanics*, 26(4): 493-500.

Ruby, P., and M.L. Hull. 1993. Response of intersegmental knee loads to foot/pedal platform degrees of freedom in cycling. *Journal of Biomechanics*, 26(11): 1327-1340.

Salai, M., T. Brosh, A. Blankstein, A. Oran, and A. Chechik. 1999. Effect of changing the saddle angle on the incidence of low back pain in recreational bicyclists. *British Journal of Sports Medicine*, 33(6): 398-400.

Sanderson, D.J., A.H. Black, and J. Montgomery. 1994. The effect of varus and valgus wedges on coronal plane knee motion during steady-rate cycling. *Clinical Journal of Sport Medicine*, 4(2): 120-124.

Van Sickle, J.R., and M.L. Hull. 2007. Is economy of competitive cyclists affected by the anterior-posterior foot position on the pedal? *Journal of Biomechanics*, 40(6): 1262-1267.

Chapter 9

Bassett, D.R., C.R. Kyle, L. Passfield, J.P. Broker, and E.R. Burke. 1999. Comparing cycling world hours records, 1967–1996: Modeling with empirical data. *Medicine and Science in Sports and Exercise*, 31: 1665-1676.

Chowdhury, A. 2012. Aerodynamics of sports fabrics and garments. PhD dissertation, School of Aerospace, Mechanical and Manufacturing Engineering, RMIT University, Melbourne, Australia.

Coggan, A. 2011. Estimation of CdA from anthropometric data. *Training and racing with a power meter journal*, www.trainingandracingwithapowermeter.com

Kyle, C. 1991. The effects of crosswinds upon time trials. *Cycling Science*, Sept/Dec: 51-56.

Martin, J.C., A.S. Gardner, M. Barras, and D. Martin. 2006. Modeling sprint cycling using field-derived parameters and forward integration. *Medicine and Science in Sports and Exercise*, 38(3): 592-597.

Martin, J., D. Milliken, J. Cobb, K. McFadden, and A. Coggan. 1998. Validation of a mathematical model for road cycling power. *Journal of Applied Biomechanics*, 14: 276-291.

Chapter 10

Barratt, P.R., A.S. Gardner, J.C. Martin, and T. Korff. (under review). Mechanical differences in muscular power production between elite and sub-elite track cyclists: The influences of strength and inter-muscular coordination.

Bini, R.R., F.P. Carpes, F. Diefenthaeler, C.B. Mota, A.C. Guimaraes, and Grupo de Estudo e Pesquisa em Ciclismo. 2008. Physiological and electromyographic responses during 40-km cycling time trial: Relationship to muscle coordination and performance. *Journal of Science and Medicine in Sport / Sports Medicine Australia*, 11(4): 363-370.

Bini, R.R., and P.A. Hume. 2014. Assessment of bilateral asymmetry in cycling using a commercial instrumented crank system and instrumented pedals. *International Journal of Sports Physiology and Performance*, 9(5): 876-881.

Carpes, F.P., F. Diefenthaeler, R.R. Bini, D. Stefanyshyn, I.E. Faria, and C.B. Mota. 2010. Does leg preference affect muscle activation and efficiency? *Journal of Electromyography and Kinesiology, Official Journal of the International Society of Electrophysiological Kinesiology*, 20(6): 1230-1236.

Carpes, F.P., M. Rossato, I.E. Faria, and C. Bolli Mota. 2007. Bilateral pedaling asymmetry during a simulated 40-km cycling time-trial. *Journal of Sports Medicine and Physical Fitness*, 47(1): 51-57.

Cannon, D.T., F.W. Kolkhorst, and D.J. Cipriani. 2007. Effect of pedaling technique on muscle activity and cycling efficiency. *European Journal of Applied Physiology*, 99(6): 659-664.

Coyle, E.F., L.S. Sidossis, J.F. Horowitz, and J.D. Beltz. 1992. Cycling efficiency is related to the percentage of type I muscle fibers. *Medicine and Science in Sports and Exercise*, 24(7): 782-788.

Daly, D.J., and P.R. Cavanagh. 1976. Asymmetry in bicycle ergometer pedalling. *Medicine and Science in Sports*, 8(3): 204-208.

Dorel, S., J.M. Drouet, A. Couturier, Y. Champoux, and F. Hug. 2009. Changes of pedaling technique and muscle coordination during an exhaustive exercise. *Medicine and Science in Sports and Exercise*, 41(6): 1277-1286.

Dorel, S., G. Guilhem, A. Couturier, and F. Hug. 2012. Adjustment of muscle coordination during an all-out sprint cycling task. *Medicine and Science in Sports and Exercise*, 44(11): 2154-2164.

Dorel, S., C.A. Hautier, O. Rambaud, D. Rouffet, E. Van Praagh, J.R. Lacour, and M. Bourdin. 2005. Torque and power-velocity relationships in cycling: Relevance to track sprint performance in world-class cyclists. *International Journal of Sports Medicine*, 26(9): 739-746.

Elmer, S.J., P.R. Barratt, T. Korff, and J.C. Martin. 2011. Joint-specific power production during submaximal and maximal cycling. *Medicine and Science in Sports and Exercise*, 43(10): 1940-1947.

Elmer, S.J., C.S. Marshall, K. Wehmanen, M. Amann, J. McDaniel, D.T. Martin, and J.C. Martin. 2012. Effects of locomotor muscle fatigue on joint-specific power production during cycling. *Medicine and Science in Sports and Exercise*, 44(8): 1504-1511.

Gardner, A.S., J.C. Martin, D.T. Martin, M. Barras, and D.G. Jenkins. 2007. Maximal torque- and power-pedaling rate relationships for elite sprint cyclists in laboratory and field tests. *European Journal of Applied Physiology*, 101(3): 287-292.

Hopker, J., D. Coleman, and L. Passfield. 2009. Changes in cycling efficiency during a competitive season. *Medicine and Science in Sports and Exercise*, 41(4): 912-919.

Hopker, J., D. Coleman, L. Passfield, and J. Wiles. 2010. The effect of training volume and intensity on competitive cyclists' efficiency. *Applied Physiology, Nutrition, and Metabolism = Physiologie Appliquee, Nutrition Et Metabolisme*, 35(1): 17-22.

Hopker, J.G., D.A. Coleman, H.C. Gregson, S.A. Jobson, T. Von der Haar, J. Wiles, and L. Passfield. 2013. The influence of training status, age, and muscle fiber type on cycling efficiency and endurance performance. *Journal of Applied Physiology (Bethesda, MD: 1985)*, 115(5): 723-729.

Hopker, J.G., D.A. Coleman, and J.D. Wiles. 2007. Differences in efficiency between trained and recreational cyclists. *Applied Physiology, Nutrition, and Metabolism = Physiologie Appliquee, Nutrition Et Metabolisme*, 32(6): 1036-1042.

Horowitz, J.F., L.S. Sidossis, and E.F. Coyle. 1994. High efficiency of type I muscle fibers improves performance. *International Journal of Sports Medicine*, 15(3): 152-157.

Hug, F., and S. Dorel. 2009. Electromyographic analysis of pedaling: A review. *Journal of Electromyography and Kinesiology*, 19(2): 182-198.

Kautz, S.A., and M.L. Hull. 1993. A theoretical basis for interpreting the force applied to the pedal in cycling. *Journal of Biomechanics*, 26(2): 155-165.

Korff, T., and L.M. Romer (2012, July). Relationship between bilateral symmetry and efficiency during submaximal cycling. Paper presented at the International Convention on Science, Education and Medicine in Sport (ICSEMIS 2012), Glasgow UK.

Korff, T., L.M. Romer, I. Mayhew, and J.C. Martin. 2007. Effect of pedaling technique on mechanical effectiveness and efficiency in cyclists. *Medicine and Science in Sports and Exercise*, 39(6): 991-995.

Martin, J.C., and N.A. Brown. 2009. Joint-specific power production and fatigue during maximal cycling. *Journal of Biomechanics*, 42(4): 474-479.

Martin, J.C., A.S. Gardner, M. Barras, and D.T. Martin. 2006. Modeling sprint cycling using field-derived parameters and forward integration. *Medicine and Science in Sports and Exercise*, 38(3): 592-597.

McDaniel, J., J.L. Durstine, G.A. Hand, and J.C. Martin. 2002. Determinants of metabolic cost during submaximal cycling. *Journal of Applied Physiology (Bethesda, MD: 1985)*, 93(3): 823-828.

Mornieux, G., A. Gollhofer, and B. Stapelfeldt. 2010. Muscle coordination while pulling up during cycling. *International Journal of Sports Medicine*, 31(12): 843-846.

Mornieux, G., B. Stapelfeldt, A. Gollhofer, and A. Belli. 2008. Effects of pedal type and pull-up action during cycling. *International Journal of Sports Medicine*, 29(10): 817-822.

Moseley, L., J. Achten, J.C. Martin, and A.E. Jeukendrup. 2004. No differences in cycling efficiency between world-class and recreational cyclists. *International Journal of Sports Medicine*, 25(5): 374-379.

Sanderson, D.J. 1990. The influence of cadence and power output on asymmetry of force application during steady-rate cycling. *Journal of Human Movement Studies*, 19: 1-9.

Sanderson, D.J., and A. Black. 2003. The effect of prolonged cycling on pedal forces. *Journal of Sports Sciences*, 21(3): 191-199.

So, R.C., K.-F. Joseph, and Y.F. Gabriel. 2005. Muscle recruitment pattern in cycling: A review. *Physical Therapy in Sport*, 6(2): 89-96.

Theurel, J., M. Crepin, M. Foissac, and J.J. Temprado. 2012. Effects of different pedalling techniques on muscle fatigue and mechanical efficiency during prolonged cycling. *Scandinavian Journal of Medicine and Science in Sports*, 22(6): 714-721.

Chapter 11

Armstrong, L.E. 2007. *Exertional heat illness*, 288. Champaign, IL: Human Kinetics.

Armstrong, L.E., D.J. Casa, M. Millard-Stafford, D.S. Moran, S.W. Pyne, and W.O. Roberts. 2007. American College of Sports Medicine position stand. Exertional heat illness during training and competition. *Medicine and Science in Sports and Exercise*, 39: 556-572.

Arngrimsson, S.A., D.S. Petitt, M.G. Stueck, D.K. Jorgensen, and K.J. Cureton. 2004. Cooling vest worn during active warm-up improves 5-km run performance in the heat. *Journal of Applied Physiology*, 96: 1867-1874.

Ball, D., C. Burrows, and A.J. Sargeant. 1999. Human power output during repeated sprint cycle exercise: The influence of thermal stress. *European Journal of Applied Physiology*, 79: 360-366.

Barnett, A., and R.J. Maughan. 1993. Response of unacclimatized males to repeated weekly bouts of exercise in the heat. *British Journal of Sports Medicine*, 27: 39-44.

Cheung, S.S., and T.M. McLellan. 1998. Heat acclimation, aerobic fitness, and hydration effects on tolerance during uncompensable heat stress. *Journal of Applied Physiology*, 84: 1731-1739.

Cheung, S.S., T.M. McLellan, and S. Tenaglia. 2000. The thermophysiology of uncompensable heat stress. Physiological manipulations and individual characteristics. *Sports Medicine*, 29: 329-359.

Cheung, S.S., and A.M. Robinson. 2004. The influence of upper-body pre-cooling on repeated sprint performance in moderate ambient temperatures. *Journal of Sports Sciences*, 22: 605-612.

Cheung, S.S., and G.G. Sleivert. 2004. Multiple triggers for hyperthermic fatigue and exhaustion. *Exercise and Sport Sciences Reviews*, 32: 100-106.

Cotter, J.D., and N.A. Taylor. 2005. The distribution of cutaneous sudomotor and alliesthesial thermosensitivity in mildly heat-stressed humans: An open-loop approach. *Journal of Physiology*, 565: 335-345.

Dawson, B.T. 1994. Exercise training in sweat clothing in cool conditions to improve heat tolerance. *Sports Medicine*, 17: 233-244.

Duffield, R., B. Dawson, D. Bishop, M. Fitzsimons, and S. Lawrence. 2003. Effect of wearing an ice cooling jacket on repeat sprint performance in warm/humid conditions. *British Journal of Sports Medicine*, 37: 164-169.

Ely, M.R., S.N. Cheuvront, W.O. Roberts, and S.J. Montain. 2007. Impact of weather on marathon-running performance. *Medicine and Science in Sports and Exercise*, 39: 487-493.

Galloway, S.D., and R.J. Maughan. 1997. Effects of ambient temperature on the capacity to perform prolonged cycle exercise in man. *Medicine and Science in Sports and Exercise*, 29: 1240-1249.

Garrett, A.T., R. Creasy, N.J. Rehrer, M.J. Patterson, and J.D. Cotter. 2012. Effectiveness of short-term heat acclimation for highly trained athletes. *European Journal of Applied Physiology*, 112: 1827-1837.

Garrett, A.T., N.G. Goosens, N.J. Rehrer, M.J. Patterson, J. Harrison, I. Sammut, and J.D. Cotter. 2014. Short-term heat acclimation is effective and may be enhanced rather than impaired by dehydration. *American Journal of Human Biology: The Official Journal of the Human Biology Council*, 26: 311-320.

Karlsen, A., L. Nybo, S.J. Nørgaard, M.V. Jensen, T. Bonne, and S. Racinais. 2015a. Time course of natural heat acclimatization in well-trained cyclists during a 2-week training camp in the heat. *Scandinavian Journal of Medicine and Science in Sports*, 25(Suppl 1): 240-249.

Karlsen, A., S. Racinais, M.V. Jensen, S.J. Nørgaard, T. Bonne, and L. Nybo. 2015b. Heat acclimatization does not improve $\dot{V}O_2$max or cycling performance in a cool climate in trained cyclists. *Scandinavian Journal of Medicine and Science in Sports*, 25(Suppl 1): 269-276.

Kenefick, R.W., S.N. Cheuvront, and M.N. Sawka. 2007. Thermoregulatory function during the marathon. *Sports Medicine*, 37: 312-315.

Lorenzo, S., J.R. Halliwill, M.N. Sawka, and C.T. Minson. 2010. Heat acclimation improves exercise performance. *Journal of Applied Physiology*, 109: 1140-1147.

Morrison, S.A., S. Cheung, and J.D. Cotter. 2014. Importance of airflow for physiologic and ergogenic effects of precooling. *Journal of Athletic Training*, 49: 632-639.

Pandolf, K.B., R.L. Burse, and R.F. Goldman. 1977. Role of physical fitness in heat acclimatization, decay and reinduction. *Ergonomics*, 20: 399-408.

Périard, J.D., S. Racinais, and M.N. Sawka. 2015. Adaptations and mechanisms of human heat acclimation: Applications for competitive athletes and sports. *Scandinavian Journal of Medicine and Science in Sports*, 25(Suppl 1): 20-38.

Roberts, W.O. 2006. Exertional heat stroke during a cool weather marathon: A case study. *Medicine and Science in Sports and Exercise*, 38: 1197-1203.

Sawka, M.N., A.J. Young, K.B. Pandolf, R.C. Dennis, and C.R. Valeri. 1992. Erythrocyte, plasma, and blood volume of healthy young men. *Medicine and Science in Sports and Exercise*, 24: 447-453.

Selkirk, G.A., and T.M. McLellan. 2001. Influence of aerobic fitness and body fatness on tolerance to uncompensable heat stress. *Journal of Applied Physiology*, 91: 2055-2063.

Sleivert, G.G., J.D. Cotter, W.S. Roberts, and M.A. Febbraio. 2001. The influence of whole-body vs. torso pre-cooling on physiological strain and performance of high-intensity exercise in the heat. *Comparative Biochemistry and Physiology—Part A: Molecular and Integrative Physiology*, 128: 657-666.

Thornley, L.J., N.S. Maxwell, and S.S. Cheung. 2003. Local tissue temperature effects on peak torque and muscular endurance during isometric knee extension. *European Journal of Applied Physiology and Occupational Physiology*, 90: 588-594.

Tucker, R., T. Marle, E.V. Lambert, and T.D. Noakes. 2006. The rate of heat storage mediates an anticipatory reduction in exercise intensity during cycling at a fixed rating of perceived exertion. *Journal of Physiology (London)*, 574: 905-915.

Tyler, C.J., and C. Sunderland. 2011. Cooling the neck region during exercise in the heat. *Journal of Athletic Training*, 46: 61-68.

Tyler, C.J., C. Sunderland, and S.S. Cheung. 2015. The effect of cooling prior to and during exercise on exercise performance and capacity in the heat: A meta-analysis. *British Journal of Sports Medicine*, 49: 7-13.

Chapter 12

Bosch-Cano, F., N. Bernard, B. Sudre, F. Gillet, M. Thibaudon, H. Richard, P.M. Badot, and P. Ruffaldi. 2011. Human exposure to allergenic pollens: A comparison between urban and rural areas. *Environmental Research*, 111(5): 619-625.

Brunekreef, B., G. Hoek, O. Breugelmans, and M. Leentvaar. 1994. Respiratory effects of low-level photochemical air pollution in amateur cyclists. *American Journal of Respiratory and Critical Care Medicine*, 150(4): 962-966.

Cutrufello, P.T., K.W. Rundell, J.M. Smoliga, and G.A. Stylianides. 2011. Inhaled whole exhaust and its effect on exercise performance and vascular function. *Inhalation Toxicology*, 23(11): 658-667.

Drinkwater, B.L., P.B. Raven, S.M. Horvath, J.A. Gliner, R.O. Ruhling, N.W. Bolduan, and S. Taquchi. 1974. Air pollution, exercise, and heat stress. *Archives of Environmental Health*, 28(4): 177-181.

Fitch, K.D. 2012. An overview of asthma and airway hyper-responsiveness in Olympic athletes. *British Journal of Sports Medicine*, 46(6): 413-416.

Giles, L.V., J.P. Brandenburg, C. Carlsten, and M.S. Koehle. 2014. Physiological responses to diesel exhaust exposure are modified by cycling intensity. *Medicine and Science in Sports and Exercise*, 46(10): 1999-2006.

Giles, L.V., C. Carlsten, and M.S. Koehle. 2012. The effect of pre-exercise diesel exhaust exposure on cycling performance and cardio-respiratory variables. *Inhalation Toxicology*, 24(12): 783-789.

Giles, L.V., and M.S. Koehle. 2013. The health effects of exercising in air pollution. *Sports Medicine*, 44(2): 223-249.

Gomes, E.C., J.E. Allgrove, G. Florida-James, and V. Stone. 2011. Effect of vitamin supplementation on lung injury and running performance in a hot, humid, and ozone-polluted environment. *Scandinavian Journal of Medicine and Science in Sports*, 21(6): e452-460.

Gomes, E.C., V. Stone, and G. Florida-James. 2010. Investigating performance and lung function in a hot, humid and ozone-polluted environment. *European Journal of Applied Physiology*, 110(1): 199-205.

Gong, H., Jr., P.W. Bradley, M.S. Simmons, and D.P. Tashkin. 1986. Impaired exercise performance and pulmonary function in elite cyclists during low-level ozone exposure in a hot environment. *American Review of Respiratory Disease*, 134(4): 726-733.

Gong, H., Jr., W.S. Linn, S.L. Terrell, K.R. Anderson, and K.W. Clark. 2001. Anti-inflammatory and lung function effects of montelukast in asthmatic volunteers exposed to sulfur dioxide. *Chest*, 119(2): 402-408.

Koch, S., M.J. Macinnis, B.C. Sporer, J.L. Rupert, and M.S. Koehle. 2013. Inhaled salbutamol does not affect athletic performance in asthmatic and non-asthmatic cyclists. *British Journal of Sports Medicine*, 49(1): 51-55.

Koike, A., K. Wasserman, Y. Armon, and D. Weiler-Ravell. 1991. The work-rate-dependent effect of carbon monoxide on ventilatory control during exercise. *Respiration Physiology*, 85(2): 169-183.

Linn, W.S., E.L. Avol, D.A. Shamoo, T.G. Venet, K.R. Anderson, J.D. Whynot, and J.D. Hackney. 1984. Asthmatics' responses to 6-hr sulfur dioxide exposures on two successive days. *Archives of Environmental Health*, 39(4): 313-319.

McCreanor, J., P. Cullinan, M.J. Nieuwenhuijsen, J. Stewart-Evans, E. Malliarou, L. Jarup, R. Harrington, M. Svartengren, I.K. Han, P. Ohman-Strickland, K.F. Chung, and J. Zhang. 2007. Respiratory effects of exposure to diesel traffic in persons with asthma. *New England Journal of Medicine*, 357(23): 2348-2358.

McKenzie, D.C., D.R. Stirling, S. Fadl, and M. Allen. 1987. The effects of salbutamol on pulmonary function in cyclists exposed to ozone: A pilot study. *Canadian Journal of Sport Sciences*, 12(1): 46-48.

Paulsen, G., K.T. Cumming, G. Holden, J. Hallén, B.R. Rønnestad, O. Sveen, A. Skaug, I. Paur, N.E. Bastani, H.N. Østgaard, C. Buer, M. Midttun, F. Freuchen, H. Wiig, E.T. Ulseth, I. Garthe, R. Blomhoff, H.B. Benestad, and T. Raastad. 2014. Vitamin C and E supplementation hampers cellular adaptation to endurance training in humans: A double-blind, randomised, controlled trial. *Journal of Physiology*, 592(Pt 8): 1887-1901.

Raub, J.A., M. Mathieu-Nolf, N.B. Hampson, and S.R. Thom. 2000. Carbon monoxide poisoning: A public health perspective. *Toxicology*, 145(1): 1-14.

Rundell, K.W., J.B. Slee, R. Caviston, and A.M. Hollenbach. 2008. Decreased lung function after inhalation of ultrafine and fine particulate matter during exercise is related to decreased total nitrate in exhaled breath condensate. *Inhalation Toxicology*, 20(1): 1-9.

Rundell, K.W., B.A. Spiering, J.M. Baumann, and T.M. Evans. 2005. Bronchoconstriction provoked by exercise in a high-particulate-matter environment is attenuated by montelukast. *Inhalation Toxicology*, 17(2): 99-105.

Scannell, C., L. Chen, R.M. Aris, I. Tager, D. Christian, R. Ferrando, B. Welch, T. Kelly, and J.R. Balmes. 1996. Greater ozone-induced inflammatory responses in subjects with asthma. *American Journal of Respiratory and Critical Care Medicine*, 154(1): 24-29.

Schelegle, E.S., and W.C. Adams. 1986. Reduced exercise time in competitive simulations consequent to low level ozone exposure. *Medicine and Science in Sports and Exercise*, 18(4): 408-414.

Sienra-Monge, J.J., M. Ramirez-Aguilar, H. Moreno-Macias, N.I. Reyes-Ruiz, B.E. Del Rio-Navarro, M.X. Ruiz-Navarro, G. Hatch, K. Crissman, R. Slade, R.B. Devlin, and I. Romieu. 2004. Antioxidant supplementation and nasal inflammatory responses among young asthmatics exposed to high levels of ozone. *Clinical and Experimental Immunology*, 138(2): 317-322.

Spektor, D.M., M. Lippmann, G.D. Thurston, P.J. Lioy, J. Stecko, G. O'Connor, E. Garshick, F.E. Speizer, and C. Hayes. 1988. Effects of ambient ozone on respiratory function in healthy adults exercising outdoors. *American Review of Respiratory Disease*, 138(4): 821-828.

Traidl-Hoffmann, C., T. Jakob, and H. Behrendt. 2009. Determinants of allergenicity. *Journal of Allergy and Clinical Immunology*, 123(3): 558-566.

Chapter 13

Ashenden, M.J., C.J. Gore, G.P. Dobson, and A.G. Hahn. 1999. "Live high, train low" does not change the total haemoglobin mass of male endurance athletes sleeping at a simulated altitude of 3000 m for 23 nights. *European Journal of Applied Physiology*, 80: 479-484.

Aughey, R.J., S.A. Clark, C.J. Gore, N.E. Townsend, A.G. Hahn, T.A. Kinsman, C. Goodman, C.M. Chow, D.T. Martin, J.A. Hawley, and M.J. McKenna. 2006. Interspersed normoxia during live high, train low interventions reverses an early reduction in muscle Na+-K+-ATPase activity in well-trained athletes. *European Journal of Applied Physiology*, 98: 299-309.

Bonetti, D.L., W.G. Hopkins, and A.E. Kilding. 2006. High-intensity kayak performance after adaptation to intermittent hypoxia. *International Journal of Sports Physiology and Performance*, 1: 246-260.

Brugniaux, J.V., L. Schmitt, P. Robach, G. Nicolet, J.P. Fouillot, S. Moutereau, F. Lasne, V. Pialoux, P. Saas, M.C. Chorvot, J. Cornolo, N.V. Olsen, and J.P. Richalet. 2006. Eighteen days of "living high, training low" stimulate erythropoiesis and enhance aerobic performance in elite middle-distance runners. *Journal of Applied Physiology*, 100: 203-211.

Buskirk, E.R., J. Kollias, R.F. Akers, E.K. Prokop, and E.P. Reategui. 1967. Maximal performance at altitude and on return from altitude in conditioned runners. *Journal of Applied Physiology*, 23: 259-266.

Faiss, R., B. Leger, J.M. Vesin, P.E. Fournier, Y. Eggel, O. Deriaz, and G.P. Millet. 2013. Significant molecular and systemic adaptations after repeated sprint training in hypoxia. *PLos One*, 8: 1-13.

Gore, C.J., A.G. Hahn, R.J. Aughey, D.T. Martin, M.J. Ashenden, S.A. Clark, A.P. Garnham, A.D. Roberts, G.J. Slater, and M.J. McKenna. 2001. Live high: train low increases muscle buffer capacity and submaximal cycling efficiency. *Acta Physiologica Scandinavica*, 173: 275-286.

Hamlin, M.J., and J. Hellemans. 2004. Effects of intermittent normobaric hypoxia on blood parameters in multi-sport endurance athletes. *Medicine and Science in Sports and Exercise*, 36 (Suppl. 5): S337.

Hinckson, E.A., and W.G. Hopkins. 2005. Changes in running endurance performance following intermittent altitude exposure simulated with tents. *European Journal of Sport Sciences*, 5: 15-24.

Hinckson, E.A., W.G. Hopkins, J.S. Fleming, T. Edwards, P. Pfitzinger, and J. Hellemans. 2005. Sea-level performance in runners using altitude tents: A field study. *Journal of Science and Medicine in Sport*, 8: 451-457.

Levine, B.D. 2002. Intermittent hypoxic training: Fact and fancy. *High Altitude Medicine and Biology*, 3: 177-193.

Levine, B.D. 2006. Should "artificial" high altitude environments be considered doping? *Scandinavian Journal of Medicine and Science in Sports*, 16: 297-301.

Levine, B.D., and J. Stray-Gundersen. 1997. "Living high-training low": Effect of moderate-altitude acclimatization with low-altitude training on performance. *Journal of Applied Physiology*, 83: 102-112.

Levine, B.D., and J. Stray-Gundersen. 2006. Dose–response of altitude training: How much altitude is enough? In *Hypoxia and exercise*, eds. Robert C.

Roach, Peter D. Wagner, and Peter H. Hackett. New York: Springer. 233-247.

Martin, D.T., A.G. Hahn, H. Lee, A.D. Roberts, J. Victor, and C.J. Gore. 2002. Effects of a 12-day "live high, train low" cycling camp on 4-min and 30-min performance. *Medicine and Science in Sports and Exercise*, 34 (Suppl. 5): S274.

McLean, S.R., J.C. Kolb, S.R. Norris, and D.J. Smith. 2006. Diurnal normobaric moderate hypoxia raises serum erythropoietin concentration but does not stimulate accelerated erythrocyte production. *European Journal of Applied Physiology*, 96: 651-658.

Millet, G.P., B. Roels, L. Schmitt, X. Woorons, and J.P. Richalet. 2010. Combining hypoxic methods for peak performance. *Sports Medicine*, 40: 1-25.

Morris, D.M., J.T. Kearney, and E.R. Burke. 2000. The effects of breathing supplemental oxygen during altitude training on cycling performance. *Journal of Science and Medicine in Sport*, 3: 165-175.

Niess, A.M., E. Fehrenbach, G. Strobel, K. Roecker, E.M. Schneider, J. Buergler, S. Fuss, R. Lehmann, H. Northoff, and H.H. Dickhuth. 2003. Evaluation of stress response to interval training at low and moderate altitudes. *Medicine and Science in Sports and Exercise*, 35: 263-269.

Nummela, A., and H. Rusko. 2000. Acclimatization to altitude and normoxic training improve 400-m running performance at sea level. *Journal of Sports Sciences*, 18: 411-419.

Ponsot, E., S.P. Dufour, J. Zoll, S. Doutrelau, B. N'Guessan, B. Geny, H. Hoppeler, E. Lampert, B. Mettauer, R. Ventura-Clapier, and R. Richard. 2006. Exercise training in normobaric hypoxia in endurance runners. II. Improvement in mitochondrial properties in skeletal muscle. *Journal of Applied Physiology*, 100: 1249-1257.

Robach, P., L. Schmitt, J.V. Brugniaux, G. Nicolet, A. Duvallet, J.P. Fouillot, S. Moutereau, F. Lasne, V. Pialoux, N.V. Olsen, and J.P. Richalet. 2006a. Living high-training low: effect on erythropoiesis and maximal aerobic performance in elite Nordic skiers. *European Journal of Applied Physiology*, 97: 695-705.

Robach, P., L. Schmitt, J.V. Brugniaux, B. Roels, G. Millet, P. Hellard, G. Nicolet, A. Duvallet, J.P. Fouillot, S. Moutereau, F. Lasne, V. Pialoux, N.V. Olsen, and J.P. Richalet. 2006b. Living high-training low: effect on erythropoiesis and aerobic performance in highly-trained swimmers. *European Journal of Applied Physiology*, 96: 423-433.

Robertson, E.Y., P.U. Saunders, D.B. Pyne, C.J. Gore, and J.M. Anson. 2010. Effectiveness of intermittent training in hypoxia combined with live high/train low. *European Journal of Applied Physiology*, 110: 379-387.

Rusko, H.K., A. Leppavuori, P. Makela, and J. Leppaluoto. 1995. Living high, training low: a new approach to altitude training at sea level in athletes. *Medicine and Science in Sports and Exercise*, 27 (Suppl. 5): S6.

Saunders, P.U., R.D. Telford, D.B. Pyne, R.B. Cunningham, C.J. Gore, A.G. Hahn, and J.A. Hawley. 2004. Improved running economy in elite runners after 20 days of simulated moderate-altitude exposure. *Journal of Applied Physiology*, 96: 931-937.

Schmidt, W. 2002. Effects of intermittent exposure to high altitude on blood volume and erythropoietic activity. *High Altitude Medicine and Biology*, 3: 167-176.

Schmitt, L., G. Millet, P. Robach, G. Nicolet, J.V. Brugniaux, J.P. Fouillot, and J.P. Richalet. 2006. Influence of "living high-training low" on aerobic performance and economy of work in elite athletes. *European Journal of Applied Physiology*, 97: 627-636.

Townsend, N.A., C.J. Gore, A.G. Hahn, M.J. McKenna, R.J. Aughey, S.A. Clark, T. Kinsman, J.A. Howley, and C.M. Chow. 2002. Living high-training low increases hypoxic ventilatory response of well-trained endurance athletes. *Journal of Applied Physiology*, 93: 1498-1505.

Vogt, M., A. Puntschart, J. Geiser, C. Zuleger, R. Billeter, and H. Hoppeler. 2001. Molecular adaptations in human skeletal muscle to endurance training under simulated hypoxic conditions. *Journal of Applied Physiology*, 91: 173-182.

Wilber, R.L. 2004. Current practices and trends in altitude training. In *Altitude training and athletic performance*. Champaign, IL: Human Kinetics, pp. 183-223.

Wilber, R.L. 2007. Application of altitude/hypoxic training by elite athletes. *Medicine and Science in Sports and Exercise*, 39: 1610-1624.

Wilber, R.L., and Y.P. Pitsiladis. 2012. Kenyan and Ethiopian distance runners: What makes them so good? *International Journal of Sport Physiology and Performance*, 7: 92-102.

Wilber, R.L., P.L. Holm, D.M. Morris, G.M. Dallam, and S.D. Callan. 2003. Effect of F_IO_2 on physiological responses and cycling performance at moderate altitude. *Medicine and Science in Sport and Exercise*, 35: 1153-1159.

Wilber, R.L., P.L. Holm, D.M. Morris, G.M. Dallam, A.W. Subudhi, D.M. Murray, and S.D. Callan. 2004. Effect of F_IO_2 on oxidative stress during interval training at moderate altitude. *Medicine and Science in Sports and Exercise*, 36: 1888-1894.

Wilber, R.L., J. Im, P.L. Holm, C.D. Toms, D.M. Morris, G.M. Dallam, J.R. Trombold, and B. Chance. 2005. Effect of F_IO_2 on hemoglobin/myoglobin-deoxygenation during high-intensity exercise at moderate altitude. *Medicine and Science in Sports and Exercise*, 37 (Suppl. 5): S297.

Chapter 15

Bazzano, L.A., T. Hu, K. Reynolds, L. Yao, C. Bunol, Y. Liu, C.S. Chen, M.J. Klag, P.K. Whelton, and J. He. 2014. Effects of low-carbohydrate and low-fat diets:

A randomized trial. *Annals of Internal Medicine*, 161(5): 309-318.

Beals, K.A. 2013. *Nutrition and the female athlete: From research to practice.* Boca Raton, FL: CRC Press.

Brooks, G.A., and J. Mercier. 1994. Balance of carbohydrate and lipid utilization during exercise: The "crossover" concept. *Journal of Applied Physiology (1985),* 76(6): 2253-2261.

Bryhn, M. 2015. Prevention of sports injuries by marine omega-3 fatty acids. *Journal of the American College of Nutrition,* 34(Suppl 1): 60-61.

Burke, L. 2009. *Clinical sports nutrition.* 4th ed. Sydney: McGraw-Hill Australia.

Close, G.L., J. Leckey, M. Patterson, W. Bradley, D.J. Owens, W.D. Fraser, and J.P. Morton. 2013. The effects of vitamin D(3) supplementation on serum total 25[OH]D concentration and physical performance: A randomised dose-response study. *British Journal of Sports Medicine,* 47(11): 692-696.

de Souza, R.J., A. Mente, A. Maroleanu, A.I. Cozma, V. Ha, T. Kishibe, E. Uleryk, P. Budylowski, H. Schünemann, J. Beyene, and S.S. Anand. 2015. Intake of saturated and trans unsaturated fatty acids and risk of all cause mortality, cardiovascular disease, and type 2 diabetes: Systematic review and meta-analysis of observational studies. *BMJ,* 351: h3978.

Feinman, R.D., W.K. Pogozelski, A. Astrup, R.K. Bernstein, E.J. Fine, E.C. Westman, A. Accurso, L. Frassetto, B.A. Gower, S.I. McFarlane, J.V. Nielsen, T. Krarup, L. Saslow, K.S. Roth, M.C. Vernon, J.S. Volek, G.B. Wilshire, A. Dahlqvist, R. Sundberg, A. Childers, K. Morrison, A.H. Manninen, H.M. Dashti, R.J. Wood, J. Wortman, and and N. Worm. 2015. Dietary carbohydrate restriction as the first approach in diabetes management: Critical review and evidence base. *Nutrition,* 31(1): 1-13.

Girgis, C.M., R.J. Clifton-Bligh, N. Turner, S.L. Lau, and J.E. Gunton. 2014. Effects of vitamin D in skeletal muscle: Falls, strength, athletic performance and insulin sensitivity. *Clinical Endocrinology (Oxford),* 80(2): 169-181.

Haakonssen, E.C., M. Barras, L.M. Burke, D.G. Jenkins, and D.T. Martin. 2016. Body composition in female road and track endurance cyclists: Normative values and typical changes in female road and track endurance cyclists. *European Journal of Sport Science,* 16(6): 645-653.

Hawley, J.A. 2011. Fat adaptation science: Low-carbohydrate, high-fat diets to alter fuel utilization and promote training adaptation. *Nestlé Nutrition Institute Workshop Series,* 69: 59-71; discussion 71.

Holick, M.F., N.C. Binkley, H.A. Bischoff-Ferrari, C.M. Gordon, D.A. Hanley, R.P. Heaney, M.H. Murad, C.M. Weaver, and Endocrine Society. 2011. Evaluation, treatment, and prevention of vitamin D deficiency: An Endocrine Society clinical practice guideline. *Journal of Clinical Endocrinology and Metabolism,* 96(7): 1911-1930.

Jeukendrup, A., and M. Gleeson. 2009. *Sport nutrition.* 2nd ed. Champaign, IL: Human Kinetics.

Kuipers, R.S., D.J. de Graaf, M.F. Luxwolda, M.H. Muskiet, D.A. Dijck-Brouwer, and F.A. Muskiet. 2011. Saturated fat, carbohydrates and cardiovascular disease. *Netherlands Journal of Medicine,* 69(9): 372-378.

Larson-Meyer, E. 2013. Vitamin D supplementation in athletes. *Nestlé Nutrition Institute Workshop Series,* 75: 109-121.

Lewis, E.J., P.W. Radonic, T.M. Wolever, and G.D. Wells. 2015. 21 days of mammalian omega-3 fatty acid supplementation improves aspects of neuromuscular function and performance in male athletes compared to olive oil placebo. *Journal of the International Society of Sports Nutrition,* 12: 28.

Lu, Z., T.C. Chen, A. Zhang, K.S. Persons, N. Kohn, R. Berkowitz, S. Martinello, and M.F. Holick. 2007. An evaluation of the vitamin D3 content in fish: Is the vitamin D content adequate to satisfy the dietary requirement for vitamin D. *Journal of Steroid Biochemistry and Molecular Biology,* 103(3-5): 642-644.

Mathis, S.L., R.S. Farley, D.K. Fuller, A.E. Jetton, and J.L. Caputo. 2013. The relationship between cortisol and bone mineral density in competitive male cyclists. *Journal of Sports Medicine (Hindawi Publishing Corporation),* 2013: 896821.

Mickleborough, T.D. 2013. Omega-3 polyunsaturated fatty acids in physical performance optimization. *International Journal of Sport Nutrition and Exercise Metabolism,* 23(1): 83-96.

Mountjoy, M., J. Sundgot-Borgen, L. Burke, S. Carter, N. Constantini, C. Lebrun, N. Meyer, R. Sherman, K. Steffen, R. Budgett, and A. Ljungqvist. 2014. The IOC consensus statement: Beyond the female athlete triad—relative energy deficiency in sport (RED-S). *British Journal of Sports Medicine,* 48(7): 491-497.

National Institutes of Health. 2015. *Exercise for your bone health.* www.niams.nih.gov/Health_Info/Bone/Bone_Health/Exercise/exercise_bone_health.pdf

National Institutes of Health, Office of Dietary Supplements. 2014. *Vitamin D fact sheet for health professionals.* www.ods.od.nih.gov/factsheets/VitaminD-HealthProfessional/#h3

Nattiv, A., A.B. Loucks, M.M. Manore, C.F. Sanborn, J. Sundgot-Borgen, M.P. Warren, and American College of Sports Medicine. 2007. American College of Sports Medicine position stand. The female athlete triad. *Medicine and Science in Sports and Exercise,* 39(10): 1867-1882.

Nichols, J.F., J.E. Palmer, and S.S. Levy. 2003. Low bone mineral density in highly trained male master cyclists. *Osteoporosis International,* 14(8): 644-649.

Penteado, V.S., C.H. Castro, M.M. Pinheiro, M. Santana, S. Bertolino, M.T. de Mello, and V.L. Szejnfeld. 2010. Diet, body composition, and bone mass in well-trained cyclists. *Journal of Clinical Densitometry*, 13(1): 43-50.

Phillips, S.M. 2014. A brief review of higher dietary protein diets in weight loss: A focus on athletes. *Sports Medicine*, 44(Suppl 2): S149-S153.

Prioreschi, A., T. Oosthuyse, I. Avidon, and J. McVeigh. 2012. Whole body vibration increases hip bone mineral density in road cyclists. *International Journal of Sports Medicine*, 33(8): 593-599.

Rector, R.S., R. Rogers, M. Ruebel, and P.S. Hinton. 2008. Participation in road cycling vs. running is associated with lower bone mineral density in men. *Metabolism*, 57(2): 226-232.

Seebohar, B. 2011. *Nutrition periodization for athletes: Taking traditional sports nutrition to the next level.* 2nd ed. Boulder, CO: Bull.

Seebohar, B. 2014. *Metabolic efficiency training: Teaching the body to burn more fat.* 2nd ed. Fuel4mance, LLC.

Shuler, F.D., M.K. Wingate, G.H. Moore, and C. Giangarra. 2012. Sports health benefits of vitamin D. *Sports Health*, 4(6): 496-501.

Siri-Tarino, P.W., S. Chiu, N. Bergeron, and R.M. Krauss. 2015. Saturated fats versus polyunsaturated fats versus carbohydrates for cardiovascular disease prevention and treatment. *Annual Review of Nutrition*, 35: 517-543.

Siri-Tarino, P.W., Q. Sun, F.B. Hu, and R.M. Krauss. 2010. Saturated fatty acids and risk of coronary heart disease: Modulation by replacement nutrients. *Current Atherosclerosis Reports*, 12(6): 384-390.

Stewart, A.D., and J. Hannan. 2000. Total and regional bone density in male runners, cyclists, and controls. *Medicine and Science in Sports and Exercise*, 32(8): 1373-1377.

U.S. Department of Agriculture, A.R.S., Nutrient Data Laboratory. 2015. *USDA national nutrient database for standard reference, release 28.* www.ars.usda.gov/nea/bhnrc/ndl

U.S. Department of Agriculture, Agricultural Research Service, Nutrient Data Laboratory. 2016. *USDA national nutrient database for standard reference, release 28.* Version Current: May 2016. https://ndb.nal.usda.gov/ndb/foods

Vannice, G., and H. Rasmussen. 2014. Position of the academy of nutrition and dietetics: Dietary fatty acids for healthy adults. *Journal of the Academy of Nutrition and Dietetics*, 114(1): 136-153.

Viner, R.T., M. Harris, J.R. Berning, and N.L. Meyer. 2015. Energy availability and dietary patterns of adult male and female competitive cyclists with lower than expected bone mineral density. *International Journal of Sport Nutrition and Exercise Metabolism*, 25(6): 594-602.

Vitamin D Council. 2010. *For health professionals: Position statement on supplementation, blood levels and sun exposure.* www.vitamindcouncil.org/further-topics/for-health-professionals-position-statement-on-supplementation-blood-levels-and-sun-exposure/

Chapter 16

Beals, K.A. 2013. *Nutrition and the female athlete: From research to practice.* Boca Raton, FL: CRC Press.

Burke, L.M., J.A. Hawley, S.H. Wong, A.E. Jeukendrup. 2011. Carbohydrates for training and competition. *Journal of Sports Sciences*, 29(Suppl 1): S17-S27.

Bussau, V.A., T.J. Fairchild, A. Rao, P. Steele, and P.A. Fournier. 2002. Carbohydrate loading in human muscle: An improved 1 day protocol. *European Journal of Applied Physiology*, 87(3): 290-295.

Cox, G.R., S.A. Clark, A.J. Cox, S.L. Halson, M. Hargreaves, J.A. Hawley, N. Jeacocke, R.J. Snow, W.K. Yeo, and L.M. Burke. 2010. Daily training with high carbohydrate availability increases exogenous carbohydrate oxidation during endurance cycling. *Journal of Applied Physiology (1985)*, 109(1): 126-134.

de Ataide e Silva, T., M.E. Di Cavalcanti Alves de Souza, J.F. de Amorim, C.G. Stathis, C.G. Leandro, and A.E. Lima-Silva. 2014. Can carbohydrate mouth rinse improve performance during exercise? A systematic review. *Nutrients*, 6(1): 1-10.

Doering, T.M., P.R. Reaburn, S.M. Phillips, and D.G. Jenkins. 2016. Post-exercise dietary protein strategies to maximize skeletal muscle repair and remodeling in masters endurance athletes: A review. *International Journal of Sport Nutrition and Exercise Metabolism*, 26(2): 168-178.

Goran, M.I., L. Tappy, and K.-A. Lê. 2014. *Dietary sugars and health.* Boca Raton, FL: CRC Press.

Hansen, A.K., C.P. Fischer, P. Plomgaard, J.L. Andersen, B. Saltin, and B.K. Pedersen. 2005. Skeletal muscle adaptation: Training twice every second day vs. training once daily. *Journal of Applied Physiology (1985)*, 98(1): 93-99.

Hausswirth, C., and Y. Le Meur. 2011. Physiological and nutritional aspects of post-exercise recovery: Specific recommendations for female athletes. *Sports Medicine*, 41(10): 861-882.

Hulston, C.J., M.C. Venables, C.H. Mann, C. Martin, A. Philp, K. Baar, and A.E. Jeukendrup. 2010. Training with low muscle glycogen enhances fat metabolism in well-trained cyclists. *Medicine and Science in Sports and Exercise*, 42(11): 2046-2055.

Jeukendrup, A.E. 2010. Carbohydrate and exercise performance: The role of multiple transportable carbohydrates. *Current Opinion in Clinical Nutrition and Metabolic Care*, 13(4): 452-457.

Jeukendrup, A. 2014. A step towards personalized sports nutrition: Carbohydrate intake during exercise. *Sports Medicine*, 44(Suppl 1): S25-S33.

Jeukendrup, A.E., and J. McLaughlin. 2011. Carbohydrate ingestion during exercise: Effects on performance, training adaptations and trainability of the gut. *Nestlé Nutrition Institute Workshop Series*, 69: 1-12; discussion 13.

McArdle, W.D., F.I. Katch, and V.L. Katch. 2009. *Exercise physiology: Nutrition, energy, and human performance.* 7th ed. Baltimore: Lippincott Williams & Wilkins.

Marquet, L.A., J. Brisswalter, J. Louis, E. Tiollier, L.M. Burke, J.A. Hawley, and C. Hausswirth. 2016. Enhanced endurance performance by periodization of carbohydrate intake: "Sleep low" strategy. *Medicine and Science in Sports and Exercise*, 48(4): 663.

Morton, R.W., C. McGlory, and S.M. Phillips. 2015. Nutritional interventions to augment resistance training-induced skeletal muscle hypertrophy. *Frontiers in Physiology*, 6: 245.

Pfeiffer, B., T. Stellingwerff, A.B. Hodgson, R. Randell, K. Pöttgen, P. Res, and A.E. Jeukendrup. 2012. Nutritional intake and gastrointestinal problems during competitive endurance events. *Medicine and Science in Sports and Exercise*, 44(2): 344-351.

Phillips, S.M. 2014. A brief review of critical processes in exercise-induced muscular hypertrophy. *Sports Medicine*, 44(Suppl 1): S71.

Phillips, S.M., S. Findlay, M. Kavaliauskas, and M.C. Grant. 2014. The influence of serial carbohydrate mouth rinsing on power output during a cycle sprint. *Journal of Sports Science and Medicine*, 13(2): 252.

Schoenfeld, B.J., A.A. Aragon, C.D. Wilborn, J.W. Krieger, and G.T. Sonmez. 2014. Body composition changes associated with fasted versus nonfasted aerobic exercise. *Journal of the International Society of Sports Nutrition*, 11(1): 54.

Seebohar, B. 2011. *Nutrition periodization for athletes: Taking traditional sports nutrition to the next level.* 2nd ed. Boulder, CO: Bull.

Sinclair, J., L. Bottoms, C. Flynn, E. Bradley, G. Alexander, S. McCullagh, T. Finn, and H.T. Hurst. 2014. The effect of different durations of carbohydrate mouth rinse on cycling performance. *European Journal of Sport Science*, 14(3): 259.

Sun, S.Z., and M.W. Empie. 2012. Fructose metabolism in humans: What isotopic tracer studies tell us. *Nutrition and Metabolism (London)*, 9(1): 89.

Thomas, D.T., K.A. Erdman, and L.M. Burke. 2016. Position of the Academy of Nutrition and Dietetics, Dietitians of Canada, and the American College of Sports Medicine: Nutrition and athletic performance. *Journal of the Academy of Nutrition and Dietetics*, 116(3): 501.

van Wijck, K., K. Lenaerts, J. Grootjans, K.A. Wijnands, M. Poeze, L. van Loon, C.H. Dejong, and W.A. Buurman. 2012. Physiology and pathophysiology of splanchnic hypoperfusion and intestinal injury during exercise: Strategies for evaluation and prevention. *American Journal of Physiology—Gastrointestinal and Liver Physiology*, 303(2): G155-G168.

van Loon, L.J. 2014. Is there a need for protein ingestion during exercise. *Sports Medicine*, 44(Suppl 1): S105-S111.

Chapter 17

Armstrong, L.E., and C.M. Maresh. 1998. Effects of training, environment, and host factors on the sweating response to exercise. *International Journal of Sports Medicine*, 19(Suppl 2): S103-S105.

Beis, L.Y., M. Wright-Whyte, B. Fudge, T. Noakes, and Y.P. Pitsiladis. 2012. Drinking behaviors of elite male runners during marathon competition. *Clinical Journal of Sport Medicine: Official Journal of the Canadian Academy of Sport Medicine*, 22: 254-261.

Castellani, J.W., S.R. Muza, S.N. Cheuvront, I.V. Sils, C.S. Fulco, R.W. Kenefick, B.A. Beidleman, and M.N. Sawka. 2010. Effect of hypohydration and altitude exposure on aerobic exercise performance and acute mountain sickness. *Journal of Applied Physiology*, 109: 1792-1800.

Cheung, S.S., G.W. McGarr, M.M. Mallette, P.J. Wallace, C.L. Watson, I.M. Kim, and M.J. Greenway. 2015. Separate and combined effects of dehydration and thirst sensation on exercise performance in the heat. *Scandinavian Journal of Medicine and Science in Sports*, 25(Suppl 1): 104-111.

Cheuvront, S.N., R. Carter III, J.W. Castellani, and M.N. Sawka. 2005. Hypohydration impairs endurance exercise performance in temperate but not cold air. *Journal of Applied Physiology*, 99: 1972-1976.

Cheuvront, S.N., and R.W. Kenefick. 2014. Dehydration: Physiology, assessment, and performance effects. *Comprehensive Physiology*, 4(1): 257-285.

Costill, D.L., R. Cote, and W. Fink. 1976. Muscle water and electrolytes following varied levels of dehydration in man. *Journal of Applied Physiology*, 40: 6-11.

Gagge, A.P., J.A. Stolwijk, and J.D. Hardy. 1967. Comfort and thermal sensations and associated physiological responses at various ambient temperatures. *Environmental Research*, 1: 1-20.

Gisolfi, C.V., R.D. Summers, H.P. Schedl, and T.L. Bleiler. 1995. Effect of sodium concentration in a carbohydrate-electrolyte solution on intestinal absorption. *Medicine and Science in Sports and Exercise*, 27: 1414-1420.

Goulet, E.D.B. 2011. Effect of exercise-induced dehydration on time-trial exercise performance: A meta-analysis. *British Journal of Sports Medicine*, 45: 1149-1156.

Harrison, M.H. 1985. Effects of thermal stress and exercise on blood volume in humans. *Physiological Reviews*, 65: 149-208.

Hew-Butler, T., M.H. Rosner, S. Fowkes-Godek, J.P. Dugas, M.D. Hoffman, D.P. Lewis, R.J. Maughan, K.C. Miller, S.J. Montain, N.J. Rehrer, W.O. Roberts, I.R. Rogers, A.J. Siegel, K.J. Stuempfle, J.M. Winger, and J.G. Verbalis. 2015. Statement of the third international exercise-associated hyponatremia consensus development conference, Carlsbad, California, 2015. *Clinical Journal of Sport Medicine*, 25: 303-320.

Hunt, J.B., E.J. Elliott, P.D. Fairclough, M.L. Clark, and M.J.G. Farthing. 1992. Water and solute absorption from hypotonic glucose-electrolyte solutions in human jejunum. *Gut*, 33: 479-483.

Kenefick, R.W., S.N. Cheuvront, L.J. Palombo, B.R. Ely, and M.N. Sawka. 2010. Skin temperature modifies the impact of hypohydration on aerobic performance. *Journal of Applied Physiology*, 109: 79-86.

Kirby, C.R., and V.A. Convertino. 1986. Plasma aldosterone and sweat sodium concentrations after exercise and heat acclimation. *Journal of Applied Physiology*, 61: 967-970.

Marsh, S.A., and D.G. Jenkins. 2002. Physiological responses to the menstrual cycle: Implications for the development of heat illness in female athletes. *Sports Medicine*, 32: 601-614.

Merry, T.L., P.N. Ainslie, and J.D. Cotter. 2010. Effects of aerobic fitness on hypohydration-induced physiological strain and exercise impairment. *Acta Physiologica*, 198: 179-190.

Montain, S.J., and E.F. Coyle. 1992. Influence of graded dehydration on hyperthermia and cardiovascular drift during exercise. *Journal of Applied Physiology*, 73: 1340-1350.

Mora-Rodriguez, R., N. Hamouti, J. Del Coso, and J.F. Ortega. 2013. Fluid ingestion is more effective in preventing hyperthermia in aerobically trained than untrained individuals during exercise in the heat. *Applied Physiology, Nutrition, and Metabolism*, 38: 73-80.

Noakes, T. 2012. *Waterlogged: The serious problem of overhydration in endurance sports*. Champaign, IL: Human Kinetics.

Nose, H., G.W. Mack, X. Shi, and E.R. Nadel. 1988. Involvement of sodium retention hormones during rehydration in humans. *Journal of Applied Physiology*, 65: 332-336.

Oian, P., A. Tollan, H.O. Fadnes, H. Noddeland, and J.M. Maltau. 1987. Transcapillary fluid dynamics during the menstrual cycle. *American Journal of Obstetrics and Gynecology*, 156: 952-955.

Rogers, J., R.W. Summers, and G.P. Lambert. 2005. Gastric emptying and intestinal absorption of a low-carbohydrate sport drink during exercise. *International Journal of Sport Nutrition and Exercise Metabolism*, 15: 220-235.

Sawka, M.N. 1992. Physiological consequences of hypohydration: Exercise performance and thermoregulation. *Medicine and Science in Sports and Exercise*, 24: 657-670.

Sawka, M.N., L.M. Burke, E.R. Eichner, R.J. Maughan, S.J. Montain, and N.S. Stachenfeld. 2007. American college of sports medicine position stand. Exercise and fluid replacement. *Medicine and Science in Sports and Exercise*, 39: 377-390.

Sawka, M.N., S.N. Cheuvront, and R.W. Kenefick. 2012. High skin temperature and hypohydration impair aerobic performance. *Experimental Physiology*, 97: 327-332.

Sawka, M.N., R.R. Gonzalez, A.J. Young, R.C. Dennis, C.R. Valeri, and K.B. Pandolf. 1989. Control of thermoregulatory sweating during exercise in the heat. *American Journal of Physiology*, 257: R311-R316.

Shi, X., R.W. Summers, H.P. Schedl, R.T. Chang, G.P. Lambert, and C.V. Gisolfi. 1994. Effects of solution osmolality on absorption of select fluid replacement solutions in human duodenojejunum. *Journal of Applied Physiology*, 77: 1178-1184.

Stachenfeld, N.S., L. DiPietro, C.A. Kokoszka, C. Silva, D.L. Keefe, and E.R. Nadel. 1999. Physiological variability of fluid-regulation hormones in young women. *Journal of Applied Physiology*, 86: 1092-1096.

Tucker, R. 2009. The anticipatory regulation of performance: The physiological basis for pacing strategies and the development of a perception-based model for exercise performance. *British Journal of Sports Medicine*, 43: 392-400.

Vrijens, D.M., and N.J. Rehrer. 1999. Sodium-free fluid ingestion decreases plasma sodium during exercise in the heat. *Journal of Applied Physiology*, 86: 1847-1851.

Chapter 18

Angell, P.J., N. Chester, N. Sculthorpe, G. Whyte, K. George, and J. Somauroo. 2012. Performance enhancing drug abuse and cardiovascular risk in athletes: Implications for the clinician. *British Journal of Sports Medicine*, 46(Suppl 1): i78-i84.

Bloodworth, A., and M. McNamee. 2010. Clean Olympians? Doping and anti-doping: The views of talented young British athletes. *International Journal of Drug Policy*, 21: 276-282.

Bloodworth, A.J., A. Petróczi, R. Bailey, G. Pearce, and M.J. McNamee. 2012. Doping and supplementation: The attitudes of talented young athletes. *Scandinavian Journal of Medicine and Science in Sports*, 22(2): 293-301.

Catlin, D., K. Fitch, and A. Ljungqvist. 2008. Medicine and science in the fight against doping in sport. *Journal of Internal Medicine*, 264: 99-114.

Davis, N.J. 2013. Neurodoping: Brain stimulation as a performance-enhancing measure. *Sports Medicine*, 43(8): 649-653.

Dunn, M., J.O. Thomas, W. Swift, and L. Burns. 2012. Elite athletes' estimates of the prevalence of illicit drug use: Evidence for the false consensus effect. *Drug and Alcohol Review*, 31(1): 27-32.

Erdman, K.A., T.S. Fung, P.K. Doyle-Baker, M.J. Verhoef, and R.A. Reimer. 2007. Dietary supplementation of high-performance Canadian athletes by age and gender. *Clinical Journal of Sports Medicine*, 17(6): 458-464.

Kim, J., S.K. Kang, H.S. Jung, Y.S. Chun, J. Trilk, and S.H. Jung. 2011. Dietary supplementation patterns of Korean Olympic athletes participating in the Beijing 2008 Summer Olympic Games. *International Journal of Sport Nutrition and Exercise Metabolism*, 21(2): 166-174.

Lentillon-Kaestner, V., and C. Carstairs. 2010. Doping use among young elite cyclists: A qualitative psychosociological approach. *Scandinavian Journal of Medicine and Science in Sports*, 20: 336-345.

Lentillon-Kaestner, V., M. Hagger, and S. Hardcastle. 2012. Health and doping in elite-level cycling. *Scandinavian Journal of Medicine and Science in Sports*, 22: 596-606.

Morente-Sánchez, J., M. Leruite, M. Mateo-March, and M. Zabala. 2014. Spanish cycling and attitudes towards doping of different stakeholders involved. *Journal of Science and Cycling*, 3(1): 21-25.

Morente-Sánchez, J., and M. Zabala. 2013. Doping in sport: A review of elite athletes' attitudes, beliefs, and knowledge. *Sports Medicine*, 43(6): 395-411.

Nieper, A. 2005. Nutritional supplement practices in UK junior national track and field athletes. *British Journal of Sports Medicine*, 39(9): 645-649.

Outram, S.M., and B. Stewart. 2015. Condemning and condoning: Elite amateur cyclists' perspectives on drug use and professional cycling. *International Journal of Drug Policy*, 26(7): 682-687.

Petróczi, A, and E. Aidman. 2009. Measuring explicit attitude toward doping: Review of the psychometric properties of the performance enhancement attitude scale. *Psychology of Sport and Exercise*, 10: 390-396.

Pitsch, W., E. Emrich, and M. Kleinm. 2007. Doping in elite sports in Germany: Results of a www survey. *European Journal for Sport and Society*, 4(2): 89-102.

Pope, H.G., R.I. Wood, A. Rogol, F. Nyberg, L. Bowers, and S. Bhasin. 2013. Adverse health consequences of performance-enhancing drugs: An Endocrine Society scientific statement. *Endocrine Reviews*, 35(3): 341-375.

Schumacher, Y.O. and R. Palfreeman. 2012. The fight against doping in cycling. In *Performance cycling: The science of success*, ed. J. Hopker and S. Jobson, 282-294. London: Bloomsbury.

Spivak, J.L. 2001. Erythropoietin use and abuse. In *Hypoxia,* ed. R.C. Roach, P.D. Wagner, and P.H. Hackett, 207-224. New York: Springer US.

Striegel, H., G. Vollkommer, and H.H. Dickhuth. 2002. Combating drug use in competitive sports: An analysis from the athletes' perspective. *Journal of Sports Medicine and Physical Fitness*, 42(3): 354-359.

Tangen, J.O., and G. Breivik. 2001. Doping games and drug abuse. *Sportwissenschaft*, 31: 188-198.

Uvacsek, M., T. Nepusz, D.P. Naughton, J. Mazanov, M.Z. Ránky, and A. Petróczi. 2011. Self-admitted behavior and perceived use of performance-enhancing vs. psychoactive drugs among competitive athletes. *Scandinavian Journal of Medicine and Science in Sports*, 21(2): 224-234.

Vest Christiansen, A. 2005. The legacy of Festina: Patterns of drug use in European cycling since 1998. *Sport in History*, 25(3): 497-514.

Waddington, I., and A. Smith. 2009. *An introduction to drugs in sport. Addicted to winning?* London and New York: Routledge.

Zabala, M., and G. Atkinson. 2012. Looking for the "athlete 2.0": A collaborative challenge. *Journal of Science and Cycling*, 1: 1-2.

Zabala, M., L. Sanz, J. Durán, and J. Morente-Sánchez. 2009. Doping and professional road cycling: Perspective of cyclists versus team managers. *Journal of Sports Science and Medicine*, 8: 102-103.

Zabala, M., and M. Mateo. 2015. Data, science and ethics around athletes' performance: $\dot{V}O_2$max does not win the Tour de France. *Journal of Science and Cycling*, 4(3): 1-2.

Zabala, M., J. Morente-Sánchez, M. Mateo-March, and D. Sanabria. 2016. Relationship between self-reported doping behavior and psychosocial factors in adult amateur cyclists. *Sport Psychologist*, 30: 68-75.

Zorzoli, M. 2011. Biological passport parameters. *Journal of Human Sport and Exercise*, 6(2): 205-217.

Chapter 19

Baker, S.P., B. O'Neill, W. Haddon, and W.B. Long. 1974. The injury severity score: A method for describing patients with multiple injuries and evaluating emergency care. *Journal of Trauma*, 14(3): 187-196.

Barrios, C., N. De Bernardo, P. Vera, C. Laiz, and M. Hadala. 2011. Clinical patterns and injury exposure rates in elite road cycling are changing over the last decade. *British Journal of Sports Medicine*, 45: 310-384.

Barrios, C., D. Sala, N. Terrados, and J.R. Valenti. 1997. Traumatic and overuse injuries in elite professional cyclists. *Sports Exercise and Injury*, 3(4): 176-179.

Bohlmann, T. 1981. Injuries in competitive cycling. *Physician and Sportsmedicine*, 9: 117-124.

Brøgger-Jensen, T., I. Hvass, and S. Bugge. 1990. Injuries at the BMX Cycling European Championship, 1989. *British Journal of Sports Medicine*, 24(4): 269-270.

Callaghan, M.J., and C. Jarvis. 1996. Evaluation of elite British cyclists: The role of the squad medical. *British Journal of Sports Medicine*, 30: 349-353.

Chow, T.K., and R.L. Kronisch. 2002. Mechanisms of injury in competitive off-road bicycling. *Wilderness and Environmental Medicine*, 13(1): 27-30.

Clarsen, B., R. Bahr, M.W. Heymans, M. Engedahl, G. Midtsundstad, L. Rosenlund, G. Thorsen, and G. Myklebust. 2014. The prevalence and impact of overuse injuries in five Norwegian sports: Application of a new surveillance method. *Scandinavian Journal of Medicine and Science in Sports*, March: 1-8.

Clarsen, B., T. Krosshaug, and R. Bahr. 2010. Overuse injuries in professional road cyclists. *American Journal of Sports Medicine*, 38(12): 2494-2501.

De Bernardo, N., C. Barrios, P. Vera, C. Laíz, and M. Hadala. 2012. Incidence and risk for traumatic and overuse injuries in top-level road cyclists. *Journal of Sports Sciences*, 30(10): 1047-1053.

Greve, M.W., and M.R. Modabber. 2012. An epidemic of traumatic brain injury in professional cycling: A call to action. *Clinical Journal of Sport Medicine*, 22(2): 81-82.

Holmes, J.C., A.L. Pruitt, and N.J. Whalen. 1994. Lower extremity overuse in bicycling. *Clinics in Sports Medicine*, 13(1): 187-205.

Joint Committee on Injury Scaling. 1980. *The Abbreviated Injury Scale (AIS)*. Arlington Heights, IL.

Kronisch, R.L., T.K. Chow, L.M. Simon, and P.F. Wong. 1996. Acute injuries in off-road bicycle racing. *American Journal of Sports Medicine*, 24(1): 88-93.

McCrory, P., W.H. Meeuwisse, M. Aubry, B. Cantu, J. Dvorák, R.J. Echemendia, L. Engebretsen, K. Johnston, J.S. Kutcher, M. Raftery, A. Sills, B.W. Benson, G.A. Davis, R.G. Ellenbogen, K. Guskiewicz, S.A. Herring, G.L. Iverson, B.D. Jordan, J. Kissick, M. McCrea, A.S. McIntosh, D. Maddocks, M. Makdissi, L. Purcell, M. Putukian, K. Schneider, C.H. Tator, and M. Turner. 2013. Consensus statement on concussion in sport: The 4th International Conference on Concussion in Sport held in Zurich, November 2012. *British Journal of Sports Medicine*, 47(5): 250-258.

Mellion, M.B. 1991. Common cycling injuries: Management and prevention. *Sports Medicine (Auckland, NZ)*, 11(1): 52-70.

Pfeiffer, R. 1993. Injuries in NORBA pro/elite category off-road bicycle competitors. *Cycling Science* 5(1): 21-24.

Pfeiffer, R. 1994. Off-road bicycle racing injuries—The NORBA pro/elite category: Care and prevention. *Clinics in Sports Medicine*, 13(1): 207-218.

Thompson, D.C., F. Rivara, and R. Thompson. 1999. Helmets for preventing head and facial injuries in bicyclists. *Cochrane Database of Systematic Reviews*, DOI10.1002/14651858.CD001855.

Van der Walt, A., D. van Rensburg, L. Fletcher, C.C. Grant, and A.J. van der Walt. 2014. Non-traumatic injury profile of amateur cyclists. *South African Journal of Sports Medicine*, 26(4): 199-122.

Wilber, C.A., G.J. Holland, R.E. Madison, and S.F. Loy. 1995. An epidemiological analysis of overuse injuries among recreational cyclists. *International Journal of Sports Medicine*, 16(3): 201-206.

Chapter 20

Aboyans, V., M.H. Criqui, P. Abraham, M.A. Allison, M.A. Creager, C. Diehm, F.G. Fowkes, W.R. Hiatt, B. Jönsson, P. Lacroix, B. Marin, M.M. McDermott, L. Norgren, R.L. Pande, P.M. Preux, H.E. Stoffers, D. Treat-Jacobson, American Heart Association Council on Peripheral Vascular Disease, Council on Epidemiology and Prevention, Council on Clinical Cardiology, Council on Cardiovascular Nursing, Council on Cardiovascular Radiology and Intervention, and Council on Cardiovascular Surgery and Anesthesia. 2012. Measurement and interpretation of the ankle-brachial index: A scientific statement from the American Heart Association. *Circulation*, 126(24): 2890-2909.

Akuthota, V., C. Plastaras, K. Lindberg, J. Tobey, J. Press, and C. Garvan. 2005. The effect of long-distance bicycling on ulnar and median nerves: An electrophysiologic evaluation of cyclist palsy. *American Journal of Sports Medicine*, 33(8): 1224-1230.

Andersen, K.V., and G. Bovim. 1997. Impotence and nerve entrapment in long distance amateur cyclists. *Acta Neurologica Scandinavica*, 95(4): 233-240.

Barrios, C., N. De Bernardo, P. Vera, C. Laiz, and M. Hadala. 2011. Clinical patterns and injury exposure rates in elite road cycling are changing over the last decade. *British Journal of Sports Medicine*, 45: 310-384.

Barrios, C., D. Sala, N. Terrados, and J.R. Valenti. 1997. Traumatic and overuse injuries in elite professional cyclists. *Sports Exercise and Injury*, 3(4): 176-179.

Bini, R., P.A. Hume, and J.L. Croft. 2011. Effects of bicycle saddle height on knee injury risk and cycling performance. *Sports Medicine*, 11(6): 463-476.

Callaghan, M.J., and C. Jarvis. 1996. Evaluation of elite British cyclists: The role of the squad medical. *British Journal of Sports Medicine*, 30: 349-353.

Clarsen, B., T. Krosshaug, and R. Bahr. 2010. Overuse injuries in professional road cyclists. *American Journal of Sports Medicine*, 38(12): 2494-2501.

Ericson, M.O., and R. Nisell. 1986. Tibiofemoral joint forces during ergometric cycling. *American Journal of Sports Medicine*, 14(4): 285-290.

Ericson, M.O., and R. Nisell. 1987. Patellofemoral joint forces during ergometric cycling. *Physical Therapy*, 67(9): 1365-1369.

Feugier, P., J. Chevalier, and Edouard Herriot Hospital. 2004. Endofibrosis of the iliac arteries: An underestimated problem. *Acta Chirurgica Belgica*, 104: 635-640.

Gemery, J.M., A.K. Nangia, A.C. Mamourian, and S.K. Reid. 2007. Digital three-dimensional modelling of the male pelvis and bicycle seats: Impact of rider position and seat design on potential penile hypoxia and erectile dysfunction. *BJU International*, 99(1): 135-140.

Holmes, J.C., A.L. Pruitt, and N.J. Whalen. 1994. Lower extremity overuse in bicycling. *Clinics in Sports Medicine*, 13(1): 187-205.

Jozsa, L., and P. Kannus. 1997. *Human tendons: Anatomy, physiology, and pathology*. Champaign, IL: Human Kinetics.

Lowe, B.D., S.M. Schrader, and M.J. Breitenstein. 2004. Effect of bicycle saddle designs on the pressure to the perineum of the bicyclist. *Medicine and Science in Sports and Exercise*, 36(6): 1055-1062.

Malliaras, P., C.J. Barton, N.D. Reeves, and H. Langberg. 2013. Achilles and patellar tendinopathy loading programmes: A systematic review comparing clinical outcomes and identifying potential mechanisms for effectiveness. *Sports Medicine (Auckland, NZ)*, 43(4): 267-286.

Marsden, M., and M. Schwellnus. 2010. Lower back pain in cyclists: A review of epidemiology, pathomechanics and risk factors. *International SportMed Journal*, 11(1): 216-225.

McCrory, P., W.H. Meeuwisse, M. Aubry, B. Cantu, J. Dvorák, R.J. Echemendia, L. Engebretsen, K. Johnston, J.S. Kutcher, M. Raftery, A. Sills, B.W. Benson, G.A. Davis, R.G. Ellenbogen, K. Guskiewicz, S.A. Herring, G.L. Iverson, B.D. Jordan, J. Kissick, M. McCrea, A.S. McIntosh, D. Maddocks,

M. Makdissi, L. Purcell, M. Putukian, K. Schneider, C.H. Tator, and M. Turner. 2013. Consensus statement on concussion in sport: The 4th International Conference on Concussion in Sport Held in Zurich, November 2012. *British Journal of Sports Medicine*, 47(5): 250-258.

McKee, R.C., D.B. Whelan, E.H. Schemitsch, and M.D. McKee. 2012. Operative versus nonoperative care of displaced midshaft clavicular fractures: A meta-analysis of randomized clinical trials. *Journal of Bone and Joint Surgery. American Volume*, 94(8): 675-684.

Mellion, M.B. 1991. Common cycling injuries: Management and prevention. *Sports Medicine (Auckland, NZ)*, 11(1): 52-70.

Rockwood, C.A., G.R. Williams, and D.C. Young. 1996. Fractures in adults. In *Fractures in adults*, 4th ed., ed. J.D. Heckman, C.A. Rockwood, D.P. Green, and R.W. Bucholz. 1341-1413. Philadelphia: Lippincott-Raven.

Slane, J., M. Timmerman, H. Ploeg, and D. Thelen. 2011. The influence of glove and hand position on pressure over the ulnar nerve during cycling. *Clinical Biomechanics*, 26(6): 642-648.

Sommer, F., D. Konig, C. Graft, U. Schwarzer, C. Bertram, T. Klotz, and U. Engelmann. 2001. Impotence and genital numbness in cyclists. *International Journal of Sports Medicine*, 22(6): 410-413.

Spears, I.R., N.K. Cummins, Z. Brenchley, C. Donohue, C. Turnbull, S. Burton, and G.A. Macho. 2003. The effect of saddle design on stresses in the perineum during cycling. *Medicine and Science in Sports and Exercise*, 35(9): 1620-1625.

Thompson, D.C., F. Rivara, and R. Thompson. 1999. Helmets for preventing head and facial injuries in bicyclists. *Cochrane Database of Systematic Reviews*, DOI10.1002/14651858.CD001855.

Vink, A., M.H. Bender, G. Schep, D.F. van Wichen, R.A. de Weger, G. Pasterkamp, and F.L. Moll. 2008. Histopathological comparison between endofibrosis of the high-performance cyclist and atherosclerosis in the external iliac artery. *Journal of Vascular Surgery*, 48(6): 1458-1463.

Virtanen, K.J., A.O.V. Malmivaara, V.M. Remes, and M.P. Paavola. 2012. Operative and nonoperative treatment of clavicle fractures in adults. *Acta Orthopaedica*, 83(1): 65-73.

Visnes, H., and R. Bahr. 2007. The evolution of eccentric training as treatment for patellar tendinopathy (jumper's knee): A critical review of exercise programmes. *British Journal of Sports Medicine*, 41(4): 217-223.

Chapter 21

Acevedo, E., K. Rinehardt, and R. Kraemer. 1994. Perceived exertion and affect at varying intensities of running. *Research Quarterly for Exercise and Sport*, 65: 372-376.

Armstrong, L., and J. Van Heest. 2002. The unknown mechanisms of the overtraining syndrome. Clues from depression and psychoneuroimmunology. *Sports Medicine*, 32: 185-209.

Barron, G., T. Noakes, W. Levy, C. Smidt, and R. Millar. 1985. Hypothalamic dysfunction in overtrained athletes. *Journal of Clinical Endocrinology and Metabolism*, 60: 803-806.

Budgett, R., E. Newsholme, M. Lehmann, C. Sharp, D. Jones, T. Peto, D. Collins, R. Nerurkar, and P. White. 2000. Redefining the overtraining syndrome as the unexplained underperformance syndrome. *British Journal of Sports Medicine*, 34: 67-68.

Callister, R., R.J. Callister, S. Fleck, and G. Dudley. 1990. Physiological and performance responses to overtraining in elite judo athletes. *Medicine and Science in Sports and Exercise*, 22: 816-824.

Chatard, J., D. Atlaoui, G. Lac, M. Duclos, S. Hooper, and L. MacKinnon. 2002. Cortisol, DHEA, performance and training in elite swimmers. *International Journal of Sports Medicine*, 23: 510-515.

Cumps, E., J. Pockelé, and R. Meeusen. 2004. Blits on-line: An uniform injury registration system. Proceedings International Conference on IT and Sport. Koln, September 15-17, 2004.

De Schutter, G., L. Buyse, R. Meeusen, and B. Roelands. 2004. Hormonal responses to a high-intensity training period in Army recruits. *Medicine and Science in Sports and Exercise*, 36: S295.

Foster, C. 1998. Monitoring training in athletes with reference to overtraining syndrome. *Medicine and Science in Sports and Exercise*, 30: 1164-1168.

Foster, C., E. Daines, L. Hector, A. Snyder, and R. Welsh. 1996. Athletic performance in relation to training load. *Wisconsin Medical Journal*, 95: 370-374.

Foster, C., A. Snyder, N. Thompson, and K. Kuettel. 1988. Normalisation of the blood lactate Profile. *International Journal of Sports Medicine*, 9: 198-200.

Hall, H., M. Flynn, K. Carroll, P. Brolinson, S. Shapiro, and B. Bushman. 1999. Effects of intensified training and detraining on testicular function. *Clinical Journal of Sports Medicine*, 9: 203-208.

Halson, S.L., M.W. Bridge, R. Meeusen, B. Busschaert, M. Gleeson, D.A. Jones, and A.E. Jeukendrup. 2002. Time course of performance changes and fatigue markers during intensified training in trained cyclists. *Journal of Applied Physiology*, 93(3): 947-956.

Halson, S., G. Lancaster, A. Jeukendrup, and M. Gleeson. 2003. Immunological responses to overreaching in cyclists. *Medicine and Science in Sports and Exercise*, 35(5): 854-861.

Halson, S., and A. Jeukendrup. 2004. Does overtraining exist? An analysis of overreaching and overtraining research. *Sports Medicine*, 34: 967-981.

Hooper, S., L. Mackinnon, R. Gordon, and A. Bachmann. 1993. Hormonal responses of elite swimmers to overtraining. *Medicine and Science in Sports and Exercise*, 25(6): 741-747.

Hooper, S.L., L.T. MacKinnon, A. Howard, R.D. Gordon, and A.W. Bachmann. 1995. Markers for monitoring overtraining and recovery. *Medicine and Science in Sports and Exercise*, 27: 106-112.

Hooper, S., L. MacKinnon, and A. Howard. 1999. Physiological and psychometric variables for monitoring recovery during tapering for major competition. *Medicine and Science in Sports and Exercise*, 31(8): 1205-1210.

Hopkins, W. 1991. Quantification of training in competitive sports. Methods and Applications. *Sports Medicine*, 12: 161-83.

Jeukendrup, A.E., M.K. Hesselink, A.C. Snyder, H. Kuipers, and H.A. Keizer. 1992. Physiological changes in male competitive cyclists after two weeks of intensified training. *International Journal of Sports Medicine*, 13: 534-541.

Kellmann, M. 2002. *Enhancing recovery: Preventing underperformance in athletes*. Champaign, IL: Human Kinetics.

Kellmann, M., and K-L. Gunther. 2000. Changes in stress and recovery in elite rowers during preparation for the Olympic Games. *Medicine and Science in Sports and Exercise*, 32(3): 676-683.

Knopfli, B., R. Calvert, O. Bar-Or, B. Villiger, and S. Von Duvillard. 2001. Competition performance and basal nocturnal catecholamine excretion in cross-country skiers. *Medicine and Science in Sports and Exercise*, 33(7): 1228-1232.

Kreider, R., A.C. Fry, and M. O'Toole. 1998. Overtraining in sport: Terms, definitions, and prevalence. In *Overtraining in sport*, ed. R. Kreider, A.C. Fry, and M. O'Toole, vii-ix. Champaign, IL: Human Kinetics.

Kubesch, S., V. Bretschneider, R. Freudenmann, N. Weidenhammer, M. Lehmann, M. Spitzer, and G. Gron. 2003. Aerobic endurance exercise improves executive functions in depressed patients. *Journal of Clinical Psychiatry*, 64(9):1005-1012.

Kuipers, H., and H. Keizer. 1988. Overtraining in elite athletes. *Sports Medicine*, 6: 79-92.

Lehmann, M., C. Foster, U. Gastmann, H. Keizer, and J. Steinacker. 1999. Definitions, types, symptoms, findings, underlying mechanisms, and frequency of overtraining and overtraining syndrome. In *Overload, performance incompetence, and regeneration in sport*, ed. M. Lehmann, C. Foster, U. Gastmann, H. Keizer, and J. Steinacker, 1-6. New York: Kluwer Academic/Plenum.

Le Meur, Y., C. Hausswirth, F. Natta, A. Couturier, F. Bignet, and P.P. Vidal. 2013a. A multidisciplinary approach to overreaching detection in endurance trained athletes. *Journal of Applied Physiology*, 114: 411-420.

Le Meur, Y., A. Pichon, K. Schaal, L. Schmitt, J. Louis, J. Gueneron, P.P. Vidal, and C. Hausswirth. 2013b. Evidence of parasympathetic hyperactivity in functionally overreached athletes. *Medicine and Science in Sports and Exercise* 45(11): 2061-2071.

Lemyre, N. 2005. Determinants of burnout in elite athletes. PhD thesis, Norwegian University of Sport and Physical Education.

Manetta, J., J. Brun, L. Maimoun, O. Galy, O. Coste, F. Maso, J. Raibaut, C. Benezis, G. Lac, and J. Mercier. 2002. Carbohydrate dependence during hard-intensity exercise in trained cyclists in the competitive season: Importance of training status. *International Journal of Sports Medicine*, 23: 516-523.

Maso, F., G. Lac, O. Michaux, and A. Robert. 2003. Corrélations entre scores au questionnaire de la Société française de médecine du sport et concentrations de cortisol et testostérone salivaires lors du suivi d'une équipe de rugby de haut niveau. *Science and Sports*, 18: 299-301.

Meeusen, R., M. Duclos, C. Foster, A. Fry, M. Gleeson, D. Nieman, J. Raglin, G. Rietjens, J. Steinacker, A. Urhausen, European College of Sport Science, and American College of Sports Medicine. 2013. Prevention, diagnosis and the treatment of the overtraining syndrome: Joint consensus statement of the European College of Sport Science and the American College of Sports Medicine. *Medicine and Science in Sports and Exercise*, 45(1): 186-205.

Meeusen, R., M. Duclos, M. Gleeson, G. Rietjens, J. Steinacker, and A. Urhausen. 2006. Prevention, diagnosis and the treatment of the overtraining syndrome. *European Journal of Sport Science*, 6(1): 1-14.

Meeusen, R., E. Nederhof, L. Buyse, B. Roelands, G. de Schutter, and M.F. Piacentini. 2010. Diagnosing overtraining in athletes using the two-bout exercise protocol. *British Journal of Sports Medicine*, 44: 642-648.

Meeusen, R., M.F. Piacentini, B. Busschaert, L. Buyse, G. De Schutter, and J. Stray-Gundersen. 2004. Hormonal responses in athletes: The use of a two bout exercise protocol to detect subtle differences in (over)training status. *European Journal of Applied Physiology*, 91: 140-146.

Morgan, W.P., D.R. Brown, J.S. Raglin, P.J. O'Connor, and K.A. Ellickson. 1987. Psychological monitoring of overtraining and staleness. *British Journal of Sports Medicine*, 21(3): 107-114.

Morgan, W., D. Costill, M. Flynn, J. Raglin, and P. O'Connor. 1988. Mood disturbance following increased training in swimmers. *Medicine and Science in Sports and Exercise*, 20: 408-414.

Nindl, B., C. Leone, W. Tharion, R. Johnson, J. Castellani, J. Patton, and S. Montain. 2002. Physical performance responses during 72h of military operations. *Medicine and Science in Sports and Exercise*, 34(11): 1814-1822.

O'Connor, P., W. Morgan, and J. Raglin. 1991. Psychobiologic effect of 3d of increased training in female and male swimmers. *Medicine and Science in Sports and Exercise*, 23(9): 1055-1061.

Passelergue, P., and G. Lac. 1999. Saliva cortisol, testosterone and T/C ratio variations during a wrestling competition and during the post-competitive recovery period. *International Journal of Sports Medicine*, 20: 109-113.

Petibois, C., G. Cazorla, J. Pootmans, and G. Déléris. 2003. Biochemical aspects of overtraining in endurance sports. The metabolism alteration process syndrome. *Sports Medicine*, 33(2): 83-94.

Pichot, V., T. Busso, F. Roche, M. Garet, F. Costes, D. Duverney, J-R. Lacour, and J-C. Barthélémy. 2002. Autonomic adaptations to intensive and overload training periods: A laboratory study. *Medicine and Science in Sports and Exercise*, 34(10): 1660-1666.

Pockelé, J., E. Cumps, F. Piacentini, and R. Meeusen. 2004. Blits on-line training diary for the early detection of overreaching and overtraining. Proceedings International Conference on IT and Sport. Koln, September 15-17, 2004.

Rietjens, G., H. Kuipers, J. Adam, W. Saris, E. Van Breda, D. Van Hamont, and H. Keizer. 2005. Physiological, biochemical and psychological markers of strenuous training-induced fatigue. *International Journal of Sports Medicine*, 26: 16-26.

Steinacker, J.M., W. Lormes, Y. Liu, A. Opitz-Gress, B. Baller, K. Günther, U. Gastmann, K.G. Petersen, M. Lehmann, and D. Altenburg. 2000. Training of junior rowers before world championships. Effects on performance, mood state and selected hormonal and metabolic responses. *Journal of Physical Fitness and Sports Medicine*, 40: 327-335.

Steinacker, J.M., W. Lormes, S. Reissnecker, and Y. Liu. 2004. New aspects of the hormone and cytokine response to training. *European Journal of Applied Physiology*, 91: 382-393.

Steinacker, J.M., and M. Lehmann. 2002. Clinical findings and mechanisms of stress and recovery in athletes. In *Enhancing recovery: Preventing underperformance in athletes*, ed. M. Kellmann, 103-118. Champaign, IL: Human Kinetics.

Urhausen, A., H. Gabriel, and W. Kindermann. 1995. Blood hormones as markers of training stress and overtraining. *Sports Medicine*, 20: 251-276.

Urhausen, A., H. Gabriel, and W. Kindermann. 1998. Impaired pituitary hormonal response to exhaustive exercise in overtrained endurance athletes. *Medicine and Science in Sports and Exercise*, 30: 407-414.

Urhausen, A., H. Gabriel, B. Weiler, and W. Kindermann. 1998. Ergometric and psychological findings during overtraining: A long-term follow-up study in endurance athletes. *International Journal of Sports Medicine*, 19: 114-120.

Urhausen, A., and W. Kindermann. 2002. Diagnosis of overtraining—What tools do we have? *Sports Medicine*, 32: 95-102.

Uusitalo, A.L.T., P. Huttunen, Y. Hanin, A.J. Uusitalo, and H. Rusko. 1998. Hormonal responses to endurance training and overtraining in female athletes. *Clinical Journal of Sports Medicine*, 8: 178-186.

Uusitalo, A.L.T., A.J. Uusitalo, and H.K. Rusko. 1998. Exhaustive endurance training for 6-9 weeks did not induce changes in intrinsic heart rate and cardiac autonomic modulation in female athletes. *International Journal of Sports Medicine*, 19:532-540.

Ventura, N., H. Hoppeler, R. Seiler, A. Binggeli, P. Mullis, and M. Vogt. 2003. The response of trained athletes to six weeks of endurance training in hypoxia or normoxia. *International Journal of Sports Medicine*, 24: 166-172.

Chapter 22

Ahlman, K., and M.J. Karvonen. 1961. Weight reduction by sweating in wrestlers, and its effect on physical fitness. *Journal of Sports Medicine and Physical Fitness*, 1: 58-62.

Argus, C.K., M.W. Driller, T.R. Ebert, D.T. Martin, and S.L. Halson. 2013. The effects of 4 different recovery strategies on repeat sprint-cycling performance. *International Journal of Sports Physiology and Performance*, 8(5): 542-548.

Babault, N., C. Cometti, N.A. Maffiuletti, and G. Delay. 2011. Does electrical stimulation enhance post-exercise performance recovery? *European Journal of Applied Physiology*, 111(10): 2501-2507.

Barnett, A. 2006. Using recovery modalities between training session in elite athletes: Does it help? *Sports Medicine*, 36(9): 781-796.

Bleakley, C.M., F. Bieuzen, G.W. Davison, and J.T. Costello. 2014. Whole-body cryotherapy: Empiricle evidence and theoretical perspectives. *Open Access Journal of Sports Medicine*, 10(5): 25-36.

Costello, J.T., L.A. Algar, and A.E. Donnelly. 2012. Effects of whole-body cryotherapy (–110 °C) on proprioception and indices of muscle damage. *Scandinavian Journal of Medicine and Science in Sports*, 22(2): 190-198.

Crampton, D., B. Donne, S.A. Warmington, and M. Egana. 2013. Cycling time to failure is better maintained by cold than contrast or thermoneutral lower-body water immersion in normothermia. *European Journal of Applied Physiology*, 113(12): 3059-3067.

de Glanville, K.M., and M.J. Hamlin. 2012. Positive effect of lower body compression garments on subsequent 40-kM cycling time trial performance. *Journal of Strength and Conditioning Research*, 26(2): 480-486.

Driller, M.W., and S.L. Halson. 2013. The effects of wearing lower body compression garments during a cycling performance test. *International Journal of Sports Physiology and Performance*, 8(3): 300-306.

Halson, S.L. 2013. Sleep and the elite athlete. *Sport Science Exchange*, 26(113): 1-4.

Halson, S.L., J. Bartram, N. West, J. Stephens, C.K. Argus, M.W. Driller, C. Sargent, M. Lastella, W.G. Hopkins, and D.T. Martin. 2014. Does hydrotherapy help or hinder adaptation to training in competitive cyclists? *Medicine and Science in Sports and Exercise*, 46(8): 1631-1639.

Hausswirth, C., J. Louis, F. Bieuzen, H. Pournot, J. Fournier, J. Filliard, and J. Brisswalter. 2011. Effects of whole-body cryotherapy vs. far-intrared vs. passive modalities on recovery from exercise-induced muscle damage in highly-trained runners. *PLoS One*, 6(12): e27749.

Maffiuletti, N.A. 2010. Physiological and methodological considerations for the use of neuromuscular electrical stimulation. *European Journal of Applied Physiology*, 110(2): 223-234.

Magnusson, P., and P. Renstrom. 2006. The European College of Sports Sciences position statement: The role of stretching exercises in sports. *European Journal of Sport Science*, 6(2): 87-91.

Morgan, P.M., A.J. Salacinski, and M.A. Stults-Kolehmainen. 2013. The acute effects of flotation restricted environmental stimulation technique on recovery from maximal eccentric exercise. *Journal of Strength and Conditioning Research*, 27(12): 3467-3474.

Pournot, H., F.O. Bieuzen, J. Louis, J-R. Fillard, E. Barbiche, and C. Hausswirth. 2011. Time-course of changes in inflammatory response after whole-body cryotherapy multi exposures following severe exercise. *PLoS One*, 6(7): e22748.

Reilly, T., and B. Edwards. 2007. Altered sleep-wake cycles and physical performance in athletes. *Physiology and Behavior* 90(2-3): 274-284.

Ridge, B.R. 1986. Physiological response to combinations of exercise and sauna. *Australian Journal of Science and Medicine in Sport*, 18(4): 25-28.

Schroeder, A.N., and T.M. Best. 2015. Is self myofascial release an effective preexercise and recovery strategy? A literature review. *Current Sports Medicine Reports*, 14(3): 200-208.

Scoon, G., W. Hopkins, S. Mayhew, and J. Cotter. 2007. Effect of post-exercise sauna bathing on the endurance performance of competitive male runners. *Journal of Science and Medicine in Sport*, 10(4): 259-262.

Sutkowy, P., A. Wonźiak, T. Boraczyński, C. Mila-Kierzenkowska, and M. Boraczyński. 2014. The effect of a single Finnish sauna bath after aerobic exercise on the oxidative status in healthy men. *Scandinavian Journal of Clinical and Laboratory Investigation*, 74(2): 89-94.

Taoutaou, Z., P. Granier, B. Mercier, J. Mercier, S. Ahmaidi, and C. Prefaut. 1996. Lactate kinetics during passive and partially active recovery in endurance and sprint athletes. *European Journal of Applied Physiology and Occupational Physiology*, 73(5): 465-470.

Turner, J.W., and T.H. Fine. 1983. Effects of relaxation associated with brief restricted environmental stimulation therapy (REST) on plasma cortisol, ACTH, and LH. *Applied Psychophysiology and Biofeedback*, 8(1): 115-126.

Vaile, J., S. Halson, N. Gill, and B. Dawson. 2008a. Effect of hydrotherapy on recovery from fatigue. *International Journal of Sports Medicine*, 29(7): 539-544.

Vaile, J., S. Halson, N. Gill, and B. Dawson. 2008b. Effect of hydrotherapy on signs and symptoms of delayed onset muscle soreness. *European Journal of Applied Physiology*, 102(4): 447-455.

Versey, N., S. Halson, and B. Dawson. 2011. Effect of contrast water therapy duration on recovery of cycling performance: a dose-response study. *European Journal of Applied Physiology*, 111(1): 37-46.

Versey, N.G., S.L. Halson, and B.T. Dawson. 2012. Effect of contrast water therapy duration on recovery of running performance. *International Journal of Sports Physiology and Performance*, 7(2): 130-140.

Versey, N.G., S.L. Halson, and B.T. Dawson. 2013. Water immersion recovery for athletes: Effect on exercise performance and practical recommendations. *Sports Medicine*, 43(11): 1101-1130.

Waterhouse, J., G. Atkinson, B. Edwards, and T. Reilly. 2007. The role of a short post-lunch nap in improving cognitive, motor and sprint performance in participants with partial sleep deprivation. *Journal of Sports Sciences*, 25(14): 1557-1566.

Chapter 23

Bailey, R., D. Collins, P. Ford, A. MacNamara, M. Toms, and G. Pearce. 2010. Participant development in sport: An academic review. *Sports Coach UK*, 4: 1-134.

Baker, J., S. Cobley, and J. Fraser-Thomas. 2009. What do we know about early sport specialization? Not much! *High Ability Studies*, 20(1): 77-89.

Balyi, I., R. Way, and C. Higgs. 2013. *Long-term athlete development*. Champaign, IL: Human Kinetics.

Bergeron, M.F., M. Mountjoy, N. Armstrong, M. Chia, J. Côté, C.A. Emery, A. Faigenbaum, G. Hall, S. Kriemler, M. Léglise, and R.M. Malina. 2015. International Olympic Committee consensus statement on youth athletic development. *British Journal of Sports Medicine*, 49(13): 843-851.

Brenner, J.S. 2007. Overuse injuries, overtraining, and burnout in child and adolescent athletes. *Pediatrics*, 119(6): 1242-1245.

Butcher, J., K.J. Lindner, and D.P. Johns. 2002. Withdrawal from competitive youth sport: A retrospective ten-year study. *Journal of Sport Behavior*, 25(2): 145-163.

Conroy, D.E., and J.D. Coatsworth. 2006. Coach training as a strategy for promoting youth social development. *Sport Psychologist*, 20(2): 128.

Côté, J., J. Baker, and B. Abernethy. 2007. Practice and play in the development of sport expertise. *Handbook of Sport Psychology*, 3: 184-202.

Csikszentmihalyi, M., K. Rathunde, and S. Whalen. 1997. *Talented teens: The roots of success and failure*. Oxford: Oxford University Press.

Durand-Bush, N., and J. Salmela. 2002. The development and maintenance of expert athletic performance: Perceptions of world and Olympic champions. *Journal of Applied Sport Psychology*, 14: 154-171.

Dweck, C. 2006. *Mindset: The new psychology of success*. New York: Random House.

Fraser-Thomas, J., J. Cote, and J. Deakin. 2008. Examining adolescent sport dropout and prolonged engagement from a developmental perspective. *Journal of Applied Sport Psychology*, 20(3): 318-333.

Gladwell, M. 2008. *Outliers: The secret of success*. New York: Little, Brown.

Gould, D., K. Dieffenbach, and A. Moffett. 2002. Psychological characteristics and their development in Olympic champions. *Journal of Applied Sport Psychology*, 14: 172-204.

Gustafsson, H., G. Kentta, P. Hassmén, and C. Lundqvist. 2007. Prevalence of burnout in competitive adolescent athletes. *Sport Psychologist*, 21(1): 21.

Helsen, W.F., J. Van Winckel, and A.M. Williams. 2005. The relative age effect in youth soccer across Europe. *Journal of Sports Sciences*, 23(6): 629-636.

Henderson, N. 2013. Application of talent development. Lecture presented at the National Coaching Conference in Colorado Springs, Colorado.

Hill, M. 2007. Achievement and athletics: Issues and concerns for state boards of education. *State Education Standard*, 8(1): 22-31.

Kaufman, S.B., and A.L. Duckworth. 2015. *World-class expertise: A developmental model*. WIREs Cognitive Science. doi: 10.1002/wcs.1365

Malina, R.M. 2010. Early sport specialization: roots, effectiveness, risks. *Current Sports Medicine Reports*, 9(6): 364-371.

Musch, J., and S. Grondin. 2001. Unequal competition as an impediment to personal development: A review of the relative age effect in sport. *Developmental Review*, 21(2): 147-167.

Raedeke, T.D., K. Lunney, and K. Venables. 2002. Understanding athletes burnout: Coach perspectives. *Journal of Sport Behavior*, 25(2): 181.

Smith, R.E., F.L. Smoll, and S.P. Cumming. 2007. Effects of a motivational climate in intervention for coaches on young athletes' sport performance anxiety. *Journal of Sport and Exercise Psychology*, 29: 39-59.

Smoll, F., S. Cumming, and R. Smith. 2011. Enhancing coach-parent relationships in youth sports: Increasing harmony and minimizing hassle. *International Journal of Sports Science and Coaching*, 6(1): 13-26.

Stebelsky, R.H.B.G. 1991. "Born to play ball." The relative age effect and Major League Baseball. *Sociology of Sport Journal*, 8: 146-151.

Ward, P., N.J. Hodges, A.M. Williams, and J.L. Starkes. 2004. Deliberate practice and expert performance. In *Skill acquisition in sport: Research, theory and practice*, ed. M. Williams and N. Hodges. New York: Routledge..

Whitehead, M., ed. 2010. *Physical literacy: Throughout the lifecourse*. London: Routledge.

Chapter 24

Bass, B.M., and B.J. Avolio. 1994. *Improving organizational effectiveness through transformational leadership*. Thousand Oaks, CA: Sage.

Bass, B.M., B.J. Avolio, D.I. Jung, and Y. Berson. 2003. Predicting unit performance by assessing transformational and transactional leadership. *Journal of Applied Psychology*, 88: 207-218.

Baumeister, R.F., S.E. Ainsworth, and K.D. Vohs. 2015. Are groups more or less than the sum of their members? The moderating role of individual identification. *Behavioral and brain sciences/target articles under commentary*. Published online: May, 2015. DOI: http://dx.doi.org/10.1017/S0140525X15000618.

Beal, D.J., R.R. Cohen, M.J. Burke, and C.L. McLendon. 2003. Cohesion and performance in groups: A meta-analytic clarification of construct relations. *Journal of Applied Psychology*, 88: 989-1004.

Beauchamp, M.R., S.R. Bray, A. Fielding, and M.A. Eys. 2005. A multilevel investigation of the relationship between role ambiguity and role efficacy in sport. *Psychology of Sport and Exercise*, 6: 289-302.

Beauchamp, M.R., and M.A. Eys. 2014. *Group dynamics in exercise and sport psychology*. 2nd ed. New York: Routledge.

Beauchamp, M.R., and M.A. Eys. 2015. Leadership in sport and exercise. In *Sport and exercise psychology: A Canadian perspective*, 3rd ed., ed. P.R.E. Crocker, 199-226. Toronto: Pearson.

Carron, A.V., and L.R. Brawley. 2000. Cohesion: Conceptual and measurement issues. *Small Group Research*, 31: 89-106.

Carron, A.V., M. Eys, and L.J. Martin. 2012. Cohesion: Its nature and measurement. In *Handbook of measurement in sport and exercise psychology*, ed. G. Tenenbaum, R. Eklund, and A. Kamata, 411-422. Champaign, IL: Human Kinetics.

Carron, A.V., L.J. Martin, and T.M. Loughead. 2012. Teamwork and performance. In *The Oxford handbook of sport and performance psychology*, ed. S.M. Murphy, 309-332. New York: Oxford University Press.

Chelladurai, P. 1993. Leadership. In *Handbook of research on sport psychology*, ed. R.N. Singer, M. Murphey, and L.K. Tennant, 647-671. New York: Macmillan.

Chelladurai, P. 2012. Leadership and manifestations of sport. In *The Oxford handbook of sport and performance psychology*, ed. S.M. Murphy, 328-342. New York: Oxford University Press.

Conger, J.A. 1989. *The charismatic leader: Behind the mystique of exceptional leadership*. San Francisco, CA: Jossey-Bass.

Cope, C.J., M.A. Eys, M.R. Beauchamp, R.J. Schinke, and G. Bosselut. 2011. Informal roles on sport teams. *International Journal of Sport and Exercise Psychology*, 9: 19-30.

Delise, L., C.A. Gorman, A.M. Brooks, J.R. Rentsch, and D. Steele-Johnson. 2010. The effects of team training on team outcomes: A meta-analysis. *Performance Improvement Quarterly*, 22: 53-80.

Dietz, H.M.S., D. van Knippenberg, G. Hirst, and S. Restubog. 2015. Outperforming whom? A multilevel study of performance-prove goal orientation, performance, and the moderating role of shared team identification. *Journal of Applied Psychology*, 100: 1811-1824.

D'Innocenzo, L., J.E. Mathieu, and M.R. Kukenberger. 2016. A meta-analysis of different forms of shared leadership-team performance relations. *Journal of Management*, 42(7): 1964-1991.

Eckel, C.C., and P.J. Grossman. 2004. Managing diversity by creating team identity. *Journal of Economic Behavior and Organization*, 58: 317-392.

Eys, M.A., M.R. Beauchamp, and S.R. Bray. 2006. A review of team roles in sport. In *Literature reviews in sport psychology*, ed. S. Hanton and S.D. Mellalieu, 227-255. New York: Nova Science.

Hackman, J.R., and N. Katz. 2010. Group behavior and performance. In *The handbook of social psychology*, ed. S.T. Fiske, D.T. Gilbert, and G. Lindzey, 1208-1251. Hoboken, NJ: Wiley.

Hardy, C.J., and R.K. Crace. 1997. Foundations of team building: Introduction to the team building primer. *Journal of Applied Sport Psychology*, 9: 1-10.

Hogg, M.A. 1992. *The social psychology of group cohesiveness: From attraction to social identity*. New York: University Press.

Hogg, M.A. 2001. A social identity theory of leadership. *Personality and Social Psychology Review*, 5: 184-200.

Hogg, M.A. 2012. Social identity and the psychology of groups. In *Handbook of self and identity*, 2nd ed., ed. M.R. Leary and J.P. Tangney, 502-519. New York: Guilford.

Hogg, M.A., D. van Knippenberg, and D.E. Rast III. 2012. The social identity theory of leadership: Theoretical origins, research findings, and conceptual developments. *European Review of Social Psychology*, 23: 258-304.

Horcajo, J., and R. De la Vega. 2014. Changing doping-related attitudes in soccer players: How can we get stable and persistent changes? *European Journal of Sport Science*, 14: 839-846.

Horcajo, J., and R. De la Vega. 2016. La convicción en las actitudes relacionadas con el dopaje: Un estudio experimental con entrenadores de fútbol. [Conviction in doping-related attitudes: An experimental study with soccer coaches]. *Revista de Psicología del Deporte*, 25: 57-64.

Horcajo, J., and A. Luttrell. 2016. The effects of elaboration on the strength of doping-related attitudes: Resistance to change and behavioral intentions. *Journal of Sport and Exercise Psychology*, 38(3): 236-246.

Hornsey, M.J. 2008. Social identity theory and self-categorization theory: A historical review. *Social and Personality Psychology Compass*, 2: 204-222.

Ilgen, D.R., J.R. Hollenbeck, M. Johnson, and D. Jundt. 2005. Teams in organizations: From I-P-O models to IMOI models. *Annual Review of Psychology*, 56: 517-544.

Kerr, N.L., and R.S. Tindale. 2004. Group performance and decision making. *Annual Review of Psychology*, 55: 623-655.

Klein, C., D. DiazGranados, E. Salas, H. Le, C.S. Burke, R. Lyons, and G.F. Goodwin. 2009. Does team building work? *Small Group Research*, 40: 181-222.

Kramer, W., A.L. Thayer, and E. Salas. 2013. Goal setting in teams. In *New developments in goal setting and task performance*, ed. E.A. Locke and G.P. Latham, 287-310. New York: Routledge.

LePine, J.A., R.F. Piccolo, C.L. Jackson, J.E. Mathieu, and J.R. Saul. 2008. A meta-analysis of teamwork processes: Tests of a multidimensional model and relationships with team effectiveness criteria. *Personnel Psychology*, 61: 273-307.

Levine, J., and R. Moreland. 1998. Small groups. In *The handbook of social psychology*, ed. D.T. Gilbert, S.T. Fiske, and G. Lindzey, 415-469. New York: McGraw-Hill.

Loughead, T.M., and A.V. Carron. 2004. The mediating role of cohesion in the leader behavior-satisfaction relationship. *Psychology of Sport and Exercise*, 5: 355-371.

Martin, L.J., A.V. Carron, and S.M. Burke. 2009. Team building interventions in sport: A meta-analysis. *Sport and Exercise Psychology Review*, 5: 3-18.

Mathieu, J., M.T. Maynard, T. Rapp, and L. Gilson. 2008. Team effectiveness 1997–2007: A review of recent advancements and a glimpse into the future. *Journal of Management*, 34: 410-476.

McEwan, D., and M.R. Beauchamp. 2014. Teamwork in sport: A theoretical and integrative review. *International Review of Sport and Exercise Psychology*, 7: 229-250.

McGrath, J.E., H. Arrow, and J.L. Berdahl. 2000. The study of groups: Past, present, and future. *Personality and Social Psychology Review*, 4: 95-105.

Munroe, K., P. Estabrooks, P. Dennis, and A.V. Carron. 1999. A phenomenological analysis of group norms in sport teams. *Sport Psychologist*, 13: 171-182.

Petty, R.E., and P. Briñol. 2012. The elaboration likelihood model. In *Handbook of theories of social psychology*, ed. P.A.M. Van Lange, A. Kruglanski, and E.T. Higgins, 224-245. London: Sage.

Petty, R.E., and J.T. Cacioppo. 1986. *Communication and persuasion: Central and peripheral routes to attitude change*. New York: Springer/Verlag.

Postmes, T., S.A. Haslam, and R.I. Swaab. 2005. Social influence in small groups: An interactive model of social identity formation. *European Review of Social Psychology*, 16: 1-42.

Salas, E., M.A. Rosen, C.S. Burke, and G.F. Goodwin. 2009. The wisdom of collectives in organizations: An update of the teamwork competencies. In *Team effectiveness in complex organizations. Cross-disciplinary perspectives and approaches*, ed. E. Salas, G.F. Goodwin, and C.S. Burke, 39-79. New York: New York Psychology Press.

Salas, E., S.I. Tannenbaum, K. Kraiger, and K.A. Smith-Jentsch. 2012. The science of training and development in organizations: What matters in practice. *Psychological Science in the Public Interest*, 13: 74-101.

Shuffler, M.L., D. DiazGranados, and E. Salas. 2011. There's a science for that: Team development interventions in organizations. *Current Directions in Psychological Science*, 20: 365-372.

Smoll F.L., and R.E. Smith. 1989. Leadership behaviors in sport: A theoretical model and research paradigm. *Journal of Applied Social Psychology*, 19: 1522-1551.

Swaab, R., T. Postmes, I. Van Beest, and R. Spears. 2007. Shared cognition as a product of and precursor to, shared identity in negotiations. *Personality and Social Psychology Bulletin*, 33: 187-199.

Tajfel, H., and J.C. Turner. 1986. The social identity theory of intergroup behavior. In *The psychology of intergroup relations*, ed. S. Worchel and W.G. Austin, 7-24. Chicago: Nelson-Hall.

Turner, J.C. 1987. *Rediscovering the social group: A self-categorization theory*. Oxford: Blackwell.

van Knippenberg, D., and N. Ellemers. 2003. Social identity and group performance: Identification as the key to group-oriented efforts. In *Social identity at work: Developing theory for organizational practice*, ed. S.A. Haslam, D. van Knippenberg, M.J. Platow, and N. Ellemers, 29-42. New York: Psychology Press.

van Knippenberg, D., and M.C. Schippers. 2007. Work group diversity. *Annual Review of Psychology*, 58: 515-541.

Weinberg, R., and D. Gould. 2015. *Foundations of sport and exercise psychology*. 6th ed. Champaign, IL: Human Kinetics.

Widmeyer, W.N., and K. Ducharme. 1997. Team building through team goal setting. *Journal of Applied Sport Psychology*, 9: 97-113.

Worchel, S., H. Rothberger, A. Day, D. Hart, and J. Butemeyer. 1998. Social identity and individual productivity within groups. *British Journal of Social Psychology*, 37: 389-413.

Zabala, M., and G. Atkinson. 2012. Looking for the "athlete 2.0": A collaborative challenge. *Journal of Science and Cycling*, 1: 1-2.

Chapter 25

Catalano, E.M. 1987. *The chronic pain control workbook*. Oakland, CA: New Harbinger.

Caudill, D., R. Weinberg, and A. Jackson. 1983. Psyching-up and track athletes: A preliminary investigation. *Journal of Sport Psychology*, 5: 231-235.

Cousins, M.J., and G.D. Phillips. 1985. Acute pain management. *Clinics in Critical Care Medicine*, 8: 82-117.

Cresswell, S., and J. Hodge. 2004. Coping skills: Role of trait sport confidence and trait anxiety. *Perceptual and Motor Skills*, 98(2): 433-438.

Duda, J.L., and D.C. Treasure. 2001. Toward optimal motivation in sport. In *Applied sport psychology*, ed. J.M. Williams. Mountain View, CA: Mayfield.

Edwards, T., and L. Hardy. 1996. The interactive effects of intensity and direction of cognitive and somatic anxiety and self-confidence upon performance. *Journal of Sport and Exercise Psychology*, 18: 296-312.

Hanton, S., S.D. Mellalieu, and R. Hall. 2004. Self-confidence and anxiety interpretation: A qualitative investigation. *Psychology of Sport and Exercise*, 5: 477-495.

Heil, J. 1993. *Psychology of sport injury*. Champaign, IL: Human Kinetics.

Jacobson, E. 1938. *Progressive relaxation*. Chicago: University of Chicago Press.

Kress, J. 1998. A naturalistic investigation of former Olympic cyclists' cognitive strategies for coping with exertion pain during performance. Unpublished doctorial dissertation. Lawrence, KS.

Landers, D.M. and S.H. Boucher. 1986. Arousal-performance relationships. In *Applied sport psychology*, ed. J.M. Williams. Mountain View, CA: Mayfield.

Laird, J.D. 1974. Self-attribution of emotion: The effects of expressive behavior on the quality of emotional experience. *Journal of Personality and Social Psychology*, 29: 475-486.

Leventhal, H., and D. Everhart. 1979. Emotion, pain, and physical illness. In *Emotions in personality and psychopathology*, ed. C. E. Izard. New York: Plenum.

Manzon, L.G., G.W. Mondin, B. Clark, and T. Schneider. 2005. Confidence. In *Applying sport psychology*, ed. J. Taylor and G. Wilson. Champaign, IL: Human Kinetics.

Raglin, J.S., and Y.L. Hanin. 1999. Competitive anxiety. In *Emotions in sport*, ed. Y.L. Hanin. Champaign, IL: Human Kinetics.

Ravizza, K. 2001. Increasing awareness for sport performance. In *Applied sport psychology*, ed. J.M. Williams. Mountain View, CA: Mayfield.

Rian, C.B. 1990. Principles and practices of sports medicine. Unpublished manuscript.

Seligman, M. 1991. *Learned optimism*. New York: Knopf.

Taylor, J. 2001. *Prime sport: The triumph of the athlete mind*. New York: Universe.

Taylor, J., and G.S. Wilson. 2002. Intensity regulation and sport performance. In *Exploring sport and exercise psychology*, 2nd ed., ed. J. Van Raalte and B. Brewer. Washington, DC: American Psychological Association.

Taylor, J., and J. Kress. 2006. Psychology of cycling. In *The sport psychologist's handbook: A guide to sport specific performance enhancement*, ed. J. Dosil, New York: Wiley.

Taylor, J., and G. Wilson, ed. 2005. *Applying sport psychology: Four perspectives*. Champaign, IL: Human Kinetics.

Taylor, J., and S. Taylor. 1998. Pain education and management in the rehabilitation from sports injury. *Sport Psychologist*, 12: 68-88.

Thompson, S.C. 1981. Will it hurt less if I can control it? A complex answer to a simple question. *Psychological Bulletin*, 90: 89-101.

Williams, J.M. and D.V. Harris. 1988. Relaxation and energizing techniques of regulation arousal. In *Applied sport psychology*, ed. J.M. Williams. Mountain View, CA: Mayfield.

Williams, J.M., and V. Krane. 2001. Psychological characteristics of peak performance. In *Applied sport psychology*, ed. J.M. Williams. Mountain View, CA: Mayfield.

Wilson, G., J. Taylor, F. Gundersen, and T. Brahm. 2005. Intensity. In *Applying sport psychology: Four perspectives*, ed. J. Taylor and G.S. Wilson. Champaign, IL: Human Kinetics.

Zajonc, R.B. 1965. Social facilitation. *Science*, 149: 269-274.

Zinsser, N., L. Bunker, and J.M. William. 2001. Cognitive techniques for building confidence and enhancing performance. In *Applied sport psychology*, ed. J.M. Williams. Mountain View, CA: Mayfield.

Chapter 26

Allen, H., and A. Coggan. 2010. *Training and racing with a power meter*. 2nd ed. Boulder, CO: VeloPress.

Borg, G. 1998. *Borg's Perceived Exertion and Pain Scales*. Champaign, IL: Human Kinetics.

Coyle, E., A.R. Coggan, M.K. Hopper, and T.J. Walters. 1988. Determinants of endurance in well-trained cyclists. *Journal of Applied Physiology*, 64: 2622-2630.

Karsten, B., S.A. Jobson, J. Hopker, A. Jimenez, and C. Beedie. 2014. High agreement between laboratory and field estimates of critical power in cycling. *International Journal of Sports Medicine*, 35: 298-303.

Lamberts, R.P., J. Swart, T.D. Noakes, and M.I. Lambert. 2011. A novel submaximal cycle test to monitor fatigue and predict cycling performance. *British Journal of Sports Medicine*, 45: 797-804.

Loftin, M., and B. Warren. 1994. Comparison of a simulated 16.1-km time trial, VO_2max and related factors in cyclists with different ventilatory thresholds. *International Journal of Sports Medicine*, 15: 498-503.

Pinot, J., and F. Grappe. 2011. The record power profile to assess performance in elite cycling. *International Journal of Sports Medicine*, 32: 839-844.

Quod, M.J., D.T. Martin, J.C. Martin, and P.B. Laursen. 2010. The power profile predicts road cycling MMP. *International Journal of Sports Medicine*, 31: 394-401.

Chapter 27

Issurin, V. 2008. Block periodization versus traditional training theory: A review. *Journal of Sports Medicine and Physical Fitness*, 48(1): 65-75.

Laursen, P.B. 2010. Training for intense exercise performance: High-intensity or high-volume training? *Scandinavian Journal of Medicine and Science in Sports*, 20(Suppl 2): 1-10.

Plews, D.J., P.B. Laursen, A.E. Kilding, and M. Buchheit. 2014. Heart rate variability and training intensity distribution in elite rowers. *International Journal of Sports Physiology and Performance*, 9(6): 1026-1032.

Quod, M.J., D.T. Martin, J.C. Martin, and P.B. Laursen. 2010. The power profile predicts road cycling MMP. *International Journal of Sports Medicine*, 31(6): 397-401.

Seiler, K.S., and G.O. Kjerland. 2006. Quantifying training intensity distribution in elite endurance athletes: Is there evidence for an "optimal" distribution? *Scandinavian Journal of Medicine and Science in Sports*, 16(1): 49-56.

Stanley, J., J.M. Peake, and M. Buchheit. 2013. Cardiac parasympathetic reactivation following exercise: Implications for training prescription. *Sports Medicine*, 43(12): 1259-1277.

Stoggl, T., and B. Sperlich. 2014. Polarized training has greater impact on key endurance variables than threshold, high intensity, or high volume training. *Frontiers in Physiology*, 5: 33.

Chapter 28

Bompa, T., and G.G. Haff. 2009. *Periodization: Theory and methodology of training*. 5th ed. Champaign, IL: Human Kinetics.

Breil, F.A., S.N. Weber, S. Koller, H. Hoppeler, and M. Vogt. 2010. Block training periodization in alpine skiing: Effects of 11-day HIT on VO_2max and per-

formance. *European Journal of Applied Physiology*, 109: 1077-1086.

Chapple, T. 2006. *Base building for cyclists: A new foundation for endurance and performance*. Boulder, CO: VeloPress.

Clark, B., V.P. Costa, B.J. O'Brien, L.G. Guglielmo, and C.D. Paton. 2014. Effects of a seven day overload-period of high-intensity training on performance and physiology of competitive cyclists. *PLoS One*, 9: e115308.

Friel, J. 1996. *Cyclist's training bible*. Boulder, CO: VeloPress.

García-Pallarés, J., M. García-Fernández, L. Sánchez-Medina, and M. Izquierdo. 2010. Performance changes in world-class kayakers following two different training periodization models. *European Journal of Applied Physiology*, 110: 99-107.

Issurin, V. 2008. Block periodization versus traditional training theory: A review. *Journal of Sports Medicine and Physical Fitness*, 48: 65-75.

Issurin, V.B. 2016. Benefits and limitations of Block periodized Training approaches to athletes' preparation: A review. *Sports Medicine*, 46(3): 329-338.

Issurin, V.B. 2010. New horizons for the methodology and physiology of training periodization. *Sports Medicine*, 40: 189-206.

Kiely, J. 2012. Periodization paradigms in the 21st century: Evidence-led or tradition-driven? *International Journal of Sports Physiology and Performance*, 7: 242-250.

Matvejev, L. 1977. *Fundamentals of sport training*. Moscow, Russia: Fizkultura I Sport. (Translated from Russian by A.P. Zdornykh. Moscow, Russia: 1981).

Midgley, A.W., L.R. McNaughton, and M. Wilkinson. 2006. Is there an optimal training intensity for enhancing the maximal oxygen uptake of distance runners? Empirical research findings, current opinions, physiological rationale and practical recommendations. *Sports Medicine*, 36: 117-132.

Mujika, I. 2009. *Tapering and peaking for optimal performance*. Champaign, IL: Human Kinetics.

Mujika, I., and P. Laursen. 2012. Training methodology and periodisation for cycling. In *Performance cycling: The science of success*, ed. J. Hopker and S. Jobson, 58-65. London: Bloomsbury..

Rønnestad, B.R., S. Ellefsen, H. Nygaard, E.E. Zacharoff, O. Vikmoen, J. Hansen, and J. Hallén. 2014. Effects of 12 weeks of block periodization on performance and performance indices in well-trained cyclists. *Scandinavian Journal of Medicine and Science in Sports*, 24: 327-335.

Rønnestad, B.R., J. Hansen, and S. Ellefsen. 2014. Block periodization of high-intensity aerobic intervals provides superior training effects in trained cyclists. *Scandinavian Journal of Medicine and Science in Sports*, 24: 34-42.

Rønnestad, B.R., J. Hansen, G. Vegge, and I. Mujika. 2016. Short-term performance peaking in an elite cross-country mountain biker. *Journal of Sports Sciences*, Aug 1: 1-4.

Seiler, K.S., and G.Ø. Kjerland. 2006. Quantifying training intensity distribution in elite endurance athletes: Is there evidence for an "optimal" distribution? *Scandinavian Journal of Medicine and Science in Sports*, 16: 49-56.

Seiler, S. 2010. What is best practice for training intensity and duration distribution in endurance athletes? *International Journal of Sports Physiology and Performance*, 5: 276-291.

Shephard, R.J. 1968. Intensity, duration and frequency of exercise as determinants of the response to a training regime. *Internationale Zetischrift Fur Angewandte Physiologie Einschliesslich Arbeitsphysiologie*, 26: 272-278.

Strohacker, K., D. Fazzino, W.L. Breslin, and X. Xu. 2015. The use of periodization in exercise prescriptions for inactive adults: A systematic review. *Preventive Medicine Reports*, 2: 385-396.

Wenger, H.A., and G.J. Bell. 1986. The interactions of intensity, frequency and duration of exercise training in altering cardiorespiratory fitness. *Sports Medicine*, 3: 346-356.

Chapter 29

Allen, H., and A. Coggan. 2010. *Training and racing with a power meter.* Boulder, CO: VeloPress.

Chapter 30

Allen, H., and A. Coggan. 2010. *Training and racing with a power meter.* Boulder, CO: VeloPress.

Balouchestani, M., and S. Krishnan. 2014. Effective low-power wearable wireless surface EMG sensor design based on analog-compressed sensing. *Sensors (Basel)*, 14(12): 24305-24328.

Borden, J., and M. Lambert. 2006. A theoretical basis of monitoring fatigue: A practical approach for coaches. *International Journal of Sports Science and Coaching*, 1(4): 371-388.

Borresen, J., and M. Lambert. 2008. Quantifying training load: A comparison of subjective and objective methods. *International Journal of Sports Physiology and Performance*, 3: 16-30.

Ebert, T., D. Martin, B. Stephens, and R. Withers. 2006. Power output during a professional men's road-cycling tour. *International Journal of Sports Physiology and Performance*, 1(4): 324-335.

Foster, C. 1998. Monitoring training in athletes with reference to overtraining syndrome. *Medicine and Science in Sports and Exercise*, 30: 1164-1168.

Halson, S. 2014. Monitoring training load to understand fatigue in athletes. *Sports Medicine*, 44(Suppl 2): 139-147.

Hayes, P.R., and M.D. Quinn. 2009. A mathematical model for quantifying training. *European Journal of Applied Physiology*, 106(6): 839-847.

Martin, D., and M. Andersen. 2000. Heart rate-perceived exertion relationship during training and taper. *Journal of Sports Medicine and Physical Fitness*, 40: 201-208.

Manzi, V., C. Castagna, E. Padua, M. Lombardo, S. D'Ottavio, M. Massaro, M. Volterrani, and F. Iellamo. 2009a. Dose-response relationship of autonomic nervous system responses to individualized training impulse in marathon runners. *American Journal of Physiology—Heart and Circulatory Physiology*, 296(6): H1733-H1740.

Manzi, V., F. Iellamo, F. Impellizzeri, S. D'Ottavio, and C. Castagna. 2009b. Relation between individualized training impulses and performance in distance runners. *Medicine and Science in Sports and Exercise*, 41(11): 2090-2096.

Chapter 31

Aagaard, P., J.L. Andersen, M. Bennekou, B. Larsson, J.L. Olesen, R. Crameri, S.P. Magnusson, and M. Kjaer. 2011. Effects of resistance training on endurance capacity and muscle fiber composition in young top-level cyclists. *Scandinavian Journal of Medicine and Science in Sports*, 21: e298-e307.

Atkinson, G., R. Davison, A. Jeukendrup, and L. Passfield. 2003. Science and cycling: Current knowledge and future directions for research. *Journal of Sports Sciences*, 21: 767-787.

Barrett-O'Keefe, Z., J. Helgerud, P.D. Wagner, and R.S. Richardson. 2012. Maximal strength training and increased work efficiency: Contribution from the trained muscle bed. *Journal of Applied Physiology*, 113: 1846-1851.

Bastiaans, J.J., A.B. van Diemen, T. Veneberg, and A.E. Jeukendrup. 2001. The effects of replacing a portion of endurance training by explosive strength training on performance in trained cyclists. *European Journal of Applied Physiology*, 86: 79-84.

Bishop, D., D.G. Jenkins, L.T. Mackinnon, M. McEniery, and M.F. Carey. 1999. The effects of strength training on endurance performance and muscle characteristics. *Medicine and Science in Sports and Exercise*, 31: 886-891.

Costill, D.L. 1967. The relationship between selected physiological variables and distance running performance. *Journal of Sports Medicine and Physical Fitness*, 7: 61-66.

Coyle, E.F., M.E. Feltner, S.A. Kautz, M.T. Hamilton, S.J. Montain, A.M. Baylor, L.D. Abraham, and G.W. Petrek. 1991. Physiological and biomechanical factors associated with elite endurance cycling performance. *Medicine and Science in Sports and Exercise*, 23: 93-107.

Fitts, R.H., D.L. Costill, and P.R. Gardetto. 1989. Effect of swim exercise training on human muscle fiber function. *Journal of Applied Physiology*, 66: 465-475.

Hawley, J.A., and T.D. Noakes. 1992. Peak power output predicts maximal oxygen uptake and performance time in trained cyclists. *European Journal of Applied Physiology and Occupational Physiology*, 65: 79-83.

Hawley, J.A. 2009. Molecular responses to strength and endurance training: Are they incompatible? *Applied Physiology, Nutrition, and Metabolism*, 34: 355-361.

Heggelund, J., M.S. Fimland, J. Helgerud, and J. Hoff. 2013. Maximal strength training improves work economy, rate of force development and maximal strength more than conventional strength training. *European Journal of Applied Physiology*, 113: 1565-1573.

Hickson, R.C., B.A. Dvorak, E.M. Gorostiaga, T.T. Kurowski, and C. Foster. 1988. Potential for strength and endurance training to amplify endurance performance. *Journal of Applied Physiology*, 65: 2285-2290.

Hickson, R.C., M.A. Rosenkoetter, and M.M. Brown. 1980. Strength training effects on aerobic power and short-term endurance. *Medicine and Science in Sports and Exercise*, 12: 36-39.

Izquierdo, M., J. Ibanez, K. Hakkinen, W.J. Kraemer, M. Ruesta, and E.M. Gorostiaga. 2004. Maximal strength and power, muscle mass, endurance and serum hormones in weightlifters and road cyclists. *Journal of Sports Sciences*, 22: 465-478.

Jones, A.M., and H. Carter. 2000. The effect of endurance training on parameters of aerobic fitness. *Sports Medicine*, 29: 373-386.

Jones, T.W., G. Howatson, M. Russell, and D.N. French. 2013. Performance and neuromuscular adaptations following differing ratios of concurrent strength and endurance training. *Journal of Strength and Conditioning Research*, 27(12): 3342-3351.

Joyner, M.J., and E.F. Coyle. 2008. Endurance exercise performance: The physiology of champions. *Journal of Physiology*, 586: 35-44.

Koninckx, E., M. Van Leemputte, and P. Hespel. 2010. Effect of isokinetic cycling versus weight training on maximal power output and endurance performance in cycling. *European Journal of Applied Physiology*, 109: 699-708.

Kraemer, W.J., J.F. Patton, S.E. Gordon, E.A. Harman, M.R. Deschenes, K. Reynolds, R.U. Newton, N.T. Triplett, and J.E. Dziados. 1995. Compatibility of high-intensity strength and endurance training on hormonal and skeletal-muscle adaptations. *Journal of Applied Physiology*, 78: 976-989.

Kristoffersen, M., H. Gundersen, S. Leirdal, and V.V. Iversen. 2014. Low cadence interval training at moderate intensity does not improve cycling performance in highly trained veteran cyclists. *Frontiers in Physiology*, 5: 34.

Levin, G.T., M.R. Mcguigan, and P.B. Laursen. 2009. Effect of concurrent resistance and endurance training on physiologic and performance parameters of well-trained endurance cyclists. *Journal of Strength and Conditioning Research*, 23: 2280-2286.

Losnegard, T., K. Mikkelsen, B.R. Rønnestad, J. Hallén, B. Rud, and T. Raastad. 2011. The effect of heavy strength training on muscle mass and physical performance in elite cross country skiers. *Scandinavian Journal of Medicine and Science in Sports*, 21: 389-401.

Louis, J., C. Hausswirth, C. Easthope, and J. Brisswalter. 2012. Strength training improves cycling efficiency in master endurance athletes. *European Journal of Applied Physiology*, 112: 631-640.

Lucía, A., J. Pardo, A. Durántez, J. Hoyos, and J.L. Chicharro. 1998. Physiological differences between professional and elite road cyclists. *International Journal of Sports Medicine*, 19(5): 342-348.

McCarthy, J.P., J.C. Agre, B.K. Graf, M.A. Pozniak, and A.C. Vailas. 1995. Compatibility of adaptive responses with combining strength and endurance training. *Medicine and Science in Sports and Exercise*, 27: 429-436.

Rønnestad, B.R., E.A. Hansen, and T. Raastad. 2010a. Effect of heavy strength training on thigh muscle cross-sectional area, performance determinants, and performance in well-trained cyclists. *European Journal of Applied Physiology*, 108: 965-975.

Rønnestad, B.R., E.A. Hansen, and T. Raastad. 2010b. In-season strength maintenance training increases well-trained cyclists' performance *European Journal of Applied Physiology*, 110: 1269-1282.

Rønnestad, B.R., E.A. Hansen, and T. Raastad. 2012. High volume of endurance training impairs adaptations to 12 weeks of strength training in well-trained endurance athletes. *European Journal of Applied Physiology*, 112: 1457-1466.

Rønnestad, B.R., E.A. Hansen, and T. Raastad. 2011. Strength training improves 5-min all-out performance following 185 min of cycling. *Scandinavian Journal of Medicine and Science in Sports*, 21: 250-259.

Rønnestad, B.R., J. Hansen, I. Hollan, and S. Ellefsen. 2015. Strength training improves performance and pedaling characteristics in elite cyclists. *Scandinavian Journal of Medicine and Science in Sports*, 25(1): e89-e98.

Støren, Ø., K. Ulevåg, M.H. Larsen, E.M. Støa, and J. Helgerud. 2013. Physiological determinants of the cycling time trial. *Journal of Strength and Conditioning Research*, 27(9): 2366-2373.

Sunde, A., O. Støren, M. Bjerkaas, M.H. Larsen, J. Hoff, and J. Helgerud. 2010. Maximal strength training improves cycling economy in competitive cyclists. *Journal of Strength and Conditioning Research*, 24: 2157-2165.

Taipale, R.S., J. Mikkola, A. Nummela, V. Vesterinen, B. Capostagno, S. Walker, D. Gitonga, W.J. Kraemer, and K. Häkkinen. 2010. Strength training in endurance runners. *International Journal of Sports Medicine*, 31: 468-476.

Tokmakidis, S.P., L.A. Leger, and T.C. Pilianidis. 1998. Failure to obtain a unique threshold on the blood lactate concentration curve during exercise. *European Journal of Applied Physiology and Occupational Physiology*, 77: 333-342.

Vikmoen, O., B.R. Rønnestad, S. Ellefsen, and T. Raastad. 2014. Strength training improves running and cycling performance. Abstract, European College of Sports Science Conference July 2-5, 2014.

Vikmoen, O., S. Ellefsen, Ø. Trøen, I. Hollan, M. Hanestadhaugen, T. Raastad, and B.R. Rønnestad. 2016. Strength training improves cycling performance, fractional utilization of VO$_2$max and cycling economy in female cyclists. *Scandinavian Journal of Medicine and Science in Sports*, 26: 384-396.

Chapter 32

Aaron, E.A., K.C. Seow, B.D. Johnson, and J.A. Dempsey. 1992. Oxygen cost of exercise hyperpnea: Implications for performance. *Journal of Applied Physiology*, 72: 1818-1825.

Amann, M., L.T. Proctor, J.J. Sebranek, M.W. Eldridge, D.F. Pegelow, and J.A. Dempsey. 2008. Somatosensory feedback from the limbs exerts inhibitory influences on central neural drive during whole body endurance exercise. *Journal of Applied Physiology*, 105(6): 1714-1724.

Dempsey, J.A., L. Romer, J. Rodman, J. Miller, and C. Smith. 2006. Consequences of exercise-induced respiratory muscle work. *Respiratory Physiology and Neurobiology*, 151: 242-250.

Elliott, A.D., and F. Grace. 2010. An examination of exercise mode on ventilatory patterns during incremental exercise. *European Journal of Applied Physiology*, 110: 557-562.

HajGhanbari, B., C. Yamabayashi, T.R. Buna, J.D. Coelho, K.D. Freedman, T.A. Morton, S.A. Palmer, M.A. Toy, C. Walsh, A.W. Sheel, and W.D. Reid. 2013. Effects of respiratory muscle training on performance in athletes: A systematic review with meta-analyses. *Journal of Strength and Conditioning Research*, 27: 1643-1663.

Harms, C.A., T.J. Wetter, C.M. St Croix, D.F. Pegelow, and J.A. Dempsey. 2000. Effects of respiratory muscle work on exercise performance. *Journal of Applied Physiology*, 89: 131-138.

Illi, S.K., U. Held, I. Frank, and C.M. Spengler. 2012. Effect of respiratory muscle training on exercise performance in healthy individuals: A systematic review and meta-analysis. *Sports Medicine*, 42: 707-724.

Johnson, B.D., M.A. Babcock, O.E. Suman, and J.A. Dempsey. 1993. Exercise-induced diaphragmatic fatigue in healthy humans. *Journal of Physiology*, 460: 385-405.

McConnell, A.K., and L.M. Romer. 2004. Dyspnoea in health and obstructive pulmonary disease: The role of respiratory muscle function and training. *Sports Medicine*, 34: 117-132.

McConnell, A.K., and M. Lomax. 2006. The influence of inspiratory muscle work history and specific inspiratory muscle training upon human limb muscle fatigue. *Journal of Physiology*, 577: 445-457.

Morton, D.P., and R. Callister. 2000. Characteristics and etiology of exercise-related transient abdominal pain. *Medicine and Science in Sports and Exercise*, 32: 432-438.

Morton, D.P., and R. Callister. 2002. Factors influencing exercise-related transient abdominal pain. *Medicine and Science in Sports and Exercise*, 34: 745-749.

Origenes, M.M. IV, S.E. Blank, and R.B. Schoene. 1993. Exercise ventilatory response to upright and aeroposture cycling. *Medicine and Science in Sports and Exercise*, 25: 608-612.

Romer, L.M., A.K. McConnell, and D.A. Jones. 2002a. Effects of inspiratory muscle training on time-trial performance in trained cyclists. *Journal of Sports Science*, 20: 547-562.

Romer, L.M., A.K. McConnell, and D.A. Jones. 2002b. Inspiratory muscle fatigue in trained cyclists: Effects of inspiratory muscle training. *Medicine and Science in Sports and Exercise*, 34: 785-792.

Romer, L.M., and A.K. McConnell. 2003. Specificity and reversibility of inspiratory muscle training. *Medicine and Science in Sports and Exercise*, 35: 237-244.

Sheel, A.W., I. Lama, P. Potvin, K.D. Coutts, and D.C. McKenzie. 1996. Comparison of aero-bars versus traditional cycling postures on physiological parameters during submaximal cycling. *Canadian Journal of Applied Physiology*, 21: 16-22.

Sheel, A.W., and L.M. Romer. 2012. Ventilation and respiratory mechanics. *Comprehensive Physiology*, 2: 1093-1142.

Tanner, D.A., J.W. Duke, and J.M. Stager. 2014. Ventilatory patterns differ between maximal running and cycling. *Respiratory Physiology and Neurobiology*, 191: 9-16.

Taylor, B.J., and L.M. Romer. 2008. Effect of expiratory muscle fatigue on exercise tolerance and locomotor muscle fatigue in healthy humans. *Journal of Applied Physiology*, 104: 1442-1451.

Verges, S., O. Lenherr, A.C. Haner, C. Schulz, and C.M. Spengler. 2007. Increased fatigue resistance of respiratory muscles during exercise after respiratory muscle endurance training. *American Journal of Physiology—Regulatory, Integrative and Comparative Physiology*, 292: R1246-R1253.

Witt, J.D., J.A. Guenette, J.L. Rupert, D.C. McKenzie, and A.W. Sheel. 2007. Inspiratory muscle training attenuates the human respiratory muscle metaboreflex. *Journal of Physiology*, 584: 1019-1028.

Chapter 33

Atkinson, G., C. Todd, T. Reilly, and J. Waterhouse. 2005. Diurnal variation in cycling performance: Influence of warm-up. *Journal of Sports Sciences*, 23: 321-329.

Bishop, D. 2003. Warm up II: Performance changes following active warm up and how to structure the warm up. *Sports Medicine*, 33: 483-498.

Bishop, D., and N.S. Maxwell. 2009. Effects of active warm up on thermoregulation and intermittent-sprint performance in hot conditions. *Journal of Science and Medicine in Sport*, 12: 196-204.

Burnley, M., J.H. Doust, H. Carter, and A.M. Jones. 2001. Effects of prior exercise and recovery duration on oxygen uptake kinetics during heavy exercise in humans. *Experimental Physiology*, 86: 417-425.

Burnley, M., J.H. Doust, and A.M. Jones. 2002. Effects of prior heavy exercise, prior sprint exercise and passive warming on oxygen uptake kinetics during heavy exercise in humans. *European Journal of Applied Physiology*, 87: 424-432.

Burnley, M., J.H. Doust, and A.M. Jones. 2005. Effects of prior warm-up regime on severe-intensity cycling performance. *Medicine and Science in Sports and Exercise*, 37: 838-845.

Burnley, M., A.M. Jones, H. Carter, and J.H. Doust. 2000. Effects of prior heavy exercise on phase II pulmonary oxygen uptake kinetics during heavy exercise. *Journal of Applied Physiology*, 89: 1387-1396.

Christensen, P.M., and J. Bangsbo. 2015. Warm-up strategy and high-intensity endurance performance in trained cyclist. *International Journal of Sports Physiology and Performance*, 10: 353-360.

Dos-Santos, R.C., C.R.M. Costa, F. Di Masi, and A.L.B. Silveira. 2014. Effects of pre-exercise activities on progressive cycling test performance and autonomic response. *Journal of Exercise Physiology*, 17: 84-94.

Faulkner, S.H., R.A. Ferguson, N. Gerrett, M. Hupperets, S.G. Hodder, and G. Havenith. 2013. Reducing muscle temperature drop after warm-up improves sprint cycling performance. *Medicine and Science in Sports and Exercise*, 45: 359-365.

Faulkner, S.H., M. Hupperets, S.G. Hodder, and G. Havenith. 2015. Conductive and evaporative precooling lowers mean skin temperature and improves time trial performance in the heat. *Scandinavian Journal of Medicine and Science in Sports*, 25: 183-189.

Fradkin, A.J., T.R. Zazryn, and J.M. Smoliga. 2010. Effects of warming-up on physical performance: A systematic review with meta-analysis. *Journal of Strength and Conditioning Research*, 24: 140-148.

Galloway, S.D., and R.J. Maughan. 1997. Effects of ambient temperature on the capacity to perform prolonged cycle exercise in man. *Medicine and Science in Sports and Exercise*, 29: 1240-1249.

Gray, S.C., G. Devito, and M.A. Nimmo. 2002. Effect of active warm-up on metabolism prior to and during intense dynamic exercise. *Medicine and Science in Sports and Exercise*, 34: 2091-2096.

Gray, S., and M. Nimmo. 2001. Effects of active, passive or no warm-up on metabolism and performance during high-intensity exercise. *Journal of Sports Sciences*, 19: 693-700.

Hajoglou, A., C. Foster, J.J. De Koning, A. Lucia, T.W. Kernozek, and J.P. Porcari. 2005. Effect of warm-up on cycle time trial performance. *Medicine and Science in Sports and Exercise*, 37: 1608-1614.

Hedrick, A. 1992. Physiological responses to warm-up. *Strength and Conditioning Journal*, 14: 25-27.

Johnson, M.A., I.R. Gregson, D.E. Mills, J.T. Gonzalez, and G.R. Sharpe. 2014. Inspiratory muscle warm-up does not improve cycling time-trial performance. *European Journal of Applied Physiology*, 114: 1821-1830.

Jones, A.M., K. Koppo, and M. Burnley. 2003. Effects of prior exercise on metabolic and gas exchange responses to exercise. *Sports Medicine*, 33: 949-971.

Lee, J.F., K.M. Christmas, D.R. Machin, B.D. McLean, and E.F. Coyle. 2015. Warm skin alters cardiovascular responses to cycling after preheating and precooling. *Medicine and Science in Sports and Exercise*, 47: 1168-1176.

Levels, K., L.P.J. Teunissen, A. de Haan, J.J. de Koning, B. van Os, and H.A.M. Daanen. 2013. Effect of warm-up and precooling on pacing during a 15-km cycling time trial in the heat. *International Journal of Sports Physiology and Performance*, 8: 307-311.

Maughan, R.J., H. Otani, and P. Watson. 2012. Influence of relative humidity on prolonged exercise capacity in a warm environment. *European Journal of Applied Physiology*, 112: 2313-2321.

Olsen, O., M. Sjøhaug, M. van Beekvelt, and P.J. Mork. 2012. The effect of warm-up and cool-down exercise on delayed onset muscle soreness in the quadriceps muscle: A randomized controlled trial. *Journal of Human Kinetics*, 12: 59-68.

Passfield, L., and J.H. Doust. 2000. Changes in cycling efficiency and performance after endurance exercise. *Medicine and Science in Sports and Exercise*, 32: 1935-1941.

Racinais, S., S. Blonc, and O. Hue. 2005. Effects of active warm-up and diurnal increase in temperature on muscular power. *Medicine and Science in Sports and Exercise*, 37: 2134-2139.

Safran, M.R., A.V. Seaber, and W.E. Garrett. 1989. Warm-up and muscular injury prevention: An update. *Sports Medicine*, 8: 239-249.

Stewart, D., A. Macaluso, and G. De Vito. 2003. The effect of an active warm-up on surface EMG and muscle performance in healthy humans. *European Journal of Applied Physiology*, 89: 509-513.

Teles, M.C., I.A. Fonseca, J.B. Martins, M.M. de Carvalho, M. Xavier, S.J. Costa, N.C. de Avelar, V.G. Ribeiro, F.S. Salvador, L. Augusto, V.A. Mendonça, and A.C. Lacerda. 2015. Comparison between whole-body vibration, light-emitting diode, and cycling warm-up on high-intensity physical performance during sprint bicycle exercise. *Journal of Strength and Conditioning Research*, 29: 1542-1550.

Tomaras, E.K., and B.R. MacIntosh. 2011. Less is more: Standard warm-up causes fatigue and less warm-up permits greater cycling power output. *Journal of Applied Physiology*, 111: 228-235.

Wittekind, A., C.E. Cooper, C.E. Elwell, T.S. Leung, and R. Beneke. 2012. Warm-up effects on muscle oxygenation, metabolism and sprint cycling performance. *European Journal of Applied Physiology*, 112: 3129-3139.

Wittekind, A., and R. Beneke. 2011. Metabolic and performance effects of warm-up intensity on sprint cycling. *Scandinavian Journal of Medicine and Science in Sports*, 21: e201-e207.

Chapter 34

Andersen, J.C. 2005. Stretching before and after exercise: Effect on muscle soreness and injury risk. *Journal of Athletic Training*, 40: 218-220.

Asplund, C., C. Webb, and T. Barkdull. 2005. Neck and back pain in bicycling. *Current Sports Medicine Reports*, 4: 271-274.

Beach, T.A., R.J. Parkinson, J.P. Stothart, and J.P. Callaghan. 2005. Effects of prolonged sitting on the passive flexion stiffness of the in vivo lumbar spine. *Spine Journal*, 5:145-154.

Behm, D.G., A. Bambury, F. Cahill, and K. Power. 2004. Effect of acute static stretching on force, balance, reaction time, and movement time. *Medicine and Science in Sports and Exercise*, 36: 1397-1402.

Bini, R., and F. Diefenthaeler. 2010. Kinetics and kinematics analysis of incremental cycling to exhaustion. *Sports Biomechanics*, 9: 223-235.

Cunha, A.C., T.N. Burke, F.J. França, and A.P. Marques. 2008. Effect of global posture reeducation and of static stretching on pain, range of motion, and quality of life in women with chronic neck pain: A randomized clinical trial. *Clinics*, 63: 763-770.

Curry, B.S., D. Chengkalath, G.J. Crouch, M. Romance, and P.J. Manns. 2009. Acute effects of dynamic stretching, static stretching, and light aerobic activity on muscular performance in women. *Journal of Strength and Conditioning Research*, 23(6): 1811-1819.

De Vey Mesdagh, K. 1998. Personal perspective: In search of an optimum cycling posture. *Applied Ergonomics*, 29: 325-334.

Dorado, C., J. Sanchís-Moysi, and J.A. Calbet. 2004. Effects of recovery mode on performance, O_2 uptake, and O_2 deficit during high-intensity intermittent exercise. *Canadian Journal of Applied Physiology*, 29: 227-244.

Esposito, F., E. Cè, and E. Limonta. 2012. Cycling efficiency and time exhaustion are reduced after acute passive stretching administration. *Scandinavian Journal of Medicine and Science in Sports*, 22: 737-745.

Ingraham, S.J. 2003. The role of flexibility in injury prevention and athletic performance: Have we stretched the truth? *Minnesota Medicine*, 86: 58-61.

Khalil, T.M., S.S. Asfour, L.M. Martinez, S.M. Waly, R.S. Rosomoff, and H.L. Rosomoff. 1992. Stretching in the rehabilitation of low-back pain patients. *Spine*, 17: 311-317.

Kingsley, J.D., R.A. Zakrajsek, T.W. Nesser, and M.J. Gage. 2013. The effect of motor imagery and static stretching on anaerobic performance in trained cyclists. *Journal of Strength and Conditioning Research*, 27: 265-269.

Marsden, M.. 2010. Lower back pain in cyclists: A review of epidemiology, pathomechanics and risk factors. *International SportMed Journal*, 11: 216-225.

McGill, S. 2007. *Low back disorders: Evidence-based prevention and rehabilitation*. Champaign, IL: Human Kinetics.

McGorry, R.W., and J.H. Lin. 2012. Flexion relaxation and its relation to pain and function over the duration of a back pain episode. *PLoS One*, 7: e39207.

McHugh, M.P., and C.H. Cosgrave. 2010. To stretch or not to stretch: The role of stretching in injury prevention and performance. *Scandinavian Journal of Medicine and Science in Sports*, 20: 169-181.

Mika, A., P. Mika, B. Fernhall, and V.B. Unnithan. 2007. Comparison of recovery strategies on muscle performance after fatiguing exercise. *American Journal of Physical Medicine and Rehabilitation*, 86: 474-481.

Miladi, I., A. Temfemo, S.H. Mandengué, and S. Ahmaidi. 2011. Effect of recovery mode on exercise time to exhaustion, cardiorespiratory responses, and blood lactate after prior, intermittent supramaximal exercise. *Journal of Strength and Conditioning Research*, 25: 205-210.

Muyor, J.M., P.A. López-Miñarro, and F. Alacid. 2011a. A comparison of the thoracic spine in the sagittal plane between elite cyclists and non-athlete subjects. *Journal of Back and Musculoskeletal Rehabilitation*, 24: 129-135.

Muyor, J.M., P.A. López-Miñarro, and F. Alacid. 2011b. Spinal posture of thoracic and lumbar spine and pelvic tilt in highly trained cyclists. *Journal of Sports Science and Medicine*, 10: 355-361.

Muyor, J.M., P.A. López-Miñarro, and F. Alacid. 2011c. Spinal posture of thoracic and lumbar spine in master 40 cyclists. *International Journal of Morphology*, 29: 727-732.

Muyor, J.M., P.A. López-Miñarro, and F. Alacid. 2011d. Influence of hamstring muscles enxtensibility on spinal curvatures and pelvic tilt in highly trained cyclists. *Journal of Human Kinetics*, 29: 15-23.

Muyor, J.M., P.A. López-Miñarro, and F. Alacid. 2013a. Comparison of sagittal lumbar curvature between elite cyclists and non-athletes. *Science and Sports*, 28: e167-e173.

Muyor, J.M., P.A. López-Miñarro, and F. Alacid. 2013b. The relationship between hamstring muscle extensibility and spinal postures varies with the degree of knee extension. *Journal of Applied Biomechanics*, 29: 678-686.

Muyor, J.M., P.A. López-Miñarro, F. Alacid, and A.J. Casimiro. 2012. Evolution of spinal morphology and pelvic tilt in cyclists of different ages: A cross sectional study. *International Journal of Morphology*, 30: 199-204.

O'Connor, D.M., M.J. Crowe, and W.L. Spinks. 2006. Effects of static stretching on leg power during cycling. *Journal of Sports Medicine and Physical Fitness*, 46: 52-56.

Peck, E., G. Chomko, D.V. Gaz, and A.M. Farrell. 2014. The effects of stretching on performance. *Current Sports Medicine Reports*, 13: 179-185.

Polga, D.J., B.P. Beaubien, P.M. Kallemeier, K.P. Schelhas, W.D. Lee, G.R. Buttermann, and K.B. Wood. 2004. Measurement of *in vivo* intradiscal pressure in healthy thoracic intervertebral disc. *Spine*, 29: 1320-1324.

Rajabi, R., A. Freemont, and P. Doherty. 2000. The investigation of cycling position on thoracic spine: A novel method of measuring thoracic kyphosis in the standing position. *Archives of Physiology and Biochemistry*, 1: 142.

Ratamess, N. 2012. *ACSM's foundations of strength training and conditioning*. Philadelphia: Lippincott Williams & Wilkins.

Salai, M., T. Brosh, A. Blankstein, A. Oran, and A. Chechik. 1999. Effect of changing the saddle angle on the incidence of low back pain in recreational bicyclists. *British Journal of Sports Medicine*, 33: 398-400.

Solomonow, M., B.H. Zhou, R.V. Baratta, and E. Burger E. 2003. Biomechanics and electromyography of a cumulative lumbar disorder: Response to static flexion. *Clinical Biomechanics*, 18: 890-898.

Taylor, D.C., J.D. Dalton, A.V. Seaber, and W.E. Garret. 1990. Viscoelastic properties of muscle-tendon units: The biomechanical effects of stretching. *American Journal of Sports Medicine*, 18: 300-309.

Usabiaga, J., R. Crespo, I. Iza, J. Aramendi, N. Terrados, and J.J. Poza. 2007. Adaptation of the lumbar spine to different positions in the bicycle racing. *Spine*, 22: 1965-1969.

Wilke, H.J., P. Neef, M. Caimi, T. Hoogland, and L.E. Claes. 1999. New in vivo measurements of pressures in the intervertebral disc in daily life. *Spine*, 24: 755-762.

Wolfe, A.E., L.E. Brown, J.W. Corburn, R.D. Kersey, and M. Bottaro. 2011. Timer course of the effects of static stretching on cycling economy. *Journal of Strength and Conditioning Research*, 25: 2980-2984.

Yoo, W.G. 2013. Effect of thoracic stretching, thoracic extension exercise and exercises for cervical and scapular posture on thoracic kyphosis angle and upper thoracic pain. *Journal of Physical Therapy Science*, 25: 1509-1510.

Chapter 35

Abbiss, C.R., and P.B. Laursen. 2005. Models to explain fatigue during prolonged endurance cycling. *Sports Medicine*, 10: 865-898.

Abbiss, C.R., and P.B. Laursen. 2008. Describing and understanding pacing strategies during athletic competition. *Sports Medicine*, 3: 239-252.

Abbiss, C.R., P. Menaspa, V. Villerius, and D.T. Martin. 2013a. Invited commentary: Distribution of power output when establishing a breakaway in cycling.

International Journal of Sports Physiology and Performance, 8(4): 452-455.

Abbiss, C.R., M.L. Ross, L.A. Garvican, N. Ross, T. Pottgiesser, J. Gregory, and D.T. Martin. 2013b. The distribution of pace adopted by cyclists during a cross-country mountain bike World Championships. *Journal of Sports Sciences*, 7: 787-794.

Aisbett, B., P. Le Rossignol, G.K. McConell, C.R. Abbiss, and R. Snow. 2009a. Effects of starting strategy on 5-min cycling time-trial performance. *Journal of Sports Sciences*, 11: 1201-1209.

Aisbett, B., P. Lerossignol, G.K. McConell, C.R. Abbiss, and R. Snow. 2009b. Influence of all-out and fast start on 5-min cycling time trial performance. *Medicine and Science in Sports and Exercise*, 10: 1965-1971.

Allen, H., and A. Coggan. 2010. *Training and racing with a power meter*. 2nd ed. Boulder, CO: VeloPress.

Atkinson, G., and A. Brunskill. 2000. Pacing strategies during a cycling time trial with simulated headwinds and tailwinds. *Ergonomics*, 10: 1449-1460.

Atkinson, G., O. Peacock, and M. Law. 2007. Acceptability of power variation during a simulated hilly time trial. *International Journal of Sports Medicine*, 2: 157-163.

Atkinson, G., O. Peacock, and L. Passfield. 2007. Variable versus constant power strategies during cycling time-trials: Prediction of time savings using an up-to-date mathematical model. *Journal of Sports Sciences*, 9: 1001-1009.

Baron, B., F. Moullan, F. Deruelle, and T.D. Noakes. 2011. The role of emotions on pacing strategies and performance in middle and long duration sport events. *British Journal of Sports Medicine*, 6: 511-517.

Billat, L.V., J.P. Koralsztein, and R.H. Morton. 1999. Time in human endurance models - from empirical models to physiological models. *Sports Medicine*, 6: 359-379.

Bishop, D., D. Bonetti, and B. Dawson. 2002. The influence of pacing strategy on VO_2 and supramaximal kayak performance. *Medicine and Science in Sports and Exercise*, 6: 1041-1047.

Candau, R.B., F. Grappe, M. Menard, B. Barbier, G.Y. Millet, M.D. Hoffman, A.R. Belli, and J.D. Rouillon. 1999. Simplified deceleration method for assessment of resistive forces in cycling. *Medicine and Science in Sports and Exercise*, 10: 1441-1447.

CyclingPowerLab. 2008–2014. Power models: Variable power pacing model. www.cyclingpowerlab.com/timetrialpacingstrategy.aspx

de Koning, J.J., M.F. Bobbert, and C. Foster. 1999. Determination of optimal pacing strategy in track cycling with an energy flow model. *Journal of Science and Medicine in Sport*, 3: 266-277.

di Prampero, P.E., G. Cortili, P. Mognoni, and F. Saibene. 1979. Equation of motion of a cyclist. *Journal of Applied Physiology*, 1: 201-206.

Edwards, A.M., and R.C. Polman. 2013. Pacing and awareness: brain regulation of physical activity. *Sports Medicine*, 11: 1057-1064.

Foster, C., J. Hoyos, C. Earnest, and A. Lucia. 2005. Regulation of energy expenditure during prolonged athletic competition. *Medicine and Science in Sports and Exercise*, 4: 670-675.

Foster, C., M. Schrager, A.C. Snyder, and N.N. Thompson. 1994. Pacing strategy and athletic performance. *Sports Medicine*, 2: 77-85.

Fukuba, Y., and B.J. Whipp. 1999. A metabolic limit on the ability to make up for lost time in endurance events. *Journal of Applied Physiology*, 2: 853-861.

Hettinga, F.J., J.J. De Koning, and C. Foster. 2009. VO_2 response in supramaximal cycling time trial exercise of 750 to 4000 m. *Medicine and Science in Sports and Exercise*, 1: 230-236.

Keller, J.B. 1974. Optimal velocity in a race. *American Mathematical Monthly*, 5: 474-480.

Le Meur, Y., C. Hausswirth, S. Dorel, F. Bignet, J. Brisswalter, and T. Bernard. 2009. Influence of gender on pacing adopted by elite triathletes during a competition. *European Journal of Applied Physiology*, 4: 535-545.

Menaspà, P., F.M. Impellizzeri, E.C. Haakonssen, D.T. Martin, and C.R. Abbiss. 2014. Consistency of commercial devices for measuring elevation gain. *International Journal of Sports Physiology and Performance*, 9(5): 884-886.

Menaspà, P., M. Quod, D.T. Martin, J. Victor, and C.R. Abbiss. 2013. Physiological demands of road sprinting in professional and U23 cycling. A pilot study. *Journal of Science in Cycling*, 2: 35-39.

Morton, R.H. 2006. The critical power and related whole-body bioenergetic models. *European Journal of Applied Physiology*, 4: 339-354.

Noakes, T.D., A. St Clair Gibson, and E.V. Lambert. 2005. From catastrophe to complexity: A novel model of integrative central neural regulation of effort and fatigue during exercise in humans. Summary and conclusions. *British Journal of Sports Medicine*, 2: 120-124.

Simmons, A. 2008. *Quantifying the effective application of pacing strategies in cycling time trial events: The Pacing Optimisation Index (POI)*. Richard Stern Training.

St. Clair Gibson, A., E.V. Lambert, L.H.G. Rauch, R. Tucker, D.A. Baden, C. Foster, and T.D. Noakes. 2006. The role of information processing between the brain and peripheral physiological systems in pacing and perception of effort. *Sports Medicine*, 8: 705-722.

Swain, D.P. 1997. A model for optimizing cycling performance by varying power on hills and in wind. *Medicine and Science in Sports and Exercise*, 8: 1104-1108.

van Ingen Schenau, G.J., J.J. de Koning, and G. de Groot. 1992. The distribution of anaerobic energy in 1000 and 4000 metre cycling bouts. *International Journal of Sports Medicine*, 6: 447-451.

Wilberg, R.B., and J. Pratt. 1988. A survey of the race profiles of cyclists in the pursuit and kilo track events. *Canadian Journal of Sport Sciences*, 4: 208-213.

Chapter 37

Baron, R. 2001. Aerobic and anaerobic characteristics of off-road cyclists. *Medicine and Science in Sports and Exercise*, 33(8): 1387-1393.

Burr, J.F., C. Taylor Drury, A.C. Ivey, and D.E.R. Warburton. 2012. Physiological demands of downhill mountain biking. *Journal of Sports Sciences*, 30(6): 1777-1785.

Gregory, J., D. Johns, and J. Walls. 2007. Relative vs absolute physiological measures as predictors of mountain bike cross-country race performance. *Journal of Strength and Conditioning Research*, 21(1): 17-22.

Hurst, H.T., and S. Atkins. 2002. The physiological demands of downhill mountain biking as determined by heart rate monitoring. *Proceedings of the 7th Annual Congress of the European College of Sports Sciences*.

Hurst, H.T., and S. Atkins. 2006. Power output of field-based downhill mountain biking. *Journal of Sports Sciences*, 24(10): 1047-1053.

Hurst, H.T., M. Swarén, K. Hébert-Losier, F. Ericsson, and H-C. Holmberg. 2012a. Anaerobic power and cadence characteristics of elite cross-country and downhill mountain bikers. *Proceedings of the 17th Annual Congress of the European College of Sports Sciences*.

Hurst, H.T., M. Swaren, K. Herber-Losier, F. Ericsson, J. Sinclair, S. Atkins, and H-C. Holmberg. 2013. GPS-based evaluation of activity profiles in elite downhill mountain biking and the influence of course terrain. *Journal of Science and Cycling*, 2(1): 25-32.

Hurst, H.T., M. Swaren, K. Herber-Losier, F. Ericsson, J. Sinclair, S. Atkins, and H-C. Holmberg. 2012b. Influence of course type on upper body muscle activity in elite cross-country and downhill mountain bikers during off road downhill cycling. *Journal of Cycling Science*, 1(2): 2-9.

Impellizzeri, F., and S. Marcora. 2007. The physiology of mountain biking. *Sports Medicine*, 37(1): 59-71.

Impellizzeri, F., E. Rampinini, A. Sassi, P. Mognoni, and S. Marcora. 2005. Physiological correlates to off-road cycling performance. *Journal of Sports Sciences*, 23(1): 41-47.

Impellizzeri, F., A. Sassi, M. Rodriguez-Alonso, P. Mognoni, and S. Marcora. 2002. Exercise intensity during off-road cycling competitions. *Medicine and Science in Sports and Exercise*, 34(11): 1808-1813.

Lee, H., D.T. Martin, J.M. Anson, D. Grundy, and A.G. Hahn. 2002. Physiological characteristics of successful mountain bikers and professional road cyclists. *Journal of Sports Sciences*, 20: 1001-1008.

Lucía, A., J. Hoyos, and J.L. Chicharro. 2001. Physiology of professional road cycling. *Sports Medicine*, 31(5): 325-337.

MacRae, H.S.H., K.J. Hise, and P.J. Allen. 2000. Effects of front and dual suspension mountain bike systems on uphill cycling performance. *Medicine and Science in Sports and Exercise*, 32(7): 1276-1280.

Padilla, S., I. Mujika, G. Cuesta, and J.J. Goiriena. 1999. Level ground and uphill cycling ability in professional road cycling. *Medicine and Science in Sports and Exercise*, 31(6): 878-885.

Patterson, R.P., and M.I. Moreno. 1990. Bicycle pedalling forces as a function of pedalling rate and power output. *Medicine and Science in Sports and Exercise*, 22(4): 512-516.

Seifert, J.G., M.J. Luetkemeier, M.K. Spencer, D. Miller, and E.R. Burke. 1997. The effects of mountain bike suspension systems on energy expenditure, physical exertion, and time trial performance during mountain bicycling. *International Journal of Sports Medicine*, 18(3): 197-200.

Sperlich, B., S. Achtzehn, M. Buhr, C. Zinner, S. Zelle, and H-C. Holmberg. 2012. Salivary cortisol, heart rate, and blood lactate responses during elite downhill mountain bike racing. *International Journal of Sports Physiology and Performance*, 7(1): 47-52.

Stapelfeldt, B., A. Schwirtz, Y.O. Schumacher, and M. Hillebrecht. 2004. Workload demands in mountain bike racing. *International Journal of Sports Medicine*, 25: 294-300.

Warner, S., J. Shaw, and G. Dalsky. 2002. Bone mineral density of competitive male mountain and road cyclists. *Bone*, 30(1): 281-286.

Wilber, R.L., K.M. Zawadzki, J.T. Kearney, M.P. Shannon, and D. Disalvo. 1997. Physiological profile of elite off-road and road cyclists. *Medicine and Science in Sports and Exercise*, 29(8): 1090-1094.

Wingo, J.E., D.J. Casa, E.M. Berger, W.O. Dellis, J.C. Knight, and J.M. McClung. 2004. Influence of a pre-exercise glycerol hydration beverage on performance and physiologic function during mountain-bike races in the heat. *Journal of Athletic Training*, 39(2): 169-175.

Chapter 38

Aisbett, B., P. Le Rossignol, G.K. McConell, C.R. Abbiss, and R. Snow. 2009a. Effects of starting strategy on 5-min cycling time-trial performance. *Journal of Sports Sciences*, 27(11): 1201-1209.

Aisbett, B., P. Lerossignol, G.K. McConnell, and C.R. Abbiss. 2009b. Influence of all-out and fast start on 5-min cycling time trial performance. *Medicine and Science in Sports and Exercise*, 41(10): 1965-1971.

Balsom, P.D., J.Y. Seger, B. Sjödin, and B. Ekblom. 1992. Physiological responses to maximal intensity intermittent exercise. *European Journal of Applied Physiology and Occupational Physiology*, 65(2): 144-149.

Bassett, D.R., Jr., C.R. Kyle, L. Passfield, J.P. Broker, and E.R. Burke. 1999. Comparing cycling world hour records, 1967-1996: Modeling with empirical data. *Medicine and Science in Sports and Exercise*, 31(11): 1665-1676.

Broker, J.P., C.R. Kyle, and E.R. Burke. 1999. Racing cyclist power requirements in the 4000-m individual and team pursuits. *Medicine and Science in Sports and Exercise*, 31(11): 1677-1685.

Coyle, E.F., M.E. Feltner, S.A. Kautz, M.T. Hamilton, S.J. Montain, A.M. Baylor, L.D. Abraham, and G.W. Petrek. 1991. Physiological and biomechanical factors associated with elite endurance cycling performance. *Medicine and Science in Sports and Exercise*, 23(1): 93-107.

Craig, N.P., and K.I. Norton. 2001. Characteristics of track cycling. *Sports Medicine*, 31(7): 457-468.

Craig, N.P., K.I. Norton, P.C. Bourdon, S.M. Woolford, T. Stanef, B. Squires, T.S. Olds, R.A.J. Conyers, and C.B.V. Walsh. 1993. Aerobic and anaerobic indices contributing to track endurance cycling performance. *European Journal of Applied Physiology and Occupational Physiology*, 67(2): 150-158.

Craig, N.P., K.I. Norton, R.A. Conyers, S.M. Woolford, P.C. Bourdon, T. Stanef, and C.B. Walsh. 1995a. Influence of test duration and event specificity on maximal accumulated oxygen deficit of high performance track cyclists. *International Journal of Sports Medicine*, 16(8): 534-540.

Craig, N.P., K.I. Norton, R.A.J. Conyers, S.M. Woolford, P.C. Bourdon, and C.B.V. Walsh. 1995b. Influence of test duration and event specificity on maximal accumulated oxygen deficit on high performance track cyclists. *International Journal of Sports Medicine*, 16(8): 534-540.

Craig, N.P., F.S. Pyke, and K.I. Norton. 1989. Specificity of test duration when assessing the anaerobic lactacid capacity of high-performance track cyclists. *International Journal of Sports Medicine*, 10(4): 237-242.

Dorel, S., C.A. Hautier, O. Rambaud, D. Rouffet, E. Van Praagh, J.R. Lacour, and M. Bourdin. 2005. Torque and power-velocity relationships in cycling: Relevance to track sprint performance in world-class cyclists. *International Journal of Sports Medicine*, 26(9): 739-746.

Driss, T., and H. Vandewalle. 2013. The measurement of maximal (anaerobic) power output on a cycle ergometer: A critical review. *BioMed Research International*, 589361.

Gardner, A.S., J.C. Martin, D.T. Martin, M. Barras, and D.G. Jenkins. 2007. Maximal torque- and power-pedaling rate relationships for elite sprint cyclists in laboratory and field tests. *European Journal of Applied Physiology*, 101(3): 287-292.

Glaister, M., M.H. Stone, A.M. Stewart, M.G. Hughes, and G.L. Moir. 2006. Aerobic and anaerobic correlates of multiple sprint cycling performance. *Journal of Strength and Conditioning Research*, 20(4): 792-798.

Haakonssen, E.C., M. Barras, L.M. Burke, D.G. Jenkins, and D.T. Martin. 2016. Body composition of female road and track endurance cyclists: Normative values and typical changes in female road and track endurance cyclists. *European Journal of Sport Science*, 16(6): 1-9.

Hettinga, F., J.J. De Koning, and C. Foster. 2009. $\dot{V}O_2$ response in supramaximal cycling time trial exercise of 750 to 4000m. *Medicine and Science in Sports and Exercise*, 41(1): 230- 236.

Hettinga, F.J., J.J. De Koning, E. Meijer, L. Teunissen, and C. Foster. 2007. Biodynamics: Effect of pacing strategy on energy expenditure during a 1500-m cycling time trial. *Medicine and Science in Sports and Exercise*, 39(12): 2212-2218.

Jeukendrup, A.E., N.P. Craig, and J.A. Hawley. 2000. The bioenergetics of world class cycling. *Journal of Science and Medicine in Sport*, 3(4): 414-433.

McLean, B.D., and A.W. Parker. 1989. An anthropometric analysis of elite Australian track cyclists. *Journal of Sports Sciences*, 7(3): 247-255.

Miura, A., C. Shiragiku, Y. Hirotoshi, A. Kitano, M.Y. Endo, T.J. Barstow, R.H. Morton, and Y. Fukuba. 2009. The effect of prior heavy exercise on the parameters of the power-duration curve for cycle ergometry. *Applied Physiology, Nutrition, and Metabolism*, 34(6): 1001-1007.

Mujika, I., and S. Padilla. 2001. Physiological and performance characteristics of male professional road cyclists. *Sports Medicine*, 31(7): 479-487.

Ofoghi, B., J. Zeleznikow, D. Dwyer, and C. Macmahon. 2013. Modelling and analysing track cycling Omnium performances using statistical and machine learning techniques. *Journal of Sports Sciences*, 31(9): 954-962.

Padilla, S., I. Mujika, F. Angulo, and J.J. Goiriena. 2000. Scientific approach to the 1-h cycling world record: A case study. *Journal of Applied Physiology*, 89(4): 1522-1527.

Palmer, C.D., A.M. Jones, G.J. Kennedy, and J. Cotter. 2009. Effects of prior heavy exercise on energy supply and 4000-m cycling performance. *Medicine and Science in Sports and Exercise*, 41(1): 221-229.

Schumacher, Y.O., and P. Mueller. 2002. The 4000-m team pursuit cycling world record: Theoretical and practical aspects. *Medicine and Science in Sports and Exercise*, 34(6): 1029-1036.

Chapter 39

Bertucci, W.M., and C. Hourde. 2011. Laboratory testing and field performance in BMX riders. *Journal of Sports Science and Medicine*, 10(2): 417-419.

Bertucci, W., C. Hourde, A. Manolova, and F. Vettoretti. 2007. Mechanical performance factors of the BMX acceleration phase in trained riders. *Science and Sports*, 22(3-4): 179-181.

Blasco-Lafarga, C., A. Montoya-Vieco, I. Martinez-Navarro, M. Mateo-March, and J.E. Gallach. 2013. Six hundred meter-run and broken 800's contribution to pacing improvement in eight hundred meter-athletics: Role of expertise and training implications. *Journal of Strength and Conditioning Research*, 27(9): 2405-2413.

Campillo, P., T. Doremus, and J.M. Hespel. 2007. Pedaling analysis in BMX by telemetric collection of mechanic variables. *Brazilian Journal of Biomotricity*, 1(2): 15-27.

Chiementin, X., S. Crequy, and W. Bertucci. 2012. New statistic analysis for BMX rider. *Computer Methods in Biomechanics and Biomedical Engineering*, 15(suppl. 1): 261-262.

Chiementin, X., S. Crequy, L. Rasolofondraibe, and W. Bertucci. 2012. New performance indicators for BMX riders. *Computer Methods in Biomechanics and Biomedical Engineering*, 15(suppl. 1): 218-219.

Córdova, A., G. Villa, J. Seco, and I. Latasa. 2009. *Preliminary report on Q-Rings. Analysis of physiological and biomechanical effects of oval variable geared chainrings (Q-Rings) in comparison to conventional circular chainrings*. University of Vallodolid, Spain.

Debraux, P., A.V. Manolova, M. Soudain-Pineau, C. Hourde, and W. Bertucci. 2013. Maximal torque and power pedaling rate relationships for high level BMX riders in field tests. *Journal of Science and Cycling*, 2(1): 51-57.

Herman, C.W., S.J. McGregor, H. Allen, and E.M. Bollt. 2009. Power capabilities of elite Bicycle Motocross (BMX) racers during field testing in preparation for 2008 Olympics: 2321: Board #209 May 28 3:30 PM–5:00 PM. *Medicine and Science in Sports and Exercise*, 41(5): 306-307.

Louis, J., F. Billaut, T. Bernad, F. Vettoretti, C. Hausswirth, and J. Brisswalter. 2013. Physiological demands of a simulated BMX competition. *International Journal of Sports and Medicine*, 34(6): 491-496.

Mateo-March, M., C. Blasco-Lafarga, D. Doran, R.C. Romero-Rodríguez, and M. Zabala. 2012a. Notational analysis of European, World, and Olympic BMX cycling races. *Journal of Sports Science and Medicine*, 11: 502-509.

Mateo-March, M., E. Fernández-Peña, C. Blasco-Lafarga, J. Morente-Sánchez, and M. Zabala. 2014. Does a non-circular chainring improve performance in the bicycle motocross cycling start sprint? *Journal of Sports Science and Medicine*, 13: 97-104.

Mateo-March, M., M. Zabala, C. Blasco-Lafarga, and J. Guzman. 2012b. Blood lactate concentration versus design and difficulty of the track in BMX. *Revista Internacional de Medicina y Ciencias de la Actividad Física y del Deporte*, 12(45): 52-65.

Mateo-March, M., M. Zabala, and J.J. González-Badillo. 2012. Effects of the orientation of the maximum torque point with a Q-Rin non-circular chainring system on the BMX cycling sprint performance. *Science and Sports*, 27(3): e15-e19.

Mateo, M., C. Blasco-Lafarga, and M. Zabala. 2011. Pedaling power and speed production vs. technical factors and track difficulty in bicycle motocross cycling. *Journal of Strength Conditioning Research*, 25(12): 3248-3256.

Mateo, M., and M. Zabala. 2007. Optimización del rendimiento en la salida ciclista de BMX mediante la técnica slingshot [Improvement of performance of BMX cycling gate start by using slingshot technique] www.efdeportes.com/efd111/optimizaciondel-rendimiento-en-la-salida-ciclista-de-bmx.htm. (In Spanish:English abstract). *Lecturas: EF y Deportes, 111.*

Romero-Rodríguez, R.C., M. Mateo-March, and M. Zabala. 2013. The dilemma of using flat vs. clip pedals since early ages in BMX cycling: Influence of age and previous experience. *Science and Sports*, 28(3): e71-e76.

Rylands, L., and S.J. Roberts. 2014. Relationship between starting and finishing position in World Cup BMX racing. *International Journal of Performance Analysis in Sport*, 14(1): 14-23.

Rylands, L.P., S.J. Roberts, and H.T. Hurst. 2016. Effect of gear ratio on peak power and time to peak power in BMX cyclists. *European Journal of Sport Science*, 1-5.

Rylands, L.P., S.J. Roberts, H.T. Hurst, and I. Bentley. 2016. Effect of cadence selection on peak power and time of power production in elite BMX riders: A laboratory based study. *Journal of Sports Sciences*, 1-5

UCI (Union Cycliste Internationale). 2014. *BMX track guide.* www.uci.ch/mm/Document/News/NewsGeneral/16/58/58/UCIBMXtrackdesignguideline_v5_140326_Neutral.pdf

Zabala, M., B. Requena, C. Sánchez-Muñoz, J.J. González-Badillo, I. García, V. Ööpik, and M. Pääsuke. 2008. Effects of sodium bicarbonate ingestion on performance and perceptual responses in a laboratory-simulated BMX cycling qualification series. *Journal of Strength and Conditioning Research*, 22(5): 1645-1653.

Zabala, M., C. Sánchez-Muñoz, and A. Gutiérrez. 2009. [BMX cycling disicipline] La especialidad ciclista de BMX. In *Medicina y fisiología del ciclismo.* vol. I, ed. N. Médica. Madrid: FEMEDE, Spanish Federation of Sports Medicine.

Zabala, M., C. Sánchez-Muñoz, and M. Mateo. 2009. Effects of the administration of feedback on performance of the BMX cycling gate start. *Journal of Sports Science and Medicine*, 8(3): 393-400.

Chapter 40

Almond, C.S., A.Y. Shin, E.B. Fortescue, R.C. Mannix, D. Wypij, B.A. Binstadt, C.N. Duncan, D.P. Olson, A.E. Salerno, J.W. Newburger, and D.S. Greenes. 2005. Hyponatremia among runners in the Boston Marathon. *New England Journal of Medicine*, 352: 1550-1556.

Armstrong, L.E., D.J. Casa, H. Emmanuel, M.S. Ganio, J.F. Klau, E.C. Lee, C.M. Maresh, B.P. McDermott, R.L. Stearns, J.L. Vingren, J.E. Wingo, K.H. Williamson, and L.M. Yamamoto. 2012. Nutritional, physiological, and perceptual responses during a summer ultraendurance cycling event. *Journal of Strength and Conditioning Research*, 26: 307-318.

Armstrong, L.E., E.C. Johnson, M.S. Ganio, D.A. Judelson, J.L. Vingren, B.R. Kupchak, L.J. Kunces, C.X. Muñoz, A.L. McKenzie, and K.H. Williamson. 2015a. Effective body water and body mass changes during summer ultra-endurance road cycling. *Journal of Sports Sciences*, 33: 125-135.

Armstrong, L.E., E.C. Johnson, A.L. McKenzie, L.A. Ellis, and K.H. Williamson. 2015b. Endurance cyclist fluid intake, hydration status, thirst, and thermal sensations: Gender differences. *International Journal of Sport Nutrition and Exercise Metabolism*, 26: 161-197.

Ultraendurance cycling in a hot environment: Thirst, fluid consumption, and water balance. *Journal of Strength and Conditioning Research*, 29: 869-876.

Bescós, R., F.A. Rodríguez, X. Iglesias, B. Knechtle, A. Benítez, M. Marina, J.M. Padullés, P. Torrado, J. Vazquez, and T. Rosemann. 2012a. Nutritional behavior of cyclists during a 24-hour team relay race: A field study report. *Journal of the International Society of Sports Nutrition*, 9: 3.

Bescós, R., F.A. Rodríguez, X. Iglesias, A. Benítez, M. Marina, J.M. Padullés, P. Torrado, J. Vázquez, and B. Knechtle. 2012b. High energy deficit in an ultraendurance athlete in a 24-hour ultracycling race. *Baylor University Medical Center Proceedings*, 25: 124-128.

Bircher, S., A. Enggist, T. Jehle, and B. Knechtle. 2006. Effects of an extreme endurance race on energy balance and body composition: A case study. *Journal of Sports Science and Medicine*, 5: 154-162.

Bischof, M., B. Knechtle, C.A. Rüst, P. Knechtle, and T. Rosemann. 2013. Changes in skinfold thicknesses and body fat in ultra-endurance cyclists. *Asian Journal of Sports Medicine*, 4: 15-22.

Burke, L.M. 2001. Nutritional practices of male and female endurance cyclists. *Sports Medicine*, 31: 521-532.

Black, K.E., P.M. Skidmore, and R.C. Brown. 2012. Energy intakes of ultraendurance cyclists during competition: An observational study. *International Journal of Sport Nutrition and Exercise Metabolism*, 22: 19-23.

Chlíbková, D., B. Knechtle, T. Rosemann, A. Zákovská, and I. Tomášková. 2014. The prevalence of exercise-associated hyponatremia in 24-hour ultra-mountain bikers, 24-hour ultra-runners and multi-stage ultra-mountain bikers in the Czech Republic. *Journal of the International Society of Sports Nutrition*, 11: 3.

Francescato, M.P., and P.E. Di Prampero. 2002. Energy expenditure during an ultra-endurance cycling race. *Journal of Sports Medicine and Physical Fitness*, 42: 1-7.

García-Rovés, P.M., N. Terrados, S.F. Fernández, and A.M. Patterson. 1998. Macronutrients intake of top level cyclists during continuous competition: Change in the feeding pattern. *International Journal of Sports Medicine*, 19: 61-67.

Geesmann, B., J. Mester., and K. Koehler. 2014. Energy balance, macronutrient intake and hydration status during a 1,230-km ultra-endurance bike marathon. *International Journal of Sport Nutrition and Exercise Metabolism*, 24(5): 497-506.

Haupt, S., B. Knechtle, P. Knechtle, C.A. Rüst, T. Rosemann, and R. Lepers. 2013. The age-related performance decline in ultraendurance mountain biking. *Research in Sports Medicine*, 21: 146-158.

Heidenfelder, A., T. Rosemann, C.A. Rüst, and B. Knechtle. 2016. Pacing strategies of ultracyclists in the "Race Across America." *International Journal of Sports Physiology and Performance*, 11: 319-327.

Hoffman, M.D., and K. Fogard. 2012. Demographic characteristics of 161-km ultramarathon runners. *Research in Sports Medicine*, 20: 59-69.

Hulton, A.T., I. Lahart, K.L. Williams, R. Godfrey, S. Charlesworth, M. Wilson, C. Pedlar, and G. Whyte. 2010. Energy expenditure in the Race Across America (RAAM). *International Journal of Sports Medicine*, 31: 463-467.

Jeukendrup, A.E. 2011. Nutrition for endurance sports: Marathon, triathlon, and road cycling. *Journal of Sports Sciences*, 29(suppl 1): S91-S99.

Kipps, C., S. Sharma, and D.T. Pedoe. 2011. The incidence of exercise-associated hyponatraemia in the London marathon. *British Journal of Sports Medicine*, 45: 14-19.

Knechtle, B., N.L. Bragazzi, T. Rosemann, and C.A. Rüst. 2015. Pacing in a self-paced world record attempt in 24-h road cycling. *SpringerPlus*, 4: 650.

Knechtle, B., A. Enggist, and T. Jehle. 2005. Energy turnover at the Race Across America (RAAM): A case report. *International Journal of Sports Medicine*, 26: 499-503.

Knechtle, B., A. Wirth, P. Knechtle, and T. Rosemann. 2009. An ultra-cycling race leads to no decrease in skeletal muscle mass. *International Journal of Sports Medicine*, 30: 163-167.

Knechtle, B., M. Gnädinger, P. Knechtle, R. Imoberdorf, G. Kohler, P. Ballmer, T. Rosemann, and O. Senn. 2011. Prevalence of exercise-associated hyponatremia in male ultraendurance athletes. *Clinical Journal of Sport Medicine*, 21: 226-232.

Knechtle, B., A. Wirth, P. Knechtle, C.A. Rüst, and T. Rosemann. 2012a. A comparison of ultra-endurance cyclists in a qualifying ultra-cycling race for Paris–Brest–Paris and Race Across America-Swiss

cycling marathon. *Perceptual and Motor Skills*, 114: 96-110.

Knechtle, B., A. Wirth, P. Knechtle, C.A. Rüst, T. Rosemann, and R. Lepers. 2012b. No improvement in race performance by naps in male ultra-endurance cyclists in a 600-km ultra-cycling race. *Chinese Journal of Physiology*, 55: 125-133.

Lahart, I.M., A.M. Lane, A. Hulton, K. Williams, R. Godfrey, C. Pedlar, M.G. Wilson, and G.P. Whyte. 2013. Challenges in maintaining emotion regulation in a sleep and energy deprived state induced by the 4800km ultra-endurance bicycle race: The Race Across America (RAAM). *Journal of Sports Science and Medicine*, 12: 481-488.

Lindeman, A.K. 1991. Nutrient intake of an ultraendurance cyclist. *International Journal of Sport Nutrition*, 1: 79-85.

Luk, H.-Y., D.E. Levitt, E.C. Lee, M.S. Ganio, B.P. McDermott, B.R. Kupchak, B.K. McFarlin, D.W. Hill, L.E. Armstrong, and J.L. Vingren. 2016. Pro- and anti-inflammatory cytokine responses to a 164-km road cycle ride in a hot environment. *European Journal of Applied Physiology*, 116(10): 2007-2015.

Moyen, N.E., M.S. Ganio, L.D. Wiersma, S.A. Kavouras, M. Gray, B.R. McDermott, J.D. Adams, A.P. Binns, D.A. Judelson, A.M. McKenzie, E.C. Johnson, C.X. Muñoz, L.J. Kunces, and L.E. Armstrong. 2015. Hydration status affects mood state and pain sensation during ultra-endurance cycling. *Journal of Sports Sciences*, 33: 1962-1969.

Pozzi, L., B. Knechtle, P. Knechtle, T. Rosemann, R. Lepers, and C.A. Rüst. 2014. Sex and age-related differences in performance in a 24-hour ultra-cycling draft-legal event: A cross-sectional data analysis. *BMC Sports Science, Medicine and Rehabilitation*, 15(6): 19.

Reaburn, P., and B. Dascombe. 2008. Endurance performance in masters athletes. *European Review of Aging and Physical Activity*, 5: 31-42.

Rüst, C.A., B. Knechtle, P. Knechtle, and T. Rosemann. 2012. No case of exercise-associated hyponatraemia in top male ultra-endurance cyclists: The "Swiss Cycling Marathon." *European Journal of Applied Physiology*, 112: 689-697.

Rüst, C.A., B. Knechtle, T. Rosemann, and R. Lepers. 2013. Men cross America faster than women: The "Race Across America" from 1982 to 2012. *International Journal of Sports Physiology and Performance*, 8: 611-617.

Rüst, C.A., T. Rosemann, R. Lepers, and B. Knechtle. 2015. Gender difference in cycling speed and age of winning performers in ultra-cycling—the 508-mile "Furnace Creek" from 1983 to 2012. *Journal of Sports Sciences*, 33: 198-210.

Salihu, L., C.A. Rüst, T. Rosemann, and B. Knechtle. 2016. Sex difference in draft-legal ultra-distance events—a comparison between ultra-swimming and ultra-cycling. *Chinese Journal of Physiology*, 59: 87-99.

Shoak, M.A., B. Knechtle, P. Knechtle, C.A. Rüst, T. Rosemann, and R. Lepers. 2013. Participation and performance trends in ultracycling. *Open Access Journal of Sports Medicine,* 4: 41-51.

Sigg, K., B. Knechtle, C.A. Rüst, P. Knechtle, R. Lepers, and T. Rosemann. 2012. Central European triathletes dominate Double Iron ultratriathlon: Analysis of participation and performance 1985-2011. *Open Access Journal of Sports Medicine,* 3: 159-168.

Stewart, I.B., and K.L. Stewart. 2007. Energy balance during two days of continuous stationary cycling. *Journal of the International Society of Sports Nutrition,* 4: 15.

Vingren, J.L., R.G.Jr. Budnar, A.L. McKenzie, A.A. Duplanty, H.-Y. Luk, D.E. Levitt, and L.E. Armstrong. 2016. The acute testosterone, growth hormone, cortisol and interleukin-6 response to 164-km road cycling in a hot environment. *Journal of Sports Sciences,* 34: 694-699.

Wirnitzer, K.C., and E. Kornexl. 2014. Energy and macronutrient intake of a female vegan cyclist during an 8-day mountain bike stage race. *Baylor University Medical Center Proceedings,* 27(1): 42-45.

Zaryski, C., and D.J. Smith. 2005. Training principles and issues for ultra-endurance athletes. *Current Sports Medicine Reports,* 4: 165-170.

Zingg, M., B. Knechtle, C.A. Rüst, T. Rosemann, and R. Lepers. 2013. Age and gender difference in nondrafting ultra-endurance cycling performance: The "Swiss Cycling Marathon." *Extreme Physiology and Medicine,* 2: 18.

Index

A

Abbreviated Injury Scale (AIS) 236-237, 240
Absolute Record (UCI category) 461
acceleration, metabolic cost of 431-432
accelerometry 452, 454
acclimation, heat 134, 137-138, 219
acclimatization, heat 134, 136, 138
acromioclavicular joint separation 257-258
actin 67-68
α-actinin-3 R577X gene 21
active recovery 272, 275-276, 368
active relaxation 324
active shortening of muscle 71
active stretch 71
active warm-up 405-406
acute mountain sickness 162
ADAMS 224, 232
adaptations
    fat 184-185
    heat 134-138, 141
    strength-training 383-384
    training 354
adductor stretch 420
adenosine triphosphate–phosphocreatine system 13-14, 17
adolescence 293-294
adrenocorticotropic hormone 267
adventure bikes 30
adversity 320-321
aerobic capacity
    of cross-country mountain riders 445
    description of 16
    of downhill mountain riders 449-450
    of endurance track riders 465
aerobic fitness 133-134
aerobic metabolism 15-17
aerodynamic drag area 6-7, 95-96, 99, 102
aerodynamic drag (CdA)
    aero field testing of 100-101
    anthropometric estimation of 103
    body position effects on 104, 107-108

case study of 107-109
computational fluid dynamics for measuring 103
description of 93-95
dimpling effects on 98
drafting effects on 106-107
equipment effects on 104-106
helmet effects on 105, 107-108
Martin regression method for 101-102
measurement of 98-103
projected frontal area and 96, 98-99
reduction of 103-107
virtual elevation method for measuring 102
wind tunnel measurement of 99-100, 106
aerodynamics
    airfoils 96-97
    dimpling effects on 97-98
    importance of 92-93
    low-back pain and 248
    of simple shapes 93-98
    texturing effects on 97-98, 105
aero field testing 100-101
aero helmet 105, 107-108
aero road helmet 105, 107-108
aerosols 143
AICAR 225
airfoils 96-97
air pollutants
    aerosols 143
    carbon monoxide 143-145, 148
    categories of 143
    health effects of 145-146
    nitrogen dioxide 143-144, 146
    ozone 143-146
    particulate matter 142-145
    sulfur dioxide 143-146
air pollution
    anemia secondary to 148
    asthma secondary to 148-150
    cycling/cycling performance affected by 146-147
    definition of 142
    exercise-induced bronchoconstriction secondary to 148-150
    health effects of 145-146
    heat and 147
    medical issues related to 147-150

recommendations for avoiding 151
urban and rural sources of 145
vocal cord dysfunction secondary to 150-151
air resistance 5-7
AIS (Abbreviated Injury Scale) 236-237, 240
albuterol 149
aldosterone 218
Allen and Coggan's functional threshold power test 331, 336
all-rounders 4
ALPHA (Athlete Learning Program About Health and Antidoping) 228
altitude or hypoxic training
    algorithms for 153
    artificially induced hypoxic conditions for 166-168
    live high and train high model of 152-154
    live high and train low model of 154-158, 160, 168
    live low and train high model of 158-160, 168
    maximal oxygen consumption benefits of 152, 160
    physiological responses 162
    recommendations for 159-161
    summary of 167-168
    World Anti-Doping Agency policy on 166-167
altitude or hypoxic training camp
    adjustments in training during 163
    description of 161
    iron status measurements before 161, 163
    return to sea level after 163-166
aluminum frame 27-28, 40-42
American National Standards Institute 256
amino acids 186, 200
anaerobic capacity 369, 384, 464
anaerobic glycolysis 14-15
anemia 148
angiotensin I-converting enzyme gene 21
Animal-derived protein 186, 188
ankle position 87

About the Editors

Stephen Cheung, PhD, is the science and training editor for *PezCycling News*, focusing on translating the latest scientific research into practical guidance for both cyclists and coaches. He coauthored *Cutting-Edge Cycling* (Human Kinetics, 2012) and has written more than 100 articles that cover respiratory training, altitude training, precooling and fatigue in the heat, hydration, optimal cadence, pacing strategies, jet lag, supplements, hypoxic stress, and the reliability of exercise testing protocols.

Cheung holds a Canada Research Chair in environmental ergonomics at Brock University, where his research focuses on the effects of thermal and altitude stress on human physiology and performance. The author of *Advanced Environmental Exercise Physiology* (Human Kinetics, 2010), Cheung helped to establish the sport science support network for the Canadian Sport Centre in Atlantic Canada and has consulted with world champion cyclists along with the Canadian national rowing and snowboard teams on specific sport performance projects. He has also served as a cycling official and as a board member of the Canadian Cycling Association. Cheung lives in Fonthill, Ontario.

Mikel Zabala, PhD, is director of the Cycling Research Center in Granada, Spain, and editor in chief of the *Journal of Science and Cycling*. His research interests are cycling performance and doping prevention. He is a senior lecturer on the faculty of sport sciences at the University of Granada, teaching students who are seeking advanced degrees in cycling. He has authored numerous scientific papers about cycling and training and coached a number of international professional cyclists, serving as performance director for the renowned Movistar professional cycling team since 2012.

Beginning his career as a professional motocross rider and amateur bike racer, Zabala still competes as a masters cyclist. In 1999, he began working as a coach for the Spanish Cycling Federation and later served as manager of Spain's national mountain biking team. He currently works with the Spanish Cycling Federation as a project director, coordinating their doping prevention efforts. In 2013, he was named director of teaching and research for the Spanish Cycling Federation.

About the Contributors

Chris R. Abbiss, PhD, is an associate professor in human and exercise physiology within the School of Medical and Health Sciences at Edith Cowan University. His research interests center on human physiology and exercise performance, focusing on cycling, fatigue, thermoregulation, pacing strategies, training modalities, and recovery. Throughout his career he has worked closely with, and provided applied sport science services to, several professional cycling organizations. Because of this work he has published over 80 scientific manuscripts aimed at better understanding human physiology and exercise performance.

Hunter Allen, legendary cycling coach, is coauthor of *Training and Racing With a Power Meter* and *Cutting-Edge Cycling*, codeveloper of TrainingPeaks' WKO+ software, and CEO and founder of Peaks Coaching Group (PCG). Widely known as one of the top experts in the world in coaching endurance athletes using power meters, Hunter Allen's goal has always been to teach athletes how to maximize their training and racing potential through professional analysis of their power data. This purpose goes hand in hand with his philosophy that a power meter helps athletes discover their true

strengths and weaknesses, quantitatively assess their training improvements, and refine and maximize the focus of their training. Hunter has presented the training with power principles to coaches and athletes in over 200 seminars in more than 20 countries and continues to travel and teach each year. He also runs a thriving coaching business, manages cycling camps, and teaches webinars along with coaching his personal clients. For the past 15 years, PCG has been a leader in the industry in the field of power training for endurance cyclists. This unique opportunity has given Hunter the ability to review thousands of power files and racer profiles and develop an artful science of power training and coaching.

Marco Arkesteijn, PhD, is a lecturer in sport and exercise biomechanics at Aberystwyth University, United Kingdom. His PhD research focused on the effect of cycling technique on endurance-cycling performance. A particular focus therein was on the relationship between muscle activation, force production on the pedals, and the energy cost of cycling. He currently has several publications looking at uphill cycling and the effect of turbo trainer cycling on pedaling technique and efficiency.

Paul Barratt, PhD, is a sport biomechanist with more than 10 years of experience at the cutting edge of cycling science and technology. Over three Olympic campaigns with the English Institute of Sport and the Great Britain Cycling Team, he has delivered innovative, performance-influencing support to countless World and Olympic champions across track cycling, road cycling, mountain bike, and BMX disciplines. During this period, he has also been heavily involved in the Great Britain Cycling Team's outstanding research and development program, the Secret Squirrel Club.

Kate Bennett, PsyD, is a clinical sport psychologist and the director of Athlete Insight, PC. She devotes her practice to the clinical and performance needs of athletes. Dr. Bennett worked with Team SmartStop during their breakout season in 2014. Currently, she works individually with continental, pro-continental, and World Tour professional road cyclists as well as professional mountain bikers and cyclocross riders. Before becoming a psychologist, Dr. Bennett was an athletic trainer and cycling coach. During her coaching career, she coached several state and national champions and earned two national championships herself. Dr. Bennett presented at both the American Psychological Association and Association for Applied Sport Psychology annual conferences. Additionally, she regularly conducts sport psychology workshops for teams and individuals interested in excelling athletically by maximizing their mental game.

Rodrigo Rico Bini, PhD, is a lecturer on human biomechanics at the School of Physical Education of the Army in Brazil. Currently, Rodrigo is a member of the scientific board of the Brazilian Society of Biomechanics. Rodrigo is also the deputy editor of *Journal of Physical Education of the Army* and an associate editor of *Journal of Science and Cycling*. He is a member of the editorial boards of *Sports Biomechanics Journal*, *European Journal of Sport Science*, and the journal *Medicine*. Rodrigo is also coeditor of and contributor to *Biomechanics of Cycling*, published in 2014. Rodrigo has published more than 50 articles, most involving studies on cycling biomechanics.

Cristina Blasco-Lafarga combines researching tasks with lecturing on physical conditioning and exercise training at the University of Valencia, where she received her doctoral degree in 2008. After 15 years of teaching physical education in high school and a broad period of training elite sport people (from 1992 to today), in the last 6 years she has focused her studies on sport performance analysis, autonomic cardiac regulation, and complex systems and exercise training for the elderly. Dr. Blasco-Lafarga has published papers in prestigious journals on physiology, physical conditioning, training, and aging.

Todd M. Carver, MS, is based in Boulder, Colorado, and works as the head of human performance for Specialized Bicycles. In 2007 he cofounded the Retül Bike Fitting System that is widely used across the industry today. Todd holds a master's of science degree in integrative physiology from the University of Colorado and for the last 15 years has used his knowledge of cycling science to help professional and amateur riders improve performance and prevent injury. In his free time, Todd enjoys spending time with his wife and two boys, cycling, and skiing.

Kevin De Pauw graduated in July 2005 from the Vrije Universiteit Brussel (Brussels, Belgium) as master in physical education. Since May 2006 Kevin has been employed at the Research Group of Human Physiology, and he started his PhD project in February 2010 on cycling, recover, and the brain. Currently he is a postdoctoral researcher in the research group Human Physiology of the VUB and performs research in the field of human-robot interactions with emphasis on the physical and mental load. He is the author of 17 papers in scientific journals with an international referee system.

Kristen Dieffenbach, PhD, is an assistant professor of athletic coaching education at West Virginia University and is a consultant certified by the Association of Applied Sport Psychology. Currently, she is the coaching education representative on the NASPE Sport Steering Committee and is on the board for the National Council for Accreditation of Coaching Education. She also serves as an advisory board member with the USA Cycling Coaching Education Committee. Kristen is a professional coach with a category 1 (elite) USA Cycling license and a level II endurance specialization from USA Track and Field. She has coached for over 15 years at the high school, collegiate, recreational, and elite levels.

Dirk Friel is an ex-pro cyclist, cycling coach, entrepreneur, and cofounder of Peaksware and TrainingPeaks.com. Dirk started TrainingPeaks in 1999 when he was coaching with his father, Joe Friel, and recognized a need for coaching software to make the process of tracking, analyzing, and planning training programs more efficient and effective. Peaksware, LLC, was founded several years later to take the principles developed at TrainingPeaks and apply them to helping people achieve their best through deliberate practice independent of their specific goals. Today, Peaksware serves endurance athletes and

team sports as well as music instructors and students through software tools that connect creators, performers, and instructors. Dirk's primary role with Peaksware is to shape future products that serve coaches and instructors in an effort to allow them to offer better service to their athletes and students. Dirk lives in Boulder, Colorado, where he continues to coach, race bikes, ski, and enjoy the outdoors with his wife and daughter.

Andy Froncioni is a PhD in aerospace and mechanical engineering and is lead aerodynamicist for Alphamantis Technologies, a leader in cycling aerodynamics that has 12 aero test centers worldwide. The company has provided telemetry equipment to Team Sky and for numerous hour record attempts. Andy has been an aerodynamics consultant for Cycling Canada, USA Cycling, Cycling Australia, and the French Cycling Federation. His expertise includes bike position optimization and cycling performance analysis for solo and team efforts.

Luisa Giles is a faculty member in the Department of Sport Science at Douglas College in New Westminster, British Columbia. Luisa earned her doctorate degree from the University of British Columbia where her research and training were funded through Health Canada, the Fraser Basin Council, the Canadian Academy of Sports and Exercise Medicine, the Ministry of Environment, and the University of British Columbia. Dr. Giles' training and research focused on the cardiorespiratory responses to exercising in air pollution. Luisa formerly worked as a sport scientist with the Canadian BMX team and a knowl-

edge translation scientist at the National Collaborating Centre for Environmental Health. Luisa has served as a scientific advisor to the Clean Air Champions and as a director for the BC Environmental and Occupations Health Research Network and the AllerGen Students and New Professionals Network. Dr. Giles was formerly a member of the technical committee for the Canadian Standards Agency on Residential Carbon Monoxide Alarming Devices and the Federal, Provincial, and Territorial Indoor Air Quality and Health Group. Outside work, Luisa enjoys rock climbing, running, hiking, skiing, mountain biking, and growing vegetables.

Dina Griffin is a Colorado-based, board-certified specialist in sport dietetics and a registered dietitian nutritionist who has worked in the health and fitness industry for 10 years. She specializes in optimizing health and athletic performance for endurance athletes of all levels. Her work in the cycling community includes providing customized nutrition coaching for competitive road and off-road cyclists, ultracyclists, and randonneurs. Living in the mountains near Boulder, Colorado, Dina has completed numerous cycling events and races. She therefore has a personal understanding of the nutrition challenges encountered by various types of cyclists. She is an Ironman finisher and Leadville 100 run finisher and has competed in many other ultraevents.

Shona L. Halson is a senior physiologist at the Australian Institute of Sport, where her role involves service provision, education, and scientific research. She has a PhD in exercise physiology and has been involved in conducting research into the areas of recovery, fatigue, sleep, and travel. She is an associate editor of the *International Journal of Sports Physiology and Performance*. Shona was selected as the director of the Australian Olympic Committee Recovery Centre for the 2008 Beijing Olympic Games, the 2012 London Olympic Games, and the Rio 2016 Olympic Games. She has published numerous peer-reviewed articles and has authored several book chapters on sleep, fatigue, and recovery.

Dr. **James Hopker** is a senior lecturer in the School of Sport and Exercise Sciences at the University of Kent. He has a PhD in exercise physiology, for which he investigated the effects of training on cycling efficiency. Since completing his PhD, James has published an extensive amount of research connected with various aspects of cycling science such as cycling efficiency, training individualization, and the optimization of performance. These projects have engaged riders of all ranges of abilities from across the United Kingdom.

Javier Horcajo received his PhD in psychology from Universidad Autónoma de Madrid, where he works as professor in social psychology. His research focuses mainly on the factors and processes responsible for changes in attitudes and their practical application to social topics, health, and sport. Part of this work has resulted in several articles published in leading journals, such as *Psychological Science, Journal of Personality and Social Psychology*, and *Journal of Sport and Exercise Psychology*. He combines this academic activity and the psychological skills of training and coaching into professional cycling.

Dr. **Howard T. Hurst** is a senior lecturer in sport and exercise physiology at the University of Central Lancashire, Preston, UK. He completed his PhD in 2010, which investigated the effectiveness of acute hypoxic exposures for repeated sprint-cycling performance. Dr. Hurst has coauthored numerous scientific papers on the physiological and biomechanical demands of downhill and cross-country mountain biking along with several papers on the demands of BMX. He is a member of the International Society for the Advancement of Kinanthropometry and a registered sport nutritionist with the Association for Nutrition, and he has written a number of papers

on the use of ergogenic aids on cycling performance. Dr. Hurst has worked with a number of national and international bodies including British Cycling as a coauthor of several coaching handbooks. He has collaborated with the Swedish National Cycling Federation and Swedish Olympic Committee to investigate upper-body muscle activity in cross-country MTB in the lead-up to the London 2012 Olympic Games and has worked with the Cycling Ireland BMX development squads. Previously, he worked as a mountain bike coach. In his spare time, he still competes regularly in triathlon, running, and mountain bike events.

Franco M. Impellizzeri (MS, PhD) is senior research fellow at the Schulthess Clinic (Zurich). His main areas of research in sport are training, testing, and research methods. He has worked for 10 years as head of research at the MAPEI Sport Research Centre (Italy), which was created to support the professional cycling team. He was also responsible for the training and testing of elite and top-professional level athletes, especially cyclists and mountain bikers. Franco Impellizzeri has published more than 130 papers in peer-reviewed journals. He is a member of the Skeptics Society and a member of the editorial boards of various scientific journals. He is associate editor of the *International Journal of Sports Physiology and Performance* and editor-in-chief of *Science and Medicine in Football*.

Professor **Simon Jobson** is a sport and exercise physiologist known for his work in the field of cycling science. Simon has published research findings in many areas related to cycling performance including efficiency, allometric scaling, and the ecological validity of laboratory testing. Simon's research applies mathematical techniques to the study of athletic training more generally. This work seeks to optimize the effectiveness of athletic training to maximize benefits for both elite athletes and recreational exercisers. As a BASES-accredited sport and exercise scientist, Simon applies the findings of his research when providing sport science support for many top athletes.

Beat Knechtle is a Swiss primary care physician working at the Gesundheitszentrum St. Gallen, Switzerland, and the Institute of Primary Care, University of Zurich, Switzerland. For more than 20 years, he has competed in ultradistance races in swimming, cycling, running, and triathlon. Because of his sporting pursuits, his main interests in research are predictive variables in ultraendurance, nutrition, and fluid metabolism in ultraendurance performance, and the age of peak athletic performance.

Michael Koehle MD, PhD is an associate professor in both sport medicine and kinesiology at the University of British Columbia. He practices sport and exercise medicine at the Allan McGavin Sport Medicine Centre. His research program combines exercise and environmental physiology ranging from basic mechanistic research to clinical field studies in remote environments and applied research for high-performance sport. Key research areas include high-altitude medicine and physiology, and the physiology of exercise in polluted air. As a physiologist, he runs the Environmental Physiology Laboratory at the University of British Columbia and works closely with the Canadian Sport Institute Pacific in applied sport science research. As a physician, he works with a number of elite and professional cyclists and triathletes.

Thomas Korff, PhD, is a senior lecturer at Brunel University, London. His main research interests are the biomechanics of child development and the biomechanics of cycling. Regarding the former, he has been investigating the mechanical determinants of movement in children. Specifically, he looked at the effect of developmental changes in segmental growth as well as the mechanical structure of muscles and tendons on muscular force production and movement performance in children. Regarding his cycling research, Thomas has been investigating the mechanical determinants of maximal and submaximal cycling performance. Thomas' work has been published in high-quality journals such as *Journal of Applied Physiology, Journal of Experimental Biology, Journal of Biomechanics*, and *Medicine and Science in Sport and Exercise*.

Paul B. Laursen earned his undergraduate and master's degrees in exercise science from the University of British Columbia (Canada, 2000) and his PhD in exercise physiology from the University of Queensland (Australia, 2004). His research interests include training program design, pacing, fatigue, recovery, hydration, thermoregulation, and athlete health. He has published more than 100 refereed manuscripts, and his work has been cited more than 5,000 times. Paul was an associate professor of exercise physiology at Edith Cowan University (Western Australia, 2004–2009), where he supervised

a number of doctoral candidates directly involved with national sport programs through the Australian Institute of Sport. He then worked as physiology manager for High Performance Sport New Zealand, where he led physiological support for the national Olympic sporting organizations of priority in New Zealand. He is currently an adjunct professor of exercise physiology at AUT University, New Zealand. He is also a high-performance consultant, author, entrepreneur, and coach to elite endurance athletes. Laursen is based in Revelstoke, British Columbia, Canada.

Victor Lun, MSc, MD, practices sport medicine at the University of Calgary (U of C) Sport Medicine Centre. He is the team physician for the U of C Dinos football team and a number of Canadian national teams, including long track speed skating, men's artistic gymnastics, water polo, and athletics and a consulting physician for the Canadian Sport Institute Calgary. Dr. Lun was a member of the Canadian Health and Science Team at the 2008 Beijing Summer Olympic Games and 2010 Vancouver Winter Olympic Games. Dr. Lun is a clinical assistant professor in the U of C Department of Family Medicine and director of the U of C Enhanced Skills Sport and Exercise Medicine Residency Program.

Manuel Mateo-March has been working for many years on different lines, always focused on sport performance in various cycling disciplines. He is currently working as the team manager of the Spanish BMX national team (Spanish Cycling Federation) as well as working as a coach in Movistar Cycling Team since 2013. Lecturer of mountain biking in the La Creueta Institute of Onil, he is the associate director of the Cycling Research Center. He has written scientific papers about cycling and training and is deputy editor-in-chief of *Journal of Science and Cycling*.

Dr. **Romain Meeusen**, PhD, is head of the Human Physiology Research Group at the Vrije Universiteit Brussel. His research interest is focused on exercise and the brain in health and disease, exploring the influence of neurotransmitters on human performance, training, and rehabilitation. He teaches exercise physiology, training and coaching, and sports physiotherapy. He is past president of the Belgian Society of Kinesiology, the Belgian Federation of Sports Physiotherapy, and the Society of Kinesiology Belgium. He is a former board member of the European College of Sport  Science (ECSS) (2000–2013) and the American College of Sports Medicine (ACSM) (2010–2013). He is director of the Human Performance Lab of the Vrije Universiteit Brussel, where he works with several top athletes, and he is scientific advisor of the Lotto Cycling Institute (Lotto–Soudal professional cycling team).

Dr. **Paolo Menaspà** completed a PhD at Edith Cowan University in 2015 and is now a postdoctoral research fellow. He was awarded the 2015 Australian Institute of Sport Withers PhD Scholar Award for "having conducted exercise physiology research that has had a substantial impact on Australian sport." Paolo's research is primarily focused on examining road-cycling performance, including analysis of professional competitions. In conducting his research, he collaborates with national sport organizations such as Cycling Australia and professional cycling teams. Paolo was a member of the Australian team at the Rio Olympic Games, supporting the men's and women's road-cycling teams as a sport scientist.

José M. Muyor has a PhD in sport sciences. Currently, he is associate professor in the faculty of education sciences and scientific assessor at the Laboratory of Kinesiology, Biomechanics, and Ergonomics in the Research Central Services at the University of Almería (Spain). His studies are focused on biomechanics in cycling, spinal morphology, hamstring muscle extensibility, and posture in athletes.

Dr. **Pantelis Nikolaidis** is a Greek sport scientist who specializes in sports physiology. He studied sport science at the University of Athens (2001) and then focused on exercise physiology at the University of Prague as a scholar of the state scholarship foundation (PhD, 2008). Since 2008 he has run a private exercise physiology laboratory and collaborated with many sport clubs and athletes, mostly in the region of Athens and Piraeus (Greece). He has published more than 100 peer-reviewed scientific papers and has been a reviewer for more than 40 international scientific journals.

Carli M. Peters is a PhD student in the School of Kinesiology at the University of British Columbia, Vancouver, BC, Canada. Carli works in the Health and Integrative Physiology Laboratory under the supervision of Dr. A. W. Sheel. Her research interests include the assessment of respiratory muscle fatigue and airway remodeling in elite athletes.

Daniel J. Plews earned his undergraduate and master's degrees at Loughborough and Leeds Metropolitan Universities in the United Kingdom and a PhD from the Auckland University of Technology, New Zealand. His research focus during his PhD was on the practical application of heart rate variability to monitor training adaptation. Dan is the lead performance physiologist for Rowing New Zealand, which has been the number one rowing nation in the world for the past 3 years. Before that, Dan worked in Singapore, where he was the founder, team manager, and coach for the OCBC Singapore Professional Continental Cycling Team. In his spare time, he coaches professional Ironman-distance triathletes and competes himself. He has a personal best time of 3 hours, 57 minutes for the Half Ironman distance.

Bent R. Rønnestad, PhD, is a professor in exercise physiology at the Section for Sports Science, Lillehammer University College, Norway. He is a consultant for the Norwegian Olympic Federation, providing physiological research and supervision for endurance athletes and team sports. Major research interests of his research group include optimizing strength and endurance training for sport performance. Bent R. Rønnestad has published more than 50 international peer-reviewed research articles and textbook chapters.

Dr. **Larry Ruff** supervises the Manufacturing Innovation Learning Laboratory and teaches courses in manufacturing at Rensselaer Polytechnic Institute in Troy, New York. His background in bicycling started with the purchase of a Schwinn Varsity at age 14. Dr. Ruff started working in bicycle shops at age 16, and this activity led to racing and working with a local frame builder. He has designed and built frames for his own use and collects and restores vintage race bikes. He owned a bicycle shop for over a decade. Dr. Ruff has designed and built equipment to test bicycle frames and forks. This equipment has allowed him to do deflection, fatigue, and vibration testing for his own research and industrial sponsors. Dr. Ruff and some students have been working to solve manufacturing problems for several smaller bicycle companies.

Daniel Schade has been involved in moving sport biomechanics forward for more than 15 years. After graduating in sport science from the University of Münster and writing his final thesis on the analysis of saddle pressure mapping on custom saddles, he cofounded the cycling biomechanics brand gebioMized. He now works as a biomechanical researcher and develops sports analysis technology, such as tools for pressure mapping, motion capturing, and force analysis. His focus is on cycling, and he has more than 10 years of fitting experience. Daniel uses his expertise when providing biomechanical support to several pro tour teams, such as Trek–Segafredo, Movistar, Trek Factory Racing, Katusha, and HTC Highroad.

A. William Sheel, PhD, is a professor of exercise physiology in the School of Kinesiology at the University of British Columbia, Canada. His research interests focus on understanding the physiological basis and importance of cardiorespiratory interactions in various conditions such as exercise, disease, and hypoxia. Elite cyclists feature prominently in his program of research.

Rodney Siegel earned his undergraduate and honors degrees in exercise and sport science from Deakin University in Melbourne, Australia, before completing a PhD in exercise physiology at Edith Cowan University in Perth, Western Australia. His research focus has involved thermoregulation and practical strategies to enhance endurance performance in the heat, such as cooling, hydration, and heat acclimation. From 2011 to 2014, Rodney was the lead performance physiologist for the New Zealand canoe (sprint and slalom), sailing, and speed skating programs. He is now a sport scientist at the Victorian Institute of Sport in Melbourne, Australia, working with the rowing and triathlon programs. From his work in these roles, Rodney has developed a fascination for understanding and developing methods that maximize training adaptation in athletes wishing to improve their performance.

Dr. **Stacy T. Sims** has contributed to the environmental exercise physiology and sport nutrition field for more than 15 years as both an athlete and a scientist. Her personal interest in sex differences and performance has been the priority of her academic and consulting career; she is always looking at true physiology to apply innovative solutions in the sport nutrition world. Before joining the University of Waikato at the new Adams Centre for High Performance as a senior research fellow, Stacy cofounded and created a successful sport nutrition company based on sex differences while maintaining a strong applied research track. Stacy served as an exercise physiologist and nutrition scientist at Stanford University from 2007 to 2012, specializing in the role of sex differences in environmental and nutritional considerations for recovery and performance. Preceding her work at Stanford, she was a senior research scientist in clothing and textile sciences at Otago University, where she transferred her PhD work in sex differences related to hydration and exercise in the heat to investigating the interactions of human performance, fabrics, and extreme environmental conditions. An elite athlete herself, Stacy has extensive experience working with athletes at the highest levels of sport worldwide, from the Olympics to the Tour de France.

Jim Taylor, PhD, is an internationally recognized authority on the psychology of cycling. Jim has been the team psychologist for the Subaru/Gary Fisher and Trek/VW professional mountain bike teams. He works with cyclists and other endurance athletes from top juniors to age-groupers to Tour de France competitors. Jim has written 15 books, has published more than 750 articles in popular and professional publications, and has given more than 1,000 workshops throughout North and South America, Europe, and the Middle East. He is a former world-ranked alpine ski racer, a second-degree black belt in karate, a sub-3-hour marathon runner, a two-time Ironman triathlete, and an avid road cyclist and mountain biker.

Nathan G. Versey is a physiologist at the Australian Institute of Sport. He works with a range of elite athletes, coaches, and support staff, primarily in the areas of postexercise recovery, fatigue, sleep, and travel. He completed a PhD in exercise physiology, specifically hydrotherapy recovery for athletes, and now supervises and conducts applied research. Nathan has written a number of peer-reviewed articles on recovery for athletes.

Randall L. Wilber, PhD, FACSM, is a senior sport physiologist at the U.S. Olympic Training Center in Colorado Springs and has worked at the United States Olympic Committee (USOC) for 24 years. He works closely with Team USA athletes and coaches in the areas of altitude training, heat and humidity acclimatization, blood chemistry analysis, overtraining, international air travel (jet lag), and exercise-induced asthma. Wilber has worked with several U.S. Olympic medalists including Michael Phelps, Katie Ledecky, Missy Franklin, Allison Schmitt, Chase Kalisz, Conor Dwyer, and Ryan Lochte from USA Swimming, as well as Meb Keflezighi, Galen Rupp, Joe Kovacs, Jeff Henderson, Matthew Centrowitz, Evan Jager, Emma Coburn, Jenny Simpson, Leo Manzano, Deena Kastor, and Shalane Flanagan from USA Track and Field. In USA Triathlon, Wilber has worked with Olympic medalists Gwen Jorgensen and Susan Williams and world champions Barb Lindquist, Sheila Taormina, Siri Lindley, and Hunter Kemper. He has been a staff member of Team USA at four Summer Olympics (Athens 2004, Beijing 2008, London 2012, Rio de Janeiro 2016), four Winter Olympics (Salt Lake City 2002, Torino 2006, Vancouver 2010, Sochi 2014), two Pan American Games (Santo Domingo 2003, Rio de Janeiro 2007), and multiple world championships. In addition, Wilber serves as a consultant to the U.S. Navy SEALs on issues related to combat performance at high altitude. Wilber has written more than 35 papers in peer-reviewed scientific journals and has written several book chapters in the areas of sports medicine and sport science. He wrote the book *Altitude Training and Athletic Performance* (Human Kinetics, 2004) and coauthored *Exercise-Induced Asthma: Pathophysiology and Treatment* (Human Kinetics, 2002). Wilber was recognized as a fellow of the American College of Sports Medicine (ACSM) in 1998 and currently serves as chair of the ACSM Olympic and Paralympic Sports Medicine and Sport Science Committee.

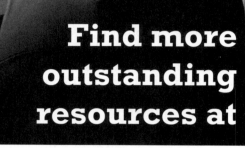